Lomax, Becky,
Yellowstone & Grand
Teton /
2018.
33305241210677
ca   04/09/18

D0201405

YELLOWSTONE & GRAND TETON

BECKY LOMAX

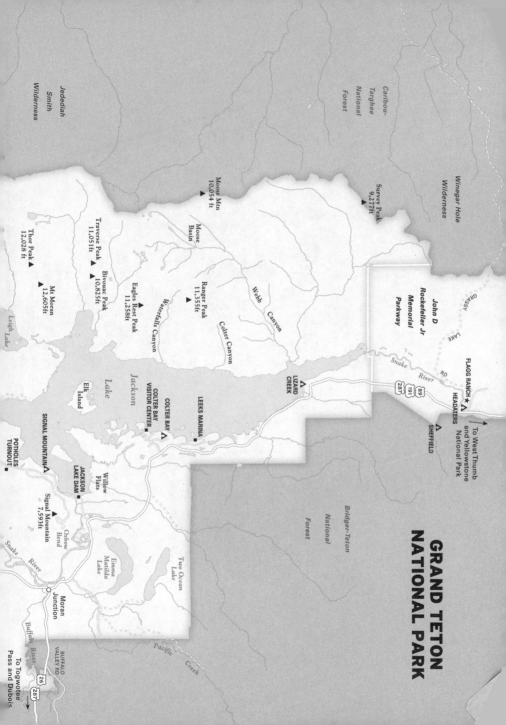

GRAND TETON NATIONAL PARK

Jedediah
Smith
Wilderness

Caribou-
Targhee
National
Forest

Winegar Hole
Wilderness

Survey Peak
9,277ft

Moose Mtn
10,054 ft

Moose
Basin

John D
Rockefeller Jr
Memorial
Parkway

GRASSY

LAKE

FLAGG RANCH ★
HEADATERS

RD

Snake   River

HEADATERS

89
191
287

SHEFFIELD

To West Thumb
and Yellowstone
National Park

Thor Peak
12,028 ft

Traverse Peak
11,051ft

Bivouac Peak
10,825ft

Ranger Peak
11,355ft

Webb

Canyon

Mt Moran
12,605ft

Eagles Rest Peak
11,258ft

Waterfalls Canyon

Colter Canyon

Leigh
Lake

Jackson

Elk
Island

Lake

LIZARD
CREEK

COLTER BAY
VISITOR CENTER

COLTER BAY

LEEKS MARINA

Bridger-Teton

National

Forest

SIGNAL MOUNTAIN

POTHOLES
TURNOUT

JACKSON
LAKE DAM

Willow
Flats

Signal Mountain
7,593ft

Oxbow
Bend

Emma
Matilda
Lake

Two Ocean
Lake

Snake

River

Moran
Junction

Buffalo   River

BUFFALO
VALLEY RD

Pacific   Creek

26
287

To Togwotee
Pass and Dubois

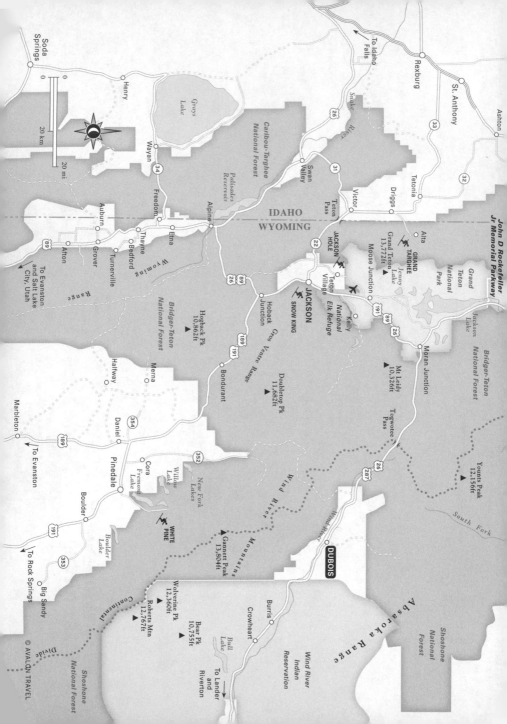

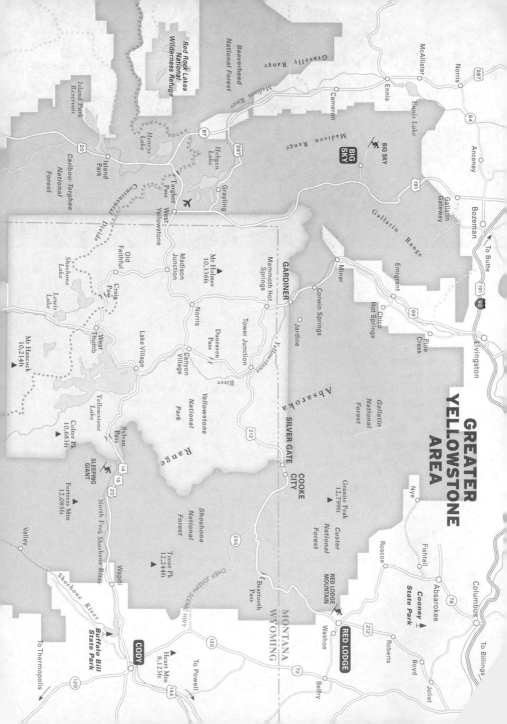

GREATER YELLOWSTONE AREA

Contents

**Discover Yellowstone
and Grand Teton** **10**
 10 Top Experiences **14**
 Planning Your Trip 22
 • Beat the Crowds 24
 • If You're Looking For............ 25
 • Yellowstone In-Park Lodging..... 28
 • Grand Teton In-Park Lodging..... 29
 The Best of Yellowstone
 and Grand Teton............... 31
 • One Day in Yellowstone 32
 Best Hikes 35
 • One Day in Grand Teton
 and Jackson Hole.............. 36
 Geologic Wonders 38
 • Wildlife-Watching Hot Spots..... 39
 • Winter Fun.................... 40

North Yellowstone **41**
 Exploring North Yellowstone 45
 Sights 49
 Recreation...................... 56
 Entertainment and Shopping 70
 Food 71
 Accommodations 75

 Camping....................... 80
 Transportation and Services 83

**Old Faithful and
West Yellowstone** **84**
 Exploring Old Faithful
 and West Yellowstone.......... 88
 Sights 93
 Recreation...................... 102
 Entertainment and Shopping 117
 Food 119
 Accommodations 123
 Camping....................... 128
 Transportation and Services 131

Canyon and Lake Country **133**
 Exploring Canyon and
 Lake Country................. 137
 Sights 141
 Recreation...................... 148
 Entertainment and Shopping 170
 Food 171
 Accommodations 173
 Camping....................... 174
 Transportation and Services 177

North Grand Teton............**178**
Exploring North Grand Teton 182
Sights 185
Recreation...................... 189
Entertainment and Shopping 207
Food 208
Accommodations 211
Camping....................... 213
Transportation and Services 216

South Grand Teton............**218**
Exploring South Grand Teton 222
Sights 227
Recreation...................... 234
Entertainment and Shopping 254
Food 255
Accommodations 256
Camping....................... 259
Transportation and Services 260

Jackson Hole...................**262**
Exploring Jackson Hole............ 266
Sights 269
Recreation...................... 276
Entertainment and Shopping 285
Food 288
Accommodations 294
Camping....................... 300
Transportation and Services 301

Teton Valley...................... 303

Gateways......................**312**
Big Sky, Montana................. 315
Red Lodge, Montana.............. 329
Cody, Wyoming.................. 340
Dubois, Wyoming 357

Background **360**
The Landscape 361
Plants and Animals 374
History......................... 380
Local Culture.................... 387

Essentials **389**
Getting There 390
Getting Around.................. 398
Recreation...................... 402
Visas and Officialdom 410
Travel Tips 410
Health and Safety 413

Resources **417**
Suggested Reading............... 417
Internet Resources 421

Index **423**

Lis of Maps....................**432**

DISCOVER

Yellowstone and Grand Teton

Welcome to the land of fire and ice. The earth's tremendous forces have made Yellowstone and Grand Teton National Parks a volatile landscape. The parks bear the marks of ancient seas, volcanic heat, tectonic upthrusting, and ice scouring. Even today, they shake and roar.

In Yellowstone National Park, rumblings of a supervolcano boil to the surface—spewing, spitting, oozing, and bubbling. Steam rolls from vivid-colored pools, muddy cauldrons burp smelly gases, and blasts of hot water shoot high into the air. The cantankerous landscape gushes with spouters like iconic Old Faithful.

In Grand Teton National Park, toothy spires claw the sky in one of the newest mountain ranges in the Rockies. Glaciers have chewed the terrain, leaving lakes, bowls, and canyons to explore. Towering thousands of feet high to culminate in the Grand Teton, mountains dwarf all that roams across the floor of Jackson Hole.

Clockwise from top left: Old Faithful Inn; Colter Bay Marina; yurt camp at Grand Canyon of the Yellowstone; black bear; the Chapel of the Transfiguration; Morning Glory Pool.

Throughout the Greater Yellowstone area, sagebrush prairies make wildlife easy to spot. Bison, elk, antelope, wolves, and even grizzly bears enchant visitors. Blue-ribbon trout fishing streams, hiking trails, alpine lakes, bicycle paths, white water rivers, and epic ski slopes all create a four-season recreation paradise to explore. The town of Jackson, which anchors the Jackson Hole valley, offers an urban base of operations for the region's myriad recreational bounty.

Come to Yellowstone and Grand Teton National Parks—for the classic experience of the West.

Clockwise from top left: elk antler arch in Jackson; skiers tour Grand Canyon of the Yellowstone; elk; Excelsior Geyser.

10 TOP
EXPERIENCES

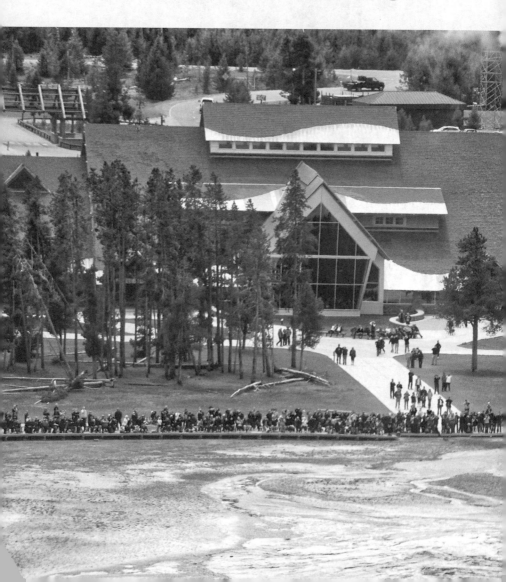

1 **Old Faithful Geyser:** Watch Yellowstone's most reliable geyser shoot up to 8,400 gallons of hot water as high as 185 feet (page 97).

2 **Grand Prismatic Spring:** Gaze at the largest and most colorful hot spring in Yellowstone from Midway Geyser Basin or on the Fairy Falls Trail (page 96).

3 **Wildlife-Watching:** See bison herds, elk, pronghorn antelope, bears, wolves, and bighorn sheep in Yellowstone's Lamar Valley (page 54) and Hayden Valley (page 143).

4 **Mammoth Hot Springs:** Stroll the boardwalks amid these travertine terraces as sulfur fills the air (page 50).

5 **Grand Canyon of the Yellowstone:** Admire this giant chasm from scenic rim overlooks or on hikes to the Upper and Lower Falls (page 141).

>>>

6 **Winter Snowcoach Tours:** Ride through Yellowstone's wintry landscape to Old Faithful or the Grand Canyon of the Yellowstone (page 91).

>>>

7 **Mormon Row:** These ranch buildings from the 1890s sit backdropped by the craggy Tetons (page 233).

>>>

9 **Grand Teton:** View the grandeur of the 13,770-foot Grand Teton from Teton Glacier Turnout or Bradley Lake (page 227).

<<<

8 **Hike the Tetons:** The towering Tetons beg exploration. Get up close with a hike to Hidden Falls and Inspiration Point (page 238) or backpack the Teton Crest (page 246).

>>>

10 **River Rafting:** Raft the Wild and Scenic Snake River (page 203) through the Tetons and or paddle Jackson Lake at Colter Bay (page 202).

Planning Your Trip

Where to Go

North Yellowstone

From the **North Entrance** near **Gardiner** to the **Northeast Entrance** at **Silver Gate** and **Cooke City,** a two-lane park road snakes east across North Yellowstone. Anchored in the west by **Mammoth Hot Springs,** the road follows the **Yellowstone River** past sagebrush plateaus to **Tower-Roosevelt,** through the remote **Lamar Valley,** and across the Absaroka Mountains. This is the only park road that remains open year-round, providing **winter access**. The **Mammoth Campground** is also open year-round.

Old Faithful and West Yellowstone

The town of **West Yellowstone** hosts the **busiest park entrance** and the **most services.**

Fountain Paint Pots

As the road enters the park, it follows the Madison and Gibbon Rivers, passing campgrounds at **Madison** and **Norris.** South of Madison, it is geyser paradise: volcanic features include **Fountain Paint Pots,** the **Grand Prismatic Spring,** and the most famous hydrothermal of all—**Old Faithful Geyser.** The Old Faithful area is home to three park lodges, including the architecturally rustic **Old Faithful Inn.**

Canyon and Lake Country

The park hub of **Canyon Village** links Yellowstone's east and west sides. Here, the Yellowstone River cuts deep into the **Grand Canyon of the Yellowstone.** Prominent points and rim-side hikes yield epic views of the plunging waterfalls below. South of Canyon Village, the road follows the Yellowstone River

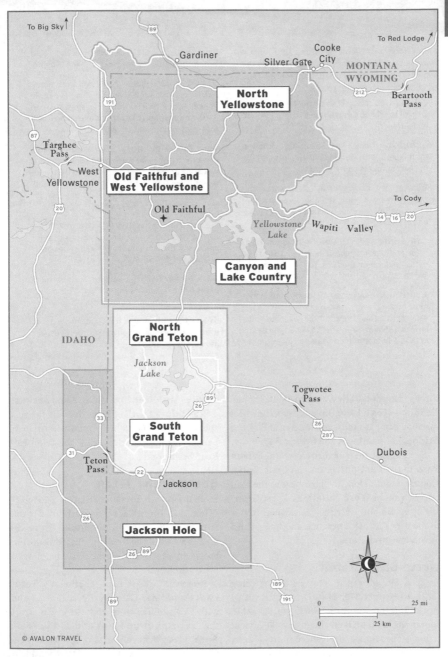

To Big Sky

89

To Red Lodge

Gardiner

Cooke City

Silver Gate

MONTANA

WYOMING

191

212

Beartooth Pass

North Yellowstone

87

Targhee Pass

West Yellowstone

Old Faithful and West Yellowstone

20

Old Faithful

Yellowstone Lake

Wapiti Valley

To Cody

14 16 20

Canyon and Lake Country

IDAHO

North Grand Teton

Jackson Lake

89

26

Togwotee Pass

26

South Grand Teton

33

287

Dubois

31

Teton Pass

22

Jackson

26

Jackson Hole

26 89

189

89

191

0   25 mi

0   25 km

© AVALON TRAVEL

Beat the Crowds

Yellowstone and Grand Teton top four million visitors annually. Most come in summer when the huge parking lots fill to maximum capacity. Here are some tips to beat the crowds:

- Visit in **June** or **September,** while most kids are still in school. Crowds thin in comparison to midsummer.

- **Avoid July,** which has the heaviest visitation for the park, with clogged parking lots and the thickest numbers on trails and boardwalks.

- Try **May** or **October.** May offers a chance to watch newborn bison and elk calves. October brings on fall colors and active bears in hyperphasia.

- Go in **winter.** Enjoy the beauty of the icy landscape and prolific steam in the geyser basins due to the colder temperatures. You may even have Old Faithful to yourself.

- **Avoid midday hours** (10am-4pm), when most of the crowds are out in force. Utilize the early morning and late afternoon-evening hours instead. Hit Midway and the Lower Geyser Basins in the early morning en route to Norris Geyser Basin by 10am. Visit the Upper Geyser Basin (Old Faithful, Black Sands, and Biscuit) in the evening.

- **Visit Old Faithful at sunrise.** In summer, sunrise occurs 5am-6:30am. While most people are still rubbing sleep from their eyes, you can check the eruption predictions and score front-row seats in time for Old Faithful to blow.

- **Tour in the evening.** After an early dinner, explore the geyser basins until sunset occurs, which is 8pm-9:30pm in summer. You'll encounter far fewer people on the boardwalks and will have several hours for exploring hot pools, fumaroles, mud pots, and geysers.

- **Go wildlife watching in the morning and evening.** Though most visitors look for animals as they tour midday, wildlife is more active around dawn and dusk.

- **Park early.** Trailhead parking lots at popular paths fill up by late morning. Plan to be at your trailhead by 8am-9am or earlier.

- **Stop at picnic areas** for restroom breaks, as the geyser basins and Canyon restrooms usually have lengthy lines.

through **Hayden Valley,** prime wildlife habitat. At **Yellowstone Lake,** miles of shoreline host marinas, campgrounds, and lodging at **Fishing Bridge, Lake Village,** and **Bridge Bay.**

Heading east, the park road crosses the **Sylvan Pass** to the **East Entrance** and on to **Cody.** Continue south along the lakeshore as the road curves around **West Thumb** and past **Grant Village,** climbing over the Continental Divide to the park's **South Entrance** and into **Grand Teton National Park.**

North Grand Teton

Rugged Mt. Moran greets visitors entering **Grand Teton National Park** along **John D. Rockefeller, Jr. Memorial Parkway.** Below Mt. Moran sits **Jackson Lake,** home to a native trout fishery. The lake's eastern shore sports lodges, hiking, horseback riding, marinas, and visitor services at **Colter Bay Village** and **Jackson Lake Lodge.** South of Jackson Lake, the road splits east past wildlife-rich **Oxbow Bend** to the park's **Moran Entrance,** while the Teton Park Road heads south.

South Grand Teton

From the **Moran Entrance,** Highways 26/89/191 offer year-round access south to **Moose Junction.** Floaters on the **Snake River** can take in views of the toothy peaks, while history buffs will want to explore the scenic buildings of **Mormon Row.**

From the Jackson Lake Junction, the **Teton Park Road** (May-Oct.) tours past **Jenny Lake,** with views of Teewinot and Mt. Owen. Trails such as **Inspiration Point and Hidden Falls** climb through canyons to take in waterfalls and lakes while the rugged **Teton Crest Trail** trips

If You're Looking For...

- **Backpacking:** Plan a route along the Teton Crest Trail in Grand Teton.

- **Bicycling:** Bike to Fairy Falls and Lone Star Geyser in Yellowstone. In Grand Teton, cycle the Multi-Use Pathway.

- **Boating:** Boat around Frank Island in Yellowstone Lake or around Elk Island in Jackson Lake.

- **Fishing:** Cast for wild trout in Yellowstone Lake or Jackson Lake, or aim for Slough Creek, Lamar River, Madison River, or Snake River.

- **Hiking:** Walk to the summit of Mt. Washburn in Yellowstone, or hike Paintbrush Canyon in Grand Teton.

- **Kayaking and Canoeing:** Paddle across Lewis Lake and up the thoroughfare to Shoshone Lake in Yellowstone. In Grand Teton, paddle String Lake or around the islands in Colter Bay on Jackson Lake.

- **Rafting:** Raft the Yellowstone and Gallatin Rivers outside the park. In Grand Teton, float the Snake River.

- **Wildflowers:** Drive Sylvan Pass in Yellowstone for lupine-lined roads, hike Grand View Point in Grand Teton for pink sticky geranium, or backpack Alaska Basin for prolific wildflower displays in August, including white columbine.

- **Winter Activities:** Take a snowcoach to Old Faithful, or ski at Jackson Hole Mountain Resort.

National Elk Refuge is one of the best places for wildlife-watching.

In **Teton Village,** snow season brings skiing and snowboarding to **Jackson Hole Mountain Resort,** where visitors can ride the **Aerial Tram** to the 10,000-foot summit of Rendezvous Mountain.

West of the Tetons, the **Teton Valley** stretches into Idaho and back, with tiny towns like **Victor** and **Driggs.** The **Grand Targhee Resort** balances hiking, sightseeing, and biking in summer with skiing in winter.

Gateways

Big Sky, Montana is the closest gateway to Yellowstone with access to the park's North and West Entrances. **Red Lodge, Montana** serves as the eastern springboard for the scenic Beartooth Highway to Yellowstone's Northeast Entrance. **Cody, Wyoming** offers a Wild West base of operations for Yellowstone's East Entrance. In Wyoming's Wind River Valley, **Dubois** is a stop on the way to Yellowstone's South Entrance and Grand Teton's Moran Entrance—a route that crosses the Continental Divide at **Togwotee Pass.**

the Jackson Hole Aerial Tram

through thin air along the mountain spines. Teton Park Road terminates at the southern **Moose Entrance.**

Jackson Hole

Jackson Hole is a year-round recreation Mecca. The valley encompasses the towns of Moran, Moose, Kelly, Wilson, Teton Village, and Jackson, as well as **Bridger-Teton** and **Caribou-Targhee National Forests.**

The town of **Jackson** serves as a base for adventures, with year-round services and accommodations, and famous Western saloons like the **Million Dollar Cowboy Bar.** The nearby

Fairy Falls freeze in winter

When to Go

High Season
SUMMER (JUNE-AUG.)
Summer sees the most visitors, with **July** and **August** luring the biggest crowds. All park **lodges**, **campgrounds**, and **visitors centers** are open. **June** through **early July** buzzes with mosquitoes, while July through early August brings on rampant wildflowers. **August** also yields the best high-elevation hiking in the Tetons, and warmer days produce less steam for better hot spring viewing in Yellowstone. Most **park roads are open**.

WINTER (DEC.-MAR.)
In winter, deep snows turn the parks white. Alpine skiers gravitate to Jackson Hole while cross-country skiers tackle groomed and untracked trails in both parks. Most **park roads are closed** (Nov.-late Apr.), with the exception of the park road between Yellowstone's North and Northeast Entrances. Touring in Yellowstone is via guided **snowcoach** or **snowmobile,** while lodging is available at **Mammoth Hot Springs** and **Old Faithful.**

Off Season
SPRING (MAR.-MAY)
Mid-April offers **car-free park roads** to cyclists before roads open to vehicles in late April or May. As the snow melts, fields of yellow glacier lilies emerge. Come in **May** for bison calving season, or **June** to spot bighorn sheep ewes with newborn lambs and grizzly bears foraging along Yellowstone Lake. By May, most **park roads start to open** and **visitor services return.** Days may be rainy and cold, and some trails remain snow-covered into June.

FALL (SEPT.-NOV.)
Cooler, bug-free days yielsd pleasant hiking with **thinner crowds.** Come in late **September** for the elk rut, when bulls gather harems to prove their dominance and their bugles break the nighttime quiet. Sporadic snowstorms can **close park roads** and **services are limited**.

Before You Go

Park Fees and Passes

For each park, the **entrance fee** is **$30** per vehicle ($25 motorcycles, $15 pedestrians and cyclists) and is good for seven days. Visitors planning to enter both parks can buy a **joint pass** ($50 per vehicle, $40 motorcycles, $20 pedestrians and cyclists).

Other fee options include the **Annual Park Pass** ($60) for Yellowstone or Grand Teton, and the **Interagency Annual Pass** ($80), which is good for all national parks and federal fee areas. U.S. fourth graders, disabled, and military personnel can get free interagency passes, and seniors can buy lifetime interagency passes ($80).

Entrance Stations

YELLOWSTONE NATIONAL PARK

Yellowstone has five entrance stations:

- **North Entrance** (U.S. 89, near Gardiner) is open **year-round** and provides the closest access to Mammoth Hot Springs.

- **Northeast Entrance** (Hwy. 212, west of Silver Gate) provides access to Tower-Roosevelt and the Lamar Valley. Winter snow may temporarily close this entrance. Roads east of Cooke City shut down in winter due to snow.

- **West Entrance** (Hwy. 20, West Yellowstone), the busiest entrance in the park, opens mid-April to early November and only admits snowcoaches and snowmobiles in winter.

- **East Entrance** (U.S. 20), located between Fishing Bridge and Cody, Wyoming, opens mid-May to early November.

- **South Entrance** (U.S. 89/191/287), located on the border between Yellowstone and Grand Teton, opens mid-May to early November.

GRAND TETON NATIONAL PARK

Grand Teton has three entrance stations:

- **Moran Entrance** (Hwy. 26/89/191 and Hwy. 26/287) is open **year-round** and offers access from the east.

- **Granite Canyon Entrance** is on the south entrance to the Moose-Wilson Road between Teton Village and Moose. Seasonal access varies.

- **Moose Entrance** (Teton Park Rd.) provides access to the southern region of the park and is open **year-round**.

Reservations

To guarantee lodging, camping, tours, or dinner reservations for anytime in **summer,** make reservations at least **one year in advance.** For **winter** travel plans, make reservations **6-12 months in advance.**

YELLOWSTONE

Xanterra (866/439-7375 or 307/344-7311, www.yellowstonenationalparklodges.com) operates two winter lodges (Mammoth and Old Faithful Snow Lodge), nine summer lodges (Canyon Lodge, Grant Village, Lake Lodge, Lake Yellowstone Hotel, Mammoth Springs Hotel, Old Faithful Inn, Old Faithful Lodge, Snow Lodge, and Roosevelt Lodge), and five campgrounds (Madison, Grant Village, Canyon, Bridge Bay, and Fishing Bridge RV Park).

GRAND TETON

Grand Teton Lodging Company (800/628-9988 or 307/543-2811, www.gtlc.com) operates four summer lodges (Jackson Lake Lodge, Colter Bay Village, Jenny Lake Lodge, and Headwaters Lodge) and two campgrounds (Headwaters and Colter Bay RV Park).

JACKSON HOLE

For reservations at Jackson Hole Mountain Resort and in the town of Jackson, contact **Jackson Hole Central Reservations** (800/333-7766 or 307/733-2292, www.jacksonhole.com) or **Jackson Hole Reservations Company** (800/329-9205 or 307/733-6331, www.jackson-hole.net).

Yellowstone In-Park Lodging

	Location	Price	Season	Amenities
Mammoth Campground	Mammoth Hot Springs	$20	year-round	campsites
Mammoth Hot Springs Hotel	Mammoth Hot Springs	$100-290, suites $560	late Apr.-early Oct.; mid-Dec.-early Mar.	hotel rooms, cabins, restaurant
Tower Fall Campground	Tower-Roosevelt	$15	late May-late Sept.	campsites
Roosevelt Lodge and Cabins	Tower-Roosevelt	$96-155	early June-early Sept.	cabins, restaurant
Slough Creek Campground	Northeast Entrance	$15	mid-June-early Sept.	campsites
Pebble Creek Campground	Northeast Entrance	$15	mid-June-late Sept.	campsites
Madison Campground	Madison	$25	May-mid-Oct.	campsites
Indian Creek Campground	Mammoth to Norris	$15	mid-June-mid-Sept	campsites
Norris Campground	Norris	$20	mid-May-late Sept.	campsites
Old Faithful Lodge	Old Faithful	$96-160	mid-May-early Oct.	cabins, restaurant
Snow Lodge	Old Faithful	$123-325	late Apr.-mid-Oct.; mid-Dec.-Feb.	hotel rooms, cabins, restaurants
Old Faithful Inn	Old Faithful	$144-335, suites $670-715	early May-mid-Oct.	hotel rooms, restaurants
Canyon Campground	Canyon Village	$30	late May-late Sept.	campsites, showers
Canyon Lodge and Cabins	Canyon Village	$175-330, suites $625	late May-late Sept.	hotel rooms, cabins, restaurants
Fishing Bridge RV Park	Fishing Bridge	$50	early May-late Sept.	RV hookups
Bridge Bay Campground	Lake Village	$25	late May-early Sept.	campsites, marina
Lake Lodge Cabins	Lake Village	$95-235	early June-late Sept.	motel rooms, cabins, restaurant
Lake Yellowstone Hotel and Cabins	Lake Village	$190-550, suites $740-890	mid-May-early Oct.	hotel rooms, cabins, restaurant
Grant Village Campground	Grant Village	$30	mid-June-mid-Sept.	campsites
Grant Village Lodge	Grant Village	$255	late May-late Sept.	hotel rooms, restaurants
Lewis Lake Campground	South Entrance Road	$15	mid-June-Oct.	campsites

Grand Teton In-Park Lodging

	Location	Price	Season	Amenities
Grassy Lake Road	John D. Rockefeller, Jr. Memorial Parkway	free	June-Sept.	primitive campsites
Lizard Creek	John D. Rockefeller, Jr. Memorial Parkway	$23	June-early Sept.	campsites
Headwaters Campground & RV	John D. Rockefeller, Jr. Memorial Parkway	$38-75	June-Sept.	Campsites, RV hookups, camping cabins
Headwaters Lodge & Cabins at Flagg Ranch	John D. Rockefeller, Jr. Memorial Parkway	$227-330	June-Sept.	motel rooms, cabins, camper cabins, restaurant
Colter Bay Campground	Colter Bay	$30-75	mid-May-Oct.	Campsites, RV hookups
Colter Bay Tent Village	Colter Bay	$72-75	late May-early Sept.	tent cabins
Colter Bay Cabins	Colter Bay	$175-280	late May-early Oct.	cabins
Jackson Lake Lodge	Jackson Lake	$320-835	late May-early Oct.	hotel rooms, cottages, restaurant
Signal Mountain Campground	Signal Mountain	$31-52	mid-May-mid-Oct.	campsites
Signal Mountain Lodge	Signal Mountain	$211-430	mid-May-mid-Oct.	motel rooms, cabins, restaurants
Jenny Lake Campground	Jenny Lake	$28	early May-late Sept	tent-only campsites
Jenny Lake Lodge	Jenny Lake	$758-1,050	June-early Oct.	cabins, restaurant
Gros Ventre Campground	Moose	$28-52	early May-early Oct.	Campsites, RV elec. hookups
Dornan's Spur Ranch Cabins	Moose	$200-360	May-Oct. and Dec.-Mar.	cabins, restaurants
Triangle X Ranch	Moose to Moran	rates vary	mid-May-mid-Oct. and late Dec.-mid-Mar.	dude ranch

In the Parks

Visitor Centers

YELLOWSTONE

Out of the eight visitor centers, the largest ones are **Old Faithful Visitor Education Center** (307/344-2751, Old Faithful Village) and **Canyon Visitor Education Center** (307/344-2550, Canyon Village).

GRAND TETON

The main visitor center is the **Craig Thomas Discovery & Visitor Center** (307/739-3399) in the South Teton section of the park.

Campgrounds

YELLOWSTONE

Of the 12 campgrounds in Yellowstone, the largest five accept **reservations** (Xanterra, 307/344-7311 or 866/439-7375, www.yellowstonenationalparklodges.com):

- **Madison** (278 sites, early May-mid-Oct.) located at Madison Junction.
- **Canyon** (270 sites, late May-mid-Sept.) in Canyon Village.
- **Fishing Bridge RV Park** (340 sites, early May-late Sept.) in Fishing Bridge.
- **Bridge Bay** (432 sites, late May-early Sept.) near Lake Village.
- **Grant Village** (430 sites, late June-late Sept.) on the West Thumb of Lake Yellowstone.

Campers without reservations should head to the park's **first-come, first-served campgrounds:** Mammoth (85 sites, year-round), Indian Creek (70 sites, mid-June-mid-Sept.), Norris (100 sites, late May-late Sept.), Tower Fall (31 sites, late May-late Sept.), Slough Creek (23 sites, mid-June-early Oct.), Pebble Creek (27 sites, mid-June-late Sept.), or Lewis Lake (85 sites, mid-June-early Nov.).

GRAND TETON

Grand Teton's five campgrounds are all **first-come, first-served** and include Lizard Creek (60 sites, mid-June-early Sept.), Signal Mountain (81 sites, early May-mid-Oct.), Jenny Lake (49 sites, early May-late Sept.), Gros Ventre (350 sites, early May-early Oct.), and Colter Bay (350 sites, mid-May-late Sept.).

Colter Bay RV Park (Colter Bay Village, 800/628-9988, www.gtlc.com, mid-May-late Sept.) and **Headwaters Campground & RV** (Flagg Ranch, 307/543-2861 or 800/443-2311, www.gtlc.com, late May-Sept.) accept reservations 6-9 months in advance.

Backpackers should reserve a **backcountry camping permit** in advance (Yellowstone, www.nps.gov/yell, $35, Jan.; Grand Teton, www.recreation.gov, early Jan.-mid-May, $45). Permits are also available first-come, first-served (Yellowstone, 48 hours in advance, $3/person/night; Grand Teton, 24 hours in advance, $35/trip).

Getting Around

YELLOWSTONE

In summer, **you'll need a vehicle** to get around. There is **no park shuttle.** In winter, visitors can ride snowcoaches or snowmobiles from West Yellowstone, Mammoth, or Flagg Ranch into the park.

GRAND TETON

Alltrans (307/733-3135, www.jacksonholealltrans.com) runs several times daily from Jackson to popular park destinations in summer.

Norris Geyser Basin

The Best of Yellowstone and Grand Teton

From spouting geysers to toothy mountains, a romp through Yellowstone and Grand Teton wraps up with a smash-bang ending in Jackson Hole.

Yellowstone

DAY 1

From the **North Entrance** in Gardiner, drive through the **Roosevelt Arch** to enter Yellowstone National Park. Cross the **45th Parallel** into the steaming landscape at **Mammoth Hot Springs** and stop to stroll the boardwalk through colorful travertine terraces. Back in the car, drive south through the **Golden Gate** to **Swan Lake**, a high plateau with elk and bison. Continuing south, pull over at **Roaring Mountain** to see, hear, and smell the volcanic action, then stop at **Norris Geyser Basin** to tour the hottest and fastest-changing geothermals in the park. From Norris, head east on the park road toward **Canyon Village,** where

you'll spend three nights (book accommodations or campsites one year in advance).

DAY 2

In the morning, drive to **Artist Point** and park (get there before 10am to snag a spot), then hit the South Rim Trail along the **Grand Canyon of the Yellowstone,** following the scenic path down to the **Upper Falls Overlook**. Climb down (then back up) the steel steps of **Uncle Tom's Trail** to get wet in the mist from the **Lower Falls**.

After lunch in Canyon Village, drive north over **Dunraven Pass** and gaze up at **Mt. Washburn,** the highest peak in the park. Just south of Tower Junction, pull over to view **Tower Fall** as it spills into the Yellowstone River. Continue down the curvy descent to Tower-Roosevelt, then turn northeast into the **Lamar Valley** for wildlife-watching. Look for elk, antelope, bison, bears, and wolves, and bring binoculars to spy bighorn

One Day in Yellowstone

bison jam

With 2.2 million acres and half of the world's geothermal features, how do you see Yellowstone with limited time? Focus on the southern Grand Loop Road. The route takes in wildlife watching, the park's biggest waterfall, and geysers.

HAYDEN VALLEY

From Yellowstone's East or South Entrance, aim for Hayden Valley north of Fishing Bridge. Crazy bison jams alternate with placid waterways containing trumpeter swans and moose.

GRAND CANYON OF THE YELLOWSTONE

Take the North Rim Road to hike down the switchbacks to Brink of the Lower Falls where the waterfall's thunder shakes the ground. Farther on the North Rim, stop at Lookout Point for a classic front view of the Lower Falls.

LOWER GEYSER BASIN

Back on Grand Loop, head west toward Norris and then south, to drop into the supervolcano caldera. After descending the Gibbon River to Madison Junction, climb along the aptly named Firehole River that leads to steaming volcanic basins. In the Lower Geyser Basin, stop to see Great Fountain Geyser, if it is erupting.

MIDWAY GEYSER BASIN

At Midway Geyser Basin, tour the boardwalk to the colorful Grand Prismatic Spring, the park's largest hot spring.

UPPER GEYSER BASIN

In Upper Geyser Basin, plan your visit around Old Faithful's eruption. See the iconic geyser and tack on a walk of Geyser Hill. Dine in the historic Old Faithful Inn, departing near dusk to drive back to Madison Junction. Turning west, follow the Madison River downstream to watch elk in the meadows before exiting the park at West Yellowstone.

sheep and mountain goats on the flanks of the Absaroka Mountains. Return to Canyon Village for the night.

DAY 3

Today, explore the steaming geothermal features of Yellowstone's caldera. From Canyon, head west toward Norris, then drive south past Madison to drop into the crater's geyser basin. Park at **Old Faithful** and make a beeline for **Old Faithful Visitor Education Center.** Time your day based on the center's geyser eruption predictions. Follow the **Upper Geyser Basin** boardwalks north to see colorful **Morning Glory Pool** while waiting for famous Old Faithful to blow.

After reveling in the majesty of Old Faithful, return to the park road and drive north to tour the other nearby geyser basins. Don't miss **Midway Geyser Basin,** which features the radiant **Grand Prismatic Spring.** In the **Lower Geyser Basin,** drive along Firehole Lake Drive to **Fountain Paint Pots,** which contains four types of geothermal features. Once you've had your fill of geysers, return to Canyon Village.

Yellowstone and Grand Teton
DAY 4

It's your last day in Yellowstone—and your first day in Grand Teton. Begin by driving south through **Hayden Valley,** keeping an eye out for bison and trumpeter swans. Stop to walk the lower loop of **Mud Volcano** amid the sputtering, growling geothermals. At **Yellowstone Lake,** tour historic **Lake Yellowstone Hotel** and the **West Thumb Geyser Basin,** known for its crystal-blue hot pools, cone geysers, and paint pots. Just before exiting Yellowstone, the **Lewis River** descends to join the **Snake River,** Grand Teton's iconic river.

At the **South Entrance,** you'll enter Grand Teton National Park on Highway 89/191/287. Continuing south, the road passes through the remains of the 2016 Berry Fire as it nears the Flagg Ranch Information Station. Just before reaching the north shore of **Jackson Lake,** look west for the first view of the jagged **Teton Mountains.** Stop at **Jackson Lake Lodge,** where you'll spend the next two nights.

Old Faithful

Lake Yellowstone Hotel

Mormon Row

Grand Teton

DAY 5

In the morning, sign up for a two-hour **horse-back ride** at Jackson Lake Lodge for fantastic views of the Teton Range. Back at the lodge, enjoy lunch in the **Mural Room,** then drive north to **Colter Bay** to walk the two-mile loop along the **Lakeshore Trail.** Return to Jackson Lake Lodge for the evening.

DAY 6

Get an early start for the drive south along **Teton Park Road** to **Jenny Lake,** where you'll park and hop aboard the boat shuttle to cross the lake. Once on the shore's terra firma, follow the **Jenny Lake Loop** to 200-foot **Hidden Falls.** Continue on a ledge that cuts through a rock cliff to **Inspiration Point** with views overlooking Jenny Lake and Jackson Hole.

After soaking in the scenery, either hike back or take the boat shuttle across the lake to return to the Jenny Lake Visitor Center where you left your car. Back on the road, drive south to **Moose** and tour the exhibits at the **Craig Thomas Discovery & Visitor Center.** Take a

sunset drive to **Mormon Row** for history and **wildlife-watching** before returning to Jackson Lake Lodge.

Jackson Hole

DAY 7

Exit the park and head south to **Jackson** for the final day. Wander through the **National Museum of Wildlife Art,** walk through the antler archways in **Jackson Town Square,** and dance the night away in the **Million Dollar Cowboy Bar.**

IF YOU HAVE MORE TIME

Before hitting Jackson, take an early-morning drive south on the **Moose-Wilson Road,** stopping at the **Laurance S. Rockefeller Preserve.** Continue south, keeping your eyes peeled for wildlife, then turn east to visit **Teton Village.** Climb aboard Jackson Hole Mountain Resort's **Aerial Tram** to be whisked to 10,450 feet atop **Rendezvous Mountain** to survey the Tetons and Jackson Hole. Enjoy a late brunch of waffles at **Corbet's Cabin** before descending to Jackson.

Best Hikes

Yellowstone National Park

FAIRY FALLS

Traipse **5.8 miles round-trip** through open meadows and a young lodgepole forest to reach the 197-foot **Fairy Falls.** From a narrow slot, the falls plunge into a deep pool. In winter, the falls are draped with icicles.

OLD FAITHFUL OBSERVATION POINT

Climb **2.1 miles round-trip** up a couple switchbacks to a point where you can look down on **Old Faithful Geyser.** Crowds below look tiny, and the viewpoint gives a different angle on the erupting geyser. Descend via a different route to complete the loop.

SOUTH RIM TRAIL
AND POINT SUBLIME

On the south rim of the **Grand Canyon of the Yellowstone,** this **5.1-mile round-trip** trail takes in multiple viewpoints with side trips. On **Uncle Tom's Trail,** a steel staircase plunges more than 300 steps to the base of Lower Yellowstone Falls. The route continues to **Artist Point** and on the less-traveled route to **Point Sublime.**

MT. WASHBURN

A **5-mile round-trip** climb leads to the 10,243-foot summit of **Mt. Washburn** for 360-degree panoramic views. It's a grunt, but the lookout provides huge rewards.

CHAIN OF LAKES

For fishing and wildflowers, hike **8 miles round-trip** to **Cascade** and **Grebe Lakes.** With a shuttle and strong route-finding skills, hikers can add on **Wolf** and **Ice Lakes.**

Grand Teton National Park

GRAND VIEW POINT

Take in this scenic viewpoint of the Teton

Mt. Washburn Lookout, the highest point in Yellowstone

To avoid that "dash and see" tourist feeling, target a few activities that soak up the oh-so-grand Teton ramparts.

MOOSE

Begin by heading to Moose to orient yourself at the Craig Thomas Discovery & Visitor Center. Then, pop across the road to meet your guide for a float trip on the Snake River. While floating, you'll see bald eagles as the twisting river shifts your viewpoint of the sky-scraping Teton Mountains.

JENNY LAKE

After floating back to Moose, drive north on the Teton Park Road, stopping at the Teton Glacier interpretive site to gaze on the Grand Teton. Then, drive to Jenny Lake and walk from the interpretive plaza to the lake overlooks to soak up the views.

SIGNAL MOUNTAIN

Then, aim northward for Signal Mountain, driving to the two overlooks at the summit. One yields big views of Jackson Lake and the Teton Mountains while the other looks northward, taking in the Two Oceans Plateau and Teton Wilderness.

DOWNTOWN JACKSON

Before dusk, drive the Outside Road to Jackson. As the sun goes down, the antler arches at Jackson Town Square twinkle white, and the lights flash

the Million Dollar Cowboy Bar

neon on the Million Dollar Cowboy Bar. Tour galleries, shops, bars, and breweries, or settle into Bin 22 for toasting your adventures with wine tasting and small plates.

the Craig Thomas Discovery & Visitor Center

Mountains from multiple trailheads. Shorter **3-mile routes** go from Jackson Lake Lodge while a **13.2-mile loop** takes in the viewpoint plus **Two Oceans** and **Emma Matilda Lakes.**

National Park is a **7.2-mile round-trip** climb that takes in **Hidden Falls** before summiting **Inspiration Point,** a rocky outcrop at 7,200 feet with impressive views of Jackson Hole.

PAINTBRUSH CANYON-CASCADE CANYON

A long day takes hikers up **Paintbrush Canyon** to the 10,700-foot-high **Paintbrush Divide** before dropping to **Solitude Lake** and heading straight toward the **Grand Teton.** The **20-mile-loop** finishes by plunging down **Cascade Canyon.**

HIDDEN FALLS AND INSPIRATION POINT

The **most popular hike** in Grand Teton

SURPRISE AND AMPHITHEATER LAKES

A hefty dose of switchbacks climbs into a sub-alpine basin below Grand Teton. The **10.2-mile round-trip** hike yields rewards of dazzling **Surprise** and **Amphitheater Lakes,** both tucked in hanging valleys.

HERON POND AND SWAN LAKE

The virtually flat **2.6-mile loop** goes to the sheltered **Heron Pond,** where you can see American **pelicans, beaver,** and **moose.**

the view from Inspiration Point

Geologic Wonders

Yellowstone and Grand Teton National Parks are chock full of geologic wonders. These are the ones for the record books.

Geothermals

Norris Geyser Basin is the hottest hydrothermal basin with temperatures 1,087 feet below the surface measured at 459°F (237°C). At 115,000 years in age, it is also the oldest as well as the most dynamic geothermal basin, with constantly changing features. Dormant **Terrace Mountain** at Mammoth Hot Springs is the oldest thermal in the park.

Geysers

The most famous geyser anywhere, **Old Faithful** acquired its name thanks to its regular eruptions—an average of one every 88 minutes since 2013 (but the geyser can erupt at intervals of 45-120 minutes). **Upper Geyser Basin,** which houses Old Faithful, has the most geysers in the park, with 410. In Norris Geyser Basin, **Steamboat Geyser** is the world's tallest geyser, spouting up to 300 feet. **Echinus Geyser** is the largest acidic geyser, but its eruptions are becoming more rare.

Mud Pots

In the Lower Geyser Basin, **Pocket Basin Mud Pots** has the largest concentration of mud pots in the park. Iron oxides tint the **Fountain Paint Pots** pink, beige, and gray, while **Artist Paintpots** spew pastels.

Fumaroles

In Norris Geyser Basin, **Black Growler** is known for its grumbling noise. It reaches temperatures of 300°F (149°C). **Roaring Mountain** is a mountainside collection of fumaroles that earned its name from its constant hissing.

Hot Springs

In the Midway Geyser Basin, **Grand Prismatic Springs** is the largest hot spring at 370 feet in diameter and 121 feet deep. It radiates stunning colors from its blue center to orange and brown rays.

Supervolcano Caldera

The rim of Yellowstone's caldera is larger than the Lower Grand Loop Road. Stand near the rim at **Lake Butte,** near **Gibbon Falls,** and near **Lewis Falls.**

Teton Fault

The 44-mile-long **Teton Fault** runs along the base of the Teton Mountains with a 30,000-foot offset where the mountains rise and Jackson Hole sinks.

Glacial Features

In the Tetons, **Cascade Canyon** shows the U-shape of glacial carving and the glacier's terminal moraine that impounded Jenny Lake.

Canyons

Grand Canyon of the Yellowstone shows the V-shape of fast-carving water, thanks to repeated floods from collapsing ice dams. The **Snake River** through Jackson Hole is carved by the river's slower erosion.

Minerva Terrace at Mammoth Hot Springs

Look for yellow-bellied marmots sun-soaking on rocks.

Grab the binoculars and spotting scopes. Wildlife-watching is rampant in the Greater Yellowstone Ecosystem.

YELLOWSTONE

Swan Lake Flat: South of Mammoth, Swan Lake Flat in Gardners Hole yields frequent sightings of bears, birds, elk, bison, and wolves.

Lamar Valley: Driving into Lamar Valley catapults visitors back to the days of Lewis and Clark with a seemingly endless herd of bison. Pronghorn antelope feed between the bison, and wolves cruise through looking for the old or infirm. You can also spot bighorn sheep and mountain goats near cliffs on the surrounding mountains.

Madison River: In fall, watch bugling bull elk round up harems of cows. Bison often block traffic on the road. Deer munch grass on the fringes of the meadows, and trumpeter swans float in slow-moving eddies.

Hayden Valley: Spot larger animals in Hayden Valley as well as trumpeter swans. Bison feed next to the Yellowstone River, and grizzly bears and moose use the area, too. Look for harlequin ducks in early summer at LeHardy Rapids.

Tower-Roosevelt: Bighorn sheep cluster in the cliffs for safety from predators around the Tower Fall area.

Mammoth Hot Springs: In the village of Mammoth Hot Springs, elk hang out on the lawns.

Fishing Bridge: During spawning season in June and July on the Yellowstone River, stand on the historic Fishing Bridge to see hundreds of wild cutthroat trout, plus bald eagles and grizzly bears as they fish.

Pelican Creek: In spring, Pelican Creek turns into a prime bear feeding area. Look also for bald eagles and moose.

GRAND TETON

Oxbow Bend: Below Jackson Lake Dam where the Snake River slows into convoluted backwaters, the habitat attracts moose, river otters, muskrats, songbirds, American pelicans, and bald eagles.

Mormon Row-Antelope Flats: Look for bison, pronghorn, coyote, sage grouse, and raptors such as American kestrels and northern harriers.

Teton Park Road: The sage meadows attract elk and bison. Look for raptors overhead.

Moose-Wilson Road: The wetlands on the road are home to beaver and moose while berry bushes and wild fruit trees attract grizzly bears.

Death Canyon: Spot yellow-bellied marmots scampering around the rocks.

JACKSON HOLE

On the **National Elk Refuge,** thousands of elk winter before returning to the mountains. The refuge is also habitat for mountain lions, trumpeter swans, bighorn sheep, and raptors.

Winter Fun

bison in winter

Most lodges and roads inside Yellowstone and Grand Teton close in winter, which means solitude is guaranteed for those who enter these winter wonderlands.

- **Cross-country ski** or **snowshoe** on groomed roads or ungroomed snow-buried trails in both parks.

- **Wildlife-watching** in each park offers opportunities to see bison, elk, wolves, coyote, bobcats, moose, and raptors appear.

- Heated **snowcoaches** tour Yellowstone departing from Mammoth, West Yellowstone, and Flagg Ranch to visit Old Faithful or Grand Canyon of the Yellowstone.

- Overnight at **Mammoth Hot Springs Hotel** or Old Faithful's **Snow Lodge.**

- Stay in **Yellowstone Expedition's yurt camp** for cross-country ski or snowshoe tours.

- **Snowmobile** to Old Faithful or Grand Canyon of the Yellowstone on guided trips from West Yellowstone, Mammoth, or Flagg Ranch.

- **Downhill ski** or **snowboard** at Jackson Hole Mountain Resort, Snow King Mountain, Grand Targhee Resort, or Big Sky Resort.

- **Skate or ski** on groomed trails at Rendezvous Trails (West Yellowstone), Lone Mountain Ranch (Big Sky), Grand Targhee (Teton Valley), Teton Pines (Jackson Hole), and Teton Park Road (between Taggart Trailhead and Jenny Lake).

- **Ice climb** at Exum Ice Park in Jackson or hire a professional guide for **backcountry skiing** or **ice climbing** inside Grand Teton.

- **Sleigh rides** in Jackson Hole or Big Sky Resort.

- Watch elk and bighorn sheep in the **National Elk Refuge** in Jackson Hole.

North Yellowstone

Exploring North Yellowstone . . . 45

Sights 49

Recreation 56

Entertainment and Shopping . . . 70

Food 71

Accommodations 75

Camping 80

Transportation and Services 83

Look for ★ to find recommended sights, activities, dining, and lodging.

Highlights

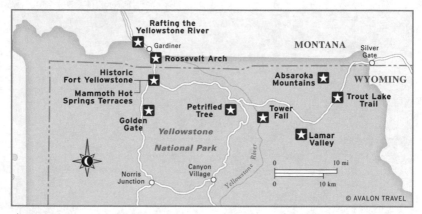

★ **Roosevelt Arch:** Built in 1903, the Roosevelt Arch offers an impressive entrance into Yellowstone National Park (page 49).

★ **Historic Fort Yellowstone:** Tour the stone building of the visitor center and walk the street of this former cavalry outpost while watching resident elk graze on the parade grounds (page 50).

★ **Mammoth Hot Springs Terraces:** Walk the lower formations of these otherworldly travertine terraces and drive through the dormant upper terraces (page 50).

★ **Golden Gate:** The road through Golden Gate climbs 1,500 feet in three miles to crest Kingman Pass, offering views of the amazing landscape (page 51).

★ **Petrified Tree:** A lone petrified tree trunk stands as a testament to ancient redwoods that used to populate Yellowstone in a wetter climate (page 53).

★ **Tower Fall:** This 132-foot-tall waterfall drops through a fantastical collection of rhyolite pinnacles (page 53).

★ **Lamar Valley:** Huge bison herds, elk, pronghorn antelope, bears, wolves, bighorn sheep, and raptors range across the valley known as "America's Serengeti." (page 54).

★ **Absaroka Mountains:** Forming the eastern boundary of Yellowstone, these mountains climb higher than 12,000 feet (page 55).

★ **Trout Lake Trail:** This short but steep grunt climbs to an idyllic subalpine lake surrounded by wildflower meadows and forest (page 63).

★ **Rafting the Yellowstone River:** Raft through the multicolored rock formations of Yankee Jim Canyon on the last major free-flowing river in the Lower 48 (page 65).

B alancing volcanic features and high mountains, North Yellowstone clings to the park's Montana-Wyoming border.

Slicing across North Yellowstone between the high Gallatin and Absaroka Mountains, sagebrush plateaus proliferate with wildlife. Elk hang out on the lawns in Mammoth Hot Springs. Bears and wolves hunt at Swan Lake Flat in Gardners Hole. Vast herds of bison congregate in Lamar Valley. Pronghorn race through sagebrush, bighorn sheep feed on steep slopes, and, higher yet, mountain goats walk the cliffs. Bring binoculars and spotting scopes for watching the action.

Beneath the landscape, hot water boils to the earth's surface. It spews out steaming in Mammoth Hot Springs, creating otherworldly sculptures of ever-changing colorful travertine. Soak up the smells, sounds, and sights on its boardwalks.

Between wildlife and hot springs, the Yellowstone River plunges through the narrow canyons alternating with pools in the flats. As the longest free-flowing river in the Lower 48, it provides clean passage for native trout to lure anglers to its waters.

Several small communities provide visitor services. Mammoth, a village once known as Fort Yellowstone, houses the visitors center, hotel, and restaurants. Five miles north, Gardiner borders the park's North Entrance, and serves as the capital for rafting, floating, and fishing the Yellowstone River. The tiny mountain outposts of Silver Gate and Cooke City flank the park's Northeast Entrance and anchor the Beartooth Highway.

PLANNING YOUR TIME

The road between Gardiner-Mammoth and Silver Gate-Cooke City remains open all year. In summer, most visitors spend a day or two in the northern section of the park to see Mammoth Hot Springs, raft the Yellowstone River, and watch wildlife. In winter, Gardiner and Mammoth can be a destination for several days of cross-country skiing, snowmobiling, and snowcoach touring.

Previous: Canary Springs at Mammoth Hot Springs; hiking Specimen Ridge. **Above:** a bison in Lamar.

North Yellowstone

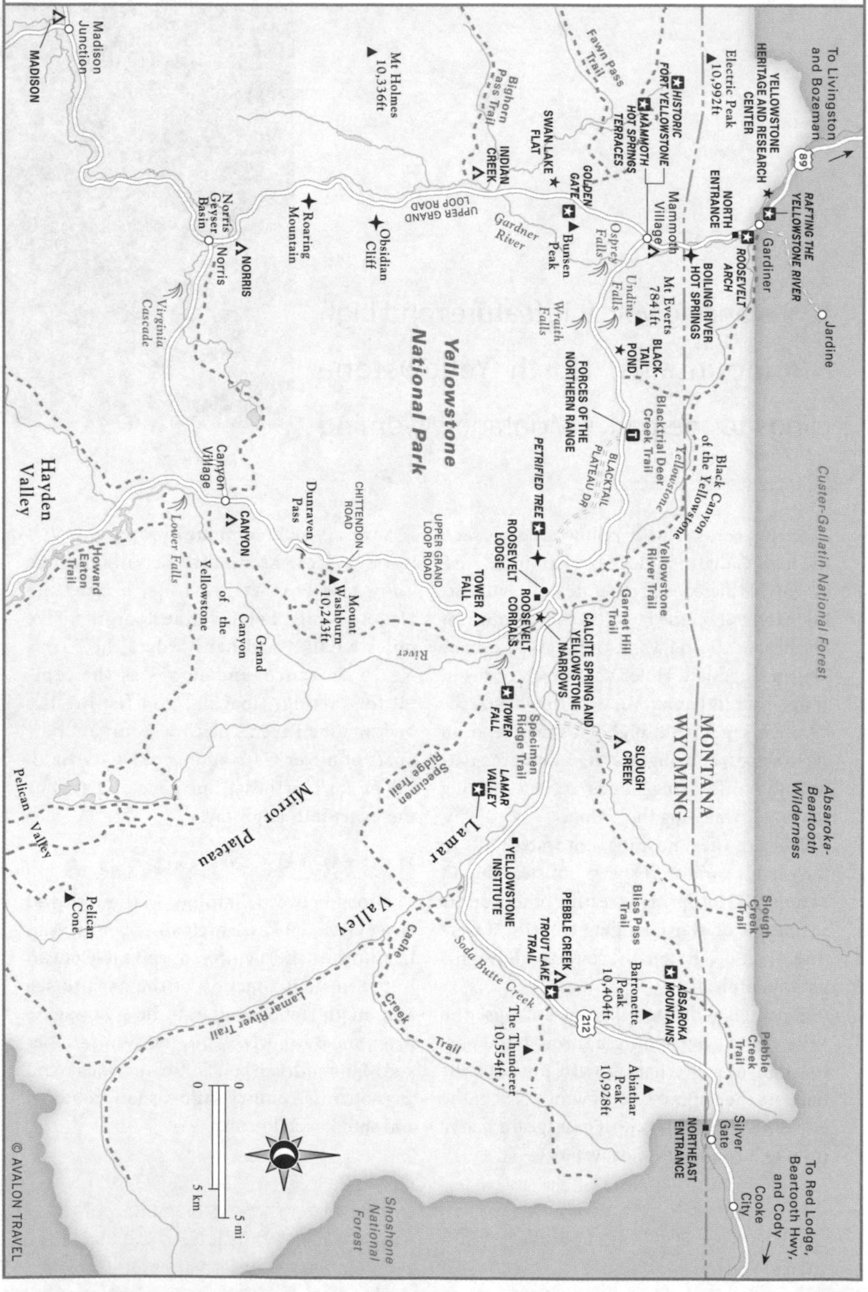

MADISON

Madison Junction

Mt. Holmes 10,336ft

Electric Peak 10,992ft

Bighorn Pass Trail

Fawn Pass Trail

YELLOWSTONE HERITAGE AND RESEARCH CENTER

To Livingston and Bozeman

89

RAFTING THE YELLOWSTONE RIVER

HISTORIC FORT YELLOWSTONE

MAMMOTH HOT SPRINGS TERRACES

SWAN LAKE FLAT

INDIAN CREEK

GOLDEN GATE

Mammoth Village

NORTH ENTRANCE

ROOSEVELT ARCH

Gardiner

Jardine

Norris Geyser Basin

Roaring Mountain

Obsidian Cliff

UPPER GRAND LOOP ROAD

Bunsen Peak

Osprey Falls

Gardner River

Undine Falls

Mt. Everts 7841ft

BOILING RIVER HOT SPRINGS

BLACK TAIL POND

NORRIS

Virginia Cascade

Yellowstone National Park

Wraith Falls

FORCES OF THE NORTHERN RANGE

Blacktail Deer Creek Trail

BLACKTAIL PLATEAU DR.

Black Canyon of the Yellowstone

Yellowstone River

Custer-Gallatin National Forest

Absaroka-Beartooth Wilderness

Hayden Valley

Canyon Village

CANYON

Dunraven Pass

CHITTENDEN ROAD

Mount Washburn 10,243ft

UPPER GRAND LOOP ROAD

PETRIFIED TREE

ROOSEVELT LODGE

TOWER FALL

ROOSEVELT CORRALS

CALCITE SPRING AND YELLOWSTONE NARROWS

Garnet Hill Trail

Yellowstone River Trail

MONTANA

WYOMING

Slough Creek Trail

Lower Falls

Grand Canyon of the Yellowstone

Yellowstone River

Mirror Plateau

Speciman Ridge Trail

TOWER FALL

LAMAR VALLEY

YELLOWSTONE INSTITUTE

SLOUGH CREEK

Bliss Pass Trail

Pebble Creek Trail

Pelican Valley

Pelican Cone

Howard Eaton Trail

Speciman Ridge Trail

Lamar Valley

Cache Creek

Soda Butte Creek

PEBBLE CREEK

TROUT LAKE

ABSAROKA MOUNTAINS

Barronette Peak 10,404ft

212

The Thunderer 10,554ft

Abiathar Peak 10,928ft

NORTHEAST ENTRANCE

Silver Gate

Cooke City

To Red Lodge, Beartooth Hwy., and Cooke and Cody

Lamar River Trail

Shoshone National Forest

0 5 mi
0 5 km

© AVALON TRAVEL

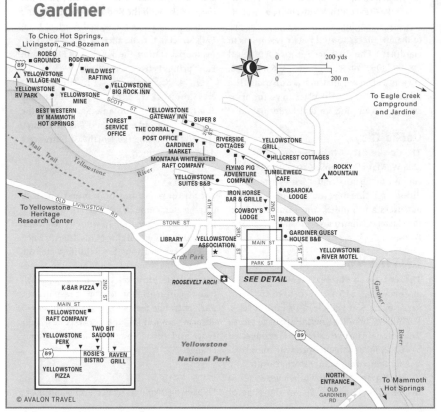

Exploring North Yellowstone

VISITORS CENTERS
Albright Visitor Center

The renovated **Albright Visitor Center** (307/344-2263, 8am-7pm daily June-Sept., 9am-5pm daily Oct.-May) is located in Mammoth Hot Springs, with elk often hanging out on the front lawn. One of the historic buildings from the days when the U.S. Cavalry ran the park, the red-tiled roof, brick structure, and large-columned veranda retain the look of Fort Yellowstone when it served as quarters for bachelor officers. The visitors center has park maps, trail information, brochures, updates, and a **backcountry office** (8am-4:30pm daily June-Aug.) with permits for backcountry camping, boating, and fishing. In 2016, new exhibits were added on cultural history, wildlife, and the northern area of the park. **Yellowstone Forever** (406/848-2400, www.yellowstone.org) operates a small bookstore inside.

Gardiner

The **Gardiner Chamber of Commerce** (216 Park St., Gardiner, 406/848-7971, www.gardinerchamber.com) maintains an information center. While it lacks exhibits, it is a good place to get information on Gardiner, the Custer-Gallatin National Forest, and the Absaroka-Beartooth Wilderness, as well as recreation, lodging, and dining. (It is also one of the few places to find public restrooms in Gardiner.) The **Custer-Gallatin National Forest** (805 Scott St., Gardiner, 406/848-7485, www.fs.usda.gov/gallatin) has a district office in Gardiner, and is the place to go for maps and forest, camping, and trail information.

Cooke City

The **Cooke City Chamber of Commerce** (206 W. Main St., Cooke City, 406/838-2495) runs a tiny visitors center with current conditions on the Beartooth Highway, local outfitters and guides, and information on the Custer-Gallatin and Shoshone National Forests.

ENTRANCE STATIONS

Two **entrance stations** ($30 vehicle, $25 motorcycles, $15 hike-in/bike-in; joint parks pass: $50 vehicle, $40 motorcycles, $20 hike-in/bike-in) provide access to North Yellowstone. The two entrances are connected by a 52-mile road that is open year-round (except for temporary winter storm closures).

The **North Entrance** (open year-round) sits on U.S. Highway 89 on the edge of Gardiner, Montana. Smaller vehicles can enter the park through the Roosevelt Arch; RVs and trailers should take the signed shortcut from Park Street to the entrance station. After passing the pay station, the park hub of Mammoth Hot Springs is five miles south.

On U.S. Highway 212, the remote **Northeast Entrance** is west of Silver Gate and Cooke City, Montana. Snow closes the roads east of Cooke City (mid-Oct.-late May), effectively making the Northeast Entrance a dead end in winter.

TOURS

For all tours (winter or summer), plan to bring water, cameras, and layers of clothing for changeable weather. In winter, add gloves, a hat, and winter walking boots. Clarify when making reservations for wildlife-watching tours whether binoculars and spotting scopes are available. Most tours do not include lunch (ask to confirm), but do stop at restaurants. Park entrance fees and guide gratuities (15 percent) are not included in the rates. Tour costs and times vary seasonally and may change.

Bus Tours

Departing from Gardiner and Mammoth,

Gardiner's main street

the **Yellowstone in a Day** tour (Xanterra, 307/344-7311 or 866/439-7375, www.yellowstonenationalparklodges.com, 7:30am-6:30pm daily mid-June-mid-Sept., $118-125 adults, $59-62 children 3-11) circles the 142-mile Grand Loop Road to hit the big places: Old Faithful, Yellowstone Lake, and Grand Canyon of the Yellowstone.

Stagecoach Adventure

For a taste of early western travel, take a stagecoach tour with the **Stagecoach Adventure** (Xanterra, 307/344-7311 or 866/439-7375, www.yellowstonenationalparklodges.com, daily early June-early Sept., $15 adults, $8 children 3-11). From the Roosevelt Corrals, the half-hour ride in a replica stagecoach gives a glimpse into the park's history, and authenticity comes from the dust. The brave can ride up top.

Wildlife Tours

Yellowstone Forever Institute (406/848-2400, www.yellowstone.org) offers expert-led educational tours year-round. Naturalist guides take you to various locations aboard institute buses to watch wildlife. While some programs are high energy, others are more like tours. Private tours, one-day, and multiday programs are available with varied locations and rates. Multi-day programs base from park hotels, Lamar Buffalo Ranch Field Campus, or Yellowstone Overlook Field Campus (Gardiner, Montana).

Xanterra (307/344-7311 or 866/439-7375, www.yellowstonenationalparklodges.com) operates wildlife watching tours in summer and winter. Reservations are required. In summer, vintage 1930 touring sedans hold 13 passengers and feature roll-back canvas tops for easy wildlife-watching. Children age 3-11 are half price. **Wake Up to Wildlife** (daily late May-mid-Sept., $95) departs from Mammoth Hotel (6:15am-11:30am) or Roosevelt Lodge (7am-11am) to explore the Lamar Valley. Juice and muffins are included for breakfast. **Evening Wildlife Encounters** (4:15pm-8:30pm daily late May-mid-Aug.,

3:45pm-8pm daily mid-Aug.-mid-Sept., $67) depart from Mammoth on a tour of Tower-Roosevelt and Lamar Valley. In winter, tours depart from Mammoth Hotel in vans and buses for wildlife-watching in Lamar Valley. Juice and muffins for breakfast are included. **Wake Up to Winter Wildlife** (6:45am-11am daily mid-Dec.-early Mar., $76) offers a four-hour option while the **Lamar Valley Wildlife Tour** (7am-2pm Mon., Thurs., and Sat. mid-Dec.-Feb., $130) extends to seven hours.

Winter Tours

Mid-December through early March, visitors can tour the snow-buried roads of Yellowstone in heated snowcoaches, which are converted vans or buses with huge tires or tracks, or on snowmobiles. Reservations are required. Snowcoach fares for children are half price. Plan to tip your guides 15 percent.

From Mammoth Hot Springs Hotel, **Xanterra** (307/344-7311 or 866/439-7375, www.yellowstonenationalparklodges.com) leads winter snowcoach tours. The **Grand Canyon Day Tour** (8:15am-5pm Tues., Thurs., and Sat., $204) visits Norris Geyser Basin and the Grand Canyon of the Yellowstone. Bring a lunch or order one the night before from the Mammoth Hot Springs Dining Room. The **Norris Geyser Basin Tour** (12:30pm-5:30pm Tues., Thurs., and Sat.-Sun., $89) visits the geothermal basin south of Mammoth.

Departing from Gardiner, **Yellowstone Year-Round Safaris** (905 Scott St., Gardiner, 406/848-7311 or 800/828-9080, www.yellowstoneyearroundsafaris.com, 7am-5:30pm daily mid-Dec.-Feb., $180) guides full-day snowcoach tours to Old Faithful or the Grand Canyon of the Yellowstone. The company also guides snowmobile tours ($315-350) to both locations. Sack lunches are provided.

DRIVING TOURS
Gardiner to Cooke City
52 MILES

The road between the **North Entrance Station** at Gardiner and the **Northeast**

Entrance Station at Silver Gate and Cooke City is the only road in Yellowstone **open year-round** to private cars and RVs. The road is plowed in winter, but snowstorms can cause temporary closures in the fall, winter, and spring. For current road conditions, call 307/344-2117. Plan on about **2 hours** (one way) for this tour. Add on more time for stops.

The two-lane road starts as U.S. Highway 89 in Gardiner, Montana on Park Street. Drive under the **Roosevelt Arch** (RVs take the signed shortcut) to reach the entrance station. The road then climbs five miles south through ancient mudflows, crossing the **45th Parallel** at the bridge over the Gardner River about half way, then hitting the Montana/Wyoming state line.

From **Mammoth Hot Springs to Tower Junction** (18 miles, 45 min.) the route follows **Grand Loop Road.** Stop to see **Undine Falls** and the **Petrified Tree.** Between the two sights, **Blacktail Plateau Drive** (6 miles, 30 min., July-early Nov., no RVs or trailers) offers a scenic detour on a curvy, dirt, one-way road. The route gains territorial views, goes through fire successions, and is good habitat for elk, bears, and bison.

From Tower Junction to the Northeast Entrance (29 miles, 60 min.), the route crosses the **Yellowstone River** into **Lamar Valley** and swings northeast along **Soda Butte Creek** into the **Absaroka Mountains.** After Pebble Creek, the road climbs into narrow **Ice Box Canyon,** flanked by frozen waterfalls in winter-early spring. At the Northeast Entrance, the road exits Yellowstone and enters the tiny blink-and-you-miss-it villages of **Silver Gate** and **Cooke City.** In winter (Nov.-May), the route dead-ends at Cooke City due to snowbound roads, but in summer,

you can connect with the 68-mile Beartooth Highway (late May-Oct.).

Upper Grand Loop Road
70 MILES

Upper Grand Loop Road links **Mammoth Hot Springs** with **Norris Geyser Basin, Canyon Village,** and **Tower-Roosevelt.** The road east from Mammoth to Tower Junction (18 miles, 45 min.) is open year-round; all other segments of the Upper Grand Loop Road are closed in winter. You can drive the entire loop (late May-early Nov.) in three hours; stops and side trips add time.

Between Mammoth Hot Springs and Norris Junction (21 miles, 45 min., late Apr.-early Nov.), U.S. Highway 89 serves as the **park road.** From Mammoth, the road climbs south through the hoodoos, monster travertine boulders formed by a landslide on Terrace Mountain. It then crawls along the cliffs of **Golden Gate** before topping out at **Swan Lake Flat,** where you can often spot wolves and bison. Continuing south, you'll pass **Obsidian Cliff,** a site of geological, Native American, and historical significance. Stop again at **Roaring Mountain** to listen to the thermal activity and look for trumpeter swans in nearby **Twin Lakes.** Your first leg ends at the **Norris Geyser Basin,** a hotbed of geothermal activity.

From the Norris Junction, the park road turns east toward **Canyon Village** (12 miles, 30 min., late Apr.-early Nov.). Continue the loop north from Canyon Village to reach **Tower Junction** (19 miles, 45 min., late May-early Nov.). The road climbs over Dunraven Pass before descending to Tower Fall and the Tower-Roosevelt area before returning west to Mammoth.

Sights

NORTH ENTRANCE

Bordering the national park, **Gardiner, Montana,** is a small town of about 875 permanent residents that sees 700,000 visitors, mostly in summer. The Yellowstone River runs through the middle of town, making it the rafting capital for those visiting the park. The Roosevelt Arch sits on the south edge of town, marking the historic park entrance.

Yellowstone Heritage and Research Center

Located in Gardiner, the **Yellowstone Heritage and Research Center** (20 Old Yellowstone Trail, 307/344-2664, 8am-5pm Mon.-Fri.) houses the park archives and library, museum collections, historian, archaeology lab, and herbarium. The lobby rotates small exhibits, but the facility is primarily for research and storage for 5.3 million archived items, including 30 historical vehicles. Public tours are available by reservation (307/344-2264, 2pm Wed. in summer, free).

★ Roosevelt Arch

Roosevelt Arch may be one of the best human-built park entrances in the country. The original entrance road crosses under the stone-and-mortar arch dedicated to President Theodore Roosevelt, who laid the cornerstone in 1903. Reconstruction of Park Street, the viewing park and amphitheater, and the arch area for the 2016 anniversary of the National Park Service has improved access for photographing the arch. The reconstruction also re-opened walkway doors. A signed shortcut road lets large RVs bypass the narrow entrance through the arch, but cars can still drive through it. To walk around the arch and **Arch Park,** park on Park Street.

45th Parallel

On U.S. Highway 89, the **45th Parallel** marks the latitude halfway between the North Pole and the equator. A tiny pullout and sign allows for a photo-op. Find it 2.5 miles south of Gardiner and 2.5 miles north of Mammoth Hot Springs.

Roosevelt Arch is the historic entrance to Yellowstone.

Mammoth Hot Springs

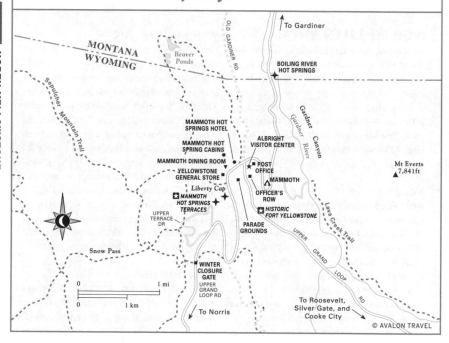

To Gardiner

MONTANA
WYOMING

Beaver
Ponds

OLD GARDINER RD

BOILING RIVER
HOT SPRINGS

Sepulcher Mountain Trail

Gardner Canyon

Gardner River

MAMMOTH HOT
SPRINGS HOTEL

MAMMOTH HOT
SPRING CABINS

ALBRIGHT
VISITOR CENTER

Mt Everts
▲ 7,841ft

MAMMOTH DINING ROOM

YELLOWSTONE
GENERAL STORE

■ POST
OFFICE

Liberty Cap

MAMMOTH

☒ MAMMOTH
HOT SPRINGS
TERRACES

OFFICER'S
ROW

UPPER
TERRACE
DR

☒ HISTORIC
FORT YELLOWSTONE

Lava Creek Trail

PARADE
GROUNDS

Snow Pass

UPPER GRAND LOOP

WINTER
CLOSURE
GATE

UPPER
GRAND
LOOP RD

0   1 mi

0   1 km

To Norris

To Roosevelt,
Silver Gate, and
Cooke City

© AVALON TRAVEL

MAMMOTH HOT SPRINGS

Open year-round, Mammoth Village is home to the Albright Visitor Center, Mammoth Hot Springs Hotel, historic Fort Yellowstone, a campground, a picnic area, and other services. But the main attractions are the stately elk that often lounge on lawns and the fantastical sculptures of the hot springs travertine terraces. Mammoth is not a spa, nor does it have developed hot springs for soaking.

★ Historic Fort Yellowstone

In the pre-National Park Service decades, the village of Mammoth was **Fort Yellowstone** when the U.S. Cavalry managed the park. A self-guided walking tour visits the streets of stone buildings erected by the army between 1891 and 1916. Start at **Albright Visitor Center** (307/344-2263, 9am-5pm daily year-round), once the Bachelor Officer's Quarters,

where you can pick up an interpretive brochure ($1). Across from the visitors center, the **parade grounds** (sometimes called the drill field) are covered with sagebrush and wandering bison or elk. Walk down the row of houses to see the **Captain's Quarters, Field Officer's Quarters,** and **Officer's Quarters.** Today, most of the buildings house park service personnel and their families or serve as supply depots and offices; as such, they are not open to the public. Additional sights include the **granary, chapel, hospital, blacksmith,** and **stables.**

★ Mammoth Hot Springs Terraces
LOWER TERRACE

Raised boardwalks and stairways loop 1.75 miles through the lower terrace of **Mammoth Hot Springs,** where limestone creates travertine terraces. The boardwalks offer an opportunity to view the changing calcium carbonate sculptures, and sulfur fills the air. From the parking lot, be ready to climb 300 feet in elevation to reach the Upper Terrace.

Access the boardwalk at one of three lower parking lots on the park road south of Mammoth Village, or walk there from the Albright Visitor Center. To start, follow the northwest boardwalk to see **Liberty Cap,** a 37-foot-tall dormant hot springs cone. Across the street from Liberty Cap is **Opal Spring,** which amasses a new foot of travertine every year. Past Liberty Cap, a spur on the right leads to the colorful **Palette Spring,** where thermophiles create orange and brown colors. Continue on the main boardwalk to circle the loop around **Minerva Terrace,** known for its striking travertine sculptures that alternate between watery and dry. **Cleopatra, Mound,** and **Jupiter Terraces** flank the stair climbs to the overlook at the Upper Terrace Drive parking lot. A spur boardwalk with steps heads left to the striking orange and brilliant white sinter **Canary Spring.**

UPPER TERRACE

At Mammoth Hot Springs, the 0.75-mile, one-way, single-lane **Upper Terrace Drive** (mid-May-early Nov.) snakes through unique limestone features created from once-active hydrothermals. From several locations, walk to overlooks for views of the Gallatin Mountains, the village below, the lower terraces, and **Canary Spring.** Drive by the striking **Orange Spring Mound.** The narrow, curvy loop drive squeezes between firs and junipers; trailers or RVs over 25 feet are prohibited. Locate the entrance to the Upper Terrace about two miles south of Mammoth Village on the road toward Norris.

MAMMOTH TO NORRIS

From Mammoth Hot Springs in the north, U.S. Highway 89 (mid-Apr.-early Nov.) leads 21 miles south to Norris, which is anchored by a campground and geyser basin.

★ Golden Gate

Driving south from Mammoth, the curvy road climbs 1,500 feet in three miles on a cliff-clinging viaduct to reach Kingman Pass. The passage through Glen Creek Canyon is known as the **Golden Gate,** named for the vivid color of yellow lichens on the rhyolite cliffs. While the road has been rebuilt several times, its first incarnation in 1884 was a rickety wooden trestle bridge. A unique **rock pillar,** which was moved with each reconstruction of the road, sits at the bottom of the climb, while

Boardwalks tour the Mammoth Hot Springs Terraces.

at the top, **Rustic Falls** sprays down 47 feet of natural stair-step stones. **Bunsen Peak,** a cone volcano, looms above. Find an overlook on the east side of the road between the rock pillar and falls to view them.

Swan Lake Flat

Wildlife frequents **Swan Lake Flat,** and so do wildlife-watchers. Bring the binoculars, cameras, and telephoto lenses. Located on the Grand Loop Road about five miles south of Mammoth (look for a small parking lot on the west side), the sagebrush prairie of Swan Lake Flat in Gardners Hole offers a great chance to see gray wolves, grizzly bears, and elk. Tiny Swan Lake, which once filled the entire flat, often houses trumpeter swans in summer, along with other waterfowl. The vast, open, high-elevation valley makes for a broad arena, where almost any movement is visible. In winter, look for bison.

Obsidian Cliff

Located between Mammoth and Norris on the east side of Grand Loop Road, the half-mile-long **Obsidian Cliff,** a National Historic Landmark and archaeological site, resulted from a 180,000-year-old rhyolite lava flow that crystallized. Look closely to see the shiny black volcanic glass bits of obsidian in the layers, but do so with binoculars or from a car as the site is closed to exploring. Early natives in the area quarried the sharp obsidian for making knives, arrowheads, and other tools. North of the cliff on the west side of the road, the **Obsidian Cliff interpretive kiosk** is one of the first interpretive exhibits created by the National Park Service.

Roaring Mountain

Five miles north of Norris Geyser Basin, the seemingly barren hillside of **Roaring Mountain** is riddled with fumaroles. Steam billows from multiple vents across the hillside. While the roar has lessened considerably in the past century, you can still hear the hissing when you get out of your vehicle at the

Golden Gate

interpretive site, which was revamped in 2015. Excessive tree-killing heat, gases, and billowing steam make the hillside look like the aftermath of a fire. Some thermophiles survive in this toxic environment. Steam is more visible in early morning, evening, or winter.

MAMMOTH TO TOWER-ROOSEVELT

From the village at Mammoth Hot Springs, the **Upper Grand Loop Road** heads east for 19 miles across the Blacktail Deer Plateau to Tower Junction. Bison jams and congested traffic are common along this road.

Undine Falls

Drive four miles east on the Grand Loop Road and look for a pullout for Undine Falls on the north side of the road. Lava Creek drops over a lava cliff formed about 700,000 years ago; **Undine Falls,** named for water spirits in German mythology, cascades 60 feet down three shelves.

Blacktail Pond

Blacktail Pond offers an opportunity for wildlife-watching, particularly for sandhill cranes, Canada geese, waterfowl, and bald eagles in spring; you can also spot pronghorn and bison. Look for a pullout on the north side of the road about six miles east of Mammoth.

Forces of the Northern Range

About two miles east of Blacktail Pond and eight miles east of Mammoth, look for an interpretive boardwalk on the north side of Grand Loop Road. This easy 0.5-mile board-walk loop tours the Northern Range through an open sagebrush plateau, aspens, and younger lodgepole pines. The **self-guided interpretive loop** is one of the best ways to learn about northern Yellowstone's wildlife, wildflowers, trees, geology, landscape, and scenery.

★ Petrified Tree

Tucked off a side road about 0.8 mile west of Tower Junction, a lone **Petrified Tree** trunk stands on a steep hillside. Once a giant ancient redwood, the now-petrified tree is a clue to the wetter forests that covered the area prior to a supervolcano eruption. A 0.25-mile path leads to the solidified tree. (Ravaged by souvenir seekers, this specimen is now fenced off for protection.)

TOWER-ROOSEVELT
Calcite Spring

The **Calcite Spring** loop connects 0.2 mile of boardwalks with platforms. From the overlook above the **Narrows of the Yellowstone River**, you can see basalt columns from lava across the gorge, the springs at the river level, and the **Yellowstone River** about 500 feet below. The calcite spring itself emits minerals that color the slope white and yellow. The parking lot is 1.6 miles south of Tower Junction.

★ Tower Fall

Tower Fall plunges 132 feet from its brink between rhyolite spires, dropping from a

petrified tree

Tower Fall

hanging valley into a ribbon that spews in a long freefall. An overlook, located 0.1 mile from the Tower Fall parking lot, offers the best view. Due to a washout in 2004, the viewing platform and trail to the base of the falls are closed. Find the site 2.3 miles south of Tower Junction.

NORTHEAST ENTRANCE
Yellowstone River

The **Yellowstone River** tumbles through the Narrows of the Yellowstone, slicing between the Buffalo and Blacktail Deer Plateaus, before plunging through the Black Canyon of the Yellowstone and exiting the park at Gardiner. About 0.7-mile on the Northeast Entrance Road northeast of Tower Junction, the road plunges to a high bridge crossing the river. On the north side of the road, a pullout is just before the bridge and a trailhead just after. These offer the best spots for viewing the river far below. Be cautious walking on the bridge due to traffic and a lack of walkway.

Slough Creek

Slough Creek is often packed with wildlife-watchers sporting scopes. The dirt Slough Creek Road has a few pullouts that offer a vast territorial view where you can spy wolves, bears, bighorn sheep, bison, and pronghorn. Bring binoculars, but you may be able to sneak a peek through someone else's scope. Most wildlife-watchers enjoy sharing what they are seeing. To get there from Tower Junction, drive 5.8 miles east on the Northeast Entrance Road and turn left onto Slough Creek Road.

★ Lamar Valley

Park guides often refer to the massive **Lamar Valley** as America's Serengeti due to its hefty numbers of wildlife. The Lamar River flows through the sagebrush valley where immense herds of bison feed. Between herds, look for pronghorn, bighorn sheep, elk, bears, coyotes, and wolves. The valley also provides rich hunting grounds for predators. In late fall, listen for bighorn sheep crash-butting heads or elk bugling as displays of dominance. The **Yellowstone Forever Institute's** Lamar Buffalo Ranch Field Campus is also located in this valley. (Access is via registered programs only at www.yellowstone.org.)

From Tower Junction, follow the Northeast Entrance Road east past the turnoff for Slough Creek. Multiple pullouts along the road allow for observation. Wildlife is most active at dawn and dusk; bring spotting scopes, cameras, and binoculars.

herds of bison in Lamar Valley

Exploring the Yellowstone River

The 692-mile Yellowstone River is the park's longest river and the last free-flowing major river in the Lower 48. From Yellowstone Lake, it gushes through the **Grand Canyon of the Yellowstone** before squeezing through the **Narrows** and plunging through the **Black Canyon of the Yellowstone** to Gardiner and Montana's **Yankee Jim Canyon**. So how can visitors best enjoy it?

- **Sightseeing:** To see the Yellowstone River with minimal effort, go to the bridges in Gardiner or northeast of Tower Junction. Also, the boardwalk overlooking Calcite Springs looks 500 feet down to the blue water.

- **Hiking:** Several hiking trails overlook the Yellowstone River: the **Narrows of the Yellowstone**, **Garnet Hill**, and **Black Canyon of the Yellowstone**.

- **Fishing:** In Montana, the bulk of the river has been classified as **blue-ribbon trout fishing**, the highest rating for the state's fisheries. The lack of dams aids in promoting movement of trout from the upper to lower elevations. Among the trout, anglers can catch native Yellowstone cutthroat. Inside the park, anglers don waders for fishing or cast from the shore in the reaches around the bridge east of Tower Junction, Garnet Hill Loop Trail, Black Canyon of the Yellowstone, and outside the park at fishing access sites west of Gardiner. Below Gardiner, fishing companies take anglers fly-fishing via rafts or dories.

- **Rafting:** Inside the park, no floating is permitted on the river. But outside the park, Class I-IV white water attracts rafters and kayakers. **Yankee Jim Canyon** provides four river miles of rugged scenery and splashy fun. **Gardiner** has five rafting companies that get people on the river for scenic floats or white-water paddling.

Soda Butte

As the Northeast Entrance Road swings north from the Lamar Valley, it follows **Soda Butte Creek,** a popular fly-fishing stream for its ease of access and productive trout fishery. The creek is named for the extinct geyser that left a large white cone called **Soda Butte**. Look for the interpretive sign and pullout on the east side of the road.

★ Absaroka Mountains

In Yellowstone's northeast corner, the **Absaroka Mountains** (pronounced Ab-zor-ka) stretch into high rugged peaks more than 11,000 feet high. From Soda Butte, drive northwest for 14 miles on the Northeast Entrance Road to tour the mountains. As the road climbs past **Pebble Creek** and swings east, it squeezes through **Ice Box Canyon**, where Soda Butte Creek has carved a narrow passageway. In winter and early spring, the canyon displays frozen walls from water seeps. Past the canyon, the road climbs a high-elevation, forested valley tucked below **Barronette Peak**, which spouts with waterfalls in May. Scan its precipitous cliffs for mountain goats. With fewer visitors, this region of the park offers solitude.

Soda Butte Creek in the Absaroka Mountains

Recreation

DAY HIKES

National Park Service rangers lead free, **guided hikes** (www.nps.gov/yell, daily or several times weekly, early June-early Sept.) that tour the Mammoth Hot Springs Terraces and Wraith Falls. They provide educational details on the natural history of the travertine terraces at the hot springs and the ecology of the Wraith Falls environment. Check in at the Albright Visitor Center for a current schedule and location of where to meet.

Guided Hikes

Expert-led educational hikes are also available through **Yellowstone Forever Institute** (406/848-2400, www.yellowstone.org, year-round). Private tours, one-day, and multi-day programs are available with varied rates. Hiking programs include day hikes and backpacking trips. Some of the hiking programs operate out of the institute's cabin complex in Lamar Valley.

Operating out of Gardiner, **Yellowstone YearRound Adventures** (406/585-9041,

North Yellowstone Hikes

Trail	Effort	Distance	Duration	Features
Wraith Falls	Easy	0.8 mi rt	45 min	waterfall
Trout Lake Trail	Easy	1.2 mi rt	1 hr	lake
Lost Lake Loop	Moderate	4 mi rt	2.5 hr	lake, petrified tree, waterfall
Garnet Hill	Moderate	8 mi rt	4 hr	wildlife & views
Narrows of the Yellowstone River	Moderate	4 mi rt	2.5 hr	scenery & hot springs
Slough Creek	Moderate	4 mi rt	3 hr	fishing
Grizzly Lake	Moderate	4.2 mi rt	3 hr	lake
Beaver Pond Loop	Moderate	5 mi one-way	2.5 hr	scenery
Hellroaring Creek	Moderately strenuous	4 mi rt	3 hr	scenery, fishing
Specimen Ridge	Strenuous	3 mi rt	3-4 hr	petrified trees
Bunsen Peak and Osprey Falls	Strenuous	4.2-11.6 mi rt	3-7 hr	views, waterfall
Blacktail Deer Creek	Strenuous	7.4 mi rt	4-5 hr	scenery
Sepulcher Mountain	Strenuous	12.5 mi rt	7 hr	views
Black Canyon of the Yellowstone	Strenuous	13.5-16.9 mi rt	7-9 hr	river

Bunsen Peak Trail

of an old beaver pond split by a dam and then descends through open sagebrush meadows, Douglas fir forests, and aspen groves. The route ends on the Old Gardiner Road behind the Mammoth Hotel.

Mammoth to Norris
BUNSEN PEAK AND OSPREY FALLS

Distance: 4.2 miles round-trip or 6.6-11.6-mile loop
Duration: 3-7 hours
Elevation change: 1,278-2,058 feet
Effort: strenuous
Trailhead: Old Bunsen Peak Road Trailhead, 4.8 miles south of Mammoth on the east side of Grand Loop Road

The peak, a volcanic cone named for Robert Bunsen, who invented the Bunsen burner, contains a summit weather station with the building and connecting power lines posing a minor disruption to the wilderness feel. In summer, go early to nab a parking spot at the popular trailhead.

Starting in a sagebrush meadow, the trail climbs through steep forests, meadows, and 1988 burns to the 8,564-foot summit. Shortly after starting the climb, spot the Golden Gate from above along with Glen Creek Canyon hoodoos. The trail winds back and forth around the mountain, passing **Cathedral Rock** at 1.4 miles, where views plunge to Mammoth Hot Springs. Steep switchbacks then lead across talus slopes to the summit. The reward is the view of Electric Peak in the Gallatin Range and Gardners Hole. For the shortest hike, retrace your route back down. Or, for an alternative, drop eastward 1.4 steep miles through a burn zone to the **Old Bunsen Peak Road,** turning right to circle three gentle miles (shared by bikers) around the south of **Bunsen Peak** (6.6 miles total).

Strong hikers can lengthen the loop with a descent and return climb to see 150-foot **Osprey Falls** on the Gardner River. Descend eastward from the peak to the Old Bunsen Peak Road, then turn left to find the Osprey Falls Trailhead. From the trailhead, a 1.4-mile trail traverses the edge of Sheepeater Canyon

---

www.yellowstoneyearround.com, from $455 for 1-4 people) guides hikes for families and private small groups. Rates include the licensed guide, transportation to the trailhead from Gardiner, lunch, and snacks.

Mammoth
BEAVER POND LOOP

Distance: 5 miles one-way
Duration: 2.5 hours
Elevation change: 380 feet
Effort: moderate
Trailhead: in Mammoth Hot Springs between Liberty Cap and the stone house

Blooming with arrowleaf balsamroot, bluebells, and larkspur in June, Beaver Pond Loop is a good early-season hike when higher country still has snow. The route's meadows offer broad vistas of Bunsen Peak, Gardiner, and the Absaroka Mountains. Start with a one-mile climb up Clematis Creek. At the signed junction, turn right; the trail alternates between rolling, flat, or downhill terrain. About halfway, the trail waltzes along the shoreline with the basalt-columned Sheepeater Cliffs visible on the opposite side. Drop down steep, narrow, sunny switchbacks into the ravine below the falls. After climbing the 780 feet back up, follow the old road south around Bunsen Peak to return to your vehicle. Those wanting to avoid the Bunsen Peak climb can hike out and back on the old road to see Osprey Falls (8.8 miles, 780 feet elevation gain).

SEPULCHER MOUNTAIN

Distance: 12.5 miles round-trip
Duration: 7 hours
Elevation change: 2,366 feet
Effort: strenuous
Trailhead: Glen Creek Trailhead opposite Old Bunsen Peak Road Trailhead, 4.8 miles south of Mammoth

Sepulcher Mountain attracts hikers out for big views without the crowds of Bunsen Peak. But since the trail uses the same crowded parking lot at Bunsen Peak, you'll need to get an early start. The trail begins with a gentle 1.8-mile walk through sagebrush meadows below **Terrace Mountain,** home to bighorn sheep. Continue through several junctions where trails turn off to Fawn Pass, Snow Pass, and Sportsman Lake Trail. After the third turnoff, begin climbing the switchbacks up an open mountainside with views of Electric Peak. With less than 0.5 mile to go, the trail enters a forest before popping out on the summit for views of the Absaroka Mountains. A jaunt along the 9,652-foot **summit** yields more views, including the Yellowstone River and Gardiner far below.

Continue the loop by following the cliff edge and then descending through pines and meadows overlooking Mammoth Hot Springs. At the junction with the Clagett Butte Trail, turn right to climb uphill to the **Snow Pass Trail.** Turn right again for one mile to cross Snow Pass. Turn left to return back to Glen Creek Trailhead.

As an alternate descent for a point-to-point

hike, the route connects with trails to Mammoth Hot Springs. The Snow Pass Trail ends at the Upper Terrace, and the Clagett Butte Trail links to the trailhead adjacent to Liberty Cap.

GRIZZLY LAKE

Distance: 4.2 miles round-trip
Duration: 3 hours
Elevation change: 725 feet
Effort: moderate
Trailhead: a pullout on the west side of Grand Loop Road, 16 miles south of Mammoth

Start by crossing **Obsidian Creek** on a footbridge, one of many log bridges in the first 0.5 mile through this boggy marsh. Leaving the meadows, the trail climbs through a 1988 fire zone. Turn around for views of the valley you just crossed. On the ascent, the trail breaks into a meadow before reentering the burn with new lodgepoles. The trail then descends to **Grizzly Lake,** where anglers can fish for brook trout and yellow lilies grow along the shores.

Mammoth to Tower Junction
WRAITH FALLS

Distance: 0.8 mile round-trip
Duration: 45 minutes
Elevation change: 74 feet
Effort: easy
Trailhead: a pullout on the south side of Grand Loop Road, 0.5 mile east of Lava Creek Picnic Area east of Mammoth

Launch onto this trail by walking through a sagebrush-scented meadow blooming with columbine and buckwheat in early summer. An intermittent **boardwalk** crosses small streams and marshes. The route tucks in between coniferous tree islands, crosses Lupine Creek, and climbs one switchback to reach the viewing platform. The 79-foot **Wraith Falls** cascades down a wide-angled rock face squeezed into a canyon. In June, the water fills the full width, but by September, the water thins to appear like two parallel falls.

BLACKTAIL DEER CREEK

Distance: 7.4 miles round-trip
Duration: 4-5 hours
Elevation change: 1,340 feet
Effort: strenuous
Trailhead: Blacktail Deer Creek Trailhead on Grand Loop Road, 6.7 miles east of Mammoth

From the trailhead on the east end of **Blacktail Pond,** the route plunges to the Yellowstone River and the Black Canyon of the Yellowstone. On summer days, the treeless trail can be hot, especially on the return climb back up to the trailhead.

After crossing the Blacktail Pond valley, the trail climbs 130 feet in elevation over a sagebrush hill before dropping northward, passing the **Rescue Creek Trail** junction at 0.7 mile. The trail parallels **Blacktail Deer Creek** in its descent down the ravine to reach the suspension bridge at the **Yellowstone River.** The return climb is 1,210 feet in elevation back up. You can also add on another 0.5-mile round-trip to see **Crevice Lake.**

HELLROARING CREEK

Distance: 4 miles round-trip
Duration: 3 hours
Elevation change: 643 feet
Effort: moderately strenuous
Trailhead: Hellroaring Trailhead on Grand Loop Road, 3.5 miles west of Tower Junction

The trail takes a steep drop to the Yellowstone River and crosses the Buffalo Plateau to reach Hellroaring Creek, a prized angler destination. It requires a hefty climb on a hot, dusty, dry trail to return to the trailhead. The trail is popular with horseback riders, so be ready for manure and flies.

A one-mile plunge through a semi-forested hillside passes the **Garnet Hill Loop** junction before reaching the **suspension bridge** over the Yellowstone River. Cross the river and continue across the open, sagebrush Buffalo Plateau for 1.1 miles, passing a junction with the **Buffalo Plateau** and **Coyote Creek Trail.** Above **Hellroaring Creek,** the trail reaches the east-west path where you can go either direction. Go left

and then take the first spur right for the fastest access to the creek.

BLACK CANYON OF THE YELLOWSTONE

Distance: 13.5-16.9 miles round-trip
Duration: 7-9 hours
Elevation change: 2,036 feet
Effort: strenuous
Trailhead: Hellroaring Trailhead on Grand Loop Road, 3.5 miles west of Tower Junction

This point-to-point hike used to go to Gardiner, but that trailhead is now closed. Most hikers combine the **Hellroaring Creek Trail** and the **Yellowstone River Trail** through the Black Canyon, and climb out via **Blacktail Deer Creek.** You'll need two cars to set up a shuttle as the trailheads are eight miles apart. Carry plenty of water, be prepared for heat and dust, and take a map to aid with route-finding due to multiple side trails.

To connect the two trails when you reach **Hellroaring Creek,** you have two options. In late season when the water is low, drop to the river, ford it, and climb to the trail heading downstream to reach the Yellowstone River. In early summer when the water is too high, turn east instead to hike 3.7 miles northeast, crossing the river via **Hellroaring Creek Bridge** to reconnect with the trail on the opposite side. At the junction, head straight north for the **Yellowstone River Trail** through the Black Canyon, climbing and dropping multiple times above the river. In 6.9 miles, take the **Blacktail Deer Creek Trail** junction for 0.8 mile to reach the suspension bridge to cross back over the Yellowstone River and climb to the **Blacktail Deer Creek Trailhead.**

Tower-Roosevelt

LOST LAKE LOOP

Distance: 4 miles round-trip
Duration: 2.5 hours
Elevation change: 608 feet
Effort: moderate
Trailhead: behind Roosevelt Lodge, the Petrified Tree parking lot, or Tower Fall Campground

Hikers can start this trail from a variety of

Black Canyon of the Yellowstone

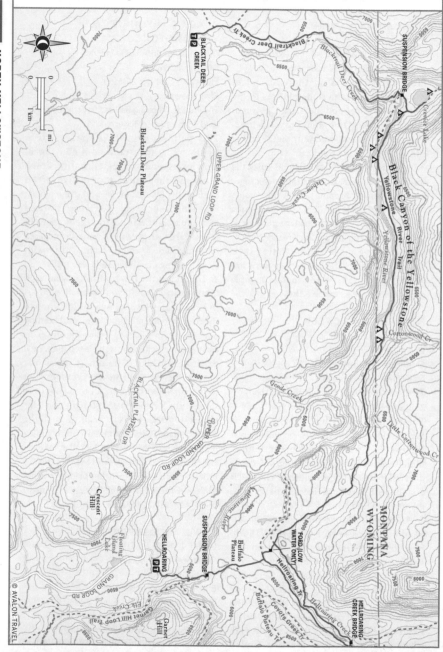

© AVALON TRAVEL

Lost Lake Loop

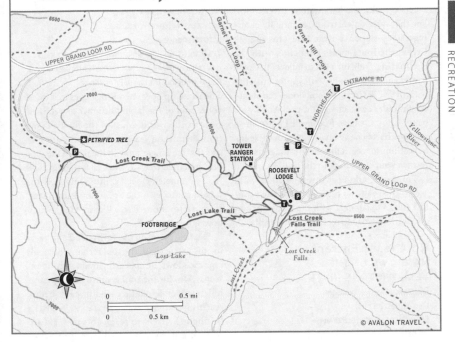

trailheads, and it has plenty of things to see: a waterfall, the small lake, Petrified Tree, and views of the Absaroka Mountains. The trail is also used by horses, which means you'll encounter manure and flies. If you run into horses, step to the downhill side of the trail unless the wrangler instructs otherwise. Remain still until they have passed.

From behind Roosevelt Lodge, take the left spur to the **Lost Creek Falls Trail** that climbs up a pine-shaded ravine to the 40-foot falls. Return to the junction to continue up the **Lost Lake Trail.** Switchbacks head up the steep hill to reach the small bridge at the lake's outlet. The trail rims the lake until it heads west through another ravine to **Petrified Tree.** From the Petrified Tree parking lot, the trail mounts a hill east to a sagebrush meadow before dropping to swing behind **Tower Ranger Station** and then around to Roosevelt Lodge.

GARNET HILL

Distance: 8 miles round-trip
Duration: 4 hours
Elevation change: 580 feet
Effort: moderate
Trailheads: Minimal parking is across the road from the main trailhead 0.3 mile northeast of Tower Junction on the Northeast Entrance Road. Alternate parking is at Tower Junction on the service road south of Upper Grand Loop Rd. between the gas station and Roosevelt Lodge entrance road.

Often frequented by pronghorn, bison, and elk, the trail loops through sagebrush and glacial erratics for its start and finish. Due to the wide-open terrain, plan to hike early on hot days. The north end of the loop passes through cooler forests flanking the Yellowstone River and Elk Creek before gaining elevation on the returns.

From the trailhead, hike 0.5 mile to a junction where you can go either direction to circle the forested bluff of Garnet Hill. Starting on the eastern side of the loop, the trail soon meets up with the Yellowstone River to follow the water downstream, eventually entering a steep-sloped canyon. After crossing Elk Creek, the route meets a junction with the Hellroaring Trail; turn left to follow Elk Creek upstream. In Pleasant Valley after crossing back over Elk Creek, several horse and stagecoach routes connect with the trail. You'll also pass Yancy's, where Roosevelt Lodge hosts outdoor barbecues. Stay left at all of these intersections to return to your first junction and retrace your steps back to the trailhead.

For those parking at Tower Junction, walk across the road and take the stagecoach trail to Yancy's to connect with the loop. You can also walk the road to reach the main trailhead.

Northeast Entrance
NARROWS OF THE YELLOWSTONE RIVER

Distance: 4 miles round-trip
Duration: 2.5 hours
Elevation change: 393 feet
Effort: easy
Trailhead: Yellowstone River Picnic Area Trailhead, 1.2 miles east of Tower Junction on the Northeast Entrance Road

A steep grunt uphill through sagebrush meadows with pink sticky geranium and arrowleaf balsamroot leads to the east rim of the Narrows of the Yellowstone River. The trail saunters along the rim above the deep canyon with several viewpoints. In one mile, the trail overlooks **Calcite Springs.** As it traverses a ridge 500 feet above the Yellowstone River, the route affords spectacular views of the narrows, sculpted minarets, and columnar basalt. It's also a good place to spot bighorn sheep, osprey, and peregrine falcons. Pronghorn cross the ridge, and marmots live in the rocks. In two miles, you'll reach a **four-way trail junction,** which is where most hikers turn around. Those with gumption add on a 0.8-mile drop to the Yellowstone River and back on the spur trail that plunges steeply 0.4 mile to the historic **Bannock Indian Ford.**

SPECIMEN RIDGE

Distance: 3 miles round-trip
Duration: 3-4 hours
Elevation change: 1,024 feet
Effort: strenuous
Trailhead: Look for a hiker symbol at a pullout 4.5 miles east of Tower Junction on the Northeast Entrance Road just before the Lamar River Bridge

The route up Specimen Ridge goes to a fossil zone, part of the largest number of petrified trees in the world. Most of the fossils come from 50 million years ago, and some are species that no longer grow in the park. One toppled petrified tree stretches 20 feet long and 8 feet in diameter. Do not confuse this unmaintained route with the Specimen Ridge Trail from Yellowstone River Picnic Area, which does not go to the fossils.

Starting off on an **old faint road** and veering off to the right, the route tromps through sage meadows, disappearing frequently in wet seeps. Aim for the trail grunting straight uphill. It will cross multiple wildlife paths before reaching a small forest. The trail switchbacks through the trees to reach an **open ridge.** A rock outcropping marks the **petrified redwood tree trunks** area, and sweeping views span the bison herds in Lamar Valley and the Absaroka Mountains.

SLOUGH CREEK

Distance: 4 miles round-trip
Duration: 3 hours
Elevation change: 597 feet
Effort: moderate
Trailhead: 1.8 miles north on Slough Creek Road

Slough Creek Trail is a lengthy route that climbs up through the Absaroka Mountains, exits the park, and connects with trails entering the **Absaroka-Beartooth Wilderness** and a private ranch. It attracts anglers, horseback riders, and backpackers. To reach the first meadow of the outstanding fishing stream, climb 423 feet up through the open Douglas fir forest and small meadows until the trail drops to a giant meadow surrounding Slough Creek. The return hike climbs 174 feet over the hill back to the trailhead.

★ TROUT LAKE TRAIL

Distance: 1.2 miles round-trip
Duration: 1 hour
Elevation change: 220 feet
Effort: easy
Trailhead: a small pullout with limited parking on the Northeast Entrance Road, 3 miles north of Soda Butte Trailhead and 1.5 miles south of Pebble Creek Campground

An idyllic little lake sitting at about 7,000 feet in elevation, **Trout Lake** is actually the largest of three small lakes tucked near the Northeast Entrance Road in the **Absaroka Mountains.** From the trailhead, the path catapults vertically through a Douglas fir forest to the lake. About 0.3 mile up the trail, the **route splits** to circle the lake. Go either way. The trail circles the shoreline, which is semi-forested on the east shore and open meadows on the west shore. In early summer, phlox blankets the hillsides, cutthroat trout spawn in the inlet stream, and osprey hang around to fish. Short unmaintained trails connect with Shrimp and Buck Lakes.

BACKPACKING

Backpackers must obtain **permits** ($3/person, children 8 and younger free) for assigned backcountry campsites. Permits are available in person 48 hours in advance from the backcountry offices. For more information, see the *Essentials* chapter.

Mt. Holmes
21.2 MILES

The Gallatin Mountains have the best backpacking in the northern part of the park. Until July, snow can clog the upper elevations of the 21.2-mile round-trip route to 10,336-foot **Mt. Holmes** in the Gallatin Range. After that, the route is usually accessible. Camp for two nights at **Winter Creek** (campsite 1C4 or 1C5), near the junction for Trilobite Lake. The next day, climb to the unstaffed lookout on the summit for immense views. Due to bear concentration, the park service recommends having four people in your party. Campsites are usually snow-free by mid-June or so, but Mt. Holmes can retain snow until mid-July or later.

Black Canyon of the Yellowstone
20 MILES

Since the closure of the west end of the Black Canyon of the Yellowstone Trail at Gardiner, point-to-point backpacking trips in the canyon go from **Hellroaring Creek Trailhead** to **Blacktail Creek Trailhead.** Plan three days for the 16.5-mile trip, and mentally prepare for the ascent up on the last day. Watch for ticks. Choose from 19 **campsites** on the route, but the best flank the Yellowstone River (1R1, 1R2, 1Y4-1Y9) in a three-mile stretch where anglers can fish. Due to the short mileage on the middle day, explore the Yellowstone River Trail running west downstream through the Black Canyon, but note that it is only maintained for about two miles. With lower elevation, this backpack trip is usually viable in early May, but hikers must use the longer Hellroaring Bridge route rather than the shortcut ford that isn't safe until August.

Bliss Pass
19-21 MILES

In the Absaroka Mountains, 9,360-foot grassy Bliss Pass yields rugged mountain views and walking through a combo of river valleys, subalpine meadows, and forest. The pass connects Pebble Creek with Slough Creek on a point-to-point hike. The three trailheads of **Slough Creek, Pebble Creek,** and **Warm Creek** access the route, but the eastern trailheads make for 1,000 feet less of elevation climbing. Challenges with this trip include fords and setting up a car shuttle. No backcountry campsites are on the central cross over Bliss Pass; look for them along the Slough Creek or on upper and lower Pebble Creek. To be close to the Bliss Pass Trail, stay in **campsites** 2S3 or 2S4 on Slough Creek and 3P2 or 3P3 on Pebble Creek. Bliss Pass is snow-free by mid-July or so; fording the creeks is easier in August.

BIKING

Biking is not permitted on trails, but is allowed on dirt roads. **Flying Pig Adventure Company** (511 Scott St., Gardiner, 866/264-8448, www.flyingpigrafting.com, $80-175) guides mountain bike tours and provides bikes and helmets.

Late March-mid-April, roads open to bicyclists, but remain closed to vehicles, offering car-free riding from Mammoth to Norris and from Tower Junction to Tower Fall. Bring your own bike; rentals are not available.

At Gardiner, the **old rail trail** (5 miles one-way, Apr.-mid-Nov.) parallels the Yellowstone River. The level, kid-friendly trail can be hot in summer. Find the trailhead 0.1 mile west of the Yellowstone Heritage and Research Center. For 1,500 feet of climbing or descending, the **Old Gardiner Road** (5 miles one-way, late Apr.-early Nov.) connects Gardiner with Mammoth Hot Springs. While cars can only go downhill from Mammoth, bikers can go both directions. Road access is behind Mammoth Hot Springs Hotel or at the North Park Entrance Station.

South of Mammoth, **Bunsen Peak Loop** (6 miles one-way, May-early Nov.) starts from Bunsen Peak Trailhead to circle Bunsen Peak's east side. The trail drops through employee housing before joining the Grand Loop Road between the Upper and Lower Terraces.

On the Grand Loop Road 9.5 miles east of Mammoth, **Blacktail Plateau Drive** (6 miles one-way, mid-July-early Nov.) rolls through higher-elevation terrain with wildlife. Vehicles can only go eastbound, but bicyclists can travel in both directions.

HORSEBACK RIDING

Many companies can help you saddle up in a western tradition. You don't need cowboy gear, but do wear long pants, sturdy shoes (no sandals), and a hat for sun or wind protection. Children must be 5-8 years old (exact minimum age varies). Per person rates run $40-55 for one hour and $60-75 for two hours. Three-hour and half-day trips cost $110-130, while full-day rides cost $220-230. Make

cycling near Tower Fall

reservations in advance and tip your wrangler 15 percent for day trips, 20 percent for overnights.

Inside the Park

From the Roosevelt Corrals, wranglers lead **Saddle Up** (Xanterra, 307/344-7311 or 866/439-7375, www.yellowstonenationalparklodges.com, daily early June-early Sept.) tours. The one-hour ride (departure times vary through summer, $50) goes around sagebrush flats, while the two-hour ride (9:15am daily, $73) makes Lost Lake a destination.

Yellowstone Wilderness Outfitters (406/223-3300, www.yellowstone.ws, daily June-Sept.) guides half-day ($128), full-day ($225), and overnight ($1,400-2,700) pack trips to various park destinations. Guides with degrees in wildlife biology lead rides to places with superb wildlife-watching. The outfitter also partners with a rafting company for a saddle-paddle trip ($170) with horseback portions inside the park.

Outside the Park

Around Gardiner, outfitters guide trail rides in Custer-Gallatin National Forest. **Hell's A-Roaring Outfitters** (164 Crevice Rd., Jardine, 406/848-7578, www.hellsaroarinoutfitters.com, daily May-Sept., $45-220) kicks off the annual season on Memorial Day weekend, when ranch staff wrangle their 100 horses through the town streets. From the Johnson ranch, located about six miles north of Gardiner, they lead one-hour, two-hour, half-day, and full-day horseback rides through high sagebrush and grass plains with views into Yellowstone. Overnight rides go into the Absaroka-Beartooth Wilderness. Since they only take reservations via email or phone, it's easier to book trips online through their partner, **Flying Pig Adventure Company** (511 Scott St., Gardiner, 866/264-8448, www.flyingpigrafting.com). Flying Pig and four other rafting companies in Gardiner also offer paddle-saddle combo trips ($78-100).

Trail rides from Cooke City tour the Absaroka Mountains. **Skyline Guest Ranch** (31 Kersey Lake Rd., Cooke City, 406/838-2380 or 877/238-8885, www.flyfishyellowstone.com, Mon.-Sat. June-early Sept., $40-155) leads horseback trail rides for one, two, or three hours; the half-day ride to Rock Island Lake includes lunch. Make reservations up to three days in advance.

WATER SPORTS

Yellowstone National Park does not permit rafting and kayaking inside the park; all Yellowstone River floats take place outside the park in Gardiner.

★ Rafting the Yellowstone River

The **Yellowstone River** (Class I-IV) flows through Gardiner and Yankee Jim Canyon, where wave trains throw up a rolling kick for white-water rafting. Below the canyon, the river settles into a calmer pace, better for scenic floats. While floating, you have an excellent chance of seeing wildlife from the river. Most of the shorter white-water trips are good for families looking for some thrills and splashing, but not a frightening ride.

There are no raft or kayak rentals available in Gardiner, but if you have your own raft or kayak, you can float the Yellowstone River. No permits are needed. Find the put-in at Queen of the Waters Fishing Access near Gardiner and take-out 7.2 miles downstream at Tom Miner Bridge. For longer floats, river access sites lie every few miles en route to Livingston.

Trail rides depart from the Roosevelt corrals.

The Yellowstone River carries rafters through Yankee Jim Canyon.

GUIDES

In Gardiner, several rafting companies guide trips **May-September** on the Yellowstone River. With comparable rates, most offer scenic floats ($42-47), half-day ($42-47) and full-day ($85-95) white-water trips, and paddle-saddle combos ($78-100). For more splash, opt for smaller boats that hold 4-6 paddlers or inflatable kayaks ($10-25 more per person). Rates for children 12 and younger are about $10-20 less. Half-day white-water trips cover eight miles in 2-3 hours and depart multiple times daily. Full-day white-water trips combine rafting and floating with lunch, while covering about 18 miles of river. Life jackets are supplied. In cooler shoulder seasons, companies provide wetsuits, booties, and splash tops. Some include those in the fees; some do not. Professional photographers shoot photos of your raft bouncing through white water; the photos are then available for purchase.

Reservations are recommended, and most companies accept online booking. Some companies may have weight or minimum age restrictions. Plan to tip your river guide 15 percent for day trips and 20 percent for overnights. In addition to the regular rafting lineup, the following companies add specialties:

Flying Pig Adventure Company (511 Scott St., 888/687-1276, www.flyingpigrafting.com) launches behind their camp store down a long stairway to the river. They also run overnight trips ($560).

Montana Whitewater (603 Scott St., 800/799-4465, www.montanawhitewater.com) takes out small boats and inflatable kayaks. Montana Whitewater also has raft-zipline packages ($90-120).

Wild West Rafting (220 W. Park St., 406/848-2252 or 800/862-0557, www.wildwestrafting.com) adds on small boats and inflatable kayaks.

Yellowstone Raft Company (111 2nd St., 406/848-7777 or 800/858-7781, www.yellowstoneraft.com) has sit-on-top kayak options ($60-135).

Fishing
INSIDE THE PARK

In the northern region of the park, multiple rivers harbor wild trout. **Gardner River, Slough Creek, Soda Butte Creek,** and **Lamar River** offer iconic places to fly-fish. The deeper, wider, and bigger **Yellowstone River** adds more pools for casting. Hiking anglers can also find fishing with less pressure on **Blacktail Deer Creek,** and **Hellroaring**

Creek, but the Trout Lake inlet stream is closed to fishing. Runoff usually clears from streams in early July. With no float tubes permitted, cast from shore or wade-fish. To help native trout conservation, kill all nonnative fish including brook and rainbow trout in the Lamar River drainage above the Lamar River Bridge and Slough Creek drainage above the campground.

For kids, smaller creeks work best for fishing. Take them to the picnic areas at the Gardner River or Lava Creek, or near the campgrounds of Slough, Indian, or Pebble Creeks. Joffe and Trout Lakes are smaller lakes where kids can have fun fishing, too.

Inside Yellowstone, a **fishing permit** is required for anglers 16 years and older ($18 for three days, $25 seven days, $40 season). For permit information and regulations, see the *Essentials* chapter.

OUTSIDE THE PARK

Outside Yellowstone, you'll need a **Montana fishing license** (http://fwp.mt.gov, $15-31 for residents, $25-81 for nonresidents). For fishing east of Cooke City, you'll need a **Wyoming fishing license** (residents: $3 youth, $6 adults daily, $24 adults annual; nonresidents: $15 youth, $14 adults daily, $92 adults annual). For information, see the *Essentials* chapter.

Guided trips inside the park are wade-fishing; guided raft, drift boat fishing, and powerboat fishing are only outside the park. Trips for 1-2 people cost $375-425 for a half day and $475-525 for a full day. Trips are for beginners through experts; beginners can get lessons. **Parks' Fly Shop** (202 S. 2nd St., Gardiner, 406/848-7314, www.parksflyshop.com, daily year-round) has flies, tackle, gear, and Montana fishing licenses. They also guide wade-fishing, float, and powerboat fishing trips. **Flying Pig Store and Fly Shop** (204 Park St., Gardiner, 888/792-9193, www.flying-pigrafting.com, daily May-mid-Oct.) carries flies, tackle, and gear, rents rods and waders, and sells Yellowstone fishing permits. They also guide wade-fishing, float, and horseback angling trips. The **Cooke City Store** (101 Main St., Cooke City, 406/838-2234, http://cookecitystore.com) sells tackle and licenses for Montana, Wyoming, and Yellowstone.

Swimming

The natural **Boiling River Hot Springs** (dawn-dusk midsummer-late spring, free)

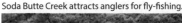
Soda Butte Creek attracts anglers for fly-fishing.

spills into the Gardner River, where you can soak your cares away. Since the Boiling River water is scalding hot, soak in the Gardner River, where its frigid water tempers the thermally heated stream. Finding the line between the hot and cold is tough; usually one side of your body sizzles while the other freezes. Exercise caution due to temperature extremes, slippery rocks, and strong currents. Please respect this thermal site; you'll see plenty of wear from abuse. Swimsuits are required. Suit up before you go as changing facilities are not available. Bring a towel and water shoes.

Located midway between Gardiner and Mammoth, find the unmarked turnoff to the Boiling River Trailhead on the east side of U.S. Highway 89, about 200 feet south of the bridge over the Gardner River. Hike 0.5 mile to two stair-step entrances and the soaking area.

THRILL SPORTS

At Yellowstone Ranch, **Yellowstone Zip** (603 Scott St., Gardiner, 800/799-4465, www.yellowstonezip.com, June-Aug., $60-100 adults, $10 less for kids) has zipline tours whizzing through the forest and tiptoeing along sky bridges. The longest lines fly 1,200 feet and the highest is 200 feet. Rates include the shuttle from the meeting location at Montana Whitewater to the historic ranch outside Gardiner. The company also packages rafting with ziplining.

WINTER SPORTS
Cross-Country Skiing and Snowshoeing

Winter transforms Yellowstone into a prime cross-country ski and snowshoe locale. All unplowed roads become trails, which allows for experiencing them differently than in summer. With the exception of the plowed road between Gardiner, Mammoth, and Cooke City, all other roads closed to wheeled vehicles are open for skiing. Some have snowcoach and snowmobile traffic. Winter trail maps are located online (www.nps.gov/yell) and at Albright Visitor Center.

Around Mammoth Hot Springs, **Upper Terrace Loop**, **Bunsen Peak Trail**, and **Blacktail Plateau Trail** are groomed for cross-country skiing. Other trails for skiers are the **Snow Pass, Sheepeater,** and **Indian Creek-Bighorn Loop** trails. Warming huts sit at the Indian Creek and Upper Terrace Trailheads. Parking to access all trails is at Upper Terrace Loop and the lower Bunsen Peak Trailhead. The **Old Gardiner Road**

soaking in the Gardner River

parksflyshop.com, $15-30 per day) rents cross-country ski and snowshoe packages.

SHUTTLES AND TOURS

From Mammoth, **ski shuttles** (Xanterra, 307/344-7311 or 866/439-7375, www.yellowstonenationalparklodges.com, Sat.-Sun. mid-Dec.-Feb., $38 each way, kids half price) go to **Indian Creek.** Catch the snowcoach both directions for skiing Indian Creek Trails or one way to ski back to Mammoth.

Park naturalists guide two-hour **snowshoe tours** (Sun. late Dec.-Feb., free) around Upper Terrace Drive in winter. **Yellowstone Forever Institute** (406/848-2400, www.yellowstone.org) offers expert-led educational ski and snowshoe trips starting from Gardiner, Mammoth, or Lamar Valley. Private tours, one-day, and multiday programs are available with varied rates.

Snowmobile tours launch from Mammoth Hot Springs.

Trail, located behind the hotel, and **Upper Terrace Loop** provide good snowshoeing.

By parking at Petrified Tree or Tower Junction, skiers and snowshoers can tour the **Lost Lake Trail** or ski 2.3 miles up Grand Loop Road to **Tower Fall.**

In the northeast corner of Yellowstone, unplowed roads and snow-buried trails provide touring routes. The **Barronette** and **Bannock Trails** parallel Soda Butte Creek, the latter trail connected with an unplowed road that runs between Silver Gate and Cooke City.

RENTALS

In Mammoth Hot Springs, find winter gear rentals in the **Bear Den Ski Shop** (7:30am-5pm daily mid-Dec.-Feb.). You can rent gear for a half day, full day, or three days for $2-22 per item: snowshoes, gaiters, cross-country skis, poles, ski boots, and Yaktrax. A full-day ski package costs $27. The shop offers repairs, wax, and lessons. In Gardiner, **Parks' Fly Shop** (202 S. 2nd St., 406/848-7314, www.

Snowmobiling

Yellowstone's snowmobile season runs **mid-December-early March** with travel only on roads. Inside the park at Mammoth, the most popular route departs from the snowmobile staging area at the **Upper Terrace Trailhead** and travels the Grand Loop Road south to Old Faithful or Grand Canyon of the Yellowstone. Outside the park from Cooke City, snowmobilers travel the snow-buried **Beartooth Highway** (U.S. Hwy. 212) and other forest roads December-May. Snowmobiling in the Custer-Gallatin and Shoshone National Forests is not restricted to roadways.

GUIDED TOURS

From Mammoth, **Yellowstone Year-Round Safaris** (905 Scott St., 406/848-7311 or 800/828-9080, www.yellowstoneyearroundsafaris.com, $315-360 per machine) leads full-day snowmobile tours. Rates include helmets, snowmobile suits, gloves, shuttles, and trail lunches; fees do not include park entrance or tips for guides (15 percent). Daily tours head to Old Faithful or Grand Canyon of the Yellowstone.

SELF-GUIDED
To snowmobile without a guide, you must enter the **permit lottery** (www.recreation. gov, early Sept.-early Oct.). Regulations for trips and machine types are online (www. nps.gov/yell). Rentals ($200-250) include snowsuits and helmets. They also have age limits and license requirements. Avalanche gear (beacons, probes, shovels, and airbags) usually costs $50. In Gardiner, rent from **Yellowstone Year-Round Safaris**. In Cooke City, rent snowmobiles from **Cooke City Motorsports** (203 Eaton St., 406/838-2231, www.cookecitymotorsports.com).

Entertainment and Shopping

INSIDE THE PARK
Ranger Programs
The amphitheater at **Mammoth Campground** (8pm-9:30pm daily early June-mid-Sept.) hosts free rotating evening programs. The 45-minute presentations illustrate Yellowstone wildlife, cultural history, flora, and natural history. In winter, naturalist talks take place in the **Mammoth Hot Springs Hotel** (8pm Thurs.-Sat. late Dec.-late Feb.) in the map room.

Shopping
Gift shops in the lodges and **Yellowstone General Stores** (406/586-7593, www.yellowstonegift.com, 7:30am-9:30pm daily) offer places to shop in **Mammoth Hot Springs** (year-round) and adjacent to **Roosevelt Lodge** (June-Aug.). A **Yellowstone Forever** (406/848-2400, www.yellowstone.org) store is located in the Albright Visitor Center at Mammoth.

GARDINER
While people hunker down in Mammoth for the night, the action kicks up at a couple of western saloons in Gardiner. You can dance to live music at the **Two Bit Saloon** (107 2nd St. S., 406/848-7743, www.twobitsaloon.com, 9am-2am daily) on select nights.

Gardiner's annual **rodeo** (100 U.S. 89 S., www.northernrodeo.com, June) is held over two days at the Jim Duffy Arena. A parade kicks off the events, which include calf roping, barrel racing, and bareback bronco riding. Sponsored by the Northern Rodeo Association and Gardiner Rodeo Club, the competitions run Friday and Saturday evenings and are open to the public.

Gardiner has a handful of shops concentrated on Park Street adjacent to the Roosevelt Arch. Art and photography galleries contain western works, and bookstores feature local and regional authors. You'll also find gift, jewelry, and clothing shops. **Yellowstone Forever** (308 Park St., 406/848-2400, www.yellowstone.org) runs a shop that sells books on park history, geology, wildlife, science, flora, and photography, plus field guides and recreation guidebooks.

COOKE CITY
Cooke City Store (101 Main St., 406/838-2234, http://cookecitystore.com, 8am-8pm daily May-Sept.) is listed on the National Register of Historic Places due to its start in 1886. Today, it serves as a general mercantile carrying groceries, sporting goods, maps, books, hardware, and gifts.

Food

INSIDE THE PARK

Xanterra (307/344-7311 or 866/439-7375, www.yellowstonenationalparklodges.com) operates the park lodge restaurants, grills, and cookouts. In winter, dinner reservations are accepted at Mammoth Hotel Dining Room; in summer, reservations are mandatory for the Old West Dinner Cookout. In all park restaurants, casual dress is common. No dresses, heels, or ties needed.

Mammoth Hot Springs

Located across from the Mammoth Hot Springs Hotel, the Mammoth Hotel Dining Room (307/344-7311 or 866/439-7375, www.yellowstonenationalparklodges.com, breakfast 6:30am-10am, lunch 11:30am-2:30pm daily early May-early Oct. and late Dec.-early Mar., dinner 5pm-10pm daily early May-early Oct., 5:30pm-8pm or 9pm daily late Dec.-early Mar., $9-30) overlooks the parade grounds where wildlife often adds entertainment. This certified-green restaurant changes menus between winter and summer, but both seasons offer a variety of light and healthy small-plate, vegan, and gluten-free options alongside classic full meals. Kids have their own menu. Breakfast is from the menu or, in summer, from the large all-you-can-eat buffet ($13 adults, $7 kids). Lunches feature soup, salad, sandwiches, and burgers. Local specialties include wild-game chili and bison tacos or burgers. In summer, dinner is first-come, first-served; in winter, make reservations through Xanterra. Fish, pastas, and Montana farm-raised meats comprise the dinner menu. Beer, wine, and cocktails are also served, and the restaurant makes to-go breakfasts or lunches.

With an a la carte menu, Mammoth Terrace Grill (307/344-7311 or 866/439-7375, www.yellowstonenationalparklodges.com, 7am-9pm daily late Apr.-mid-Oct., hours vary seasonally, $3-10) serves breakfast, lunch, dinner, light snacks, ice cream, sandwiches, burgers, and kiddie meals. Breakfast choices narrow to continental selections in spring or fall; in summer, expect hot meals.

Yellowstone Mammoth General Store (DNC Parks and Resorts, 1 Mammoth Upper Loop Rd., 406/586-7593, www.yellowstone-vacations.com, 7:30am-9:30pm daily in summer, shorter hours in winter) serves hot dogs, snacks, and Montana-made Wilcoxson's ice cream.

Roosevelt Lodge

With a cowboy-friendly menu and a lobby bar, dining at Roosevelt Lodge just feels western. Lauded by many locals as the best food in the park, ★ Roosevelt Lodge Dining Room (307/344-7311 or 866/439-7375, www.yellowstonenationalparklodges.com, 7am-10am and 11:30am-9:30pm daily early June-Sept., $10-28) designs menu items for flexibility with plenty of size, toppings, sides, and gluten-free choices. Breakfast skillets, Tex-Mex, wild game, and smoked barbecue ribs are house specialties. At 4:30pm, the menu expands with additional western-style dinner options. Seating is first-come, first-served, and a kiddie menu is available. You can also order to-go lunches ($15).

The Old West Dinner Cookout (307/344-7311 or 866/439-7375, www.yellowstonenationalparklodges.com, rides start at dusk daily early June-mid-Sept., $63-94 adults, $50-86 children ages 8-11) is adventure dining. Guests saddle up or ride a wagon from the Roosevelt Corrals to Yancy's Hole. At the cookout, wranglers grill up steaks to order and serve up traditional cookout sides along with coffee cooked on a fire. (With advance notice, vegetarian options can replace the steak.) Check-in times at the Roosevelt Corral range between 2:45pm-4:45pm (hours vary seasonally). Horseback rides take 1-2 hours to reach the site; the wagon ride takes 30-45 minutes. All return rides take 30 minutes. Reservations are required.

Located adjacent to the Roosevelt Lodge, the **Roosevelt Store** (7:30am-9:30pm daily early June-Aug.) has a small grocery.

Tower Fall

At Tower Fall, **Yellowstone Tower Fall General Store** (7:30am-9:30pm daily mid-May-mid-Sept.) has a snack bar that sells hot dogs, ice cream, chips, drinks, and snacks. Outdoor picnic tables are available.

OUTSIDE THE PARK
Gardiner

Due to limited dining inside the park, many people drive 15 minutes from Mammoth to Gardiner for dinner. Most restaurants shorten their hours or days in winter, so call ahead to confirm when they are open. Summer visitors pay a 3 percent resort tax added to meals.

CAFÉS

Yellowstone Perk (208 Park St., 406/848-9430, 7am-10pm daily in summer, shorter hours in winter) is a small shop tucked inside the Gardiner Pharmacy that serves espresso drinks and Livingston-made Wilcoxson's ice cream in homemade waffle cones. Internet access is also available.

Part bookstore and part eatery, the **Tumbleweed Café** (501 Scott St., 406/848-2225, http://tumbleweedbooksandcafe.weebly.com, 7am-9pm daily May-Oct., 9am-6pm daily Nov.-Apr., $4-11) serves light homemade meals for breakfast, lunch, and dinner; choose from cereal, breakfast burritos, wraps, paninis, salads, soups, and espresso. You can also find gluten-free, vegan, and vegetarian options, as well as baked goodies and to-go items, such as a sack lunch ($11) to take into the park.

In the style of a mom-and-pop drive-in, **The Corral** (711 Scott Street, 406/848-7627, Mon.-Sat. 6am-10:30am, 11am-10pm, $9-20) is an old-time staple with indoor and outdoor seating. Come for locally sourced, organic bison or elk burgers with fresh fixings. They

also serve salmon burgers, beef burgers, sandwiches, shakes made from local Wilcoxson's ice cream, hand-cut fries, and organic salads.

BARBECUE

With owners from southern Georgia, **Cowboy's Lodge and Grille** (208 Stone St., 406/848-9175, http://cowboyslodge.com, 11am-9pm daily year-round, $10-34) dishes up southern barbecue in a small and rustic log cabin restaurant that houses a stuffed mountain lion perched in the rafters. The lunch and dinner menu specializes in medium portions (rather than huge cowboy-type meals) with barbecued meat, chicken, brisket, or ribs served with traditional sides; opt for the combo platter to taste different sauces. Also on the menu are hand-cut fries (including sweet potato fries), chicken pot pie, bean stew, beer, and wine.

MEXICAN

A small café, ★ **Yellowstone Grill** (404 Scott St., 406/848-9433, 7am-2pm Tues.-Sun. summer, 7am-2pm Wed.-Sun. winter, $8-17) is a combo bakery-grill-Mexican food restaurant that serves fresh breakfast and lunch. South-of-the-border fare includes burritos, quesadillas, and tacos, though you can also choose from omelets, hash, blueberry pancakes, soups, salads, wraps, burgers, and espresso. The baked goods specialty is caramel cinnamon rolls.

PIZZA

For a small town, Gardiner has multiple pizza options. Visitors can pair up a pie with a local microbrew or wine, or grab a pizza to go. Open since 1953, **KBar Pizza** (202 Main St., 406/848-9995, www.kbarpizza.com, 11am-11pm daily summer, 4pm-9pm Fri.-Sun. winter, $10-30) bakes pizzas in a vintage deck oven with wheat or gluten-free crusts. Their Crazy Woman pizza has a kicky spice. **Yellowstone Pizza Company** (210 Park St., 406/848-9991, http://yellowstonepizza-company.com, 11am-10pm daily May-Oct., $10-30) dishes up 12-inch pizzas cooked in a brick oven with regular or gluten-free crust. Elk or bison pizza is the house specialty. You can also get salads or pasta-of-the-day. In summer, outdoor dining on the upstairs deck yields views of the Roosevelt Arch.

PUBS

With the only outside deck overlooking the Yellowstone River, the **Iron Horse Bar & Grille** (200 Spring St., 406/848-7666, 11am-midnight daily May-Sept., $8-26) allows viewing of the river and peaks while dining. Specialties include elk tacos, bison burgers, grilled bison meatloaf, bison shepherd's pie, trout, fries, local microbrews, and huckleberry margaritas. Lunch usually runs until 4pm, while dinner is served until 9pm. Bar food is available until midnight. There is also indoor seating, pool tables in the pub, and takeout available.

The **Two Bit Saloon & Grill** (107 2nd St., 406/848-7743, www.twobitsaloon.com, 9am-2am daily year-round, $6-18) serves western food: biscuits and gravy, eggs, burgers, sandwiches, and a few Tex-Mex dishes. This longtime Gardiner staple is the place to go for an elk burger and a regional Montana microbrew, or to start the day with a pick-me-up cocktail. Breakfast is served until 11:30am, followed by a lunch and dinner menu that lasts until 9pm; families are welcome until 10pm. The saloon also has slot machines and billiards, plus occasional live music.

FINE DINING

The tiny ★ **Raven Grill** (220 W. Park St., 406/848-7600, 5pm-10pm daily mid-Apr.-mid-Oct., $17-40) sits right outside the park entrance in view of the Roosevelt Arch and Electric Peak. The restaurant is crammed with minimal diner-style seating and a few outdoor tables, making reservations a good idea. Though primarily a steakhouse with grilled meats (beef, bison, elk rib eye, chicken, seafood) and elk burgers, it also serves wild-game pastas and small plates.

Located seven miles north of Gardiner, the ★ **Lighthouse Restaurant** (752 Hwy. 89 S., 406/848-2138, www.lrmts.com, 5:30pm-11pm Wed.-Mon. late May-late Sept., $12-29) may have the outside appearance of a ramshackle dive, but inside is food

Yellowstone Grill

of a much higher caliber. Choose from locally sourced, organic, and fresh entrees of burgers (beef, bison, lamb), fish, and steaks (beef, bison, or elk). Eclectic house specialties are big on flavor with Southeast Asian twists and unique sauces.

COWBOY COOKOUT

Hell's A-Roarin' (164 Crevice Rd., 406/848-7578, www.hellsaroarinoutfitters.com, Sun.-Fri. late May-mid-Aug., $48 adults, $30 children) hosts an evening cookout at their ranch with views of Yellowstone across the valley. The cowboy steak cookout takes place around a campfire and is accompanied by potatoes, salad, cornbread, dessert, beverages, and marshmallow roasting. You can also add on a one-hour horseback ride (fee). Since the ranch only accepts reservations by phone or email, make cookout reservations online via their partner, **Flying Pig Adventure Company** (www.flyingpigrafting.com).

GROCERIES

While you won't find big box grocers, the **Gardiner Market** (701 Scott St., 406/848-7524, www.gardinermarket.com, 7am-11pm daily in summer, 7am-8pm daily winter) sells fresh produce and meat, frozen and baked goods, convenience food, deli items, and beer and wine. It also has a Montana State Liquor Store for the stronger stuff. The closest full-size supermarket is Albertson's in Livingston.

Silver Gate and Cooke City

Two small stores carry limited groceries, beer, and wine: **Cooke City Store** (101 Main St., Cooke City, 406/838-2234, http://cookecitystore.com, 8am-8pm daily May-Sept.) and **Silver Gate General Store** (109 U.S. Hwy 212, Silver City, 406/838-2371, www.pineedgecabins.com, 8am-10pm daily May-Oct.). Stop in at the ★ **Bearclaw Bakery** (303 E. Main, Cooke City, 406/838-2040, 5am-11am Tues.-Sun. late May-Sept., hours vary in winter, $4-9) for breakfast burritos, eggs with sides, biscuits and gravy, cinnamon rolls, bear claws, blueberry scones, cookies, and breads. The house specialty is Bearclaw French toast. Go early or you may not get a seat in the tiny restaurant, which also serves as the front room for an automobile and snowmobile shop.

Housed in a 1940s log cabin, the **Beartooth Café** (14 Main St., Cooke City, 406/838-2475, www.beartoothcafe.com, 11am-10pm daily late May-late Sept., $8-30) is a Cooke City institution run by a fourth-generation family. Meals are made from scratch,

Raven Grill

including appetizers and desserts, and served al fresco on a deck filled with flowers and umbrella tables. Lunch (served until 5pm) includes sandwiches and burgers, while dinner (served after 5pm) rolls out burgers, steaks, prime rib, dinner salads, and pasta. Wine or an extensive selection of 120 beers can accompany your meal. A kiddie menu and vegetarian choices are also available.

In a log cabin more than 75 years old, the **Log Cabin Café** (106 Hwy. 212, Silver Gate, 406/838-2367, www.thelogcabincafe.com, 5:30am-10pm daily May-Oct. $8-33) serves breakfast, lunch, and dinner. Find fresh-ground organic coffee, homemade hash browns, and grilled pumpkin bread with Montana honey for breakfast followed by soups, salads, burgers, and wraps for lunch. Pies, desserts, baked goods, and soups are homemade. Fresh produce is mostly organic, and grass-fed, free-range beef is sourced locally for dinner steaks. Trout is also served for breakfast and dinner. Beer and wine are available.

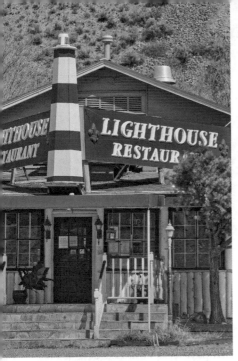

Lighthouse Restaurant

Accommodations

Park accommodations may range widely, but there is no upscale lodging. In-park lodging fills up first and fast. For amenities such as TVs, wireless Internet, and air-conditioning, stay in Gardiner. Those planning to drive the Beartooth Highway and explore more remote sections of Yellowstone's northeast corner should lodge in Silver Gate or Cooke City.

INSIDE THE PARK
Reservations
Xanterra (307/344-7311 or 866/439-7375, www.yellowstonenationalparklodges.com) runs all the lodges inside Yellowstone. Reservations are recommended 13 months in advance for summer and holidays in winter, especially for rooms with en suite baths. Cancellations may free up last-minute bookings, but with limited choices.

In keeping with the historical ambience, most in-park rooms and cabins lack televisions, radios, telephones, and air-conditioning. If you are a light sleeper, bring earplugs; if you are traveling during midsummer heat, you may want to bring a fan with an extension cord (very few are available from the front desks). ADA rooms are limited. Lodging rates listed are for two people; add $17-20 per each additional person. Some of the cabins permit pets for an added fee of $25. In-park utility fees and taxes add on about 14 percent.

Mammoth Hot Springs
MAMMOTH HOT SPRINGS HOTEL
In a busy tourist center, ★ **Mammoth Hot Springs Hotel** (1 Grand Loop Rd., late Apr.-mid-Oct. and mid-Dec.-early Mar., $100-290 rooms and cabins, $560 suites) is a

large complex with almost 100 hotel rooms and 125 cabins. The U.S. Cavalry built the north wing of the four-story hotel in 1911; the main lobby and remainder of the hotel were erected in 1936. In 2017, a $7.9 million renovation upgraded public spaces; in 2018, private bathrooms will be added to all hotel guest rooms. The historic attraction off the lobby is the Map Room, containing a large wooden U.S. map constructed in 1937. The map is made from 2,544 pieces of 15 different kinds of wood from nine countries. The hotel is within walking distance from the Albright Visitor Center, travertine terrace boardwalks, trailheads, a gift shop, a post office, and two restaurants. Xanterra charges about $5 per hour, $12 per day, or $25 for three days for Internet access, available only in the map room. In winter, Mammoth is the only hotel in the park accessible by private vehicles on plowed roads.

The hotel has **multiple types of accommodations:** hotel rooms with or without private baths, two-room suites, one- or two-room rustic cabins with sinks but no bathrooms, cabins with baths, and hot tub cabins. Hotel rooms and cabins without baths have access to shared community facilities. Rustic cabins have one queen or one queen

and two doubles. Hotel rooms and larger cabins have two queens. Shower stalls throughout the hotel and cabins tend to be small, and walls are thin. An elevator accesses the upper floors of the hotel. Two high-end suites have a bedroom with two queen beds plus a sitting room with a couch, chairs, trundle bed, television, and telephone. Four cabins have the added perk of fenced private hot tubs. In winter, only hotel rooms, the two suites, and the hot tub cabins are available.

Tower-Roosevelt
ROOSEVELT LODGE AND CABINS
At Tower Junction on Grand Loop Road, **Roosevelt Lodge and Cabins** (Grand Loop Rd. at junction with Northeast Entrance Rd., early June-early Sept., $96-155) sits near the Roosevelt Corrals, Tower Fall, Petrified Tree, and Lamar Valley. The 1920s lodge derives its name from a nearby campsite used by President Theodore Roosevelt, and the locale is perfect for dawn and dusk wildlife-watching drives. The lodge has a gift shop, dining room, and a lineup of cane rockers on the front porch that overlooks the dusty parking lot. Two types of small bucolic cabins surround the lodge. Spartan **Roughrider cabins** contain one or two double beds and

Roosevelt Lodge has rustic cabins.

wood-burning stoves for heat (two Presto Logs included), but require walking to the nearby community toilet-and-shower house. **Frontier cabins** come with an en suite toilet, shower, sink, and usually two double beds. Walk to the neighboring corral for trail rides, wagon rides, and Old West Dinner Cookouts. With no Internet, the western atmosphere has more backwoods authenticity.

OUTSIDE THE PARK
Gardiner

Flanking the park boundary and the Yellowstone River, Gardiner bustles in summer with tourists. Located five miles from Mammoth, the town makes a good base for exploring Yellowstone's north end with easy access to rafting, fly-fishing, restaurants, bars, and shops. Most of Gardiner's lodging properties, including several national chain motels, rim the highway through town on the north side of the bridge crossing the Yellowstone River. The most popular chain motels are **Rodeway Inn & Suites** (109 Hellroaring St., 406/848-7520 or 866/238-4218, www.choicehotels.com, May-Sept., $240-300) and **Best Western by Mammoth Hot Springs** (905 Scott St. W., 406/848-7311, www.bestwestern.com, year-round, $110-300). Find a full listing of Gardiner lodging options online (www.visitgardinermt.com).

Most rooms in Gardiner have televisions, wireless Internet (although perhaps not strong enough for major streaming or downloading), phones, and air-conditioning. Rates are highest June-September, then lower in fall, winter, and spring. Add on a 7 percent Montana bed tax year-round; for June-September stays, add on 3 percent more for the Gardiner Resort Tax. For summer or winter holiday lodging, make reservations 9-12 months in advance.

HOSTEL
North Yellowstone Lodge and Hostel (1083 U.S. Hwy. 89, 406/823-9683, www.northyellowstonehostel.com, mid-May-Sept.) sits 10 miles north of Gardiner in a quiet apple orchard on a Yellowstone River beach.

Accommodations are in shared dorm rooms with bunk beds ($49/person) and private rooms for 2-4 people ($120-140) with a queen bed and set of bunks. Shared bath facilities are down the hall. Private rooms come with linens, but you'll need a sleeping bag for the dorm beds or add $5 for linens. The lodge has a communal kitchen, dining room, living room, and recreation room.

MOTELS
★ **Yellowstone Gateway Inn** (103 Bigelow Ln., 406/848-7100, http://yellowstonegatewayinn.com, year-round, $80-375) has 16 suites with full kitchens, 1-2 bedrooms, a living room, framed wildlife photographs, and access to communal barbecue grills. Each unit sleeps 2-8 people. The master bedroom has a king bed, while the second bedroom has a queen. One or two sofa beds, with specially made, comfortable mattresses, are in the living room. The ground-level suites include a few steps up to the door, and each unit has a tiny outdoor patio with seating; some have views of Electric Peak. A grocery store is across the street for stocking the kitchen.

Located on the west end of town, the two-story **Yellowstone Village Inn and Suites** (1102 Scott St., 406/848-7417, www.yellowstonevinn.com, mid-Apr.-Oct., $140-250) offers simple hotel rooms and suites with 1-3 bedrooms, full kitchens, and living rooms. Hotel rooms and suites contain one king or queen bed, two queens, or one of each. The inn has an indoor pool, basketball court, and free continental breakfast.

Adjacent to the Yellowstone River, the **Yellowstone River Motel** (14 Park St., 406/848-7303 or 888/797-4837, www.yellowstonerivermotel.com, Apr.-Oct., $80-165) is a two-story, 38-room, no-frills property with an additional three-bedroom unit with a full kitchen. Rooms in the older wing have small but revamped bathrooms. The newer wing has larger rooms at higher rates. Communal outdoor areas include a patio overlooking the river, a charcoal grill, and picnic tables.

Built in 2016, **Yellowstone Big Rock**

Inn (902 Scott St. W., 406/848-7414, www. yellowstonebigrockinn.com, May-early Oct., $175-260) claims views of Electric Peak in Yellowstone. Rooms have two queens, mini-fridges, and microwaves. Suites have two queens and full kitchens.

BED-AND-BREAKFASTS

The **Gardiner Guest House B&B** (112 Main St. E., 406/848-9414, www.gardiner-guesthouse.com, year-round, $70-150) offers three rooms in a 1903 Victorian house, plus a backyard cabin, with en suite or shared bathrooms. Most rooms have one queen bed, except for Room 2, which has an antique double bed. Room 3 features an additional single bed. Amenities include full breakfasts and late-night snacks.

The **Yellowstone Suites Bed and Breakfast** (506 4th St. S., 406/848-7937 or 800/948-7937, www.yellowstonesuites.com, Feb.-Oct., $140-195) sits three blocks from the Roosevelt Arch in a restored 1904 stone home with a covered porch that allows guests to enjoy the garden. Located on the 2nd and 3rd floors, two guest rooms have one queen bed each with shared baths, while two other rooms feature queen beds and private baths. The Roosevelt Room has an additional single bed. There is no elevator.

Located four miles north of Gardiner, **Yellowstone Basin Inn** (4 Maiden Basin Dr., 406/848-7080, http://yellowstonebasininn. com, May-mid-Oct., $160-435) has 11 rooms or suites, each one unique and themed after the Montana outdoors. Studios and three-bedroom apartments with full kitchens and king and queen beds sleep 2-5 people each. Amenities include an outdoor hot tub, home-cooked hot breakfasts, and to-go lunches in summer.

CABINS AND TEPEES

On the Yellowstone River, ★ **Riverside Cottages** (521 Scott St. W., 406/848-7719 or 877/774-2836, www.riversidecottages.com, year-round, $90-330) has a hot tub and a large wooden deck with seating that overlooks the

Riverside Cottages

river; a wooden stairway drops to the shore. Park peaks provide the backdrop. Cottages and balcony suites have full kitchens. Balcony suites are newer, while some of the tiny older cabins have thin walls. Efficiency rooms feature microwaves and mini-fridges.

About four miles north of Gardiner, ★ **Dreamcatcher Tipi Hotel** (20 Maiden Basin Dr., 406/848-9447 or 844/313-7684, www.dreamcatchertipihotel.com, mid-May-Sept., $360) appeals to those wanting to sleep in a tepee but with modern glamping comforts. Ten tepees have king or double beds, unique high-end furnishings, electric fireplaces, in-room safes, and private bathhouses with heated floors. Roast marshmallows at night around the community fire.

Silver Gate and Cooke City

Located just outside the Northeast Entrance to Yellowstone, the tiny villages of Silver Gate and Cooke City are backwoods throwbacks to another era, where the tourists quickly outnumber the locals. Because the towns sit at 7,500 feet in elevation, the altitude may bother some people, causing labored breathing or fitful sleeping. Make reservations for July-August and winter holidays.

Find complete lodging listings at Cooke City Chamber of Commerce (www.cookecitychamber.org).

MOTELS

Basic no-frills motels line the main drag of U.S. Highway 212 in Cooke City. Most are open year-round. **Super 8** (303 E. Main St., Cooke City, 406/838-2070 or 877/338-2070, www.super8.com, $110-200) is the only chain motel in town. **Alpine Motel** (105 E. Main St., Cooke City, 406/838-2262 or 888/838-1190, www.cookecityalpine.com, $115-165) has rooms with one or two queen beds, plus a microwave and mini-fridge, or two-bedroom suites with full kitchens. **High Country Motel** (113 W. Main St., Cooke City,

406/838-2272, www.highcountrymotelandcabins.com, May-mid Oct., mid-Dec.-Mar., $110-150) has 1-2 queen beds in 11 motel rooms and four 1950s log cabins. Some rooms have kitchens. **Soda Butte Lodge** (209 Hwy. 212, Cooke City, 406/838-2251, www.cookecity.com, $100-160) has 32 motel rooms in a two- and three-story building with no elevator. Room choices include a king bed or two or three queen beds. A restaurant and saloon are part of the complex.

CABINS

Pine Edge Cabins (107 and 109 U.S. Hwy. 212, Silver Gate, 406/838-2371, www.pineedgecabins.com, year-round, $145-350) is a collection of 29 log cabins, five motel rooms, and a general store that rents spotting scopes for wildlife-watching. Three different cabin complexes are available, most with full kitchens. At the upper prices, the newer Silver Gate Cabins have kitchens and one or two queen beds (some with additional bunk beds or sofa beds). The mid-range Pine Edge Cabins have one or two double beds, with some additional bunks. Most of the older and lower-priced Whispering Pines Cabins have one or two double beds and access to a wood-fired sauna. Motel rooms have one queen bed.

GUEST RANCH

In a quiet three-story log lodge set amid firs, **Skyline Guest Ranch** (31 Kersey Lake Rd., Cooke City, 406/838-2380 or 877/238-8885, www.flyfishyellowstone.com, winter and summer, $130-180) operates a bed-and-breakfast along with an outfitting service for horseback riding, hunting, fishing, and snowmobiling. Six guest rooms include private bathrooms and one or two queen beds. Communal areas include a hot tub, picnic tables, outdoor grill, living room, and dining room. In winter, the ranch is only accessible via snowmobile.

Camping

INSIDE THE PARK

This region of Yellowstone has smaller campgrounds than elsewhere in the park. With the exception of Mammoth Campground, each offers a quiet place to get away from crowds. Reservations are not accepted; all campgrounds are **first-come, first-served.** Amenities include potable water, picnic tables, bear boxes for food storage, fire rings with grills, and flush or vault toilets, but no showers. Accessible sites are available at Mammoth and Indian Creek Campgrounds. Check online (www.nps.gov/yell) to see what time the campgrounds filled on the previous day and then aim to grab a campsite before then. In midsummer, campgrounds can fill before 8am.

Mammoth Hot Springs

At 6,200 feet, **Mammoth Campground** (year-round, $20) clusters its 85 campsites on an open sagebrush hillside with scattered trees. This is the only campground in the northern region of the park with flush toilets and where generators are permitted (8am-8pm). Most campsites have pull-through parking to accommodate RVs (some can fit combinations up to 75 feet), and 51 sites have tent pads. Campers can walk to trailheads, Mammoth Hot Springs Terraces, restaurants, and shops. Though it can be windy or hot in midsummer, most campsites get broad scenery of Gardner River Canyon. The access road to Mammoth Hot Springs circles the campground, which makes daytime traffic noise a factor. In winter, RVs are limited to 30 feet.

Mammoth to Norris

Eight miles south of Mammoth Hot Springs, **Indian Creek Campground** (mid-June-mid-Sept., $15) has 70 sites, vault toilets, and a quiet ambience with views of Electric Peak in the Gallatin Range. This is a place to hear the haunting hoot of owls or bugling elk in fall.

Most campsites are tucked into the forest with parking pads (35 feet or less). At 7,300 feet, the campground offers quick access to Swan Lake Flat for wildlife-watching, the trailhead to Bighorn Pass, and Bunsen Peak

Tower-Roosevelt

Set on a steep hillside above Tower Fall, **Tower Fall Campground** (late May-late Sept., $15) has 31 campsites with parking pads (30 feet or shorter), plus a hairpin turn to negotiate. Some sites sit in the open while others tuck under large pines. At 6,600 feet in elevation, hiking up or down the hill to vault toilets or to the hand-cranked water pump may have you huffing and puffing. A trail drops from the campground to the Tower Fall observation area, but be prepared to climb back uphill. Horseback trail rides and a restaurant are two miles north at Roosevelt Lodge. The amphitheater has evening naturalist talks.

Northeast Entrance

★ **Slough Creek Campground** (mid-June-early Sept., $15) is prized for its remoteness, solitude, wildlife-watching, and fishing. Lined up along Slough Creek at 6,250 feet in elevation, the 23 campsites vary from open sagebrush meadows to shady conifers. Prime campsites include creek frontage within sound of the water. All sites have less than 30-foot parking pads; amenities include hand pumps for water and vault toilets. This primitive campground is accessed via the dirt Slough Creek Road, five miles east of Tower Junction on the Northeast Entrance Road.

North of Lamar Valley at 6,900 feet elevation, **Pebble Creek Campground** (mid-June-late Sept., $15) loops through forest-flanked wildflower meadows. Some of the 27 campsites are open with views of the surrounding Absaroka Mountains, and a few are walk-in tent-only sites. Facilities include a hand pump for water and vault toilets.

Nearby, you can access the trailhead to Trout Lake, fishing in Soda Butte Creek, wildlife-watching in Lamar Valley, or Silver Gate and Cooke City. The campground is located along the Northeast Entrance Road, 13 miles past Slough Creek Road.

OUTSIDE THE PARK
Gardiner
PRIVATE CAMPGROUNDS

Gardiner has two commercial campgrounds. Facilities include picnic tables, wireless Internet, cable TV, laundries, flush toilets, showers, and hookups for sewer, water, and electricity. Add a 10 percent tax to all rates.

Rocky Mountain Campground (14 Jardine Rd., 406/848-7251 or 877/534-6931, www.rockymountainrvpark.com, May-Sept., $47-70) perches on a bluff in downtown Gardiner, within walking distance to shopping, restaurants, groceries, and the Roosevelt Arch. With 71 RV campsites, the sunny campground commands views of the town. A few campsites tuck under the shade of large trees, but all stack up in parking-lot fashion and lack privacy. RVs are limited to 45 feet. Facilities include a community campfire area, miniature golf, and a disposal station.

Yellowstone RV Park (117 Hwy. 89 S., 406/848-7496, www.venturewestinc.com/ YellowstoneRVPark.htm, May-Oct., $59-70 RV, $38 tents) sits farther from the main action of town, but overlooks the Yellowstone River. Two rows of 46 RV sites line up like a parking lot. The campsites are open, sunny, and speckled with a few low trees. Expect to hear both the river and the highway; winds also frequently blow through the canyon. The campground can accommodate a few tents and RVs up to 70 feet.

FOREST SERVICE CAMPGROUNDS
Custer-Gallatin National Forest (Gardiner Ranger District, 406/848-7375, www.fs.usda. gov/custergallatin, first-come first-served year-round, $7 for one vehicle, $3 each additional vehicle) operates two campgrounds near Gardiner that work for overflow camping

in a pinch or places to stay before heading into the park. Sites have picnic tables, fire rings with grills, bear boxes, and vault toilets. There is no drinking water, so be prepared to filter creek water or bring your own.

Three miles north of Gardiner along Jardine Road, **Eagle Creek Campground** has commanding views across the valley into Yellowstone. Set on an open hillside, the 16 campsites have no shade or privacy, and many sites are sloped. Eagle Creek runs along the west side of the campground, surrounded by brush, aspens, and willows. RVs are limited to 40 feet, and there is a corral adjacent to the campground. Eagle Creek fills early on summer weekends and holidays.

About 15 miles north of Gardiner along U.S. Highway 89, **Canyon Campground** has 17 arid campsites in Yankee Jim Canyon set amid huge clustered boulders and junipers. Sites 3, 4, and 6 tuck back into mini-canyons for more privacy. This campground is best for tents and small RVs (up to 48 feet), as navigation requires squeezing between boulders. Watch for rattlesnakes.

Cooke City

Along U.S. Highway 212 east of Cooke City are three **Custer-Gallatin National Forest** (Gardiner Ranger District, 406/848-7375, www.fs.usda.gov/gallatin, July-early Sept., $7-9 first vehicle, $3 additional car) campgrounds, each set at around 8,000 feet in elevation and within 4-7 miles of the Northeast Entrance to Yellowstone. Facilities at each campground include picnic tables, fire rings with grills, bear boxes, vault toilets, and drinking water. The forest canopy has thinned out due to bark beetle infestations, opening up the campgrounds to sunlight and views. Campsites are first-come, first-served and fit RVs up to 48 feet. Due to the prevalence of bears, the campgrounds permit hard-sided RVs only (no tents).

Overlooking burbling Soda Butte Creek, **Soda Butte Campground** has 27 campsites. Surrounded by pink sticky geranium and white cow parsnip, the campground is

Where Can I Find . . .?

- **Banks and ATMs:** An ATM is available in Mammoth Village and in Gardiner at First Interstate Bank (903 Scott St. W., 406/848-7474).

- **Cell Service:** Verizon service is available in the village of Mammoth Hot Springs. Tower-Roosevelt does not have cell service. Outside the park, Gardiner has cell service, but Cooke City does not.

- **Day Care:** Little People's Learning Center (330 Lower Mammoth, 307/344-9011, http://little-peopleslearningcenter.blogspot.com, 6:45am-5:45pm Mon.-Fri. summer, hours vary seasonally, $6-10/hour, $42-70/day) offers drop-in day care for ages six weeks-school age with 24-hour advance notice and immunization records.

- **Gas and Garage Services:** Gas stations (406/848-7548) are located at Mammoth (mid-May-mid-Oct.) and Tower Junction (June-Sept.). You can pay at the pump 24 hours a day with a credit card; in summer, you can also pay with cash. Outside the park, Gardiner and Cooke City have gas stations; head to Gardiner for auto repairs.

- **Internet Service:** Internet is available at the Mammoth Hot Springs Hotel lounge ($5/hour) and Albright Visitor Center (free). Outside the park, Cooke City's visitors center has wireless Internet, as do most hotels in Gardiner.

- **Laundry:** The closest laundry services are at Gardiner Laundry (111 E. Main St., Gardiner, 406/223-9936) and North Entrance Washtub (209 Main St., Gardiner, 406/848-9870), which also has public showers.

- **Pet-Friendly Lodging:** Available in Mammoth Hot Springs Hotel and Roosevelt Lodge.

- **Post Office:** A year-round post office (8:30am-5pm Mon.-Fri.) is located in Mammoth Village next to the Albright Visitor Center. There is also a post office in Gardiner (707 Scott St. W., 406/848-7579).

- **Showers:** Pay showers are located in the Mammoth Hot Springs Hotel (May-Oct.) and at the Roosevelt Lodge (June-Sept.) at Tower Junction.

six miles from the Northeast Entrance and one mile east of Cooke City.

One mile east of Soda Butte, on the north side of the highway, is neighboring **Colter Campground** with 18 campsites. Set in new-growth forest and meadows with views of the Absaroka Mountains, the campground is seven miles from the Northeast Entrance and two miles east of Cooke City.

Transportation and Services

DRIVING

Gardiner is located on U.S. Highway 89, which becomes Park Street approaching the North Entrance to Yellowstone. From Gardiner, the North Entrance Road (U.S. 89, open year-round) runs five miles south to Mammoth Village.

From Mammoth Village, the two-lane Grand Loop Road travels east for 19 miles across the Blacktail Deer Plateau to Tower Junction and the park hub of Roosevelt. At Tower Junction, the Northeast Entrance Road continues 30 miles east to the Northeast Entrance. These roads are open year-round, and are the only park roads accessible by private cars and RVs in winter. Snowstorms can cause temporary closures during fall, winter, and spring. Call for current road conditions (307/344-2117). In winter, plowing terminates just east of Cooke City where snow closes Highways 212 and 296. While this stretch of road offers prime wildlife-watching, the two-lane road is often clogged with "bison jams" (bison herds crossing the road), as well as traffic from stopped vehicles and dazed tourists taking photos. The drive from Mammoth to Tower Junction can take one hour or more in summer; the Northeast Entrance Road can take also take up to one hour.

Find parking streetside in towns and villages or in parking lots at trailheads, lodges, picnic areas, and campgrounds in Yellowstone. Covered parking is not available at motels in Gardiner, Mammoth, Roosevelt, or Cooke City.

SHUTTLES

There is no public transportation between Gardiner, Mammoth Village, and Cooke City. Karst Stage (800/287-4759, www.karststage.com) provides shuttle services to and from the Bozeman, Montana airport and to Gardiner or Mammoth Village.

EMERGENCY SERVICES

Inside the park, medical emergencies can be treated at the Mammoth Clinic (Mammoth Village, 307/344-7965). You can also get help at the ranger stations located at Tower Junction and at the park entrance at Gardiner. Neither Gardiner nor Cooke City has a medical clinic, but they do have emergency medical services (dial 911).

The nearest hospital is Livingston HealthCare Hospital (32 Alpenglow Ln., Livingston, MT, 406/823-6262, www.livingstonhealthcare.org), 54 miles north along U.S. Highway 89, or head to their Livingston HealthCare Urgent Care (104 Centennial Dr., Ste. 103, 406/222-0030, 11am-10pm Mon.-Fri., 9am-5pm Sat.-Sun.).

The nearest hospital to Cooke City is West Park Hospital (707 Sheridan Ave., Cody, WY, 307/527-7501, www.westparkhospital.org), located 78 long and winding miles south in Cody. However, road closures can prevent access in winter, in which case you must drive 112 miles north to Livingston instead.

Old Faithful and West Yellowstone

Exploring Old Faithful
    and West Yellowstone......... 88
Sights 93
Recreation..................... 102
Entertainment and Shopping ...117

Food 119
Accommodations.............. 123
Camping 128
Transportation and Services ... 131

The western arc of Yellowstone's supervolcano houses a string of geyser basins that contain some of the world's most active hydrothermal features.

Paint pots simmer with colorful microscopic creatures. Mud pots bubble like witches' cauldrons. Fumaroles blow off steam, and geysers spout scalding water. Rumbling with geothermal gusto, Upper Geyser Basin has the largest concentration of geysers. Old Faithful draws crowds for its regular eruptions, and hot pools yield mesmerizing colors. Midway Geyser Basin houses two of Yellowstone's largest geothermal features: Grand Prismatic Spring and Excelsior Geyser. Lower Geyser Basin spreads across the largest piece of landscape, almost 11 square miles of steaming portals from the earth's bowels. Norris Geyser Basin harbors the hottest hydrothermals and Steamboat Geyser, the world's tallest geyser.

For those exploring this bubbling landscape, Old Faithful and West Yellowstone house visitor services, restaurants, and lodging; Madison and Norris have the camping. Between them, fishing abounds, particularly in the trout-rich waters of the Firehole, Madison, and Gallatin Rivers.

Wildlife is easy to spot, even in winter. Bison wander through the geyser basins, and elk herds gather along the Madison River with the bulls bugling in fall. Carnivores follow the herds. Raptors fly overhead.

This supervolcano arc is one of the most active geothermal zones in Yellowstone; it is also the most popular. Old Faithful and West Yellowstone buzz with throngs of visitors in summer. But nowhere else in the world will you see such utter uniqueness.

PLANNING YOUR TIME

Wildlife-watching and geothermal activity go on year-round in Yellowstone. What alters is access and crowds. **High season is July-August**. June and September are still busy, but with fewer hordes. To avoid crowds, go in spring or late fall. **Park roads close** to private vehicles **November-mid-April**. During **winter high season** (mid-Dec.-mid-Mar.) only snowmobiles and snowcoaches are permitted on the roads in to Old Faithful. West Yellowstone is open

---

Previous: Grand Prismatic Spring; fishing for trout in the Madison River. **Above:** Great Fountain Geyser.

Look for ★ to find recommended
sights, activities, dining, and lodging.

Highlights

★ **Old Faithful Visitor Education Center:** Learn how geothermal features work and what scientists are discovering (page 89).

★ **Winter Snowcoach Tours:** See the volcanic landscape of the park in winter for a steaming clash of heat and ice (page 91).

★ **Wildlife Watching:** Elk and bison dominate the Madison River valley, spilling northeast into the Gibbon River drainage (page 94).

★ **Fountain Paint Pots:** This 0.5-mile interpretive boardwalk loop visits all four of Yellowstone's different volcanic features (page 94).

★ **Great Fountain Geyser:** The only predictable eruption in Lower Geyser Basin blows for one hour to heights of 75-220 feet (page 95).

★ **Grand Prismatic Spring:** Vivid blue water surrounded by radiating browns and oranges comprise the largest hot springs in the United States (page 96).

★ **Old Faithful Geyser:** This geyser spews hot water 145 feet into the air about every 90 minutes (page 97).

★ **Old Faithful Inn:** The log lobby of this 1904 masterpiece holds an 85-foot-tall stone fireplace, the centerpiece of one of the first "parkitecture" inns (page 100).

★ **Norris Geyser Basin:** Walk through the hottest and most changeable geothermal basin in the park (page 101).

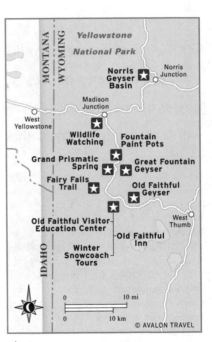

★ **Fairy Falls Trail:** Hike to this 197-foot-tall waterfall as it plummets over a cliff and sprays down rock steps to collect in a cold pool (page 106).

Old Faithful and West Yellowstone

To Big Sky
and Bozeman

Fawn Pass
Trail

To Mammoth
Hot Springs

Bighorn Pass
Trail

Gardner
River

191

Custer-Gallatin

National

Forest

To Earthquake Lake
Visitor Center, Ennis,
and Butte

287

RAINBOW
POINT

191

287

Gneiss Creek
Trail

YELLOWSTONE

NATIONAL

PARK

Mt Holmes
10,336ft

Obsidian
Cliff

Roaring
Mountain

NORRIS

Ice
Lake

NORRIS GEYSER
BASIN

Norris
Junction

20

BAKERS
HOLE

Upper
Madison
Valley
Trail

Monument
Geyser Basin

Gibbon R.

Artists
Paintpots

Virginia
Cascade

To
Canyon
Village

West
Yellowstone

Madison River

Harlequin
Lake

Madison
Junction

TERRACE
SPRING

GRIZZLY AND WOLF
DISCOVERY CENTER

WEST
ENTRANCE

WILDLIFE
WATCHING

MADISON

MADISON INFO STATION

FIREHOLE
CANYON DR

Gibbon
Falls

MONTANA

WYOMING

Mt Haynes
8,235ft

Firehole
Falls

GRAND

LOOP

Mary

Mountain

Trail

National Park
Mountain
7,549ft

FOUNTAIN
FLAT DRIVE

RD

Sentinel Meadows

Queen's
Laundry

Lower
Geyser
Basin

FOUNTAIN
PAINT POTS

FIREHOLE
LAKE DRIVE

Midway Geyser
Basin

GREAT FOUNTAIN
GEYSER

GRAND PRISMATIC SPRING

Upper
Geyser
Basin

FAIRY FALLS TRAIL

MALLARD
LAKE

Caribou-Targhee

National

Forest

Continental

Black Sand
Basin

Isa
Lake

WINTER
SNOWCOACH
TOURS

OLD
FAITHFUL
GEYSER

Craig
Pass

Summit
Lake Trail

OLD
FAITHFUL
INN

Lone Star
Geyser

West
Thumb

West Boundary Trail

IDAHO

Divide

Firehole River

North
Shore Trail

Shoshone
Lake

Delacy Creek Trail

Shoshone
Geyser Basin

Shoshone Lake Trail

0   5 mi

0   5 km

Bechler River
Trail

Lewis
Lake

© AVALON TRAVEL

year-round, but **Old Faithful (mid-Apr.-early Nov. and mid-Dec.-mid-Mar.)** is a seasonal destination.

At the **Lower, Middle,** and **Upper Geyser Basins,** crowds thicken midday. For greater solitude, visit early or late in the day. For the best touring experience, pack a picnic lunch so you won't be pressed by hunger to forgo sightseeing in favor of finding a restaurant. Most visitors who drive the **Grand Loop** in one day do so because they have limited time. You'll find exploring the route more enjoyable with **multiple days** of touring.

Summer

For geothermal activity, you'll want to schedule visiting some sights based on when geysers erupt. Stop at visitors centers or use the park's Yellowstone Geyser App to **check eruption schedules;** then plan excursions based on the predicted eruptions. For Old Faithful, crowds gather 30 minutes before eruptions to claim front-row seating.

In **July** and **August,** get an early start. When parking lots max out (10am-4pm), you may have to circle around to find a parking spot, or go elsewhere and come back. Restrooms will have long waiting lines.

For **Old Faithful lodging,** make reservations one year in advance to guarantee getting your preferred room. For **West Yellowstone lodging,** book 6-12 months in advance for July-August. You can find last-minute lodging in summer, but may have limited options.

Winter

In winter, when **park roads are closed for driving,** West Yellowstone serves as the biggest hub to access Old Faithful on day trips. **Make reservations six months in advance** for snowcoach and snowmobile tours.

At Old Faithful, only the **Snow Lodge** is open for about 10 weeks in winter. Book at least **six months in advance** or as early as March 15 for winter holidays. You can book snowcoach transportation with Xantera when boking lodging; however, their snowcoaches only launch from Mammoth.

Spring and Fall

A less hectic time to travel, spring and fall may be hampered by snow squalls. **Late March-mid-April** and **early November** offers a few weeks when cyclists can ride the plowed road without cars. Cooler temperatures produce more steam in the geyser basins.

Exploring Old Faithful and West Yellowstone

VISITORS CENTERS
West Yellowstone Visitor Information Center

The **West Yellowstone Visitor Information Center** (30 Yellowstone Ave., West Yellowstone, 307/344-2876, www.nps.gov/yell, 8am-8pm daily late May-early Sept., 8am-4pm daily mid-Dec.-late Apr., spring, and fall) is located in West Yellowstone (outside the park) at the corner of Canyon Street and the park entrance road. Inside is the **West Yellowstone Chamber of Commerce** (406/646-7701, www.destinationyellowstone.com) and a National Park Service desk. At the park service desk, you can get maps, ranger programs, and naturalist-led tour schedules, as well as information on campgrounds, backcountry permits (8am-4:30pm daily June-Aug.), wildlife, and geothermal hot spots. Restrooms are also available.

Madison Information Station

A National Historic Landmark, the small **Madison Information Station**

(307/244-2821, www.nps.gov/yell, 9am-6pm daily late May-early Sept.) is housed in a historic cabin overlooking the Madison River near Madison Junction. Also known as the **Madison Junior Ranger Station,** this is where naturalists put on short presentations about wildlife and ecology for families. Visitors can get maps and information, and there is a tiny bookstore in one corner. In winter, a wood-sided trailer in the adjacent parking lot serves as the information station (and sells hot chocolate).

Norris Geyser Basin Museum & Information Station

Located at the entrance to Norris Geyser Basin, the **Norris Geyser Basin Museum & Information Station** (307/344-2812, www.nps.gov/yell, 9am-6pm daily late May-Sept., spring, and fall) houses exhibits on geothermal features and offers information on naturalist-led tours, camping, sightseeing, and wildlife. Rangers lead several programs, including walks into the geyser basin. Completed in 1930, the log-and-stone building is a National Historic Landmark. A **Yellowstone Forever** bookstore (406/848-2400, www.yellowstone.org) is housed in an adjacent building.

★ Old Faithful Visitor Education Center

The **Old Faithful Visitor Education Center** (307/344-2751, www.nps.gov/yell, 8am-8pm daily late Apr.-early Nov., 9am-5pm daily mid-Dec.-Feb., hours vary in spring and fall), located adjacent to Old Faithful Geyser, is the place to learn about geysers, hot springs, mud pots, and fumaroles. Visitors can get maps, park information, and schedules for naturalist-led tours, including tours of the facility. The center also shows a rotating lineup of films about the park with stunning photography that features geysers, wildlife, park history, and ecology. The daily film schedule is posted outside the theater. Current research exhibits reveal what scientists are discovering, while a special kids' room takes a hands-on approach for young scientists. Kids can get Junior Ranger booklets ($3) and are sworn in after completion to receive a patch. Geyser eruption predictions are also available (304/344-2751, @Twitter.com/GeyserNPS). **Yellowstone Forever** (406/848-2400, www.yellowstone.org) runs a bookstore inside.

ENTRANCE STATION

Located on U.S. Highway 20 on the east edge of West Yellowstone, Montana, the **West**

Old Faithful Visitor Education Center

Entrance ($30/vehicle, $25 motorcycles, $15 hike-in/bike-in; joint parks pass: $50/vehicle, $40 motorcycles, $20 hike-in/bike-in) is the busiest entrance in the park. From the West Entrance, the park hub of Madison lies 14 miles east and Old Faithful 30 miles southeast. The West Entrance is open to cars and RVs mid-April-early November; in winter (mid-Dec.-mid-Mar.), the road closes and is accessible only to snowmobiles and snowcoaches.

In summer, the West Entrance sees more than 100,000 visitors each month; in July, more than 4,000 visitors enter each *day* (that's more than double some of the other park entrance stations). The crowds are due to West Yellowstone's high volume of lodging and close proximity to Old Faithful. If visiting in summer (especially July), stop at the West Yellowstone Visitor Information Center in West Yellowstone first to buy your park entrance pass, which will allow you to enter the faster entrance line for vehicles with passes (usually the left lane). In summer, plan to enter the park before 9:30am or after 3pm as cars clog the four entrance lanes midday, often creating 30-minute waits as traffic backs up into town.

Summer and winter tours in Yellowstone require reservations. For July, August, or winter, book tours 6-12 months in advance and make lodging reservations at the same time. You can also call a day ahead to pick up spare seats. Generally, rates for trips do not include entrance fees into the park, lunch, or tips for guides (15 percent). Bring binoculars, cameras, clothing layers for warmth, a water bottle, a thermos of hot drinks (optional), snacks, and park passes. A full list of West Yellowstone bus tours is available at West Yellowstone Chamber of Commerce (406/646-7701, www.destinationyellowstone.com).

Bus Tours
FROM OLD FAITHFUL INN

Several Xanterra tours (307/344-7311 or 866/439-7375, www.yellowstonenationalpark-lodges.com) visit the central geyser basins or drive the Grand Loop Road. Geyser Gazers (4:15pm-6pm daily late May-mid-Oct., $30) tours Midway Geyser Basin and Firehole Lake Drive in historic yellow buses from the 1930s with rollback canvas tops that allow for stand-up viewing when stopped. All other tours use buses or vans.

Firehole Basin Adventure (12:45pm-4pm daily late May-mid-Sept., $57) and Twilight on the Firehole (2-hour tour, departs 5:45pm-7:15pm daily late May-mid-Sept., $39) visit steamy thermal features. Yellowstone in a Day (8:15am-6pm daily late May-early Oct., $118) circles the 142-mile Grand Loop Road with stops at Yellowstone Lake, Grand Canyon of the Yellowstone, and Mammoth Hot Springs. Circle of Fire (8:15am-4:30pm daily late May-early Oct., $85) hits Yellowstone Lake, Hayden Valley, Grand Canyon of the Yellowstone, and Fountain Paint Pots on the south Grand Loop Road. Picture Perfect Photo Safari (5-hour tour, departs 5:45am-6:15am daily mid-May-Sept., $98) takes advantage of early morning light for photographing geothermal features and wildlife.

FROM WEST YELLOWSTONE

Multiple West Yellowstone companies run full-day sightseeing tours (depart 8am-9am, spring, summer, and fall, $75-110 adults). Interpretive guides drive buses or vans, stopping for geyser basins, scenery, and wildlife. Most tours concentrate on circling Lower Grand Loop Road to take in Old Faithful, Yellowstone Lake, Grand Canyon of the Yellowstone, wildlife, and several geyser basins. Upper Grand Loop tours go to Mammoth Hot Springs, Tower Fall, Dunraven Pass, and Grand Canyon of the Yellowstone. Some companies offer discounts for seniors and kids.

- Buffalo Bus Touring Company (415 Yellowstone Ave., 406/646-9564 or 800/426-7669, www.yellowstonevacations.com, late Apr.-early Nov.) offers full-day tours in yellow mini-buses or big buses, both with large

Snowcoaches tour the park in winter.

Upper Grand Loop to see wildlife around Mammoth Hot Springs, Lamar Valley, and Dunraven Pass.

- **Yellowstone Alpen Guides** (555 Yellowstone Ave., 406/646-9591 or 800/858-3502, www.yellowstoneguides.com) runs daily wildlife tours that include a bison stew picnic dinner.
- **See Yellowstone Tours** (217 Yellowstone Ave., 800/221-1151, www.seeyellowstone. com) runs evening tours (depart 1pm daily) with bison stew picnic dinners and morning tours with picnic lunches (depart 7am Mon., Wed., and Fri.).

★ Winter Snowcoach Tours

When snow covers the geyser basins, every pore in the landscape emits copious steam, creating an otherworldly peek at nature. Due to colder winter temperatures, the scenes take on more drama than in summer. Designed for snow travel, snowcoaches are heated sightseeing buses or vans equipped with tracks, skis, or huge wheels. Some of the vans on tracks sway and bounce, especially for backseat riders. Historic 10-passenger Bombardiers are a very loud, but fun, nostalgic ride with pop-open roof hatches for easy wildlife-viewing. Led by interpretive guides, coaches stop at sights where visitors can photograph geysers or wildlife. Wear warm layers of winter clothing and boots for walking in snow.

FROM OLD FAITHFUL

From the Old Faithful Snow Lodge, **Xanterra** (307/344-7311 or 866/439-7375, www.yellowstonenationalparklodges.com, mid-Dec.-early Mar., kids age 3-11 half price) offers snowcoach mini-bus tours and ski trips. Shorter daily tours ($54-97) go wildlife-watching, evening stargazing, and geyser exploring; destinations include West Thumb Geyser Basin, Firehole Basin, and Madison River. Full-day tours ($247-276) visit Grand Canyon of the Yellowstone or go on a photo safari; order box lunches one day prior.

windows. Tours circle Lower Grand Loop Road (daily) and Upper Grand Loop Road (Mon., Wed., and Fri.-Sat.).

- **See Yellowstone Tours** (217 Yellowstone Ave., 800/221-1151, www.seeyellowstone. com, early May-Sept) drives sightseeing vans with large windows on morning or evening tours around the Lower Grand Loop, Upper Grand Loop, or to Grand Teton National Park. Picnic lunches are included.
- **Yellowstone Alpen Guides** (555 Yellowstone Ave., 406/646-9591 or 800/858-3502, www.yellowstoneguides.com, May-Sept.) circles Lower Grand Loop daily.

Wildlife Safaris

Wildlife safari tours (mid-May-Sept., $95 adults, $85 kids, $90 seniors, includes picnic lunches or dinners) take advantage of mornings and evenings for the optimum chance of seeing bison, elk, bears, moose, and wolves. From West Yellowstone, tours head for the

FROM WEST YELLOWSTONE

Several companies run full-day snowcoach tours **mid-December-mid-March**. Tours depart West Yellowstone 8am-9am daily and last 8-9 hours. Some companies offer discounts for seniors and kids.

- **Buffalo Bus Touring Company** (415 Yellowstone Ave., 406/646-9564 or 800/426-7669, www.yellowstonevacations. com, $120-130) operates a fleet of six-passenger Chevy Suburbans and 30-passenger sightseeing coaches. Daily tours go to Old Faithful. Snowcoach tours visit Grand Canyon of the Yellowstone (departing four days weekly).

- **See Yellowstone Tours** (217 Yellowstone Ave., 800/221-1151, www.seeyellowstone. com, $145) drives oversized vans with large windows or Bombardiers on daily tours to Old Faithful and Grand Canyon of the Yellowstone.

- **Yellowstone Alpen Guides** (555 Yellowstone Ave., 406/646-9591 or 800/858-3502, www.yellowstoneguides. com, $145-160) drive Bombardiers daily to Old Faithful or Grand Canyon of the Yellowstone.

DRIVING TOURS
West Entrance Road
14 MILES

For an evening wildlife-watching drive, take the West Entrance Road (14 miles, 30 min., late Apr.-early Nov.) west from **West Yellowstone** to **Madison Junction.** The road parallels the Madison River, with sprawling meadows that fill with bison in summer and elk herds in fall. Pullouts allow places to watch, but don't become so enamored by the megafauna that you miss eagles in the trees or bobcats hunting along the river.

Lower Grand Loop Road
96 MILES

Lower Grand Loop Road links **Madison, Norris, Canyon Village, West Thumb,** and **Old Faithful** to take in loads of wildlife-watching plus Norris Geyser Basin, Grand Canyon of the Yellowstone, Hayden Valley, Yellowstone Lake, West Thumb Geyser Basin, and the Old Faithful complex. Driving the entire loop (mid-May-early Nov.) will take four hours; add more time for scenic stops and walks along the geyser basins.

Follow the West Entrance Road from Madison Junction to Norris Junction (14 miles, 30 min., mid-Apr.-early Nov.). From Madison, the road loops past **Terrace Springs** to parallel the **Gibbon River.** Look for bison and elk in **Gibbon Meadows.** The road climbs north through a canyon housing **Gibbon Falls** as it ascends out of the supervolcano caldera. **Beryl Spring** pops out in the upper meadows near **Artists Paintpots** before reaching the **Norris Geyser Basin**.

Zip east over the forested road from Norris to **Canyon Village** (12 miles, 30 min., late Apr.-early Nov.). From Canyon Village, the road passes the Grand Canyon of the Yellowstone to head south along the Yellowstone River, curving around the shores of Yellowstone Lake to **West Thumb** (37 miles, 90 min., mid May-early Nov.).

From West Thumb, head west to Old Faithful (17 miles, 45 min., mid-May-early Nov.). The route bounces twice over the **Continental Divide,** the highest point at 8,391 feet. **Isa Lake**, located at **Craig Pass**, has the unique status of flowing toward both the Pacific Ocean and the Gulf of Mexico. After descending Craig Pass, the road passes **Old Faithful** and the **Upper Geyser Basin** before completing the loop north to Madison (16 miles, 45 min. late Apr.-early Nov.).

Geyser Basin Tour
16 MILES

The Lower Grand Loop Road climbs south along the Firehole River from Madison Junction to Old Faithful (45 min., mid-Apr.-early Nov.), passing through the **Lower Geyser Basin,** which houses **Fountain Paint Pots, Firehole Lake,** and **Great Fountain Geyser,** before passing **Midway**

Geyser Basin. The road then enters **Upper Geyser Basin**, reaching **Biscuit Basin** first, then **Black Sand Basin**, before the **Old Faithful Complex**. Steam plumes from most of the basins are visible from the road. Bison herds frequent the area; prepare for stopped traffic. Three short spur roads allow scenic side tours.

FIREHOLE CANYON DRIVE

At 0.5 mile south of Madison Junction, **Firehole Canyon Drive** (2 miles, 15 min., mid-Apr.-early Nov., no RVs or trailers) cuts off on the west side of the Grand Loop Road. This one-way, steep and narrow road goes to a scenic overlook of the 40-foot **Firehole Falls** and 800-foot-thick lava flows; however, there are minimal places to pull over for photos.

FOUNTAIN FLAT DRIVE

Find **Fountain Flat Drive** (1 mile, late May-early Nov.) on the west side of the Grand Loop Road about 10.4 miles south of Madison Junction and 3.5 miles north of Old Faithful. The short drive is a good place for **wildlife-watching,** particularly elk and bison in June; it has the **Nez Perce Picnic Area** at its start and several pullouts en route. Turn around when the two-way drive dead-ends. Bear activity keeps the road closed in spring.

FIREHOLE LAKE DRIVE

Located about 9.3 miles south of Madison Junction and 6.8 miles north of Old Faithful, the one-way **Firehole Lake Drive** (3.3 miles, 30 min., late May-early Nov., no RVs or trailers) is accessed off the east side of the Grand Loop Road. The drive passes eight thermal features, including the brown **Firehole Lake,** the largest hot springs on the road, and **Great Fountain Geyser.** The nearby **White Dome Geyser** erupts at 15-30-minute intervals. The *Fountain Paint Pot Trail Guide* ($1, available at visitors centers) includes interpretive information on Firehole Lake Drive. Bear activity keeps the road closed in spring.

Sights

WEST YELLOWSTONE

With the park entrance on its eastern edge, West Yellowstone is the largest tourist town on Yellowstone's boundary. Part of the town retains its mom-and-pop souvenir shops, which crowd in summer with scads of visitors. In winter, it serves as a cross-country ski, snowmobile, and snowcoach tour headquarters. It is home to Rendezvous Ski Trails, Grizzly and Wolf Discovery Center, and Yellowstone Nature Connection. For the park's history, the **Yellowstone Historic Center** (104 Yellowstone Ave., 406/646-1100, www.yellowstonehistoriccenter.org, 9am-6pm daily mid-May-mid-Oct., 9am-9pm daily in summer, $2-6) has hands-on exhibits on stagecoaches, railroads, and early pioneers. The museum also runs walking tours, ranger talks, films, and a children's program.

The **Grizzly and Wolf Discovery Center** (201 S. Canyon St., West Yellowstone, 406/646-7001 or 800/257-2570, www.grizzlydiscoveryctr.com, 8:30am-8:30pm daily mid-May-early Sept., hours vary in fall, winter, and spring, $12 adults, $11 seniors, $7 kids, free for children under 4) provides a place to watch wildlife up close and learn about grizzly bear, wolf, and raptor behaviors. (The grizzlies don't hibernate because they are fed.) Admission is good for two consecutive days, so you can visit multiple times. Sometimes a discount coupon is available online.

MADISON JUNCTION

The confluence of the Gibbon and Firehole Rivers forms the Madison River at Madison Junction. Adjacent to the river, Madison Campground tucks below National Park Mountain. The junction is 14 miles from the

West Entrance, 16 miles from Old Faithful, and 14 miles from Norris.

Firehole River and Falls

An outstanding trout fishery, the **Firehole River** gets its name from the adjacent geyser basins pouring in scalding water; the resulting steam makes it look like the land is on fire. The 21-mile Firehole River ends at the confluence with the Gibbon River to form the Madison River at Madison Junction. Along the way, the river drops through three waterfalls, most notably the 40-foot-high frothy-white **Firehole Falls** (Firehole Canyon Dr.). Traveling south on the park road toward Old Faithful allows views of the river in the Upper, Midway, and Lower Geyser Basins.

★ Wildlife-Watching

Wildlife-watching is equally as captivating as watching geysers blow. Along the **Madison River** and the **West Entrance Road,** pull-outs permit viewing bison, elk, deer, and raptors. The **Madison Junior Ranger Station** (access via the Madison Picnic Area parking lot) is another good vantage point. In fall, bull elk often round up harems along the river, with the bulls' bugling echoing across the valley.

Maintain a safe distance (at least 75-100 feet) from all wildlife and give them plenty of room. The animals may look tame, but gorings continue to occur when people get too close, especially while trying to take selfies or photos of others posed with bison.

LOWER GEYSER BASIN
★ Fountain Paint Pots

Eight miles south of Madison Junction (or north of Old Faithful), **Fountain Paint Pots** is a 0.5-mile interpretive boardwalk loop that includes all four hydrothermal features in the park: geysers, mud pots, hot springs, and fumaroles. Pick up the *Fountain Paint Pot Trail Guide* ($1) at the start of the trail.

At the boardwalk junction, look left into the blue **Celestine Pool** or right for the colorful bacterial mats of thermophiles formed

In fall, bull elk bugle in Madison River Valley.

Fountain Paint Pots burble with colored mud.

Lower and Midway Geyser Basins

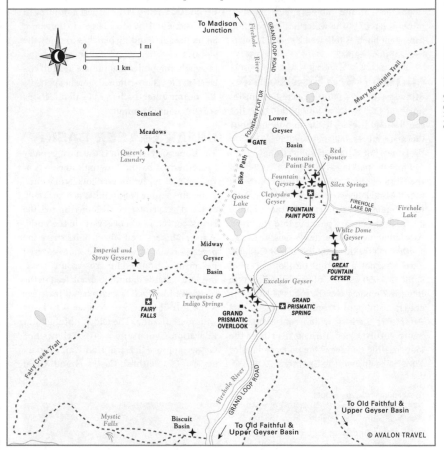

in the runoff from the silica-rich, turquoise **Silex Spring** straight ahead. The trail then divides around pink and gray **Fountain Paint Pot,** bubbling more in the liquid clay of early summer, but thicker by fall. (Its clay was used to paint the former hotel across the road.) The trail splits to circle **Red Spouter,** named for the red clay that acts like a mud pot, hot springs, or steam vent based on changing water amounts throughout the year. As the boardwalk continues west downhill, several geysers spurt and fume. When **Fountain Geyser** erupts, it can shoot water 20-50 feet in the air for longer than 20 minutes. The smaller neighboring **Clepsydra Geyser,** which sputters nonstop from several vents, can pause when Fountain erupts.

★ Great Fountain Geyser

Located on the one-way Firehole Lake Drive (9.3 miles south of Madison Junction and 6.8 miles north of Old Faithful), **Great Fountain Geyser** shoots 75-220 feet high every 10-14 hours. Unlike Old Faithful's short durations, Great Fountain's eruptions last about an hour, with short bursts of water interspersed between quiet periods. The geyser ushers in a long, dramatic prelude to erupting. Water floods the vent, and bubbles appear about 30 minutes later. As the water boils into giant three-foot bubbles followed by one big burp, the eruption begins.

MIDWAY GEYSER BASIN

Midway Geyser Basin is located 6.5 miles north of Old Faithful and about 10 miles south of Madison. The basin only has four thermal features, but they are huge. Two are the largest hot springs in Yellowstone.

From the parking area (on the west side of the Grand Loop Road), head south to walk over the bridge across the Firehole River. Start the 0.7-mile loop, admiring the thermophile colors in the stream pouring into the river. After climbing up a boardwalk switchback, go south along the dormant **Excelsior Geyser.** Excelsior is now a stunning turquoise hot pool spilling 4,050 gallons of water per minute into the Firehole River. Beyond the Excelsior crater, steam pours from the larger **Grand Prismatic Spring,** which commands the high point of the loop. Turn north to finish the loop, passing the clear blue pools of smaller **Turquoise** and **Indigo Springs.**

★ Grand Prismatic Spring

At 370 feet across and 121 feet deep, **Grand Prismatic Spring** is the largest hot spring in Yellowstone and the third-largest in the world. Sit on the surrounding benches to enjoy the glorious hues: fiery arms of orange, gold, and brown thermophiles that radiate in a full circle from the yellow-rimmed, blue hot pool. Its 160-degree water discharges in all directions at 560 gallons per minute.

UPPER GEYSER BASIN

The Upper Geyser Basin is the most popular hydrothermal basin, drawing thousands of visitors each day in summer but few in winter. It contains a maze of four miles of boardwalk, dirt, and paved interpretive loops through the largest concentration of geysers in the world. Walkers, bikers, and wheelchairs share the paved portion; in winter, the snow-covered pavement is groomed for cross-country skiing. Often, herds of buffalo or elk feed in the meadows in between geothermal features. Signs at trail junctions have maps to assist with route-finding. The Old Faithful Visitor Education Center and a NPS Yellowstone Geyser app predict eruption times for six geysers: Old Faithful, Castle, Grand, Great

Great Fountain Geyser erupts.

Prismatic Spring

Upper Geyser Basin
GEYSER HILL LOOP

From the Old Faithful viewing area, head east across the Firehole River to climb the boardwalk and stairs that ring **Geyser Hill,** which is sprinkled with several active geysers. Geyser Hill is a 1.3-mile walk from the visitors center, and a boardwalk connects it with the Firehole River Loops.

On the south section of this loop, turn left to view **Beehive Geyser,** which can shoot up 200 feet, but has an irregular schedule. The smaller nearby **Anemone** and **Plume Geysers** erupt regularly, the first about every 10 minutes and the second hourly. Continue north past Beehive to find the clear blue **Heart Spring** near the cones of the interconnected **Lion Group,** a family of geysers called Little Cub, Big Cub, Lioness, and Lion, the latter of which heralds eruptions with a roar. Turn right to access the upper part of this loop. Admire the radiant color and ledges of **Doublet Pool.** From here, a spur trail heads north to **Solitary Geyser,** which surges with short, six-foot bursts every 4-8 minutes.

FIREHOLE RIVER LOOP

Northwest of Geyser Hill, the bigger Firehole River Loop crosses two bridges to take in the famous hot pools of the Upper Geyser Basin, plus more geysers, fumaroles, and springs.

At the southern start of this loop is **Castle Geyser,** a cone geyser built into the largest sinter formation in the world. About every 14 hours, Castle Geyser erupts for 20 minutes and then pumps out copious steam. Continue north and turn right to cross the Firehole River and reach **Grand Geyser,** a predictable fountain geyser that throws water 200 feet skyward in several short bursts. To the north sit a pair of interconnected hot springs, **Beauty Pool** and **Chromatic Pool.** When the water level rises in one, it drops in the other.

As the boardwalk crosses the river again, you might get to see the erratic **Giant Geyser** throw water up 300 feet. At the junction with the paved trail, **Grotto Geyser** squirts water

Fountain, Daisy, and Riverside. Pick up the interpretive *Old Faithful Trail Guide* ($1) at the visitors center.

★ Old Faithful Geyser

Old Faithful Geyser anchors the Upper Geyser Basin. When Old Faithful erupts, it shoots up to 8,400 gallons of hot water as high as 185 feet. It's not the tallest geyser in the park, but it is one of the most regular, erupting about every 90 minutes for 1.5-5 minutes. Often, the geyser sputters for up to 20 minutes before the eruption. A quiet interval between eruptions correlates to the length of the previous eruption. Expect massive crowds of people in summer, with benches surrounding the geyser filling 30 minutes in advance. Winter eruptions see only a handful of people. Old Faithful is located behind the Old Faithful Visitor Education Center, which posts eruption times. A 0.7-mile rubberized and pavement loop circles the famous geyser.

Upper Geyser Basin

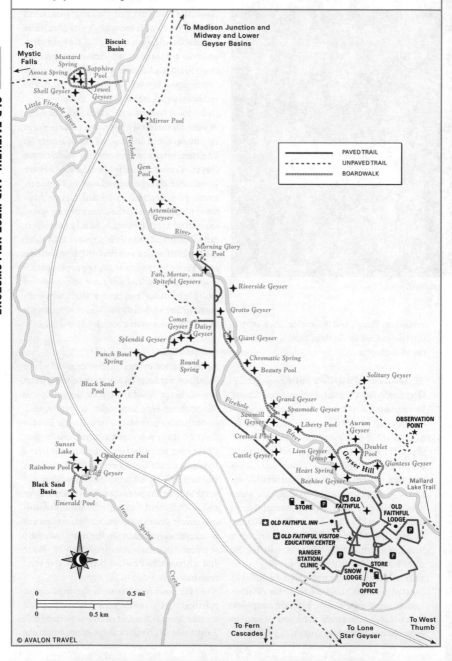

To Mystic Falls

Biscuit Basin

To Madison Junction and Midway and Lower Geyser Basins

Mustard Spring

Avoca Spring

Sapphire Pool

Shell Geyser

Jewel Geyser

Little Firehole River

Firehole

Mirror Pool

Gem Pool

Artemisia Geyser

River

Morning Glory Pool

Fan, Mortar, and Spiteful Geysers

Riverside Geyser

Grotto Geyser

Comet Geyser

Daisy Geyser

Giant Geyser

Splendid Geyser

Punch Bowl Spring

Round Spring

Chromatic Spring

Beauty Pool

Solitary Geyser

Black Sand Pool

Firehole

Grand Geyser

Spasmodic Geyser

OBSERVATION POINT

Sawmill Geyser

Liberty Pool

Aurum Geyser

River

Sunset Lake

Opalescent Pool

Crested Pool

Castle Geyser

Lion Geyser Group

Doublet Pool

Geyser Hill

Giantess Geyser

Rainbow Pool

Cliff Geyser

Black Sand Basin

Emerald Pool

Heart Spring

Beehive Geyser

Mallard Lake Trail

STORE

OLD FAITHFUL

OLD FAITHFUL LODGE

OLD FAITHFUL INN

OLD FAITHFUL VISITOR EDUCATION CENTER

RANGER STATION/ CLINIC

SNOW LODGE

STORE

POST OFFICE

Iron Spring Creek

PAVED TRAIL

UNPAVED TRAIL

BOARDWALK

0   0.5 mi

0   0.5 km

© AVALON TRAVEL

To Fern Cascades

To Lone Star Geyser

To West Thumb

Old Faithful Geyser erupts every 90 minutes.

footbridge, the boardwalk tours past **Black Opal Pool, Wall Pool,** and **Sapphire Pool.** The latter is the most commanding feature, a hot pool of crystal-clear 200-degree blue water that once used to be a geyser. At the junction, go either way to circle the basin. Highlights on the upper loop include the yellow **Mustard Spring** and **Jewel Geyser,** which shoots water up to 20 feet in the air about every 10 minutes, a short enough time to wait to see it.

Biscuit Basin is located on the park road, two miles north of the Old Faithful turnoff and south of the Midway Geyser Basin. From the Old Faithful Visitor Education Center, it is a 5.9-mile round-trip hike to the basin. From the paved trail, take the Daisy Geyser Loop junction and turn west. At the next junction, turn north to reach Grand Loop Road. A trail continues on the opposite side to reach the back of the geyser basin. (Bikes must turn right onto the road to reach the parking lot.)

Black Sand Basin

In the Upper Geyser Basin, **Black Sand Basin** has a 0.6-mile boardwalk across Iron Spring Creek with two short spurs that tour past small geysers and colorful hot pools. The basin acquired its name from the bits of obsidian that speckle the area. On the creek's edge, **Cliff Geyser** blows water up to 40 feet from a small crater. Eruptions last 0.5-3 hours, with copious steam spewing out. At the boardwalk junction, turn right to see **Sunset Lake,** named for its yellow-orange rim, and left to see **Emerald Pool,** colored from its algae. Before hopping back in the car, walk a tiny spur off the north corner of the parking lot to see **Opalescent Pool,** fed by the almost constantly erupting **Spouter Geyser,** which flooded an area of lodgepoles. The dead trees are now known as **Bobby sox trees** due to the white socks around their silica-soaked trunk bases.

Reach Black Sand Basin by driving 0.5 mile northwest of Old Faithful. It's also possible to hike there (4.4 miles round-trip) from Old Faithful Visitor Education Center. From the paved trail, turn left to take the Daisy Geyser

from its odd-shaped cone for sometimes up to 24 hours. Continue north on the paved trail to **Riverside Geyser,** which shoots an arc of water at six-hour intervals over the Firehole for about 20 minutes. The striking green, orange, and yellow **Morning Glory Pool** marks the turnaround point.

DAISY GEYSER BASIN LOOP

From the paved trail on the west side of the Firehole River, the **Daisy Geyser Basin** loops through smaller, but unique features. **Daisy Geyser** erupts every 2-3 hours with water spewing out to 75 feet. As the paved trail turns west, **Punch Bowl** boils in its 12-foot-diameter raised sinter bowl.

Biscuit Basin

One of several hydrothermal basins in Upper Geyser Basin, **Biscuit Basin** holds a collection of smaller geothermal features, accessed by a 0.7-mile boardwalk that ascends into the basin to circle hot pools, geysers, and fumaroles. After crossing the Firehole River on a

Loop cutoff. After touring past the basin geysers and pools, cross Grand Loop Road to reach Black Sand Basin.

★ Old Faithful Inn

Built in 1903-1904 from surrounding logs, tree limbs, and rhyolite stone, **Old Faithful Inn** is worthy of wows. With a steep-pitched roof and gabled dormers, the lobby vaults five stories high and is centered around an 85-foot-tall stone fireplace and handcrafted clock built from wood, copper, and iron. Today, this National Historic Landmark houses 327 guest rooms in two wings. Walk around the lobby balcony to take in all the historical intricacies, and watch Old Faithful Geyser erupt from the deck. Daily **tours** (hours vary daily early May-early Oct., free) are available.

MADISON TO NORRIS
Gibbon Falls

On the road between Madison Junction and Norris, **Gibbon Falls** plunges 84 feet into the Gibbon River. The cascade-type falls froth from every rock ledge. The falls used to be a barrier for migrating fish, but now introduced species such as arctic grayling and rainbow trout populate the upper reaches of the Gibbon River and Grebe Lake at its headwaters. From the signed large parking area on the east side of the road, walk to the interpretive viewpoints to see the falls.

Artists Paintpots

Located 3.7 miles south of Norris Junction, **Artists Paintpots** gets its name from its bubbling gray mud pots. A sunny gravel, dirt, boardwalk, and stair-step trail (one mile) starts by cutting through lodgepoles recovering from the 1988 fire. The path tours past small geysers, fumaroles, light blue pools, and red crusts. Thermophiles (organisms that proliferate in hot water) add the bright colors. Stinky hydrogen sulfide gas leaks from underground, and the mud pots burp and spurt.

At the junction, turn in either direction; the remainder of the trail loops around the side of **Paintpot Hill.** The base of the hill holds bubbling hot springs, clear hot pools, and streams with thermophiles. Geothermal features at the bottom of the loop have more water, while the famous paint pots at the top are formed of thicker clay; they emit gasses that scent the air. By late summer, the mud pots thicken or dry up when less water feeds them.

Old Faithfull Inn

NORRIS

Located 14 miles from Madison Junction, 30 miles from Old Faithful, and 28 miles from the West Entrance, Norris houses a large double geyser basin with boardwalks, two museums, and a campground. The **Norris Geyser Basin Museum & Information Station** (307/344-2812, 9am-6pm daily late May-Sept.) and a **Yellowstone Forever** bookstore (406/848-2400, www.yellowstone.org) anchor the visitor services.

★ Norris Geyser Basin

Of Yellowstone's thermal basins, **Norris Geyser Basin** is the hottest, measuring 459°F at 1,087 feet below the surface. With features 115,000 years old, it is the oldest geothermal basin. The most vigorous of the park's geyser basins, Norris has some features that change daily, many due to earthquakes. It also contains rare acidic geysers; you'll smell the rotten egg stench.

Interpretive boardwalks and paths tour two hydrothermal basins: Back Basin and Porcelain Basin. The *Norris Geyser Basin Trail Guide* ($1, available at visitors centers) can aid in touring the site. Explore the boardwalks and trails in three ways: self-guided, with a ranger-led walk, or on a one-mile trail from Norris Campground. Due to the changing nature of the basin, boardwalks can be closed for reconstruction.

BACK BASIN

The thinly forested **Back Basin** double-loop (1.5 miles) houses two geysers that each hold world records: the tallest geyser and the largest acidic geyser. Heading south from the museum, the boardwalk first reaches **Emerald Spring** with its striking blue color created from the yellow sulfur minerals, near-boiling water, and colorful thermophiles. Continue south to unpredictable **Steamboat Geyser,** which shoots small bursts of water up to 40 feet in the air (its world-record eruptions of 300-400 feet happen infrequently). The geyser links underground to the blue-green **Cistern Spring,** which puts out so much sinter that

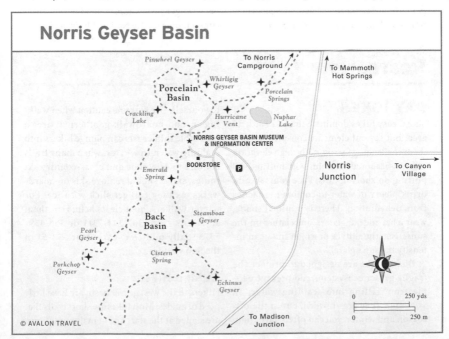

Norris Geyser Basin

Pinwheel Geyser

To Norris Campground

To Mammoth Hot Springs

Whirligig Geyser

Porcelain Basin

Porcelain Springs

Crackling Lake

Hurricane Vent

Nuphar Lake

NORRIS GEYSER BASIN MUSEUM & INFORMATION CENTER

BOOKSTORE

P

Norris Junction

To Canyon Village

Emerald Spring

Back Basin

Steamboat Geyser

Pearl Geyser

Cistern Spring

Porkchop Geyser

Echinus Geyser

0   250 yds
0   250 m

To Madison Junction

© AVALON TRAVEL

pipes often clog and force water to the surface in new pools. Turn left to stay on this outer loop as it winds past the red-orange rimmed pool of Echinus Geyser. With unpredictable eruptions, it's the world's largest acidic geyser—on par with vinegar. After passing several fumaroles, geysers, hot springs, and mud pots, Porkchop Geyser roils turquoise water but is more like a hot spring (it hasn't erupted since 1989). Due to superheating in this evolving basin, the park service rerouted the boardwalk to Pearl Geyser to avoid the 200-degree ground.

This outer loop completes at the junction near Palpitator Spring. Continue north through the Back Basin past Minute and Monarch Geyers, to return to the museum junction and connect with the Porcelain Basin.

PORCELAIN BASIN

The wide-open Porcelain Basin is named for its color. Two loops of the 0.5-mile boardwalk cross the acidic basin that contains the park's highest concentration of silica; thermophiles add brilliant splashes of green or red.

From the museum junction, turn left past turquoise Crackling Lake, a hot pool that bubbles along the edges of the basin. The loop brings you to the defunct Pinwheel Geyser and active Whirligig Geyser, which spills into a runoff stream full of orange iron oxide and green thermophiles. A smaller boardwalk loop heads left past roaring Hurricane Vent and colorful Porcelain Springs, a changeable hot pool that waffles from water action to dry. Complete the loop and return to the museum by heading south, or follow the trail from Porcelain Springs to the Museum of the National Park Ranger.

Museum of the National Park Ranger

Tiny **Museum of the National Park Ranger** (307/344-7353, www.nps.gov/yell, 9am-5pm daily late May-Sept., free) is located in an 1886 historic log cabin near the Norris Campground. Staffed by volunteer retired rangers, the museum houses a small collection of photos that show the evolution of the park ranger profession. A small auditorium runs a movie on the National Park Service.

Recreation

DAY HIKES

Short, easy hikes dominate the Old Faithful area, but several elements conspire to turn them challenging for some. The high elevation can cause labored breathing with huffing and puffing on short uphills. Pace yourself and drink plenty of water to combat headaches from dehydration. There is minimal shade; wear a hat and sunglasses, and slather on the sunscreen (the altitude or winter snow can intensify the sun's glare).

Boardwalks are designed to protect the fragile geyser ecosystems and prevent people from falling into scalding water. In summer, they are crowded, but in the off-season and winter, you can often have them

to yourself. Use extreme caution when walking in non-boardwalk geothermal areas; breakable thin crusts can plunge hikers into scalding water. In winter, when many trails convert to snowshoe and cross-country ski routes, skiers should remove skis on boardwalks, as they can get slick with ice. For winter walkers, boot cleats help; rent them at Bear's Den (307/344-7311 or 866/439-7375, daily mid-Dec.-early Mar., $3-5) in the Snow Lodge.

Guided Hikes

Hikers in the west geyser basin arc have little need of guides. Most hikes are short trails that are signed at the start and at major junctions.

Old Faithful and West Yellowstone Hikes

Trail	Effort	Distance	Duration	Features
Ice Lake	Easy	0.6 mi rt	30 min	lake
Harlequin Lake	Easy	0.6 mi rt	1 hr	lake, wildlife
Lone Star Geyser	Easy	4.8-8.2 mi rt	3-5 hr	geyser
Fairy Falls and Grand Prismatic Overlook	Easy	1.5-9 mi rt	1-5 hr	waterfall, scenic hot springs overlook
Sentinel Meadows and Queens Laundry	Easy to moderate	3.8 mi rt	2 hr	thermals
Howard Eaton	Easy to strenuous	7-18.2 mi	4-10 hr	geyser basin
Observation Point	Moderate	2.1 mi rt	1 hr	overlook
Mystic Falls and Biscuit Basin Overlook	Moderate	2.4-8 mi rt	1-4 hr	waterfall, thermals
Spring Creek	Moderate	2-12.4 mi rt	1.5-6 hr	scenery
Mallard Lake	Moderate	7-8.4 mi rt	4 hr	lake
Monument Geyser Basin	Strenuous	2.8 mi rt	2.5 hr	thermals

However, private, park-licensed guides (www.nps.gov/yell) are available for hikes beyond the geyser boardwalks.

Yellowstone's naturalist rangers lead free daily interpretive hikes in the Old Faithful area. Walks usually meet at Old Faithful Visitor Education Center or the trailhead. In summer, guided walks explore Old Faithful, Mystic Falls, Lone Star Geyser, Fairy Falls, Queen's Laundry, and Shoshone Lake. In winter, rangers lead snowshoe hikes in the Old Faithful area and West Yellowstone. Check the visitors centers for schedules. Reservations are required for some hikes (307/344-2750 or in person at the visitors center). Guided hikes and walks also go from Madison area trailheads and Norris Geyser Basin.

Madison

HARLEQUIN LAKE

Distance: 0.6 mile round-trip
Duration: 1 hour
Elevation change: 102 feet
Effort: easy
Trailhead: West Entrance Road, 1.9 miles west of Madison Junction. Park in the pullout on the south side of the road opposite the trailhead.

This easy walk is popular with families and campers staying at Madison Campground. Potential wildlife sightings include elk in June and fall or beaver and waterfowl at the lake. A short ascent through a lodgepole corridor climbs north up a hill to swing west and reach the south shore of Harlequin Lake. Copious yellow pond lilies, water rushes, and cattails rim the shallow 10-acre fishless lake

Volcanic Facts

GEYSERS

Geysers are all about clogged plumbing. Similar to hot springs, geysers have underground pipes that let boiling water bubble up to the surface. But contrary to free-flowing hot springs, geyser pipes constrict, producing a backup of water and bubbles. When the pressure becomes too great, the explosion occurs. Yellowstone has more than 450 active geysers that produce two eruption patterns: **Cone geysers** shoot water into the air in a narrow stream, and **fountain geysers** spray water in multiple directions, usually from a pool.

Where can you see the two types of geysers?

· To see cone geyser action, catch **Riverside** and **Castle Geysers** erupting in Upper Geyser Basin. For one of the best examples of a fountain geyser, watch **Great Fountain Geyser** erupt in Lower Geyser Basin.

How can you know when geysers will erupt?

· Park rangers predict **eruption schedules** for Old Faithful, Castle, Great Fountain, Riverside, Grand, and Daisy Geysers. Find eruption times posted at visitors centers and on the NPS Yellowstone Geyser app.

MAGMA

The stove that heats Yellowstone is actually a stacked three-pot burner: a **magma chamber** on top of a huge **magma reservoir** on top of the **Yellowstone Hotspot Plume.** Starting at the bottom, the **Yellowstone hotspot plume** once heated the Snake River Plain in Idaho. When the earth's crust shifted eastward, the hotspot moved under Yellowstone. At 40-plus miles below the surface, the hotspot plume sends heat upward into the lower crust of the earth, where hot rocks melt into a huge magma reservoir about 16 miles thick. The heat from the reservoir rises into the upper crust, where superheated rock melts into a magma chamber that lurks 3-9 miles below the earth's surface. It is roughly 19 miles wide by 55 miles long. Together, the chamber and reservoir have enough magma to fill the Grand Canyon 14 times.

Where can you learn more about these workings below ground?

· Tour exhibits in **Old Faithful Visitor Education Center**.

COLORS

Many of Yellowstone's geothermal features show the artistry of colors from heat-loving organisms, acidic thrivers, and minerals. **Thermophiles** are microscopic organisms (bacteria, viruses, flies, spiders, algae, fungi, or microscopic organisms) that thrive on extreme heat, seeking out water of

---

by late summer. Look for beaver-chewed trees and a beaver lodge across the lake.

Upper and Lower Geyser Basins
SENTINEL MEADOWS AND QUEEN'S LAUNDRY

Distance: 3.8 miles round-trip
Duration: 2 hours
Elevation change: 45 feet
Effort: easy to moderate
Trailhead: Fountain Flat Drive parking lot, south of Madison

From the trailhead, walk south on the old road to the bridge over the Firehole River. To the west, the riverside Ojo Caliente hot spring pours water down yellow sulfur channels. Cross the bridge to find the trail junction on the right. Turn west to walk through grasslands, crossing Fairy and Sentinel

colorful thermophiles

up to 174 degrees in hot pools and runoff streams. Photosynthetic capabilities allow some to show pigments. **Archea** are single-celled creatures (also called extremophiles) that thrive in hot, acidic waters. **Minerals** also produce color. Unfortunately, some hot pools have changed color due to the amount of coins, trinkets, and **trash** thrown in by visitors; the garbage clogs the plumbing systems and lowers the temperature.

Where can you see Yellowstone's vivid colors?

· Find thermophiles in the green, brown, orange, and red mats in the Lower, Midway, and Upper **Geyser Basins.** To see one of the most vivid color displays, go to **Grand Prismatic Spring** in Midway Geyser Basin.

· See the green or colorless archaea at **Norris Geyser Basin.**

· For mineral colors, look for orange-red iron deposits in **Norris Geyser Basin**, and pale pink and gray iron oxides in **Fountain Paint Pots**.

· You can see the effect of trash clogging at **Morning Glory Pool**; it has changed from brilliant blue to a less hot green.

Creeks. In wet seeps, the trail can disappear. At **Sentinel Meadows,** thermal features come into view; the first is **Mound Spring,** the largest. Several smaller cones spread around the meadows. (Use caution in exploring the basin, as thermal features can be dangerous.) Follow the trail south between the forest and the multiple smaller cones. The next major thermal is **Queen's Laundry Geyser,** at 1.9 miles. On top of the sinter mound is an old, roofless log structure that was built in 1881 to serve as the bathhouse for soaking in the hot spring. To protect the spring, and for safety, soaking is now discouraged.

While you can hike out and back on this trail, other options include adding on **Imperial Geyser** and **Fairy Falls** or bicycling **Fountain Flat Drive** to trailheads and locking up bikes to walk to destinations.

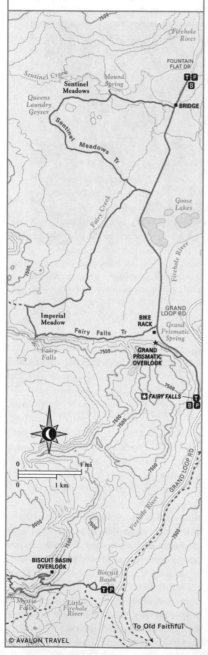

Upper and Lower Geyser Basins

Bear activity closes this trail in spring until Memorial Day weekend.

★ FAIRY FALLS AND GRAND PRISMATIC OVERLOOK

Distance: 1.5-9 miles round-trip
Duration: 1-5 hours
Elevation change: 52-129 feet
Effort: easy
Trailheads: Fairy Falls parking area off Grand Loop Road; an alternate trailhead is located at the Fountain Flat Drive parking lot
Directions: The Fairy Falls parking area is off the Grand Loop Road, 11.5 miles south of Madison Junction or 4.5 miles north of Old Faithful. The Fountain Flat Drive trailhead is 5.5 miles south of Madison Junction or 10.5 miles north of Old Faithful. On Fountain Flat Drive, continue south 0.8 mile to the trailhead parking lot.

At 197 feet, Fairy Falls is the park's fourth-highest waterfall, and it provides a scenic year-round destination for hikers, bikers, and skiers. In 2017, a spur trail en route added an overlook of Grand Prismatic Spring with its

Fairy Falls plunges 197 feet.

Mystic Falls on the Little Firehole River

hiking, biking, or skiing three miles on the old road, which is closed to vehicles. It goes south through open terrain, crossing the Firehole River and passing **Goose Lakes**. At the **Fairy Falls Trail** turnoff, there is a bike rack (bring your own bike lock), as bikes are not permitted farther.

MYSTIC FALLS AND BISCUIT BASIN OVERLOOK

Distance: 2.4-8 miles round-trip
Duration: 1-4 hours
Elevation change: 135-545 feet
Effort: moderate
Trailheads: Biscuit Basin parking area, 2 miles northwest of Old Faithful, or access from Old Faithful Visitor Education Center

At Biscuit Basin, a short boardwalk loop provides hiking access to Mystic Falls and the overlook trail. Bears close the trail in spring until **late May.** The route can be hot in summer with sparse shade.

From Biscuit Basin parking area, follow the **boardwalk trail** 0.3 mile west to the trailhead for Mystic Falls. Turn right and hike 0.4 mile through young lodgepoles and meadows to a junction. Take the left fork and ascend 0.5 mile into the canyon along the Little Firehole River to **Mystic Falls,** a 70-foot waterfall that feeds a series of cascades. To make this a **2.4-mile hike,** retrace your steps to Biscuit Basin.

For a **3.9-mile loop,** continue west from the falls to the Biscuit Basin Overlook. Climb the south-facing switchbacks to reach another junction at the forested 7,827-foot summit. Turn right to reach **Biscuit Basin Overlook** (a left turn heads to Fairy Falls). As the trail crosses the ridge and descends, you'll get multiple views of Biscuit Basin, the Firehole River valley, and steam rising across the Upper Geyser Basin. Descending the trail, take the left fork to return to Biscuit Basin.

From Old Faithful, hiking to Biscuit Basin, the falls, and the overlook is **8 miles round-trip.** Follow the trail system through the Upper Geyser Basin to connect to Biscuit Basin across Grand Loop Road.

cobalt hot spring and fiery arms of thermophiles. (To hike only to the overlook is 1.5 miles round trip.) Bears close this trail in spring until late May.

From **Fairy Falls Trailhead,** cross the Firehole River and hike the abandoned road. To climb to the new overlook of **Grand Prismatic Spring,** take the signed 0.5-mile spur to ascend 105 feet in elevation to the platform. After returning to the trail, the route westward reaches the junction with the **Fairy Falls Trail** at 1.4 miles. Turning west, hike 1.5 miles through a young lodgepole forest to the base of the falls. In summer, the falls plunge ribbon-like into a pool; in winter, it's an ice sculpture. Plan three hours for the **6.8-mile round-trip** to the falls, including Grand Prismatic Spring Overlook. In winter, cross-country skiers can catch a snowcoach shuttle from Old Faithful to ski from the parking area. To hike from Old Faithful, allow five hours for nine miles round trip.

Reaching Fairy Falls from the alternate **Fountain Flat Drive trailhead** requires

Old Faithful

OBSERVATION POINT

Distance: 2.1 miles round-trip
Duration: 1 hour
Elevation change: 237 feet
Effort: moderate
Trailhead: Old Faithful Visitor Education Center

Most hikers coordinate the walk up to Observation Point with an eruption of Old Faithful Geyser. From the overlook, you can look down on the masses of people surrounding the geyser and watch it blow, but the steam plume sometimes occludes the water spouting, depending on wind direction. In winter, when the ground is snow-covered, wear snowshoes or boot cleats (rent from the Bear's Den in the Snow Lodge). While hiking time is short, waiting for Old Faithful to erupt may be long.

From the Old Faithful Visitor Education Center, circle the east side of Old Faithful Geyser heading toward **Geyser Hill** and cross the Firehole River. After crossing the bridge, turn right at the sign for **Observation Point.** The trail switchbacks uphill for 0.5 mile, making a small loop at the top. At the point, claim your spot in the trees to watch Old Faithful erupt. In winter, you may be the only one there, but in summer, you'll join a crowd. To descend, walk down the loop then continue westward on the trail through the forest to **Solitary Geyser.** From the geyser, a dirt trail connects south with the boardwalk on Geyser Hill near Aurum Geyser. Go east on the boardwalk to retrace your route across the Firehole River and back to Old Faithful.

MALLARD LAKE

Distance: 7-8.4 miles round-trip
Duration: 4 hours
Elevation change: 867-945 feet
Effort: moderate
Trailhead: Behind the employee cabins of Old Faithful Lodge, or 3.8 miles north of Old Faithful at Mallard Creek Trailhead

Mallard Lake, a small, 34-acre lake set in the forest at 8,037 feet in elevation on the edge of the Central Plateau, is one of the few places to get away from the crowds around the geyser basins. Anglers won't find fish in its sterile waters, but wildlife sightings can include bison, elk, bears, and osprey. While lupine, harebells, and paintbrush line the trail in early summer, the air also fills with copious mosquitoes. In winter, the route serves as a cross-country ski trail.

The out-and-back trail starts from either **Old Faithful** (7 miles), the easier route, or **Mallard Creek Trailhead** (8.4 miles). Head east, crossing the **Firehole River.** You'll tromp through lodgepole regrowth from the 1988 fire and a rocky ravine with lichen-covered volcanic boulders. Newer, thicker lodgepoles create long green corridors, but high points offer peek-a-boo views of the Upper Geyser Basin. About 0.2 mile before reaching **Mallard Lake,** meet up at the junction with **Mallard Creek Trail** to drop to the forested shoreline. With a shuttle, you can do a point-to-point hike (7.3 miles) to the Mallard Creek Trailhead.

HOWARD EATON

Distance: 7-18.2 miles round-trip
Duration: 4-10 hours
Elevation change: 250-583 feet
Effort: easy to strenuous
Trailhead: On Grand Loop Road across from Old Faithful. Pick up a connecting trail south of the Snow Lodge

While this hot, dusty, forested walk has little to recommend it, the route is part of the historic 157-mile Howard Eaton loop trail through Yellowstone, dedicated in 1923. With the exception of a few sections (including this one), much of the trail today parallels the Grand Loop Road and is unmaintained with brush and downed trees. You'll find far less people on this trail than elsewhere around Old Faithful.

From Old Faithful, the 7-mile round-trip route goes southeast to climb 250 feet then drops to a junction. At the junction, turn left for 0.3 mile to reach **Lone Star Geyser.**

The longer, 18.2-mile route leads to **Shoshone Geyser Basin,** the largest backcountry geyser basin. After reaching the Lone Star Geyser junction, follow the trail southeast through loose forest broken by intermittent meadows and streams. The trail grunts 350 feet over the **Continental Divide** at 8,050-foot **Grant's Pass,** then drops to the west end of Shoshone Lake. This basin area holds 110 hydrothermal features, including hot pools and geysers. The main attraction, **Minute Man Geyser,** spouts 10-40 feet high every 1-3 minutes during active phases. There are no boardwalks touring the geyser basin, so use caution. Savvy hikers start from Lone Star Geyser Trailhead instead of Old Faithful, or ride bikes to Lone Star Geyser to chop the hiking down to 13.4 miles.

LONE STAR GEYSER
Distance: 4.8-8.2 miles round-trip
Duration: 3-5 hours

Elevation change: 65-243 feet
Effort: easy
Trailhead: Lone Star Geyser Trailhead or the adjacent Kepler Cascades parking area (park at either), 2.5 miles east of Old Faithful or Old Faithful Lodge.

From the Lone Star Geyser Trailhead, walk south along the old **asphalt service road** through conifers along the meandering Firehole River. The route passes a large meadow (scout for wildlife) before ascending a gentle hill to the geyser basin. **Lone Star Geyser,** a 12-foot-tall pink and gray sinter cone, sits tucked away, hidden from the hubbub of the Upper Geyser Basin. Spouting up to 40 feet in the air, the geyser erupts about every three hours with spurts lasting 30 minutes. If you see the geyser go off, add the date and time to the logbook in the old interpretive stand.

Hiking the trail **from Old Faithful Lodge**

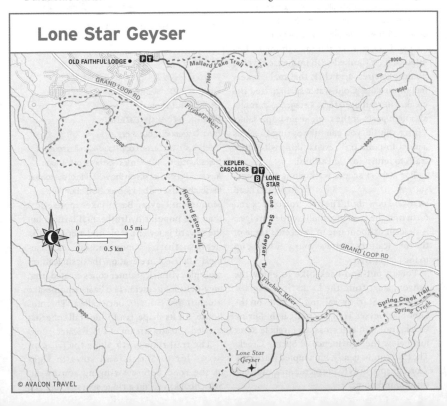

Lone Star Geyser

OLD FAITHFUL LODGE • P T
Mallard Lake Trail
GRAND LOOP RD
Firehole River
7500
KEPLER CASCADES P T LONE STAR B
Howard Eaton Trail
0   0.5 mi
0   0.5 km
Lone Star Geyser Tr
GRAND LOOP RD
Firehole River
Spring Creek Trail
Spring Creek
Lone Star Geyser
8000

© AVALON TRAVEL

almost doubles the mileage. From the southeast corner of the Old Faithful cabin complex, hop onto the **Mallard Lake Trail.** After crossing the Firehole River, turn right to follow the signage to **Kepler Cascades.** The trail climbs through forest and meadows until it parallels Grand Loop Road, then crosses to the Kepler Cascades parking lot. Locate the Lone Star Geyser Trailhead just south of the cascades. For an alternate return, take the Howard Eaton Trail 2.9 miles north back to Old Faithful.

SPRING CREEK

Distance: 2-12.4 miles round-trip
Duration: 1.5-6 hours
Elevation change: 750 feet
Effort: moderate
Trailheads: Spring Creek Picnic Area or Lone Star Geyser Trailhead
Directions: From Old Faithful, drive 5.6 miles east on the Grand Loop Road to the Spring Creek Picnic Area; or drive 2.5 miles to the Lone Star Geyser Trailhead.

The Spring Creek Trail tours a dramatic forested canyon flanked with immense rhyolite boulders, spires, and cliffs that make hikers feel minuscule. Cold-water springs feed the creek. The trail used to be a stagecoach route, although parts of the route seem impassable. With a shuttle, you can hike Spring Creek as a point-to-point trail, even linking with other trails to return to Old Faithful.

For a short scenic walk along the creek, start at **Spring Creek Picnic Area** and head westward downhill. The trail crosses back and forth over the creek on small wooden bridges. A descent of about one mile reaches some of the rock features. Retrace your steps back up to the picnic area.

For an out-and-back hike to enjoy the canyon, start from the **Lone Star Geyser Trailhead.** Start by walking 2.7 miles on the Lone Star Geyser Trail. Turn left at the Spring Creek Trail sign and cross the Firehole River just below the confluence of Spring Creek. The trail climbs gently, interrupted with a few short, steep grunts to the picnic area and your turnaround point.

Lone Star Geyser erupts about every three hours.

Norris
MONUMENT GEYSER BASIN

Distance: 2.8 miles round-trip
Duration: 2.5 hours
Elevation change: 637 feet
Effort: strenuous, but short
Trailhead: On Grand Loop Road 4.7 miles south of Norris Junction and 8.7 miles northeast of Madison Junction. Parking lot sits on the west side of the road at the south end of the bridge over the Gibbon River.

Monument Geyser Basin takes more effort than the popular hydrothermal basins, but the reward is fewer people and a boardwalk-free basin that has a more natural look. At almost 8,000 feet in elevation, the basin features multiple cylindrical sinter cones created from now-defunct geysers. The basin's namesake **Monument Geyser,** once called "Thermos Bottle" for its shape, is a 10-foot-tall cone that spewed a steady stream of 194°F water.

The trail runs north along the **Gibbon River** for 0.45 mile and stays in sight of the road before swinging southwest. Switchbacks ascend a ridge sparsely forested

Monument Geyser Basin

Gibbon Meadows

To Norris

GRAND LOOP RD

7500

7500

7500

7500

Monument Geyser Basin

8000

8000

Gibbon River

0   0.25 mi

0   0.25 km

To Madison Junction

© AVALON TRAVEL

with lodgepoles. Near the ridgetop, the trail broadens into an overlook with views of **Mt. Holmes** and **Gibbon Meadows.** As the route travels northwest, the sulfur smell heralds the barren landscape of **Monument Geyser Basin.** Use caution while exploring the cones and steam vents before retracing your steps back down the trail.

ICE LAKE
Distance: 0.6 mile round-trip
Duration: 30 minutes
Elevation change: 22 feet
Effort: easy
Trailhead: Norris-Canyon Road, 3.5 miles east of Norris

Ice Lake is a narrow lake tucked in thick lodgepole pine forest regrowth after the 1988 fires. The lake is less than a mile long and is rimmed with downed timber and pines with only a few small beach areas.

From the trailhead, hike 0.2 mile up the trail to a **junction.** Take the right fork for the quickest access. The left fork heads farther to the northwest corner of the lake and at 0.5 mile reaches a junction with the **Howard Eaton Trail.** The trail westward reaches **Norris Campground** in 4.1 miles, an alternate trailhead. The trail right goes along the north shore of **Ice Lake** to **Wolf Lake, Grebe Lake,** and **Cascade Lake.**

BACKPACKING

Backpackers must obtain **permits** ($3/person, children 8 and younger free) for assigned backcountry campsites. Permits are available in person 48 hours in advance from the backcountry offices. For more information, see the *Essentials* chapter.

Shoshone Geyser Basin
18 MILES

This two-day trip travels to **Shoshone Geyser Basin,** the largest backcountry geyser basin with 110 hydrothermal features, and **Shoshone Lake,** the second largest lake in the park. Via the Howard Eaton Trail from Old Faithful, the route crosses the **Continental Divide** at 8,050-foot **Grant's Pass** before dropping to the west end of Shoshone Lake. Plan to camp on the lake at 8R5 or 8T1 on either side of the geyser basin. Use caution touring the boardwalk-free basin to see **Minute Man Geyser;** it will spout 10-40 feet high every 1-3 minutes during active phases.

Bechler River Trail
30 MILES

The king of Yellowstone backpacking trips gets you farther away from day hiker hordes. The **Bechler River Trail** descends into Bechler River Canyon and the land of waterfalls. While you can backpack the 30-mile trail in 3-5 days point-to-point from the Lone Star Geyser Trailhead to the Bechler Ranger Station, you'll need to add eight hours for the shuttle back. To avoid the shuttle, you can hike to Colonnade Falls in the canyon and back in 5-6 days (40 miles). While overnighting at a campsite en route is necessary, aim your daily mileage allowance for the core canyon campsites (9B4-9B9), especially Ouzel, Colonnade, and Albright Falls. Due to snow and water levels, permit reservations are only available from July 15 onward. While elevation gain is minimal (980 feet), crossing the Continental Divide twice, fording multiple streams and the river adds difficulty.

BIKING
Inside the Park
ROAD CYCLING

Yellowstone park roads offer prime road cycling with rolling terrain along the Madison River, a big climb from Madison to Norris, and a slightly lesser grade to Old Faithful and the Continental Divide. Lack of road shoulders means that cyclists should be skilled enough to bike with traffic at their elbows. Plows clear pavement on the **West Entrance to Madison** (14 miles) and **Madison to Mammoth Hot Springs** (35 miles) late March-mid-April. During this time, these roads open to cyclists yet remain closed to vehicles. Confirm road status online (www. nps.gov/yell) and carry all supplies (including pepper spray for bears), as no services are open. After traffic thins in fall, riding from

West Yellowstone to Old Faithful is a prime time to hear elk bugling.

MOUNTAIN BIKING

Mountain bikes are only permitted on three shared hiker-biker routes in the Old Faithful area. These wide level remnants of old asphalt roadbeds are perfect places for family biking. **Fountain Flats Road** (4 miles, Memorial Day Weekend-early Nov.) links the Fountain Flat Drive parking lot with the Fairy Falls Trailhead (park at either end). En route between Goose Lake and Grand Prismatic Spring, park bikes in the rack to walk to Fairy Falls.

A round-trip ride connects **Old Faithful Inn** with **Biscuit Basin** (5 miles). Start at Hamilton's Store (1 Old Faithful Rd., 406/586-7593) to ride the paved path along the south side of the Firehole River for 1.2 miles. Turn left onto the second Daisy Geyser Loop entrance, then turn right onto a single-track trail that leads to Grand Loop Road near Biscuit Basin.

The **Lone Star Geyser Trail** (4.8 miles round-trip) offers a pleasant forest ride along the Firehole River to Lone Star Geyser. Park at Lone Star Geyser Trailhead or Kepler Cascades.

In Old Faithful, the **Snow Lodge**

bicycling the Fountain Flats Road

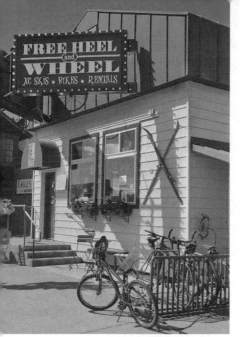

Rent bikes at Freeheel and Wheel.

(307/344-7311 or 866/439-7375, www.yellowstonenationalparklodges.com, daily late May-early Oct.) rents bikes for adults and children, including helmets ($8-10/1 hr., $20-30/4 hrs., $30-40/8 hrs.). Kiddie trailers and bike trains are available ($5-20).

Outside the Park

In West Yellowstone, mountain bikers have two trail systems. **Rendezvous Ski Trails** (www.skirunbikemt.com, mid-June-mid-Oct.) become biking and hiking trails when snow melts in June. About 15 miles of gently rolling, easy-to-intermediate trails loop through meadows and forests. Mountain bikers can also ride the **Riverside Trail** (2.8 miles round-trip) along the Madison River into the park. Locate the trailhead across from the Dude Motel (3 Madison Ave., West Yellowstone).

Freeheel and Wheel (33 Yellowstone Ave., West Yellowstone, 406/646-7744, www.freeheelandwheel.com, 9am-6pm daily year-round) rents road bikes and front suspension mountain bikes ($10/hr., $35-40/day). Helmets and kiddie trailers are available, too.

HORSEBACK RIDING

Old Faithful has no horseback riding concessionaires. Outside the park, West Yellowstone has several ranches about six miles west of town with trail rides (Mon.-Sat., mid-May-Sept.). Wear long pants and sturdy shoes, hiking boots, or cowboy boots and ask about weight and age restrictions

Creekside Trail Rides (175 Oldroyd Rd., 406/560-6913, www.creeksidetrailrides.com, 10am-6:30pm) tour the ranch's meadows. Reservations are not required for the one-hour ride ($35). Rodeo Rides (June-Aug., $40-45, reservations required) depart at 6:30pm to return in time for the included Wild West Yellowstone Rodeo.

Diamond P Ranch (2865 Targhee Pass Hwy., 406/646-0606, www.thediamondpranch.com, $70-80) guides rides into Custer Gallatin National Forest at 9:30am, 1:30pm, and 5:30 pm. Make reservations.

WATER SPORTS
Boating

Outside the park, 15-mile-long **Hebgen Lake** (8.5 miles northwest of West Yellowstone) offers boating, angling, paddling, sailing, and waterskiing. The dammed lake has several long arms, good paddling and bird-watching zones. Winds tend to kick up in the afternoon. (The lake is also the site of the 1959 earthquake that shook Yellowstone and created Quake Lake to the west.) Launch boats at **Rainbow Point Campground** (Custer-Gallatin National Forest, 406/823-6961, www.fs.usda.gov/gallatin, mid-May-mid-Sept.), which has a cement boat ramp, docks, and trailer parking. From West Yellowstone, drive five miles north on U.S. Highway 191. Turn west onto Rainbow Point Road (Forest Rd. 6954) and drive 1.7 miles to the boat launch.

Montana has amped up control efforts for aquatic invasive species (AIS). If you are bringing a boat to Hebgen Lake, you will most likely pass a boat check station, where boaters are required to stop. Clean your boat completely before bringing it to Montana.

Located on Hebgen Lake, Madison Arm Resort Marina (5475 Madison Arm Rd., West Yellowstone, 406/646-9328, www.madisonarmresort.com, $15-40/hour) rents motorized aluminum boats, paddleboards, canoes, and kayaks.

Fishing

INSIDE THE PARK

The western region of Yellowstone serves as headwaters for Montana's blue-ribbon trout streams. Inside the park, the Firehole, Madison, and lower Gibbon Rivers offer prime fly-fishing for rainbow and brown trout. Riffles and slow ambling stretches alternate with deep pools. Most of the rivers begin to clear of runoff sediments by early July, when the real fishing begins. Most anglers wade in to fish, but you can fish from shore.

For kids, two waterways near Norris, the Gibbon River at Virginia Meadows and Solfatara Creek, offer good places to gain fishing skills. Near Madison Junction, take the kids to the large meadows that flank the Madison River. For lake fishing near Old Faithful, try Goose Lake.

Only fly-fishing is permitted on the Firehole, Madison, and lower Gibbon Rivers. If you don't have a fly rod, that's okay, just attach a fly on a casting rod. Three waterways are closed to fishing: the Firehole River upstream of Old Faithful to Biscuit Basin, the Midway Foot Bridge area, and the Seven Mile Bridge area of the Madison.

Fishing permits are required for anglers 16 years and older ($18 for three days, $25 seven days, $40 season). For permit information and regulations, see the *Essentials* chapter.

OUTSIDE THE PARK

Northwest of West Yellowstone, Hebgen Lake harbors several sportfish species, especially brown trout in May and June before the streams clear up. The Madison River has classic fly-fishing. You'll need a Montana fishing license (http://fwp.mt.gov, residents: $15-31; nonresidents: $50-111) available at West Yellowstone fly shops.

West Yellowstone has fishing outfitters that guide trips inside and outside the park. Trips inside the park are wade-fishing, but outside the park, guides offer float-fishing on certain rivers. Rates run $300-350 for a half day and $500-600 for a full day for 1-3 people. Fees usually include the guide, lunch, and gear, but clarify that when you make reservations. Park entrance fees, fishing licenses, and guide tips (15-20 percent) are not included in the rates. In West Yellowstone, call the fly-fishing outfitters at Arrick's Fly Shop (37 Canyon St., 406/646-7290, www.arricks.com), Bud Lilly's Trout Shop (39 Madison Ave. W., 406/646-7801 or 800-854-9559, www.budlillys.com), or Madison River Outfitters (117 N. Canyon St., 406/646-9644 or 800/646-9644, www.madisonriveroutfitters.com).

Swimming

Geothermal features can scald, thus swimming is not permitted in the hot pools in geyser basins. A swimming hole opens on the Firehole River once high water abates in early July. On Firehole Canyon Drive (one-way), park near the outhouses and descend wooden stairs to the river. There is no lifeguard; swim at your own risk. Outside the park at Hebgen Lake, you can swim at Rainbow Point Campground.

THRILL SPORTS

In West Yellowstone, Yellowstone Aerial Adventures (105 S. Faithful St., 406/646-5171, www.yellowstoneparkzipline.com, 9am-8pm daily late May- Sept., shorter hours in fall, $49 adults, $45 kids 6-12) strings an aerial park through the treetops. Start easy and work up in difficulty through more than 50 challenges on swinging ropes, ziplines, climbing walls, nets, and aerial bridges. Kids ages 4-7 can do a special Junior Ranger Course ($29, includes parent). Make reservations online or by phone.

WINTER SPORTS
Cross-Country Skiing and Snowshoeing

Winter turns Old Faithful into an otherworldly landscape of snow broken by steam and melt-outs from geothermals. Park roads between West Yellowstone and Old Faithful are closed to wheeled vehicles, but open for skiing and snowshoeing.

The park service grooms several roads around Old Faithful for skate and classic skiing or snowshoeing. A groomed ski trail ascends a gentle grade to Lone Star Geyser, while a less-traveled loop tours through the cabins of Old Faithful Lodge with views of the Firehole River. The park service also grooms a trail from Old Faithful Inn to Morning Glory Pool, but geothermal hot spots cause melt-outs; visitors may have to remove their skis in order to walk or cross the trail on fake grass carpets.

All summer hiking trails turn into winter ski and snowshoe trails, including Biscuit Basin, Fairy Falls, Spring Creek, and trails around the geyser basins, though boardwalks can get icy. Snowcoach shuttles (by reservation only from Snow Lodge, $22-38 adults, $11-19 kids) help whittle down mileages.

GUIDES AND RENTALS

At Old Faithful's Snow Lodge, the Bear's Den (Snow Lodge, 307/344-7311 or 866/439-7375, www.yellowstonenationalparklodges.com, daily mid-Dec.-early Mar.) rents cross-country ski packages (skis, boots, and poles, $16-30), snowshoes ($13-25), and boot cleats for walking on ice ($3-5). The shop also waxes skis, repairs gear, teaches lessons, and guides ski and snowshoe trips by reservation. A guided snowshoe trip goes around Old Faithful (daily, $30-38), and a ski or snowshoe tour goes to Lone Star Geyser (Mon. and Fri., $54). Snowcoaches also go to Grand Canyon of the Yellowstone (7:45am-6pm, $276) for guided Ski Tours (Tues., Thurs., and Sun.) and Snowshoe Tours (Wed. and Sat.). Make reservations for Canyon trips when booking your lodging.

Other guides lead tours mid-December-mid-March. Park naturalists guide a two-hour snowshoe tour (Sun., free) at Old Faithful. From West Yellowstone, Yellowstone Alpen Guides (555 Yellowstone Ave., 406/646-9591 or 800/858-3502, www.yellowstoneguides.com) can shuttle skiers to Biscuit Basin to ski 2.5 miles to Old Faithful for pick up on their Old Faithful snowcoach tours.

OUTSIDE THE PARK

West Yellowstone serves as a regional destination for Nordic skiing November-March. With a reputation for stellar grooming, consistent snowpack, and a long season, Rendezvous Ski Trails (www.skirunbikemt.com) daily grooms skate and classic ski trails in Custer-Gallatin National Forest. Find the 35 kilometers of rolling trails at the log arch at the south end of Geyser Street. The trails loop around 6,800 feet elevation through meadows and forests. Purchase trail passes ($6-12) at the self-service, cash-only kiosk at the trailhead near the arch, or at the chamber of commerce, Forest Service office, or Freeheel and Wheel. The ski area launches the season with the annual Yellowstone Ski Festival at the end of November and wraps up the racing season with the annual Yellowstone Rendezvous marathon races in early March.

Because West Yellowstone sits on the park boundary, skiers and snowshoers can also tour the Riverside Trail along the Madison River inside the park. The nine-mile trail has three loops, but skiing only one loop or so shortens the distance. Sometimes you can see bison, bald eagles, trumpeter swans, and foxes.

Freeheel and Wheel (33 Yellowstone Ave., West Yellowstone, 406/646-7744, www.freeheelandwheel.com, 9am-6pm daily year-round, $10/hour, $25-30/day) rents snowshoes, pull sleds for tots, and touring, racing, and performance skate and classic skis. Call ahead to reserve equipment. The shop also repairs and waxes skis, teaches lessons, and gives guided tours by reservation.

Snowmobiling

West Yellowstone is Montana's snowmobile capital for touring the park in winter. Street-legal snow machines park in front of bars, stores, and hotels on all but the main highways. All reservations for **guided tours** ($210-350 per machine) and snowmobile **rentals** ($120-230 per machine) are made in **West Yellowstone.**

Inside the park, the snowmobile season runs **mid-December-mid-March**. You can go with commercial concessionaires or self-guided via the annual lottery for limited permits (apply in Sept.). Daily, guided snowmobile tours travel roads inside Yellowstone on new quieter, less stinky machines required by the park. Outside the park, guides lead snowmobile tours on more than 200 miles of groomed trails in Custer-Gallatin National Forest. The most popular route travels the 28-mile **Two Top Trail,** a National Recreational Snowmobile Trail that climbs 2,000 feet to view the Teton Mountains.

Tours and rentals are available through **Yellowstone Vacations** (415 Yellowstone Ave., 406/646-9564 or 800/426-7669, www.yellowstonevacations.com), **Backcountry Adventures** (224 N. Electric St., 406/646-9317 or 800/924-7669, www.backcountry-adventures.com), and **Two Top Yellowstone Winter Tours** (645 Gibbon Ave., 406/646-7802, www.twotopsnowmobile.com). Insulated snowsuits, gloves, boots, and helmets rent for $15-30. Avalanche gear (beacons, probes, shovels, and airbags, $50) may be required outside the park.

From West Yellowstone, the tour to **Old Faithful** is 65 miles round-trip. You'll have time to get off the snowmobile to tour geyser basins and walk around Old Faithful. The Grand Canyon of the Yellowstone tour is a 90-mile round-trip. Because the roads are groomed daily, you don't need previous experience. Tours into the park are limited to 10 snowmobiles and usually launch at 8am for the eight-hour ride. Rates do not include park entrance fees, meals, taxes, or 15 percent guide gratuities. Make reservations for park tours six months in advance.

For alternate staging locations, **Yellowstone Year-Round Safaris** (905 Scott St., Gardiner, 406/838-7311 or 800/828-9080, www.yellowstoneyearroundsafaris.com) leads tours from Mammoth to Old Faithful. **Old Faithful Snowmobile Tours** (Jackson, WY, 307/733-9767 or 800/253-7130, www.snowmobilingtours.com) leads trips from Flagg Ranch to Old Faithful.

Snowmobile tours depart West Yellowstone for Old Faithful.

Entertainment and Shopping

INSIDE THE PARK
Ranger Programs

Ranger naturalists present free programs at several locations. Find program schedules at visitors centers, on campground bulletin boards, in park hotels, and online. Daily daytime programs cover volcanic activity, geology, wildlife, natural history, and cultural history. **Old Faithful Visitor Education Center** (307/344-2751, www.nps.gov/yell, daily mid-Apr.-Sept. and mid-Dec.-Feb.) hosts a short 10-minute ranger talk on geysers every half hour in the afternoon near Old Faithful Geyser. At the **Madison Junior Ranger Station,** 30-minute programs run several times daily in summer and are designed for kids and their families.

For 45-minute **evening programs**, topics vary nightly. At **Old Faithful Visitor Education Center Theater** (7pm daily late May-early Sept., 7:30pm Fri.-Mon. late Dec.-Feb.), naturalists give slide presentations on geysers, wildlife, and current science. In early summer, don bug spray for mosquitoes at the campground outdoor amphitheaters. Evening ranger presentations happen at **Madison Campground Amphitheater** (9:30pm early June-early Aug., 9pm Aug.-early Sept.) and at **Norris Campground Amphitheater** (7:30pm mid-June-early Sept.). Rangers also conduct periodic programs on night sky observations and stargazing on moonless nights.

Shopping

Old Faithful has two **Yellowstone General Stores** (406/586-7593, www.visityellowstonepark.com, 7:30am-9:30pm daily) in historic buildings. In addition to food service, both shops sell clothing and gifts. Built in 1897, the **Old Faithful Basin Store** (2 Old Faithful Loop, late May-late Sept.) is located in the historic Hamilton's Store near Old Faithful Inn. South of the visitors center, **Old Faithful General Store** (1 Old Faithful Loop, May-mid-Oct.) is a 1920s building with a large fireplace and log beams.

Yellowstone Forever park stores (406/848-2400, www.yellowstone.org) are located at Old Faithful Visitor Education Center, Norris, and Madison Information Station. They sell park-themed items: games, books, maps, and souvenirs.

Gift shops (Xanterra, 307/344-7311 or 866/439-7375, www.yellowstonenationalparklodges.com) operate in Old Faithful Inn, Old Faithful Lodge, and the Snow Lodge when the hotels are open.

WEST YELLOWSTONE
Ranger Programs

The **West Yellowstone Visitor Information Center** (30 Yellowstone Ave., 307/344-2876, daily early June-early Sept.) presents free naturalist and ranger programs in summer. Families can enjoy wildlife talks (20 min., 9:30am) and ranger introductions to Yellowstone (30 min., 9am). Evening presentations (45 min., 7pm Tues., mid-June-Aug.) cover a variety of unique features in the park. Afternoon programs (30 min., 2pm daily late May-early Sept.) alternate locations between the **Yellowstone Historic Center Museum** (Sun.-Mon., Wed., and Fri.) and the **Grizzly and Wolf Discovery Center** (Tues., Thurs., and Sat.).

Entertainment

West Yellowstone nightlife heats up in western saloons and lounges. Some have live music, and the dancing rocks until 2am. Bands vary from western to rock. Find them by walking the strip to check out the scene.

With three or more shows per day in rotation, the **Yellowstone Giant Screen Theater** (101 S. Canyon St., 888/854-5862, www.yellowstonegiantscreen.com, daily in summer, Mon.-Sat. in winter, closed in spring, $7-14) gives huge visuals. The screen is six stories tall and 80 feet wide with a six-track audio system. Catch 40-minute educational films on Yellowstone, nature, and national parks hourly.

The **Playmill Theatre** (29 Madison Ave., 406/646-7757, www.playmill.com, Mon.-Sat. late May-early Sept., box office open 10am-9pm, $20-24) is a small, long-running theater that imports its cast and crew every summer for plays like *Singin' in the Rain* or *Mary Poppins*. Three plays run in repertory, usually family musicals and comedies. Showtimes vary. Discounted tickets for seniors and children are available Monday-Thursday.

Events

In true cowboy fashion, the **Yellowstone Rodeo** (175 Oldroyd Rd., 406/560-6913, www.yellowstonerodeo.com, 8pm Wed.-Sat. mid-June-Aug., Tues.-Sat. July-early Aug., $15 adults, $8 kids), located 6.5 miles west of town, stages cowpoke competitions during the summer. Rodeo events include bareback bronc riding, barrel racing, bull riding, team roping, breakaway roping, saddle bronc riding, and a calf scramble for kids. Tickets are sold at the gate, but to guarantee seating on sellout shows, buy tickets in advance online.

The annual **West Yellowstone Old Faithful Cycle Tour** (www.cycleyellowstone. com, Sept.), a one-day, 60-mile round-trip ride to raise funds for the Yellowstone Park Foundation and other organizations, happens in early October with registration open mid-June. Entry is limited to 300 riders.

West Yellowstone is home to the annual **World Snowmobile Expo** (http://snowmobileexpo.com), held for three days in March. The town packs out for high-flying snowmobile stunts, races, drags, demos, exhibits, bands, and outdoor concerts.

Shopping

During summer high season, West Yellowstone shops and galleries stay open in the evening along Canyon Street, which has several blocks of independent gift shops, candy outlets, cowboy hat and boot stores, fly shops, galleries, and eclectic stores. Most galleries specialize in western art with wildlife, mountain scenes, and geothermal landscapes. Some shops close during fall and spring off-seasons; in winter, many shops shorten business hours.

Built in 1927, the **Eagle's Store** (3 N. Canyon St., 406/646-9300, www.eagles-store. com, 8am-8pm daily) sells a gaggle of souvenirs, western and outdoor clothing, Native

Eagle's Store has an old-fashioned soda fountain.

American crafts, and tackle. It is listed on the National Register of Historic Places and also houses an old-fashioned soda fountain. For outdoor gear, check out the small **Freeheel and Wheel** (33 Yellowstone Ave., 406/646-7744, www.freeheelandwheel.com, 9am-6pm daily), which specializes in reputable bicycle, snowshoe, and cross-country ski gear, and lattes. Along with fly-fishing gear, **Madison River Outfitters** (117 N. Canyon St., 406/646-9644 or 800/646-9644, www.madisonriveroutfitters.com, 8am-6pm daily) carries tents, sleeping bags, and packs as well as outdoor clothing, wildlife-watching binoculars and scopes, and camping, backpacking, and hiking gear. Visitors can take home coffee beans locally roasted by **Morning Glory Coffee and Tea** (129 Dunraven St., 406/646-7061, www.morninggglorycoffee.net, daily 8am-5pm).

Food

INSIDE THE PARK
Old Faithful
Xanterra (307/344-7311 or 866/439-7375, www.yellowstonenationalparklodges.com) operates all lodge restaurants in Old Faithful. Only the Snow Lodge is open in winter, accessible via snowcoach. All lodges sell box lunches ($15), and casual attire is appropriate.

There are two full-service restaurants: the dining room at Old Faithful Inn and the Obsidian Room in Snow Lodge. Both venues serve beer, wine, and cocktails and have short menus with flexible choices for light eaters, as well as multi-course dinners featuring local and regional sources, along with select organic ingredients. Vegan, vegetarian, and gluten-free options and kid's menus are available.

OLD FAITHFUL INN
In the historic hotel, the ★ **Old Faithful Inn Dining Room** (early May-mid-Oct.) is an experience of ambience. The log dining room, with its immense fireplace and woven twig chairs, harkens back to another era. **Breakfast** (6:30am-10am, $6-11) serves up traditional egg and griddle dishes. You can custom-design several entrées, such as oatmeal and omelets, with toppings, fillings, and sides. **Lunch** (11:30am-2:30pm daily, $10-18) serves burgers, sandwiches, and salads. Breakfast and lunch are first-come, first-served.

Dinner (4:30pm-10pm daily in summer, $10-40) mixes lighter, flexible options with entrée specialties such as pork osso bucco, pasta, fish, and quail. Dinner reservations are required; without one, waits of one hour or longer are common. Make reservations by phone or online up to one year in advance when booking lodging at the inn. Those not staying at the inn can make reservations 60 days in advance.

For faster service, **buffets** (breakfast and lunch $14-17 adults, $7-9 kids; dinner $30 adults, $12 kids) are available for breakfast, lunch, and dinner. Lunch features a western buffet with trout, pulled pork, and barbecue-style sides. Dinner rolls out the prime rib.

The inn has two alternatives for lighter meals. The **Bear Pit Lounge** (11:30am-11pm) serves bison burgers, pub-style meals, and appetizers. The **Bear Paw Deli** (6:30am-6pm) has continental breakfast, salads, sandwiches, ice cream, and to-go items for hiking. An espresso stand is on the 2nd-floor balcony overlooking the lobby.

SNOW LODGE
The Snow Lodge has two places to eat and is the only option in winter. The modern **Obsidian Dining Room** is decorated as a contemporary lodge with gas fireplaces and trendy western chandeliers. In summer, the restaurant serves only breakfast and dinner; in winter, it also serves lunch. For **breakfast** (6:30am-10:30am daily early May-mid-Oct.,

6:30am-10am daily mid-Dec.-Feb., $6-15), the smoked salmon eggs Benedict is a specialty. A faster alternative, the breakfast buffet ($15 adults, $8 kids) is offered in summer and in winter (but only when the lodge reaches a certain capacity). **Lunch** (11:30am-3pm mid-Dec.-Feb., $10-18) has salads, burgers, sandwiches, and a few pasta entrées. For **dinner** (5pm-10:30pm daily May-mid-Oct., 5pm-9:30pm daily mid-Dec.-Feb., $10-40), salads and burgers provide lighter options, while full entrées plate trout, prime rib, duck, and pork osso bucco. Reservations are required for dinner in winter. For all meals, prepare for leisurely dining as service is frequently slow.

With everything à la carte, the **Geyser Grill** (8am-9pm daily summer, shorter hours in spring and fall, 10:30am-3:30pm daily in winter, $4-10) has burgers, sandwiches, soups and chili, fries, beer, and wine. Breakfast is served in summer.

OLD FAITHFUL LODGE

With a cafeteria and deck overlooking its namesake geyser, the **Old Faithful Lodge** (mid-May-early Oct.) is the place to go for light, quick meals, especially if you are waiting for Old Faithful to blow. You can even grab to-go sandwiches and claim your seat on the benches surrounding the geyser. The **cafeteria** (11am-9pm daily, shorter hours in spring and fall, $4-18) serves hot sandwiches, teriyaki bowls, chili, wraps, salads, desserts, and full dinners of bison meatloaf, trout, turkey, or chicken. The à la carte **Bake Shop** (6:30am-10pm daily May-Sept., 6:30am-8pm daily mid-late Sept.) serves baked goods, beverages, wraps, sandwiches, salads, breakfast sandwiches, oatmeal, and ice cream. You can order to-go, too.

CAFÉS

Two **Yellowstone General Stores** (406/586-7593, www.yellowstonevacations.com, 7:30am-8:30pm daily, $6-14) contain cafés with seated food service. **Old Faithful General Store** (May-Oct.) is located east of the Snow Lodge in a circa 1920s building with a large fireplace and log beams. It serves personal pizzas, soups and chili, hot and cold sandwiches, salads, and ice cream. The **Old Faithful Basin Store** (early May-late Sept.) is located in the historic Hamilton's Store, built in 1897 near Old Faithful Inn. The shop, which still retains its original marble fountain counter, serves ice cream, burgers, sandwiches, and salads.

You can put together hiking lunches with supplies from the two Yellowstone General Stores. For a larger grocery selection, head to West Yellowstone.

Picnicking

Between West Yellowstone, Old Faithful, and Norris, plenty of picnic areas offer places to eat an alfresco meal. Most are equipped with picnic tables and accessible restroom facilities that are sometimes vault toilets rather than flushers. Find picnic areas at the Madison River and **Madison Junction,** along the West Entrance Road. On Lower Grand Loop Road between Norris and Madison Junctions, picnic spots are at **Norris Meadows, Virginia Cascade, Gibbon Meadows, Caldera Rim, Iron Spring, Gibbon Falls,** and **Tuff Cliff.** Between Madison and the Continental Divide east of Old Faithful, look for them at **Firehole River, Nez Perce, Whiskey Flat, East Lot, Spring Creek,** and **DeLacy Creek.** The only picnic areas that permit fires are Nez Perce, Whiskey Flat, Spring Creek, and Norris Meadows.

OUTSIDE THE PARK
West Yellowstone

For a small town, West Yellowstone packs in nearly 40 restaurants, with mainstays being pizza, burger, and barbecue joints. It is also a tourist town that sees huge crowds in summer, so expect waiting lines at restaurants. About half the restaurants close in winter; those that stay open shorten hours in the off-seasons, and some take a few weeks off in early spring and early December. Many restaurants sell to-go lunches ($10-13).

CAFÉS

A town staple, **Ernie's Bakery and Deli** (406 Hwy. 20, 406/646-9467, http://erniesbakery. com, 7am-2pm daily, $6-12) is a place to go for breakfast omelets, Benedicts, and grits (until 11am) or deli sandwiches, salads, and wraps. The bakery churns out bagels, breakfast sandwiches, and espresso to-go for driving into the park, and you can get boxed lunches for travel. Coffee fans go to **Espresso West** (10 Canyon St., 406/646-0829, daily early May-late Sept., 7am-9pm) for lattes, mochas, cappuccinos, iced drinks, ice cream, and milkshakes.

AMERICAN

A family restaurant now run by the second generation, ★ **Running Bear Pancake House** (538 Madison Ave., 406/646-7703, http://runningbearph.com, 6am-2pm daily year-round, $7-14) keeps the griddle going with pancakes and omelets. Specialty French toast is made from apple-pecan and other sweet breads. Espresso with that breakfast? You bet. The lunch menu (11am-2pm daily) adds burgers, sandwiches, and salads.

Beartooth Barbecue (111 N. Canyon St., 406/646-0227, 11am-10pm daily year-round, $11-30) has draft local beers, pulled pork sammies, brisket, ribs, cheese grits, fried pickles, jalapeño poppers with huckleberry sauce, and traditional barbecue sides.

LATIN

Bringing Spain to Montana, the small ★ **Café Madriz** (311 N. Canyon St., 406/646-9245, 5pm-9pm Mon.-Sat. mid-May-Sept, $10-25) serves dinners of made-from-scratch Spanish foods including the house sangria from chef-owner Elena de Diego. Dine on hot and cold tapas, paella, and Chorizo al Inferno. For a local fave, squeeze into the Taco Bus for authentic Mexican food from **Taqueria Las Palmas** (21 N. Canyon St., 406/640-1822, 10:30am-10:30pm daily Apr.-Oct., $8-12). Eat at the old white-painted school bus with seating mostly outside on picnic tables, or get takeout to go back to your motel or campsite. The huge menu has traditional choices of meat or vegetarian tacos, enchiladas, quesadillas, carne asada, fajitas, and burritos.

ITALIAN

★ **Wild West Pizzeria and Saloon** (14 Madison Ave., 406/646-4400 or 406/646-7259, http://wildwestpizza.com, 11am-midnight daily year-round, $12-26) relies on Wheat Montana flour for its pizza dough and fresh ingredients for toppings. Pizzas come in menu-recommended combinations, or create your own. Pasta and sandwiches are also available, as well as wine and beer. They also deliver. The saloon has gambling machines and frequent live music (8pm, $3 cover) with dancing.

Pete's Rocky Mountain Pizza & Pasta (112 Canyon St., 406/646-7820, http://petesrockymountainpizza.com, 11am-10pm daily year-round, $12-26) serves create-your-own-style pizzas or Pete's designs. Lunch adds pasta and sandwiches. Dinner expands the pasta menu with lasagna, elk sausage spaghetti, and bison ravioli. Beer, wine, and Italian sodas are available. After 5pm, you can have pizza delivered to your campsite or motel.

SALOONS

After seeing bison in the park, head to the ★ **Buffalo Bar** (335 Hwy. 20, 406/646-1176, http://thebuffalobar.com, 10am-2pm daily year-round, $10-33), where the broad menu dishes up bison in many forms: nachos, tacos, burritos, burgers, chili, and meatloaf. You can also get western appetizers such as Rocky Mountain oysters and wild game sausage. The bar has Montana craft beers, wine, and cocktails. It serves breakfast until 4pm. Portions are big. It also has outdoor seating in summer, live poker on weekends, sports on big-screen TVs, pool, and a little casino action.

On the main drag, the **Slippery Otter Pub** (139 Canyon St., 406/646-7050, 11:30am-11pm daily year-round, $10-30) serves pizza, salads, bison and elk burgers, beer-battered cod and chips, and, on Friday and Saturday nights, prime rib. The pub has a broad beer and wine selection and a kids' menu, too.

a blue cheese, bacon, and bison burger at the Buffalo Bar

FINE DINING

With a cozy dining room, Serenity Bistro (38 N. Canyon St., 406/646-7660, www.serenitybistro.com, 11am-3pm and 5pm-10pm daily year-round, $13-38) expands with patio seating in summer. Soups, salads, sandwiches, burgers, and wraps make up the lunch menu. Dinner plates Montana cuisine: rib eye, elk tenderloin, quail, and pasta with suggested wine pairings. The menu has gluten-free, vegetarian, and vegan options. With extensive tapas, the menu is more conducive to ordering multiple small plates.

Located in the old first grade classroom of the 1918 West Yellowstone school, the Madison Crossing Lounge (121 Madison Ave., 406/646-7621, www.madisoncrossinglounge.com, 5pm-10pm daily May-Oct. and mid-Dec.-mid-Mar., $13-30) serves steaks, fish, burgers, chicken, and pasta. Regional microbrews, worldwide wines, whiskey, and specialty cocktails add to the fine-dining ambience. Appetizers include bison nachos.

You'll need to drive about six miles north of town to reach the Bar N Ranch (890 Buttermilk Creek Rd., 406/646-9445, www.bar-n-ranch.com, 5pm-10pm daily mid-May-Sept., $22-46) to dine in its upscale stone-and-log ranch house with mountain west decor and wildlife mounts. The restaurant specializes in steaks, bison, wild game, and fish accompanied by a worldwide wine list, Montana microbrews, and traditional cocktails.

DESSERT

Built in 1927 and listed on the National Register of Historic Places, the log Eagle's Store (3 N. Canyon St., 406/646-9300, www.eagles-store.com, 8am-8pm daily year-round, shorter hours off-season) serves ice cream, malts, and shakes from its old-fashioned soda fountain, which features some of the original leather stools, historic tiled counter, and back bar. City Creamery (105 N. Canyon St., 406/843-5515, noon-9pm daily mid-May-mid-Sept.) has homemade ice cream with rotating flavors, including huckleberry.

GROCERIES

West Yellowstone has two grocery stores; prices may be a bit higher than at your local big-city market. The Market Place (22 Madison Ave., 406/646-9600, 7am-10pm daily year-round) has takeout foods, a deli, produce, meats, and a liquor store. The Food Roundup Supermarket (107 Dunraven St., 406/646-7501, 7am-10pm daily year-round) is a larger grocery.

Accommodations

INSIDE THE PARK
Reservations

Competition for **Old Faithful reservations** (Xanterra, 307/344-7311 or 866/439-7375, www.yellowstonenationalparklodges.com, May-Oct., Snow Lodge mid-Dec.-early Mar.) is fierce. Plan ahead and **book one year in advance** for summer stays and winter holidays. You may be able to pick up last-minute reservations due to cancellations, but choices for room types will be limited.

Old Faithful has three lodging options, with 557 rooms total, all within a five-minute walk from the visitors center and Old Faithful Geyser. None of the lodges have televisions, radios, or air-conditioning. Most rooms do not have telephones, but they do have cell phone reception. Only Snow Lodge has wireless Internet. Bathrooms come in four types: tub-shower combo, shower only (shower stalls are small), shared baths down the hall, or communal toilets and showers in a separate cabin. Clarify your needs when reserving a room; a few ADA rooms and cabins are available. Rates listed are for two people; add on 14 percent tax and $18 per each additional person.

Old Faithful
OLD FAITHFUL INN

The most-requested lodge in the park, ★ **Old Faithful Inn** (early May-mid-Oct., $144-335 rooms, $670-715 suites) is a National Historic Landmark. The Old House, or the main log lodge, was built in 1903-1904, with the east wing added in 1913-1914 and west wing in 1927-1928. As such, room styles, sizes, and ambience are a throwback to the last century. It is reputed to be the largest log building in the world, with distinctive log architecture. The Old House contains the immense lobby, dining room, lounge, snack bar, gift shop, and old-style rooms, while the two wings are more modern. The deck over the portico has benches and chairs facing Old Faithful Geyser for watching eruptions.

The 327-room inn has **10 styles of rooms,** some overlooking Upper Geyser Basin and Old Faithful Geyser. Historic rooms in the Old House have fixtures with minimal outlets for charging electronics, 1-3 queen beds, and either private baths with clawfoot tubs or shared marble-and-tile baths with showers down the hall. No elevators access the upper floors of the Old House. The two more modern (but still dated) wings are 3-4 stories tall with elevators. Most of the hotel rooms have 1-3 queen beds with private baths. The east wing has rooms facing Old Faithful Geyser, although trees may block the view. Upper-end suites have sitting rooms, bedrooms with two queen beds, and private baths.

OLD FAITHFUL LODGE

Old Faithful Lodge (mid-May-early Oct., $96-160) is close to Old Faithful Geyser, but removed from the visitor center hubbub, producing a quieter location. You can sit on the lodge deck or in the lobby to watch the geyser blow. Inside, the huge stone-and-log lodge has a snack shop and a food court cafeteria.

Between the lodge and the Firehole River, 96 simple small motel-style rooms are in rustic duplex or fourplex cabins with tiny windows and no porches. From cabins 112-116 and 200-203, you can step right out the door to watch Old Faithful. Cabins 22-25 and 31-35 overlook the Firehole River. The bare-bones cabins have two double beds or one double and one single. Some have private baths; others require walking to a nearby communal bathroom and shower cabin. Sixty-seven of the cabins were renovated in 2016.

SNOW LODGE AND CABINS

Built in 1989-1999 with modern western architecture, ★ **Snow Lodge** (late

Apr.-mid-Oct. $123-325, mid-Dec.-Feb., $149-315) sits behind the visitors center with no views of the geyser basin and partially surrounded by parking lots. Snow Lodge is the most modern hotel at Old Faithful. The 134 rooms are larger and have modern-style bathrooms and furnishings. Cabins are located a few-minute walk from the lodge; you might encounter wildlife en route to breakfast. Wireless Internet is available in the lobby and main lodge ($5/hour, $12/day, $25/three days). The lodge has a restaurant, grill café, lounge, gift shop, and winter ice rink.

Hotel-style rooms with one king or two queen beds and log furnishings are in the three-story main lodge. Motel-style rooms cluster in plain duplex or quad buildings. Larger cabins have two queen beds per room with some rooms adjoining, while smaller cabins have one or two double beds. In winter, slide your bags to your room on plastic sleds, or use the bell service.

In winter, the park road to Old Faithful is closed. **Snowcoaches** ($123 adults one-way, kids half-price) travel from Mammoth to the Snow Lodge twice daily in each direction for the four-hour trip. You can also get a snowcoach from Flagg Ranch or West Yellowstone through other companies.

OUTSIDE THE PARK
West Yellowstone

On the western boundary of the park, West Yellowstone houses a mix of circa 1950 mom-and-pop motels interspersed with three-story modern hotels. More than 50 lodging properties cram into the town and sprawl throughout surrounding ranchland. Most motels have satellite television, phones, wireless Internet, air-conditioning, refrigerators, and microwaves. Due to limited lodging at Old Faithful, many visitors choose to stay in West Yellowstone, as the drive between the two places is only 30 miles.

Some motels are open year-round, while others are summer season only. Reservations are recommended six months in advance for summer, when the town packs out. Summer sees the highest prices, with rates $100-200 higher than winter, spring, and fall. Rates listed reflect the lowest and highest seasonal prices. Add on 10 percent tax.

HOSTEL

Built in 1912, the **Madison Hotel Motel and Hostel** (139 Yellowstone Ave., 406/646-7745 or 800/838-7745, www.madisonhotel-motel.com, mid-May-early Oct.) is listed on the National Register of Historic Places. The hostel ($48-50) has small, gender-separated

In winter, visitors sled their gear to Snow Lodge cabins.

West Yellowstone

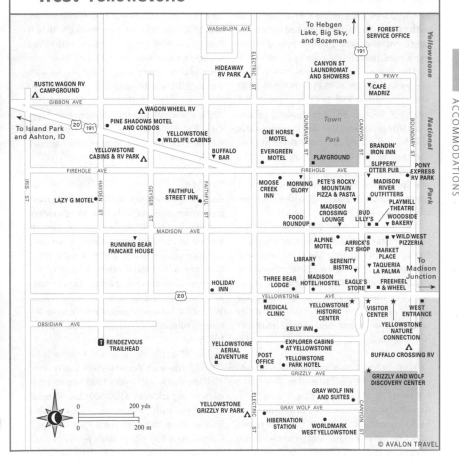

WASHBURN AVE

To Hebgen Lake, Big Sky, and Bozeman

FOREST SERVICE OFFICE

191

HIDEAWAY RV PARK

CANYON ST LAUNDROMAT AND SHOWERS

D PKWY

CAFÉ MADRIZ

RUSTIC WAGON RV CAMPGROUND

GIBBON AVE

WAGON WHEEL RV

Town Park

ELECTRIC ST

To Island Park and Ashton, ID

20 191

PINE SHADOWS MOTEL AND CONDOS

YELLOWSTONE WILDLIFE CABINS

ONE HORSE MOTEL

DUNRAVEN ST

CANYON ST

BRANDIN' IRON INN

BOUNDARY ST

Yellowstone

National

YELLOWSTONE CABINS & RV PARK

BUFFALO BAR

EVERGREEN MOTEL

PLAYGROUND

SLIPPERY OTTER PUB

PONY EXPRESS RV PARK

FIREHOLE AVE

FIREHOLE AVE

IRIS ST

HAYDEN ST

LAZY G MOTEL

GEYSER ST

FAITHFUL STREET INN

FAITHFUL ST

MOOSE CREEK INN

MORNING GLORY

PETE'S ROCKY MOUNTAIN PIZZA & PASTA

MADISON RIVER OUTFITTERS

PLAYMILL THEATRE

Park

MADISON CROSSING LOUNGE

BUD LILLY'S

WOODSIDE BAKERY

FOOD ROUNDUP

MADISON AVE

RUNNING BEAR PANCAKE HOUSE

ALPINE MOTEL

ARRICK'S FLY SHOP

WILD WEST PIZZERIA

MARKET PLACE

LIBRARY

SERENITY BISTRO

TAQUERIA LA PALMA

To Madison Junction

20

HOLIDAY INN

THREE BEAR LODGE

MADISON HOTEL/HOSTEL

EAGLE'S STORE

FREEHEEL & WHEEL

YELLOWSTONE AVE

MEDICAL CLINIC

YELLOWSTONE HISTORIC CENTER

VISITOR CENTER

WEST ENTRANCE

KELLY INN

YELLOWSTONE NATURE CONNECTION

OBSIDIAN AVE

RENDEZVOUS TRAILHEAD

YELLOWSTONE AERIAL ADVENTURE

EXPLORER CABINS AT YELLOWSTONE

POST OFFICE

YELLOWSTONE PARK HOTEL

BUFFALO CROSSING RV

GRIZZLY AVE

GRIZZLY AND WOLF DISCOVERY CENTER

0   200 yds
0   200 m

ELECTRIC ST

YELLOWSTONE GRIZZLY RV PARK

GRAY WOLF INN AND SUITES

GRAY WOLF AVE

CANYON ST

HIBERNATION STATION

WORLDMARK WEST YELLOWSTONE

© AVALON TRAVEL

second-floor dorm rooms with bunks and shared bathroom-shower facilities down the hall. The lobby has the common lounge, computers for Internet, a small refrigerator and microwave, but no kitchen for cooking. Small hotel and motel rooms ($70-180) have combos of queen, double, and single beds.

MOTELS
DNC Parks and Resorts (406/586-7593 or 877/600-4308, www.visityellowstonepark. com) runs several properties, including the Holiday Inn and Explorer Cabins, with seasonal packages that bundle up activities in Yellowstone with their lodging. Most have rooms that will take pets for an additional fee. Opposite the Grizzly and Wolf Discovery Center, the **Gray Wolf Inn and Suites** (250 S. Canyon St., year-round, $90-345) has three stories of rooms: one- or two-bedroom family suites with full kitchens, smaller suites with full kitchens, king hotel rooms, and standard two-queen hotel rooms. Some units have full kitchens. The inn serves a free continental breakfast and has an indoor pool, sauna, hot tub, and underground heated parking. Built

in 2007 on the quiet western side of town, the Yellowstone Park Hotel (201 Grizzly Ave., late Apr.-Sept. $100-395) is a three-story hotel with 66 standard hotel rooms and suites, free continental breakfast, indoor heated swimming pool, hot tub, and coin-op laundry.

The three-story ★ Kelly Inn (104 S. Canyon St., 406/646-4544 or 800/635-3559, www.yellowstonekellyinn.com, year-round, $100-365) has carved bears climbing up outside railings to stare in windows. Large rooms, which have a king or two or three queens, feature log furniture, and rates include a breakfast bar. Some suites have wet bars and whirlpool tubs. The inn has an indoor pool, hot tub, sauna, outdoor patio with gas fire pit, laundry, pet walk, and play areas.

Two longtime West Yellowstone staples sit on or near the Canyon Street activity. The Brandin' Iron Inn (201 Canyon St., 406/646-9411 or 800/217-4613, www.hotelyellowstone.com, year-round, $200-245) has 80 rooms with one queen or king, two queens, three queens, or suites with kitchens. Amenities include indoor hot tubs, complimentary hot breakfast, a ski wax room, and laundry services.

West Yellowstone abounds with relic motels from the 1950s or earlier. The ★ Alpine Motel (120 Madison Ave., 406/646-7544, http://alpinemotelwestyellowstone.com, mid-May-mid-Oct., $70-185) has small rooms with one queen or king and rooms with two queens. Bathrooms are small, and the walls are thin. It has a reputation for friendly owners and cleanliness. A renovated motel from 1931, the Evergreen Motel (229 Firehole Ave., 406/646-7655, www.theevergreenmotel.com, year-round, $100-230) is a small single-story motel with 17 rooms that have a king, queen, or two queen log beds. A laundry is available, and a few rooms have kitchens or kitchenettes. Tiny Pine Shadows Motel (229 N. Hayden St., 406/646-7541 or 800/624-5291, www.pineshadowsmotel.com, May-Mar., $90-270) also has a reputation for cleanliness. The motel has king rooms, double-queen rooms, and condos. The complex also has an on-site

laundry and outdoor picnic tables with gas barbecues. One mile from the park entrance, Lazy G Motel (123 Hayden St., 406/646-7586, http://lazygmotel.com, year-round, $90-140) has pine-walled single rooms, two-bedroom units, and kitchenettes ($20/day) in single-story and two-story wings. Picnic tables with a gas grill are outdoors. One Horse Motel (216 Dunraven St., 406/646-7677 or 800/488-2750, www.onehorsemotel.com, mid-May-Oct., $60-155) is a simple, single-story motel with a homespun look to its rooms. Laundry facilities are available.

CABINS

Cabins are common in West Yellowstone, from older minimalist log cabins to modern with frills. Instead of an out-in-the-woods ambience, the town cabins are clustered close together with views of streets. Cabins listed here are open year-round. Several of the campgrounds also have rustic cabins in summer: Yellowstone Grizzly RV Park, Wagon Wheel RV Campground, Rustic Wagon RV Campground, and Yellowstone Cabins and RV Park.

The ★ Explorer Cabins at Yellowstone (DNC Parks and Resorts, 201 Grizzly Ave., 406/586-7593 or 877/600-4308, www.visityellowstonepark.com, $120-500) has 50 modern cabins with kitchenettes. Front porches have seating, although most view the road. Community fire pits provide places to roast the s'mores supplied at check-in. Different cabin configurations include king, queen, and bunk beds.

Faithful Street Inn (120 Faithful St., 406/646-1010, www.faithfulstreetinn.com, $130-700) has nine cabins, townhomes, and houses of different configurations with 2-8 bedrooms and full kitchens. Set on a less-traveled street, they sleep 2-18 people and have clean, updated interiors, some with knotty pine walls. A minimum of 3-7 nights is required.

Yellowstone Wildlife Cabins (225 Geyser St., 406/646-7675, www.yellowstonewildlifecabins.com, $165-500) has six cabins with 1-3 bedrooms, full kitchens, and washers and dryers. A three-night minimum is required in summer. A few of the cabins are manufactured homes.

Hibernation Station (212 Gray Wolf Ave., 406/646-4200 or 800/580-3557, www.hibernationstation.com, $110-330) tucks 50 modern single and duplex log cabins around a 27-foot-long bronze dueling bull elk statue and a 30-foot waterfall with bronze mountain goats and bighorn sheep. Nine styles of cabins come with varied combinations of doubles, queens, kings, and bunks. Some cabins have jet tubs, fireplaces, and kitchenettes. In winter, a four-night minimum is required, and minimal services are available.

With 1950s-style log cabins, **Moose Creek Inn** (220 Firehole Ave. for the cabins, 119 Electric St. for the inn and check-in, 406/646-9546, www.moosecreekinn.com, $110-350) has a mix of lodging options. Log and knotty pine-walled cabins have one bath, two queen beds in separate rooms, and refrigerators and microwaves rather than kitchens. The two-story inn has a variety of hotel rooms including king, queen, two queens, two doubles, and three queens.

BED-AND-BREAKFAST

Located four miles outside town, **West Yellowstone Bed and Breakfast** (20 Crane Ln., 406/646-7754, www.westyellowstone-bandb.com, year-round, $140-210) has three rooms, each with a fireplace and log furniture. Two rooms are for 3-4 people. Rates are for two people, with each extra person at $100. Hot breakfast is served from a menu, with special diets accommodated.

LODGE

With the original lodge dating from 1932 and several rebuilds from fires, **Three Bear Lodge** (217 Yellowstone Ave., 406/646-7353 or 800/646-7353, www.threebearlodge.com, year-round, $70-310) is a survivor. Exhibits in the lodge detail the history and use of reclaimed wood and local rocks in the remodels. Large lodge rooms, including two-room Goldilocks suites for families, have mountain west decor and handcrafted reclaimed wood furnishings. More economical rooms (king, two queens, or two-room suites) are in the older single-story motel. Amenities include an outdoor heated pool (summer only), hot tubs, business center, theater, and a restaurant.

the Explorer Cabins in West Yellowstone

GUEST RANCHES

Guest ranches are one of the hallmarks of Montana. These two are located 6-18 miles outside of West Yellowstone, with breathing room and places to ride horses. On a 200-acre ranch, the **Bar N Ranch** (890 Buttermilk Rd., 406/646-0300, www.bar-n-ranch.com, mid-May-mid-Oct., $250-610) has high-end accommodations in the 9,000-square-foot main log lodge or in cabins. On-site amenities include an outdoor heated pool, hot tub, and restaurant. The lodge has seven rooms, each with different bed configurations, decor, and jetted tubs. The log cabins have one or two bedrooms, wood-burning fireplaces, baths, and personal outdoor hot tubs. On an old homestead, **Parade Rest Guest Ranch** (1279 Grayling Rd., 406/646-7217 or 800/753-5934, http://paraderestranch.com, mid-May-Sept., $300/day adults, $105-230 children 5-11) is an all-inclusive program with lodging, three meals per day, horseback riding, fly-fishing, and western cookouts. Lodging is in 15 unique cabins with 1-4 bedrooms and private baths. The dining room serves meals made from scratch.

Camping

INSIDE THE PARK

Two outstanding campgrounds sit on Yellowstone's west side. Madison is closest to Old Faithful, while Norris is closer to Mammoth and Canyon Village. Both campgrounds have flush toilets, potable water, picnic tables, fire rings with grills, food storage boxes, tent pads (at some sites), firewood and ice sales, evening ranger programs (mid-June-mid-Sept.), accessible sites, and shared biker-hiker campsites ($8/person). For hookups or showers, go to West Yellowstone.

Madison

At Madison Junction, below National Park Mountain, **Madison Campground** (307/344-7311 or 866/439-7375 advance reservations; 307/344-7901 same-day reservations, www.yellowstonenationalparklodges.com, May-mid-Oct., $25) has 278 sites on a flat plain spread around 10 loops. The

Madison Campground sits next to the Madison River.

Madison River flows past the campground, attracting anglers for iconic fly-fishing; wildlife-watchers often spot bison and elk. In fall, elk bugling fills the air. At the campground's west end, G and H loops have 65 sunny sites for tents only. Some campsites can fit RVs up to 40 feet. Make reservations nine months in advance.

Norris

Across from Norris Geyser Basin at 7,555 feet on the Upper Grand Loop's southwest corner, **Norris Campground** (first-come, first-served, mid-May-late Sept., $20) has 100 sites spread around a steep hillside. Loop A campsites are flatter and have views of surrounding meadows that often contain elk, bears, moose, or sandhill cranes. Bison often walk through campsites and bed down here. Prime walk-in tent sites line Solfatara Creek. The adjacent Museum of the National Park Ranger contains exhibits about early rangers, and nearby hiking trails lead to Norris Geyser Basin, Ice Lake, and north along Solfatara Creek. Arrive by 8am in summer to claim a campsite. RVs are limited to 30 feet.

OUTSIDE THE PARK

Campers requiring RV hookups should head to West Yellowstone where private campgrounds have flush toilets, showers, potable water, wireless Internet, dump stations, and hookups; most also have laundries. Reservations are a must for summer. Add on 7-10 percent for taxes.

West Yellowstone

Private campgrounds in West Yellowstone are surrounded by residential and commercial properties. From most, you can walk to restaurants, shopping, attractions, trailheads, fishing, the visitors center, and the park entrance. Rates are usually for two people. Add $4-10 for each additional person.

There are two campgrounds for RVs only. The largest campground, **Yellowstone Grizzly RV Park** (210 S. Electric St., 406/646-4466, www.grizzlyrv.com, May-Oct., RVs $70-85) has 261 RV campsites (limited to 80 feet). Bordered on two sides by Montana's Custer-Gallatin National Forest, the campground has landscaped gardens and lawns with aspens and lodgepole pines providing partial shade. RV sites have paved back-in or pull-through parking pads, cement walkways, and patios. They are positioned right next to each other, but are roomy enough for slide-outs and awnings. Facilities include picnic tables and barbecue grills (bring your own charcoal) plus a dog walk, game room, playground, convenience store, launderette, accessible facilities, and horseshoes.

Buffalo Crossing RV Park (101B S. Canyon St., 406/646-4300, www.buffalocrossingrvpark.com, May-mid-Oct., $40-65) tucks behind the Yellowstone Giant Screen Theater. The campground is a large gravel parking lot with a few small trees. Railroad ties divide the 15 sites (limited to 70 feet). It has a laundry and a tiny pet walk area.

If those fill, RV spots are at **Yellowstone Cabins and RV Park** (504 Hwy. 20, 406/646-9350 or 866/646-9350, www.yellowstonecabinsandrv.com, mid-May-mid-Oct., $50-60), **Pony Express RV Park** (3 Firehole Ave., 800/217-4613, www.brandiniron.com, Apr.-Oct., $50-60), and **Wagon Wheel RV** (408 Gibbon Ave., 406/646-7872, www.wagonwheelrv.com, mid-May-Sept., $50-60).

Tent campers can find grassy sites at a couple of older RV parks. **Rustic Wagon RV Campground** (637 Hwy. 20, 406/646-7387, www.rusticwagonrv.com, mid-Apr.-Oct., $47-62 RV, $47-50 tent) has 45 RV sites and 10 tent campsites. **Hideaway RV Park** (320 Electric St., 406/646-9049, www.hideawayrv.com, Apr.-Oct., RVs $50-58, tents $28-30) has 14 RV campsites and two tent campsites.

In the Vicinity

Several private campgrounds located outside West Yellowstone offer a quieter alternative to the bustle of town. Rates are for two people; add $4-6 for each additional person. In addition to full hookups, flush toilets, and wireless

Internet, the campsites have picnic tables and some fire rings.

Seven miles outside town near the rodeo and trail rides, two large adjacent campgrounds are **KOAs** (late May-Sept., RVs $38-88, tents $27-47). Set in shady pine forests and sunny mowed lawns, the campgrounds have 343 RV campsites and 104 tent campsites, a few with electricity. The main campground, **Yellowstone KOA** (3305 Targhee Pass Hwy., 406/646-7606 or 800/562-7591, www.yellowstonekoa.com), has an indoor pool, hot tub, camping kitchen, pancake breakfasts, nightly barbecue dinners, espresso kiosk, mini-golf, playground, basketball, dog walk, game room, and surrey bike rentals. Located behind the Super 8, the **Yellowstone KOA Mountainside** (1545 Targhee Pass Hwy., 406/646-7662 or 800/562-5640, www.yellowstonekoamountainside.com) has a convenience store, playground, dog park, camping kitchen, disposal station, and grills. Denny Creek flows past the back of the campground, with bridges accessing nature trails and fishing ponds.

On the south shore of the Madison Arm of Hebgen Lake, 8.5 miles outside West Yellowstone, **Madison Arm Resort** (5475 Madison Arm Rd., 406/646-9328, www.madisonarmresort.com, mid-May-Sept., RVs $45-50, tents $35-38) has 22 tent and 52 RV campsites overlooking a sandy beach, buoyed swimming area, and marina tucked into a small bay. For boating, paddling, fishing, waterskiing, and sailing, this is the place to camp. The resort rents canoes, paddleboats, kayaks, and motorized aluminum boats.

In a broad field on Bar N Ranch, about six miles north of West Yellowstone, **Yellowstone Under Canvas** (890 Buttermilk Creek Rd., 406/219-0441, www.mtundercanvas.com, late May-early Sept., $129-439) has luxury camping in safari tents, tepees, and cabin-style canvas tents. Standard tents have cots and floors; luxury tents include beds, furniture, and heat. Baths with hot water, showers, and flush toilets are in separate private facilities. Some bathrooms and showers are in tepees; others are individual rooms in trailers.

Forest Service Campgrounds

Three **Custer-Gallatin National Forest campgrounds** (Hebgen Lake Ranger District, 330 Gallatin Rd., West Yellowstone, 406/823-6961, www.fs.usda.gov/gallatin, mid-May-mid-Sept., $16-25, $6 extra vehicle) are near West Yellowstone. These sites work as backups when town campgrounds are full; with their locations and recreation, they might even be preferable. The campgrounds have picnic tables, fire rings with grills, vault and pit toilets, drinking water, bear boxes, firewood for sale, accessible campsites, and campground hosts.

Flanking the Madison River, **Baker's Hole Campground** (first-come, first-served) sits three miles north of West Yellowstone, where the trout-fishing river slows to a crawl in convoluted oxbows through willow wetlands that provide habitat for moose, birds, and mosquitoes. It has 73 first-come, first-served campsites, 33 with electrical hookups, and a 75-foot RV limit. Some sites have river frontage.

Two campgrounds are on Hebgen Lake, 10 miles from West Yellowstone. **Rainbow Point Campground** sits on an east arm of Hebgen Lake. Four loops contain 85 quiet campsites (15 with electrical hookups, 40-foot RV limit) tucked back from the lake in a thick, shady forest of tall lodgepole pines. Big, flat tent spaces are available. **Lonesomehurst Campground** sits on the South Fork Arm. Conifers dot the sunny, quiet campground with 27 campsites (five with electrical hookups, 45-foot RV limit) surrounded by arid grass and sagebrush meadows. Campsites along the east side overlook the lake; all campsites have territorial views of the Madison Range.

Reservations (877/444-6777 for advance reservations, www.recreation.gov; 406/646-1012 or 877/646-1012 for last-minute sites) are accepted for both campgrounds. Each is equipped with boat launches and Hebgen Lake is popular for swimming, paddling, waterskiing, boating, and fishing.

Transportation and Services

DRIVING

Only two-lane roads tour this area of Montana and Wyoming. Inside and outside the park, roads cut through wildlife habitats. Be on the lookout for deer, antelope, elk, and other wildlife jumping out onto the road.

Inside the park, the West Entrance is 14 miles from Madison Junction. The road from Madison Junction to Norris Junction is 14 miles northwest. From Madison Junction to Old Faithful, the drive is 16 miles south. Driving each of these roads can take 35-45 minutes due to wildlife jams and traffic. These roads close early November to mid-April.

Parking

At many of the geyser basins, **parking** lots restrict entry of RVs, buses, and trailers. This is due to small, tight parking spaces, sharp corners, and lack of turnaround area. You may need to park elsewhere and hike to access geyser basins.

OLD FAITHFUL

Driving into Old Faithful can be confusing, as one-way roads enter and depart the complex. Look for signage at junctions. For overnight visitors staying at lodges, check in first and park where the front desk directs. For day visitors, two giant parking lots are available, both equal distance from Old Faithful Geyser. They pack out in summer; row signs will help you remember where you parked. The smaller parking lot is southwest of the visitors center in between Snow Lodge and Old Faithful Inn. The larger parking lot is southwest of Old Faithful Lodge. To see Old Faithful Geyser, you must walk about five minutes or so from the parking lots, as no road passes by it. RVs are not permitted to park overnight in the lots.

WEST YELLOWSTONE

Streetside parking in West Yellowstone is crowded in summer. Rather than drive from your West Yellowstone lodging to the shopping and restaurant streets, plan to walk. RVs can find parking along Boundary Street and at the West Yellowstone Visitor Information Center on the corner of Yellowstone Avenue and Canyon Street. Hidden in the middle of four blocks are parking lots. They are difficult to see because they are surrounded by commercial businesses. Find the entrances to these parking lots on Boundary, Canyon, and Dunraven Streets between Firehole, Madison, and Yellowstone Avenues. In winter, be aware that snowmobiles are street legal on all streets except Canyon and the highways.

Car Rental

Rent cars in West Yellowstone from **Big Sky Car Rentals** (415 Yellowstone Ave., 406/646-9564 or 800/426-7669, http://yellowstonevacations.com). **Budget Car Rental** (406/646-5156, www.budget.com) has a desk in the Yellowstone Airport and an office in West Yellowstone (131 Dunraven St., 406/646-7882 or 800/231-5991, http://budget-yellowstone.com).

AIR

The **Yellowstone Airport** (WYS, 607 Airport Rd., West Yellowstone, 406/646-7631, www.yellowstoneairport.org) operates just outside of West Yellowstone in summer only. You can fly in and be at Old Faithful within a couple of hours. The airport is serviced only by Delta Air Lines from Salt Lake City (June-Sept., two flights daily Mon.-Fri., three flights daily Sat.-Sun.).

SHUTTLES

Based in West Yellowstone, **Yellowstone Road Runner** (406/640-0631, http://yellowstoneroadrunner.com) operates a year-round taxi and van service to airports (West Yellowstone, Bozeman, Jackson Hole, and Idaho Falls), campgrounds, and trailheads

Where Can I Find . . .?

- **Banks and ATMs:** ATMs are available in park lodges and at First Security Bank (106 S. Electric St., West Yellowstone, 406/646-7646).

- **Cell Service:** Verizon service is available in Old Faithful and West Yellowstone. There is no cell service in Madison or Norris.

- **Gas and Garage Services:** A gas station is located at Old Faithful (late Apr.-late Oct.). You can pay at the pump 24 hours with a credit card. West Yellowstone has gas and auto services.

- **Internet Service:** In the park, Wi-Fi is available for hotel guests only at Snow Lodge at Old Faithful.

- **Laundry:** A coin-op laundry is available in Snow Lodge (May-Oct.). In West Yellowstone, coin-op machines are available at Swan Cleaners and Laundromat (520 Madison Ave., 406/646-7892) and Canyon Street Laundromat (312 N. Canyon St., 406/646-7220).

- **Post Office:** A post office is located at Old Faithful (1000 Old Faithful, 307/545-7252, 8:30am-12:30pm and 1:30pm-5pm Mon.-Fri. early May-late Oct.) and in West Yellowstone (209 Grizzly Ave., 406/646-7704, 8:30am-5pm Mon.-Fri.).

- **Showers:** Pay showers are available at Old Faithful Inn (May-Oct.) and at Canyon Street Laundromat (312 N. Canyon St., 406/646-7220).

in Yellowstone. Their vehicles have bike racks.

EMERGENCY SERVICES

In an emergency, stop at the ranger station at Old Faithful (staffed daily). In West Yellowstone, the **Hebgen Lake Ranger District Station** (330 Gallatin Rd., 406/823-6961) is staffed weekdays only. For medical emergencies, drop in to the **Old Faithful Clinic** (Old Faithful Ranger Station, 307/545-7325, 7am-7pm summer).

Until the West Yellowstone Medical Center is constructed, the **West Yellowstone Clinic** (11 S. Electric St., 406/646-9441, Tues.-Fri., call for hours) provides the only medical service. The nearest hospitals are about 100 miles away: **Bozeman Deaconess Hospital** (915 Highland Blvd., Bozeman, MT, 406/585-5000, www.bozemandeaconess.org) and **Eastern Idaho Regional Medical Center** (3100 Channing Way, Idaho Falls, ID, 208/529-6111, http://eirmc.com).

Canyon and Lake Country

Exploring Canyon
    and Lake Country 137
Sights 141
Recreation 148
Entertainment and Shopping . . 170

Food 171
Accommodations 173
Camping 174
Transportation and Services . . . 177

Look for ★ to find recommended
sights, activities, dining, and lodging.

Highlights

★ **Canyon Visitor Education Center:**
See murals, computer-generated exhibits, films,
and a huge relief model of the park illustrating
the geologic history of Yellowstone's supervolcano (page 137).

★ **Grand Canyon of the Yellowstone:**
From 10 overlooks, view the thunderous Upper
or Lower Falls as they plummet through the colorful canyon (page 141).

★ **Fishing Bridge:** Watch cutthroat trout
spawn and perhaps see bears fishing from the
shore (page 145).

★ **Yellowstone Lake:** The largest freshwater lake above 7,000 feet in North America is an
immense body of water (page 145).

★ **West Thumb Geyser Basin:** This geyser
basin contains steaming hot pools and yields
views across Yellowstone Lake to the Absaroka
Mountains (page 146).

★ **Lewis Lake:** Yellowstone's third-largest
lake is a favorite for boaters, paddlers, and
anglers, with access to remote Shoshone Lake
(page 147).

★ **Mt. Washburn:** Hike to 10,243 feet atop
Mt. Washburn, the highest peak in Yellowstone
(page 149).

★ **South Rim Trail to Point Sublime:** Get
ready for more than 300 stair steps, the closest

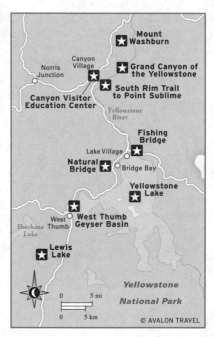

view of the Lower Falls, and unique canyon views
(page 155).

★ **Natural Bridge:** This 1.3-mile forested
trail leads to a natural rhyolite bridge of rock
spanning a canyon (page 158).

Sculpted by a glacier, water, earthquakes, and wind, the Grand Canyon of the Yellowstone is one of the park's most striking features.

Prominent points allow visitors to gape down to the Yellowstone River far below and the Upper and Lower Falls plunging over their precipices. Trails with steep stairways climb down to platforms for viewing. At Brink of the Lower Falls, you can feel the pounding of the water.

Upstream at 7,732 feet, Yellowstone Lake is the largest freshwater high-elevation lake in North America. Rimmed with a handful of steaming thermals, the lake holds islands and remote bays that offer boaters, canoers, and kayakers plenty of places for solitude. Native cutthroat and introduced lake trout appeal to sport anglers. Miles and miles of shoreline give visitors scenic drives and places to enjoy the water, but be prepared for frigid temperatures.

In addition to the canyon and lake, the area contains several other remarkable ecosystems. Mt. Washburn, one of the highest mountains in the park, is flanked with trails for hikers. For wildlife-watchers, Hayden Valley proliferates with bison, elk, trumpeter swans, and grizzly bears. Lewis Lake offers a quiet trout fishery and paddler paradise to reach Shoshone Lake.

Most of the visitor services concentrate in Canyon, Fishing Bridge, Bridge Bay, Lake, and Grant Villages, with additional campgrounds sprinkled throughout the area. Visitors to canyon and lake country get to discover a diverse landscape shaped by the powers of the earth.

PLANNING YOUR TIME

Starting the third week in **April**, you can drive into Canyon via Norris, West Yellowstone, and Mammoth. In **early May,** East and South Entrance roads open for access to Canyon and the still ice-covered Yellowstone Lake. Dunraven Pass and Craig Pass open in **late May,** with heavy snow years sometimes posing delays. In **summer,** Canyon overlook parking lots crowd with cars and tour buses between 10am and 4pm, and parking lot restrooms have long waiting lines.

Previous: Grand Canyon of the Yellowstone; Yellowstone Lake. **Above:** Gull Point.

Canyon and Lake Country

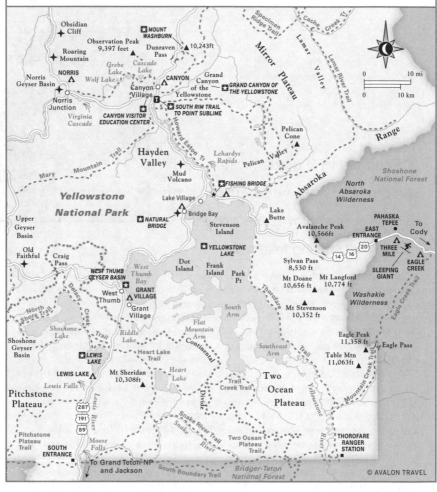

All visitor facilities, including visitors centers, restaurants, lodges, and campgrounds, are fully operational **June-early September.** A handful start the summer season in mid-May and linger into **early October.** In fall, Dunraven Pass closes in mid-October for the winter. All other roads close for the season in **early November.**

In winter, no lodging, restaurants, or facilities are open at Canyon or Yellowstone Lake (except for the Yellowstone Expeditions yurt camp). **Mid-December-mid-March,** visitors can tour the region on snowcoaches, snowmobiles, or skis. Warming huts with minimal services are in the Canyon Visitor Education Center lobby (exhibits closed), Fishing Bridge, and West Thumb. Tours originate in Mammoth, West Yellowstone, Old Faithful, or Flagg Ranch/Headwaters.

Exploring Canyon and Lake Country

VISITORS CENTERS

Four visitor information centers dot the canyon and lake area; all contain **Yellowstone Forever** stores (406/848-2400, www.yellowstone.org) selling books, field guides, and maps. Hours shorten in spring and fall.

★ Canyon Visitor Education Center

Canyon Visitor Education Center (Canyon Village, 307/344-2550, www.nps.gov/yell, 8am-8pm daily May-mid-Oct.) features films, murals, photos, and interactive exhibits that explore the powerful geologic forces of fire and ice that created Yellowstone's supervolcano. Highlights include a huge relief model of the park that traces its geologic history, a 9,000-pound rotating kugel ball that shows volcanic hotspots around the globe, and one of the world's largest lava lamps to show how magma works. You can even check the strength of the current earthquakes resounding underground. The visitors center also contains a **backcountry office** (8am-4:30pm daily June-Aug.).

Fishing Bridge Museum and Visitor Center

Located on the north end of Yellowstone Lake, the log-and-stone **Fishing Bridge Museum and Visitor Center** (307/344-2450, www.nps.gov/yell, 8am-7pm daily late May-early Oct.) tucks into the trees on the East Entrance Road, less than one mile from the historic Fishing Bridge. Built in 1931, the small museum is now a National Historic Landmark and contains bird and waterfowl specimens plus other wildlife. Their outdoor amphitheater has naturalist presentations.

West Thumb Information Center

Located on the west thumb of Yellowstone Lake, **West Thumb Information Center** (307/344-2876, www.nps.gov/yell, 9am-5pm daily late May-early Oct.) is a small, log building with exhibits on West Thumb Geyser Basin. This is where you can ask about the 100-foot-high bulge growing on the floor of Yellowstone Lake due to activity from faults and hot springs.

Grant Visitor Center

Grant Visitor Center (Grant Village, 307/344-2650, www.nps.gov/yell, 8am-7pm daily late May-early Oct.) has exhibits and a movie that detail the role of fire via the story of 1988, the fieriest summer in the park's history.

ENTRANCE STATIONS

Two **entrance stations** ($30 vehicle, $25 motorcycles, $15 hike-in/bike-in; joint parks pass: $50/vehicle, $40 motorcycles, $20 hike-in/bike-in) provide access to the Lake Yellowstone region; they are 70 miles apart. The entrance roads into the park are generally open spring-fall; winter access (mid-Dec.-early Mar.) is only via snowmobile at both entrances or by snowcoach from the south at Flagg Ranch outside the park boundary. Both roads close to vehicles early November-early May.

The **South Entrance** (mid-May-early Nov.) is located on U.S. Highway 89/191/287 south of Lewis Lake at the boundary between Yellowstone and Grand Teton National Parks. If entering the park from Grand Teton, you will drive through this entrance. The closest park hub is West Thumb, 22 miles north; the Old Faithful area is 17 miles farther west.

The **East Entrance** (late May-early Nov.) sits on the east side of Sylvan Pass on U.S. Highway 20, the road between Fishing Bridge and Cody, Wyoming (53 miles away). From the East Entrance, it is 27 miles to Lake Yellowstone and Fishing Bridge.

TOURS

Bus, wildlife, and boat tours launch from Canyon Village and Yellowstone Lake locales daily late May-late September. Some tours are in rebuilt 1930s yellow sedans that cruise the park in historic style. In winter, snowcoach tours originate at Old Faithful Snow Lodge to visit the canyon or lake sights. For all tours, make **reservations** (Xanterra, 307/344-7311 or 866/439-7375, www.yellowstonenational-parklodges.com, mid-Dec.-Feb., rates vary, half-price for children ages 3-11) up to one year in advance. Some departure and return times vary seasonally based on daylight hours.

Bus Tours

Guides drive two tours in vans or sightseeing buses. The full-day **Circle of Fire** tour (8.5 hrs., daily June-early Oct., $85) cruises the lower loop of Grand Loop Road to take in the biggies: Old Faithful, Yellowstone Lake, Hayden Valley, Grand Canyon of the Yellowstone, and Fountain Paint Pots. Departure times vary by origin locations: Canyon Village, Fishing Bridge RV Park, Lake Hotel, Bridge Bay Campground, and Grant Village. **Picture Perfect Photo Safaris** (5 hrs., daily mid-May-early Oct., $98) depart around sunrise from Lake Hotel to tour

Hayden Valley and the Grand Canyon of the Yellowstone. Led by professional photographers, the tour helps amateur and pro shutterbugs get the cool shots; and beginners receive instruction.

The evening **Yellowstone Lake Butte Sunset Tour** (2 hours, daily June-early Oct., $40) departs from Lake Hotel or Fishing Bridge RV Park in historic yellow touring sedans to watch the sunset from the 8,348-foot summit of Lake Butte.

Wildlife Tours

Dawn and dusk make for the best wildlife watching when animals are most active. Two wildlife-watching tours depart in historic yellow touring sedans. The **Wake Up to Wildlife** (5 hrs., daily June-late Sept., $95) tour leaves around sunrise from Canyon Village to explore the Lamar Valley. **Evening Wildlife Encounters** (4 hrs., daily June-mid-Sept., $70) departs from Canyon Village in the late afternoon for a ride to Dunraven Pass, Tower Fall, and the Tower Junction sagebrush flats.

Boat Tours

To get out on Yellowstone Lake, take the **Yellowstone Lake Scenic Cruise** (1 hour,

Historic yellow sedans tour the park.

departs 5-7 times daily mid-June-early Sept., $18 adults, $11 children). From Bridge Bay Marina, the *Lake Queen* circles Stevenson Island, home to osprey, eagles, ducks, herons, and other shorebirds. The interpretive tour fills you in on the lake's history, geology, and natural history while the enclosed boat shelters passengers from strong afternoon lake winds. Reservations are highly recommended midsummer. Plan to arrive at the marina 15 minutes prior to launch.

Winter Snowcoach Tours

Winter Snowcoach Tours (mid-Dec.-Feb.) depart from Old Faithful Snow Lodge in wheeled mini-buses with big windows. **Across the Great Divide** (4 hrs., departs 7:45am daily, $74) pops over the Continental Divide to walk through West Thumb Geyser Basin. **Grand Canyon Day Tours** (10 hours, departs 8:15am Mon., Wed., Fri.-Sun., $247) takes in viewpoints overlooking the famous canyon waterfalls.

DRIVING TOURS
South Entrance Road
22 MILES

The forested **South Entrance Road** (45 min., mid-May-early Nov.) connects the South Entrance of Yellowstone with West Thumb. The road passes the **Lewis River, Lewis Falls**, and **Lewis Lake**.

East Entrance Road
27 MILES

From the East Entrance Station, the **East Entrance Road** (60 min., late-May-early Nov.) climbs a steep road through cliffs overlooking Middle Creek. Near the head of the valley, a pullout affords views down into the glacier-carved terrain. Amid howling winds, 8,524-foot **Sylvan Pass** cuts through a rocky slot in the Absaroka Mountains. A small summit parking lot offers a place to scan the hillsides for bighorn sheep and peruse the long, thin waterfalls.

On the descent, use second gear to avoid burning your brakes. At **Sylvan and Eleanor Lakes**, small pullouts allow photo ops. Thick lupine flanks the road as it plunges to the paved side spur of **Lake Butte Road** (1 mile, no RVs or trailers), which goes through the remains of a 2002 forest fire to 8,348-foot **Lake Butte Overlook,** where you can look down on Yellowstone Lake and spot the Teton Mountains in the distance. After reaching the north shore of **Yellowstone Lake,** the road curves around **Steamboat Point,**

Lake Butte Overlook at Yellowstone Lake

a collection of puffing, noisy fumaroles, and **Mary Bay**, a volcanic caldera, to reach **Fishing Bridge**.

Lower Grand Loop Road
96 MILES

The **Lower Grand Loop Road** (4 hours, late May-early Nov.) links the Grand Canyon of the Yellowstone, Hayden Valley, Yellowstone Lake, West Thumb Geyser Basin, Old Faithful, and Norris Geyser Basin. Stops for touring geyser basins will add to your time.

Between Canyon Village and Fishing Bridge (16 miles, 45 min.), the road tours the ultra-scenic **Hayden Valley,** cut by the meandering **Yellowstone River.** The valley usually has scads of **wildlife:** bison, elk, deer, and sometimes bears or wolves. For the best wildlife-watching, drive through Hayden Valley in the early morning or at dusk. Expect slow going where wildlife jams stall traffic. South of Hayden Valley, the smelly volcanic features of **Mud Volcano** and **Sulphur Cauldron** shoot steam across the road. **LeHardy's Rapids** offers a place to spot harlequin ducks in early summer.

The scenic drive continues south along **Yellowstone Lake** from Fishing Bridge to West Thumb Junction (21 miles, 45 min.). Stop in Lake Village to view the historic **Lake Yellowstone Hotel**. Continuing south, the road passes **Bridge Bay** and the trailhead to **Natural Bridge**. South of Bridge Bay, the conifer-lined **Gull Point Drive** (2.1 miles, may close late May-June) leads to **Gull Point Picnic Area**, where a long sandbar extends out into the lake at Gull Point—a good place for fishing and beachcombing with views across the lake to the Absaroka Mountains. South of Gull Point Drive, multiple **picnic areas** and pullouts offer places to enjoy the lake; prepare for wind. **West Thumb Geyser Basin** is on the left just before West Thumb Junction.

From West Thumb, the Lower Grand Loop Road heads west through lodgepole pine and spruce forests toward **Old Faithful** (17 miles, 45 min.), reaching two south-side overlooks of distant **Shoshone Lake**. The route pops out twice over the **Continental Divide,** the highest point at 8,391 feet. **Isa Lake**, located at **Craig Pass**, has the unique status of flowing toward both the Pacific Ocean and the Gulf of Mexico. After Craig Pass, the road descends into **Old Faithful.**

LeHardy Rapids is a nesting spot for harlequin ducks.

Gull Point Picnic Area on Yellowstone Lake

Upper Grand Loop Road
70 MILES

Upper Grand Loop Road (3 hours) links Canyon Village with Tower Junction, Mammoth Hot Springs, and Norris. Various segments of the road open at different times in spring; private vehicles can tour the entire loop late May-early November. Stopping at geyser basins and overlooks will add more time to the drive.

Driving north from Canyon Village to Tower Junction (19 miles, 45 min.), Upper Grand Loop Road climbs to **Dunraven Pass,** which yields territorial views off either side of the pass. En route, you'll spot the lookout on the summit of **Mt. Washburn.** North of the pass, the road descends to **Tower Fall, Calcite Springs,** and **Tower Junction.** For the 7 percent grade down from the pass, shift into second gear to avoid burning your brakes.

Sights

CANYON VILLAGE

The park hub of Canyon Village sits at an east-side junction connecting Upper and Lower Grand Loop Roads. It is 12 miles east of Norris, 19 miles south of Tower Junction, and 16 miles north of Yellowstone Lake and Fishing Bridge.

Dunraven Pass and Mt. Washburn

On Upper Grand Loop Road north of Canyon Village, 8,859-foot **Dunraven Pass** is the highest drive-to point in Yellowstone. Those coming from sea level will feel sluggish and short of breath just stepping a few feet from the car at scenic pullouts. The pass crosses the Washburn Range right at the base of **Mt. Washburn.** To reach the 10,243-foot summit of Mt. Washburn and the lookout requires hiking or mountain biking.

★ Grand Canyon of the Yellowstone

South of Canyon Village are three entrances to **Grand Canyon of the Yellowstone,** the iconic, 20-mile-long canyon made from lava rhyolite. The **Yellowstone River** cuts a colorful swath 1,000 feet deep and 0.75 mile wide through the landscape. The river plunges over the **Upper Falls** before thundering down the **Lower Falls,** the tallest (and most famous) falls in the park. Roads and trails with multiple overlooks flank the North and South Rims. If you have only a few minutes, stop at **Artist Point** on the South Rim or **Lookout Point** on the North Rim.

Some overlooks have short, easy paved routes, while others have descents that require strenuous climbs back up. The 8,000-foot elevation may cause labored breathing for those coming from sea level. Prepare for crowds in summer: tour buses disgorge swarms of

Grand Canyon of the Yellowstone

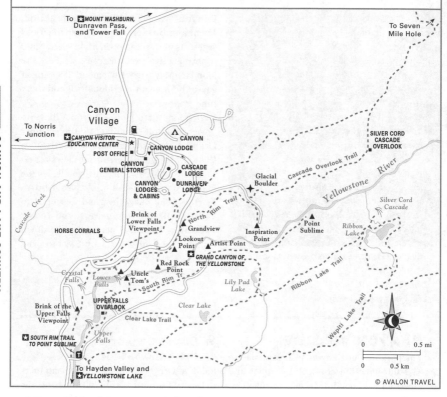

To ⭐ MOUNT WASHBURN,
Dunraven Pass,
and Tower Fall

To Seven
Mile Hole

Canyon
Village

To Norris
Junction

🅿 CANYON VISITOR
EDUCATION CENTER
POST OFFICE ■
CANYON
GENERAL STORE
CANYON
LODGES
& CABINS

CANYON
CANYON LODGE
CASCADE
LODGE
DUNRAVEN
LODGE

SILVER CORD
CASCADE
OVERLOOK

Glacial
Boulder

Cascade Overlook Trail

Yellowstone River

Silver Cord
Cascade

Cascade Creek

Brink of
Lower Falls
Viewpoint

North Rim Trail

HORSE CORRALS

Grandview
Lookout
Point
Artist Point

Inspiration
Point

Point
Sublime

Ribbon
Lake

⭐ GRAND CANYON OF
THE YELLOWSTONE

Red Rock
Point

Ribbon Lake Trail

Crystal
Falls
Lower
Falls
Uncle
Tom's

South Rim Tr.

Lily Pad
Lake

UPPER FALLS
OVERLOOK
Brink of the
Upper Falls
Viewpoint

Clear Lake

Wapiti Lake Trail

Clear Lake Trail

⭐ SOUTH RIM TRAIL
TO POINT SUBLIME

Upper
Falls

0   0.5 mi

0   0.5 km

To Hayden Valley and
⭐ YELLOWSTONE LAKE

© AVALON TRAVEL

visitors, parking lots are congested, and restrooms have long lines. Visit in early morning or evening for fewer people. Pick up a trail guide ($1) at visitors centers.

NORTH RIM

The one-way **North Rim Drive** (east side of Lower Grand Loop Rd., 1.2 miles south of Canyon Junction) visits four signed overlooks of the canyon, Yellowstone River, and the 308-foot Lower Falls. The first stop is **Brink of the Lower Falls,** where a paved walkway with stairs leads to an overlook for views. To reach the actual brink requires a steep 357-foot drop in elevation through multiple switchbacks to the platform. Underfoot, you can feel the thundering of almost 40,000 gallons of water per second plummeting over

the lip. The second stop accesses **Lookout Point** via a quick ascent to an overlook of the Lower Falls, canyon, and an osprey nest. (In early summer, rangers may set up a spotting scope to view the osprey nest.) Just before the overlook, a 0.4-mile switchback-and-stairway trail plunges 315 feet in elevation to **Red Rock Point,** a perch closer to the Lower Falls. The third stop on North Rim Drive is **Grand View,** a paved descent of 127 feet in elevation to the overlook. Near the end of North Rim Drive, turn right onto the two-lane road to reach **Inspiration Point** for the fourth and more distant view up canyon. Stairs lead to a small platform where you can see the Lower Falls upstream.

From Lower Grand Loop Road (0.4 mile

south of North Rim Dr.), turn east at the signed road to **Brink of the Upper Falls**. Walk 0.1 mile upstream to a left turn for the short descent to the platform at the brink. The falls mesmerize with a 109-foot plunge.

SOUTH RIM

From **South Rim Drive** (one mile south of Canyon Junction), cross the Chittenden Bridge to reach two main signed parking areas that have viewpoints of the canyon, Yellowstone River, Upper Falls, and Lower Falls. At **Uncle Tom's Point** (west side of the drive), park and follow the easy paved walkway to the **Upper Falls** viewpoint that faces the 109-foot waterfall. North of the parking lot, a 0.25-mile trail follows switchbacks and steel stairways to drop 500 feet in elevation to **Uncle Tom's overlook**, a small steel platform yielding the closest view of the 308-foot **Lower Falls**. Most visitors count the 328 metal stairs as they slog back up. South Rim Drive terminates at the parking lot for **Artist Point**. An easy, paved walkway leads to the classic view of the canyon and Lower Falls.

HAYDEN VALLEY

Occupying almost 50 square miles between Canyon and Fishing Bridge, **Hayden Valley** once held an arm of Yellowstone Lake. Today, it contains prime **wildlife-watching**, where bison jams are common. Look for coyote, moose, bison, elk, raptors, grizzly bears, trumpeter swans, wolves, and hordes of Canada geese. (Use the multiple pullovers to watch wildlife.) The **Yellowstone River** meanders through the sagebrush and grass valley, giving it a bucolic feel. No off-trail travel is allowed, and most waterways are closed to fishing in order to protect the sensitive area.

Mud Volcano

Before you see Mud Volcano, you'll smell the rotten-egg scent of hydrogen sulfide gas billowing from the earth. A 0.7-mile boardwalk and trail tours several thermal features; the two most prominent ones are on the lower and shorter boardwalk loop. **Mud Volcano** is a 17-foot-deep burbling pot of watery clay that especially amuses kids when they can stand the stench. Nearby, hot steam from 170°F water belches from **Dragon's Mouth Spring**. At the high end of the longer paved and stair-step boardwalk loop, **Black Dragon's Cauldron** stretches nearly 200 feet across, bubbling up from a crack with the dark color created from iron sulfides. Pick up a trail guide ($1) at Mud Volcano.

Winter visitors can spot the 100-foot-tall mountain of ice at the base of the Lower Falls.

At a pullout across the road to the north is one of the park's most acidic hot springs. On par with battery acid, **Sulphur Cauldron** boils with yellow color created from sulphur and bacteria.

LeHardys Rapids

On the Yellowstone River, **LeHardy's Rapids** (2.7 miles south of Mud Volcano; 3 miles north of Fishing Bridge) drops in a cascade broken by rocks. Boardwalk platforms allow for viewing. In early summer, cutthroat trout wriggle up the rapids to reach Fishing Bridge for annual spawning, and colorful harlequin ducks surf the white water. The viewing boardwalk closes in early spring to protect ducks during mating season.

FISHING BRIDGE

The park hub of **Fishing Bridge** (East Entrance Rd. near the junction with Lower Grand Loop Rd.) sits on the only outlet from Yellowstone Lake. Fishing Bridge Historic District is home to the 1931 **Fishing Bridge Museum and Visitor Center** (307/344-2450, www.nps.gov/yell, 8am-7pm daily late May-Sept.), a National Historic Landmark. Other facilities include Fishing Bridge RV Park, Yellowstone General Store, and a gas station.

the Upper Falls of the Grand Canyon of the Yellowstone

Lake Village (signed spur road 1.5 miles south of Fishing Bridge Junction) is a cluster of visitor services on the northwest end of Yellowstone Lake. The yellow colonial **Lake Yellowstone Hotel** is a National Historic

stairway to Red Rock Overlook of the Grand Canyon of the Yellowstone

Landmark built in 1891 that offers lodging and dining. Follow the beach road to pull over at the overlook in front of the octagonal **Yellowstone General Store,** built in 1919 and housing historical photos.

★ Fishing Bridge

Where the Yellowstone River exits Yellowstone Lake, the original log **Fishing Bridge** was erected over the waterway in 1902. The current bridge replaced it in 1937 with walkways on both sides to accommodate hordes of anglers going after cutthroat trout. Due to threats to the trout population from lake trout and overfishing, angling is no longer allowed on the bridge, but visitors can still watch spawning trout in June-early July.

Pelican Creek

Pelican Creek (East Entrance Rd.) offers prime wildlife-watching. Early mornings or evenings are best for spotting waterfowl, bald eagles, elk, moose, or bears. Twisting in slow eddies, the creek turns through a two-mile-long wetland that stretches 0.3-mile wide. Pullouts on the east end of the bridge over the creek offer the best place to scan the terrain with binoculars.

★ YELLOWSTONE LAKE

At 7,733 feet, the natural **Yellowstone Lake** is the largest water body in Yellowstone National Park and the largest high-elevation freshwater lake in North America. Its stats are impressive: 20 miles long by 15 miles wide, covering 136 square miles and diving to its deepest spot at 410 feet. With the exception of thermal areas, the lake freezes over with three feet of ice in winter and often doesn't melt out until late May or early June, which means chilly water for swimming. (Boating starts in summer.) Snowmelt causes the water to rise to its highest level in early June, flooding some south-end beaches and closing Gull Point Drive. During summer and fall, afternoon winds frequently whip the lake into whitecaps.

Located partly inside the Yellowstone Caldera, the northern section of the lake has its origins in volcanic activity and lava flows—hence **Steamboat Springs**—while the southern arms formed from glaciation. The lake's thermal activity includes geysers, fumaroles, and hot springs. West Thumb Geyser Basin is the most accessible of these; the largest is a 2,000-foot-long vent at the lake bottom that bulges up 100 feet.

The lake's six islands and shoreline attract wildlife. Look for trumpeter swans,

historic Fishing Bridge

pelicans, ducks, eagles, herons, and other shorebirds.

GRANT VILLAGE AND WEST THUMB

Near West Thumb Junction, the adjoining West Thumb Geyser Basin and Grant Village provide the most southern services in the park. In West Thumb, the **West Thumb Geyser Basin** burbles and steams with hydrothermal features. To the south, **Grant Village** has a campground, lodging, restaurants, stores, and a marina for launches onto Yellowstone Lake. The junction is located 21 miles south of Fishing Bridge, 17 miles east of Old Faithful, and 22 miles north of the South Entrance.

★ West Thumb Geyser Basin

On West Thumb Bay in Yellowstone Lake, the **West Thumb Geyser Basin** (0.1 mile northeast of West Thumb Junction) is a smaller caldera within the larger Yellowstone Caldera. The geyser basin dumps more than 3,100 gallons of hot water daily into the lake and contains three geysers and 11 hot springs, plus fumaroles and mud pots. Two loops (0.8 mile) guide visitors around the thermal features.

Explore Yellowstone Lake

Yellowstone Lake is so big that it's difficult to know how to best explore it. Here are the top ways:

- **Lake Butte Overlook** is the best place to see across the giant expanse and watch sunsets.

- **Storm Point** offers the best scenic beach walk.

- **Gull Point** is the best beach for shore-fishing and beachcombing.

- **West Thumb Geyser Basin** has the lake's best thermals.

- A *Lake Queen* **boat tour** offers the easiest way to get on the lake and around Stevenson Island.

- A **boat** is the best way to tour Frank Island, the largest island.

- Use **paddle kayaks or canoes** to see the southern arms.

The larger boardwalk loop cruises the lakeshore where early park visitors once cooked fish in **Fishing Cone.** The striking turquoise

West Thumb Geyser Basin

Yellowstone Lake

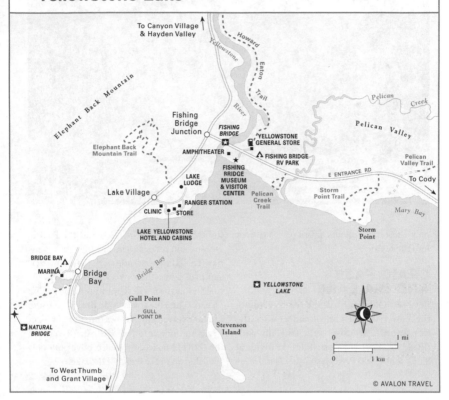

and emerald **Abyss Pool** may be one of the deepest in the park at 53 feet. **Twin Geyser** has two vents that shoot water as high as 75 feet. Many of the colorful hot pools derive their hues from heat-happy thermophiles. Pick up a trail guide ($1) on the boardwalk.

SOUTH ENTRANCE
★ Lewis Lake

Named for Meriwether Lewis of the Lewis and Clark Corps of Discovery expedition, **Lewis Lake** (10 miles south of West Thumb Junction) is Yellowstone's third-largest lake at 2,716 acres. Fed by the Lewis River from Shoshone Lake, the lake is a favorite for boaters, paddlers, and campers. A few hot springs empty into the lake, and anglers go after several species of trout that weren't originally in the fishless waters. The lake also serves as access to Shoshone Lake. Paddlers can work up the slow-moving inlet river to reach the bigger lake. Lewis Lake feeds the **Lewis River,** which tumbles over Lewis Falls and into the Snake River.

Lewis Falls

After the Lewis River departs Lewis Lake, it tumbles down the 30-foot-high **Lewis Falls,** which roars at its fullest in June with high water. The falls are viewable from the South Entrance Road, just a short distance from Lewis Lake, or from an overlook at the end of a short climb. South of the falls, the river slices through the **Lewis River Canyon,** but

Lewis Falls tumbles at sunset.

only a few tiny pullouts afford places to peer into the ravine.

CRAIG PASS AND ISA LAKE

Between Old Faithful and West Thumb, the Lower Grand Loop Road crosses the **Continental Divide** twice. Tiny, lily-pad-filled **Isa Lake,** which straddles the divide at 8,262-foot **Craig Pass,** is unique, as it drains to both the Gulf of Mexico and the Pacific Ocean—but it does so in a roundabout manner. The lake's east-side outlet stream curls southward into the Lewis River, which eventually joins the Snake River west to the Pacific Ocean. The lake's west side drains into the Firehole River, which flows into the Madison River and north to the Missouri River and the Gulf of Mexico. An interpretive pullout is available on the east end of the lake.

Recreation

DAY HIKES

Hikes vary from short stops to scenic viewpoints to long treks up river drainages or steep ascents up mountains. High elevation and the arid climate can dehydrate hikers. Take your time and drink lots of fluids to combat headaches and altitude sickness.

Some trails remain **closed until July 1** in order to minimize conflicts with grizzlies and black bears during seasons when they concentrate on food sources. Conditions such as bear activity, high water, snow, and fires can close trails at any time. For information about seasonal closures, contact the ranger stations and visitors centers, or check trails online (www.

nps.gov/yell). A small booth near the visitors center at Canyon Village rents **pepper spray** ($10/day, $28/week).

Guided Hikes

Naturalist rangers lead **free walks and hikes** (June-Sept.) in Canyon, West Thumb, and Fishing Bridge. Some walks run daily while others are offered weekly. Find schedules in park newspapers. Popular short hikes include **Storm Point, Yellowstone Lake Overlook,** and **canyon rim** trails. Yellowstone also permits multiple concessionaires (www.nps.gov/yell) to guide day hikes.

Canyon and Lake Country Hikes

Trail	Effort	Distance	Duration	Features
Duck Lake	Easy	1 mi	30 min	lake
Pelican Creek Nature Trail	Easy	1.3 mi rt	1 hr	wildlife
Storm Point	Easy	2.3 mi rt	1.5 hr	scenery
Clear Lake and Ribbon Lake	Easy	2.2-7.3 mi rt	1.5-4 hr	lakes, thermal basin
Natural Bridge	Easy	2.6 mi rt	2 hr	natural arch
Riddle Lake	Easy	4.8 mi rt	3 hr	lake, waterfowl
South Rim Trail to Point Sublime	Easy	5.1 mi rt	3 hr	scenery
Shoshone Lake via DeLacy Creek	Easy	5.8 mi rt	3-4 hr	scenery, lake
Grebe Lake	Easy	6.6 mi rt	3-4 hr	lake, waterfowl
Silver Cord Cascade	Easy	2 mi rt	1 hr	scenery, waterfall
North Rim of Grand Canyon of the Yellowstone	Easy to strenuous	3.8-6.6 mi one-way	3-4 hr	scenery, waterfalls
Cascade Lake and Observation Peak	Easy to strenuous	4.4-9.6 mi rt	2.5-5 hr	scenery, lake
Mt. Washburn	Easy to strenuous	5.4-6.4 mi rt	4 hr	scenery
Yellowstone Lake Overlook	Moderate	2 mi rt	1.5 hr	scenery
Elephant Back Mountain	Moderate	3.6 mi rt	2.5 hr	scenery
Chain of Lakes	Moderate	10.7 mi one-way	5-6 hr	scenery, lakes
Shoshone Lake via Dogshead Trail	Moderate	10.8 mi rt	5-6 hr	scenery, lake
Heart Lake	Moderately strenuous	15 mi rt	7-8 hr	lake, scenery
Avalanche Peak	Strenuous	5 mi rt	4 hr	scenery

Canyon Village
★ MT. WASHBURN

Distance: 5.4-6.4 miles round-trip
Duration: 4 hours
Elevation change: 1,400-1,483 feet
Effort: easy grade, but strenuous by elevation
Trailheads: For the south trail: Dunraven Pass

Trailhead parking area on the east side of Grand Loop Road, 5.4 miles north of Canyon Junction. For the north trail: 10.3 miles north of Canyon Junction, drive 1.3 miles up Chittenden Road to reach the parking area.

At 10,243 feet, the Mt. Washburn Lookout yields a 360-degree panorama with big views. On a clear day, hikers can see the Grand

Canyon of the Yellowstone, Yellowstone Lake, and even the Tetons. The Chittenden Trail is steeper and has a bit more elevation gain than the Dunraven Pass Trail, but both high elevation trails climb up switchbacks in a steady plod on former roads.

The **Dunraven Pass Trail** (6.4 miles, hikers only) traverses across a southern slope before swinging north at 9,100 feet. It then makes four switchbacks up a west slope to crest a long ridge for a scenic walk that finishes with a 360-degree circle to Mt. Washburn Lookout. In upper elevation cliffs and meadows, look for bighorn sheep.

The steeper **Chittenden Trail** (5.4 miles, bicycles allowed) ascends just below a ridge with a few switchbacks thrown in to work up the slope. On the final ridge, the trail swings east and then switchbacks west for the last steps to the summit of Mt. Washburn.

At the summit, **Mt. Washburn Lookout**

summit thrill on top of Yellowstone's highest peak

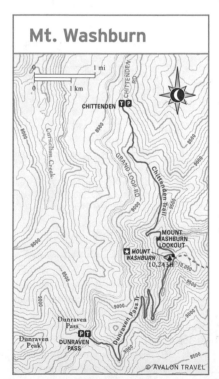

is an ugly three-story cement block covered in radio equipment. Visitors can access only two levels: an observation room with windows on three sides, interpretive displays, and a viewing scope; and a deck above. Restrooms are available.

Slopes may be **snow-covered in June** but burst with alpine wildflowers by July. Due to afternoon thunderstorms, plan to **descend before early afternoon.** Even though the treeless trail looks hot, **bring warm clothing;** the alpine tundra summit is often windy and cold. Due to the trail's popularity, you'll have company at the lookout.

CASCADE LAKE AND OBSERVATION PEAK

Distance: 4.4-9.6 miles round-trip
Duration: 2.5-5 hours
Elevation change: 60-1,389 feet
Effort: easy to strenuous
Trailhead: Cascade Picnic Area on Grand Loop Road, 1.3 miles north of Canyon Junction

Spring snowmelt can make the lower

elevations of this trail muddy in marshy areas. June and July usually bring on bluebells, prairie smoke, and elephant's head lousewort in the meadows en route to **Cascade Lake** (4.4 miles). Pack bug juice through September for copious mosquitoes.

From the trailhead, a relatively flat route crosses through large meadows made marshy by myriad streams, especially near the lake. (Some streams have footbridges, while others don't.) At 1.3 miles, the trail reaches the junction at Cascade Lake, the easternmost lake in the Chain of Lakes. Cradled in a basin surrounded by meadows, the lake is covered by lily pads on its southwest end. Look for trumpeter swans.

Since snow can still cover **Observation Peak** (9.6 miles) in June, many hikers wait until July to hike this trail. To reach the rocky 9,415-foot summit, turn north at the signed junction before Cascade Lake. Climbing 2.6 miles at a steady clip, the trail crosses a broad ridge for a long ascent through the 1988 burn area. Views stretch out for miles. From the summit, you can see Grebe Lake below and Hayden Valley stretching to the south. An old wood and stone fire **lookout** perches at the summit.

GREBE LAKE

Distance: 6.6 miles round-trip
Duration: 3-4 hours
Elevation change: 350 feet
Effort: easy
Trailhead: Grebe Lake Trailhead on Grand Loop Road, 3.8 miles west of Canyon Junction

The 156-acre Grebe Lake, the largest of the Chain of Lakes, holds rainbow trout and arctic grayling that lure anglers. Prepare for swarms of mosquitoes throughout summer.

From the trailhead, hike northward through a lodgepole forest that is fast regrowing from the 1988 fires. Portions of the trail are dusty, hot, and open, with downed timber. After arcing over a gentle hump, the trail reaches the southeast corner of **Grebe Lake** in 3.3 miles, then circles north around the lake. Meadows and marshes surround the scenic lake. When high water abates after June, beaches appear on the north shore.

An alternate route to Grebe Lake comes from **Cascade Lake**, two miles east and 100 feet lower in elevation. From Cascade Picnic Area, round-trip distance via Cascade Lake to Grebe Lake is eight miles.

CANYON AND LAKE COUNTRY
RECREATION

hiking to Grebe Lake

CHAIN OF LAKES

Distance: 10.7 miles one-way
Duration: 5-6 hours
Elevation change: 950 feet
Effort: moderate
Trailhead: Cascade Picnic Area on Grand Loop Road, 1.3 miles north of Canyon Junction

The upper Solfatara Plateau holds the Chain of Lakes, a string of four lakes: Cascade, Grebe, Wolf, and Ice. While hikers can reach each lake individually from separate trailheads, this trail connects all the lakes. It's a mosquito-infested walk most of the summer due to scads of potholes, streams, and marshes. If you're an angler, bring a rod for fishing. Hiking this trail one-way requires setting up a car shuttle at Ice Lake Trailhead.

From the Cascade Picnic Area, hike two miles west to **Cascade Lake,** then continue two more miles west to **Grebe Lake,** following signed trail junctions. From the north shore of Grebe Lake, continue 1.4 miles west to **Wolf Lake.** West of Wolf Lake, ford the Gibbon River and continue over rolling lodgepole hills for two miles to a junction. Go west at this junction toward **Ice Lake,** reaching it in another mile. After passing Ice Lake on the north side, turn left at the next junction and continue 0.5 mile west to reach the **Ice Lake Trailhead.** (You can also hike the trail in reverse.)

For those who just want to hike point-to-point to Cascade and Grebe Lake (7.5 miles), the route starts at the **Cascade Picnic Area** north of Canyon Junction and exits at the **Grebe Lake Trailhead.**

SILVER CORD CASCADE

Distance: 2 miles round trip
Duration: 1 hour
Elevation change: 150 feet
Effort: easy
Trailhead: Glacial Boulder Trailhead on the north side of the road to Inspiration Point east of Canyon Village. To reach the parking lot, loop through Inspiration Point Parking Lot to enter on the return.

For waterfall fans, this short trek on the Seven Mile Hole Trail (also called Cascade Overlook Trail) goes to viewpoints of the Grand Canyon of the Yellowstone. En route, you'll peer down into the immense canyon, but be cautious along the guardrail-less lip that has loose rock. Look to the opposite side of the canyon to find Silver Cord Cascade. The sheer rock cliffs reveal a 1,200-foot-tall slot that contains a thin ribbon waterfall.

NORTH RIM OF GRAND CANYON OF THE YELLOWSTONE

Distance: 3.8-6.6 miles one-way
Duration: 3-4 hours
Elevation change: 250-1,500 feet
Effort: easy to strenuous
Trailheads: Wapiti Lake Trailhead on South Rim Drive, on the west side of the bridge over the Yellowstone River
Directions: Park at Wapiti Picnic Area on the east side of South Rim Drive. Walk back across the Chittenden Bridge over the Yellowstone River to find the trailhead heading north.

This trail is not about backcountry solitude, but rather tremendous views of the Grand Canyon of the Yellowstone. A combination of paved and dirt trails link together multiple overlooks; some include steel stairways and boardwalks down to overlook platforms. You can start at either the north or south end to hike the entire trail, or shorten the distance by driving some segments. (In several places, the trail pops out to cross parking lots on North Rim Drive.) At several overlooks, spur trails drop down switchbacks and steep stairways to viewing platforms; all require climbing back up. Completing all the spurs adds a climb of nearly 1,500 feet in elevation and two more miles.

To start at the **south end** of the North Rim Trail, cross Chittenden Bridge to follow the Yellowstone River downstream (heading north). In 0.4 mile, the trail reaches the first viewpoint at **Brink of the Upper Falls.** A spur trail drops 42 feet to an overlook of the 109-foot falls. Continue north, passing the parking lot for Brink of the Upper Falls, to

Chain of Lakes

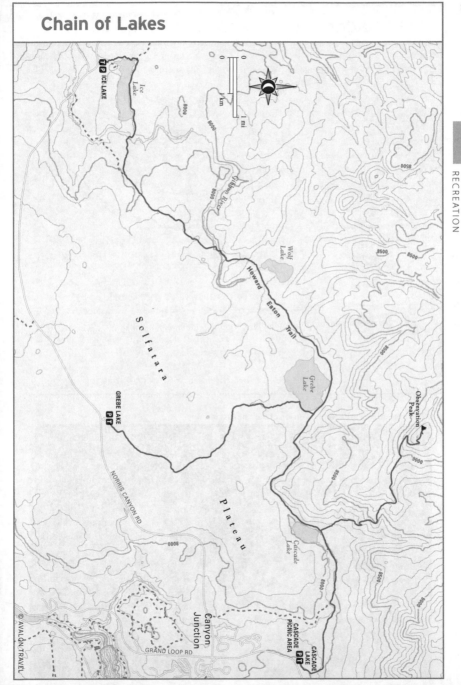

Grand Canyon of the Yellowstone Trails

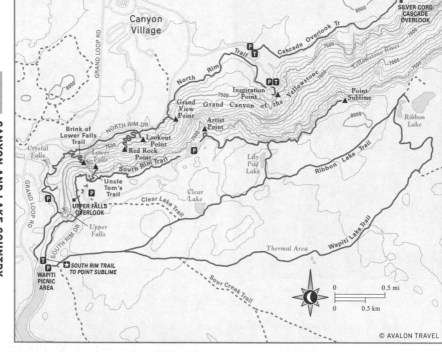

the North Rim Trail to the Grand Canyon of the Yellowstone

Point Sublime yields plummeting views of the Grand Canyon of the Yellowstone.

the 130-foot **Crystal Falls** as it spews from a slot in the North Rim cliffs. Heading northeast now, the 308-foot **Lower Falls** comes into view; follow the trail to a junction where a spur plummets 600 feet down switchbacks and stairs to the **Brink of the Lower Falls.** Climb back up the spur and continue east to the **Lookout Point Trailhead,** where a short trail climbs up 25 feet to **Lookout Point.** Just west, a longer trail plunges 500 feet in 0.4 mile down switchbacks and steep stairs to **Red Rock Point.** Returning to the North Rim Trail, continue north to **Grand View Point,** where a short paved trail drops about 150 feet to the viewpoint. Past Grand View Point, the trail curls northeast about 1.3 miles to the **Inspiration Point** parking lot. Walk through the parking lot and descend 50 feet in elevation in 0.1 mile to the classic viewpoint.

To hike the trail in reverse, start at the

north end by parking at Inspiration Point parking lot. For the 3.8-mile one-way hike, leave a car shuttle at either the Inspiration Point or Wapiti Picnic Area parking lots. Or return the way you came for a 7.6-mile out-and-back hike.

★ SOUTH RIM TRAIL
   TO POINT SUBLIME

Distance: 5.1 miles round-trip
Duration: 3 hours
Elevation change: 250-750 feet
Effort: easy to strenuous
Trailheads: South trailhead: Wapiti Picnic Area on South Rim Drive, on the east side of the bridge over the Yellowstone River. North Trailhead: Artist Point parking lot at terminus of South Rim Drive

The South Rim Trail has multiple overlooks of the Grand Canyon of the Yellowstone. From the Wapiti Picnic Area, a 0.4-mile forested walk heads north following the Yellowstone River to the first viewpoint at the **Upper Falls.** A spur trail drops 15 feet to the viewpoint. After circling north on the bluff for snippets of views, the strenuous **Uncle Tom's Trail** plunges 500 feet down paved switchbacks and 328 metal stair steps (that you have to climb back up) to an overlook. Skip this if you want the easy walk.

Past Uncle Tom's Trail, the route continues east through the forest with several viewpoints along the canyon rim until reaching the Artist Point parking lot. Walk northeast through the parking lot to reach the **Artist Point Trailhead** and continue 0.1 mile to the scenic point. From Artist Point, the dirt trail continues east 0.75 mile to **Point Sublime.** On this section, exposed overlooks (no railings) require caution as you take in the depth of the canyon. The Lower Falls drops out of view, but the canyon walls and hoodoos become far more colorful with smears of reds and pinks above the frothy blue water. The trail dead-ends at Point Sublime at a log railing where the forest claims the canyon.

CLEAR LAKE AND RIBBON LAKE

Distance: 2.2-7.3 miles round-trip
Duration: 1.5-4 hours
Elevation change: 950 feet
Effort: easy
Trailhead: Wapiti Picnic Area on South Rim Drive

This trail climbs gently to tour three small lakes, each one strikingly different. From the south end of the Wapiti Picnic Area parking lot, head east to ascend the hillside trail. The open meadows afford expansive views of Mt. Washburn and Hayden Valley. In 0.5 mile, turn left at the fork.

The **Ribbon Lake Trail** ascends a little over one mile east through the forest to **Clear Lake,** a shallow lake fed by runoff from Forest Hot Springs (hikers can turn around here for a 2.2-mile round-trip hike). After passing through the thermal zone, the trail reaches a junction. Turn north for the short jaunt to narrow **Lily Pad Lake** (3.6 miles round-trip), where lily pads can grow so thick the water is barely visible. Return to the main trail and continue east for 1.2 miles to **Ribbon Lake.** This third lake sits amid scenic meadows and forest. Follow the trail farther north to see the lake, then backtrack to the trail junction. To complete the loop, follow the trail south from Ribbon Lake to the junction with the **Wapiti Lake Trail** and turn right. This trail wanders through thermal areas, so stay on the path for safety. At 6.3 miles, the trail breaks out of the forest onto the hillside to descend to the original fork and return to the parking lot in 0.5 mile.

Other trailheads on South Rim Drive offer alternative routes to these lakes. Across the road from the parking lot at Uncle Tom's Point, the **Clear Lake Trail** climbs 0.7 mile to meet the Clear Lake-Ribbon Lake Trail. On the trail from Artist Point to Point Sublime, a trail junction leads 0.25 mile southeast past Lily Pad Lake. From that junction, it is 0.7 mile southwest to Clear Lake.

Storm Point on Yellowstone Lake

Fishing Bridge and Lake Village

PELICAN CREEK NATURE TRAIL

Distance: 1.3 miles round-trip
Duration: 1 hour
Elevation change: negligible
Effort: easy
Trailhead: The west end of Pelican Creek Bridge on the East Entrance Road, 0.9 mile east of Fishing Bridge

Starting at **Pelican Creek Bridge,** the trail cuts through the old-growth forest to the north shore of **Yellowstone Lake.** The trail then follows **Pelican Creek,** crossing to a marshy island on a boardwalk, and emerges from the forest onto a sandy obsidian beach. In early summer, the boardwalk and marsh traverse may be too wet, so stick to the forest trail. Watch for wildlife: otters, birds, ducks, pelicans, and bison. In spring, grizzly bears feed in the area.

STORM POINT

Distance: 2.3 miles round-trip
Duration: 1.5 hours
Elevation change: 40 feet
Effort: easy
Trailhead: Indian Pond pullout on the East Entrance Road, 3 miles east of Fishing Bridge

This loop hike offers wildlife-watching from an impressive point on the north shore of Yellowstone Lake. Grizzlies frequent the area, which can sometimes close the trail (check trail status at Fishing Bridge Ranger Station). Look for waterfowl at Indian Pond, marmots at Storm Point, and bison in the meadows. Winds can rage across the point, so bring an extra layer.

From the pullout at **Indian Pond,** the trail cuts across a sagebrush meadow for 0.2 mile to a fork. The left fork heads straight toward **Mary Bay,** an ancient caldera on Yellowstone Lake, before swinging into the forest to reach the rocky **Storm Point** that juts out into the lake (and takes the brunt of winds from the south). From Storm Point, you can see Stevenson Island and Mt. Sheridan in the distance. The trail continues west along broken rock and sandy bluffs reminiscent of an ocean coast with sandy beaches and driftwood. Clusters of yellow arrowleaf balsamroot flank the trail as it cuts back into the woods, where winds make the conifers clatter and creak. The trail returns to the fork in the meadow and the pullout.

ELEPHANT BACK MOUNTAIN

Distance: 3.6 miles round-trip
Duration: 2.5 hours
Elevation change: 710 feet
Effort: moderate
Trailhead: Elephant Back Trailhead on the west side of Grand Loop Road, 1 mile south of the Fishing Bridge junction

From the Grand Loop Road, this trail climbs up through a sparse lodgepole forest for 0.8 mile to a **junction.** Take the left fork to steadily ascend to the summit in a more direct line. At the 8,618-foot **summit overlook,** a small clearing in the trees has wooden benches to rest and absorb the scenery from Yellowstone Lake to the Absaroka Mountains. In the foreground are Lake Village and Lake Yellowstone Hotel; off-shore is Stevenson Island. The summit loop returns to the trail junction in 1.9 miles before returning to the trailhead.

AVALANCHE PEAK

Distance: 5 miles round-trip
Duration: 4 hours
Elevation change: 2,094 feet
Effort: strenuous
Trailhead: On the East Entrance Road, 17 miles east of the Fishing Bridge Junction. Park on the south side of the road at the west end of Eleanor Lake and find the trailhead across the road

Get an early start on this trail in order to avoid regular afternoon lightning and rain squalls, and prepare for strong winds at the summit by packing warm layers. This trail often remains covered in snow until **July;** avoid hiking in September and October due to bear activity.

Cross the East Entrance Road to find the trail catapulting straight up the mountain with minimal switchbacks. Launching in thick forest, the path climbs 2,000 feet in about one mile until breaking out of the trees across a scree slope to a **false summit.** Trails diverge around the false summit, created by hikers trying to shortcut or walk around snowfields.

The route crawls left onto an open, narrow ridge where the in-your-face views of the surrounding Absaroka peaks are the lure to continue onward. The **0.4-mile ridge** traverse leads to a stunning conclusion at the 10,566-foot summit of **Avalanche Peak.** From the summit, you'll have an impressive panorama to soak up, from the foreground Yellowstone Lake to the backbone of the Absaroka-Beartooth Wilderness and distant Tetons. On the descent, be cautious on scree; the small rocks feel like walking on marbles.

Bridge Bay
★ **NATURAL BRIDGE**

Distance: 2.6 miles round-trip
Duration: 2 hours
Elevation change: 181 feet
Effort: easy
Trailhead: Bridge Bay Marina parking lot near the entrance to the campground

This scenic loop tours Natural Bridge, a 51-foot-high sculpture of rhyolite rock that has been eroded through by Bridge Creek. The bridge is impressive, although much smaller than Utah's famed arches. Note that this trail is **closed late spring-early summer** due to grizzlies feeding on spawning trout in Bridge Creek. A bicycle route also begins south of the bridge from a separate trailhead.

From the parking lot, the trail cuts west through the forest for 0.7 mile before joining an old **paved road.** The route continues working westward for 0.4 mile, turning right at all junctions to reach an **interpretive exhibit** at the base of the loop trail. From the exhibit, a short, steep path switchbacks 0.2 mile up to the top of **Natural Bridge;** cross the creek behind the bridge to loop back down the other side. (The top of the bridge is closed in order to protect the fragile rock, but you'll see marmots run across it.)

West Thumb
DUCK LAKE

Distance: 1 mile round-trip
Duration: 30 minutes
Elevation change: 200 feet
Effort: easy
Trailhead: Duck Lake Trailhead at the north end of the West Thumb Geyser Basin parking lot

A short hike through a loose forest leads to 0.3-mile-long **Duck Lake,** a good destination for families with young kids. From the trailhead, the path crosses the road and climbs uphill. At the top of the hill, the trail crosses a power line before dropping down to the lake. The eastern lakeshore has a long **beach** with room to spread out. Wind-protected Duck Lake waters are often warmer for **swimming** than Yellowstone Lake.

YELLOWSTONE LAKE OVERLOOK

Distance: 2 miles round-trip
Duration: 1.5 hours
Elevation change: 194 feet
Effort: moderate
Trailhead: west side of the West Thumb Geyser Basin parking lot

The Lake Overlook Trail climbs from the start, beginning in a meadow and entering a forest. In 0.3 mile, the trail crosses the

Natural Bridge is a 51-foot-high rhyolite arch.

West Thumb and Grant Village

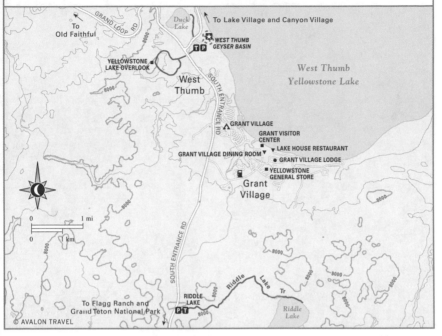

hiking Yellowstone Lake Overlook

South Entrance Road and reaches a **fork.** Turn left and continue hiking south up to a meadow with red paintbrush and yellow buckwheat in early summer; the panoramic views of the Yellowstone Lake and the Absaroka Mountains unfold. There is a **bench** to enjoy the view; a **short spur** behind the bench climbs up about 30 feet for a peekaboo view of the Tetons. Complete the loop to return to the parking lot.

Craig Pass
SHOSHONE LAKE VIA DELACY CREEK

Distance: 5.8 miles round-trip
Duration: 3-4 hours
Elevation change: 280 feet
Effort: easy
Trailhead: DeLacy Creek Trailhead on Grand Loop Road, 8.8 miles west of the West Thumb junction

Shoshone Lake is the largest backcountry lake

Shoshone Lake

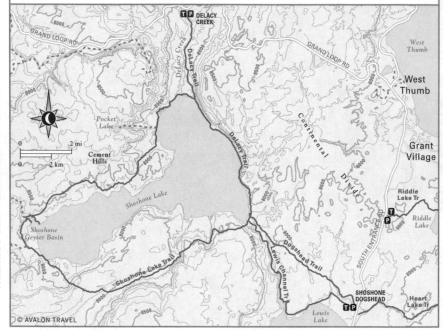

in Yellowstone. Trails reach the lake from several directions, but the **DeLacy Trail** is the shortest and easiest with a gentle uphill return. From the trailhead, the route heads 2.9 miles south to follow **DeLacy Creek,** a stream that twists through a giant meadow where anglers can find good fly-fishing for brook trout and where moose feed on willows. At **Shoshone Lake,** enjoy a pebble beach of volcanic rock. It's a scenic picnic location and a good place to wade or swim in the lake.

South Entrance
RIDDLE LAKE

Distance: 4.8 miles round-trip
Duration: 3 hours
Elevation change: 100 feet
Effort: easy
Trailhead: Riddle Lake Trailhead on the east side of the South Entrance Road, 2.3 miles south of Grant Village

The 275-acre Riddle Lake gets its name from the mystery of whether it fed two oceans due to its placement on the Continental Divide. The mystery was solved when more accurate mapping placed the lake and its outlet on the east side of the divide.

From the trailhead, the **Riddle Lake Trail** heads east. Even though this trail is fairly level, it crosses the **Continental Divide.** The route swaps between forest and marshy meadows to reach the lake's north shore. There is a sandy beach at the northeast corner of the lake to sit and enjoy the view of Mt. Sheridan and the Red Mountains. Anglers fish the lake for cutthroat trout, but much of the shoreline has marsh and lily pads.

Due to bear management, the trail is **closed in spring** (Apr. 30-July 15). Tree trunks on the trail sport claw scratches, a testament to the population of bears that inhabit the area. Closures can extend later into July

Heart Lake

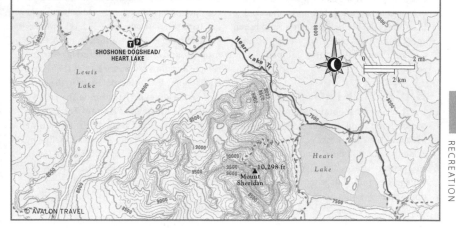

© AVALON TRAVEL

if trumpeter swans are nesting; check with a ranger station or visitors center for trail status.

SHOSHONE LAKE VIA DOGSHEAD TRAIL

Distance: 10.8 miles round-trip
Duration: 5-6 hours
Elevation change: negligible
Effort: moderate
Trailhead: Shoshone Dogshead Trailhead on the west side of the South Entrance Road, 5.3 miles south of Grant Village

When combined with the Lewis Channel Trail, the Dogshead Trail offers a loop hike to Shoshone Lake. The 4.6-mile Dogshead Trail takes a direct, hence shorter, route to the lake. The more scenic, 6.2-mile Lewis Channel follows the convolutions of the north shore of the Lewis River. Anglers head to the channel to fish for brown trout. A portion of the trail goes through burned areas from the 1988 fires. Summer brings mosquitoes.

From the **Dogshead Trail,** the route cuts 4.6 miles north through marshy zones and lodgepole forest in a fairly straight route to **Shoshone Lake.** Just before reaching the lake, the trail connects with the **Lewis Channel Trail** and the **DeLacy Creek Trail**

along the east shore. Follow the trail southward toward the lake and look for a lunch spot on the pebble beach. Return south on the **Lewis Channel Trail** for 6.2 miles; the trail requires fording one creek.

HEART LAKE

Distance: 15 miles round-trip
Duration: 7-8 hours
Elevation change: 869 feet
Effort: moderately strenuous
Trailhead: Heart Lake Trailhead on the east side of the South Entrance Road, 5.4 miles south of Grant Village

Heart Lake is the fourth-largest lake in the park, a place where anglers go after cutthroat trout. Bear management closes the Heart Lake Trail every spring until **July 1.**

Part of the 3,300-mile Continental Divide Trail, Heart Lake Trail passes through thick stands of lodgepoles and small wetland meadows to cross the Continental Divide at 8,154 feet. Climb 187 feet in elevation and descend 682 feet to the lake on the way in, then climb 682 feet on the return trip. From the trailhead, hike southeast where the landscape opens up with views, thermal areas with hot springs along **Witch Creek,** and the 10,305-foot **Mt. Sheridan** rising from the west shore of the lake. At the lake, a seasonal **backcountry ranger station** sits 250 feet from the shore, but may not be staffed. The north shore of the lake offers pebbly beaches for scenic lunch spots, lake enjoyment, and seeing **Rustic Geyser.** Ten backcountry campsites surround the lake.

BACKPACKING

Backpackers must obtain **permits** ($3/person, children 8 and younger free) for assigned backcountry campsites. Permits are available in person 48 hours in advance from the backcountry offices at Canyon Village, Lake Village, or Grant Village. For more information, see the *Essentials* chapter.

Chain of Lakes
10.7 MILES

Anglers should spend 2-3 days on the 10.7-mile **Chain of Lakes Trail**. Families with young kids and beginning backpackers also find appeal in the five campsites within two miles of the trailhead. With multiple starting, ending, and point-to-point options, trips can have short mileages. Trails connect the four lakes on the Solfatara Plateau: Cascade, Grebe, Wolf, and Ice. Camp at 4E2 on **Cascade Lake** to take a side trip up Observation Peak. **Grebe Lake** spreads four campsites (4G2, 4G3, 4G4, 4G5) around its shore. At **Wolf Lake,** campsites 4G6 and 4G7 offer more solitude than the other popular day-hike lakes. Campsite 4D3 at **Ice Lake** is reserved for campers in wheelchairs and with special needs.

Heart Lake
21 MILES

Competition for permits is keen for Heart Lake, which is closed until July 1 due to its prime grizzly habitat. For a 21-mile round-trip trek, spend two nights at **Heart Lake** and climb the steep 2,700-foot vertical trail up **Mt. Sheridan** on the middle day. Campsite 8H1 is the most secluded; campsites 8H5 and 8H6 are closest to the Mt. Sheridan Trail.

Shoshone Lake
21.4 MILES

Competition is high for multiday backpacking trips to Shoshone Lake. A level trail, accessible from several trailheads, circles 21.4 miles around Shoshone Lake and takes in the remote **Shoshone Geyser Basin,** the biggest backcountry hydrothermal basin in the park. Access the loop via the 4.6-mile **Dogshead Trail,** 6.2-mile **Lewis Channel Trail,** or the 2.9-mile **DeLacy Creek Trail.** Only nine campsites rim the lake; all are accessible by trail, including Bluff Top (8R2), Cove (8R3), and Basin Bay Point (8R5); the latter is the closest to the geyser basin.

BIKING

During spring (late Mar.-early Apr.), after roads are plowed, the **South Entrance Road to West Thumb** (22 miles) and the **East Entrance Road to Sylvan Pass** (6 miles) are open to bicycles, but remain closed to vehicles until May. In November, the roads once again close to vehicles, but remain open for bicycling. Cyclists can ride until snow covers the road.

Mountain bikes are only permitted in a few locations, mostly on old roadbeds; they are not allowed on trails. The most challenging mountain bike ride goes to **Mt. Washburn Lookout.** From the Chittenden Road parking lot, bikers grunt 2.7 miles up to the lookout. The difficulty level is compounded by the 10,243-foot summit elevation, but the return trip sails downhill. (The Dunraven Pass route is not open to bikers.)

Mountain bikers can explore shorter routes that are especially good for kids. At **Lake Village,** a one-mile slice of road runs from Lake Hotel to Grand Loop Road south of Lake Junction. Although short, the level ride is scenic along the waterfront of Yellowstone Lake. At Bridge Bay, mountain bikers can ride an old one-mile road to **Natural Bridge**. (Bikes are not allowed on the hiking trail at the site.)

HORSEBACK RIDING

Riding horses harkens back to the early days in Yellowstone. From the **Canyon Corrals** (Xanterra, 307/344-7311 or 866/439-7375, www.yellowstonenationalparklodges.com, daily late June-early Sept., $49-75), wranglers lead one-hour rides 8-9 times daily through meadows and pine forests along Cascade Creek. Two-hour rides, departing at 8:45am, go to the rim of Cascade Canyon. Find the corral one mile south of Canyon Junction.

Yellowstone Wilderness Outfitters (406/223-3300, www.yellowstone.ws, June-Sept., $1,800-2,800) guides overnight pack trips on horses. Their four-day trip goes to Heart Lake, and their 81-mile, six-day trip rides the Thorofare Trail to the Yellowstone River headwaters. Guides with degrees in wildlife biology can expand your understanding of fishing, photography, wildlife-watching, and bear safety. Rates include the horses and saddles, guides, meals, tents, and pack mules.

Wear long pants and sturdy shoes (no sandals) for riding, and make advance reservations. For short rides, tip 10-15 percent; for overnights, go to 20 percent.

WATER SPORTS
Boating

Huge Yellowstone Lake attracts boaters for sightseeing, cruising, angling, sailing, and paddling. Motorized boats are only allowed on Yellowstone Lake and Lewis Lake. Jet Skiing, parasailing, wakeboarding, waterskiing, and boats longer than 40 feet are banned. Complete boating regulations, along with permit requirements, licenses, and hazard maps are available online (www.nps.gov/yell). **Permits** are required for all boats, fishing, and backcountry boat camping.

YELLOWSTONE LAKE

With 141 miles of shoreline and six islands, Yellowstone Lake offers expansive water for boating, angling, island touring, and overnighting. Touring the east shore of the lake is best in the morning, as afternoon winds can push heavy onto the shore. In the South and Southeast Arms, no-wake zones marked by buoys reduce travel speeds.

Two marinas tuck into sheltered bays. **Bridge Bay Marina** (Xanterra, 307/344-7311 or 866/439-7375, www.yellowstonenationalparklodges.com, late May-Oct. for boat launch, daily mid-June-early Sept. for rentals and charters) has a boat launch with cement ramp, docks, moorage, rentals, store, and boat gas. The marina rents 16-foot rowboats ($10/hr.) and 18-foot boats with 40-horsepower outboard motors ($52/hr.); rentals are first-come, first-served. They also run a reservation charter service ($94/hour) for guided fishing or sightseeing. The marina has separate parking zones designated for day-use and overnighters. Located on the West Thumb, **Grant Village Marina** (mid-June-Oct.) has a boat launch with a cement ramp, docks, and boat slips, but no services.

Four docks allow places to tie up for land explorations: at the south end of Frank Island, Wolf Point, Eagle Bay, and Plover Point. Priority for tying up is for overnighters with permits; day-use boaters must be accommodating. Motorized boats can overnight at 32 primitive **campsites**; some are anchoring sites for sleeping aboard.

Be aware of **boating closures.** Thermal areas, hotel beaches, and Yellowstone Lake's outlet are closed. **Stevenson** and **Frank Islands** are closed mid-May-mid-August to protect nesting birds, although you can still tour the waters around the islands.

Those with **sailboats** should check into launch sites for keel and mast requirements. At Bridge Bay, you may need to lower the mast in order to go under a bridge to reach the lake. At Grant Village, lake levels in late summer may not be deep enough for keels.

LEWIS LAKE

Lewis Lake is prized for its beauty, quiet ambience, and fishing for brown trout. Though it is smaller than Yellowstone Lake, afternoon

Boating Permits and Safety

In Yellowstone, boating requires **permits** (Backcountry Office, 307/344-2160, www.nps.gov/yell). All boats need a permit, while some boaters will also need fishing or overnighting permits.

Boat Permit

All boats must pass an Aquatic Invasive Species (AIS) inspection before a permit can be issued. Decontaminate your boat before bringing it to Yellowstone. Fees for boat permits are based on propulsion:

- **Motorized:** $10 for 7 days, $20 for season. Jet Skiing, parasailing, wakeboarding, waterskiing, and boats longer than 40 feet are banned.

- **Nonmotorized:** $5 for 7 days, $10 for season. This includes kayaks, canoes, paddleboards, windsurfers, and float-tubes.

Fishing Permit

Permits are required for all anglers in boats.

- **Anglers ages 16 years and older:** $18 for 3 days, $25 for 7 days, $40 for season

- **Kids under age 16:** free

Overnight Permit

Permits are first-come, first-served 48 hours before departure for specific anchoring locations or shoreline campsites on Yellowstone Lake (all boats) and Shoshone Lake (nonmotorized only). Each campsite (and therefore each permit) holds 6-12 people, depending on location. On-land campsites have pit toilets and bear boxes or food-hanging bars. Where fires are permitted, fire rings are available. Bring your own water or filter lake water.

- **Backcountry camping permit:** $3/person, children under 8 free, $15 maximum/night/party

- **Reservation requests:** $25/trip, applications can be submitted online (www.nps.gov/yell/planyourvisit) starting January 1

Where to Get Permits

- **South Entrance Station** (U.S. 89/191/287)

- **Grant Village Backcountry Office** (307/344-2609, June-Sept.)

- **Bridge Bay Ranger Station** (307/242-2413, mid-May-Sept.)

Boating Safety

Be prepared for boating by consulting weather predictions at marinas, visitors centers, or ranger stations before launching. Make intelligent choices to prevent capsizing.

- **Hypothermia:** Frigid waters can be mid-30 in June and upper 50s in August.

- **Winds:** Afternoons bring on heavy winds from the west or southwest. Some raise waves to 4-foot whitecaps. Morning and evening boating can bring calmer waters (but not always). When overnighting, completely beach boats.

- **Thunderstorms:** Winds often bring squalls, thunderstorms, and lightning, usually from the west or southwest. Avoid open-water crossings; instead, stay closer to shore.

Bridge Bay Marina has boat rentals.

quiet plop of the paddle into the water offers a chance to hear the cry of an eagle in the trees or the snap of twigs from a bear walking along shore.

The water is frigid—bring a paddling jacket and pants or wetsuit. Winds crop up huge and fast on whitecaps, so stick to shoreline paddles or wait until winds subside rather than crossing open water. Since onshore winds batter eastern shores, stick to western shorelines for more sheltered paddling.

Boating regulations are available online (www.nps.gov/yell), including required boat, fishing, and backcountry camping permits. No kayak, canoe, or paddleboard rentals are available inside Yellowstone National Park. Bring your own or rent one in Jackson Hole.

YELLOWSTONE LAKE

Paddlers can launch from multiple locations to tour the shoreline of Yellowstone Lake. To launch from developed boat ramps, go to Bridge Bay Marina or Grant Village Marina. You can carry your boat or paddleboard to launch from the north shore of Yellowstone Lake at Sedge Bay or any of the picnic areas or Gull Point Drive along the west shore between Lake Village and West Thumb.

Be aware that paddling around thermal areas, hotel beaches, and wildlife preserves is restricted. In the Southeast Arm nonmotorized zone, the Molly Islands are a bird sanctuary; beaching boats is prohibited. Travel at least a half-mile out to protect this wild zone.

For prized overnight paddle trips, **campsites** are strung around the lake, with 10 coveted sites in the quiet nonmotorized zones of South and Southeast Arms. These bays with paddler-accessible campsites have abundant wildlife and birds. You can also overnight in Flat Mountain Bay and the smaller Wolf and Eagle Bays, but you will share water with motorboaters. To avoid paddling the long distance across open water, make advance reservations for a shuttle from Bridge Bay Marina. **Shuttles** (Xanterra,

winds still churn up waves. Most winds come from the west or southwest, so you'll find more sheltered boating along the west shore.

The lake connects with the larger Shoshone Lake via the **Lewis Channel;** however, motorized boats are not permitted up the channel beyond the signed closure. If you have an outboard motor, you can detach the motor and chain it up with a lock onshore at the sign to row upstream.

A **boat launch** with a cement ramp and dock is located adjacent to the Lewis Lake Campground, accessed from a well-signed turnoff on the South Entrance Road. Parking areas are designated for day-use and overnight boaters.

Canoeing, Kayaking, and Paddleboarding

Paddlesports allow boaters to access some of the most scenic waterways in Yellowstone, particularly Shoshone Lake and the South and Southeast Arms of Yellowstone Lake. The

307/344-7311 or 866/439-7375, summer shuttle office 307/242-3893, www.yellowstonenationalparklodges.com, mid-June-mid-Sept., $200/2 hrs.) can take up to six people with gear and a few canoes or kayaks. The shuttle can also be arranged to pick you up at a predetermined day, time, and location. For overnight shuttles, rental rowboats and canoes ($50-56/day) are available.

LEWIS LAKE

Higher than Yellowstone Lake, the much smaller Lewis Lake sits at 7,830 feet. While it offers pleasant day paddling, most paddlers use it as a waterway to access the Lewis Channel and Shoshone Lake, both nonmotorized zones. Unless the lake is dead calm, take a shoreline route rather than crossing open water. On many days, winds start at 10am and the trees along the western shore provide a little shelter; the eastern shore takes the brunt of winds pushing on shore.

A **boat launch** with a cement ramp and dock is located at the south end of Lewis Lake, adjacent to the campground. Park in the appropriate zone for day-use or overnight parking. A second, but more difficult launch (due to onshore winds) is along the northeast shore of the lake. Look for a parking pullout about 1.6 miles north of the boat launch; it has a short pebble-beach access.

SHOSHONE LAKE

Shoshone Lake is on every serious paddler's bucket list: It has seclusion, wildlife, a geyser basin, an access via a river channel (after paddling across Lewis Lake), and no road or motorized boat access. Lewis Channel is about three miles long as the crow flies, but river convolutions make the route longer. Paddle up the slow-moving stream for the first two miles to encounter the challenge: wading the last mile due to the water moving too fast to paddle upstream or being too shallow.

Wading the upper portion of the **Lewis Channel** is easier if you bring a 15-foot rope

the Lewis Channel to Shoshone Lake

to pull your boat. Early summer paddlers (into early July) will need a wetsuit or drysuit to sustain the cold, deep runoff of the high water season. Places can be four feet deep. If that sounds too challenging, wait until August when the water warms slightly and lowers in depth. With a sturdy pair of water shoes to protect your feet on rocks, you can wade the last mile in calf-deep water.

Shoshone Lake is divided into two sections by **the Narrows,** a pinch in the shoreline squeezing the lake to a half-mile. The Narrows provides the best place to cross open water, if you must do so. Otherwise, the southeast shore is the safest travel route; winds hammer the east shore with waves up to three feet. To visit **Shoshone Geyser Basin,** with 80 active geysers, beach boats at the landing area denoted with an orange marker. Find the area in a small bay in the northwest corner of the lake where a trail connects to the geyser basin. You can overnight at one of 16 boating **campsites** on the north or south shore.

GUIDES

Based out of Jackson, **Geyser Kayak** (307/413-6177, www.geyserkayak.com) leads day or overnight paddle trips in sea kayaks. On Yellowstone Lake, the day trips and a shorter sunset tour paddle West Thumb, including thermal features (daily mid-May-Oct., $125-175 adults, $75-125 kids under 12). Multiday trips go out July-September. Four- or six-day trips go into the Southeast Arm of Yellowstone Lake ($1,400-1,900). Three- or four-day trips paddle on Lewis and Shoshone Lakes ($1,100-1,400). Rates include kayaks, life jackets, meals, and guides. Plan to tip 15 percent for day trips and 20 percent for overnights.

Windsurfing

With strong afternoon winds, a few diehard windsurfers take to Yellowstone Lake, but most opt for warmer lakes elsewhere. Due to the cold and potential gale-force winds, the lake is not a place for beginners—only experts who have their own gear. Winds can go from zero to extreme in a few minutes, and the frigid water requires wearing a wetsuit or drysuit. Be prepared to self-rescue. Windsurfers need boating permits.

Fishing

Large lakes and blue-ribbon trout streams dominate the fishing scene. The attraction is the native Yellowstone cutthroat trout, recognized by its red slash. Unfortunately, fishing pressure and competition from lake trout have reduced the population of cutthroat to a point where its future is threatened. Catch-and-release fishing helps protect the species. Inside Yellowstone, a **fishing permit** is required for anglers 16 years and older ($18 for 3 days, $25 for 7 days, $40 season). For permit information and regulations, see the *Essentials* chapter.

LAKES

Yellowstone Lake and **Lewis Lake** work for shoreline fishing, float-tube fishing, spincasting, fly-fishing, and fishing from motorboats or rowboats. On Yellowstone Lake, the stretch of shoreline near **Gull Point** often sees a lineup of anglers, perhaps due to its ease of access and reputation for fishing, but other areas receive less fishing pressure. Take kids to protected places to drop a line: near the boat launch and campground on Lewis Lake and Gull Point Drive or Sand Point on Yellowstone Lake.

Yellowstone and Lewis Lakes have monster lake trout, which were discovered in the 1990s. Their growing population has caused a decline in native cutthroat trout due to predation and food source competition. The park service has embarked on a program to reduce lake trout numbers by having anglers kill all lake trout caught.

Lewis Lake holds prized brown trout, while Yellowstone Lake has native Yellowstone cutthroat trout along with redside shiners, longnose suckers, longnose dace, and lake chubs. Anglers can fish the lakes mid-June-early

shore angler at Yellowstone Lake

November, but should employ **catch-and-release for all cutthroat.**

On the East Entrance Road, **Sylvan Lake** is also worth fishing. From hiking destinations, anglers pull cutthroat trout from **Heart** and **Riddle Lakes.** Before hiking to an unknown lake or stream, check with rangers as some waterways are barren.

Several areas are permanently **closed to fishing.** On Yellowstone Lake, the shoreline from West Thumb Geyser Basin to Little Thumb Creek, and the marinas, harbors, and waterways from Bridge Bay and Grant Village are closed. The lower two miles of Pelican Creek are also closed.

RIVERS

While portions of the **Yellowstone River** are closed to fishing, the remainder is an outstanding trout fly-fishery with parts accessible from Grand Loop Road. Fishing season usually starts **mid-July.** Yellowstone River closures include the 1.9-mile Fishing Bridge zone, LeHardy's Rapids, and Hayden Valley including tributaries.

Along the South Entrance Road, the **Lewis River** has a reputation for 20-inch brown trout with easy access as it meanders through high meadows.

GUIDES

Bridge Bay Marina (Xanterra, 307/344-7311 or 866/439-7375, www.yellowstonenationalparklodges.com, daily mid-June-early Sept., $95/hour) runs a reservation-based fishing charter service on Yellowstone Lake. Boats can hold up to six people; only three can fish at a time. Rates include fishing rods and tackle, and a guide captain who can take you to where the fish are biting. Tip your guides 15 percent (20 percent if you catch lots of fish).

Swimming

You can swim in Yellowstone's lakes; however, it is illegal to swim near thermal features where the water is warmest. There are no designated swimming areas or lifeguards; swim at your own risk. In Yellowstone Lake, the water is a bone-chilling 35°F in June. In August, temperatures in some areas may reach the low 60s. If swimming with kids, watch for signs of hypothermia, off-shore winds, sudden whitecaps, and thunderstorms. About six miles north of West Thumb Junction, a sand bar cuts the waves and lets water get a few degrees warmer.

WINTER SPORTS
Cross-Country Skiing and Snowshoeing

At **Grand Canyon of the Yellowstone,** you can tour snowy canyon rim trails to enjoy the frozen splendor of the giant chasm; all snow-covered roads become winter ski and snowshoe routes in winter. Bring your own cross-country skis and snowshoes; rentals are only available at Old Faithful, Mammoth Hot Springs, West Yellowstone, and Jackson. Find winter trail maps online (www.nps.gov/yell) and at visitors centers. Snowcoaches are required to reach many trails, so most skiers and snowshoers tour with guides.

GUIDES

Cross-country ski and snowshoe tours of Grand Canyon of the Yellowstone depart from **Old Faithful Snow Lodge** (Xanterra, 307/344-7311 or 866/439-7375, www.yellowstonenationalparklodges.com, mid-Dec.-Feb., $276) several days weekly for a 10-hour adventure. A two-hour snowcoach ride gets you to the canyon, where a guide leads you along the canyon rim to see the Upper and Lower Falls. Ski tours go about six miles; snowshoe tours travel three miles. Advanced beginners can handle the easy routes. Lunch is included; reservations are required.

A bucket-list trip (especially for full moon), **Yellowstone Expeditions** (536 Firehole Ave., West Yellowstone, 406/646-9333 or 800/728-9333, http://yellowstoneexpeditions.com, late Dec.-early Mar., $1,100-1,900/

Yellowstone Expeditions yurt camp

person double occupancy) leads cross-country ski and snowshoe tours from their yurt camp. Located at 8,000 feet about a 0.5-mile from Grand Canyon of the Yellowstone, the camp is the only overnight winter facility on the park's east side. Two large yurts serve as the dining room and kitchen, which rolls out yummy meals. A sauna soothes muscles after skiing, and a heated restroom building has a hot shower and large pit toilet rooms. Sleeping is in two-person heated huts. Guides lead daily ski tours from camp or after a short shuttle. Packages (4, 5, or 8 days) include snowcoach transportation, lodging, sleeping bags with flannel sheets, meals, and guide service. Rental skis or snowshoes are available. January rates are lowest, when daylight hours are shortest. Plan a 20 percent gratuity for guides and camp staff.

Snowmobiling

The Yellowstone snowmobile season runs **mid-December-early March.** Several companies guide **snowmobile tours** (www.nps/gov/yell) to Grand Canyon of the Yellowstone, launching from West Yellowstone, Gardiner, Mammoth Hot Springs, and Flagg Ranch. You can go on your own with a **permit** (www.recreation. gov, early Sept.-early Oct.) from the annual lottery and an approved BAT (Best Available Technology) snowmobile. Snowmobiles rentals are only available in West Yellowstone, Gardiner, and Jackson.

Entertainment and Shopping

Summer naturalist programs (15-45 minutes daily, late May-early Sept., free) explore wildlife, geology, history, and ecology. Some programs focus on families with young kids. Programs take place at Canyon, Fishing Bridge, Lake Village, Grant Village, and West Thumb; meeting locations vary. **Fall** programs are offered daily in September. A complete list of programs is online (www.nps.gov/yell).

Evening outdoor programs (9pm or 9:30pm) are held at Canyon, Bridge Bay, Fishing Bridge, and Grant Village amphitheaters. Prepare for mosquitoes.

SHOPPING

Yellowstone General Stores (Delaware North Company, 406/586-7593, www.visityellowstonepark.com, 7:30am-9:30pm daily May-Sept.) are at Canyon Village, Fishing Bridge, Lake Village, Bridge Bay, and Grant Village. Two historic shops are worth seeing even if you don't like shopping: The **Fishing Bridge General Store** (1 East Entrance Rd.) is a relic from 1931, while the **Lake General Store** (1 Lake Loop Rd.) is a cedar octagon constructed in 1919. Most stores sell the same gifts and souvenirs, plus outdoor supplies, books, and limited groceries.

For specialty outdoor gear, **Yellowstone Adventures** (1 Canyon Village Loop Rd., mid-Apr.-early Nov.) sells hiking, camping, photography, and fishing supplies. **Bridge Bay Marina Store** (1 Bridge Bay Marina, late

the Yellowstone General Store in Lake Village

May-early Sept.) carries boating, angling, and camping supplies.

Canyon Lodge, Lake Yellowstone Hotel, Lake Lodge, and Grant Village Lodge have **gift shops** (Xanterra, 307/344-7311 or 866/439-7375, www.yellowstonenationalpark-lodges.com).

Food

INSIDE THE PARK

Dining is limited to restaurants and cafés operated by Xanterra and Delaware North Company; each concessionaire offers similar menus. In mid-June-early September, expect long waits (up to an hour or so) at some restaurants. Canyon Lodge M66 Grill, Lake Hotel Dining Room, and Grant Village Dining Room accept dinner **reservations.** In all park restaurants, dress is casual and kiddie menus are available. In spring and fall, hours may shorten.

Canyon Village

The huge Mission 66 dining facility at **Canyon Lodge** (Xanterra, 307/344-7311 or 866/439-7375, www.yellowstonenationalparklodges.com) flaunts its original 1960s color schemes and appearance. Menu items include dishes for light eaters, vegans, and vegetarians, with organic, sustainable, local, and gluten-free options. Hours and meal services lessen after mid-September.

Canyon Lodge M66 Bar and Grill (early June-late Sept.) offers table service and dining reservations. Breakfast (6:30am-10am daily, $5-12) items include egg dishes and griddle plates. The lunch (11:30am-2pm daily) menu lists burgers, sandwiches, salads, and soups. For dinner (4:30pm-10pm daily, $10-30), dine on grilled seasonal entrees of trout, bison burgers, wild game bratwurst, prime rib, or pasta. Wine, regional beers, and cocktails are served. Dinner reservations are required.

Ordering stations at **Canyon Lodge Eatery** (June-early Oct.) serve a continental breakfast (6:30am-10:30am daily, $2-6) as well as lunch and dinner (11:30am-9:30pm daily, $10-15). The wok station cooks chicken, salmon, steak, or tofu topped with veggies over greens, noodles, or rice with choices of sauces. The "Slow Food Fast" station serves stews, braises, and rotisserie chicken, plus veggies, greens, potatoes, or pasta.

Canyon Lodge Café (6am-10pm daily June-early Sept., $4-10) serves sandwiches, flatbreads, salads, snacks, beverages, beer, wine, espresso, and ice cream. It's a good place to get grab-and-go foods for breakfast, lunch, or the trail.

The ★ **Canyon General Store** (2 Canyon Village Loop Rd., 406/586-7593, www.yellowstonevacations.com, 7:30am-8:30pm daily mid-May-early Oct., $5-12) has a large soda fountain diner with red stools set around four huge peninsula counters. Music from the 1950s adds a retro feel. The diner serves breakfast until 10:30am, followed by lunch and dinner with burgers, sandwiches, fries, salads, soda fountain ice-cream treats made from Wilcoxson's from Montana, and a Junior Ranger meals for kids. An adjunct to the general store, **Yellowstone Adventures** (7:30am-9:30pm daily late Apr.-early Nov.) has a counter for frozen yogurt, hot dogs, soup, and chili.

Fishing Bridge and Lake Village

At Fishing Bridge, the circa 1931 **Fishing Bridge General Store** (1 East Entrance Rd., 406/586-7593, www.yellowstonevacations.com, 7:30am-8:30pm daily early May-mid-Oct., $5-12) has seated food service in a small diner area with breakfast until 10:30am followed by a lunch and dinner menu of sandwiches, burgers, and salads. Old-fashioned ice cream soda fountain treats headline the desserts, and kids can get Junior Ranger meals. A to-go counter serves noodles, sandwiches, ice cream, and espresso.

Dining at the lodges in **Lake Village** (Xanterra, 307/344-7311 or 866/439-7375, www.yellowstonenationalparklodges.com) ranges from light, quick meals to upscale fare. Menus include vegetarian, vegan, gluten-free, and organic options, with items for children. Surrounded on three sides by large windows with peekaboo views of the lake, the ★ **Lake Yellowstone Hotel Dining Room** (mid-May-early Oct.) clusters tables around white columns that echo the exterior architecture of the colonial building. Order **breakfast** (6:30am-10:30am daily, $5-16) off the menu; if you're in a hurry, go for the buffet. Specialties include eggs Benedict on crab cakes and a design-your-own omelet. **Lunch** (11:30am-2:30pm daily, $10-16) features burgers, wraps, sandwiches, entrée salads, a soup and salad bar, and plated entrées with sides. **Dinner** (5pm-10pm daily, $15-42) offers multiple courses with appetizers, soups, and salads followed by entrées of fresh fish, bison, steak, lamb, salads, or burgers. The wine list includes western and international vintages. Reservations are not accepted for breakfast or lunch; advance reservations *are* required for dinner and should be made when booking your lodging. (If you are not staying in Lake Yellowstone Hotel, make reservations 60 days in advance.)

The **Deli** (6:30am-9pm daily mid-May-early Oct., $4-11) serves breakfast, lunch, dinner, and desserts. Breakfast can be continental or entrées such as quiche or breakfast croissants. Lunch and dinner choices include soups, salads, sandwiches, and wraps. To-go items work for hiking lunches. Drinks include espresso, beer, and wine.

At Lake Lodge, the **Lake Lodge Cafeteria** (6:30am-9:30pm daily early June-late Sept., $6-18) has continental and à la carte breakfast items. Lunch and dinner include sandwiches, wraps, rice bowls, bison chili, pot roast, lasagna, and trout.

At **Lake General Store** (Delaware North Company, 1 Lake Loop Rd., 406/586-7593, www.yellowstonevacations.com, 7:30am-8:30pm daily mid-May-late Sept., $6-12), diners could take advantage of the million-dollar view if the restaurant had big windows—get your food to-go and take it outside to enjoy the lake. The menu features breakfast, hot sandwiches, bratwurst, chili, salads, and Junior Ranger meals for kids. The old-fashioned soda fountain serves ice cream, malts, milkshakes, and sundaes.

Grant Village

Yellowstone Lake provides a backdrop for two restaurants in **Grant Village** (Xanterra, 307/344-7311 or 866/439-7375, www.yellowstonenationalparklodges.com). Dinner reservations are accepted and required at the Lake House and should be made when booking your room in Grant Village Lodge (if staying elsewhere, make reservations 60 days in advance). Menus accommodate vegetarians, vegans, and children, with gluten-free options.

Tucked in the forest, the ★ **Grant Village Dining Room** (late May-Sept.) is a vaulted room with a wood ceiling and large-paned windows looking out on the lake. **Breakfast** (6:30am-10am daily, $5-14) can be ordered from the menu; for a quicker meal, choose the breakfast buffet. **Lunch** (11:30am-2:30pm daily, $10-15) includes salads, burgers, and sandwiches. **Dinner** (5pm-10pm daily, $16-27) starts with appetizers, salads, and soups before moving on to specialties of trout, prime rib, bison meatloaf, and eggplant. Beer, cocktails, and wine are available.

Sitting on the lake at the marina on West Thumb Bay, **Grant Village Lake House Restaurant** (late May-early Sept.) has prime window views for relishing sunrise or sunset colors glowing on the lake. Breakfast (7am-9am daily, $14) is a basic buffet, while dinner (5pm-9pm daily, $10-25) includes prime rib, wild-game meatloaf, pasta, chicken, and a few sandwiches. Local beers are on tap and wine is served. Order your food in line then wait for servers to deliver it to your table.

In the Grant General Store, the 80-seat **Grant Village Grill** (2 Grant Village Loop Rd., 406/586-7593, www.visityellowstonepark.com, 7:30am-8:30pm daily late May-mid-Sept., $5-12) serves a small menu of fast-food-style breakfast, burgers, fries, salads, and ice cream, milkshakes, and floats.

Groceries

Yellowstone General Stores (406/586-7593, www.visityellowstonepark.com) are more like large convenience marts with limited fresh produce, frozen and packaged foods, and wine and beer. They serve sundaes, root-beer floats, milkshakes, malts, and ice cream from old-style soda fountains. Stores are located at **Canyon Village, Fishing Bridge, Lake Village,** and **Grant Village** (general store and a mini-mart). For larger grocery needs, drive to Cody or Jackson for supermarkets.

Picnicking

Picnic tables are north of Canyon Village at **Dunraven Pass** or **Cascade,** the only one with fire rings. Along the Yellowstone River, picnic at **Chittenden Bridge/Wapiti Lake** or **Nez Perce Ford.**

Thirteen picnic areas rim Yellowstone Lake, offering places to enjoy the water, but hold onto the plates, as afternoons are frequently windy. All the picnic areas have tables; half have vault toilets. Picnic areas at **Grant Village** and **Bridge Bay** have fire rings. On the west shore, **Sand Point** and **Gull Point** each flank a long spit that creates a shallow pool with warmer, protected water for swimming. On the north shore, **Sedge Bay,** a blustery driftwood beach with waves crashing on shore, is best on calm days.

Accommodations

INSIDE THE PARK
Reservations

There are four in-park lodging options open in summer only. Lake Yellowstone Hotel is the most requested of the three for its location, architecture, and historical ambience. **Reservations** (Xanterra, 307/344-7311 or 866/439-7375, www.yellowstonenational-parklodges.com) are a must and should be **booked one year in advance.**

Park lodges and cabins do not have televisions, radios, or air-conditioning; a few have mini-fridges. Rooms have private bathrooms in two styles: a tub/shower combination or shower only. When booking, clarify your room needs and confirm whether there is an elevator; a few rooms and cabins meet ADA standards. Cell phone reception is usually available at the lodge or nearby. Internet access may be available for a fee ($5/hour, $12/day, $25 for 3 days). Standard rates are for two people; add 14 percent tax and $17-19 per each additional person.

Canyon Village

With more than 500 rooms in a huge complex, ★ **Canyon Lodge and Cabins** (late May-late Sept., $175-330 lodge rooms and cabins, suites $625) has hotel rooms in multistory lodges or motel rooms in cabins. It is the largest facility in the park and has the newest accommodations. Five three-story, stone-and-wood lodge buildings built in 2016 replaced the low-end cabins. These lodges have recycled glass bathroom counters, electric car charging stations, and keycard-accessed lights. Two other lodges, Cascade and Dunraven, were built in the 1990s. Rooms typically have 1-2 doubles or queens, and two-bedroom suites have a king room, queen room, and sofa-sleeper in a sitting room. Some rooms have refrigerators. All lodges, except Cascade, have elevators to access upper floors. Older cabins in four- or six-unit buildings have motel-style rooms with two queens. The complex includes several restaurants, gift shops, a visitors center, and wireless Internet in the lobby.

Lake Village

Built in 1891, ★ **Lake Yellowstone Hotel and Cabins** (mid-May-early Oct., $190-550 cabins and rooms, $740-890 suites) is a striking colonial building with tall Ionic columns, a bright yellow exterior, and an entrance facing the lake. The three-story hotel sports 15 fake balconies added in 1903 for looks rather than usability, and later additions of the portico, dining room, and sunroom gave the hotel more distinction. Named a National Historic Landmark in 2015, it is the oldest operating hotel in Yellowstone. The complex has **three types of accommodations**: hotel rooms and suites in the historic lodge, hotel rooms in an older lodge, and cabins. Historic hotel rooms include a king or 1-2 queen beds. Superior rooms face the lake, while standard rooms face the parking lot, kitchen, buildings, or trees. Two high-end suites have multiple rooms. Behind the hotel are economical options with no lake views. The two-story **Sandpiper Lodge** has hotel rooms with 1-2 double beds. The yellow 1920s duplex cabins have two double beds and small showers. Amenities include a dining room, bar, deli, a business center, and Internet in the hotel rooms.

Lake Yellowstone Hotel is a historical experience—not a luxury resort. With the history and delightful location come minimal amenities and little soundproofing between rooms. Make dinner reservations when you book, as the dining room packs out with waiting lines. The sunroom is the place to lounge with views of the lake. Nearby, a gated old roadway offers one mile of walking along the shore.

Set back from the shore of Yellowstone Lake, **Lake Lodge Cabins** (early June-late Sept., $95-235) is a complex of rustic buildings. The single-floor, log Lake Lodge has a large porch with old-style cane-and-wood rockers where you can look across a meadow to Yellowstone Lake. The classic log-raftered interior houses a lobby with two stonework fireplaces, cafeteria with wireless Internet, bar, and gift shop. Behind the lodge, 186 heated cabins accessed by paved roads come in three styles, all with private baths. Set in wild grasses and conifers on paved loops, the **Western Cabins** have 4-6 large, modern motel rooms with two queen beds. Built in the 1920s, the renovated small duplex **Frontier Cabins** and the tiny, basic **Pioneer Cabins** have 1-2 double beds. Their small baths have narrow shower stalls and no tubs, and sounds carry between rooms. Take a flashlight for walking after dark to and from the lodge.

Grant Village

Located at Grant Village at the southern end of West Thumb on Yellowstone Lake, **Grant Village Lodge** (late May-late Sept., $255) is a collection of six buildings with hotel rooms. Built in 1984, each two-story building contains 50 rooms that come in two styles with private baths and wireless Internet. Premium rooms have two double beds and a refrigerator; standard rooms have a queen bed or two doubles. Lodgepoles have grown up around the buildings, cutting off lake views. The complex includes two restaurants, a bar, and Yellowstone General Stores. A short walk drops to the beach and mostly empty marina, or to the restaurants, the visitors center, the lake, and the outdoor amphitheater (for evening ranger talks).

Camping

INSIDE THE PARK

Of the five campgrounds on the park's east side, four accept **reservations** (Xanterra, 307/344-7311 or 866/439-7375, www.yellowstonenationalparklodges.com). For summer, book reservations a year in advance at Canyon, Fishing Bridge, Bridge Bay, and Grant Village. Camping fees cover six people or one family; taxes and utility fees are added on. Call to pick up campsites from last minute cancellations.

Campgrounds have flush toilets, cold

running water, potable water, coin-op ice machines, and evening amphitheater programs. With the exception of Fishing Bridge, they also have picnic tables, fire rings, firewood for sale, dishwashing stations, bear boxes, tent pads, and shared campsites for hikers and bikers ($8/person). For RVs, only a few campsites fit rigs or combos of 40 feet or more. The only campground with full hookups for RVs is Fishing Bridge. When searching for a campsite, check daily fill times online (www. nps.gov/yell) for status updates.

Canyon Village

Canyon Campground (late May-late Sept., $30) is one of the most-requested campgrounds due to its central location. On a hillside forest of conifers, the 270 campsites squeeze into tight quarters in a dozen loops at 7,944 feet. Some of the sites are sloped. Campsites are designated for RVs, tents, or RV and tent combos. Some pull-through and back-in sites can fit RVs up to 40 feet. The campground check-in building has pay showers (two per night included), coin-op laundry, and an RV dump station, although when temperatures freeze, it shuts down. Within 0.25 mile are stores, restaurants, Grand Canyon Visitor Education Center, a post office, and a gas station with repair service; Grand Canyon of the Yellowstone is one mile away.

Fishing Bridge

On the north end of Yellowstone Lake, **Fishing Bridge RV Park** (East Entrance Rd., early May-late Sept., $48) is the closest campground to the East Entrance Station. At 7,751 feet, it is the only campground in the park with electrical, water, and sewer hookups for RVs. All of the 340 sites are double-wide backins. If you don't have huge slide-outs, you can fit a towed RV and a vehicle side by side. Hardsided units are required; tents and pop-up tent trailers are not allowed. Surrounded by a forest, the campground stacks RVs close together like a parking lot, with a few pine trees separating some of the sites. Amenities include pay showers (two per night included), coin-op laundry, store, and an RV dump station. Nearby are a gas station with vehicle repair service, a general store that carries camping supplies and groceries, and the Fishing Bridge Museum and Visitor Center.

Lake Village

At 7,784 feet, ★ **Bridge Bay Campground** (north of Bridge Bay Marina, mid-May-mid-Sept., $25) flanks a hillside across the road

Bridge Bay Campground

Where Can I Find . . .?

- **Banks and ATMS:** ATMs are in all park lodges and Yellowstone General Stores.

- **Cell Service:** Verizon service is available in Canyon Village. Verizon and AT&T service may be available around Yellowstone Lake.

- **Gas and Garage Services:** Gas stations (406/848-7548) are located at Canyon Village (early May-late Oct.), Fishing Bridge, and Grant Village (mid-May-late Sept.). You can pay at the pump 24 hours a day with a credit card.

- **Internet Service:** Wireless Internet is available at Canyon Lodge and Grant Village lodges (fee); wired service is in hotel rooms at Lake Yellowstone Hotel. Internet is not available at the visitors centers.

- **Laundry:** Coin-op laundries are located at Canyon Campground (late May-mid-Sept.), Grant Village Campground (late June-mid-Sept.), Lake Lodge (mid-June-late Sept.), and Fishing Bridge RV Park (late June-mid-Sept.).

- **Post Office:** Post offices are at Lake Village (mid-May-mid-Oct.), Grant Village (mid-May-mid-Sept.), and Canyon Village (late May-mid-Sept.).

- **Showers:** Pay showers are located at Canyon Campground (late May-mid-Sept.), Grant Village Campground (late June-mid-Sept.), and Fishing Bridge RV Park (late June-mid-Sept.).

from Yellowstone Lake. With 432 campsites in 12 loops swooping through meadows and forests, the campground is the largest in the park. The five huge front loops sit on a large, sunny, sloped meadow with some views of the water, distant Absaroka Mountains, and neighboring campers. The meadows are green in June, brown in August. The back loops circle through conifers with more shady sites. Bridge Bay Marina has a boat launch, rentals, scenic cruises, store, RV dump station, and ranger station. Separate trails for bikers and hikers lead one mile to Natural Bridge, a rock arch above Bridge Creek.

Grant Village

Set in a lodgepole forest at 7,733 feet, **Grant Village Campground** (mid-June-mid-Sept., $30) sits on West Thumb Bay of Yellowstone Lake. A paved road with paved parking pads loops through this giant campground of 430 campsites with a midsummer population larger than some Wyoming towns. A lack of understory gives views of neighboring campers. Trails lead to a large pebble and sand beach for sunbathing or swimming in chilly

water even in August. Local streams with spawning trout attract bears in spring, keeping the campground closed until mid-June. If bears are still hanging around spawning areas, nearby campground loops stay closed until bears dissipate. Within a half mile, Grant Village has stores, restaurants, pay showers, coin-op laundry, a visitors center, a post office, an RV dump station, and a marina that has cement boat launch ramps, docks, slips, and trailer parking. West Thumb Geyser Basin sits about three miles north of Grant Village. Of the lake campgrounds, this is the closest one to Old Faithful, 17 miles west over the Continental Divide.

Lewis Lake

Boaters, anglers, and paddlers favor the primitive first-come, first-served sites at ★ **Lewis Lake Campground** (South Entrance Rd., 307/344-7381, www.nps.gov/yell, mid-June-early Nov., $15). Located on Lewis Lake at 7,830 feet, this quiet campground is close to the South Entrance, hence it's the first campground for those heading north from Grand Teton National Park and

Jackson Hole. The campground flanks a forested hillside with 85 campsites and is one of the last in the park to fill; in peak season, all sites are claimed by 11am. RVs are limited to 25 feet, and generators are not allowed. The campground has vault toilets.

When temperatures reach freezing, drinking water may be shut off. Paddlers can tour up the Lewis Channel to Shoshone Lake. Near the lake's north end, trails lead to Shoshone Lake and Heart Lake. Lewis Falls sits one mile south.

Transportation and Services

DRIVING

Two-lane roads are the standard in Yellowstone. Throw in curves, wildlife, and scenery, and drivers need to pay attention. Use pullouts for sightseeing or wildlife-watching rather than stopping in the middle of the road. Traffic gets extremely congested on summer afternoons on North Rim and South Rim Drives at Grand Canyon of the Yellowstone. Avoid the mayhem by visiting earlier or later in the day. Stop at picnic areas to use toilets to avoid long restroom lines at the canyon.

Parking lots cram full between 10am and 5pm. RVs will find limited parking. At trailheads such as Dunraven Pass, and all trailheads around Grand Canyon of the Yellowstone, claim a spot before 10am.

EMERGENCY SERVICES

Ranger stations are at Bridge Bay and the South Entrance Station. For medical emergencies, **Lake Clinic** (307/242-7241, 8am-5pm daily mid-May-mid-Sept.) in Lake Village is a small facility that can handle most medical issues. For major medical emergencies, hospitals are 60-120 miles away. Head south to Jackson to **St. John's Medical Center** (625 E. Broadway, 307/733-3636, www.teton-hospital.org) or east to Cody to **West Park Hospital** (707 Sheridan Ave., 307/527-7501, www.westparkhospital.org).

North Grand Teton

Exploring North
  Grand Teton. 182
Sights 185
Recreation. 189

Entertainment
  and Shopping. 207
Food 208
Accommodations. 211
Camping 213
Transportation and Services . . . 216

The Tetons rise like no other, commanding attention from almost every location in the park.

The mountains show the results of colossal earth forces. Peaks contain ancient sea layers metamorphosed under pressure. Their height comes from upthrusting, and glaciation caused their jagged appearance.

At 12,605 feet in elevation, Mt. Moran looms over the northern Teton Mountains to plummet 6,000 feet to the shore of Jackson Lake. Its massive east face has several small active glaciers, and its trail-less access is forbidding even to climbers. Photographers can catch the image of the peak reflected in glassy water.

Once a smaller natural lake, Jackson Lake increased in size with a dam on its east side. More than 15 islands dot the lake, which serves as a foreground for the North Tetons. Marinas, campgrounds, and trails allow visitors to enjoy the shoreline. Boaters ply the waters for sightseeing, and anglers go after trout. Campgrounds and lodges rim the lake's eastern shore.

The Snake River fuels Jackson Lake and then exits to begin its lengthy journey to the Columbia River as the 13th-largest river in the United States. The river curls through Jackson Hole, where anglers and recreational rafters float the water.

A slice of John D. Rockefeller, Jr. Memorial Parkway connects the Tetons to Yellowstone. The swath extends west with one of the most remote roads in the region, the rugged gravel Grassy Lake Road. Only those with the gumption for a several-hour backwoods adventure head here.

PLANNING YOUR TIME

In **summer,** all visitors centers, campgrounds, lodges, marinas, and services are open. No wonder: That's when the weather is the warmest and the best. Most **roads open in May**. Lower-elevation trails are snow-free in June. Higher-elevation trails may not melt out until mid-July and can see snow again by September. **June** is the wettest month, followed by **July** as the driest.

Jackson Lake is at its best in summer, with the ice melting out **early May-early June.** During June's high water, anglers fish the shallows from shore. By August, lake levels

---

Previous: Grand View Point; moose at Oxbow Bend. **Above:** pelican.

Look for ★ to find recommended sights, activities, dining, and lodging.

Highlights

★ **Mt. Moran:** This 12,605-foot peak towers over Jackson Lake, with almost half its height exposed above the shore (page 186).

★ **Jackson Lake:** Backdropped by the Teton parapets, this is a unique spot for boating, paddling, fishing, or scenic cruising (page 186).

★ **Jackson Lake Lodge:** This National Historic Landmark commands a prime spot overlooking the lake (page 187).

★ **Oxbow Bend:** Watch wildlife congregate at this wetland backdropped by the Tetons (page 188).

★ **Signal Mountain:** At 7,720 feet, Signal Mountain's location yields big views (page 189).

★ **Colter Bay Lakeshore Trail:** This virtually flat trail wraps around the forested Colter Peninsula, linking rocky beaches on Jackson Lake (page 193).

★ **Grand View Point:** Climb the trail to this 7,823-foot point for a panorama of the entire valley of Jackson Hole and the Teton Mountains (page 195).

★ **Horseback Riding:** Colter Bay trail rides come with stunning views of Jackson Lake flanked by the Grand Tetons (page 199).

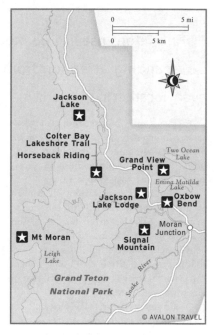

North Grand Teton

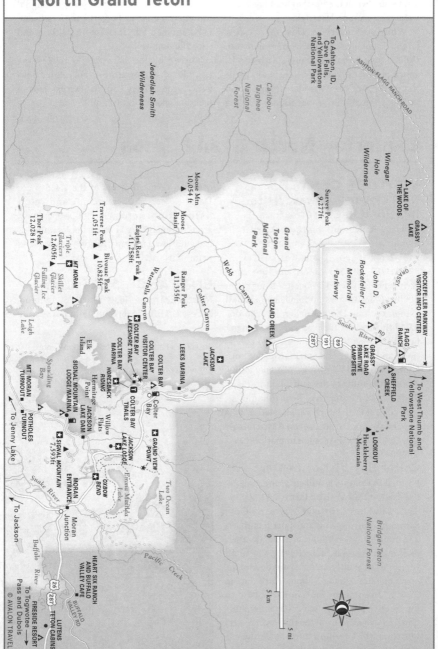

© AVALON TRAVEL

drop, and fishing moves to deeper waters. That's also when the beaches are bigger and water temperatures less frigid.

When visitor services close for **winter**, Grand Teton becomes a place of winter fun. Cold temperatures reign, along with winds, which plunge the windchill. The main highway up the park's east boundary from Jackson to Flagg Ranch is open year-round, offering wildlife-watching and scenery. **November-April,** Teton Park Road closes from Signal Mountain Lodge to Taggart Lake Trailhead. It is groomed for cross-country skiing and snowshoeing.

Snowmobiles can tour the Grassy Lake Road and South Entrance Road into Yellowstone. They can also access frozen Jackson Lake for ice fishing.

Exploring North Grand Teton

VISITORS CENTERS
Rockefeller Parkway Visitor Information Center
At Flagg Ranch on John D. Rockefeller, Jr. Memorial Parkway, **Rockefeller Parkway Visitor Information Center** (U.S. 89/191/287, 307/543-2372, 9am-4pm daily early June-early Sept.) is a one-room log cabin north of Headwaters Lodge. It has a small exhibit on John D. Rockefeller, Jr., who donated the land for the parkway. You can get information on trail conditions, road conditions, and weather, and obtain maps for both Grand Teton and Yellowstone National Parks. Anyone planning to drive the Ashton-Flagg Ranch Road (Grassy Lake Road) should get road condition updates here. The station sells a few books from **Grand Teton Association** (307/739-3606, www.grandtetonpark.org).

Colter Bay Visitor Center
Located in Colter Bay Village at the marina, the **Colter Bay Visitor Center** (307/739-3594, 8am-7pm daily mid-May-early Oct., 8am-5pm daily spring and fall) has maps and information on hiking, boating, weather, backcountry permits, and activities. The small center has an auditorium that runs documentaries on Grand Teton National Park during the day. In summer, you can participate in interpretive programs, see craft demonstrations, and go on tours of the tiny Indian Arts Museum, which features intricate beadwork, clothing, jewelry, tools, and weapons among other 46 restored pieces of the 1,416-piece David T. Vernon collection. A **Grand Teton Association** store (307/739-3606, www.grandtetonpark.org) carries books on wildlife, wildflowers, hiking, history, geology, and natural history.

ENTRANCE STATIONS
Moran Entrance ($30 vehicle, $25 motorcycles, $15 hike-in/bike-in; joint parks pass:

Rockefeller Parkway Visitor Information Center

$50 vehicle, $40 motorcycles, $20 hike-in/bike-in), just west of Moran Junction, is open year-round and provides access to North Grand Teton along with the connecting Highways 26/89/191/287. The Moran Entrance is 29 miles southeast of Yellowstone's South Entrance and 30 miles north of Jackson, Wyoming. John D. Rockefeller, Jr. Memorial Parkway has no entrance station in either direction.

TOURS
Bus Tours
Scenic bus tours (Grand Teton Lodging Company, 307/543-2811, www.gtlc.com, late May-early Oct.) offer guided narration to the sights in Grand Teton and Yellowstone National Parks. Tours depart at 8:30am from Jackson Lake Lodge. The four-hour tour of **Grand Teton** (Mon., Wed., and Fri., $75 adults, $35 kids) takes in views of the Tetons, Jenny Lake Overlook, Chapel of Transfiguration, and Oxbow Bend. The 10-hour tour of **Yellowstone National Park** (Tues., Thurs., and Sat., $130 adults, $90 kids) circles the lower Grand Loop with stops at Old Faithful, Grand Prismatic Spring, Grand Canyon of the Yellowstone, West Thumb, and Yellowstone Lake. Reservations are required. A discount is offered when booking both tours.

Boat Tours
From the marina at Colter Bay, catch a **Jackson Lake boat tour** (Grand Teton Lodging Company, 307/543-2811, www.gtlc.com, daily late May-Sept., $32-70 adults, $14-40 kids) to get out on the water and soak up the lustrous views of Mt. Moran. Scenic daytime cruises (10:15am, 1:15pm, and 3:15pm daily) go for 1.5-hour tours, each with a different theme. Cruises combined with an outdoor meal around the campfire on Elk Island go for breakfast (7:15am Fri.-Wed. summer, 8am Fri.-Wed. fall), lunch (12:15pm Mon., Wed., Fri., Sat.), and dinner (5:15pm Fri.-Wed.). Reservations are required.

Wildlife Tours
The **Teton Science School** (700 Coyote Canyon Rd., Jackson, 877/404-6626, www.tetonscience.org, daily year-round) leads half-day, full-day, and multiday wildlife expeditions in Grand Teton and Yellowstone. Taught by biologists and naturalists, the programs offer educational wildlife watching. Binoculars and spotting scopes are provided; guests ride in safari-style rigs with roof hatches that allow standing to view animals. You'll need to drive to Jackson to catch their regular half or full day expeditions. Private tours ($900/7 people, plus a pickup fee) can meet you up at Jackson Lake Lodge or Signal Lake Lodge. The school also has wildlife-watching float, hiking, or specialty seasonal trips.

DRIVING TOURS
Grassy Lake Road
52 MILES
A narrow dirt and cobble road winds west from Flagg Ranch through John D. Rockefeller, Jr. Memorial Parkway and Caribou-Targhee National Forest. The **Grassy Lake Road** (3-4 hours one-way, June-Oct.), also called **Ashton-Flagg Ranch Road,** looks like a shortcut to reach the west side of the Tetons—it's not. Top speeds reach only 15-20 mph due to bumps, ruts, potholes, dust, and washboards. Gravel added in 2014 improved the eastern parkway section, but after that, high-clearance and four-wheel-drive vehicles are best. The 2016 Berry Fire burned chunks of the eastern portion. The route has scenic primitive campsites, solitude, minimal traffic, fishing, trailheads, and wildlife such as trumpeter swans, bears, and moose. It eventually reaches pavement 12 miles before Ashton, Idaho, and is a route to connect with the remote southwest corner of Yellowstone.

Do not attempt to drive the complete road in large RVs or with big trailers, as turnarounds are few and far between. Many places squeeze into one lane with nowhere to pass. Small RVs and truck-camper combinations can handle the road most of the time,

Willow Flats offers a good viewpoint.

but you must be comfortable backing up. The road is usually snow-free **in summer,** but can flood in spring. Before driving, get current conditions at the Rockefeller Parkway Visitor Information Center at Flagg Ranch. In winter, traveling the road requires snowmobiles.

South Entrance to Moran Junction
29 MILES

A year-round, two-lane highway runs along the entire eastern flank of Grand Teton National Park. From the South Entrance of Yellowstone to Moran Junction, **Highway 89/191/287** crosses eight miles through John D. Rockefeller, Jr. Memorial Parkway before traveling 16 miles down Jackson Lake to Jackson Lake Junction. The forested **John D. Rockefeller, Jr. Memorial Parkway** (which burned in the 2016 Berry Fire) pales in comparison to the spectacular views along Jackson Lake. In the parkway, Flagg Ranch is a pit stop with food, lodging, camping, and an information center, but it does allow access to the scenic **Snake River.** Along Jackson Lake, you can stop to picnic at three designated spots, the first two with trails that drop to the shore. Between the northern two picnic areas, **Jackson Lake Overlook** affords a

dramatic view southward of the lake flanked by the massive Tetons. Of the two marinas on this road, **Colter Bay** offers the better sightseeing stop because of the visitors center and the miles of scenic walking trails around Colter Bay. A stop at **Jackson Lake Lodge** lets you peruse this National Historic Landmark. South of the lodge, **Willow Flats Overlook** gives another viewpoint of the Teton Mountains with Jackson Lake in the distance past the marshy willows. At Jackson Lake Junction, head east to stop at **Oxbow Bend Turnout,** a good place for watching birds and wildlife.

Inside Road/Outside Road Loop
43 MILES

The **Inside Road** (Teton Park Rd., 20 miles, 45 min., May-Oct.) and **Outside Road** (Hwy. 26/89/191, 23 miles, 40 min., year-round) form a large 43-mile loop with huge changing views of the Teton Mountains. Sometimes the peaks loom so close that they fill the front windshield of the vehicle. Starting at Jackson Lake Junction, take the two-lane Inside Road south. En route, it crosses the **Snake River** at **Jackson Lake Dam** and passes **Signal Mountain Lodge, Signal Mountain Summit Road,** and several scenic pullouts before reaching **Moose Junction** to shift the direction back northward on the two-lane Outside Road. At Moran Junction, turn west to return to Jackson Lake Junction. Watch for bison, elk, moose, and pronghorn on this loop, especially when driving at dusk. To protect wildlife, speed limits on the Outside Road reduce to 45 mph sunset-sunrise.

Pacific Creek Road
8 MILES

Just west of **Moran Junction,** the scenic **Pacific Creek Road** (8 miles, 35 min. roundtrip, May-early Nov.) affords wildlife-watching, especially at dawn or dusk, and views of the Tetons on the return. Turn northeast onto pavement, which ends at the park boundary and turns into a wide gravel road. The road terminates at **Pacific Creek Campground** in Bridger-Teton National Forest. A 2.4-mile side spur also reaches Two Ocean Lake inside the park.

Togwotee Pass
26 MILES

This is a drive for sunrise, sunset, and photography of the Teton Mountains. From **Moran Junction,** U.S. Highway 26 runs east to 9,658-foot **Togwotee Pass** (26 miles one-way, year-round) on the Wyoming Centennial Scenic Byway. Drive to the Continental Divide under Two Ocean Mountain. It's a scenic route up, but more impressive on the return with sunset behind the Teton Mountains.

Sights

JOHN D. ROCKEFELLER, JR. MEMORIAL PARKWAY

In 2016, the **Berry Fire** erupted on the west side of Jackson Lake to become the largest wildfire in Grand Teton National Park history. By the time winter doused the embers, the fire had scorched 20,825 acres, crossing Grassy Lake Road, the Snake River, Highway 89, and surrounding Flagg Ranch. Today, the ash provides rich nutrients for wildflower regrowth among the blackened trees. Lining John D. Rockefeller Parkway is a mosaic of different temperature burns interrupted by green survivor trees.

COLTER BAY

Colter Bay is one of those do-everything places with sights galore. You can settle in for several days without moving the car by staying in a log cabin, tent cabin, RV park, or the campground; then you can picnic, swim, hike, bike, paddle, boat, and ride horseback to see the area and enjoy Jackson Lake.

Stop in the **Colter Bay Visitor Center** (307/739-3594, 8am-7pm daily early June-early Sept., 8am-5pm daily in spring and fall) to see the small collection of Native

John D. Rockefeller Jr. Memorial Parkway

American artifacts. To see the off-shore islands, take a scenic cruise, rent a boat, or paddle by canoe or kayak (rentals available). A maze of hiking trails loop peninsulas, passing tiny lakes named for water birds, such as **Cygnet, Swan**, and **Heron**. Bikes can go on the trail to the jetty. Around Colter Bay, Jackson Lake often reflects Mt. Moran and the Teton Mountains at sunrise or sunset.

★ MT. MORAN

Despite the higher Grand Teton to the south, **Mt. Moran** dominates the scenery in the north end of Grand Teton National Park. Its 12,605-foot summit looms over Jackson Lake. Visitors coming from Yellowstone often mistake Mt. Moran's prominence for the Grand Teton. The peak acquired its name from Thomas Moran, famous for his western landscape paintings. For climbers, the peak poses multiple technical routes pioneered after the first 1922 ascent.

For sightseers to appreciate its intricacies, use binoculars to look for the **Black Dike** west below the summit. The 150-foot-wide vertical dike, an intrusion of magma from 775 million years ago, runs unseen behind the peak westward for 6-7 miles. You can also spot a tiny cap of beige marine Flathead Sandstone on the top, evidence of the ancient sea that covered the Teton rocks before uplifting and glaciation changed them into their current shape. Look closely below the summit mound to see two of the peak's five tiny glaciers. **Falling Ice Glacier** wedges in the lower Black Dike zone, while **Skillet Glacier** sits lower down on the north side. They are easier to distinguish from snow in late summer.

So where's the best view of Mt. Moran? Hike Heron Pond at Colter Bay to enjoy reflections of Mt. Moran in the water. Drive up Signal Mountain to gaze across Jackson Lake at it. Dine at Signal Mountain Lodge or Jackson Lake Lodge to enjoy its backdrop over a meal.

★ JACKSON LAKE

At 40 square miles, **Jackson Lake** is huge. Its 15-mile length runs from the Snake River in the north to Spalding Bay in the south. Lake water exits via the Jackson Lake Dam into the Snake River. Today, the water is about 438 feet deep, the natural glacial lake deepened by the dam for Idaho farm irrigation. Fifteen islands inhabit the lake, including **Elk Island,** the largest. The lake contains nonnative brown and lake trout, but real native prizes are Snake River fine-spotted cutthroat trout and mountain whitefish.

Mt. Moran has a vertical Black Dike and two glaciers, Falling Ice and Skillet.

Jackson Lake flanks the lower Teton Mountains.

You can explore the lake on a cruise and paddle its islands. **Three marinas** offer four boat launch sites (two rent boats). Kayaking and canoeing are best in the protected islands surrounding Colter Bay or below Signal Mountain. Short hikes follow the shoreline at Colter Bay and swimmers can float in the buoy-marked picnic area. Anglers can fish year-round or ice-fish in winter. For lakeview dining, eat at Signal Mountain Lodge or go alfresco at one of several picnic areas. Campers can pitch a tent at **Lizard Creek, Colter Bay,** and **Signal Mountain Campgrounds,** which have multiple beach accesses. Boaters and paddlers can find solitude at 15 primitive **backcountry campsites** that rim the lake.

★ Jackson Lake Lodge

With views of Mt. Moran and Jackson Lake, **Jackson Lake Lodge** (800/628-9988, www. gtlc.com, late May-early Oct.) is a National

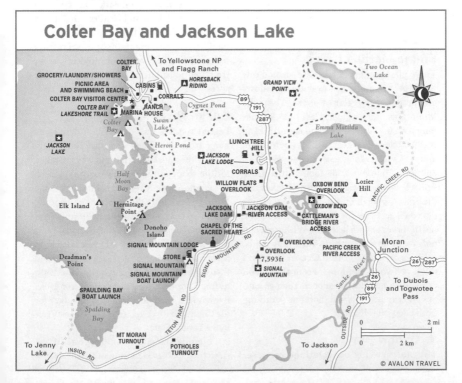

Colter Bay and Jackson Lake

COLTER BAY
To Yellowstone NP and Flagg Ranch
GROCERY/LAUNDRY/SHOWERS
PICNIC AREA AND SWIMMING BEACH
CABINS
HORESBACK RIDING
COLTER BAY VISITOR CENTER
CORRALS
COLTER BAY LAKESHORE TRAIL
RANCH MARINA HOUSE
Cygnet Pond
GRAND VIEW POINT
Two Ocean Lake
Colter Bay
Swan Lake
Heron Pond
89
191
287
Emma Matilda Lake
JACKSON LAKE
LUNCH TREE HILL
JACKSON LAKE LODGE
Half Moon Bay
CORRALS
Elk Island
Hermitage Point
WILLOW FLATS OVERLOOK
OXBOW BEND OVERLOOK
Lozier Hill
PACIFIC CREEK RD
Donoho Island
JACKSON LAKE DAM
JACKSON DAM RIVER ACCESS
OXBOW BEND
CATTLEMAN'S BRIDGE RIVER ACCESS
Deadman's Point
SIGNAL MOUNTAIN LODGE
CHAPEL OF THE SACRED HEART
OVERLOOK
PACIFIC CREEK RIVER ACCESS
Moran Junction
STORE
SIGNAL MOUNTAIN
SIGNAL MOUNTAIN BOAT LAUNCH
OVERLOOK 7,593ft
SIGNAL MOUNTAIN
Snake River
26
287
SPAULDING BAY BOAT LAUNCH
TETON PARK RD
SIGNAL MOUNTAIN RD
OUTSIDE RD
26
89
191
To Dubois and Togwotee Pass
Spalding Bay
MT MORAN TURNOUT
INSIDE RD
POTHOLES TURNOUT
To Jackson
To Jenny Lake
0   2 mi
0   2 km
© AVALON TRAVEL

Historic Landmark. Windows in the Mural Dining Room framing the Teton Mountains compete for attention with the 10 Rendezvous Murals by Carl Roters, a late 20th-century American artist. The *Trappers Bride* mural by western heritage artist Charles Banks Wilson also decorates the wall in the Blue Heron Lounge. John D. Rockefeller Jr. hand-selected the location on **Lunch Tree Hill** for its unobstructed mountain views. It was also the site where Rockefeller and Yellowstone Park superintendent Horace Albright hatched the plans to buy the mountain-front swath in Jackson Hole to preserve it from development. Commissioned by Rockefeller and built in 1955, the three-story lodge uses the modern international architecture of its era blended with artful takes on western and Native American elements. It houses a small selection of the 1,416-piece David T. Vernon collection of Native American artifacts including pottery, baskets, beadwork, weavings, and arrowheads from tribes of the Northern Rockies.

Two Ocean and Emma Matilda Lakes

These glacially carved lakes are located one mile apart in a mix of forest and meadows on the 6,800-foot flanks of the Absaroka Mountains. Both lakes are less than 3 miles long and 0.5 mile wide. A maze of hiking trails circles the lakes, cuts between them, and links to Jackson Lake Lodge. With an 800-foot climb, the 7,586-foot **Grand View Point** between the west ends of both lakes gets the best views of the Tetons and Jackson Lake, but you'll get to see the distant peaks from the north shores of both lakes too. While you can only reach **Emma Matilda** via hiking trails, vehicles can drive to **Two Ocean Lake** via the dirt Two Ocean Road. From there, you can launch nonmotorized boats such as kayaks and canoes for placid shoreline paddling. Both lakes offer fishing.

★ Oxbow Bend

The slow-moving convolutions of water through **Oxbow Bend** yield wildlife habitat and outstanding landscapes for photographers. Located one mile east of Jackson Lake Junction, Oxbow Bend is one of the best places for wildlife and bird-watching. Bring binoculars or spotting scopes to aid in viewing from the pullout. Look for river otters, beavers, or muskrats in the water, or moose foraging on willows. Squawking and grunting American pelicans add to the cacophony from songbirds, and osprey and bald eagles hunt for fish. Opt for the prime viewing at dawn or dusk, but be cautious of large animals such as bears and moose that might be using the road as a travel corridor.

Jackson Lake Dam

In 1916, Jackson Lake Dam enlarged Jackson Lake to its present size. The dam forms the outlet for the lake to spill into the Snake River. At 65 feet high, the concrete and earthen dam extends 4,920 feet. Teton Park Road crosses a portion of the dam, and visitors can park on the south side to walk out onto it. From the dam, the Teton Mountains sprout up from Jackson Lake. Below the dam, anglers cast for trout, while paddlers launch from the river access site.

Snake River

Legend says that the **Snake River** derived its name from the S-shaped gesture for salmon used by the Shoshone tribe and was mistaken for the shape of the river by early explorers. While the Snake River starts in Yellowstone National Park from three streams descending from Two Ocean Plateau, the 1,078-mile river really gets going in Grand Teton National Park. It flows south through John D. Rockefeller, Jr. Memorial Parkway to enter Jackson Lake and then departs the lake through the dam. With its first 50 miles cutting through Jackson Hole, it eventually becomes the largest tributary for the Columbia River and the 13th-longest river in the United States.

To enjoy the river, camp in one of the first four primitive campsites on Grassy

Polecat Creek outside Flagg Ranch

★ SIGNAL MOUNTAIN

At only 7,720 feet high, **Signal Mountain** cowers below the massive Tetons. Formed in part from ash falling from the Yellowstone supervolcano and a glacier leaving it as moraine, Signal Mountain rises alone above the valley of Jackson Hole with the closest peaks 10 miles away. The result is big views. Two forested routes climb 800 feet to reach the summit. Drive or bike the five-mile paved road (May-Oct.), or hike the 6.8-mile trail from Signal Mountain Lodge. The summit has two overlooks: **Jackson Point Overlook** on the south with majestic Teton Mountain views and **Emma Matilda Overlook** on the north facing the Absarokas. When driving up, be cautious of bikers enjoying the flying descent. Tiny parking areas do not have room or turn-around space for large RVs and trailers, but you can leave trailers in the base parking lot.

Signal Mountain Lodge

Located on Teton Park Road, the area around **Signal Mountain Lodge** offers views straight across Jackson Lake to Mt. Moran. While the lodge doesn't make "must-see" lists, the views from the lodge restaurants, marina, beach, parts of the campground, and the boat launch are spectacular. You can spend the night, rent a boat, walk along the beach, or camp overlooking the lake to enjoy the scenery. Donoho Point Island sits offshore; a good destination for boaters and paddlers.

Lake Road. In its reaches above and below Jackson Lake, you can raft, float, fish, or watch birds and wildlife. River accesses are located near **Flagg Ranch** and at **Jackson Lake Dam**, **Cattleman's Bridge Site** west of Oxbow Bend, and **Pacific Creek** near Moran. The waterway is prime habitat for elk, bison, deer, moose, bald eagles, and great blue herons.

Recreation

DAY HIKES

Hiking trails in the north half of Grand Teton National Park are all about getting different angles to see the Teton Mountains. Their jagged pinnacles dominate the scenery. You'll appreciate the views more if you learn what peaks you are seeing, and their distinctive shapes help in identifying them. Use the cheat sheet diagram of the Tetons in the park newspaper.

Several trail complexes offer chances to design routes based on conditions, available time, season, and interest. The park service produces non-topographical maps of two complexes that can aid in sorting out the mazes. One is available for the **Two Ocean Lake-Emma Matilda Lake-Grand View Point** complex; the other is for **Colter Bay-Hermitage Point** trails. Pick up copies of

North Grand Teton Hikes

Trail	Effort	Distance	Duration	Features
Colter Bay Lakeshore Trail	Easy	2 mi rt	1.5 hr	scenery
Polecat Creek Loop	Easy	2.5 mi rt	1.2 hr	fire regrowth
Heron Pond and Swan Lake	Easy	2.6 mi rt	1.5 hr	waterfowl, scenery
Flagg Canyon	Easy	4-5 mi rt	2-3 hr	river
Two Ocean Lake	Easy	6.4 mi rt	3 hr	lake
Grand View Point	Moderate	2.2-8.8 mi	3-5 hr	scenery
Hermitage Point	Moderate	9.7 mi rt	5 hr	lake, scenery
Emma Matilda Lake	Moderate	9.9-10.7 mi rt	5-6 hr	lake
Signal Mountain	Moderately strenuous	13.4 mi rt	6.5 hr	scenery
Huckleberry Mountain Lookout	Strenuous	11 mi rt	6 hr	scenery

these at visitors centers or online (www.nps.gov/grte).

Most trails are snow-free **late May-early November.** Be aware of your own abilities and conditioning. Elevation, wind, and sun can conspire to lead to fast cases of dehydration and altitude sickness.

Guided Hikes

In summer, rangers lead naturalist hikes daily to **Swan Lake.** Usually the hikes meet at 1pm at the flagpole in front of the Colter Bay Visitor Center for the three-mile easy walk. Plan about three hours with lots of stops to learn about wildlife, wetland communities, and flora.

John D. Rockefeller, Jr. Memorial Parkway

POLECAT CREEK LOOP

Distance: 2.5 miles round-trip
Duration: 1.2 hours
Elevation change: 80 feet
Effort: easy

Trailhead: Flagg Ranch corral

This short loop yields an option for wildlife-watching, especially in early morning or evening, but it won't feel like wilderness when it circles the employee housing and campground. The marsh can house moose and birds, but make noise for bears. The trail tours through the area of the 2016 Berry Fire, which added nutrients to the soil, boosting wildflower blooms. Start by heading west to reach **Polecat Creek,** where the trail fringes the forest with creek views. The second half loops back through the forest.

FLAGG CANYON

Distance: 4-5 miles round-trip
Duration: 2-3 hours
Elevation change: 150 feet
Effort: easy
Trailhead: Snake River Bridge River Access 0.5 mile south of Flagg Ranch on Highway 89/191/287 or Flagg Ranch Corral on the Polecat Creek Loop

From the Snake River Bridge River Access, walk across the highway eastward to catch the

Flagg Ranch Trails

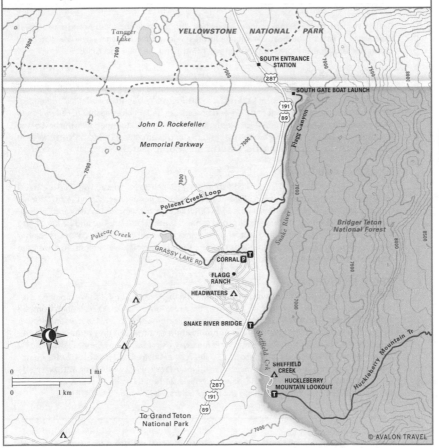

trail heading north along the **Snake River** through **Flagg Canyon.** The trail wanders upstream through an ancient lava flow, grassy meadows, and the river, but is always within sight of the road. At the north end, it climbs through the 2016 Berry Fire zone to the **South Gate Boat Launch** and Picnic Area. You can also access the trail by heading north from Flagg Ranch Corral on **Polecat Creek Loop** for 0.5 mile to a junction where a right turn crosses the highway to hook up with the trail along Snake River.

Bridger-Teton National Forest
HUCKLEBERRY MOUNTAIN LOOKOUT

Distance: 11 miles round-trip

Duration: 6 hours

Elevation change: 2,703 feet

Effort: strenuous

Trailhead: Sheffield Campground in Bridger-Teton National Forest

Directions: From Highway 89/191/287, 0.6 mile south of Flagg Ranch, turn east onto the potholed Sheffield Creek Road. Drive 0.7 mile to the trailhead.

Finding Solitude

Getting away from crowds may require some effort, but the reward is solitude and a wilderness experience. These off-the-beaten-path adventures yield gorgeous scenery, wildlife-watching, hiking, and fishing with more serenity than you'll find along the main park roads.

JACKSON LAKE

Jackson Lake is one of Grand Teton National Park's most-loved places. If you hang out in a boat along the eastern shore of Jackson Lake near the islands, you're bound to see fellow boaters, especially around the marinas. But paddlers and boaters can find private beaches to call their own by heading to the western shore, which sees far less boating traffic. To experience the best of the lake's remoteness, pick up a backcountry permit to camp overnight at **Wilcox Point, Warm Springs, Little Grassy Island,** or **Deadman's Point Island.**

GRASSY LAKE ROAD

The 52-mile Grassy Lake Road (also called Ashton-Flagg Ranch Road) puts you on a historic travel route used by Native Americans and wagons. The route snuggles between Grand Teton National Park and Yellowstone National Park in the John D. Rockefeller, Jr. Memorial Parkway and Caribou-Targhee National Forest. The rugged dirt road connects with **Grassy Lake** and **Lake of the Woods** for fishing, paddling, and motorboating (small ones only). Primitive **campsites** offer places to experience silence and perhaps hear the sound of a wolf howl at night. To drive from Flagg Ranch to Ashton, Idaho, takes about 3-4 hours.

BECHLER RIVER

In the southwest corner of Yellowstone National Park, the Bechler and Falls Rivers plunge over drops creating the land of waterfalls known as Cascade Corner. Backpackers launch from the historic **Bechler Ranger Station** to tour Bechler River through Bechler Meadows and Bechler Canyon to a series of scenic waterfalls. You can day-hike to a few, but they require round-trip distances of 17-22 miles. Near Cave Falls Picnic Area, day visitors can enjoy **Cave Falls;** it's only 20 feet tall, but 250 feet wide. A trail goes 1.3 miles further upstream to **Bechler Falls.** Campers can stay two miles away outside the park in Caribou-Targhee National Forest at **Cave Falls Campground** (June-mid-Sept., $10, $5 extra vehicle, 24-foot RV limit). The campground lines up most of its 22 campsites overlooking the river. Anglers will find superb trout fishing.

En route, the dirt road passes through a creek, which may be impassable in early summer. While this hike is outside Grand Teton National Park, you'll get views of the entire park and more. **Sheffield Creek Trail** (#027) climbs from **Sheffield Campground** to **Huckleberry Lookout,** perched at 9,638 feet. The log lookout, built in 1938 by the Civilian Conservation Corps and used by the Forest Service for spotting fires until 1957, is listed on the National Register of Historic Places. The view from the summit is big: Jackson Lake, Jackson Hole, Snake River, Teton Mountains, Yellowstone National Park, Teton Wilderness, Absaroka Mountains, and burn areas from the 2016 Berry Fire. If you're coming from sea level, the grunt may tax your lungs, but the reward is scenery galore. The trail is usually accessible June-September.

The arid, windblown trail climbs steeply through meadows and 1988 forest fire areas to **Sheffield Creek.** From here, the steepness moderates into a more reasonable, but steady sun-drenched pitch to reach **Huckleberry Ridge.** The name of the ridge indicates its flora. Ripening huckleberries in August attract bears. At a **trail sign,** where you can see the lookout to the west, depart the trail to bushwack a few hundred steep

Cave Falls in remote southwest Yellowstone

Access to the remote, uncrowded Bechler area is from two directions via gravel roads. From Flagg Ranch, drive the 52-mile, rugged, narrow dirt **Grassy Lake Road** (Ashton-Flagg Ranch Road) to five miles north of Ashton and turn east on **Cave Falls Road** (Greentimber Rd./Forest Rd. 582) for 18 miles. From Ashton, Idaho (39 miles from Driggs, ID, 55 miles from West Yellowstone, MT), drive ID-47 north and then take E-1400-N to connect with Cave Falls Road (26 miles). Cave Falls Road splits to terminate at the ranger station or Cave Falls.

BUFFALO RIVER VALLEY

Just outside Grand Teton National Park near Moran, a scenic dirt road circles through Buffalo River Valley. For a tour, drive it east to west for the best views of the distant Tetons. The valley has small **campgrounds,** fishing on the Buffalo River, dude ranches with horseback riding, and groomed cross-country skiing in winter.

yards to the ridge to pick up another trail to reach the **lookout.**

Colter Bay

★ **COLTER BAY LAKESHORE TRAIL**

Distance: 2-mile loop
Duration: 1.5 hours
Elevation change: 100 feet
Effort: easy
Trailhead: Colter Bay Visitor Center

For a short walk with minimum hills and maximum scenery, the Colter Bay Lakeshore Trail provides a double loop that follows the shoreline of the small promontory with multiple inlets. Begin on the paved trail that rims the north shore of the **marina** to tour a breakwater spit. After walking the spit, head west on the trail toward a tiny **isthmus** of rocks that connects the two parts of the peninsula. Once across the isthmus, go either way to circle the **1.1-mile loop.** Side trails reach beaches that yield views across Jackson Lake to the Teton Mountains. Upon returning to the causeway, follow your original tracks back to the visitors center, or take the other **spur trail** northeast toward the swimming beach and then return to the visitors centers on a trail paralleling the road.

HERON POND AND SWAN LAKE

Distance: 2.6 miles round-trip
Duration: 1.5 hours
Elevation change: 200 feet
Effort: easy
Trailhead: Swan, Heron, and Hermitage Point Trailhead at Colter Bay Village

A series of ponds named for birds flanks the hillside east of Colter Bay Village. They have significant growths of yellow pond lilies, leaving little visible water, but they make prime habitat for a variety of wildlife: sandhill cranes, trumpeter swans, osprey, muskrats, river otters, and great blue herons. You'll pass multiple junctions, all well signed on this forest and meadow trail. A map from the visitors center can help in navigating the junctions. Be ready for mosquitoes. Hikers can also access this loop from Jackson Lake Lodge, which will add on 10 miles round-trip.

The trail starts on an **old service road** that curves around the south edge of Colter Bay. After leaving the bay, climb over a loosely forested hill to **Heron Pond,** where the trail follows the northeastern shore to several ultra-scenic viewpoints of Mt. Moran and Rockchuck Peak in the Teton Mountains. At the southeast corner of the pond, turn left at the trail junction to reach **Swan Lake.** After following the shore northward, the trail returns to a junction where going straight will curve around **Jackson Lake Overlook** back to the trailhead.

Colter Bay Lakeshore Trail

Heron Pond

HERMITAGE POINT

Distance: 9.7 miles round-trip
Duration: 5 hours
Elevation change: 690 feet
Effort: moderate
Trailhead: Hermitage Point Trailhead at Colter Bay Village

The hike out to Hermitage Point can take in Jackson Lake Overlook, Heron Pond, and Swan Lake. Hermitage Point sits on the end of a long forest and meadow peninsula. The rocky beach at the point offers a scenic place for lunch on Jackson Lake with views of several islands, Mt. Moran, and the Teton

Grand View Trails

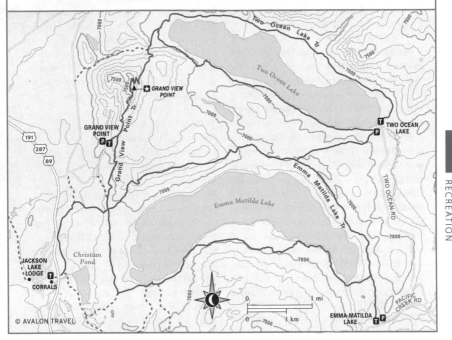

Mountains. But be prepared for winds on this treeless point, mosquitoes in early summer, and shadeless heat in midsummer. With plenty of wetlands on this trail, you'll see tracks: moose, bears, and deer. While the main trail junctions are well signed, plenty of unmarked spur trails head off to viewpoints and explorations. Pick up a map at the visitors center to aid with navigation.

For the quickest route to the point, start on the **old service road** at the trailhead. At every junction, **turn right** to reach Hermitage Point via the west side of the peninsula. The route will take you past **Jackson Lake Overlook** and **Heron Pond.** The trail goes through a lodgepole forest broken by sagebrush and wildflower meadows with lupine, paintbrush, and harebells until it emerges at **Hermitage Point.** From the point, continue up the east side of the peninsula. When you reach a broad meadow, the view eastward spans Willow Flats, Jackson Lake Lodge a

few miles away, the Absaroka Mountains, and the Teton Wilderness. At the next trail junction, **go left** to return to your previous trail and back to the trailhead via Heron Pond or Swan Lake.

Jackson Lake
★ GRAND VIEW POINT

Distance: 2.2-8.8 miles round-trip
Duration: 3-5 hours
Elevation change: 550-800 feet
Effort: moderate
Trailhead: Grand View Point
Directions: Drive 0.9 mile north of Jackson Lake Lodge on Highway 89/191/287. Take the unmarked, rough, narrow dirt road east, veering right at 0.1 mile and climbing 0.7 mile farther to the trailhead.

Multiple trailheads lead to Grand View Point, an aptly named 7,286-foot summit with huge panoramic views of Jackson Lake and the Tetons. From the signed Grand View summit, you overlook Two Ocean and Emma Matilda

Lakes. West of the summit, a large rocky bluff takes in the jagged peaks of Mt. Moran and the Cathedral group of Grand Teton, Mt. Owen, and Teewinot Mountain.

The shortest route, a **2.2-mile** out-and-back with only 550 feet of climbing, goes from the **Grand View Point** parking area to the viewpoint. From the trailhead, hike up a steep 0.2-mile connector trail to reach the **Grand View Point Trail.** The trail ascends steeply through meadows and forest.

From **Jackson Lake Lodge,** the trail is **6.1 miles** round-trip with 790 feet elevation gain. From the trailhead near the corrals, cross under the highway and gently ascend across sagebrush meadows. At **Christian Pond** (mostly grown in with greenery), take the left junction toward Grand View Point. En route to the point, you'll pass several trail junctions. At the **four-way junction,** turn left and continue straight, climbing into the forest and meadows of pink sticky geranium. Most of the elevation gain packs into the last mile.

The longest route at **8.8 miles** and 800 feet elevation gain goes from **Two Ocean Lake Trailhead.** Since Grand View Point sits above the head of the lake, hikers can loop around the lake, adding in an ascent of Grand View Point. From the trailhead, circle the north side of **Two Ocean Trail** through meadows and forest to the junction at the head of the lake. Turn right for 0.3 mile to another junction, where ascending straight up the ridge leads to Grand View summit and then the overlook. Return to the head-of-the-lake trail junction and turn right to circle back around the forested south side of Two Ocean Lake.

TWO OCEAN LAKE

Distance: 6.4 miles round-trip
Duration: 3 hours
Elevation change: 395 feet
Effort: easy
Trailhead: Two Ocean Lake Trailhead
Directions: From Highway 89/191/287 one mile north of Jackson Lake Junction, take the paved Pacific Creek Road 2 miles to a junction with Two Ocean Road. Turn left and drive 2.4 miles on dirt road to the trailhead at Two Ocean Lake.

The flat trail loops around Two Ocean Lake, a trough gouged from the Pacific Creek glacial lobe. Two Ocean Plateau, which straddles the Continental Divide, sheds water to the Pacific and Atlantic Oceans, hence the name. However, the misnamed Two Ocean Lake only drains to the Pacific. The trail travels through forests and meadows, with more

Grand View Point overlooks Two Ocean and Emma Matilda Lakes.

open meadows on the north shore and denser forest on the south shore. In June, yellow arrowleaf balsamroot dominates the meadows, while in fall, golden aspens light up the hillside. Distant views of the Tetons line the horizon. The lake is home to trumpeter swans, waterfowl, and moose. Bears move in for food sources: cow parsnip in early summer and patches of huckleberries and thimbleberries in midsummer.

From the trailhead, start on the **north-shore trail** for the bigger views first. The meadow-lined trail goes 3.4 miles with a short climb and descent to a **junction** at the head of the lake. From the junction, a steep trail grunts up to **Grand View Point.** If you tack on the point up and back, it will add 2.2 miles to your total. To continue around the lake from the junction, turn left to return three miles along the forested south side to the trailhead.

Many hikers opt to combine Two Ocean Lake with **Emma Matilda Lake** and **Grand View Point.** The distance ranges 9.3-13.2 miles depending on the routes chosen around the lakes.

EMMA MATILDA LAKE

Distance: 9.9-10.7 miles round-trip
Duration: 5-6 hours
Elevation change: 1,050 feet
Effort: moderate
Trailhead: Emma Matilda Trailhead on Pacific Creek Road or Two Ocean Lake Trailhead at Two Ocean Lake
Directions: From Highway 89/191/287 one mile north of Jackson Lake Junction, take the paved Pacific Creek Road 1.5 miles to the Emma Matilda Trailhead for the shorter loop. For the longer loop, drive 0.5 mile farther to Two Ocean Road. Turn left and drive 2.4 miles on dirt road to the trailhead at Two Ocean Lake.

Two different trailheads access Emma Matilda Lake. From the **Emma Matilda Trailhead** on Pacific Creek Road, hike **0.6 mile** to the lake. From **Two Ocean Lake Trailhead**, hike **1 mile** to the lake. Once there, the trail loops **8.7 miles** around Emma Matilda Lake. Circling the lake will take you through two lightning fire zones from burns

in 1994 and 1998 where new growth is changing the flora.

On the north shore of the lake, the trail climbs about 400 feet up a ridge that yields views of the lake backed by the Teton Mountains. A loose Douglas fir forest covers the ridge, and you can see Jackson Lake Lodge in the distance. Near the trail junction that goes to Jackson Lake Lodge, a **spur trail** cuts to **Lookout Rock** for views of the lake. From the junction, bear left to circle the south shore of the lake, where the trail travels through a dense forest of spruce and fir.

From Jackson Lake Lodge, trails link into the Emma Matilda Loop. Total distance of the loop is **10.7 miles**, but elevation gain is about 750 feet. As another alternative, many hikers opt to combine Two Ocean Lake with Emma Matilda Lake and Grand View Point. From the Two Ocean Lake Trailhead, the distance ranges 9.3-13.2 miles depending on the routes chosen around the lakes.

SIGNAL MOUNTAIN

Distance: 13.4 miles round-trip
Duration: 6.5 hours
Elevation change: 920 feet
Effort: moderately strenuous
Trailhead: At Signal Mountain Lodge, park in the main lot and walk uphill opposite employee housing to the trailhead.

Although you can drive to viewpoints on Signal Mountain, a trail also climbs to Jackson Point Overlook near the summit. Because of the mountain's island-like perch in the middle of Jackson Hole, it offers tremendous views of Jackson Lake, Jackson Hole, and the Teton Mountains despite its diminutive size in comparison to surrounding peaks. In its first mile, the trail crosses **Teton Park Road** and **Signal Mountain Road.** Once past those, you'll feel more in the wilderness.

At the **signed junction,** opt for ascending via the right fork to the ponds. This portion loops through meadows, wetlands, ponds, aspens, and conifers, a good mix of habitat for wildlife. At a second junction, the climb to the summit begins. The final ascent to

Signal Mountain

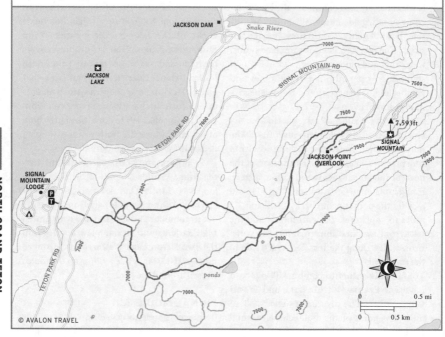

© AVALON TRAVEL

Jackson Point Overlook is steep, gaining 600 feet in one mile. Intermittent Douglas fir and aspen offer bits of shade on a hot day, and the sagebrush meadows yield bursts of wildflowers in early summer including cinquefoil and pink sticky geranium. At Jackson Point Overlook, the view is huge. Lower forested ridges below are glacial moraines from 15,000 years ago, with glacial kettles or potholes to the southeast. These features often get lost below the sweeping panorama of the Teton Mountains, Jackson Lake, Jackson Hole, and the Snake River.

BACKPACKING
Bechler River Trails
17-26 MILES

Tucked in the remote southwest corner of Yellowstone National Park are rivers riddled with waterfalls and outstanding trout fishing. This two-day trip goes to the double-drop, 100-foot-tall **Colonnade Falls** (19 miles round-trip, 9B5 campsite) at the north end of Bechler Canyon. Farther upstream sits 45-foot Iris Fall. Extend this trip by adding on a second night at Three Rivers Meadow (26 miles round-trip, 9B0 campsite) to explore **Albright Falls** and the multiple falls above Three Rivers Junction to **Twister Falls**, with two braids twisting together. The return route adds views of the Tetons.

Other two-day trips follow tributaries up Boundary Creek to 150-foot **Dunanda Falls** (17 miles round-trip, campsite 9A3), which resembles a veil, or up Mountain Ash Creek to 250-foot **Union Falls** (16 miles round-trip, campsites 9U4 or 9U5), one of the park's largest falls.

You will need a permit from the **Bechler Ranger Station** (daily 8am-4:30pm summer, www.nps.gov/yell, $3/person per night, $25 advanced reservations for campsites after mid-July), where the trailhead is located. Approved bear-resistant food storage containers are required. Be prepared for mosquitoes on the marshy trails and fording rivers. Contact the ranger station for current trail conditions. Access the trailhead via Grassy Lake Road (Flagg Ranch-Ashton Road) or from Ashton, ID, to follow Cave Falls Road to the ranger station.

BIKING

Mountain biking is not permitted on trails in Grand Teton National Park, but you can still ride several scenic dirt roads just outside the national park. Be ready for sucking dust from passing cars. Bring your own bikes, as the nearest rentals are at Moose, Teton Village, and Jackson.

Inside the Park

Road cycling has its lure with the big views of the Teton Mountains. Though the main roads have paved shoulders, most drivers are gawking at the scenery or wildlife; wear a helmet and bright colors for safety. If riding with friends, travel single file. Cyclists should be comfortable with large RVs whizzing past at their elbows, but children and families should stick to riding campground loops or to the jetty at Colter Bay. One popular ride climbs 800 feet in elevation up the paved **Signal Mountain Road** (10 miles round-trip); it's a grunt up, but you'll sail on the way down. Cyclists can camp in shared biker and hiker campsites ($10-12/person) at Headwaters, Lizard Creek, Colter Bay, and Signal Mountain Campgrounds.

Outside the Park

Eight miles east of Moran Junction, **Flagstaff Road** offers a long, scenic mountain bike ride on a dirt road through Bridger-Teton National Forest with outstanding vistas of the Tetons. **Buffalo River Valley Road** also has scenic riding past ranches and along the Buffalo River. For information and road conditions, contact **Bridger-Teton National Forest** (Blackrock Ranger District, Moran, 307/543-2386, www.fs.usda.gov/btnf).

An epic mountain bike ride over cobble and potholes, the 52-mile **Grassy Lake Road** (Ashton-Flagg Ranch Road) is an old Native American travel route that squeezes between Yellowstone and Grand Teton National Parks. On a backwoods trek through the Rockefeller Parkway and Caribou-Targhee National Forest, the route starts from Flagg Ranch to ride west through the 2016 Berry Fire zone, climbing past primitive campsites overlooking the Snake River before assuming a rolling grade. Take pepper spray for bears, and check on conditions at the Rockefeller Parkway Visitor Information Center at Flagg Ranch. The road is usually muddy in June, and August brings copious dust.

Teton Mountain Bike Tours (545 N. Cache St., Jackson, 307/733-0712 or 800/733-0788, www.tetonmtbike.com) guides half-day, full-day, and multiday mountain bike tours of the Buffalo River Valley outside Moran and on Flagstaff Road.

★ HORSEBACK RIDING

For horseback riding, wear sturdy shoes or boots and long pants. Check minimum age restrictions and maximum weights for riders when making reservations (required).

Inside the Park

Grand Teton Lodging Company (800/628-9988, reservations 307/543-2811, www.gtlc.com, daily June-early Sept., $43-80) operates three corrals at Colter Bay, Jackson Lake Lodge, and Flagg Ranch. One-hour rides cost $45-50; two-hour rides cost $67-75; kids age 7 and younger can ride ponies ($5).

Colter Bay Village corrals offers one-hour trail rides (departs at 1pm or 1:30pm) from the east side of Colter Bay Village to Jackson Lake Overlook and Heron Pond and two-hour rides that add on Swan Lake (departs at 8am or 8:30am).

Breakfast (3 hours, departs at 7:15am) and dinner (4 hours, departs at 4:15pm) **trail rides** (Sun.-Fri., $77-80 adults, $57-58 kids) go through Willow Flats to a picnic site with views of the Tetons. Vegetarian options need advance notice. A wagon takes non-horseback riders.

Horseback trail rides from **Jackson Lake Lodge corrals** get views of the Tetons. The most scenic ride (2 hours, departs at 8am or 9am) climbs to meadows above Christian Pond to reach Emma Matilda Lake with a stop at Oxbow Bend Overlook. One hour rides (departs at 2pm or 2:30pm) follow a shorter excursion.

One-hour trail rides from **Flagg Ranch corrals** (departs at 9:45am, 12:30pm, and 3pm, John D. Rockefeller Pkwy., 307/543-2861 reservations) tour through forests.

Outside the Park

Several dude ranches outside the park lead horseback trail rides through private lands and Bridger-Teton National Forest. Most ranches package trail rides with all-inclusive overnight stays. **Yellowstone Outfitters** (23590 Buffalo Valley Rd., Moran, 307/886-5421 or 307/543-2418 or 800/447-4711, http://yellowstoneoutfitters.com, daily Memorial Day-mid-Sept., $50 for two hours, $85 half day) guides trail rides from its Turpin Meadows Base Camp near Box Creek into the national forest.

WATER SPORTS

Jackson Lake offers prime boating, sailing, and windsurfing, and the Teton Mountains provide a backdrop worthy of scenic drama. Due to elevation, weather, and topography, both Jackson Lake and the Snake River can be unforgiving. Frigid waters are common in spring (35-45°F). In summer, Jackson Lake rarely warms up to 60°F. Afternoons frequently bring winds that can raise huge whitecaps on Jackson Lake; floaters on the Snake River often encounter headwinds. Morning and evening boating can bring calmer lake waters, but not always. In addition, afternoon thunderstorms can roll in unannounced. For safety on lakes, avoid open-water crossings and stay closer to shore.

You'll need multiple permits for boating or paddling excursions. Sailboats and sailboards require all the same **permits** as boats. Bring your own sailboats, boards, and gear; rentals are not available. Hand-paddled boats (except sailboats and sailboards) are permitted at **Emma Matilda** and **Two Ocean Lakes.**

Boating
JACKSON LAKE

Jackson Lake is the place to boat. Filling a trough scooped out by an ice-age glacier, Jackson Lake is so big that it takes multiple days to explore all of its nooks and crannies.

Horseback rides depart from Colter Bay Village corrals.

At full pool, the lake is 15 miles long, 7 miles wide, and more than 400 feet deep. Fifteen islands, several peninsulas, and numerous bays provide places to get away from crowds. To enjoy the solitude of your own beach, go to the west shore between Steamboat Mountain and Mt. Moran. By August, the lake level drops, which enlarges beaches.

Motorboats, nonmotorized boats, sailboats, sailboarding, and waterskiing are allowed on Jackson Lake; Jet Skis and motorized personal watercraft are not. Waterskiers and wakeboarders must be out on open water, not in channels or within 500 feet of marinas, docks, swimming beaches, and moored boats in bays. While the image of cutting lazy turns in glassy water below the sun-drenched Teton Mountains sounds idyllic, the reality is quite different. Due to chilly water, most water-skiers wear wetsuits or drysuits, and afternoons often see big waves crop up.

BOAT LAUNCHES AND MARINAS

If you have a small hand-carried watercraft, you can launch from any beach where you can haul it. Otherwise, Jackson Lake has four boat launches. Find cement ramps, docks, and trailer parking at **Leek's Marina,**

Signal Mountain Lodge, Colter Bay, and **Spalding Bay.** Designated trailer parking is signed in different locations for day-use, overnight, and long-term parking.

Spalding Bay Boat Launch has special restrictions for its rocky slope launch without a dock. Only boat trailers with single axles are permitted. A one-day parking permit (available first-come, first-served 24 hours in advance at Colter Bay Visitor Center) is required due to limited space. No overnight parking is allowed.

Jackson Lake has three marinas: **Leek's Marina** and **Signal Mountain Lodge** (307/543-2831, www.signalmountainlodge.com, daily late May-late Sept.) or **Colter Bay Marina** (Grand Teton Lodging Company, 307/543-3100 or 800/628-9988, www.gtlc.com, daily late May-late Sept.). Each has restaurants, boat services, boat gas, buoy rentals, and some boating supplies. Water levels in the lake can affect the season ending dates.

RENTALS

All boat rentals are first-come, first-served. **Colter Bay Marina** (307/543-2811 or 307/543-3100, www.gtlc.com, daily late May-late Sept., $45/hour, 2-hr. min., $185/day) rents 16-foot aluminum motorboats. **Signal**

Colter Bay Marina, Jackson Lake, and the Tetons

Permits for Boating, Floating, and Paddling

Boating, floating, or paddling in Grand Teton National Park requires a lengthy list of permits. These are not available in one location, so you may have to do a bit of running around. With prior planning, you can take care of some of them in advance.

Wyoming AIS Stickers

All boaters must purchase a Wyoming Aquatic Invasive Species **(AIS) sticker** and pass a **boat inspection** prior to launching. Roads entering Wyoming (I-80 and I-90) have inspection stations where boaters are required to stop. Drain and clean your boat before entering Wyoming.

- **AIS Fees:** If you have a motor of any type, pay the **motorized fee** ($10 Wyoming residents, $30 nonresidents). If you have a kayak, canoe, rowboat, or rubber raft longer than 10 feet, pay the **nonmotorized fee** ($5 Wyoming residents, $15 nonresidents). If you have an inflatable craft smaller than 10 feet, fishing float tube, paddleboard, or sailboard, you are **exempt** from the AIS sticker fee.

- **Where to buy AIS stickers: Colter Bay Marina** (307/543-3100 or 800/628-9988, www.gtlc.com, daily late May-late Sept.), **Signal Mountain Lodge** (307/543-2831, www.signalmountainlodge.com, daily mid-May-mid-Sept.), and **Headwaters Lodge** at Flagg Ranch (800/443-2311, www.gtlc.com, daily early June-early July). Stickers are available in the park, or in advance online through the Wyoming Game and Fish Department (307/777-4638, https://wgfd.wyo.gov), but allow several weeks for delivery.

Boating Permits

Once you have a Wyoming AIS sticker, you can get the Grand Teton National Park boating permit (for inside-park waters only).

- **Fees: Motorized boats** ($40) include boats with any type of motor, including rafts using motors between Flagg Ranch-Lizard Creek. **Nonmotorized boats** ($12) include canoes, kayaks, rowboats, paddleboards, sailboards, rafts, drift boats, and dories.

- **Where to buy permits: Colter Bay Visitor Center** (307/739-3594, 8am-7pm daily early June-early Sept., closes at 5pm spring and fall).

Mountain Lodge Marina (307/543-2831, www.signalmountainlodge.com, daily mid-May-mid-Sept., $45-130/hour, $185-675/day) rents deck cruisers and pontoon boats that hold 8-10 people. Smaller runabouts and fishing boats can fit five people.

Canoeing, Kayaking, and Paddleboarding
JACKSON LAKE

Paddlers can find fun cubbyholes to explore on **Jackson Lake,** with islands and protected bays the best places for touring. Due to big winds that can arise on Jackson Lake, avoid open-water paddles. Placid glassy-lake paddles can mutate fast into whitecaps threatening to swamp boats; take shoreline routes for safety. The most sheltered paddles are from Colter Bay Marina. Between Colter Bay and Half Moon Bay, a series of channels weaves through multiple islands. To paddle to Elk Island, launch from Signal Mountain instead, but aiming for Donoho Point and Hermitage Point to break up the open water. To paddle to east-shore locations, use Spalding Bay boat launch (permit required) to reach the base of Mt. Moran or launch from Lizard Creek Campground (minimal parking) for northwest shore paddling. Jackson Lake has 15 lake-accessed **campsites** (permit required) for overnighting, some located on islands.

- **Spalding Bay parking:** To launch at **Spalding Bay** on Jackson Lake, you'll need a **parking permit** (free) for the day (no overnight parking allowed). Permits are available first-come, first-served 24 hours in advance from the Colter Bay Visitor Center.

Backcountry Camping

Spending the night at a lake-accessed campsite requires a **backcountry camping permit** ($35 per trip, 3-night limit). Permits are assigned for specific primitive shoreline campsites that have fire rings and bear boxes; a few have tent platforms. Bring your own water or filter lake water, and pack out solid human waste.

- Advance **reservations** (307/739-3309, www.recreation.gov, early Jan.-mid-May, $45) will guarantee your campsite choice, but you must still pick up the physical permit.

- Permits are available **first-come, first-served** within 24 hours before departure. During July and August, competition for overnight camping permits on Jackson Lake has boaters lining up an hour before the backcountry office opens at 8am.

- Pick up the physical permit at **Colter Bay Visitor Center** (307/739-3594, 8am-7pm daily early June-early Sept., closes at 5pm spring and fall) by 10am on the day of your departure.

- Jackson Lake has 10 individual **campsites** (for up to 6 people) and five group campsites (for 7-12 people), all in prime lakefront locations accessible only by boat, kayak, or canoe. Five of the campsites are on islands. Coveted northwest shore campsites at Wilcox Point and Warm Springs are closest to Leek's Marina. Grassy Island, Deadman's Point, Spalding Bay, South Landing, and Hermitage Point are closest to Signal Mountain Marina and boat launch. Elk Island and Little Mackinaw Bay are closest to Colter Bay Marina and boat launch. Group campsites are at Warm Springs, South Landing, Hermitage Point, and Elk Island.

- If you want to build a fire on shore, you'll need a **fire permit** (free, available from Colter Bay Visitor Center). Fires are not allowed on the east shore, from Spalding Bay to Lizard Creek Campground.

EMMA MATILDA AND TWO OCEAN LAKES

Paddlers can access two smaller glacial lakes that don't permit motorboats. These lakes offer quiet venues for shoreline paddles, wildlife-watching, and distant scenery of the Teton Mountains. Trumpeter swans inhabit the waters, and autumn paddles yield spectacular gold hillsides of aspens. For paddling **Two Ocean Lake**, at 6,896 feet in elevation, carry your boat down a steep embankment to the east shore. The lake is less than a 0.5-mile wide, but about 2.5 miles long. To paddle **Emma Matilda Lake** requires a portage of a mile on a trail to launch. Most paddlers who go to Emma Matilda carry in ultra-lightweight boats or inflatables. The Emma Matilda shoreline is brushier and more difficult for launching, but you'll be guaranteed solitude on the water.

SNAKE RIVER

For river paddlers, the **Snake River** has Class II water above Jackson Lake from Flagg Ranch to Lizard Creek (10 miles) and from Jackson Lake Dam past Cattleman's Bridge to Pacific Creek (10 miles). While they are calmer waters, paddlers need to be skilled in maneuvering around snags and debris. Scout the swift current at the Pacific Creek take-out before launching.

RENTALS AND GUIDES

First-come, first-served rental canoes, single kayaks, and double kayaks are at **Colter Bay Marina** (307/543-2811 or 307/543-3100, www.gtlc.com, daily late May-late Sept., $20-25/hour, 2-hour min.) and **Signal Mountain Lodge Marina** (307/543-2831, www.signal-mountainlodge.com, daily mid-May-mid-Sept., $20-26/hour, 2-hour min., $79-99/day).

OARS (800/346-6277, www.oars.com, mid-June-mid-Sept.) guides multiday trips on Jackson Lake. Some are suitable for families and first-time kayakers. Two-night sea kayak trips camp overnight on Grassy Island. Other trips pair up paddling on Jackson Lake with rafting on the Snake River or kayaking Yellowstone Lake in Yellowstone National Park.

Rafting

In rafts, dories, canoes, or river kayaks, boaters can float two different sections of the **Wild and Scenic Snake River** in Grand Teton National Park: one above Jackson Lake and the other below Jackson Lake Dam. Both sections of the river yield scenery and wildlife sightings, but the Snake River below the dam adds grand views of the Tetons. Watch for great blue herons, bald eagles, and osprey fishing the river; to protect the birds, avoid stopping near nests.

Starting above the lake in John D. Rockefeller, Jr. Memorial Parkway, the 13-mile **upper Snake River** sees high water in **late May-June.** Floating from South Gate to Flagg Ranch Landing at the Snake River Bridge takes about one hour. At higher water levels, standing waves can be Class III-IV through Flagg Canyon's white water. Floating the entire route from South Gate to Lizard Creek Landing takes five hours, and the float ends with four miles of flat-water paddling through Jackson Lake. Water levels drop too low for rafting by mid-July, with exposed mudflats and gravel bars. River access is located at **South Gate Launch, Flagg Ranch Landing,** and **Lizard Creek Campground.**

Below Jackson Lake Dam, the 25-mile **lower Snake River** is **open**

Kayakers paddle the Snake River.

April-mid-December. Class I-II dam-controlled flows produce more consistent water. Floating the five miles from Jackson Lake Dam past Cattleman's Bridge to Pacific Creek (north of Moran Junction) takes about two hours. From Pacific Creek Landing to Deadman's Bar, the 10-mile stretch of river poses a more challenging 2-3 hour float due to braiding, channels, islands, logjams, and strong currents. River accesses are at **Jackson Lake Dam, Cattleman's Bridge, Pacific Creek Landing,** and **Deadman's Bar.**

Floating the Snake River requires river knowledge and is not for discount store blowup rafts (inner tubes and air mattresses are not allowed). Parts of the river require advanced rafting skills. Beginners should aim for the Jackson Lake Dam-Pacific Creek segment. Elsewhere, you'll need river savvy to navigate around logjams and maneuver in strong currents. Be ready for afternoon winds that seem to unleash upriver gales, forcing rowing against the breeze. Spring water is cold, fast, and unforgiving.

Before launching for do-it-yourself floating, check on water levels through USGS monitors (800/658-5771, http://waterdata.usgs.gov) and call (307/733-5452) for information on water flow. Find floating regulations and descriptions of different river stretches in the Grand Teton National Park floating brochure (ww.nps.gov/grte).

GUIDES

Guided trips on the Snake River depart from park lodges. The trips usually take up to four hours, including transportation. Actual float time on the river is about two hours to travel 10 miles. Float trips run about $75-80 for adults and $47-50 for kids. Five-hour trips with lunch or dinner included cost $78-90 for adults and $55-65 for kids. Rates include transportation from the lodge to the river and back. Make reservations through the lodges or when you book your stay. Plan to tip your guide 15 percent.

Floating on the upper Snake River above Jackson Lake is via **Headwaters Lodge at Flagg Ranch** (Grand Teton Lodging Company, 800/443-2311, www.gtlc.com, daily early June-early July). The 10-mile float only runs for a limited time due to water levels dropping too low. A motor gets the raft through the flat water of Jackson Lake.

Guided floating on the Snake River below Jackson Lake Dam usually goes from Pacific Creek or Deadman's Bar to Moose in the south portion of Grand Teton National Park (late May-late Sept.). The guide does the rowing; you sit back to enjoy the view. From **Jackson Lake Lodge** (Grand Teton Lodging Company, 307/543-2811 or 307/543-3100, www.gtlc.com), rafting trips depart daily at 6:45am, 8am or 8:30am, 9am, 1:30pm, 2:30pm, and 6pm. Lunch trips depart at 8:30am or 11:30am (Mon.-Sat.). Dinner trips depart at 4:30pm (Tues.-Thurs. and Sat.). From **Signal Mountain Lodge** (307/543-2831, www.signalmountainlodge.com), float trips go out at 7:30am and 5pm or 6pm.

Fishing

A good day of fishing in Grand Teton National Park yields the sun glinting off a wild trout on the line. But even if the fish aren't biting, the experience is worth it as the mountainous scenery provides such an inspirational environment for angling. Anglers can fish year-round in the park, with some areas having closures during part of the year. Fishing regulations for closures, creel limits, and specific lure and bait

fishing the Snake River below Jackson Lake Dam

requirements are available in the fishing regulations brochure (www.nps.gov/grte).

Immense **Jackson Lake** flanks the North Tetons with deep, cold water and several species of native and nonnative trout. Shore fishing is best in May when fish move to shallower water to feed. Summer offers better lake fishing from a boat. The lake is closed to fishing in October. In midwinter, anglers can ice fish on frozen portions of the lake. For ultra-remote fishing, drive the Grassy Lake Road (Ashton-Flagg Ranch Road) west from Flagg Ranch to **Grassy Lake** for cutthroat trout, rainbow, and lake trout and **Lake of the Woods** for mostly rainbows. For kids, **Two Ocean Lake** is a good place to start fishing for cutthroat trout. Portions of the shoreline are free from brush, and early summer produces the most action.

The **Snake River** feeds Jackson Lake's north end and exits the lake at the dam, providing two different stretches for fishing. Above the lake, fishing is accessed via river sites at Southgate and Flagg Ranch. Below the lake, anglers can access the river for fishing right below Jackson Lake Dam. Anglers float drift boats or rafts to fish from the dam to Cattleman's Bridge or Pacific Creek. From the Buffalo Fork confluence to Menor's Ferry, the Snake River closes annually mid-December-April.

LICENSES

To fish in Grand Teton National Park or John D. Rockefeller, Jr. Memorial Parkway requires a Wyoming state fishing license (residents: $3 youth annual, $6 adults daily, $24 adults annual; nonresident: $15 youth annual, $14 adults daily, $92 adults annual). When supervised, kids under 14 can fish for free under a parent's license or purchase a license to fish on their own. Buy licenses at Signal Mountain Marina, Colter Bay Marina, and Headwaters Lodge at Flagg Ranch.

GUIDES

Guides take anglers fishing on Jackson Lake and the Snake River. Be sure to use only guides licensed through the national park.

During late season, dropping water levels may shut down guided fishing trips, and severe weather can cancel trips, too. Rates include transportation and rods, but do not include fishing licenses, flies, or leader. Plan to tip your guide 15 percent (if you catch lots of fish, tip 20 percent).

For guided fishing on Jackson Lake, make reservations through two marinas. A minimum of two hours is needed for fishing the lake, but you can fish up to eight hours if you have the stamina. Rates run $98-110 per hour for 1-2 people. Each additional person costs $22-30 per hour. You can charter a guided fishing boat from **Colter Bay Marina** (307/543-3174 ext. 1097, www.gtlc.com, daily late May-late Sept.) or **Signal Mountain Lodge Marina** (307/543-2831, www.signalmountainlodge.com, daily mid-May-mid-Sept.). The marina also offers a four-hour trip ($295 for 1-2 people, $99 each additional person).

On the lower Snake River, each raft, drift boat, or dory can take 1-2 anglers, plus the guide. Four-hour trips usually cost around $470; full-day trips with lunch run $560. Trips depart from **Jackson Lake Lodge** (Grand Teton Lodging Company, 307/543-2811 or 307/543-3100, www.gtlc.com, daily May-Sept.).

Swimming

Jackson Lake has plenty of beaches for swimming, but there are no lifeguards and the water is frigid. Even in August, the chilly water may not hit 60°F. Frequent afternoon winds can also raise big waves. While you can swim anywhere in Jackson Lake except for marinas, **Colter Bay swimming beach** (Colter Bay Picnic Area) has a buoy-marked swimming zone for families.

WINTER SPORTS
Cross-Country Skiing and Snowshoeing

When snow settles on Grand Teton National Park, winter gear comes out. Snow-buried roads and trails turn into cross-country ski and snowshoe routes; with the snow, you can go anywhere. Trails are not marked in winter, so you're on your own for route-finding—don't assume the previous ski tracks go where you want to go. Even roadways become backcountry in winter. Bring a map, GPS, or compass, and know how to navigate.

Follow proper etiquette, and take along enough gear to survive an emergency or self-rescue. Snowshoers should travel parallel to ski tracks, but not on them. If skiing or snowshoeing where snowmobiles travel, stay to the right. If you are touring on closed roads, you won't encounter much avalanche danger, but check conditions at **Jackson Hole Avalanche Forecast** (307/733-2664, www.jhavalanche. org) to understand the snow surface.

Grand Teton has a brochure (www.nps. gov/grte) that shows popular ski and snowshoe routes, where to park vehicles, and winter wildlife closure zones. The nearest rentals and guides for cross-country skiing and snowshoeing are in Jackson.

INSIDE THE PARK

From Signal Mountain Lodge, climb six miles and 800 feet in elevation on **Signal Mountain Road** to the summit of Signal Mountain for views of the Tetons. This intermediate tour is groomed twice a week and requires the ability to ski downhill on the return trip; when the conditions are right, gravity does all the work. From the Colter Bay Visitor Center, the **Swan Lake and Heron Pond Loop** (2.6 miles round-trip) is more suitable for beginners. At Flagg Ranch, the **Polecat Creek Loop** (2.5 miles round-trip) and **South Flagg Canyon Trail** (5 miles round-trip) are easy routes with minimal climbing. You can also tour the **Grassy Lake Road** (Ashton-Flagg Ranch Road) or the road into Yellowstone National Park, but you will encounter snowmobiles.

OUTSIDE THE PARK

Outside the park east of Moran Junction, former Olympic Nordic racers groom 20 kilometers of trails for skate and classic skiing at **Turpin Meadow Ranch** (24505 Buffalo Valley Rd., 307/543-2000, $15 adults, $5 kids). Rentals run $10-30 per day, and lessons are available.

Snowmobiling

Grand Teton National Park does not permit snowmobiling on snow-buried roads, but it does allow machines on **Jackson Lake** when it is frozen. All snow machines in the park must be BAT (Best Available Technology)-approved. **Grassy Lake Road** (Ashton-Flagg Ranch Rd.) is a popular backcountry snowmobile route in winter. You don't need a guide to snowmobile on Jackson Lake or Grassy Lake Road.

GUIDES AND RENTALS

Grand Teton National Park does not permit guided snowmobile trips in the park, but Flagg Ranch serves as a winter staging area for guiding snowmobile trips into Yellowstone through the south entrance. Most guiding concessionaires and rentals are based in Jackson.

Entertainment and Shopping

RANGER PROGRAMS

Informative naturalist programs take place throughout the day at various locations around Jackson Lake. Check schedules of activities in the park newspaper (www.nps. gov/grte). At **Colter Bay Visitor Center,** the park service offers talks on the back deck, tepee demonstrations, bear safety presentations, and family-friendly programs. **Grand Teton Lodging Company** (800/628-9988, www.gtlc.com) has special programs at two of their locations. At **Jackson Lake Lodge,** visitors can join raptor presentations, grizzly bear talks, Lunch Tree Hill walks, and property tours. At **Colter Bay Village,** a walking tour explores the historic Colter Bay Cabins that used to be Jackson Hole ranch houses.

At Colter Bay, **evening ranger presentations** (7pm daily mid-June-early Sept.) take place at the outdoor amphitheater. In the visitor center auditorium, photo talks or park films start at 9pm. Stargazing and solar-gazing programs happen periodically as weather permits.

SHOPPING

There are small gift shops at **Headwaters Lodge at Flagg Ranch,** the marina and general store in **Colter Bay Village,** and **Signal Mountain Lodge. Jackson Lake Lodge** has a few gift shops that specialize in high-end clothing and jewelry, art and sculptures, and logo wear.

Food

INSIDE THE PARK

Most restaurants inside the park are first-come, first-served, with the exception of Jackson Lake Lodge Mural Room and Poolside Barbecue and Colter Bay cookouts. Expect to wait in line for seating, especially during the peak summer season. Dress is casual; however, diners in Jackson Lake Lodge's Mural Room and Signal Mountain Lodge's Peaks Restaurant tend to clean up before meals.

John D. Rockefeller, Jr. Memorial Parkway

In Headwaters Lodge, **Sheffields Restaurant & Bar** (307/543-2861 or 800/443-2311, www.gtlc.com, daily June-Sept.) offers dining in the restaurant or bar. In the restaurant, breakfast (6:30am-10am, $8-16) includes traditional griddle and egg entrées plus baked goods, trout, burritos, and tofu, or a buffet. Lunch (11am-2:30pm, $7-28) sees salads, sandwiches, burgers, and plated meals of trout or bison pot pie. Dinner (5:30pm-9:30pm, $13-32) runs the gamut from prime rib, trout, and full entrées to pasta, salads, burgers, and quick plates. The western-style **bar** (6:30am-11pm) serves light meals from a limited menu, plus local beers and liquors.

Colter Bay

Colter Bay Village has two adjacent restaurants, both run by **Grand Teton Lodging Company** (307/543-2811 or 800/628-9988, www.gtlc.com), with kids' menus and vegetarian options.

The **John Colter Café Court** (11am-10pm daily late May-early Sept., $3-10) has order-at-the-counter meals of American and Tex-Mex fare, sandwiches, salads, burgers, and hand-scooped ice cream; kids have their own menu. Beer and wine are served. Some items are premade grab-and-go for trail lunches or campsite eating, while others are made-to-order for dining at the cafeteria.

★ **Ranch House** (daily late May-Sept.) serves comfort-type food with a western flair. Eat in rustic booths while taking in historical park photos or dine at the bar where brands from area ranches are burned into the countertop. The restaurant serves local bison (from outside the national park), all-natural beef, sustainable seafood, and some locally sourced produce. Beer, wine, and cocktails are available. Breakfast and lunch buffets can speed you out the door. The breakfast (6:30am-10:30am, $7-16) menu has traditional griddle and egg entrées. Lunch (11:30am-1:30pm, $10-19) serves burgers, sandwiches, soup, salad, and comfort entrées such as mac 'n cheese or roasted chicken. For dinner (5:30pm-9pm, $11-31), go lighter with entrée salads or order prime rib, pork ribs, beef, trout, or pasta. The small bar menu (11:30am-10:30pm, $7-14) has burgers, sandwiches, chili, and appetizers.

Colter Bay cookouts are a fun way to dine outdoors western-style around a campfire with a scenic backdrop of Jackson Lake and the Tetons. The **Cookout boat cruises** (307/543-2811, June-mid-Sept., $47-70 adults, $24-40 kids) go to Elk Island. The hot by the slice. Build your own pizzas (including gluten-free) or order specialty pizzas or calzones prepared with organic flour dough. They also serve Italian sandwiches, salads, pasta, beer, wine, and hard ice cream.

Jackson Lake

JACKSON LAKE LODGE

Jackson Lake Lodge (Grand Teton Lodging Company, 307/543-3100 or 800/628-9988, www.gtlc.com, daily mid-May-early Oct.) has three distinctly different restaurants, plus outdoor dining at the pool. All facilities have kids' menus and healthy, sustainable foods that are locally sourced, plus vegetarian, gluten-free, and low-fat options. The only place to get espresso is the **Lobby Coffee Cart** (7am-4pm). Make **reservations** (307/543-3463, accepted starting late May) for the Mural Room and Poolside Barbecue.

Dining in the ★ **Mural Room** is an experience for the panoramic views of the Grand Tetons outside and the murals depicting western Native American and Wyoming trapper life inside. Dinner reservations are imperative for a window seat. For breakfast (7am-9:30am daily, $11-19), partake of the buffet or order from the menu. The buffet's Belgian waffle iron puts a moose imprint on the waffle; pastries, bread, and cinnamon rolls are baked on-site. Lunch (11:30am-1:30pm daily, $10-20) serves wild-game burgers, organic greens and bread, and entrées of trout, duck, crab, and bison. For dinner (5:30pm-9:30pm daily, $22-46), appetizers, soups, and salads lead into main courses of prime rib, elk loin, trout, duck, pheasant, and veal. Make reservations for dinner.

With big windows and a deck to gaze at the Tetons, the **Blue Heron Lounge** (11am-midnight, $5-10) has small plates, sandwiches, and salads. After 8pm, a limited menu is served. Regional beers and signature cocktails are served until midnight.

Revamped into its original 1950s diner decor, the **Pioneer Grill** serves breakfast, lunch, and dinner. Breakfast (6am-11am, $4-14) can include yogurt and house-baked

Leek's Pizzeria

breakfast (7:15am Fri.-Wed. summer, 8am Fri.-Wed. fall) has fresh eggs, trout, bacon, and pancakes. Lunch (12:15pm Mon., Wed., and Fri.-Sat.) is a picnic sack meal. Dinner (5:15pm Fri.-Wed.) serves up grilled steak and trout with all the sides. **Cookout horseback and wagon rides** (307/543-3100, Sun.-Fri. early June-early Sept., $44-80 adults, $31-58 kids) let you choose your mode of transportation to reach the picnic grounds. Breakfast (7:15am) has pancakes, eggs, bacon, sausage, and sides. Dinner (4:30pm) includes steak, trout, picnic sides, and s'mores. All cookouts require reservations.

LEEK'S MARINA

With indoor and outdoor picnic tables, **Leek's Pizzeria** (Leek's Marina, 307/543-2494, www.signalmountainlodge.com, 11am-10pm daily late May-mid-Sept., $10-26) has partial views of Jackson Lake and the Teton Mountains from its deck. The pizza, pasta, and kids' menu attracts families. You can also drop in after hiking for a cold brew and pizza pastries or full omelets or griddle entrées. Lunch and dinner menus (11am-10pm, $7-25) have soups, salads, sandwiches, wraps, burgers, and wings. The soda fountain serves homemade ice-cream milkshakes (including huckleberry) and specialty desserts. Take-out is available.

As long as the weather cooperates early June-August, the **Poolside Cantina** (11am-4pm, $5-10) serves salads, tacos, burritos, and ice-cream bars. In the evening, the café turns into the **Poolside Barbecue** (5:30pm-8pm, $28 adults, $14 kids, reservations required). The barbecue sears beef brisket, pulled pork, ribs, and chicken, with a baked potato bar, traditional sides, and desserts. Top it off by roasting s'mores over the fire and listening to live music.

Signal Mountain

At **Signal Mountain Lodge** (307/543-2831 or 800/672-6012, www.signalmountainlodge. com, daily mid-May-early Oct., hours shorten in fall), two adjacent restaurants serve meals that emphasize local sources, sustainable dining, and organic ingredients. Both have kids' menus, gluten-free and vegetarian options, and outstanding views of Jackson Lake and the north Tetons.

Relax in the lodge-style atmosphere of the **Peaks Restaurant** (5:30pm-10pm, $20-40) with Mt. Moran filling the windows. The restaurant serves upscale dinners of small plates, multiple courses, and generous western bistro entrées of trout, beef, bison, and fish. Blackberries and huckleberries doctor up the signature cocktails, or you can sip international wines or Wyoming beers. Finish with their famous blackberry pie.

With indoor dining or outdoor deck seating, ★ **Trapper Grill** (7am-10pm) has large menus with choices for families and hungry hikers. Breakfast (7am-11am, $8-14) serves eggs Benedict, skillets, and omelets. Lunch and dinner menus ($10-20) have salads, sandwiches (including banh mì), burgers, ribs, and Tex-Mex entrées such as trout tacos. Giant nachos are a post-hiking favorite. You can also order from the menus in Deadman's Bar, where the views are more limited.

Groceries

Located in Colter Bay Village, **Colter Bay General Store** (307/543-3100 or 800/628-9988, www.gtlc.com, 7:30am-9pm daily late May-late Sept.) is a small grocery with a deli where you can get sandwiches for hiking, soups to-go, fresh fruits and veggies, free-range meat and poultry, and pastries fresh from the bakery. Camping supplies, firewood, ice, snacks, beer, and wine are available.

In summer, **Headwaters Lodge at Flagg Ranch** and **Signal Mountain Lodge** carry convenience-type items with a few limited groceries.

Picnicking

Colter Bay has the only picnic area with fire rings with grills (bring your own wood). Between Lizard Creek Campground and Leek's Marina (on Hwy. 89/191/287), three picnic areas line the road. **Lakeview** is the most popular due to its water views and lake access for water play, but the rough parking lot fits only small RVs. South of Lakeview, **Arizona Island** and **Sargents Bay Picnic Areas** have parking that can fit large RVs, but no water access. **Two Ocean Lake** also has a small picnic area on the lake.

OUTSIDE THE PARK
Moran

Off the beaten path, historic **Buffalo Valley Café** (Heart Six Guest Ranch, 16945 Buffalo Valley Rd., 307/543-2062, http://heartsix.com, 7am-8pm daily May-Sept., $7-15) is a homey cowboy café serving breakfast, lunch, dinner, beer, and wine. Eat inside, in the bar, or outdoors. The deck has Tetons views if you can see beyond their giant stacked burger.

Accommodations

INSIDE THE PARK

All the in-park lodges are only open in summer. Expect rusticity without televisions, radios, or air-conditioning; only a few units at Signal Mountain Lodge offer air-conditioning. Rates are for double occupancy; add on $6-15 per additional person. Taxes run about 9 percent.

Grand Teton Lodging Company (307/543-2861 or 800/443-2311, www.gtlc. com) operates three lodging complexes at Headwaters/Flagg Ranch, Colter Bay, and Jackson Lake Lodge. **Make reservations 11 months in advance,** especially for Jackson Lake Lodge, the most popular location. You can still get last-minute reservations, but you may not have much in the way of choices.

John D. Rockefeller, Jr. Memorial Parkway

Located between Grand Teton and Yellowstone National Parks, **Headwaters Lodge & Cabins at Flagg Ranch** (June-Sept., $227-330) sits at Flagg Ranch. Much of the surrounding forest was burned in the 2016 Berry Fire, but portions are fast regrowing with wildflowers. The river-rock-and-log lodge houses the front desk, restaurant, bar, gift shop, and convenience store. Horseback rides depart from the corrals, hiking trails are nearby, and you can walk to the Snake River to fish. You can get all-day Yellowstone summer bus tours. Parking is in one large lot on the north side of all the cabins. From there, paved walkways lead to the cabins; carts are provided for moving your bags. Each cabin is actually a row of motel rooms. Standard, deluxe, and premium rooms have two queens or one king, en-suite baths, and shared front porches with rocking chairs. The standard cabins permit pets for a fee. Upper-end rooms have microwaves, mini-fridges, and newer fixtures and furniture. Flagg Ranch has no cell phone service or Wi-Fi.

In the adjacent campground, also run by Headwaters Lodge, tiny **camper cabins** (no electricity, $78) help those on a budget. The cabins are wooden boxes with a roof, walls, and windows that provide shelter from the elements and two sets of bunk beds with thin mattress pads. Bunks are doubles or a double with a twin on top. Outside, you can roast marshmallows in the fire pit and eat dinner on the picnic table. Bring your own sleeping bags or bedding, and walk to shared bathroom and shower facilities.

Colter Bay

Colter Bay Village has a visitors center, Indian arts museum, general store and grocery, two restaurants, bar, marina, corral, laundry, showers, swimming beach, boat launch, and amphitheater for naturalist ranger talks.

The 167 **Colter Bay Cabins** (late May-early Oct., $175-280) are really motel rooms without kitchens or lake views. The small, rustic cabins—relocated historic log Jackson Hole homestead buildings—have 1-2 rooms surrounded by a loose pine forest, where you can walk five minutes to the marina. These are the most popular cabins in the park due to their location and included bathrooms. Choose from three styles. For budget travelers, tiny semi-private cabins have two twins or one double with shared bath facilities accessed through a hall or in a separate building. Private one-room cabins have their own bathrooms with a shower and bed configurations (doubles and twins) that sleep 2-5 guests. Private two-room cabins have two bedrooms with different combos of double and twin beds and one bathroom. The cabins have no Wi-Fi.

For an experience reminiscent of summer camp, **Colter Bay Tent Village** (late May-early Sept., $72-75) cabins have two log walls, a wood floor, and the remaining two walls and ceiling made from canvas. Each tent cabin can sleep a family of six between pull-down bunks and two cots with thin mattresses. You stoke a fire in an old-fashioned potbelly stove to heat the interior. The outside covered patio has a picnic table, fire pit with grill, and bear box. Bring your own sleeping bags or rent bedding. Communal bathrooms a short walk away are part of the deal.

Jackson Lake

The crown of Grand Teton National Park lodging, ★ **Jackson Lake Lodge** (mid-May-early Oct., $320-410 rooms and cottages, $735-835 suites) is a National Historic Landmark built in 1955 with a dining room commanding a panoramic view of the Tetons. The modern international architecture features 60-foot-tall lobby windows and an outdoor patio designed to soak up the Tetons. Many visitors assume the lodge sits on the shore of Jackson Lake, but it sits about 1.5 miles as the bird flies from the water, and the closest access to lake activities is Colter Bay Marina. The lodge overlooks Willow Flats, which allow for unobstructed views of the mountains. The property includes several restaurants, a lounge, gift shops, Native American artifacts, playground, and a heated outdoor swimming pool (late May-Aug.). The

25-yard pool, snack cabana, and kiddie pool are located behind the lodge parking lot as an afterthought to the property. Concierges aid in setting up fly-fishing, river float, and park tour trips, and horseback rides from the on-site corral.

Jackson Lake Lodge has 385 rooms in the hotel and surrounding cottages; all have private baths and wireless Internet. Rooms come with or without views of the Teton Mountains and Jackson Lake; non-view rooms look out on conifers or buildings. Rooms are in three locations: the main lodge, separate two-story lodges, or cottages. On the 3rd floor of the main lodge, rooms have two queens. Those facing the Tetons do not have balconies. Separate from the main lodge, three two-story buildings have rooms facing the Tetons with patios or balconies. In the forest, cottages line up multiple motel rooms in single-story buildings. Rooms have a king, two queens, or two doubles. Mountain View Suite cottages add on an indoor sitting area to soak up the scenery. Some rooms have mini-fridges, and some require a two- or three-night minimum.

Signal Mountain

Sitting right on Jackson Lake, ★ **Signal Mountain Lodge** (1 Inner Park Rd.,

Colter Bay Cabins

307/543-2831, www.signalmountainlodge.com, mid-May-mid-Oct., $211-430) overlooks blue water backed by Mt. Moran and the Teton Mountains. Because it overlooks the lake, the lodge is so popular that it **takes reservations 16 months out.** The complex has two restaurants, a bar, marina, motorboat rentals, canoe and kayak rentals, laundry and showers, gift shops, campground, camp store, and wireless Internet. Guided fishing trips and white-water rafting are available. From the lodge, you can drive, mountain bike, or hike to the top of Signal Mountain.

The lodge has a variety of different room options with or without views. Rooms have various combinations of king, queens, doubles, twins, and sofa beds. Some of the units have extra amenities such as gas fireplaces, jetted tubs, microwaves, mini-fridges, and sitting areas. Older rustic log cabins can sleep 2-6 people. Motel-style rooms can sleep 2-4 people. Premier Western Rooms have wood furnishings, granite and slate bathrooms, and air-conditioning. Lakefront units have kitchenettes, balconies or shared patios, and views of Jackson Lake and the Tetons. If you want to stay right on the lake overlooking the water, these lakefront units are the only option in the park, hence their appeal.

OUTSIDE THE PARK
Moran
Outside Grand Teton National Park, Moran has a couple of lodging options, good alternatives when in-park lodging books out or in winter. Some people prefer them for the amenities. Five miles east of the Moran park entrance, **Lutens Teton Cabins** (24000 Gun Barrel Flats Rd., 307/543-2966 or 855/248-2489, www.tetoncabins.com, May-early Oct., $245-485) has two- or three-room cabins in a location with views of Mt. Moran. Located on the highway, **Hatchet Resort** (19980 E. Hwy. 287, 307/543-2413 or 877/543-2413, www.hatchetresort.com, May-Oct., $100-900) is an older revamped log lodge with a restaurant, rooms in historic wings (built in 1954, but renovated in 2014), cabins, budget rooms with shared baths, suites, and a house.

Buffalo Valley
Buffalo Valley has small dude ranches. With views of the Teton Mountains from the ranches, they offer horseback riding, fishing, and winter snowmobiling. **Heart Six Guest Ranch** (16985 Buffalo Valley Rd., 307/543-2477 or 888/543-2477, http://heartsix.com, June-Aug., mid-Dec.-mid-Mar., $100-600, 3-night min.) has guest rooms and cabins. Just 13 miles east of the entrance to Grand Teton, **Turpin Meadow Ranch** (24505 Buffalo Valley Rd., 307/543-2000, June-Oct., mid-Dec.-late Mar., $150-600/night, 2-night min. for some cabins) has one- and two-room log cabins flanking the Buffalo River with groomed cross-country ski trails in winter.

Camping

INSIDE THE PARK
Only Colter Bay RV Park and Headwaters Campground take reservations. Make **reservations a year in advance.** All other campgrounds are first-come, first-served; these fill up by noon late June-August. All campsites, except in Colter Bay RV Park, include picnic tables, fire rings, drinking water, flush toilets, and bear boxes for food storage. ADA campsites and toilets are available. Bikers and hikers can share designated campsites ($10-12 person).

John D Rockefeller, Jr. Memorial Parkway
HEADWATERS/FLAGG RANCH
Located at Flagg Ranch, **Headwaters Campground & RV** (reserve at 307/543-2861 or 800/443-2311, www.gtlc.com, June-Sept., $75 RVs with hookups, $38 tents, $5 extra

person over double occupancy) sits between Yellowstone National Park and Grand Teton National Park. Close to the Snake River, the large tourist center with a lodge, restaurant, grocery, and gas station offers guided fly-fishing, horseback riding, rafting trips, and interpretive programs. From the campground, you can fish the river, mountain bike Grassy Lake Road, and hike Polecat Loop Trail.

The forested campground with 175 campsites sits adjacent to the Snake River. Campsites vary from fully shaded under large spruces and firs to partly sunny with mountain views. RV campsites have gravel pull-throughs wide enough for slide-outs and awnings. The lack of understory yields little privacy. The eastern loops sit closest to the highway, but traffic dwindles at night. Facilities include RV hookups for sewer, water, and electricity, plus a disposal station, showers, and laundry. RV combinations are limited to 60 feet. The 2016 Berry Fire burned the forest surrounding Flagg Ranch, but not the campground.

GRASSY LAKE ROAD

In the first 10 miles of the primitive Grassy Lake Road (Ashton-Flagg Ranch Road), **Grassy Lake Road campsites** (first-come,

first-served, 307/739-3300, www.nps.gov/grte, June-Sept., free) spread out along an old wagon route. Fourteen primitive campsites are separated along the road in eight locations. Camps 1-4 command outstanding views of the Snake River and Teton Wilderness peaks, but all are prized for privacy and solitude. Facilities include picnic tables, vault toilets, bear boxes, and large spaces for tents. No drinking water is available, so you'll need to bring your own. Some sites are suitable for small RVs. You can fish for trout from several campsites, and mountain bike the road. Improvements were made to parts of the road in 2014, making access to the primitive campsites in the parkway section accessible by any rig, but parking at the campsites is limited. At some sites, the 2016 Berry Fire scorched trees, but wildflowers and grasses have already covered the forest floor once again.

LIZARD CREEK

At an ultra-scenic location, **Lizard Creek** (first-come, first-served, 307/543-2831, www.signalmountainlodge.com, early June-early Sept., $23) sits right on the north end of Jackson Lake. As an old-school campground, it still has some prime campsites overlooking the water and Teton Mountains plus walk-in

camper cabins at Headwaters Campground & RV at Flagg Ranch

campsites right on the shoreline. In early summer, fishing, launching canoes or kayaks, and swimming from the campground is prime. In late summer when lake levels drop low, huge mudflats surround the campground rather than rocky beaches. The campground has 43 RV or tent campsites and 17 walk-in tent campsites on a partly sunny hillside of spruce and lodgepole. An amphitheater has evening interpretive programs, and campground hosts are on-site. Many of the generator-free lower loop campsites overlook the lake and the Tetons. RVs are limited to 30 feet.

Cotter Bay

Located at Jackson Lake in a lodgepole forest, ★ **Colter Bay Campground** (Colter Bay Village, 800/628-9988, www.gtlc.com) is built in two sections on a bluff above the lake. The **RV park** (mid-May-early Oct., $58-75, reservations accepted) has 112 pull-through campsites with hookups for water, sewer, and electricity. No tents or fires are permitted in the RV park, but you can use your own gas or charcoal grills. RV length, including rigs and trailers, is limited to 45 feet. The larger **campground** (late May-Sept., $30, first-come, first-served) contains 350 sites (no hookups), 9 walk-in tent sites, 11 group sites, and 13 ADA campsites (hookups, $52) for tents and RVs. Some loops are generator-free zones. Sites are assigned at the staffed check-in station. If you arrive after the station closes, a whiteboard lists available sites. Reservations are available for group campsites only. **Winter camping** (Dec.-mid-Apr., $5) is possible at Colter Bay in the plowed parking lot.

Colter Bay Village houses a visitors center, amphitheater for evening naturalist programs, general store, two restaurants, coin-op laundry and showers, gas, disposal station, boat launch, swimming beach, and a marina with motorboat, canoe, and kayak rentals.

Signal Mountain

On a bluff adjacent to Signal Mountain Lodge, ★ **Signal Mountain Campground** (first-come, first-served, 307/543-2831, www. signalmountainlodge.com, mid-May-mid-Oct., $52 RVs, $31 tents) commands one of the best panoramic views of the Teton Mountains from its perch on the west shore of Jackson Lake. The campground loops around a hillside, where some of the campsites yield million-dollar views of the lake and the Tetons. There are 81 sites for tents or RVs, 4 tent-only campsites, and an ADA site with electricity ($47). A mix of fir and spruce trees provides some shade, but most small campsites are sunny midday. Low brush and trees create partial privacy. The narrow campground road and parking pads can pose challenges for RV drivers unskilled in squeezing into tight spots; RVs are limited to 30 feet. Loop 3 is generator-free.

Adjacent to the campground, Signal Mountain Lodge houses a restaurant, convenience store, gas station, and marina with guided fishing and rentals of canoes, kayaks, and motorboats. A boat launch is nearby.

OUTSIDE THE PARK

When in-park campgrounds fill up, national forest and private campgrounds east of Moran or in Bridger-Teton National Forest can work as a backup. For hookups, go to the private campground; Forest Service campgrounds are limited to vault or pit toilets, picnic tables, bear boxes, fire rings, and potable water where noted.

Private Campground

A campground for convenience located 5.6 miles east of Moran Junction, **Fireside Resort** (17800 Hwy. 287, Moran, 307/733-1980 or 800/563-6469, www.yellowstonerv.com, year-round, $70-85 hookups, $30-45 tents, $8/person over 4 people) is a sunny highway campground, but with views that give it appeal. From many campsites, the entire Teton Mountain range is visible across the horizon to the west. Buffalo Fork, good for fishing or paddling, circles around this older ex-KOA campground. The campground has 14 tent campsites, some with water and electricity, and 160 RV campsites with hookups for sewer, water, and electricity. Facilities include flush toilets, showers, laundry, store, and wireless Internet.

Forest Service Campgrounds

Bridger-Teton National Forest (Blackrock Ranger District, 307/543-2386, www.fs.usda.gov/btnf, late May-Sept., $10-12, $6 extra vehicle) has several campgrounds near Grand Teton National Park. Due to grizzly bears feeding, they may close temporarily to tents, tent campers, and tent trailers, allowing **only hard-sided RVs**. If weather permits, the campgrounds remain open later in fall, but without services. RVs are limited to 30 feet. All campgrounds are first-come, first-served.

With the turnoff located one mile south of Flagg Ranch, **Sheffield Creek Campground** cuddles below the Teton Wilderness. From the campground, a trail climbs to 9,615-foot Huckleberry Lookout. Five sunny campsites have huge territorial views. Check on access: The potholed road requires driving through a creek that may have too much water to cross in June. **Pacific Creek Campground**, located eight miles up Pacific Creek Road, has eight campsites under cottonwoods with expansive views of the surrounding mountains on the edge of the Teton Wilderness. Pacific Creek offers fly-fishing for trout, and a trail leads eight miles to Gravel Lake, tucked on the side of Pinyon Peak.

Two campgrounds sit east of Moran and the park's east entrance. Eight miles east of Moran, **Hatchet Campground** is a not-so-scenic roadside camp. In addition, the adjacent dirt Forest Road 30160 climbs a scenic drive up to a few primitive free campsites with outstanding views of the Tetons. Off the main highway on Buffalo Valley Road, **Turpin Meadow Campground** sprawls 18 pastoral campsites in sunny loops between lodgepole stands and sagebrush meadows.

In **Caribou-Targhee National Forest** (Island Park Ranger District, 208/558-7301, www.fs.usda.gov/ctnf), free primitive campsites line Grassy Lake Road (Ashton-Flagg Ranch Road). The best campsites are at **Grassy Lake** and **Lake of the Woods** due to opportunities for fishing, paddling, and solitude.

Transportation and Services

DRIVING

U.S. Highway 89/191/287 is open year-round between Yellowstone National Park and Moran Junction, Grand Teton's east entrance. From Moran, highways head east over Togwotee Pass to Dubois and Lander or south on the "Outside Road" to Jackson. Teton Park Road (also known as the Inside Road) is open year-round from Jackson Lake Junction to Signal Mountain Lodge, but closes south in winter.

Wildlife Precautions

Driving in Grand Teton National Park is on two-lane roads, some with no shoulders. Speed limits vary 25-55 mph; the nighttime speed limit is 45 mph in order to protect wildlife. U.S. Highway 26/89/191 has been the "local speedway" for getting from Jackson Lake to Jackson, often making the road a wildlife slaughterhouse. Wildlife crossing areas are rarely signed, and lighting at dusk and dawn makes spotting animals more difficult. Drive slowly at night as wildlife can be difficult to see.

SHUTTLES

Shuttles in Grand Teton are run by **Alltrans** (307/733-3135 or 800/443-6133, www.all-transparkshuttle.com, daily late May-early Oct., $15/person/day) and travel between Jackson, Moose, Jenny Lake Visitor Center, Jenny Lake Lodge, Signal Mountain Lodge, Jackson Lake Lodge, Colter Bay Village, and

Where Can I Find?

- **Banks and ATMs:** Find ATMs at Colter Bay General Store in Colter Bay Village and at Jackson Lake Lodge.

- **Cell Service:** Moran and the Jackson Lake area get limited cell phone reception, although it is best for those with Verizon. You can get cell reception at Colter Bay, Jackson Lake Lodge, and Signal Mountain Lodge.

- **Gas and Garage Services:** In summer, gas stations operate at Flagg Ranch, Colter Bay Village, Jackson Lake Lodge, Signal Mountain Lodge, and Moran. Moran is open year-round. Boat gasoline is sold at Leek's Marina, Colter Bay Marina, and Signal Mountain Lodge.

- **Internet Access:** Wi-Fi is available at Jackson Lake Lodge and Signal Mountain Lodge. Colter Bay Village has Wi-Fi available in public locations such as restaurants, launderettes, and lodging check-in lobbies.

- **Laundry:** Coin-op laundries are at Headwaters Campground at Flagg Ranch, Colter Bay, and Signal Mountain Lodge.

- **Post Office:** A post office is located in Moran (1 Central St., 8:30am-1pm and 1:30pm-4:30pm Mon.-Fri., 10am-11:30am Sat.), outside the east entrance of Grand Teton National Park.

- **Showers:** Showers ($5-8) are at Headwaters Campground at Flagg Ranch, Colter Bay, and Signal Mountain Lodge. The Signal Mountain Lodge shower house has large individual shower rooms.

Headwaters Lodge at Flagg Ranch. Shuttles run several times north and south each day. Departure times are available at the visitors centers. The one-day fee lets you get on and off the shuttle as many times as you want and wherever you want. No reservations are needed; pay with cash, Visa, or Mastercard when you board. Alltrans also provides shuttles from the Jackson Hole Airport (www.jacksonholealltrans.com) to lodges in the park.

EMERGENCY SERVICES

In an emergency, ranger stations are at Colter Bay Village, Moran Entrance Station, and Yellowstone's South Entrance Station. These stations are not staffed like visitors centers, but they can help in emergencies. **Grand**

Teton Medical Clinic (Jackson Lake Lodge, 307/543-2514, after hours 307/733-8002, http://grandtetonmedicalclinic.com, 9am-5pm daily late May-early Oct.) can take care of most situations except severe emergencies. The closest hospital, **St. John's Medical Center** (625 E. Broadway, Jackson, WY, 307/733-3636, www.tetonhospital.org), is about 30 miles south of Moran Junction.

For emergencies in the Bridger-Teton National Forest, contact **Blackrock Ranger District** (Hwy 26/287, Moran, WY, 307/543-2386, www.fs.usda.gov/btnf). For help on the Ashton-Flagg Ranch Road in Caribou-Targhee National Forest, contact **Ashton/Island Park Ranger District** (46 S. Hwy. 20, Ashton, ID, 208/652-7442, www.fs.usda.gov/ctnf).

South Grand Teton

Exploring South Grand Teton ...222

Sights 227

Recreation..................... 234

Entertainment and Shopping ...254

Food 255

Accommodations.............. 256

Camping 259

Transportation and Services ... 260

The Grand Teton crowns the Teton Mountains, the towering zenith in a range of toothy peaks spreading north and south.

From the flat sagebrush plains of Jackson Hole, the Grand shoots 7,000 feet into the sky. It lures mountain climbers, hikers, photographers, artists, and those who seek inspiration to get up close and personal. Over its skirts of peaks, the Grand rules the youngest mountains in the Rockies.

Visitors have two options: experience the peaks from the floor of Jackson Hole or hike into the mountains. Snuggled at the base of the peaks, small lakes string along the valley floor offering picturesque places to fish, paddle, and hike. High up, glacier-scoured basins house idyllic alpine lakes rimmed with meadows of wildflowers and moraines from alpine glaciers. High passes cut through the Teton Crest, and giant rock-slab ledges lead up vertical spires.

Cutting through Jackson Hole, the Wild and Scenic Snake River zigzags with changing views of the skyscraping grandeur. Families relax on the river in rubber rafts, and anglers fly-fish for trout.

Wildlife abounds in the southern Tetons.

Bison, elk, moose, pronghorn, and deer populate the fields of Jackson Hole. Bald eagles and great blue herons fish the Snake River, also home to river otters and muskrats. Grizzly bears roam the forests, and shrieking pikas inhabit high-elevation talus slopes.

PLANNING YOUR TIME

Summer packs out Jenny Lake with visitors. Parking gets tight, tent campers must claim sites early, boat tours book out, and low-elevation trails crowd with hikers. But as you climb up canyons into the Teton Mountains, the number of hikers thins. **June-early September,** all visitor services, visitors centers, lodges, and restaurants are open, and all park service and concessionaire activities run full programs. **June** brings out wildflowers around the moraine lakes along the base of the Tetons with fields of purple lupine and yellow balsamroot. By **August,** lush sagebrush grassland greens give way to golden browns, and copious early summer mosquitoes disappear as ponds dry up. In the canyons of the

---

Previous: sunset over the Teton Mountains; a moose along Moose-Wilson Road. **Above:** mountain bluebird.

Look for ★ to find recommended sights, activities, dining, and lodging.

Highlights

★ **Craig Thomas Discovery & Visitor Center:** Art and technology provide an introduction to Grand Teton National Park (page 222).

★ **Laurance S. Rockefeller Preserve Center:** Unique conservation exhibits connect you with nature through the senses (page 223).

★ **Teton Park Road:** This scenic Inner Road tours the west side of Jackson Hole, right under the Teton Mountains (page 224).

★ **Moose-Wilson Road:** This narrow road weaves through beaver, porcupine, and moose habitat (page 226).

★ **Grand Teton:** At 13,770 feet, the Grand tops all other peaks in the Teton Mountains (page 227).

★ **Jenny Lake:** Jenny Lake is flush with hiking trails and pristine water for paddling and fishing (page 227).

★ **Mormon Row:** The scenic old barns and buildings of this historic community claim expansive views of the Teton Mountains (page 233).

★ **Hidden Falls and Inspiration Point:** Hike to a rocky outcrop at 7,200 feet with views of Jackson Hole and the blue waters of Jenny Lake (page 238).

★ **Paintbrush-Cascade Loop:** Hikers rank this 19.2-mile loop, topping out at 10,720-foot Paintbrush Divide, high on their bucket lists (page 239).

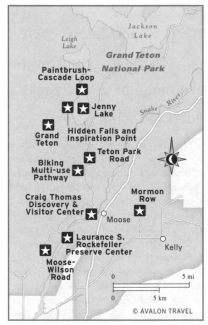

© AVALON TRAVEL

★ **Multi-Use Pathway:** Bicycle this paved pathway from Moose to Jenny Lake and back for the ultimate of riding right under the Tetons. (page 248).

South Grand Teton

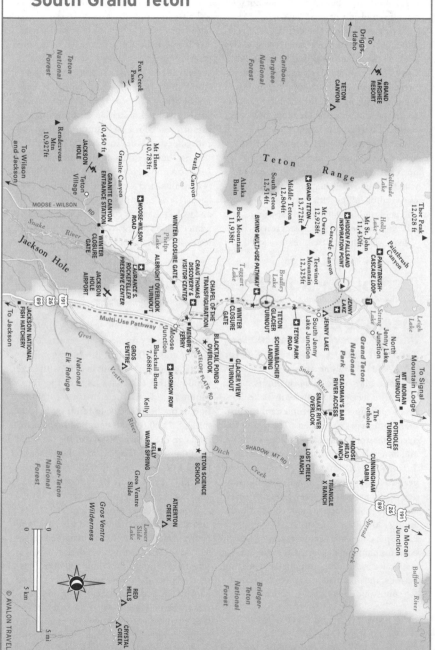

To Driggs, Idaho

Teton National Forest

Caribou-Targhee National Forest

GRAND TARGHEE RESORT

TETON CANYON

Fox Creek Pass

Teton Range

Solitude Lake

Thor Peak 12,028 ft

10,450 ft

JACKSON HOLE

Granite Canyon

Death Canyon

Alaska Basin

Mt Owen 12,928ft

GRAND TETON 13,772ft

Mt St. John 11,430ft

Holly Lake

HIDDEN FALLS AND INSPIRATION POINT

PAINTBRUSH

Leigh Lake

Rendezvous Mtn 10,927ft

Teton Village

MOOSE - WILSON RD

Mt Hunt 10,783ft

Middle Teton 12,804ft

South Teton 12,514ft

Cascade Canyon

CASCADE LOOP

Paintbrush Canyon

Cascade Lake

To Wilson and Jackson

GRANITE CANYON ENTRANCE STATION

MOOSE-WILSON ROAD

Phelps Lake

WINTER CLOSURE GATE

Buck Mountain 11,938ft

BIKING MULTI-USE PATHWAY

Teewinot Mountain 12,325ft

Bradley Lake

String Lake

JENNY LAKE

Jenny Lake

North Jenny Lake Junction

Grand Teton National Park

To Signal Mountain Lodge

MT MORAN TURNOUT

Snake River

Jackson Hole

JACKSON HOLE AIRPORT

WINTER CLOSURE GATE

ALBRIGHT OVERLOOK TURNOUT

LAURANCE S. ROCKEFELLER PRESERVE CENTER

Multi-Use Pathway

CRAIG THOMAS DISCOVERY & VISITOR CENTER

CHAPEL OF THE TRANSFIGURATION

Taggart Lake

WINTER CLOSURE GATE

GLACIER TURNOUT

TETON PARK ROAD

South Jenny Lake Junction

TETON

SCHWABACHER LANDING

Snake River

DEADMAN'S BAR RIVER ACCESS

The Potholes

To Moran Lodge

North Jenny

MT MORAN TURNOUT

POTHOLES TURNOUT

To Jackson

JACKSON NATIONAL FISH HATCHERY

89 26 191

Gros Ventre

National Elk Refuge

MENOR'S FERRY

Moose Junction

GROS VENTRE

Blacktail Butte 7,688ft

MORMON ROW

Kelly

ANTELOPE FLATS RD

BLACKTAIL PONDS OVERLOOK

GLACIER VIEW TURNOUT

SNAKE RIVER OVERLOOK

LOST CREEK RANCH

MOOSE HEAD RANCH

CUNNINGHAM CABIN

TRIANGLE X RANCH

89 26

191

To Moran Junction

Gros Ventre River

KELLY WARM SPRING

TETON SCIENCE SCHOOL

SHADOW MT RD

Ditch Creek

Spread Creek

Bridger-Teton National Forest

Gros Ventre Slide

ATHERTON CREEK

Lower Slide Lake

Gros Ventre Slide

Bridger-Teton National Forest

Gros Ventre Wilderness

RED HILLS

CRYSTAL CREEK

Buffalo River

0   5 km

0   5 mi

© AVALON TRAVEL

Tetons, waterfalls gush as snows melt, but access to high snow-buried passes may not melt out until mid-July or early August.

Spring and fall offer quieter times to visit, although weather can be erratic. If your goal is to climb the Grand Teton or hike to the Teton Crest, snow may impede travel in upper elevations. If lower-elevation hiking and sightseeing is on your agenda, the shoulder seasons are the perfect time, and the snow-clad peaks stand out dramatically against a blue sky. All roads are open, and wildlife is active. **Spring** brings the chance to see bison and pronghorn newborns, and during fall, the air fills with the sound of elk bugling. **Fall** also brings outstanding hiking with warm bug-free days and cool nights. During early spring or late fall, you may need to stay in Jackson or Teton Village when in-park facilities are closed.

When **winter** descends on Grand Teton National Park, so does the snow. Winter offers a chance for exquisite scenery: trees rimmed with frost, wind-sculpted snow, and icicles. Barring periodic blizzards, the park fills with utter quiet. **Teton Park Road,** along with several lesser roads, **closes November-April.** Only **U.S. Highway 26/89/191** remains **open year-round.** On some closed roads in winter, machine grooming lays a smooth track for cross-country skiing and snowshoeing. Most in-park **facilities are closed**, but just outside the national park, **Jackson** and **Teton Village** offer lodging, restaurants, and amenities. While bears hibernate, you can still see raptors, bison, deer, and wolves. Rangers guide snowshoe walks in winter to look for tracks, and concessionaires lead wildlife-watching tours.

Exploring South Grand Teton

VISITORS CENTERS
Jenny Lake Visitor Center

The small **Jenny Lake Visitor Center** (307/739-3392, www.nps.gov/grte, 8am-7pm daily mid-May-late Sept., shorter hours spring and fall) is located at South Jenny Lake. Stop here to pick up activity schedules, ranger program information, and maps. The center has a relief map of the park and geology exhibits, and houses a small bookstore run by **Grand Teton Association** (307/739-3606, www.grandtetonpark.org) that sells field guides and books on natural history, human history, and geology. Also located in the complex is the **Jenny Lake Ranger Station** (307/739-3343, 8am-5pm daily early June-early Sept.), which contains climbing displays. Go to the ranger station for backcountry camping and boating permits, and information on mountain climbing routes and conditions.

★ Craig Thomas Discovery & Visitor Center

The **Craig Thomas Discovery & Visitor** **Center** (307/739-3399, www.nps.gov/grte, 8am-7pm daily early Mar.-Oct., shorter hours spring and fall), called the Moose Visitor Center by locals, was built in 2007 with large windows that take advantage of the Teton Mountains. Constructed with a combination of public and private funding, the $22 million, 22,000-square-foot building has exhibits on the natural history of the park and mountaineering, large bronze wildlife sculptures, a 30-foot climbing wall, in-floor videos, kids' exhibits, and a topographic map with laser technology that shows wildlife migration and glacier progression. The theater also shows a documentary on the park, and Native Americans crafts are displayed on select days. The information desk has maps, schedules of ranger programs and hikes, current weather data from park monitors, and permits for backcountry camping and boating. A large **Grand Teton Association bookstore** (307/739-3606, www.grandtetonpark.org) sells field guides and books on wildlife, human history, and geology.

★ Laurance S. Rockefeller Preserve Center

The **Laurance S. Rockefeller Preserve Center** (307/739-3654, www.nps.gov/grte, 9am-5pm daily early June-late Sept.) is located on a 1,000-acre preserve that was once a ranch owned by the Rockefeller family. The preserve's LEED-certified building contains exhibits that appeal to the senses: visual, tactile, and auditory. Watch high-definition nature videos, view an ultra-large Phelps Lake photograph made from one-inch nature photos, and listen to natural soundscapes. Rangers lead daily programs, talks, hikes, sunrise strolls, and evening walks. Kids can check out a backpack for a journaling experience while hiking the preserve's eight miles of trails, including a loop around Phelps Lake. The parking lot is limited to 50 cars and usually fills up 10am-4pm; plan your visit early in the morning or late in the afternoon and add time for waiting in the Moose-Wilson Road queue (no RVs or trailers). In May and October, visitors can drive to the center and hike, even when the building is closed. In winter, cross-country skiers and snowshoers tour trails at the preserve.

ENTRANCE STATIONS

South Grand Teton has two entrance stations ($30 vehicle, $25 motorcycles, $15 hike-in/bike-in; joint parks pass: $50 vehicle, $40 motorcycles, $20 hike-in/bike-in); both are open year-round. The **Granite Canyon Entrance Station** (no RVs or trailers) sits just north of Teton Village on the Moose-Wilson Road. In winter, the road is only open for cars for about a half-mile for ski and snowshoe trailhead access. The **Moose Entrance Station** sits on Teton Park Road on the east side of the Snake River. U.S. 26/89/191 (open year-round) has no entrance stations.

TOURS

With the exception of boat tours, guided sightseeing tours of the Tetons originate at Jackson Lake Lodge in North Grand Teton or in Jackson. Make reservations when you make your travel plans. Park entrance passes are not included in fees. Plan to tip your guide 15 percent.

Boat Tours

Cruise around Jenny Lake to see the Teton Mountains from a different perspective; bring your camera for the views. From the

Craig Thomas Discovery & Visitor Center

dock at South Jenny Lake, **Jenny Lake Boating** (307/734-9227, www.jennylake-boating.com, daily mid-May-late Sept., $20 adults, $18 seniors, $12 kids) guides one-hour interpretive tours on open boats that hold 44 people. Guides cover tidbits about geology, history, plants, and wildlife during the shoreline loop tour. Early June–early September, three tours launch daily (11am, 2pm, and 5pm). In spring and fall, tours depart each day at noon and 2pm. Reservations by credit card are highly recommended.

Wildlife Tours

Safari-style wildlife tours get you out with expert naturalists to watch animals in their natural habitats. Guides supply binoculars, spotting scopes, and field books. You'll have to drive to Jackson to meet the tour group.

Departing from Jackson, **Teton Science School** (700 Coyote Canyon Rd., Jackson, 877/404-6626, www.tetonscience.org, year-round) leads half-day ($145 adults), full-day ($245 adults), and multiday wildlife expeditions that use customized vans with roof hatches for stand-up viewing. Full-day expeditions include lunch—a picnic in summer or a restaurant in winter. Departure times vary based on sunrise, an active time for wildlife. For pickups at lodges in the national park, you can book private tours and pay an additional pick-up fee.

Based in Jackson, **Ecotour Adventures** (307/690-9533, www.jhecotouradventures.com, year-round) runs four-hour sunrise and sunset wildlife tours ($135 adults, $99 kids). Eight-hour tours ($230 adults, $195 kids) include lunch at one of the park lodges. Departure times vary depending on daylight hours. Tours are limited to seven participants so that each person gets a window seat; roof hatches allow everyone to stand up to view and photograph wildlife. Most of the company's rigs run on biodiesel to protect air quality around wildlife.

Moose Entrance Station

DRIVING TOURS
★ Teton Park Road
20 MILES

From Jackson Lake Junction in the north to Moose in the south, the **Teton Park Road** (20 miles, May-Oct.) gives up-close views of the Teton Mountains. The road (called the Inside Road by locals) has wildlife-watching, but **closes in winter** from Signal Mountain Lodge to Taggart Lake Trailhead.

From the Craig Thomas Discovery & Visitor Center at Moose, start by driving north on Teton Park Road. Just past the Moose Entrance Station, turn right to see the **Menor's Ferry Historic District** and the small log **Chapel of the Transfiguration.** Continuing north for 3.7 miles leads to a turnoff where you can look straight up at the small **Teton Glacier.** In about three miles, stop at **South Jenny Lake** to walk from the visitors center to the lake. Continuing north on Teton Park Road, stop at the **Mt. Moran turnout** to examine the black dike and two small glaciers in its upper cliffs.

Inside-Outside Loop
43 MILES

The **Inside and Outside Roads** (Teton Park Rd. and U.S. Hwy. 26/89/191, 43 miles, 90 min. without stops, 4 hours with stops) link together in a scenic loop. Begin at the **Craig Thomas Discovery & Visitor Center** to drive the Inside Road, stopping for wildlife and sightseeing. At Jackson Lake Junction, turn east for one mile to the **Oxbow Bend Turnout.** Use binoculars to help in spotting animals and birds in the wildlife-rich wetlands. Continue east to Moran Junction and turn south onto the Outside Road. About 5.5 miles south, turn right to see the **Cunningham Cabin Historic Site.** Stop at several pullouts: **Snake River Overlook** to see the riffles of the 13th-largest river in the country, **Teton Point or Glacier View Turnouts** for panoramic mountain views, and **Blacktail Ponds Overlook** for wildlife-watching. At Moose Junction, turn right to return to the visitors center. Drive judiciously on the Outside Road. It has a reputation as a wildlife slaughter zone. To protect wildlife, speed limits drop to 45 mph at night.

Jenny Lake Road
4 MILES

The tour of **Jenny Lake Road** (4 miles, 15 min., May-Oct.) starts at North Jenny Lake. Stop at the Cathedral Group Pullout for views of three peaks: the Grand, Owen, and Teewinot. Past the String Lake Junction, Jenny Lake Road becomes one-way as it passes **Jenny Lake Lodge.** For a second peek at the Cathedral Group, go to **Jenny Lake Overlook**. When Jenny Lake is glassy, the viewpoint yields stunning photos of the water reflecting the peaks. Photos are best in the morning here. The drive loops back to Teton Park Road north of South Jenny Lake.

Antelope Flats
10 MILES

Through a flat, sagebrush plain, a loop on dirt and paved roads tours **Antelope Flats** (10 miles, 30 min.), a place of park history with wildlife-watching especially good around sunrise or dusk. Late 1800s ranches and homesteads left irrigation ditches, old buildings, and barns in **Mormon Row,** where you

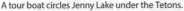

A tour boat circles Jenny Lake under the Tetons.

can take a self-guided tour. The southeast corner of the loop goes through the small burg of **Kelly,** with a population of 130 residents. Access the loop from the Gros Ventre River Road or Antelope Flats Road, both turnoffs from U.S. Highway 26/89/191. In spring, see newborn bison calves and pronghorn fawns, and in fall, watch large herds of elk cross into the National Elk Refuge to the south. Mormon Row and Antelope Flats Roads close November-April, but Gros Ventre River Road stays open year-round.

★ Moose-Wilson Road
8 MILES

Moose-Wilson Road (8 miles, 30 min., mid-May-Oct.) snuggles into the southern base of the Teton Mountains between the Granite Canyon and Moose Entrance Stations. The skinny, shoulder-less paved and gravel road has bumps, potholes, and curves. It shrinks to almost one lane in places (no vehicles over 23 feet long or trailers). Spot moose and birds at **Sawmill Ponds** and visit the **Laurance S. Rockefeller Preserve** in the road's central stretch. On busy days, the road sees about 1,000 vehicles. Drive slowly; collisions happen far too often. This corridor serves as a summer shortcut between Teton Village and

Jenny Lake Overlook

Jenny Lake, but the park plans to start a queuing system that only permits 200 vehicles at a time on the road. Go early in the day or late in the evening to avoid long lines. Expect reconstruction projects on the road through 2020, which will add a new entrance north of Moose.

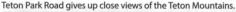

Teton Park Road gives up close views of the Teton Mountains.

Sights

INSIDE ROAD

The Inside Road (Teton Park Road) runs 20 miles from the Jackson Lake Junction south to the Moose Entrance Station. The road is open seasonally May-October.

The Teton Range

The Teton Mountains run north-south parallel to the valley of Jackson Hole. The mountains are dominated by the highest peaks, called the Cathedral Group: Grand Teton, Mt. Owen, Teewinot, Middle Teton, and South Teton. At 13,770 feet, the Grand Teton is the tallest peak in the range. Mt. Moran, at 12,605, is the most prominent peak north of the Cathedral Group. About 40 miles long, the range is the newest of the Rocky Mountains.

Enjoy the range by learning a few of its bigger landmarks; the park newspaper supplies a panorama of the peaks and identifies their summits. In summer, use binoculars to view the peaks from Mt. Moran Turnout (north of North Jenny Lake), Cathedral Group Turnout (on North Jenny Lake Rd.), or Teton Glacier Turnout on Teton Park Road. You will see tiny glaciers, black vertical dikes, and myriad toothy spires. In winter, stop at the Glacier View or Teton Point Turnouts (Hwy. 26/89/191). For photographers, sunrise photos will light up the peaks, while sunset colors will backlight their shadows. Trails up Cascade Canyon (to Hurricane Pass) or Death Canyon (to Fox Creek Pass) climb into the backbone of the mountain range along the Teton Crest Trail.

★ GRAND TETON

Like the Matterhorn, the Grand Teton spirals up into a pinnacle. You can spot its 13,770-foot pointed summit from almost everywhere in Jackson Hole. Carved by erosion from ice, water, and wind, the spire commands the highest point in the Tetons. A lure for climbers, the Grand serves as a notch in the belts of mountaineers who summit its vertical cliffs. Other than climbing, the best ways to enjoy the peak are hiking the Paintbrush Canyon-Cascade Canyon Loop, catching the sunrise glow on camera from Jenny Lake, and eyeballing its crags through binoculars at the Teton Glacier Turnout on Teton Park Road.

The Potholes

Best seen from Teton Park Road, The Potholes (Potholes Pullout north of Jenny Lake, road closed in winter) are glacial kettles. (Kettles are large depressions or potholes in the landscape.) They are evidence of a huge 2,000-foot-deep glacier that once covered Jackson Hole. As the glacier melted, pieces broke off, and where those chunks melted, they created kettles; some are filled with trees, like the one at the pullout. The Potholes Pullout is located on the south side of the road, between Signal Mountain and North Jenny Lake.

Teton Glacier ✓

Peek at Teton Glacier below the north face of Grand Teton at the Teton Glacier Turnout on Teton Park Road (2.8 miles south of Jenny Lake and 4 miles north of Moose). The ice field is the park's largest remaining glacier and one of 12 that are named. Less than 53 acres in size, it is shrinking annually. Its terminal moraine is visible below the glacier, marking the original size where it deposited rock debris. By mid-summer, when the blanket of the past winter's snow melts, its crevasses are visible.

★ JENNY LAKE

Tucked below the Grand Teton, Jenny Lake is a placid place of beauty. The two-mile-long, 250-foot-deep lake was created behind a moraine in a glacial depression. The lake beckons photographers and artists to capture its grandeur, but it's also a place where visitors can lodge or camp and spend days hiking, biking, boating, paddling, fishing, swimming, climbing, backpacking, and wildlife-watching. South Jenny Lake houses a small visitors center, ranger station, store, and campground, and has scenic boat tours.

Jenny Lake Historic District contains a homestead cabin that serves as the ranger station. The interpretive plaza orients you to the mountains; lake trails range from short, easy jaunts to long, uphill grunts with immense views. To see the lake, walk the 0.5-mile, wheelchair-accessible Discovery Loop from the interpretive plaza. It takes in two overlooks—Outlet and Big Lake—and accesses stairs down to Rock Beach for wading. South of Outlet Overlook, Aspen Overlook and Gateway Plaza lead to the boat dock for tours, shuttles, and paddling rentals.

Jenny Lake

A moose feeds along the Moose-Wilson Road.

MOOSE
Menor's Ferry

Located on a spur road north of the Moose Entrance Station, **Menor's Ferry Historic District** preserves buildings from the 1890s. Its location at a narrowing of the Snake River allowed for a ferry to cart people back and forth. In summer, rangers guide 45-minute walks through the district each afternoon, usually meeting at 2:30pm at the general store. You can also do a self-guided tour of the cabins, barns, smokehouse, farm implements, wagons, a replica ferry (rideable in late summer), and a **general store** (operated by Grand Teton Association, 307/739-3606, www.grandtetonpark.org, 9am-4:30pm daily late May-late Sept.). The **Maud Noble Cabin** hosted some of the 1923 talks to create Grand Teton National Park. Menor's Ferry Historic District has coverage for free cell phone tours of the area.

Chapel of the Transfiguration

On the road to Menor's Ferry, a small log chapel was built to frame a view of the

Jenny Lake Area

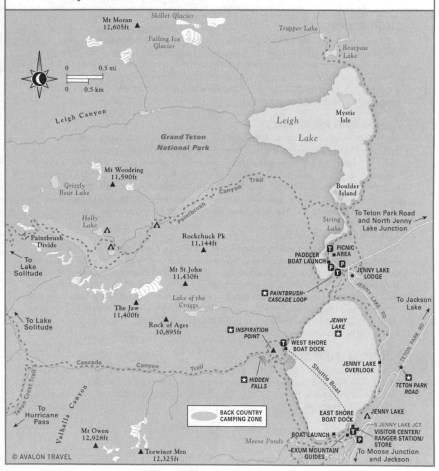

Mt Moran
12,605ft ▲

Skillet Glacier

Falling Ice
Glacier

Trapper Lake

Bearpaw
Lake

Leigh Canyon

0   0.5 mi

0   0.5 km

Leigh
Lake

Mystic
Isle

Grand Teton
National Park

Mt Woodring
11,590ft ▲

Grizzly
Bear Lake

Paintbrush   Canyon   Trail

Boulder
Island

To Teton Park Road
and North Jenny
Lake Junction

Holly
Lake

String
Lake

Paintbrush
Divide

Rockchuck Pk
11,144ft ▲

PICNIC
AREA

PADDLER
BOAT LAUNCH

To
Lake
Solitude

Mt St John
11,430ft ▲

JENNY LAKE
LODGE

To Jackson
Lake

★ PAINTBRUSH-
CASCADE LOOP

The Jaw
11,400ft ▲

Lake of the
Craggs

JENNY
LAKE ★

To Lake
Solitude

Rock of Ages
10,895ft ▲

★ INSPIRATION
POINT

WEST SHORE
BOAT DOCK

JENNY LAKE
OVERLOOK

Cascade   Canyon   Trail

Shuttle Boat

★ TETON PARK
ROAD

★ HIDDEN
FALLS

To
Hurricane
Pass

BACK COUNTRY
CAMPING ZONE

EAST SHORE
BOAT DOCK

JENNY LAKE

S JENNY LAKE JCT

Mt Owen
12,928ft ▲

Moose Ponds

BOAT LAUNCH

VISITOR CENTER/
RANGER STATION/
STORE

© AVALON TRAVEL

▲ Teewinot Mtn
12,325ft

EXUM MOUNTAIN
GUIDES

To Moose Junction
and Jackson

Cathedral Group of the Teton Mountains. Built in 1925 to serve homesteaders in Jackson Hole, the 50-foot-long **Chapel of the Transfiguration** substituted one of its stained-glass windows for a clear window over the altar that looks squarely at the Grand Teton. **St. John's Episcopal Church** (http://stjohnsjackson.diowy.org) in Jackson owns the building, which is listed on the National Register of Historic Places. Services are held Sunday mornings in summer. The chapel is open for visiting, but please be respectful of those using it for worship.

The Murie Ranch

Located at the north end of Moose-Wilson Road, the **Murie Center** (1 Murie Ranch Rd., Moose, 307/739-2246, www.muriecenter.org, 9am-5pm, free) is a National Historic Landmark where the Murie family had their 77-acre ranch. The Muries, a family of four

Fun for Kids

JUNIOR RANGERS

Kids can learn about Grand Teton National Park and earn a Junior Ranger patch or badge. Stop by a visitors center to pick up *The Grand Adventure*, the Junior Ranger activity guide. To receive the patch or badge, kids need to complete the activities in the guide geared toward their age group, attend a ranger-led program, and go on a hike. (A second ranger-led program can take the place of the hike.) Once completed, kids bring the guide to a visitors center to receive their patch or badge and be sworn in as Junior Rangers.

CAMPS AND PROGRAMS

The **Teton Science School** (700 Coyote Canyon Rd., Jackson, WY, 877/404-6626, www.teton-science.org, year-round) offers multiday summer camps and single-day programs for kids. Children from kindergarten through grade 12 can participate in summer camps that take place on the campus north of Kelly or at various locations in the park. Some programs use hiking, canoeing, and camping as vehicles for learning about the science of the Tetons and wildlife. Programs are hands-on and experiential rather than classroom based; some emphasize outdoor skills. The school also runs family adventures based on seasonal wildlife activity.

KID-FRIENDLY HIKES

For successful hiking trips with kids, take water and snacks, even if the hike is short. Kids also should carry their own packs as soon as possible, even if it only holds a windbreaker. Rewards of ice cream after a good hike are always welcome, as is swimming in lakes on a hot day. While kids often don't care about scenery, they do love water, wildlife, and spotting animal tracks. Plenty of short trails offer good destinations for kids. For kids ages 3-6, walk **String Lake Loop** or **Hidden Falls** (via boat shuttle), **Taggart Lake**, or **Phelps Lake**. For kids ages 7-12, bump up the mileage and difficulty with the **Jenny Lake Loop, Bradley-Taggart Lakes Loop,** and **Phelps Lake Loop.**

YOUNG NATURALISTS

At the **Laurance S. Rockefeller Preserve Center,** kids ages 6-12 can check out a Nature Explorer's Backpack for journaling while exploring trails at the center. Families can also check out naturalist backpacks from the **Craig Thomas Discovery & Visitor Center** for kids' activities while outdoors.

---

conservationists, sought to protect nature for its importance to the human spirit. Today, the center serves as a learning center for Teton Science School. Visitors can pick up a guide on the Muries' front porch for a one-mile walking tour or tour inside one of the ranch cabins with docents (2:30pm Mon.-Fri. in summer).

OUTSIDE ROAD

U.S. Highway 26/89/191 (open year-round) connects the hubs of Moran and Moose, which are 18 miles apart. Access this road from Jackson in the south or via Highway 287 in the north.

Cunningham Cabin Historic Site

Listed on the National Register of Historic Places, the **Cunningham Cabin Historic Site** offers a glimpse into the original homesteads in Jackson Hole. Built in 1888, the log cabin served as a home, smithy, and barn for the small Cunningham ranch. Featuring a sod roof and two rooms connected by a breezeway, the cabin is the only standing building from pre-park days. A 0.3-mile self-guided interpretive walk tours other ranch foundations. The ranch is accessed via a short road marked with a sign.

Moose Area

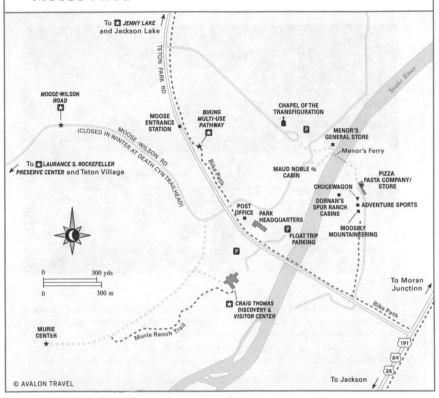

To ★ JENNY LAKE and Jackson Lake

TETON PARK RD

MOOSE-WILSON ROAD ★

MOOSE ENTRANCE STATION

MOOSE-WILSON RD (CLOSED IN WINTER AT DEATH CYN TRAILHEAD)

To ★ LAURANCE S. ROCKEFELLER PRESERVE CENTER and Teton Village

BIKING MULTI-USE PATHWAY ★

Bike Path

Snake River

CHAPEL OF THE TRANSFIGURATION

P

MENOR'S GENERAL STORE

Menor's Ferry

MAUD NOBLE CABIN

PIZZA PASTA COMPANY/ STORE

CHUCKWAGON

DORNAN'S SPUR RANCH CABINS

ADVENTURE SPORTS

POST OFFICE

PARK HEADQUARTERS

P

FLOAT TRIP PARKING

MOOSELY MOUNTAINEERING

P

0   300 yds

0   300 m

To Moran Junction

Bike Path

★ CRAIG THOMAS DISCOVERY & VISITOR CENTER

MURIE CENTER ★

Murie Ranch Trail

191

89

26

© AVALON TRAVEL

To Jackson

The Chapel of Transfiguration makes the most of its setting.

Teton Facts

Lake Solitude

While glaciers helped carve the dramatic spires, freeze-thawing water and winds continue to shape the pinnacles. If that's all there was, the Tetons would be like many other high peaks in the Rocky Mountains—but they are unique. How can you best explore these peaks?

- The highest peak in the Teton Mountains is the **Grand Teton** at 13,770 feet. You can climb it, but most visitors just gaze at it from trails, Jenny Lake Boat Tours, or Teton Park Road.

- Twelve peaks in the Teton Range stretch up to 12,000 feet or more (you can climb all of these).

- Ten glaciers that formed during the Little Ice Age still cling to the Teton Mountains. See the 53-acre **Teton Glacier** from Teton Glacier Turnout on Teton Park Road.

- Part of what makes the Tetons so spectacular is their prominence, or the amount of land jutting above the valley floor. It's close to 7,000 feet. When the Teton fault started shoving the peaks up in elevation, instead of creating foothills, the easternmost layer of rock fell, forming a gigantic valley, or hole, known today as Jackson Hole. Take in the prominence between Jackson Hole and the Teton summits by climbing, hiking, or sightseeing from the Inside and Outside Roads.

- Seven **moraine lakes** tuck at the base of the Teton Range. You can drive to Jenny Lake and String Lake, but you'll need to hike to reach Leigh, Bradley, Taggart, or Phelps Lakes.

- The Teton Mountains cradle more than 100 alpine lakes. Some of them, such as **Solitude** or **Avalanche,** can be reached by trail.

- More than 200 miles of trails wander through the Teton Mountains. Hikers can ascend four of its canyons: **Paintbrush, Cascade, Death,** and **Granite.**

- Be savvy with how you refer to the mountains. Rather than calling them the "Grand Tetons," use the proper name for the range, which is the **"Teton Mountains"** or **"Tetons."** The Grand Teton refers to the highest peak in the range.

the 1888 Cunningham Cabin

Schwabachers Landing

Bring binoculars and spotting scopes to **Schwabachers Landing** for wildlife-watching (best in early morning or late evening). The beaver ponds and slough provide outstanding birding and moose habitat; photographers frequently shoot sunrise reflection photos of the Teton Mountains. The 1.1-mile paved and potholed gravel Schwabacher Road accesses the landing from Highway 26/89/191 between Glacier View and Teton Point Turnouts.

Snake River Overlook

Through Jackson Hole, the Snake River winds from Jackson Lake Dam to where it exits the national park south of Moose. The river sees high water in June, but by August, a multitude of islands and gravel bars emerge. The river corridor provides prime habitat for songbirds, bald eagles, great blue herons, raptors, bears, bison, and ungulates. From the **Snake River Overlook**, you can walk along the bluff to snap photos of the winding river channel below the Teton Mountains. Find the lighting on the Tetons best in morning.

Blacktail Ponds Overlook

Stop at **Blacktail Ponds Overlook** with a pair of binoculars or a spotting scope for wildlife-watching (best in early morning or late evening). Moose often feed in the ponds, and the habitat is good for osprey, waterfowl, and songbirds. Active beavers maintain the dams, which keep the ponds in water. The overlook is located 1.3 miles north of Moose Junction.

Antelope Flats Road

Antelope Flats actually refers to the entire plateau (not just the road) and offers outstanding wildlife-watching for bison, pronghorn, moose, coyote, and raptors such as northern harriers or American kestrels. Due to its location near the National Elk Refuge, elk migrate through in spring and fall. It's also a good area in spring to spot bison and pronghorn newborns. The best wildlife-watching is in the early morning or late evening. The road also provides access to scenic Mormon Row.

★ Mormon Row

Located in the southeast corner of the park, **Mormon Row** (off Antelope Flats Road) is a treat for history buffs, photographers, and wildlife fans. The tract was originally a Mormon ranch settlement that started in the 1890s and grew to 27 homesteads. Today, Mormon Row is on the National Register of

Historic cabins and barns are in scenic locations on Mormon Row.

Historic Places. It retains six clusters of buildings, one ruin, and the famous Moulton barn that appears in the foreground of so many photos of the Grand Teton. Even amateur photographers can capture impressive images of historic buildings backdropped by the Teton Range. Pick up a self-guided tour brochure near the pink house.

Recreation

DAY HIKES

Hiking in the Teton Mountains yields a mix of mountainous canyons, alpine basins, and high passes. With the exception of paths that circle the moraine lakes along the base, all trails climb up—seriously up! Visitors coming from sea level will feel the altitude and experience heavy breathing. Slow your hiking pace to adjust to a steady rhythm, rather than stopping every 10 feet to catch your breath. Drink plenty of water (more than you would at home), as hydration helps ward off headaches and nausea from altitude sickness.

Most lower-elevation trails along the base of the Tetons are snow-free by **late May,** but trails that crest high passes above 9,000 feet may be buried in snow until **late July.** Until then, ice axes are necessary for safe travel. Accidents and fatalities in the Tetons are due to improper use (or no use) of ice axes when traversing steep snowfields. Weather conditions for high-elevation hikes are usually best mid-July-August, but expect afternoon thundershowers and lightning. By September, snow returns to the high passes.

Guided Hikes

Grand Teton National Park does not permit guided hikes led by concessionaires, but **naturalist rangers** lead short hikes (2-3 hours, 2-4 miles, daily in summer, free) to various scenic destinations along the base of the Teton Mountains. These hikes are loaded with interpretive stops and are great for families. Current schedules are listed in the park newspaper available at entrance stations and visitors centers. Reservations are only needed for the hike to Hidden Falls and Inspiration Point (limit of 25 people, boat shuttle fee) and can be made at Jenny Lake Visitor Center.

South Grand Teton Hikes

Trail	Effort	Distance	Duration	Features
String and Leigh Lakes	Easy	3.7 mi rt	2 hr	lakes, scenery
Taggart and Bradley Lakes	Easy to moderate	3-5.9 mi rt	2-4 hr	lakes, scenery
Phelps Lake	Easy to moderate	1.8-9.9 mi	2-5 hr	lake, scenery
Jenny Lake Loop	Moderate	7.1 mi rt	3.5 hr	lake, scenery
Hidden Falls and Inspiration Point	Moderately strenuous	2.4-7.2 mi rt	1.5-4 hr	waterfall, scenery
Amphitheater Lake and Garnet Canyon	Strenuous	10.1 mi rt	6 hr	lakes, scenery
Granite Canyon and Marion Lake	Strenuous	11.8-18.5 mi rt	7-10 hr	lake, scenery
Cascade Canyon, Lake Solitude, and Hurricane Pass	Strenuous	13.6-23.8 mi rt	7-13 hr	lakes, scenery, high pass
Paintbrush-Cascade Loop	Very strenuous	13-19.2 mi rt	7-13 hr	lakes, scenery, high pass
Death Canyon, Static Peak Divide, and Fox Creek Pass	Very strenuous	16.3-18.4 mi rt	9-12 hr	scenery, high pass

Inside Road
TAGGART AND BRADLEY LAKES

Distance: 3-5.9 miles round-trip
Duration: 2-4 hours
Elevation change: 400-900 feet
Effort: easy to moderate
Trailhead: Taggart Lake Trailhead off Teton Park Road between Jenny Lake and Moose

Two lower-elevation lakes cower around 7,000 feet at the base of Avalanche and Garnet Canyons. For a shorter three-mile hike, go to Taggart Lake and back. It's scenic, but the longer 5.9-mile loop adds on Bradley Lake, where you can stare straight up at Grand Teton. When the lake is glassy, the Grand reflects like a mirror. Get an early start in order to claim a parking spot at this popular trailhead. Anglers fish both lakes, and on hot days, both lakes make good swimming holes.

A hiker returns from Bradley Lake.

Taggart and Bradley Lakes

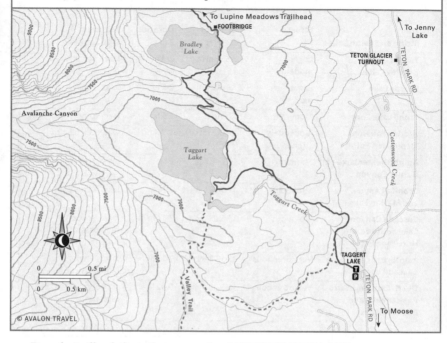

From the trailhead, the trail curves north to cross a tumbling stream before ascending through conifers and meadows growing on glacial moraines to a **signed junction** at 1.1 miles. If you are planning to hike both lakes, you will loop back to this junction. To reach **Taggart,** turn left to hike 0.5 mile to the lake. Explore the small peninsula to the south for a place to enjoy the water and views.

To continue the loop to **Bradley Lake,** circle north around the shore of Taggart Lake to climb two switchbacks that crest a forested glacial moraine. After dropping to a **signed junction,** turn left to visit Bradley Lake. Beaches flank the east shore while the north side contains a footbridge crossing the outlet. After the lake, retrace your steps back to the last junction and take the fork heading left to climb over the moraine again and complete the loop to the first junction to return to the trailhead.

AMPHITHEATER LAKE AND GARNET CANYON

Distance: 10.1 miles round-trip

Duration: 6 hours

Elevation change: 2,966 feet

Effort: strenuous

Trailhead: Lupine Meadows Trailhead off Teton Park Road south of Jenny Lake

At 9,714 feet, Surprise and Amphitheater Lakes cluster 0.2 mile apart in a high, narrow subalpine basin on an eastern ridge extending from Grand Teton. Since this out-and-back trail provides access for many technical climbing routes, you may see people loaded with ropes, helmets, and gear on the Garnet Canyon spur. Start early, as the sun-soaked climb can be hot midday.

Begin by hiking 1.7 miles on a trail that ascends a moraine ridge to the junction with the **Taggart Lake Trail.** At the junction, continue uphill to follow switchbacks that climb

Amphitheater Lake and Garnet Canyon

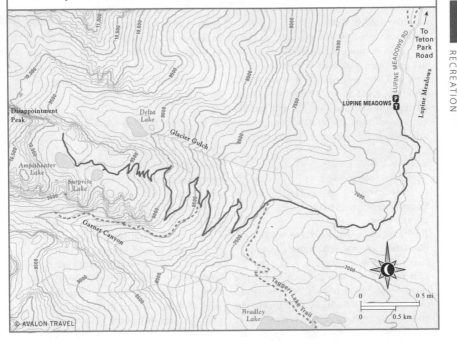

steeply on the open, east-facing slope. Views of Jackson Hole get bigger the higher you go; Bradley Lake is below to the south.

After the fourth switchback, a trail cuts left into **Garnet Canyon** for 1.1 miles until it fizzles out in a boulder field. From there, it offers good views of Middle Teton, the park's third-highest peak. (Adding on this spur increases the total distance by 2.2 miles round-trip.)

To reach the lakes, follow the switchbacks as they climb through a broken forest of white-bark pines and whortleberry. Nearing the lake basin, look up for views of the Grand Teton. At **Surprise Lake,** descend to the shore and enjoy the lake, or circle the lake's east shore to its outlet to overlook Jackson Hole. The main trail passes above the north side of Surprise Lake to climb into the small hanging valley housing **Amphitheater Lake,** tucked at the base of Disappointment Peak. After the lake, a rough trail climbs north 0.2 mile to grab a

Amphitheater Lake tucks into a narrow rocky bowl.

partial view of the Grand, glacial moraine, and immense cliffs.

Jenny Lake Area

For hikes in the Jenny Lake area, you can trim mileage with a **boat shuttle** (307/734-9227, www.jennylakeboating.com, 7am-7pm daily mid-May-Sept., shorter hours in shoulder seasons, $15 adults, $8 kids round-trip; $9 adults, $6 kids one-way). Reservations are not required; just show up at the east- or west-side dock. Shuttles run every 10-15 minutes.

JENNY LAKE LOOP

Distance: 7.1 miles round-trip
Duration: 3.5 hours
Elevation change: 456 feet
Effort: moderate
Trailhead: String Lake Trailhead or Jenny Lake Village. Plan to arrive early to claim a parking spot at the popular trailheads.

This trail loops completely around Jenny Lake; part of the path is paved near the visitors center, but most of the trail is dirt. Unless you hike in early morning or late evening, expect to meet crowds in midsummer. All trail junctions are well signed; unsigned spur trails cut to the lakeshore for views or fishing.

From the **Jenny Lake Visitor Center,** take the north trail heading to Big Lake Overlook. From there, turn right to circle the lake counterclockwise. You'll pass Rock Beach, a short **spur trail** (for those staying at Jenny Lake Campground), and eventually **Jenny Lake Overlook** as the trail cuts 3 miles between the lake and North Jenny Lake Drive.

When the trail reaches **String Lake Trailhead,** head 0.3 mile west, crossing a bridge over the String Lake outlet stream. At the junction, head left for 1.7 miles above the north shore of Jenny Lake through the remains of the 1999 Alder Fire. You'll pass large boulders (glacial erratics) before reaching multiple trail junctions. Continue straight as trails junction to **Cascade Canyon,** the boat dock (2 trails), **Hidden Falls,** and **Inspiration Point.** After crossing Cascade Creek on a **wooden bridge,** you'll reach another junction. Continue straight for 1.5 miles south along the shore of Jenny Lake, passing two junctions with the upper traverse followed by two junctions for **Moose Pond Loop;** stay left at all junctions. Pass the boat launch to reach the **bridge** crossing the Jenny Lake outlet at the tour boat dock.

★ HIDDEN FALLS AND INSPIRATION POINT

Distance: 2.4-7.2 miles round-trip
Duration: 1.5-4 hours
Elevation change: 1,250 feet
Effort: moderately strenuous
Trailhead: Jenny Lake Visitor Center

Hidden Falls, a 200-foot tumbler in Cascade Canyon, and Inspiration Point, a rocky knoll at 7,257 feet, squeeze between Mt. Teewinot and Mt. St. John. Given the point's perch, the scope of views from the summit lives up to its name. You'll look straight down on the blue waters of Jenny Lake, up to the peaks on both sides, and across Jackson Hole to the Gros Ventre Mountains. Hordes of hikers clog this trail, except in early morning or late in the day. The $18 million Jenny Lake project upgraded the eroded trails in 2015-2017 with 5,000 linear feet of stonework. The boat shuttle (fee) reduces this hike to a 2.4-mile loop from the west boat dock.

From the **visitor center,** head west toward the **boat dock** and cross the **bridge** at the outlet of Jenny Lake at Cottonwood Creek. Continue 0.9 mile west along the south shore of Jenny Lake, passing the boat launch and two junctions for **Moose Pond Loop.** At the second Moose Pond Loop junction, take either the upper or lower trails to reach Hidden Falls Trail; the lower trail walks 1.5 mile along the scenic lakeshore. Before reaching the Chasm Bridge over Cascade Creek, you'll come to a junction for **Hidden Falls.** Turn left to ascend the south side of Cascade Creek, passing one of the oldest trees in the park. At the next junction, continue straight to reach the spur that goes to Hidden Falls

hikers on the trail to Inspiration Point

STRING AND LEIGH LAKES

Distance: 3.7 miles round-trip
Duration: 2 hours
Elevation change: 325 feet
Effort: easy
Trailhead: String Lake Trailhead from North Jenny Lake

This trail circles String Lake and takes in the southern tip of Leigh Lake; it's a less crowded loop than Jenny Lake. Hike counterclockwise to get the big views down the western side of the loop.

Start from the **String Lake Trailhead** and hike 1.4 miles north along the forested eastern shore of String Lake. Stop frequently along the shallow sand-bottomed lake to look for moose and waterfowl. To the north, Mt. Moran rises into view while Teewinot Mountain pokes above the trees southward. At the south end of Leigh Lake, a trail junction splits right and continues up the east side of Leigh Lake to Bearpaw Lake. Stay straight instead to follow a **short spur** to the edge of the deeper **Leigh Lake** for the views.

Return to the junction and head west to cross the **bridge** at the rocky outlet of Leigh Lake. Enjoy the view of Boulder Island from the bridge, then continue westward as the trail climbs 0.7 mile through a lodgepole forest to a second **junction**. Turn left to break out of the woods and onto the open slopes of **Rockchuck Peak** and Mt. St. John with views of Teewinot Mountain. The trail gradually descends 1.6 miles to the foot of String Lake where it meets the **Jenny Lake Trail.** Turn left and cross the **bridge** at the outlet of String Lake to return to the String Lake Trailhead.

Hikers can add on to this trail with a round-trip walk to Leigh Lake (1.8 miles) or by going past Leigh Lake to Bearpaw Lake (8 miles round-trip).

★ PAINTBRUSH-CASCADE LOOP

Distance: 13 miles round-trip to Holly Lake; 17 miles round-trip to Paintbrush Divide; 19.2 miles round-trip for Paintbrush-Cascade Loop.
Duration: 7-13 hours

Overlook. Hikers wanting to skip Inspiration Point can drop back one junction to loop across Cascade Creek on the middle bridge and descend the creek's north side to the **Chasm Bridge** over a frothy spillway and the return trail.

To continue to Inspiration Point from the overlook, cross the two upper **bridges** below the falls for more views, then climb four south-facing switchbacks to **Inspiration Point**. (The slope can get hot in mid-summer; mornings are best for hiking to the point.) At Inspiration Point, plenty of other trails cut off to various viewpoints and places for lunch. From the point, retrace your steps back to the visitor center or loop west to connect with the **Cascade Canyon Horse Trail** and descend the north side of the canyon toward Jenny Lake. After reaching the **Jenny Lake Trail**, turn south, passing two boat dock junctions and crossing the lower bridge over Cascade Creek to reach the junction for the lakeshore trail back to the visitor center. Retrace your earlier steps.

Elevation change: 4,350 feet

Effort: very strenuous

Trailhead: String Lake Trailhead at North Jenny Lake

The Paintbrush-Cascade Loop is a trail for long-distance hikers and backpackers. Spectacular scenery, wildlife, and in-your-face views of the Grand Teton are only a few of its rewards. Crossing through multiple ecosystems, the grueling route climbs Paintbrush Canyon to Holly Lake, then crests the 10,720-foot Paintbrush Divide to drop to Lake Solitude before connecting with Cascade Canyon for the descent back to the trailhead. Until late July, you may need an ice ax for crossing the divide. For those who only want to explore part of the route, Holly Lake (13 miles, 2,600 vertical feet) and Paintbrush Divide (17 miles round-trip, 4,350 vertical feet) make outstanding destinations in their own right. For hiking the full loop, plan to depart at dawn for maximum daylight.

From the trailhead, follow the path up the east side of **String Lake.** At the junction at **Leigh Lake,** turn left and cross the rocky stream. At the next junction, turn right to circle around the north side of Rockchuck Peak and climb into **Paintbrush Canyon.** The trail goes through conifer forests interrupted by giant talus fields and avalanche paths before switchbacking up through wildflower meadows and boulders to crest into a hanging valley. Listen for the "eeep" of pikas that live around the boulders. At the next trail junction, go right to **Holly Lake** or straight for a more direct route to Paintbrush Divide.

The trail to Holly Lake ascends through broken meadows to reach the idyllic alpine lake that tucks into a tight cirque filled with wildflower meadows and talus slopes. A small point on the southwest shore offers a place to relax and enjoy the scenery. From the lake, an **unmarked path** heads directly up to join the route to **Paintbrush Divide.** The trail climbs steadily 1.7 miles upward, leaving the small pockets of trees behind and entering alpine scree slopes, where steep snow can linger late into summer. After passing the junction to **Grizzly Bear Lake,** the trail swings north across the slope to switchback steeply under a cliff face and pop out at the summit of Paintbrush Divide. The trail trots along the pass, soaking up views in both directions.

To continue on the full loop to Cascade Canyon, follow the trail as it descends 2.4 miles of switchbacks to **Lake Solitude**, a larger turquoise lake flanked by wildflower meadows in August. The Grand Teton comes into view to the south. From the lake, the trail

Hikers climb Paintbrush Divide after a fall snow.

heads 2.4 miles through meadows straight toward the Grand before dropping into the forest to reach the fork in **Cascade Canyon.** From the fork, descend 6.8 miles and 1,950 feet via **Cascade Canyon Trail,** turning north at the base to skirt Jenny Lake back to the String Lake parking lot.

CASCADE CANYON, LAKE SOLITUDE, AND HURRICANE PASS

Distance: 13.6 miles round-trip to Fork of Cascade Canyon; 18.4 miles round-trip to Lake Solitude; 23.8 miles round-trip to Hurricane Pass
Duration: 7-13 hours
Elevation change: 1,950-4,200 feet
Effort: strenuous to extremely strenuous
Trailhead: Jenny Lake Visitor Center or String Lake parking lot

Cascade Canyon Trail ascends a U-shaped glaciated canyon on the north side of Grand Teton. During the ascent, perspective changes on the Cathedral Group (Teewinot, Grand Teton, Mt. Owen), and lower-elevation cliffs and spires often occlude their summits. Starting at String Lake parking lot instead of Jenny Lake Visitor Center reduces total round-trip distance by 0.6 mile.

To ascend Cascade Canyon from either trailhead, circle around **Jenny Lake** to the west side. Start climbing via **Hidden Lake and Inspiration Point** or take the horse trail up the north side of the canyon. Once in the canyon, the number of hikers thins on the climb through wildflower meadows and forest to reach the fork. During the ascent, the trail contacts Cascade Creek at various points; look for harlequin ducks or moose in early summer. The trail also cuts across countless avalanche paths where bears feed. Most hikers go 6.8 miles to the Fork of Cascade Canyon where the creek splits in two directions. The turn-around point is not a summit or lake destination, but the trail is nonetheless scenic.

From the Fork of Cascade Canyon, take the **North Fork of Cascade Creek** to go 2.4 miles to **Lake Solitude.** Ascending through conifers and avalanche slopes, the trail eventually breaks into meadows. Broken forests and meadows flank the U-shaped, glacially carved valley that cradles the lake at 9,035 feet. Views southward stare straight at the Grand. The total elevation gain to the lake is 2,955 feet.

To reach **Hurricane Pass** at 10,400 feet on the Teton Crest, follow the **South Fork of Cascade Creek** 5.1 miles to climb through broken conifer forests as the trail arcs below Grand Teton. Eventually, the trail leaves tree line in favor of scree fields, wildflower

Hurricane Pass takes in Grand, Middle, and South Tetons.

meadows, and glacial moraine. As the trail switchbacks to the pass, Schoolroom Glacier comes into view along with its milky turquoise lake tucked inside its moraine. The total climb of 4,200 feet yields a stunning in-your-face view of the Grand, Middle, and South Tetons.

Moose

The park service has proposed a queuing system to limit 200 vehicles at a time on the **Moose-Wilson Road** (no RVs or trailers). Once implemented, this will affect reaching trailheads on this road. Enter the road by 8am to avoid long waits and to claim a parking spot in the limited trailhead lots. Death Canyon Trailhead is scheduled to undergo reconstruction into 2020 to lower the trailhead; this will add one mile (each way) to current trail mileages.

PHELPS LAKE

Distance: 1.8-9.9 miles round-trip
Duration: 2-5 hours
Elevation change: 350-975 feet
Effort: easy to moderate
Trailhead: Laurance S. Rockefeller Preserve Center or Death Canyon Trailhead on Moose-Wilson Road north of Granite Canyon Entrance.
Directions: To reach Death Canyon Trailhead from the signed turnoff, drive one mile on pavement followed by one mile of rugged rock, mud, and dirt road (high-clearance vehicles only). Park at the end of the pavement or at a pullout on the dirt road (add 1 mile to walk the dirt road).

A maze of trails surrounds the low-elevation Phelps Lake in the Laurance S. Rockefeller Preserve, a special area where hiking the trails is more about the experience than reaching destinations. Visiting the preserve's center adds to the hiking experience. Trails circle the lake, which sits at 6,645 feet at the bottom of Open and Death Canyons. From various viewpoints around the lake, hikers are rewarded with stunning views of the Teton Mountains. The lake provides a year-round destination, although you'll need skis or snowshoes in winter.

Phelps Lake

Most hikers opt to park at the **Laurance S. Rockefeller Preserve Center.** Arrive before 9am to claim a parking spot in the small 50-car lot that is designed to limit crowds and create a climate of solitude. If it's full, you'll need to hike via the Death Canyon Trailhead. From the center, you can design your own route through the maze of trails. Junctions are well signed to help in selecting routes. The shortest and easiest route to Phelps Lake is the **Lake Creek-Woodland Trail Loop** (3.1 miles). The loop tours forests and meadows on both sides of a creek, offering opportunities to watch moose. At the lake, enjoy contemplation from several different constructed rock-slab overlooks. The **Aspen Ridge-Boulder Ridge Loop** (5.8 miles) climbs through large talus fields and aspens that shimmer gold in fall to reach Phelps Lake. The longest hike, the **Phelps Lake Loop** (6.6 miles), climbs via Lake Creek to reach the lake and then loops around the lake for a changing perspective on the Teton Mountains.

Phelps Lake and Death Canyon

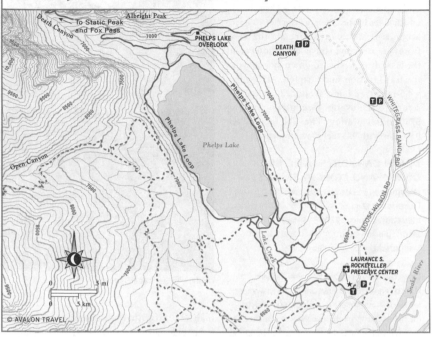

Lake Creek in Laurance S. Rockefeller Preserve

From **Death Canyon Trailhead,** climb 400 feet in 0.9 mile through Douglas firs and aspens to **Phelps Lake Overlook**, which takes in the lake plus the Gros Ventre Mountains. You can appreciate the view from here, or drop to the lake. To descend to the lake, drop westward down switchbacks to a trail junction, and turn left. At the lake, a 4.5-mile trail loops around the lake. The return to the overlook requires climbing 575 feet in elevation. The lake loop tallies 9.9 miles with 975 feet elevation gain.

DEATH CANYON, STATIC PEAK DIVIDE, AND FOX CREEK PASS

Distance: 16.3-18.4 miles round-trip
Duration: 9-12 hours
Elevation change: 2,800-5,250 feet
Effort: very strenuous
Trailhead: Death Canyon Trailhead on Moose-Wilson Road
Directions: To reach Death Canyon Trailhead from the signed turnoff, drive one mile on pavement followed by one mile of rugged rock, mud, and dirt road (high-clearance vehicles only). Park at the end of the pavement or at a pullout on the dirt road (add one mile walking the dirt road).

climbing to Static Peak Divide

With the exception of hiking to Phelps Lake Overlook and Phelps Lake, Death Canyon is a place to go to get away from hordes of people. Destinations require lengthy hikes with major elevation gain. Rewards are huge with views of glaciated canyons, alpine wonderlands, and vertical rock walls. The two main destinations are Static Peak Divide with 5,250 feet of elevation gain, and Fox Creek Pass on the Teton Crest with 18.4 miles of hiking round-trip. Both have knee-pounding returns. Many hikers opt for backpacking for these trails, although strong hikers can do them in a day. You may need ice axes for steep snowfields that linger well into August in the upper elevations.

The climb starts by going through lodgepoles to **Phelps Lake Overlook** and dropping three switchbacks to reach a **junction.** From here, the trail traverses 2.2 miles along the base of **Albright Peak** to squeeze through the boulder-strewn canyon carved by a glacier 15,000 years ago. Flanked by immense rock walls, the trail steepens through avalanche swaths, talus fields, and coniferous forests to reach a **patrol cabin**, listed on the National Register of Historic Places for a 7.9-mile destination.

From the junction at the patrol cabin, take the north fork up the ultra-steep trail that climbs 4.1 miles up the rocky scree and cliff ridge to the 10,790-foot **Static Peak Divide**. Views up-valley take in Fox Pass and Death Canyon Shelf. Another 300 feet in elevation follows a climber's trail to the summit for views of Buck Mountain and Grand Teton. For the 9,570-foot **Fox Creek Pass,** take the south fork to follow the less steep trail through meadows and sparse trees 5.5 miles along Death Canyon Creek. This fork eventually reaches the **Teton Crest** and the pass, with miles of immense meadows below Spearhead Mountain.

Granite Canyon and Marion Lake

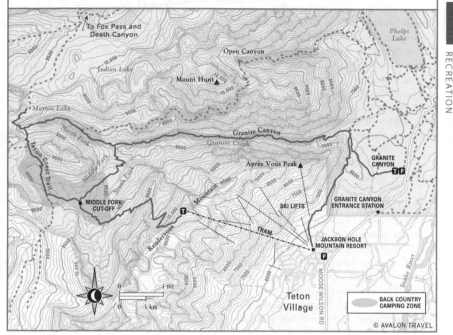

© AVALON TRAVEL

GRANITE CANYON AND MARION LAKE

Distance: 11.8-18.5 miles round-trip

Duration: 7-10 hours

Elevation change: 3,000-4,100 feet

Effort: strenuous

Trailhead: Granite Canyon Trailhead on Moose-Wilson Road; or at Jackson Hole Mountain Resort south of Granite Canyon Entrance.

You can hike 18.5 miles round-trip up Granite Canyon with 3,700 feet of elevation gain to reach Marion Lake on the Teton Crest, or take advantage of riding the tram (fee) outside the park at Jackson Hole Mountain Resort to chop off miles. After riding the tram to the 10,450-foot summit of Rendezvous Mountain, you can hike out to Marion Lake and back, reducing the round-trip distance to 11.8 miles. You can also use the tram for hiking about 12 miles one-way, either up or down 4,100 feet,

through Granite Canyon. Upper elevations can hold snow late into July; an ice ax may be necessary.

From Granite Canyon Trailhead, climb 1.6 miles uphill to reach a signed four-way junction. Continue straight up Granite Canyon 4.7 miles to a second junction. From here, you can ascend 5.2 miles south to the top of the Jackson Hole Mountain Resort tram on the summit of Rendezvous Mountain. Alternatively, hike west 4.1 miles to the Teton Crest Trail. Located 0.6 mile northwest of the junction, Marion Lake snuggles at 9,200 feet against a limestone wall.

From the summit of **Rendezvous Mountain,** start the knee-pounding descent by hiking left along the ridge followed by a service road to reach the boundary of Grand Teton National Park. After crossing into the park, switchback down Rendezvous Mountain to reach the first junction at 3.9

miles, the decision point for Marion Lake or Granite Canyon. To go to **Marion Lake,** turn left on the **Middle Fork Cutoff** to connect with the **Teton Crest Trail.** The route has steep ups and downs through alpine wildflower meadows to reach Marion Lake. To descend into **Granite Canyon** instead, go right to a second junction at 5.6 miles. Turn down-canyon to plunge into the lower-elevation forest, where you'll hit a four-way junction at 10.3 miles. Turn sharp right for 2.4 miles to return to Jackson Hole Mountain Resort or head 1.6 miles down Granite Creek to the Granite Canyon Trailhead if you set up a car shuttle.

BACKPACKING

In the popular backpacking areas of the Tetons, some campsites are assigned while others are designated to a backcountry camping zone. All backpackers are required to carry food in a **bear canister** (permit offices have loaners) and have a backcountry camping **permit.** Apply online (www.recreation.gov, apply early Jan.-mid-May, $45/trip) to guarantee your permit in advance. First-come, first-served permits ($35/trip) are available in person 24 hours before departure. Competition for walk-in permits is high in July and August; a waiting line usually forms at the Jenny Lake Ranger Station or Craig Thomas Discovery & Visitor Center one hour before the 8am opening. For more details, read the backcountry camping brochure online (www.nps.gov/grte).

Paintbrush Canyon-Cascade Canyon
19 MILES

The Paintbrush Canyon-Cascade Canyon loop (19.2 miles) is a stunning three-day backpacking trip. Outstanding scenery, the high Paintbrush Divide, and Lake Solitude highlight the route. **Camp** one night each at Holly Lake (use Upper Paintbrush zone as alternate) and North Fork Cascade zone.

Teton Crest Trail
34-58 MILES

The king of backpacking trips is the **Teton Crest Trail,** a high-elevation romp demanding major elevation gains and descents. The route crosses Fox Creek Pass, Death Canyon Shelf, Mt. Meek Pass, Alaska Basin, Hurricane Pass, and Paintbrush Divide at 9,600-10,720 feet. Traversing the trail north, the central Tetons dominate the scenery. The **38-mile point-to-point** route requires a shuttle between trailheads (Granite Canyon and String Lake), or you can complete the loop by adding on the Valley Trail (20 miles) to link them on foot. Many crest hikers chop off the 4,000-plus foot climb up Granite Canyon by taking the aerial tram (fee) at Jackson Hole Mountain Resort to join the Teton Crest Trail 3.8 miles from Rendezvous Mountain. (Taking the tram reduces total distance to 34 miles.) For the **58-mile point-to-point** trip (5 days), plan to camp at Marian Lake (use Upper Granite as alternate), Death Canyon Shelf, South Fork Cascade, and Upper Paintbrush. For those adding on the Valley Trail, start and end your trip at Jenny Lake and do the lowland trail first with a night at Bradley Lake in order to finish with the stunning trek through the alpine.

CLIMBING

Technical climbing skills are required to reach eight of the Teton summits. If you do not possess the skills, do not attempt to summit peaks; hire a guide service instead. Climbing permits are not required, but you will need a **backcountry camping permit** to camp overnight. Most of the prominent peaks seen from Jackson Hole can be climbed in one extremely long day.

Weather is a consideration. Spring is rainy, accompanied by thawing ice and snow that produce copious rockfall and wet slab avalanches. **Mid-July-August** offers the best weather, but afternoons frequently see sporadic rains and potential lightning. By late August, snow usually starts to appear at high elevations and continues to accumulate through fall. Winter brings heavy snow, frigid temperatures, high winds, and avalanches. Be prepared with the appropriate gear, as even summer can snap into extremes with cold, snow, wind, and rain.

Due to rockfall year-round, climbers must wear helmets. Until late July, ice axes (and the skill to use them correctly) may be necessary in high elevations on steep snowfields to access rock routes.

Grand Teton

Climbing Grand Teton involves 14 miles of hiking and 6,545 feet of ascent and descent. Most climbers take an ultra-long day from the valley floor. More than 35 climbing routes lead to the summit with countless variations, and climbers pioneer new routes almost every year. The most popular and famous route for climbing the Grand is the exposed Upper Exum Ridge, considered a classic in mountaineering.

The fastest time for climbing and descending, at 2:53, was set in 2012 by a climbing ranger. Although controversy surrounds the Grand's first ascent, documentation points to a team of four summiting in 1898. A duo reached the top in 1873, although they may have summited The Enclosure instead. Either way, archaeological evidence indicates that Native Americans most likely reached the summit before both groups. Since 1971, ski and snowboard descents have been added to the record books.

Self-Guided Climbing

Jenny Lake Ranger Station (307/739-3343, 8am-5pm daily June-mid-Sept.) is the only place to go for current climbing conditions and information. The rangers are actual climbers who know the area, risks, difficulties, routes, and what type of experience you need for different climbs. To help you plan climbs, the ranger station has guidebooks, maps, and photographs of peaks with routes. The climbing rangers also update conditions and mountaineering scene information online (www.tetonclimbing.blogspot.com). The ranger station has a voluntary climbing register, too. Check current conditions (307/739-3309) for climbs year-round. Above all, be prepared to self-rescue.

Mountaineering routes in the Tetons can be snow, ice, or rock, or a mix of all three. Two guidebooks are worth consulting: *Teton Classics: 50 Selected Climbs in Grand Teton National Park* by Richard Rossiter, and *A Climber's Guide to the Teton Range* by Leigh N. Ortenburger and Reynold G. Jackson. Both are available through Grand Teton Association (307/739-3606, www.grandtetonpark.org) online or at association bookstores in the park, including at Jenny Lake.

Guides and Schools

Two companies guide climbs and ski mountaineering trips year-round in Grand Teton National Park; the main climbing camps, school, and guided climbs happen in summer. Each leads climbs up Grand Teton, as well as other technical peaks. In most cases, the companies will supply all the technical climbing gear.

Launched in 1931 by Glen Exum (who solo pioneered the most famous and common route up Grand Teton) and Paul Petzoldt (who started the National Outdoor Leadership School (NOLS)), Exum Mountain Guides (307/733-2297, http://exumguides.com) leads climbs for individuals, first-timers, experts, groups, families, and kids. Their office at South Jenny Lake provides climbing instruction, camps, and kids' camps. Private guides can go one-on-one with you to the summit of the Grand, or you can go with a group (after successfully passing prerequisites).

Based in Jackson, Jackson Hole Mountain Guides (307/733-4979, www.jhmg.com) leads multiday trips up Grand Teton, even for beginners. Single-day climbs summit other peaks such as Middle Teton, South Teton, and Teewinot.

BIKING

Summer offers the best cycling weather, but prepare for potential dousing from afternoon thundershowers and strong winds. If biking paved roads, go in the early morning or late afternoon to avoid peak midday traffic. While cyclists can ride all park roads, shoulders are narrow and giant RVs will zoom by; ride single file to allow room for large RVs to pass. For safety and visibility, wear a helmet and bright colors (most drivers are looking at the peaks or wildlife rather than cyclists).

Road Biking

For riding on mostly paved shoulders, the **Inside-Outside Loop** (43 miles) starts from Moose to travel up Teton Park Road, connecting Jackson Lake Junction, Moran Junction, and U.S. Highway 26/89/191. **Jenny Lake Scenic Drive** (3 miles) offers a family-friendly ride with a designated bike lane. Though the road is one-way for vehicles, bicyclists can ride in both directions.

The Multi-Use Pathway parallels Teton Park Road.

Two paved roads offer prized riding: **Teton Park Road** (14.5 miles), between Taggart Trailhead and Signal Mountain Lodge, and **Moose-Wilson Road** (7.3 miles), between Granite Canyon Trailhead and Moose. The roadways are plowed free of snow in early April, when they open to bikes yet remain closed to vehicles until May 1.

★ MULTI-USE PATHWAY

The most popular bike ride is the **Multi-Use Pathway** (29 miles, dawn-dusk, snow-covered in winter), a paved cycling and walking path that parallels the roads between Jenny Lake, Moose, Antelope Flats Road, and Jackson. The mostly level path is perfect for cyclists who don't want to contend with RV traffic and for families with kids. Use caution, as wildlife (including bison) also walk on the trail; pathways intersect with road crossings. The southern section, from Jackson to Gros Ventre Junction, closes November-April for migrating elk. For the most scenic ride, the Moose-Jenny Lake Pathway (7.7 miles) saunters just below the Tetons.

Mountain Biking

Mountain bikes are not permitted on trails. Mountain bikers are relegated to paved paths or dirt roads. Unfortunately, passing vehicles churn up mounds of dust on dirt roads, which afternoon rains then turn muddy.

Antelope Flats Road offers biking with sagebrush and scenery, but prepare for high winds due to the wide-open plain. Extend the ride by touring the historic Mormon Row or Shadow Mountain in Bridger-Teton National Forest, which has single-track trails. Consult with Dornan's **Adventure Sports** (12170 Dornan Rd., Moose, 307/733-3307, http://dornans.com) for route conditions and details.

Guides and Rentals

Located on the Multi-Use Pathway, Dornan's **Adventure Sports** (12170 Dornan Rd., Moose, 307/733-3307, http://dornans.com, 8am-6pm daily early May-late Sept., $30-70 adults, $22-35 kids) rents road bikes and mountain bikes by the hour, half-day, full day, and week; rates include helmets. You can also rent Trailalongs and Burleys for towing kids, or bike racks for hauling gear to ride elsewhere.

Teton Mountain Bike Tours (307/733-0712 or 800/733-0788, www.tetonmtnbike.com, year-round) guides everything from family-friendly to challenging half-day, full-day, and multiday bike tours—even winter tours on fat tires. Half-day family rides through Antelope Flats ($78/person) and full-day Teton Tours ($130/person) cruise paved and dirt roads.

WATER SPORTS

Two permits are required for boating and most paddling. Boaters must pick up a State of Wyoming **Aquatic Invasive Species (AIS) sticker** and pass a boat inspection (Wyoming Game and Fish, 307/777-4638, https://wgfd.wyo.gov, Wyoming residents: $10 motorized, $5 nonmotorized; nonresidents: $30 motorized, $15 nonmotorized). Inflatable watercraft smaller than 10 feet and paddleboards are exempt. Then, to buy Grand Teton National Park **boat permits** (motorized $40, nonmotorized $12), go to Jenny Lake Ranger Station or any visitors center.

Boating

Boating on **Jenny Lake** is a quiet, idyllic experience, as only motorboats with 10 horsepower or less are permitted, plus any hand-propelled boats. Sailboats, sailboards, waterskiing, and Jet Skis are not allowed. The boat launch is located on **Lupine Meadows Road.** After crossing the bridge over Cottonwood Creek, turn right to reach the dirt ramp and small loop for trailer parking.

Canoeing, Kayaking, and Paddleboarding

Late May-October, paddlers have access to idyllic lakes tucked up against the base of the Teton Mountains. While Jenny Lake permits small-horsepower motorboats, all other lakes are limited to hand-propelled watercraft, making them perfect for paddleboarding. North of Jenny Lake, **String Lake** connects via a portage to **Leigh Lake. Phelps, Taggart, Bradley,** and **Bearpaw Lakes** are also open to paddlers, but require portaging boats a distance to reach the water. Mornings offer a calmer time to paddle, with the best days yielding smooth, glassy reflections. Afternoons often bring winds and sometimes thundershowers.

Jenny Lake Boating rents kayaks for paddling on Jenny Lake.

To reach the Jenny Lake boat launch, turn right from Teton Park Road onto Lupine Meadows Road and turn right again immediately after the bridge over Cottonwood Creek. String Lake has a canoe and kayak launch site, located in the second parking lot on the left on the String Lake Picnic Area road north of Jenny Lake Road. All other lakes require carrying boats from trailhead parking lots.

Paddlers with skills on Class II moving water can tackle 10 miles of the **Snake River** from the put-in at Deadman's Bar to Moose, a section with outstanding scenery and wildlife. Strong currents, braided channels, and logjams require advanced river savvy.

LEIGH LAKE OVERNIGHT

North of Jenny Lake, String Lake connects via a 600-foot portage through a rocky, shallow stream to peaceful **Leigh Lake**, where paddlers can overnight in solitude at eight prime **campsites.** Eastern shore campsites capture dramatic mountain reflections on the water; western shore campsites do not have trail access, thus guaranteeing more privacy. A **backcountry camping permit** is required; walk-in permits ($35/trip) from the Jenny Lake Ranger Station or the Craig Thomas Discovery & Visitor Center are released 24 hours prior to departure. Advance **reservations** (www.recreation.gov, early Jan.-mid-May, $45/trip) help guarantee a spot.

RENTALS

Jenny Lake Boating (Jenny Lake boathouse, 307/734-9227, www.jennylakeboating.com, 7am-7pm daily mid-June-mid-Sept., shorter hours in fall) rents two-person kayaks and canoes that can carry three people ($20/hour, $75/day, children under 5 not permitted). Reservations are not accepted. Rates include life jackets and paddles.

Dornan's **Adventure Sports** (12170 Dornan Rd., Moose, 307/733-3307, http://dornans.com, 8am-6pm daily early May-late Sept., $22-25/hour, $50-60/day) rents canoes, one- and two-person kayaks, and paddleboards. Rates include life jackets, paddles, and pads and straps for carrying boats on your vehicle. The shop also rents boat trailers.

Rafting

Boaters can float the **Wild and Scenic Snake River** in rafts, dories, canoes, or river kayaks. Starting below Jackson Lake Dam, the river runs 25 miles to Moose Landing. It yields scenery, including grand views of the Teton Mountains. Wildlife is also attracted to the

A guided rafting trip floats past historic Menor's Ferry.

water; watch for great blue herons, bald eagles, and osprey fishing the river (to protect the birds, avoid stopping in the eagle nest closure area). On shore, you can also spot bison, deer, elk, and bears.

While rafts can float spring, summer, and fall, the shoulder seasons are cold, rainy, and snowy. June sees the highest water when it is swift, muddy, and cold. **Summer** offers the best time for floating. From Jackson Lake Dam to Menor's Ferry, the river closes annually (Dec. 15-Apr. 1) to floating. Before launching, check water levels at river landings, permit offices, and through USGS monitors (800/658-5771, http://waterdata.usgs.gov). A park service brochure is available in visitors centers and online (www.nps.gov/grte).

River access is at Pacific Creek, Deadman's Bar, and Moose Landing. Most floats put in at **Deadman's Bar** and take out at **Moose Landing** (10 miles, 2 hours), an advanced section of the river. The Class II water requires river savvy to deal with strong currents, waves, logjams, and braiding into multiple channels with islands. The river maze breaks into many small streams, and these braided channels change during summer, demanding knowledge of safer routes. In afternoons, expect to encounter strong upriver winds. You can also continue rafting beyond the park boundary to Wilson Bridge.

GUIDES

On the Snake River, most companies guide multiple daytime **float trips** (daily mid-May-Sept., $80 adults, $50-60 kids). The guide does all the rowing and maneuvering; you get to sit back to absorb the views of the peaks and look for wildlife. From Moose, transportation is via bus or van to Deadman's Bar for launching; trips end back in Moose. With shuttles, the total trip takes about three hours, with two hours on a raft that holds 10-12 people. Some companies offer daytime, sunrise, dinner, or sunset floats; most have minimum age limits, but are family-friendly. Rates include life jackets and transportation to and from the river.

Reservations are required; plan to tip your guide 15 percent.

Barker-Ewing Scenic Float Trips (307/733-1800 or 800/365-1800, www.barkerewing.com) has a reservation desk in the grocery at Dornan's in Moose and offers daytime trips. **Triangle X-National Park Float Trips** (307/733-5500, http://nationalparkfloattrips.com) meets guests in Moose or at their ranch and offers sunrise, sunset, daytime, and dinner floats. Based in Jackson, **Solitude Float Trips** (307/733-2871 or 888/704-2800, www.grand-teton-scenic-floats.com) meets guests in Moose for daytime or sunrise trips.

Fishing

Grand Teton National Park is one of those places that combines stunning scenery with exceptional fishing. While spin-casting works, fly-fishing is the iconic method. Waters swim with native cutthroat and introduced brown, rainbow, and lake trout. Only artificial flies and lures are allowed for fishing in the southern section of Grand Teton. Fishing regulations for closures, creel limits, and lure and bait requirements are available online (www.nps.gov/grte).

The **Snake River** flows southward through the park, providing plenty of locations for fishing along its 25 miles from Jackson Lake Dam to Moose Landing. While you can fish from shore or wade into the river to fish, the best way to fish is from a drift boat or raft. The river is the place to fish for the unique indigenous Snake River fine-spotted cutthroat trout; however, conscientious anglers catch-and-release only. Most anglers use dry-flies to attract the wild trout that can get up to 18 inches.

On the river, runoff usually hits mid-May-June. In deep snowpack years, with long cool springs, runoff can last through July and even nip into August. After runoff, when the river clears, the fishing gets good. Many anglers consider **September** to be the best month for fishing. Trout fishing season on the Snake runs **April-October** (catch-and-release only

Nov.-Mar.). Tributaries to the Snake River also offer fishing. **Cottonwood Creek** and **Ditch Creek** open August-October for fishing. Most other streams plunging through the canyons of the Teton Mountains are open April-October.

Below the Tetons, seven moraine lakes tuck up against the base of the mountains and offer fishing. Fishing pressure is pretty hefty on **Jenny** and **String Lakes,** due to their drive-up access and number of visitors. **Leigh, Bradley, Taggart,** and **Phelps Lakes** offer fishing at the end of short hikes, although you may need to work around shoreline brush to good sites. Take the kids to **Jenny Lake** to learn to fish. Hiking up to alpine lakes in the Teton Mountains can also yield rewarding fishing. However, you'll most likely reach the lakes midday; morning and evening fishing are usually better, and some lakes are barren.

Fishing in Grand Teton National Park requires a **Wyoming state fishing license** (residents: $3 youth annual, $6 adults daily, $24 adults annual; nonresident: $15 youth annual, $14 adults daily, $92 adults annual), available for sale at Dornan's in Moose. For float tubes, pick up a Grand Teton National Park **boating permit** ($12) at visitors centers.

GUIDES

Only licensed guides are allowed to lead fishing trips in Grand Teton. Since the better fishing is on the **Snake River**, that's where most of the guided trips go. The river is perfect for beginners or experts; guides will coach beginners in mastering where to cast and techniques. Boats, life jackets, waders, reels, and rods are provided, but you will need to purchase your fishing license and sometimes flies and leader. Many of the guide companies are based in Jackson but meet clients at Moose or elsewhere in the park. One or two anglers and a guide can go in a drift boat, dory, or raft. Companies provide transportation to and from the river; full-day trips usually include lunch.

Half-day trips cost $450-495; full day trips run $555-595. Plan to tip your guide 15 percent (20 percent if you catch lots of fish). Reservations are required. Guided Snake River fishing trips are offered through **Snake River Angler** (10 Moose St., Moose, 307/733-3699, www.snakeriverangler.com) and **Triangle X** (307/733-5500, www.trianglex.com).

Swimming

Swimming is allowed in all park waters; however, most are chilly and there are no lifeguards or designated swimming areas. **String Lake** is shallow, so water tends to heat up a little warmer there than elsewhere, making it more pleasant. Swimming access is from the picnic area. Due to strong currents and logjams, the park service discourages swimming in the Snake River.

WINTER SPORTS

In southern Grand Teton National Park, winter sports consist of the silent sports: backcountry skiing, cross-country skiing, and snowshoeing. Snowmobiling and snow-biking on roads buried in snow are not permitted. Venturing into Grand Teton National Park in winter demands preparedness and attention to weather and snowpack. While most park roads convert to touring trails and are not in avalanche zones, they can see whiteouts, high winds, and frigid temperatures. Prepare accordingly to prevent exposure and hypothermia. Traveling into mountain canyons or skinning up peaks to ski down will increase exposure to avalanches. Take the appropriate survival and avalanche gear along and be prepared to self-rescue.

While you can ski or snowshoe anywhere, the park closes several zones in winter to protect wildlife, including the Snake River bottom. Check on **park closures** online (www.nps.gov/grte) or in the winter edition of the park's official newspaper. A good resource for snow conditions all over the park is compiled and updated periodically by the **Jenny**

Lake climbing rangers (http://tetonclimbing.blogspot.com). Check for avalanche conditions updated daily through the **Jackson Hole Avalanche Center** (307/733-2664, www.jhavalanche.org).

Skiing and Snowshoeing

In winter, some roads in the national park close to vehicles, which means they turn into cross-country ski and snowshoe routes. From the Taggart Lake Trailhead to Signal Mountain Lodge, **Teton Park Road** (14 miles, mid-Dec.-mid-Mar.) becomes a winter ski and snowshoe trail to frozen Jenny Lake. The road is groomed twice a week. Follow protocol on the groomed trail: Snowshoers should walk on the smooth grooming, not the tracks cut for skiing. Find current conditions and grooming reports online at **Jackson Hole Nordic** (http://jhnordic.com).

The closed **Moose-Wilson Road** offers a road tour through a forest, but the road is not groomed. Be ready to break your own trail or follow previous tracks from skiers and snowshoers. From the Granite Canyon Trailhead, you can tour the road north to the Laurance S. Rockefeller Preserve Center (closed in winter) and circle Phelps Lake on trails. **Taggart and Bradley Lakes** make good trail destinations for those who want to get off the roads. Because it is one of the few trailheads that drivers can access in winter, the lakes are a popular destination.

The Tetons lure skilled backcountry skiers and ski mountaineers. Winter ascents of peaks demand skiing for access, and ski descents yield untracked snow. Some skiers traverse the Teton Crest. Avalanche gear and training is required. If you don't have the skills, hire a guide.

GUIDES AND RENTALS

In winter, rangers guide interpretive **snowshoe walks** (307/739-3399, www.nps.gov/grte, late Dec.-mid-Mar., free) on historic wooden snowshoes. The two-hour tours meet at the Taggart Lake Trailhead; look for tracks, play with snow science, and examine the ecology of winter. Dress in layers, bring water and a pack, and wear snow boots or sturdy hiking boots. Reservations are required starting in early December. Snowshoes are available for rent ($5 adults, $2 kids).

Several companies are licensed to guide winter tours in the national park and instruct avalanche courses. Most trips are scheduled on demand. Consider pairing up with other visitors to reduce rates. **Hole Hiking Experience** (866/733-4453, www.holehike.com) offers 2-6-hour cross-country ski and snowshoe trips, some in tandem with wildlife-watching, sleigh rides, or dogsledding. **Teton Backcountry Guides** (307/353-2900, http://tetonbackcountryguides.com) leads full-day backcountry skiing, cross-country skiing, or snowshoe tours. **Exum Mountain Guides** (307/733-2297, www.exumguides.com) leads one-day backcountry ski trips, ski mountaineering excursions, and ski camps. **Jackson Hole Mountain Guides** (307/733-4979, www.jhmg.com) also leads one-day backcountry ski trips, ski mountaineering expeditions, and ice climbing in Death Canyon.

Dornan's Trading Post (12170 Dornan Rd., Moose, 307/733-3307 or 307/733-2415, ext. 302, http://dornans.com, 9am-5pm daily Dec.-Mar., $18-25/day) rents cross-country skis and snowshoes by the day or week. You can also rent backcountry skis, cross-country skis, and snowshoes for adults and kids in Jackson and Teton Village.

Menor's Ferry Historic District

Entertainment and Shopping

RANGER PROGRAMS

One of the best ways to learn about Grand Teton National Park is through the **free ranger programs** offered spring, summer, and fall at the Jenny Lake Visitor Center, Craig Thomas Discovery and Visitor Center, and Laurance S. Rockefeller Preserve. Short programs last 20 minutes, while longer ones run 30-45 minutes. Topics range from map chats and nature presentations to bear safety. Families with kids will enjoy **Critter Chats** at the Laurance S. Rockefeller Preserve and the **Twilight Talks** at Gros Ventre Amphitheater. Check current schedules and locations in the park newspaper or online (www.nps.gov/grte).

SHOPPING

A handful of gift shops dot the southern portion of the national park at Jenny Lake, Dornan's at Moose, and the Menor's Ferry General Store. **Grand Teton Association** (307/739-3606, www.grandtetonpark.org) bookstores are located in visitors centers and the Menor's Ferry General Store. At Dornan's, **Moosely Mountaineering** (12170 Dornan Rd., 307/739-1801, 9am-8pm daily mid-May-Sept.) sells camping, hiking, and mountaineering gear from the Jackson staple Skinny Skis.

Food

Casual attire is standard for all restaurants, with the exception of dressing for dinner at Jenny Lake Lodge. With limited dining options inside the park, many visitors drive to Jackson or Teton Village for dinner. Evening drives back to lodging or campsites add on wildlife-watching or catching the sunset over the Tetons.

INSIDE THE PARK
Jenny Lake

The dining room at ★ **Jenny Lake Lodge** (400 Jenny Lake Loop, 307/733-4647 and 800/628- 9988, www.gtlc.com, June-early Oct.) is an experience in itself. The log lodge hosts an intimate restaurant with views of the Teton peaks for a romantic setting. Local and Wyoming food sources are used, and the wine list spans the world. Vegetarian, gluten-free, vegan, organic, all-natural, and low-fat options are available. Breakfast (7:30am-10:30am daily, $28) is a gourmet prix fixe menu; you can select all options to go with your entrée. Brunch (11:30am-1:30pm daily, $10-16) features egg dishes, burgers, salads, and entrées

such as trout. Dinner (6pm-9pm daily, $90) is a five-course prix fixe affair with menus rotating on a five-night schedule. **Reservations** (307/543-3351) are recommended for breakfast and lunch and are required for dinner. The restaurant recommends that diners wear jackets, slacks, and dress attire. Guests staying at the lodge can make dinner reservations when they book their lodging; non-guests can make reservations beginning on March 1.

At South Jenny Lake, the **general store** (307/543-2811, www.gtlc.com, 8am-7pm daily mid-May-mid-Sept.) carries a few convenience foods and minimal camping supplies. The closest supermarkets are in Jackson.

Moose

Dornan's (307/733-2415, www.dornans.com, Dec.-Mar. and May-Oct.) has two restaurants in their complex, plus a deli. All have kid-friendly menu options.

Pizza Pasta Company (11:30am-9:30pm daily, shorter hours in winter, $9-25) serves pasta, pizza, calzones, hot subs, panini, soups, and salads. Breads, pastas, and pizza dough

Jenny Lake Lodge

are made fresh daily. Rooftop seating (adults only) and patio dining have outstanding views of the Tetons. Indoor seating is sometimes crowded and noisy, but there's a fireplace for cold days. Order in line at the food counter and wait for the staff to deliver to the table. Beer, wine, and cocktails are ordered separately from the **Spur Bar.**

Summers bring on the old-time ★ **Chuckwagon** (307/733-2415, ext. 203, mid-June-Labor Day) for cowboy fare in a covered outdoor pavilion with picnic tables and mountain views. You can even eat in a tepee! Breakfast (7am-11am daily, $8-10) includes eggs, biscuits and gravy, French toast, and sourdough pancakes. Lunch (noon-3pm daily, $8-15) offers sandwiches and burgers on fresh-baked breads, soups, and salads. Dinner (5pm-9pm Sun.-Thurs., $20-32) is a western barbecue with sides plus choice of entrée: Wyoming beef short ribs cooked in a Dutch oven over a wood fire, barbecue chicken, baby back pork ribs, or blackened Idaho red trout. On Sundays, strip steak and prime rib are added to the menu. Beer and wine are served. Mondays feature hootenannies, while Tuesday-Thursday nights have live music.

The small **Moose Trading Post & Deli** (9am-5pm daily winter, 8am-8pm daily summer) makes made-to-order deli sandwiches. Dine at one of a few indoor tables or take your meal to-go for hikes. The store also sells groceries, freeze-dried meals, trail mix, cheeses, and baked goods. A wine shop is on-site, and espresso and ice cream are sold June-August.

Picnicking

Teton Park Road has two picnic areas. Between the Moose Entrance Station and Jenny Lake, the **Cottonwood Creek Picnic Area** sits roadside on Cottonwood Creek opposite the Taggart Lake Trailhead. The more scenic picnic area is at **String Lake,** accessed via North Jenny Lake. Both have picnic tables and vault toilets; String Lake also has fire rings with grills.

Accommodations

INSIDE THE PARK

Lodging inside the south end of Grand Teton National Park is limited to a few cabin complexes, ranches, and campgrounds. These fill fast, especially in midsummer. **Advance reservations are a must;** book one year ahead. Just south of the park boundaries, Jackson and Teton Village have a full slate of lodging options with more amenities than in the park.

In general, inside park lodging is rustic with minimal amenities. Televisions, air-conditioning, mini-fridges, microwaves, and wireless Internet are not available, unless specified.

Jenny Lake
JENNY LAKE LODGE
Secluded in the woods at North Jenny Lake, ★ **Jenny Lake Lodge** (400 Jenny Lake Loop, 307/733-4647 and 800/628-9988, www.gtlc.com, June-early Oct., $758-1,050) offers a slice of old-style rustic luxury and is the highest priced lodging inside Grand Teton National Park. Breakfast, lunch, and activities are included in the price, but you can stay for less without the meals and activities when cabins are available. The 37 log cabins, built in 1920, have been revamped to an upscale historical feel, but still have old-fashioned rockers on porches for soaking up views. Twice-a-day housekeeping includes water and ice delivery. Visitors often mistakenly assume the lodge sits right on the lake; it does not. But from many of the cabin decks or windows, the tops of the Tetons poke up above the tall pines. The complex includes a dining room that specializes in gourmet and multi-course meals. Hiking trails depart from the lodge, and South Jenny Lake offers scenic

cruises, kayak and canoe rentals, a visitors center, stores, and the Multi-Use Pathway for bicycling. The lodge has cruiser-style bicycles and horseback riding for guests.

Lodging is in **three types of log cabins:** freestanding cabins, duplex cabins that share a common porch, and cabin suites. All the cabins have western furnishings, private bathrooms, wireless Internet, handmade quilts, and down comforters. Freestanding cabins have a king or two queens. Duplex cabins have a queen and twin bed. Suites have one bedroom with a king or two queens and a sitting room with a sofa bed and wood-burning stove. One suite has a jetted tub.

AAC CLIMBER'S RANCH

Three miles south of Jenny Lake on Teton Park Road, the American Alpine Club operates the **American Alpine Club Climber's Ranch** (307/733-7271 summer, 303/384-0110 fall-spring, http://americanalpineclub.org, 8am-8pm early June-mid-Sept., $16 ACC members, $25 nonmembers), which was originally built in 1924 as the Double Diamond Dude Ranch and its dining hall is listed on the National Register of Historic Places. You don't have to be a climber to stay here, but you must supply your own sleeping bag, pad, cook gear, food, towels, and other personal gear. Facilities include small co-ed log cabins that sleep 4-6 people each on wooden bunks dorm-style, separate bathroom and shower houses for women and men, an outdoor cook shelter with dishwashing sinks and picnic tables, and a lounge. A booster strengthens cell phone signals. Ice is for sale, and bear boxes and coolers are provided for food storage. You may be sharing a cabin with a climber rustling around in the middle of the night to pound down trail miles before sunrise, or with a family that has kids.

Moose

DORNAN'S SPUR RANCH CABINS

Located on the Snake River, the multi-generational family-owned-and-operated **Dornan's Spur Ranch Cabins** (307/733-2522, www.

dornans.com, May-Oct. and Dec.-Mar. $200-360) can sleep 4-6 people. The 12 one- and two-bedroom cabins built in 1992 have full kitchens. Some are duplexes, and most have covered decks with barbecue grills and views of the Tetons, which light up at sunrise. Beds come with down comforters, and furniture is handcrafted. They are part of a 10-acre complex that includes a grocery, deli with ice cream and espresso, gift shop, wine shop, gas station, two restaurants, and a bar. Their Adventure Sports center rents bikes, canoes, kayaks, paddleboards, cross-country skis, and snowshoes in the appropriate seasons, and fly-fishing and rafting trips are available on-site. A paved path connects to the Multi-Use Pathway to ride bikes to Jenny Lake or Antelope Flats Road.

MOULTON RANCH CABINS

Five cabins in a historic and ultra-scenic location are at the ★ **Moulton Ranch Cabins** (202 Mormon Row Rd., Kelly, 307/733-3749, www.moultonranchcabins.com, late May-Sept., $110-300). Located 3.7 miles northwest of Moose amid the historic buildings on Mormon Row, the rustic cabins can sleep two, four, or six people. Three of the cabins have en suite bathrooms, while two have private bathrooms in separate buildings; most have kitchenettes. The cabins have combos of queen, double, sofa, and twin beds. The ranch has outstanding Teton Mountain views. The owners request a three-night minimum stay.

Moose to Moran

Several guest ranches line the national park west of the Snake River. Most inholdings are private properties owned prior to the creation of the national park. Find these on **U.S. Highway 26/89/191** between Moose and Moran Junction. From these ranches, the views of the Teton Mountains provide an exquisite backdrop for horseback riding, which is one of the main reasons to stay at a ranch. Rates are all-inclusive with lodging, meals, and horseback riding. Bring long pants and sturdy shoes for riding. The ranches are also

Moulton Ranch on Mormon Row

home to elk, pronghorn, bison, bears, and wolves. Both ranches charge more for paying by credit card.

The ★ **Triangle X Ranch** (2 Triangle X Ranch Rd., 307/733-2183, http://trianglex.com, mid-May-mid-Oct. and late Dec.-mid-Mar.) is a dude ranch operated for five generations by the Turner family. Lodging is in one-, two-, or three-bedroom log cabins with private bathrooms. Early June-late August is peak season for the ranch, when seven-night stays, Sunday to Sunday, are the program ($1,865-2,660 per person weekly). Outside of peak season, four-night stays are available (mid-May-early June and Sept.-Oct., $266-298 per person per day). Winter season ($140 per person per night) has cross-country skiing and snowshoeing (no horseback riding).

North of the Cunningham Cabin, ★ **Moose Head Ranch** (21255 N. Hwy. 89, 307/733-3141 summer, 850/877-1431 off season, www.mooseheadranch.com, early June-mid-Aug., $430-760 per person per night) is a 1925 family-run homestead and dude ranch. Log cabins for guests surround the main lodge, where gourmet breakfasts and lunches are served buffet-style and dinner dresses up fish and game entrées. Sunday nights have cookouts. The ranch has fly-fishing and swimming ponds.

OUTSIDE THE PARK

Opposite the Snake River Overlook, ★ **Lost Creek Ranch and Spa** (1 Old Ranch Rd., Moose, 307/733-3435, http://lostcreek.com, mid-June-mid-Sept., $5,600-14,500/cabin or suite/week, $800 per added guest after 2 or 4 people) has dude ranch activities tucked in between the national park and national forest. Lodging is in two-bedroom cabins with living rooms, one-bedroom duplex cabins, and king suites that sleep 1-8 people. The ranch has tennis courts, a hot tub, a heated swimming pool, kids' programs, yoga classes, spa treatments, horseback riding, and meals served family-style in the dining room.

Camping

INSIDE THE PARK

Two **campgrounds** (307/543-3100, www.nps.gov/grte) offer diverse experiences. Facilities include picnic tables, fire rings with grills, bear boxes, drinking water, garbage service, and firewood for sale. All campsites are **first-come, first-served**. Shared hiker and biker campsites cost $12 per person.

Jenny Lake

The most-coveted campground in the park, **Jenny Lake Campground** (early May-late Sept., $28) has front-row seating with exceptional scenery right below the Teton Mountains. You can park the car and hike for days. Trails lead to Hidden Falls, Inspiration Point, Leigh Lake, Cascade Canyon, and Paintbrush Canyon, plus peaks for climbing. Jenny Lake also has scenic cruises, kayak and canoe rentals, fishing, paddling, and the paved Multi-Use Pathway running south to Moose.

In a hilly, loose pine forest with big boulders, the campground has 49 **tent-only** campsites including several walk-in sites.

RVs, pop-ups, trailers, truck campers, and generators are prohibited, and vehicles must be smaller than 8 feet wide and 14 feet long. Each site allows a maximum of two tents, one vehicle or two motorcycles, and six people. Bathroom facilities are vault toilets. Locate the campground by turning from Teton Park Road into South Jenny Lake and veering right. The campground fills by 9am midsummer, but you may need to start trolling for a site around 7am.

Moose

On the Gros Ventre River along the southeast national park boundary, **Gros Ventre Campground** (early May-early Oct., $28 tents, $52 RVs w/hookups) sits opposite the National Elk Refuge. Unfortunately, the Gros Ventre River often becomes a barren riverbed mid-July-September when water is diverted for irrigation, and Black Butte blocks some of the Teton Mountains. However, the campground is a haven for moose. Gros Ventre Road makes for mellow bicycling where you might see bison and elk. Because

popular Jenny Lake Campground

the campground sits 12 miles from Jackson, you can pop into town for dinner and watch wildlife on the return trip. Gros Ventre is often the last campground to fill in the park, usually by dinnertime. Stop at the office to get a campsite.

The largest campground in Grand Teton, Gros Ventre has 350 RV and tent sites plus five group sites. Amenities include flush toilets, a dump station, and an amphitheater for evening interpretive programs. Seven huge loops circle the flat, sagebrush plateau under large cottonwood trees that lack understory for privacy but provide shade. Each campsite can fit two vehicles, two tents, and six people. Ten ADA campsites are available. A limited number of campsites can accommodate large RVs and trailers; 36 sites have electrical hookups. Certain loops are designated for generator use. Make **reservations** (307/543-3100 or 800/628-9988) for large groups.

Transportation and Services

DRIVING

Two-lane paved roads are the norm in Grand Teton National Park. While they are relatively straight compared to some of the curvy roads in portions of Yellowstone, they still require attention when driving. Animals travel in road corridors and can jump out unexpectedly in front of cars. Even though speed limits range 25-55 mph in the park, speed limits drop to 45 mph after dark to protect bison, bears, wolves, and other wildlife. Secondary roads are dirt, such as Antelope Flats Road and Mormon Row. In winter, most of the Teton Park Road and Moose-Wilson Road closes to vehicles; U.S. Highway 26/89/191 is plowed and remains open. Weather can make for whiteouts, and roads can be icy. Check conditions for park roads (307/739-3682).

During July and August, **parking** lots at trailheads pack out. On the Moose-Wilson Road, the Death Canyon and Granite Canyon parking lots fill up early, as do the Jenny Lake parking lots at South Jenny Lake, String Lake Trailhead, and Lupine Meadows Trailhead. Arrive early (before 9am) to claim a spot. The

Moose frequent Gros Ventre Campground.

Where Can I Find . . .?

- **Banks and ATMs:** ATMs are located at Dornan's in Moose and outside the park in Teton Village and Jackson.

- **Cell Service:** Verizon has the widest coverage across Jackson Hole, including Jenny Lake and Moose.

- **Gas and Garage Services:** At Moose, Dornan's has gas available year-round. Pumps are open 24 hours a day with a credit card. Other gas stations are in Jackson and Wilson.

- **Internet Access:** Wireless Internet is available at the Craig Thomas Discovery & Visitor Center at Moose.

- **Post Office:** Post offices are in Moose (3 Teton Park Rd., 307/733-3336, 9am-1pm and 1:30pm-5pm Mon.-Fri., 10am-11:30am Sat.) and in Kelly (4486 Lower Gros Ventre Rd., 10am-2pm Mon.-Fri., 10am-noon Sat.) near Mormon Row.

- **Showers:** The nearest public showers and laundry are at Signal Mountain Lodge or outside the park in Jackson.

Laurance S. Rockefeller Preserve Center limits parking to 50 cars.

SHUTTLES

Shuttles are run by **Alltrans, Inc.** (307/733-3135 or 800/443-6133, www.all-transparkshuttle.com, daily late May-late Sept., $15/person/day) between Jackson, Moose, Jenny Lake Visitor Center, Jenny Lake Lodge, Signal Mountain Lodge, Jackson Lake Lodge, Colter Bay Village, and Headwaters Lodge at Flagg Ranch. Shuttles run several times north and south each day, but do not travel on Moose-Wilson Road. Departure times are available online or at visitors centers. A one-day fee lets you get on and off the shuttle as many times as you want and wherever you want. Reservations are not accepted; pay with cash, Visa, or Mastercard when you board. Alltrans also provides shuttles from the Jackson Hole Airport (www.jacksonholealltrans.com).

Jenny Lake Boating (307/734-9227, www.jennylakeboating.com, 7am-7pm daily early June-early Sept., 10am-4pm daily mid-May-early June and mid-late Sept.; round-trip: $15 adults, $12 seniors, $8 kids; one way: $9 adults, $6 kids) runs shuttles from the boat dock on Jenny Lake near the visitors center. Boats travel to the base of Mt. Teewinot to connect with multiple hiking trails around Jenny Lake and to Hidden Falls, Inspiration Point, and Cascade Canyon. Shuttles run every 10-15 minutes throughout the day. The last boat leaves the dock at the posted closing time. Reservations are not required.

EMERGENCY SERVICES

If you have an emergency, contact **Jenny Lake Ranger Station** (307/739-3343, 8am-5pm early June-early Sept.). The closest medical facility is **St. John's Medical Center** (625 E. Broadway, Jackson, 307/733-3636, www.tetonhospital.org).

Jackson Hole

Exploring Jackson Hole 266

Sights 269

Recreation 276

Entertainment
and Shopping 285

Food 288

Accommodations 294

Camping 300

Transportation and Services . . . 301

Teton Valley 303

HOWDY STRANGER YONDER IS JACKSON HOLE THE LAST OF THE OLD WEST

Jackson Hole is a year-round playground, with the best mountain recreation: camping, hiking, fishing, rafting, biking, and skiing.

At Jackson Hole's south end, the town of Jackson is the main southern portal for exploring Grand Teton and Yellowstone National Parks. From its antler arches in the Jackson Town Square to the iconic Million Dollar Cowboy Bar, the town melds the Old West with modern places to stay and dine. Local breweries, galleries, shops, music, theater, and coffee shops let you explore the culture, while a trip to the National Elk Refuge in winter lets you count up hundreds of elk.

On the west side of Jackson Hole, Teton Village snuggles just outside Grand Teton National Park. The village is home to upscale hotels and restaurants that cluster at the base of Jackson Hole Mountain Resort. In winter, the resort's steep 4,139-foot vertical lures skiers and snowboarders. In summer, the tram whisks sightseers and hikers to the summit of Rendezvous Mountain for stunning views of Jackson Hole and the Tetons.

Caribou-Targhee National Forest and neighboring Teton Valley act as a back door into the Teton Mountains. Quiet and less crowded than Jackson Hole, the small town of Driggs serves as the gateway to the Tetons for four seasons of recreation. Grand Targhee Resort has the uncrowded slopes for skiing and snowboarding in winter. In summer, the resort swaps into a mountain biking mecca and home for long-running summer music festivals.

PLANNING YOUR TIME

Swarms of visitors descend on Jackson in **summer** when the national parks are in full swing, hiking trails dry out, rivers offer white-water rafting and fishing, and the thermometer hangs around 70-80°F. Lodging properties have the **highest prices of the year** in summer. To guarantee what you want, **book flights and lodging 6-12 months in advance.**

To avoid the big crowds and take advantage of lower lodging prices, travel in **April-May** or **September-October.** While the weather may be more unpredictable, wildlife-watching is often prime during migrations, mating, and birthing. Temperatures range

---

Previous: wildflowers in Alaska Basin; welcome sign at Teton Pass. **Above:** blooming arrowleaf balsamroot.

Highlights

★ **Jackson Town Square:** The town square is famous for its four antler archways, stagecoach rides, and shootouts on summer evenings (page 269).

★ **Million Dollar Cowboy Bar:** Walk into this historic bar and you've suddenly entered the Old West (page 269).

★ **National Museum of Wildlife Art:** This museum houses a collection of art that matches the natural environment (page 271).

★ **National Elk Refuge:** The refuge provides a winter home for elk, plus bighorn sheep, pronghorn, wolves, and trumpeter swans (page 271).

★ **Aerial Tram:** The tram whips skiers, snowboarders, hikers, and sightseers up 10,450-foot Rendezvous Mountain (page 273).

★ **Jackson Hole Mountain Resort:** This world-class resort attracts expert skiers and snowboarders (page 283).

★ **Teton Pass:** Relish the steep 10 percent grade as the road climbs to 8,432 feet, squeezing over the Teton Crest (page 303).

★ **Alaska Basin:** Backpackers hike to the Teton Crest for prolific wildflower displays, mountaintop views, and sparkling lakes (page 305).

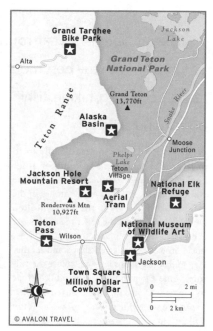

★ **Grand Targhee Bike Park:** Mountain bikers ride the lift to reach trails that come with backside Grand Teton views (page 307).

Jackson Hole

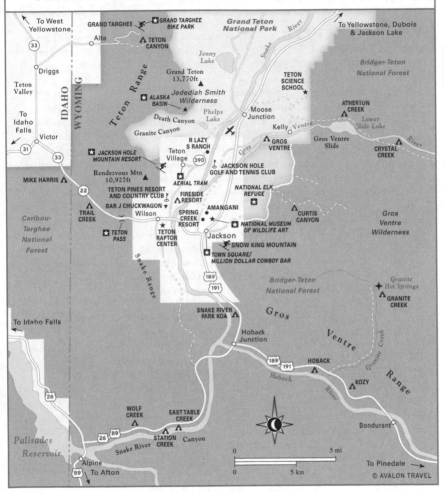

50-70°F, but sometimes cold winds can turn rain into snow, and the mercury plunges to 30°F. Fall delivers brilliant colors with aspens turning gold.

Winter brings on skiing, snowboarding, snowmobiling, ice climbing, cross-country skiing, and snowshoeing. While the winter season runs **Thanksgiving-early April**, high season includes all holidays and school vacations: Christmas, New Year's, Martin Luther King Jr. weekend, Presidents' Day week, and school spring breaks. Prices go up for those holiday periods. To avoid the crowds, **plan midweek trips** outside of the holidays. **January** and **February** usually bring the coldest weather, while **March** often delivers big dumps of snow.

Winter highs in Jackson Hole hang mostly in the 20s and 30s, but drop lower at night. Mountain temperatures plunge even lower. Ice and snow can impinge driving, especially over Teton Pass.

Exploring Jackson Hole

VISITORS CENTER
Jackson Hole and Greater Yellowstone Visitor Center

Located a half mile north of the Jackson Town Square at the southeast corner of the National Elk Refuge, the **Jackson Hole and Greater Yellowstone Visitor Center** (532 N. Cache St., 307/733-3316, www.jacksonholechamber.com, 8am-7pm daily in summer, 9am-5pm daily in winter) has interpretive displays on the elk refuge and information for visitors. The interagency center represents the **National Elk Refuge** (www.fws.gov/refuge), **Grand Teton National Park** (www.nps.gov/grte), **Bridger-Teton National Forest** (www.fs.usda.gov/btnf), and **Jackson Chamber of Commerce** (www.jacksonholechamber.com). Information is available on camping, lodging, wildlife-watching, activities, events, and road conditions for all four agencies. You can pick up maps and permits; the center also rents bear canisters and panniers. **Grand Teton Association** (307/739-3606, www.grandtetonpark.org) operates a bookstore in the visitors center that sells books on wildlife, wildflowers, history, natural history, geology, and hiking. In winter, get tickets for sleigh rides on the National Elk Refuge. The center also puts on educational programs and has Junior Ranger activity booklets for kids.

TOURS

From Jackson, you can get sightseeing and wildlife tours. For trips that go into the parks, entrance fees are additional. Plan to tip your guides 15 percent.

Stagecoach Tours

From the Stage Stop building on the south side of the Jackson Town Square, **stagecoach rides** (25 E. Broadway, Jackson, 307/733-3316, www.jacksonholechamber.com, 9am-9pm daily late May-Sept., $4-6) tour through the historic part of town. Two mules pull the authentic red stagecoach that departs every 15 minutes. You'll get the real feel on the bench seats during the 10-minute ride.

Summer Sightseeing Tours

Summer sightseeing tours (mid-May-mid-Oct., $195-330) depart from Jackson in small buses or vans. Tours go to popular sightseeing destinations and stop for wildlife-watching. Some companies offer pickups at your hotel and cheaper rates for kids. **Buffalo Roam Park Tours** (307/413-0954, www.buffaloroamtours.com) guides van tours in Grand Teton or Yellowstone National Parks. **Teton Science School** (700 Coyote Canyon Rd., Jackson, 877/404-6626, www.tetonscience.org) tours the lower loop in Yellowstone National Park.

Wildlife Tours

Most of the Jackson-based tour companies guide wildlife safaris year-round. Routes vary depending on where wildlife congregates seasonally: the National Elk Refuge, national forests, or Grand Teton National Park. Wildlife-watching tours to Yellowstone run May-October. Tour companies bring the spotting scopes and binoculars. Half-day, full-day, multiday, and specialty tours depart daily, with sunrise and sunset tours offering the best wildlife-watching. Most companies will pick up at your hotel. Rates run $150-350 per person per day.

Departing from Jackson or Teton Village, **Teton Science School** (700 Coyote Canyon Rd., Jackson, 877/404-6626, www.tetonscience.org) leads wildlife expeditions in customized vans with roof hatches for stand-up viewing. Full-day expeditions include lunch—a picnic in summer or stopping at a restaurant in winter.

Several Jackson-based companies also guide wildlife tours: **BrushBuck Tours** (307/699-2999 or 888/282-5868, www.

Orientation to Jackson Hole

Visitors can get confused about Jackson Hole. Don't get lost on your vacation by misinterpreting the local geography. Here's a guide to what is where:

Jackson Hole: A hole is an older term for a valley. Jackson Hole refers to the 80-mile-long by 15-mile-wide valley paralleling the Teton Mountains. It includes Jackson Lake, portions of Grand Teton National Park, and the towns of Moran, Moose, Kelly, Wilson, Teton Village, and Jackson.

Jackson: The town of Jackson, the largest town in Jackson Hole, sits at the south end of Jackson Hole.

Jackson Hole Mountain Resort: Jackson Hole Mountain Resort sits in Teton Village, a resort town in Jackson Hole. It is 12 miles from Jackson and one mile from Grand Teton National Park.

Teton Valley: Teton Valley is on the less-traveled west side of the Teton Mountains in Idaho. It contains tiny towns like Victor and Driggs. Teton Valley is the back door or west side access into the Teton Mountains and into Grand Teton National Park.

Teton Pass: While Teton Pass is in the Teton Mountains, it is not in Grand Teton National Park—it is south of the park. Teton Pass connects Jackson Hole to Teton Valley.

Gros Ventre Mountains: Named for the Gros Ventre Indians and French for "big belly," the Gros Ventre Mountains flank the eastern side of Jackson Hole. Far older than the younger Tetons, the more eroded rounded peaks hold Bridger-Teton National Forest and the Gros Ventre Wilderness.

Greater Yellowstone Ecosystem: This geographic term arose from the fact that national park boundaries are artificial. They do not define the ecosystem, especially as used by wildlife in seasonal migrations. The Greater Yellowstone Ecosystem includes Yellowstone National Park, Grand Teton National Park, Jackson Hole, John D. Rockefeller, Jr. Memorial Parkway, National Elk Refuge, four national forests (Custer-Gallatin, Caribou-Targhee, Bridger-Teton, and Shoshone), and Teton Valley.

brushbucktours.com), **Eco Tour Adventures** (307/690-9533, www.jacksonholewildlifetours.com), and **Jackson Hole Wildlife Safaris** (307/690-6402, http://jacksonholewildlifesafaris.com).

Photo Tours

Local photographers with **The Hole Picture Photo Safaris** (208/709-3250, www.theholepicturesafaris.com) or **Alpenglow Tours** (307/739-1914, www.alpenglowtours.com) can take you to the best spots in Grand Teton or Yellowstone National Parks to nab those professional-looking photos and offer tips on how to shoot scenery and wildlife. Sunrise and sunset tours capture the colorful skies.

Winter Sleigh Rides

At the National Elk Refuge, **horse-drawn** sleighs (Double H Bar, Inc., 307/733-0277 or 800/772-5386, www.bar5.com, 10am-4pm daily mid-Dec.-early Apr., $21 adults, $15 kids) go on winter tours to see wildlife. The sleighs tour among the elk herd, providing opportunities to watch the stately ungulates and shoot photos. Pick up tickets at the **Jackson Hole and Greater Yellowstone Visitor Center** (532 N. Cache St., 307/733-3316), where you'll meet for the free shuttle to the sleigh ride area. Wear warm clothing layers including a hat, gloves, and snow boots.

Scenic Flights

Fly Jackson Hole (1250 E. Jackson Hole Airport Rd., Jackson, 844/359-5499, www.flyjacksonhole.com, $350-450 per person) has 60- to 90-minute flights over the Tetons, as well as family and alpenglow flights.

Stagecoach rides tour through Jackson in summer.

DRIVING TOURS
National Elk Refuge
3.5 MILES

Driving into the **National Elk Refuge** (675 E. Broadway, 307/733-9212, www.fws.gov/refuge/National_Elk_Refuge, 3.5 miles, 30 min. round trip, Dec.-Apr.) offers wildlife-watching when bison, bighorn sheep, pronghorn, and thousands of elk winter here. Drivers are not allowed to stop on the narrow road with no shoulders, but can use five pullouts for wildlife-watching and photography. Ice or snow drifts can cover the road, and visibility may be limited by blowing snow or fog. Refuge Road is at the east end of Broadway.

Southern Jackson Hole Loop
33 MILES

A 33-mile loop circles the southern portion of Jackson Hole, connecting Jackson, Moose, and Teton Village (33 miles, 3 hours, May-Oct.). From Jackson or Teton Village, drive the loop clockwise or counterclockwise; the latter yields impressive views of the Teton Mountains. From Jackson, the loop starts on U.S. 26/89/191, passing the **National Wildlife Refuge.** At Moose Junction, turn left to cross the Snake River and turn left again onto the **Moose-Wilson Road** (no RVs or trailers). After exiting the national park and passing **Teton Village,** continue south on the Moose-Wilson Road to Highway 22. Turn left to return to Jackson.

The park has plans to change the road's route to the north side of the entrance station into **Grand Teton National Park** (fee) and start a queue system to regulate the number of cars on Moose-Wilson Road; to confirm changes, consult online (www.nps.gov/grte). Going early or late can help you avoid long lines.

Sights

JACKSON

★ Jackson Town Square

In downtown Jackson, the **Jackson Town Square** is a year-round attraction. Four antler arches, each made from 2,000 tightly intertwined elk antlers, serve as entrances at the square's four corners. In summer, their sunbleached white is striking. In winter, holiday lights wrap the arches in glitter. Each May, the Boy Scouts hold their **annual elk antler auction** (www.elkfest.org) in the park, selling off shed antlers collected from the National Elk Refuge. Horse-drawn **stagecoaches** (daily Memorial Day-Labor Day) give tours from the square. A **gunfight reenactment** (6pm Mon.-Sat., www.jacksonholechamber. com, free) is held in summer. The event is put on by the Jackson Hole Playhouse, a tradition since 1956. Jackson Town Square is between Broadway and Deloney Avenues and Cache and Center Streets.

★ Million Dollar Cowboy Bar

A landmark in downtown Jackson since 1937, but in a building that dates to the 1890s, the **Million Dollar Cowboy Bar** (25 N. Cache St., 307/733-2207, www.milliondollarcowboybar. com, 11am-1am or 2am daily year-round) can be recognized by its neon sign of a cowboy on a horse. Knobbled pine trims out the bar, and saddles with saddle blankets serve as stools. Cowboy murals, wildlife mounts, ranch gear, and western artifacts make the bar look more like a museum than a watering hole.

Snow King Mountain

In summer, **Snow King Mountain** (100 E. Snow King Ave., Jackson, 307/734-3194 or 307/734-9442, http://snowkingmountain. com, 10am-9pm daily late May-early Sept., hours shorten spring and fall, $21 adults, $16 seniors and kids, children under 6 free) offers **scenic chairlift rides** that zip riders to the 7,799-foot summit of Snow King Mountain. With big 360-degree views, the summit is the best place to gaze down on the town below. Views also extend across Jackson Hole to the Teton Mountains.

Elk antler arches mark the corners of Jackson Town Square.

Jackson

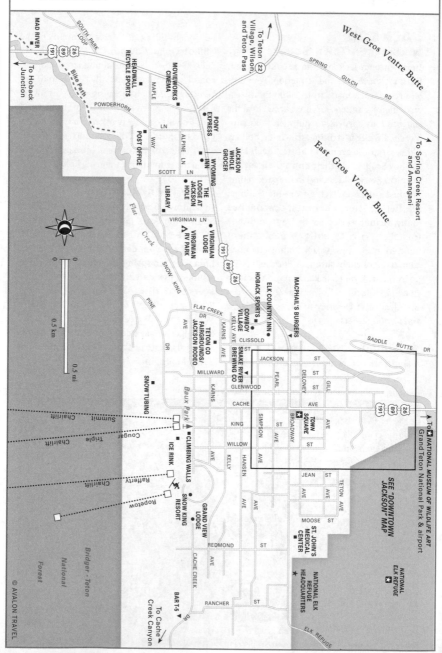

West Gros Ventre Butte

East Gros Ventre Butte

MAD RIVER

HEADWALL RECYCLE SPORTS

SOUTH PARK LOOP

191 89 26

To Hoback Junction

To Teton Village, Wilson, and Teton Pass

22

SPRING GULCH RD

To Spring Creek Resort and Amangani

POWDERHORN

MOVIEWORKS CINEMA

PONY EXPRESS

MAPLE LN

ALPINE LN

SCOTT LN

WAY

POST OFFICE

JACKSON WHOLE GROCER

WYOMING INN

THE LODGE AT JACKSON HOLE

LIBRARY

VIRGINIAN LN

VIRGINIAN RV PARK

VIRGINIAN LODGE

191 89 26

Flat Creek

SNOW KING AVE

PINE DR

FLAT CREEK DR

KARNS AVE

TETON CO FAIRGROUNDS/ JACKSON RODEO

MILLWARD

KARNS

Baux Park

SNOWTUBING

Summit Chairlift

Cougar

Triple Chairlift

Rafferty Chairlift

Ropetow

Bridger - Teton National Forest

© AVALON TRAVEL

ICE RINK

CLIMBING WALLS

SNOW KING RESORT

GRAND VIEW LODGE

CACHE CREEK DR

REDMOND

RANCHER ST

BART-5 DR

To Cache Creek Canyon

HOBACK SPORTS

ELK COUNTRY INN

COWBOY VILLAGE

KELLY AVE

CLISSOLD

MACPHAIL'S BURGERS

SNAKE RIVER BREWING CO

GLENWOOD

CACHE

KING ST

WILLOW ST

HANSEN AVE

JACKSON ST

PEARL ST

DELONEY ST

GILL AVE

PEARL AVE

SIMPSON AVE

BROADWAY

TOWN SQUARE

SADDLE BUTTE DR

191 89 26

To NATIONAL MUSEUM OF WILDLIFE ART, Grand Teton National Park & airport

SEE "DOWNTOWN JACKSON MAP"

JEAN AVE

TETON AVE

MOOSE ST

ST. JOHN'S MEDICAL CENTER

NATIONAL ELK REFUGE HEADQUARTERS

NATIONAL ELK REFUGE

ELK REFUGE

0   0.5 km

0   0.5 mi

the Million Dollar Cowboy Bar

★ National Museum of Wildlife Art

Located 2.5 miles north of Jackson, the **National Museum of Wildlife Art** (2820 Rungius Rd., 307/733-5771, www.wildlifeart. org, 9am-5pm Tues.-Sat., 11am-5pm Sun. year-round, $14 adults, $12 seniors, $2-6 kids) fuses its stone architecture into the landscape, but looks like an old fort. Walk the perimeter trails to view 30 outdoor sculptures of elk, bison, eagles, fish, and moose. Inside, 14 galleries hold paintings, drawings, and sculptures of wildlife from North America and Europe. A kids' room has hands-on activities; use the audio wands or mobile apps for interpretive info. Be sure to see Robert Bateman's painting of a bison called *Chief*, the largest collection of Carl Rungius in the United States, and Ken Bunn's *Silent Pursuit*, a mountain lion poised to pounce on unsuspecting visitors in the lobby.

★ National Elk Refuge

The 27,500-acre **National Elk Refuge** (www. fws.gov/refuge) borders the town of Jackson and is one of the best places to see wildlife year-round. The refuge was established to preserve the Jackson elk herd. About 70 percent of the herd winters at the refuge (about 7,000 elk). In early spring, **bull elk** shed their antlers and then migrate from the refuge to

the National Museum of Wildlife Art

Downtown Jackson

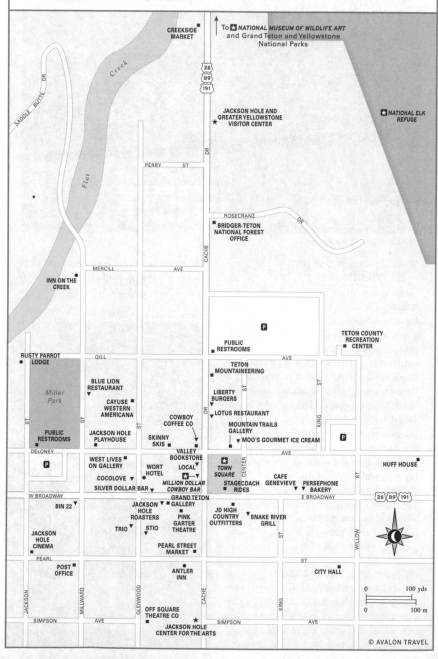

CREEKSIDE MARKET

To ★ NATIONAL MUSEUM OF WILDLIFE ART
and Grand Teton and Yellowstone
National Parks

26
89
191

Creek

SADDLE BUTTE DR

Flat

JACKSON HOLE AND
GREATER YELLOWSTONE
★ VISITOR CENTER

★ NATIONAL ELK
REFUGE

PERRY ST

CACHE DR

ROSECRANZ DR

BRIDGER-TETON
NATIONAL FOREST
OFFICE

MERCILL AVE

INN ON THE
CREEK

P

PUBLIC
RESTROOMS

TETON COUNTY
RECREATION
CENTER

RUSTY PARROT
LODGE

GILL AVE

Miller
Park

ST

TETON
MOUNTAINEERING

BLUE LION
RESTAURANT

CAYUSE
WESTERN
AMERICANA

LIBERTY
BURGERS

LOTUS RESTAURANT

KING ST

P

PUBLIC
RESTROOMS

JACKSON HOLE
PLAYHOUSE

COWBOY
COFFEE CO

SKINNY
SKIS

MOUNTAIN TRAILS
GALLERY

MOO'S GOURMET ICE CREAM

DELONEY

P

WEST LIVES
ON GALLERY

VALLEY
BOOKSTORE

WORT
HOTEL

LOCAL

★
TOWN
SQUARE

AVE

HUFF HOUSE

COCOLOVE

SILVER DOLLAR BAR

MILLION DOLLAR
COWBOY BAR

STAGECOACH
RIDES

CAFE
GENEVIEVE

PERSEPHONE
BAKERY

W BROADWAY

CENTER ST

E BROADWAY

26 89 191

BIN 22

JACKSON
HOLE
ROASTERS

GRAND TETON
GALLERY

PINK
GARTER
THEATRE

JD HIGH
COUNTRY
OUTFITTERS

SNAKE RIVER
GRILL

WILLOW ST

JACKSON
HOLE
CINEMA

TRIO

STIO

PEARL STREET
MARKET

PEARL

POST
OFFICE

ANTLER
INN

CITY HALL

JACKSON ST

MILLWARD AVE

GLENWOOD ST

CACHE ST

KING ST

0   100 yds

0   100 m

OFF SQUARE
THEATRE CO

★ JACKSON HOLE
CENTER FOR THE ARTS

SIMPSON AVE

SIMPSON AVE

© AVALON TRAVEL

Watch wildlife at the National Elk Refuge.

summer at higher elevations. The elk return in late fall. Biologists have noted changes in migratory patterns, with larger numbers choosing to spend summers close to the refuge. Elk calving happens in late spring (Apr.-May).

As the elk depart the refuge in spring, **migrating birds** arrive: songbirds, waterfowl, great blue herons, and trumpeter swans. In winter, about 100 trumpeter swans make the refuge wetlands home, and many stick around for nesting. The refuge has about 175 avian species.

Bison, pronghorn, and **mule deer** also call the refuge home—spot them from the Refuge Road past Miller Butte. The Pinnacle Peak Pack of **wolves** finds the refuge a sustainable habitat where they are thriving. Refuge biologists have radio-collared several of the canines to study their movements and assess their impacts on the elk herd.

Winter is the best season for watching wildlife at the refuge, when many animals migrate to lower valley elevations that amass 65 inches of snow (instead of the 500 inches in the mountains).

Start your visit at the **Jackson Hole and Greater Yellowstone Visitor Center** (532 N. Cache St., 307/733-3316, 8am-7pm daily summer, 9am-5pm daily winter), where you can buy tickets for a sleigh ride (in winter) on the refuge and plan a visit to the historic **Miller Ranch** (10am-4pm daily late May-mid-Sept., free).

Two roads tour the refuge year-round. From Jackson, U.S. 26/89/191 parallels the western boundary of the refuge. A pullover for wildlife-watching is just north of the Jackson Hole and Greater Yellowstone Visitor Center; another is 4.3 miles north. From the east end of Broadway Street, the 3.5-mile dirt Refuge Road tours through the refuge. The **Multi-Use Pathway** (May-Oct.) offers a bike-friendly way to tour along the refuge border and look for wildlife.

The refuge also has annual **bison and elk hunts** to manage the herd populations. Hunters with Wyoming hunting licenses can apply for a permit to hunt bison or elk. Details on the seasons and application process are available online.

WILSON
Teton Raptor Center

Injured raptors in Jackson Hole are taken for rehabilitation to the **Teton Raptor Center** (5450 W. Hwy. 22, Wilson, 307/203-2551, http://tetonraptorcenter.org, $18 adults, $15 kids and seniors) on the historic Hardeman Ranch. During the center's one-hour outdoor programs (2pm Wed.-Sat. June-Sept., 2pm Sat. Oct.-May, reservations required), you can meet the resident birds of prey and learn about raptors in Greater Yellowstone.

TETON VILLAGE
★ Aerial Tram

At Jackson Hole Mountain Resort, the **Aerial Tram** (3265 W. Village Dr., Teton Village, 307/733-2292 or 888/333-7766, www.jacksonhole.com, 9am-6pm daily late May-early

Oct., 9am-5pm spring and fall, $38 adults, $30 seniors, $25 juniors, $87 family, kids 5 and under free) is the easiest way to get on top of a mountain in the Tetons. The tram, which saves you huffing up 4,139 vertical feet, goes to the 10,450-foot summit of Rendezvous Mountain overlooking Grand Teton National Park. At the summit, most people feel sluggish or lightheaded from the elevation, but the view makes you forget any discomfort. You'll stare down at Jackson Hole and north across the Teton summits to the Grand. You can take photos, walk to viewpoints, eat waffles at tiny Corbet's Cabin, hike trails into Grand Teton National Park, or hike down to the base. Buy discounted tickets online.

BRIDGER-TETON NATIONAL FOREST

Bridger-Teton National Forest (www.fs.usda.gov/btnf) surrounds Jackson Hole. The forest offers hiking, mountain biking, whitewater rafting and kayaking, horseback riding, and camping, but you can drive to only a few lakes for boating and paddling. For sightseeing, drive cross Teton Pass from Jackson Hole to Teton Valley or head into the Gros Ventre Mountains.

Gros Ventre Mountains

Often ignored because of the higher, more jagged Teton Mountains, the **Gros Ventre Mountains** flank the eastern slopes of Jackson Hole. The older, more rounded and eroded mountains hold several high peaks taller than 11,000 feet. One of the most prominent peaks seen from the floor of Jackson Hole is **Sheep Mountain.** Its upper cliffs have gained the name **"Sleeping Indian"** due to the shape that looks like the profile of a person sleeping. View the Sleeping Indian from an overlook about one mile north of Jackson Hole Airport. To explore the Gros Ventre Mountains, drive to see where the 1927 landslide formed Lower Slide Lake or tour up Granite Creek Road to Granite Hot Springs.

LOWER SLIDE LAKE

In the Gros Ventre Mountains, **Lower Slide Lake** is the place to go for watersports. En route to the lake, **Slide Lake Overlook** is a must-see for geology buffs. The **Gros Ventre Landslide** of 1925 created Lower Slide Lake. Two years later, in 1925, the impoundment failed and flooded Jackson Hole from Kelly to Wilson. Above the lake's north side, orange rocky hillsides add a splash of color.

Ride the aerial tram to the summit of Rendezvous Mountain.

the Gros Ventre Range

To reach Lower Slide Lake, drive to Gros Ventre Junction north of Jackson. Turn right onto Gros Ventre Road until it passes Kelly, swings north, and then turns right to climb into the mountains. Ascend the curvy paved (but potholed and bumpy) road over a summit to the interpretive overlook above Lower Slide Lake. Pavement ends at Atherton Creek Campground. From there, the dirt road continues to follow the Gros Ventre River.

GRANITE HOT SPRINGS

Granite Hot Springs (end of Granite Creek Rd./Forest Rd. 30500, 307/690-6323, www. fs.usda.gov/btnf, 10am-6pm daily mid-May-Oct. and early Dec.-early Apr., hours shorten midwinter, $5-9) offers soaking in a cement pool built by the Civilian Conservation Corps in the 1930s. Beneath rocky outcrops, the hot springs heat to 93°F in summer (when rain and snowmelt dilute the hot water) and to 112°F in winter. Primitive hot pools also sit

the pool at Granite Hot Springs

below Granite Falls. The facility has changing rooms (no lockers), pit toilets, and a nearby Forest Service campground. Getting here requires a bumpy drive along a dirt road. In winter, access is only via snowmobiling, skiing, dogsledding, or fat-tire bikes.

To reach Granite Hot Springs from Jackson (34 miles), drive south on U.S. Highway 26/89/189/191 for 13 miles to Hoback Junction. Turn left to follow U.S. Highway 189/191 east for 15 miles. Turn left onto the gravel, two-lane Granite Creek Road (Forest Rd. 30500) and enjoy the 11-mile tour through aspen-rimmed meadows to the road's terminus.

Recreation

DAY HIKES

Trails run up mountains in the Bridger-Teton National Forest (www.fs.usda.gov/btnf). For hiking maps, stop by the **Jackson Hole and Greater Yellowstone Visitor Center** (532 N. Cache St., Jackson, 307/733-3316, 8am-7pm daily summer, 9am-5pm daily winter).

Guides and Equipment

Based in Jackson, **Hole Hiking Experience** (866/733-4453, www.holehike.com, year-round, $245-450/1-2 people, $90-180/pp for more than 2 people) guides day hikes, mixed programs (hiking with rafting or other activities), and customized multiday backpacking trips. The hikes in Bridger-Teton and Caribou-Targhee National Forests are led by seasoned naturalists. Day hikes run four, six, or eight hours; there are reduced rates for kids. Transportation to trailheads, snacks, and lunch for longer trips are included.

Jackson Hole Mountain Resort (3265 W. Village Dr., Teton Village, 307/733-2292 or 888/333-7766, www.jacksonhole.com, $310-420/1-5 people, reservations required) guides day hikes. Resort tram tickets are an extra fee.

To rent hiking gear, go to **Teton Mountaineering** (170 N. Cache Dr., Jackson, 307/733-3595, www.tetonmtn.com, $3-20/item/day). They rent day packs, backpacks, ice axes, crampons, kid carriers, bear canisters, trekking poles, boots, tents, sleeping bags, and sleeping pads. Weeklong gear rentals are priced for five days.

Jackson

SNOW KING MOUNTAIN

Distance: 3.6 miles round-trip
Duration: 3-4 hours
Elevation change: 1,500 feet
Effort: strenuous, but short
Trailhead: at the corner of Snow King Avenue and Cache Street

Hiking up Snow King Mountain in Bridger-Teton National Forest is something locals do for exercise, but it's also a worthy climb for scenery. The 360-degree view from the summit takes in the Tetons, National Elk Refuge, Gros Ventre Mountains, Sleeping Indian, and the town of Jackson. Prepare for a grunt and carry water as the route climbs 1,571 vertical feet. To avoid the knee-pounding descent, take the chairlift down from **Snow King Mountain** (100 E. Snow King Ave., 307/734-3194 or 307/734-9442, http://snowkingmountain.com, 9am-6pm daily late May-early Sept., $5).

From the base area, find the **Snow King Summit Trail** above the ticket office at the chairlift. The trail is a combination of trail and service roads. Climb up three switchbacks, passing the Sink or Swim Trail, to a signed junction with a mountain road. Turn west and traverse across the slope to the end of a switchback, where the steep work begins. Climb up three more switchbacks on the dirt road. The route crests out on the ridge, where a dirt road reaches the summit and the top of the chairlift. Alternate trails also go to the summit.

Teton Village

Hikers at **Jackson Hole Mountain Resort** (3265 W. Village Dr., 307/739-2654, www.jacksonhole.com) in Bridger-Teton National Forest can take a one-hour wildflower walk or long grueling climbs. Bridger Gondola (mid-June-early Sept.) and the **Aerial Tram** (9am-6pm daily late May-early Oct., $25-38) provide elevation gains in the high country without the grunt from Teton Village. From the summit, a trail drops into Granite Canyon in Grand Teton National Park. Those who hike to the top can ride the lift down for free. On upper elevation trails, prepare for exposure to sun, heat, wind, snow, and thunderstorms. Snow may linger on trails into July. To combat altitude sickness, drink lots of water and take your time, especially on ascents. Trail descriptions and maps are online.

RENDEZVOUS MOUNTAIN

Distance: 15-16 miles round-trip
Duration: 8-10 hours
Elevation change: 4,139 feet
Effort: extremely strenuous
Trailhead: Jackson Hole Mountain Resort in Teton Village

It's one long ascent to climb the 10,450-foot Rendezvous Mountain at Jackson Hole Mountain Resort. To chop the mileage in half, most people hike to the summit and take the tram back down. Other hikers take the tram up to drop the knee-pounding descent instead.

Take the **Wildflower Trail** (4 miles, 2-3 hrs.) as it switchbacks up ski slopes to reach the top of the gondola at 9,127 feet. As you ascend the mostly open meadows, the views get bigger and bigger. The trail intersects with Summit Trail service road several times; cross it and look for the trail continuing up. At the top of the gondola, you can stop for snacks, cold drinks, or lunch on the patio. Those who want to bail on the ascent here can take the gondola back down. From the top of the gondola, two routes climb to the summit of Rendezvous Mountain. The gentler **Summit Trail** (3 miles, 2 hrs.) mostly follows service roads with less steep grades to connect with the **Top of the World Loop** to reach the tram. The steeper **Cirque Trail** (1.8 miles, 1.5 hrs.) has more exposure along cliffs. From the 360-degree summit, views east take in Jackson Hole, the Snake River, and Gros Ventre Mountains. To the north, the peaks of Grand Teton National Park line up, including

See Grand Teton from summit of Rendezvous Mountain.

Grand Teton. At the top, hikers can reward themselves with waffles at **Corbet's Cabin** (9am-4pm daily late May-early Oct.). Descend via foot or tram.

CIRQUE TRAIL
Distance: 1.8 miles one-way
Duration: 1.5 hours
Elevation change: 1,323 feet
Effort: moderate down, strenuous up
Trailhead: summit of Rendezvous Mountain at Jackson Hole Mountain Resort

The Cirque Trail connects the top of the Aerial Tram with Bridger Gondola. Most hikers take the tram up and hike down to the gondola before riding back down to Teton Village, but reversing the route works, too, if you want more challenge. From below Corbet's Cabin, follow the trail in a steep descent of a ridge. Stop en route to look down the dizzying Corbet's Couloir. After short switchbacks descend a boulder spine with rough block steps, the trail swings north into the cirque below the couloir. It drops through steep wildflower meadows and under dramatic cliffs to the top of the gondola. Views sweep across Jackson Hole on the entire route. To add more scenery, extend the hike from the junction above the gondola onto **Casper Ridge** (1.75 mi rt., 1.5 hr.).

ROCK SPRINGS LOOP
Distance: 4.3 miles round-trip
Duration: 2.5 hours
Elevation change: 1,000 feet
Effort: moderately strenuous
Trailhead: summit of Rendezvous Mountain at Jackson Hole Mountain Resort

From the top of the tram on Rendezvous Mountain, hike a combination of service roads and trails to take in views of Jackson Hole, the Gros Ventre Mountains, and the Tetons. Begin by taking the **Top of the World Loop** (a service road) along the ridge southward. Those looking for a short jaunt (0.5 mile round-trip) can just walk the loop back to the summit. En route, you'll pass spur trails going to **Green River Overlook, Rock Springs Overlook,** and **Cody Bowl Overlook.**

From the lower end of the loop, continue downhill following the signed route across Rendezvous Bowl into wildflower meadows alternating with forest patches. Listen at talus slopes for the high-pitched "eep" from pikas. After passing wet seeps of Rock Springs, the

The Cirque Trail drops from the top of the tram to Bridger Gondola.

route climbs back to the summit via a service road.

Bridger-Teton National Forest
GOODWIN LAKE

Distance: 6 miles round-trip
Duration: 4 hours
Elevation change: 1,393 feet
Effort: moderate
Trailhead: Goodwin Lake Trailhead
Directions: From the east end of Broadway Street in Jackson, drive northeast on the Elk Refuge Road for 3.7 miles. Turn north and drive one mile, then turn east onto Curtis Canyon. Turn right for 4.3 miles, switchbacking past the campground. At Sheep Creek Junction, stay right for 0.2 mile, then veer left onto Forest Road 30440 for 0.8 mile to reach the trailhead. High-clearance rigs are best on the washboard and pothole road.

At 9,516 feet, Goodwin Lake sits below Jackson Peak in the Gros Ventre Wilderness. The well-traveled trail is mostly snow-free by the end of June and busy in midsummer (get an early start to claim a parking spot at the trailhead). For anglers, the lake holds brook trout.

Starting in a loose forest, the trail breaks out to climb a sagebrush hillside in 0.5 mile. Be sure to look back over your shoulder to see the Tetons. The trail travels south through forest on a steep ascent. After crossing into the wilderness, the route reaches a **rocky slope** at 2.3 miles and climbs through talus breaks. After crossing a dry creek at 2.8 miles, the trail reaches west shore of **Goodwin Lake.**

For bigger views, add a climb to 10,741-foot **Jackson Peak** (4 miles round-trip, 1,225 feet elevation change). From the lake, take the trail southward; at the rock cairn, follow the unmaintained trail to the top for impressive 360-degree views.

BACKPACKING
Teton Crest Trail
45 MILES

While many backpackers limit **Teton Crest Trail** routes to the national park section, the full route encompasses more of the crest south of the park. The 45-mile (4-5-day) trek starts near Teton Pass at Phillips Pass Trailhead and finishes at String Lake Trailhead. It combines trails from Bridger-Teton and Caribou-Targhee National Forests with trails in Grand Teton National Park. Some Teton Crest Trail hikers prefer to gain elevation by launching from **Jackson Hole Mountain Resort** (307/739-2654, www.jacksonhole.com); taking the Aerial Tram (fee) whisks backpackers up to the 10,450-foot summit of Rendezvous Mountain.

Permits are not needed in the national forests, but are required for camping in the national park sections (www.nps.gov/grte). Carry food in approved bear canisters.

MOUNTAIN CLIMBING

Jackson Hole Mountain Resort's Via Ferrata (3265 W. Village Dr., 307/739-2779, www.jacksonhole.com, daily summer, $115/1.5 hrs., $170/3.5 hrs., from $350 for private guides) gives thrillseekers a guided mountain climbing experience on granite walls. The route moves between suspended metal bridges, carved steps, ladders, and iron rungs. For safety, climbers clip themselves in to cables.

For rock, ice, and mountain climbing, **Jackson Hole Mountain Guides** (1325 S. Highway 89, Suite 104, 307/733-4979 or 800/239-7642, http://jhmg.com) leads trips up the Grand Teton, Mt. Moran, and other park summits. Guides also teach safety and technique classes.

BIKING
Road Biking

Although Highway 22 has no bike lane to ascend **Teton Pass,** it's the prime ride for cyclists who like climbing. Start early to beat traffic. From Wilson, a paved bike trail parallels the highway to join Trail Gulch Road, an abandoned road with some remaining rough pavement that switchbacks up the pass.

Road cyclists can get off the narrow, shoulderless highways and onto paved pathways that parallel roads. About 56 miles of the **Jackson Hole Pathway** (www.

friendsofpathways.org) system connects Jackson with Teton Village, the National Elk Refuge, and Moose and Jenny Lakes in Grand Teton National Park; maps are available online. The pathway along the elk refuge is usually closed in winter for wildlife protection, and only a few sections are plowed in winter. The pathways are multiuse, so prepare to meet walkers and, in places, equestrians.

Mountain Biking

Single-track trails abound in Bridger-Teton National Forest surrounding Jackson. The closest riding complex is the **Snow King Trails,** where mountain bikers can ride to the summit of Snow King or loop the **Skyline Trail** and **Cache-Game Trails.** Teton Pass also has several routes, including **Old Pass Road,** for those who want to climb to or descend from the pass. Some trails are for downhill mountain biking only, while others are multiuse. Maps (www.friendsofpathways.org) specify which trails are open to specific user groups.

Jackson Hole Mountain Resort (3265 W. Village Dr., Teton Village, 307/739-2687, www.jacksonhole.com, mid-June-late Sept.) has lift-accessed mountain biking via the five-minute Teewinot Lift. Six trails have jump tracks, banked corners, and skills features for beginners through advanced riders. Rent bikes from Jackson Hole Sports, located in the Bridger Center. The bike park package ($120/half day) includes rental, lift access, helmet, and protective pads. Tours and lessons are available.

Rentals

Several shops rent bikes in Jackson and Teton Village. Most carry mountain bikes, pathway bikes, and kids' bikes, plus trailers for tots. Rentals come with helmets and sometimes bike locks. In addition to renting bikes and bike racks, **Hoback Sports** (520 W. Broadway Ave., Jackson, 307/733-5335, http://hobacksports.com) also does tuning and repairs. For biking the Snow King or Cache-Game Trails, go to **Snow King Mountain Sports** (402

E. Snow King Ave., Jackson, 307/201-5096, http://snowkingmountain.com).

HORSEBACK RIDING

In summer, Jackson Hole is all about horseback riding. You don't need a cowboy hat and boots, but wear long pants, sturdy shoes, and a sun hat. Make reservations in advance and plan to tip your wrangler 15 percent.

Spring Creek Ranch (1800 Spirit Dance Rd., Jackson, 307/733-9209, www.springcreekranch.com, $50/1 hr., $70/2 hrs., $160/half day) guides trail rides on East Gros Ventre Butte with 360-degree views of Jackson Hole.

In Teton Village across the street from Snake River Lodge, **Teton Village Trail Rides** (307/733-2674, www.tetonvillagetrailrides.com, daily in summer, $40/1 hr., $60/2 hrs., $100/4 hrs.) tour routes on the historic Snake River Ranch. Starting at 8am, one-hour rides depart every hour; two-hour rides depart every two hours. Wranglers also lead four-hour rides on Munger Mountain, located about 10 miles south of Teton Village.

WATER SPORTS

Boaters need to have current **registration** and an Aquatic Invasive Species (AIS) sticker, available after passing an inspection (Wyoming Game and Fish, https://wgfd.wyo.gov, Wyoming residents: $10 motorized, $5 nonmotorized; nonresidents: $30 motorized, $15 nonmotorized). The only exemption is for inflatable boats shorter than 10 feet, paddleboards, and sailboards. Forest Service permits are not needed for rafting day trips (unless you have a large group), but you will need a Wyoming AIS sticker.

Rendezvous River Sports (945 W. Broadway, Jackson, 307/733-2471, www.jacksonholekayak.com) rents canoes, stand-up paddleboards, and touring, river, inflatable, and tandem kayaks ($30-60/day). For rivers, rentals include rafts, play boats, surfboards, and trailers ($25-105/day). The company also rents wetsuits, paddle jackets, dry suits, booties, spray skirts, helmets, throw bags, pumps, and PFDs and offers lessons in kayaking or paddleboarding or guided tours in inflatable kayaks.

Boating

In the Gros Ventre Mountains, five-mile-long **Lower Slide Lake** formed from a natural landslide in 1925. The lake has a boat launch with a dock and trailer parking on the east end adjacent to Atherton Campground. It is usually calm in the morning for paddling and fishing, but in the afternoon winds crop up, making it a favorite with windsurfers and small sailboats. Use caution around the lake's standing dead trees, where the forest once grew. To get to the lake, turn right on Gros Ventre Road north of Jackson.

River Rafting and Kayaking

The Snake River is a prime waterway for floating, rafting, and kayaking. The stretch from Grand Teton Park to Hoback Junction provides meandering Class I-II floating with river accesses at Moose, Wilson Bridge, and South Park Bridge. South of Jackson, a trail for kayakers accesses King's Wave for surfing.

SNAKE RIVER CANYON

With easy access along U.S. Highway 89 (25 miles south of Jackson), the Class III+ Snake River jounces through steep-walled **Snake River Canyon** (also called Hoback or Alpine Canyon). It's one of the classic day trips for white water, but don't expect wilderness; its popularity can line the river length with boats, and parking areas crowd at access sites. From the put-in at West Table southwest of Hoback Junction, the white-water section runs 7.4 miles to the Sheep Gulch take-out. You'll hit rapids such as Double D, Haircut Rock, Blind Canyon, and Big Kahuna. Several surf waves provide play boat places for kayakers, but there are also several rapids where rafts frequently flip the unskilled and unwary. A trail above Big Kahuna allows faster access to the big waves for play boating and river surfing. Spring high water can increase the difficulty of this classic rafting river; the river is usually runnable May-September. Easier float sections are upriver from West Table.

A detailed description of the rapids is available from **American Whitewater** (www.americanwhitewater.org), with information on put-ins, take-outs, and river permits from Bridger-Teton National Forest (www.fs.usda.gov/btnf). For diehard boaters who want repeated days, the canyon lines with several Forest Service campgrounds.

Dave Hansen Whitewater takes daily rafting trips down the Snake River.

GUIDES

Whitewater trips (8 miles, mid-May-late Sept., $79-99 adults, $59-89 kids) through Snake River Canyon take four hours round-trip from Jackson. Smaller rafts (6-8 people, higher rates) give more splash, while large rafts can fit up to 10-16 people. Forest Service fees may not be included in the rates; inquire when booking. Most companies have 4-5 departures daily for white-water trips; full-day trips start with floating and end with the white water. Scenic floats and trips with meals (breakfast, lunch, or dinner) are also available. Photographers are stationed on the river and can provide photos for a fee.

Bridger-Teton National Forest licenses all the commercial trips on the Snake River. Four companies operate out of Jackson, providing transportation to and from Snake River Canyon in their rafting rates: **Mad River Boat Trips** (1255 S. Hwy. 89, 307/733-6203 or 800/458-7238, http://mad-river.com), **Dave Hansen Whitewater** (225 W. Broadway, 307/733-6295 or 800/732-6295, www.davehansenwhitewater.com), **Jackson Hole Whitewater** (650 W. Broadway, 307/733-1007 or 888/700-7238, http://jhww.com), and **Lewis and Clark Expeditions** (335 N. Cache Dr., 800/824-5375, www.lewisandclarkriverrafting.com).

Fishing

Fly-fishing anglers gravitate to Jackson Hole for trout fishing, especially for fine-spotted cutthroat trout in the **Snake River**, south of Grand Teton National Park. Dry-fly fishing is best in early spring and after the waters clear in mid-July. Anglers must use catch-and-release tactics. Fishing in the **Gros Ventre River** comes on in early July and runs through August above Lower Slide Lake. In late summer, the river dries up below Kelly. Local fishing outfitters and shops can provide advice on the best flies to use.

Anglers must buy a Wyoming state **fishing license** (https://wgfd.wyo.gov, residents: $3 youth annual, $6 adults daily, $24 adults annual; nonresident: $15 youth annual, $14 adults daily, $92 adults annual), available at fly shops.

GUIDES

For beginners, **Jackson Hole Fly Fishing School** (445 Wister Ave., Jackson, 307/699-3440, www.jhflyfishingschool.com) teaches the basics of casting, mending, and reeling in fish. They offer a 90-minute introductory class ($70 adults, $60 kids) and half-day schools ($180-190 adults, $140-150 kids) for floating or stream fishing.

Fishing **guides** (daily May-Oct., $450-500 half day, $575-600 full day for 2 people) abound in Jackson Hole for wade-fishing or float-fishing. Float trips can take a maximum of two anglers per boat and guide. Full-day trips often include lunch. In Jackson, you can stop in the shops of multiple anglers to book trips: **Reel Deal Anglers** (2070 Cedar Loop, 307/739-7020, www.reeldealanglers.com), **Snake River Angler** (185 Center St., 307/733-3699, http://snakeriverangler.com), **Jackson Hole Anglers** (90 Montana Rd., 307/690-5717, http://jacksonholeanglers.com), and **Fish the Fly** (7255 N. Spring Gulch, 307/690-1139, www.fishthefly.com). **Grand Fishing Adventures** (307/734-9684, www.grandfishing.com) operates out of Teton Village Sports in Teton Village.

Swimming

The **Teton County Recreation Center** (155 E. Gill St., Jackson, 307/739-9025, www.tetonparksandrec.org, year-round, 6am-8pm Mon.-Fri., noon-8pm Sat., noon-7pm Sun., $5-7) has a swimming pool with a waterslide and waterfall, fitness facilities, and locker rooms with showers. Call to confirm hours for lap swimming or open swim.

THRILL SPORTS

In summer, **Snow King Mountain** (330 E. Snow King Ave., Jackson, 307/733-5200, http://snowkingmountain.com, daily late May-early Sept.) turns into a play zone for families. The miniature golf course has 18 holes with fun obstacles. A pair of parallel alpine slides offers families the opportunity to race each other down the mountain (although the slides must close during rainstorms), and the mountain coaster has a one-mile descent on a track. A bungee trampoline gets kids airborne, and the Treetop Adventure Park has four courses of high ropes and aerial thrills. A free bouldering park is at the base of the mountain.

In summer, **Jackson Hole Mountain Resort** (3265 W. Village Dr., Teton Village, 307/739-2779 or 307/739-2654, www.jacksonhole.com, daily late May-early Oct.) turns into a family adventure land. The Grand Adventure Park drapes trees with a maze of ziplines, cargo nets, balance beams, freefall drops, and different levels of challenges. A bungee trampoline offers flying thrills, and the family can play a nine-hole, 3,150-foot-long disc golf course, or climb towers.

GOLF AND TENNIS

The golf season in Jackson Hole runs daily May through mid-October. Don't be surprised if a moose walks across the fairway. Club rentals run $50-75. Lessons are available through the pro shops.

North of the National Elk Refuge, **Jackson Hole Golf and Tennis Club** (5000 Spring Gulch Rd., Jackson, 307/733-3111, www.jhgtc.com, $70-190) is an 18-hole course redesigned by Robert Trent Jones Jr. It's a semi-private club, but guests can book tee times after the first two hours in the day (book one month in advance by phone or online). Tennis is private.

Teton Pines Resort and Country Club (3450 N. Clubhouse Dr., Wilson, 307/733-1005, www.tetonpines.com, $70-160) is the closest golf and tennis club to Teton Village. The 18-hole semi-private golf course was designed by Arnold Palmer and Ed Seay. Nonmembers can make tee times for noon or later; a few tee times are available online, but you may have better luck by phone. Tennis (307/733-9248, 8:30am-7:30pm Mon.-Thurs., shorter hours Fri.-Sun., year-round, $14-28/person by reservation only) aficionados can play outdoors on six hard courts and two clay courts or indoors.

WINTER SPORTS
Skiing and Snowboarding

Snow King Mountain (100 E. Snow King Ave., Jackson, 307/734-3194, http://snowking-mountain.com, early Dec.-Mar., $28-58) is not usually a choice for diehard destination skiers and snowboarders, but families like its smaller size (400 acres, 3 lifts), night skiing, half-day afternoon rates, terrain park, and tubing.

★ JACKSON HOLE MOUNTAIN RESORT

With big vertical, steep chutes, and a reputation as a big, bad experts-only ski area, **Jackson Hole Mountain Resort** (3265 W. Village Dr., Teton Village, 307/733-2292, www.jacksonhole.com, late Nov.-early Apr., $105-150 adults, discounts for seniors, juniors, and advance online purchase) in reality has only 50 percent of its terrain devoted to advanced runs. The rest is rolling groomers for beginners and intermediates. The resort's 4,139 vertical feet has 15 lifts spread across 2,500 acres, including the Aerial Tram that goes to the 10,450-foot summit of Rendezvous Mountain. The average year delivers 450 inches of snowfall. Lift tickets are pricey, but there are cheaper rates online and with lodging packages. The resort offers lessons and has several terrain parks, restaurants, and rental shops.

HELI- AND SNOWCAT SKIING

Heli- and snowcat skiing can rack up 12,000-15,000 vertical feet in places where you have elbow room in big bowls, glades, and steeps. **High Mountain Heli-Skiing** (Teton Village, 307/733-3274, www.heliskijackson.com, mid-Dec.-Mar., $1,375/pp) has access to five mountain ranges surrounding Jackson Hole. A trip usually gets in six runs per day and trips can also be packaged with lodging. Reservations are required.

BACKCOUNTRY SKIING

The Tetons are a backcountry ski mecca. Slap on a pair of skins and grab the transceiver, beacon, and probe to head out for skiing. Teton Pass, Jackson Hole Mountain Resort side country, and hike-to terrain beyond the boundaries of Grand Targhee Resort are the most popular places to go. Consult with experts at **Teton Mountaineering** (170 N. Cache Dr., Jackson, 307/733-3595, http://tetonmtn.com) when renting gear and check on **avalanche conditions** (Bridger Teton Avalanche Center, 307/733-2664, http://jhavalanche.org) before you go. Guides from **Jackson Hole Mountain Resort** (307/739-2779, www.jacksonhole.com) lead trips that exit resort boundaries and go to Teton Pass.

Cross-Country Skiing and Snowshoeing

Located four miles south of Jackson Hole Mountain Resort, **Teton Pines Nordic Center** (www.tetonpinesnordiccenter.com, daily mid-Nov.-early Mar., $10-15) grooms 16 kilometers of trails daily for skate and classic skiing on rolling golf course terrain. Rentals and lessons are available, and a ski shop is on site.

Jackson Hole Nordic (http://jhnordic.com) provides information on local trails and grooming reports for skiing or snowshoeing. One of the most scenic places to snowshoe is from the summit of **Teton Pass.** Follow Forest Road 019 south for about three-quarters of a mile (1.5 miles round-trip); it's short but big on scenery. A trail continues from the end of the road, but you'll need avalanche gear to proceed.

RENTALS AND GUIDES

Skinny Skis (65 W. Deloney, Jackson, 307/733-6094 or 888/733-7205, www.skinnyskis.com, $15-30/day) rents snowshoes and packages for ski touring, metal-edge touring, and skate-skiing. The shop also waxes and tunes skis.

Hole Hiking Experience (Jackson, 866/733-4453, www.holehike.com, daily in winter, $80-175/pp) guides cross-country ski trips (half or full day) and snowshoe tours (2-6 hours). They also have trips that combine snowshoeing with wildlife-watching or other activities.

Snowmobiling

Snowmobile routes tour the Gros Ventre Mountains. A unique trip goes to the **Granite Hot Springs** (20 miles round-trip, early Dec.-early Apr.) in Bridger-Teton National Forest. The tour follows snow-buried Granite Creek Road (Forest Rd. 30500) up Granite Creek to the hot springs. The route is suitable for beginning snowmobilers. **Togwotee Lodge** (1050 S. Hwy. 89, Jackson, 866/278-4245, www.togwoteelodge.com, $275-350) guides trips to the hot springs with pickups in Jackson. The company also guides snowmobile tours into Yellowstone ($325-500). Reservations are required.

For those who can go on their own, snowmobile rentals are available from **Leisure Sports** (1075 S. Hwy. 89, Jackson, 307/733-3040, www.jacksonholefun.com) or **Jackson Hole Adventure Rentals** (1060 S. Hwy. 89, Jackson, 307/733-5678 or 877/773-5678, http://jhadventure.com). Rentals run about $165-250 per day; winter suits cost $5-20 per item. Snowmobile trailers are also available.

Ice-Skating

A free outdoor ice rink operates at the Town Square in Jackson. **Grand Teton Skating Association** (noon-8pm daily mid-Dec.-Feb., $5) rents skates. **Snow King Sports** (100 E. Snow King Ave., 307/201-1633, https://snowkingsec.com, daily mid-Oct.-Mar., $5 rentals) has indoor public skating ($6-8) and open hockey or figure skating sessions ($10).

Tubing

King Tubes (Snow King Mountain, 100 E. Snow King Ave., Jackson, 307/734-9442, http://snowkingmountain.com, 2pm-7pm Tues.-Fri., 11am-7pm Sat.-Sun. early Dec.-Mar., $15-20/pp 1 hr., $5/additional hours) requires no skill on the snow to have some fun sliding. A rope tow pulls you and your tube up a hill where you can then sail down.

Dogsledding

Dogsled tours (late Nov.-early Apr.) take place on the fringes of Jackson Hole and require longer drives or shuttles to reach their locations. Reservations are required, with pick-ups available in Jackson. Owned by eight-time Iditarod veteran Frank Teasley, **Jackson**

Hole Iditarod Sled Dog Tours (307/733-7388 or 800/554-7388, http://jhsleddog.com) runs trips to Granite Hot Springs in Bridger-Teton National Forest.

Entertainment and Shopping

NIGHTLIFE
Jackson
Most of the nightlife in Jackson takes place in venues surrounding Jackson Town Square. Top stop is the **Million Dollar Cowboy Bar** (25 N. Cache St., 307/733-2207, www.milliondollarcowboybar.com, 11am-2am daily year-round), crowned with its neon cowboy on a horse. The bar is decked out with knobbled-pine trim, inlaid silver coins, saddles with saddle blankets as stools, cowboy murals, wildlife mounts, and western artifacts. It's a place to shoot pool, and live music makes patrons take to the dance floor. The beer is made by Grand Teton Brewing Company; Jack Daniel's whiskey comes by the barrel. The **Million Dollar Cowboy Steakhouse** (307/733-4790, www.jhcowboysteakhouse.com) downstairs serves western food.

The **Silver Dollar Bar** (50 N. Glenwood St., 307/733-2190 or 800/322-2727, www.worthotel.com, 11am-2am) at the landmark Wort Hotel, mixes an authentic historic western ambience of oil paintings, murals, and bronzes with live entertainment. The bar counter is inlaid with 2,032 uncirculated silver dollars from 1921. Music plays on multiple nights weekly.

Part of the nightlife buzz around Jackson Town Square, the **Pink Garter Theatre** (50 W. Broadway Ave., 307/733-1500, www.pinkgartertheatre.com) hosts visiting bands—from hip-hop to string—in the standing-room-only venue, as well as films with full seating. The **Jackson Hole Center for the Arts** (265 Cache St., 307/734-8956, www.jhcenterforthearts.org) houses a 500-seat theater that hosts concerts, plays, ballets, film tours, and other performances.

Located near the Jackson Town Square, the **Jackson Hole Playhouse and Saddle Rock Saloon** (145 W. Deloney Ave., 307/733-6994, www.jacksonplayhouse.com, $20-55 shows, $40-85 with dinner) puts on nightly theater performances in summer, fall, and late winter; summer usually features classic Broadway musicals. **Off Square Theatre Company** (240 S. Glenwood St., 307/733-4900, www.offsquare.org) stages four musicals and plays annually, put on by local actors at various venues in town.

Jackson Hole Cinemas (307/733-2939, www.jacksonholecinemas.com) runs two theaters in Jackson: **Jackson Hole Twin Cinema** (295 W. Pearl St.) and **Movieworks Cinema** (860 S. Hwy. 89).

In winter, expert astronomers host public **stargazing** events (www.wyomingstargazing.org) on the lawn in front of the Center for the Arts (7:30pm-9:30pm Fri. Nov.-May) or at Rendezvous Park in Wilson (9pm-11pm Fri. June-Oct.). Their huge telescope focuses on star clusters, planets, and nebulae.

Teton Village
The **Mangy Moose Saloon** (3200 W. McCollister Dr., 307/733-4913, http://mangymoose.com, 11am-close daily late May-early Oct. and Nov.-mid-Apr.) has an après-ski saloon vibe. Drink local microbrews next to the namesake mangy moose, order a spicy margarita made with jalapeños, and rock to live music. Loud, and at times raucous, the bar frequently makes the list of top après-ski bars in the country. It's located at the base of Jackson Hole Mountain Resort. **Jackson Hole Mountain Resort** (3265 W. Village Dr., 307/733-2292 or 888/333-7766, www.jacksonhole.com, 5pm

Sun. in summer) sponsors free outdoor family concerts below the Tram.

FESTIVALS AND EVENTS
Spring
In the early 1950s, elk antlers were used to build the first arch in the Jackson Town Square. Boy Scouts began collecting the antlers in the late 1950s; a decade later, they started the annual **Boy Scout Antler Auction** (Jackson Town Square, www.fws.gov/refuge/National_Elk_Refuge, May). Commonly known as Elkfest, the event takes place the Saturday before Memorial Day weekend. Registered bidders can purchase elk antlers collected from the National Elk Refuge; 75 percent of the proceeds go back to the refuge.

Summer
The **Jackson Hole Rodeo** (Teton County Fairgrounds, 447 Snow King Ave., Jackson, 307/733-7927, www.jhrodeo.com, 8pm-10pm Wed. and Fri.-Sat. late May-early Sept., $15-35) offers a chance to see local cowboys and cowgirls in action; events include bronc and bull riding, roping, and barrel racing. Kids can participate in a calf scramble to nab a ribbon off its tail. Three types of seating are available in the grandstands: reserved, roof-covered general admission, and uncovered general admission. Be prepared for rain, or book a covered seat. Buy discounted tickets in advance online to avoid the ticket lines at the rodeo grounds. Arrive at 7:15pm to claim a seat in the general admission zones.

For 10 days in late July, the **Teton County Fair** (Teton County Fairgrounds, 447 Snow King Ave., Jackson, 307/733-5289, www.tetoncountyfair.com, 5pm-midnight Wed.-Fri., 2pm-midnight Sat.-Sun.) hosts carnival rides, rodeos, farm animal shows, pig wrestling, food booths, and other county fair fun.

The **Grand Teton Music Festival** (Walk Festival Hall, 3330 Cody Ln., Teton Village, 307/733-1128, http://gtmf.org, July-mid-Aug., $25-55) draws musicians and conductors from top symphonies across the country and soloists from around the world. Concerts run five nights weekly. Single tickets go on sale in March (online or by phone) and are available in person at the box office (10am-5pm Mon.-Sat.) in late June.

Fall
For 11 days, Jackson is home to the **Jackson Hole Fall Arts Festival** (locations vary, 307/733-3316, www.jacksonholechamber.com, mid-Sept.), which features about 50 events that highlight western, wildlife, Native American, and landscape works from nationally and internationally known artists. Music, food, and wine events take place throughout town and at local ranches; gallery walks tour downtown exhibitions. Some events are free; others charge a fee.

Winter
As Wyoming's Iditarod, the **International Pedigree Stage Stop Sled Dog Race** (Jackson Town Square, Jackson, www.wyomingstagestop.org, late Jan.-early Feb.) pits sled dogs and mushers in an eight-stage race across 350 miles. Starting in downtown Jackson, this two-mile leg goes through town lined with onlookers. The public can meet teams in the morning; festivities launch the event and take place around Jackson Town Square. The party continues at Snow King Mountain, with fireworks and a torchlight parade.

The whine of snowmobiles fills Jackson for four days in late March when the Jackson Hole Snow Devils put on their annual **Snowmobile Hillclimb** (Snow King Mountain, 100 E. Snow King Ave., Jackson, 307/734-9653, www.snowdevils.org, 8am-6pm late Mar., $15). Crowds show up to watch the carnage as snowmobiles race up 1,500 vertical feet that steepens to 45 degrees. Those who fail roll back down the slope.

SHOPPING
Jackson
Shopping ranges from art galleries and outdoor shops to bookstores. More than 25 art

Cowboy Attire

While photos of Jackson Hole show plenty of cowboy hats, you don't have to own a cowboy hat to visit Wyoming, attend a rodeo, or walk into the Million Dollar Cowboy Bar. In fact, you don't even have to buy one as a souvenir. But if you want to go cowboy or cowgirl, check out the hats at **Jackson Hole Hat Company** (45 W. Deloney St., Jackson, 307/733-7687, www.jhhatco.com, 10am-6pm Mon.-Sat., noon-5pm Sun.). The company hand-makes custom hats and sells other famous brands. If you want the total cowboy look with hat and boots, head to **Beaver Creek Hats & Leather** (36 E. Broadway, Jackson, 307/733-1999, www.beavercreekhats.com, 10am-6pm daily), where you can also tack on boots and other western accessories. The **Boot Barn** (840 W. Broadway, Jackson, 307/733-0247, www.bootbarn.com, 9am-8pm Mon.-Sat., 11am-6pm Sun.) has the biggest selection of boots, hats, and western garb, but it's also a chain store found in about half the states in the United States.

Cowboy culture flavors Jackson Hole, but most people wear casual modern outdoor clothing with a few plaid flannel shirts thrown in here and there. With the exception of upscale restaurants, you'll see people walk into cafés, brewpubs, restaurants, and bars while wearing ski clothing and snow boots in winter and hiking boots and gear in summer. After all, Jackson Hole is all about the mountain outdoors.

Folks dress in layers to adapt to the changeable weather that can happen during one day. Rain shells double as wind protection, especially in spring and fall. Gloves and hats protect extremities from frostbite or just getting cold. Even in summer, rain shells, layers, hats, and gloves may be necessary when a cold front blows in. That gear can also work in winter with the addition of warmer layers underneath. Jeans or Carhartts are also ubiquitous, especially for indoor activities, dining, and some outdoor activities such as horseback riding. But jeans soak up water from rain or snow like a sponge. For the wetter, colder seasons and summer hiking, quick-dry layers and rain pants will better protect you from the elements.

galleries cluster in town, providing a combination of fine, western, Native American, and modern art in a variety of mediums. Most of the galleries are located in the few downtown blocks surrounding the Jackson Town Square. **Jackson Hole Gallery Association** (http://jacksonholegalleryassociation.com) organizes art walks. Most shop hours shorten during off-season.

Galleries around Jackson Town Square sell handmade jewelry, woodcarvings, furniture, bronze sculptures, photography, and crafts from local artisans and internationally acclaimed artists. For traditional and innovative regional Western art, visit **Grand Teton Gallery** (130 W. Broadway, 307/201-1172, https://thegrandjh.com, 10am-6pm Mon.-Wed. and Fri.-Sat., 10am-8pm Thurs., 10am-5pm Sun.), **Mountain Trails Gallery** (155 North Center St., 307/734-8150, www.mtntrails.net, 10am-9pm daily), and **West Lives On Gallery** (55 N. Glenwood St. and 75 N. Glenwood St., 307/734-2888, http://westliveson.com, 9am-6pm Mon.-Sat., 10am-6pm Sun.). **Cayuse Western Americana** (255 N. Glenwood St., 307/739-1940, http://cayusewa.com, 10am-6pm Mon.-Sat.) is the place to go for antique cowboy items and Native American art. **MADE** (125 N. Cache, 307/690-7957, www.madejacksonhole.com, 10am-6pm daily) carries the handcrafted art of 125 local and regional artists.

Valley Book Store (125 N. Cache Dr., 307/733-4533, www.valleybookstore.com, 9am-7pm Mon.-Sat., 10am-6pm Sun.) is an independent bookstore that carries a good collection of field guides, trail guides, and books about the region, national parks, natural history, and recreation. The store also carries books by local authors.

You can get outfitted in Jackson for outdoor recreation. **Skinny Skis** (65 W. Deloney Ave., 307/733-6094 or 888/733-7205, www.skinnyskis.com, 9am-8pm Mon.-Sat.,

9am-7pm Sun.) sells gear for cross-country skate and classic skiing, snowshoeing, hiking, backpacking, trail running, and climbing. **Teton Mountaineering** (170 N. Cache St., 307/733-3595 or 800/850-3595, www.tetonmtn.com, 8:30am-8pm daily) is one of the oldest mountaineering shops in Jackson with gear for backcountry skiing, rock climbing, backpacking, and mountaineering. **Hoback Sports** (520 W. Broadway, 307/733-5335, www.hobacksports.com, 10am-6pm daily) carries downhill skis, snowboards, mountain bikes, and accessories. For hiking, fishing, skiing, snowboarding, and camping gear, go to **JD High Country Outfitters** (50 E. Broadway, 307/733-3270, http://jdhcoutfitters.com, 9am-7pm daily). **Stio** (10 E. Broadway, 307/201-1890, www.stio.com, 9am-8pm daily)

carries outdoor mountain clothing for hiking, climbing, skiing, snowboarding, or bicycling. You can also buy recycled gear through **Headwall Recycle Sports** (520 S. Hwy. 89, 307/734-8022, www.headwallsports.com, 9am-7pm daily); they carry outdoor gear for hiking, camping, skiing, snowboarding, and biking.

Teton Village

In Teton Village, stores are geared toward ski and snowboard shops in winter and hiking in summer. **Teton Village Sports** (3285 W. Village Dr., 307/733-2181, www.tetonvillagesports.com, 9am-6pm daily) carries high-quality outdoor clothing, Jackson Hole Mountain Resort logo wear, and outdoor gear for skiing, snowboarding, and hiking.

Food

Dining in Jackson Hole is a culinary treat. While many restaurants lean heavily toward Wyoming bison, game, and fish, innovative cuisine is common. Even the meat-heavy menus have yummy vegan, vegetarian, or gluten-free alternatives. Make reservations for dinner or you may have a very long wait.

JACKSON

Most restaurants and cafés are open year-round; some shorten hours or days in spring, fall, and winter. Expect meal prices to be spendy (due to Jackson's resort town status), but not as high as in Teton Village.

Cafés

★ **Persephone Bakery** (145 E. Broadway, 307/200-6708, http://persephonebakery.com, 7am-6pm Mon.-Sat., 7am-5pm Sun., $4-15) churns out rustic artisan breads and crispy pastries—classic croissants, brioche, and scones. Stop in for a baked treat with an espresso or unique meals such as the small herbed omelets or sweet potato and Brussels sprout hash. Breakfast toast and lunch

sandwiches come on their bread. The tiny bakery café serves breakfast (7am-3pm) and lunch (10:30am-3pm).

Tucked into a historic log cabin with indoor and outdoor seating, **Café Genevieve** (135 E. Broadway, 307/732-1910, https://genevievejh.com, 8am-5:30pm daily, $9-40) delivers yummy foods with southern flair. Breakfast includes waffles, frittatas, or eggs Benedict with house-made Cajun sausage. Lunch features sandwiches, burgers, and salads. Happy hour cocktails and appetizers, including pig candy (candied bacon), fill in before dinner brings on an eclectic mix of steaks, jambalaya, fish, and burgers.

American

People drive miles to get **MacPhail's Burgers** (399 W. Broadway, 307/733-8744, http://macphailsburgers.com, 11:30am-9pm Mon.-Sat., $14-31). This high-end venue uses fresh ingredients daily: They grind their own Angus beef, bake their own buns, and cut their own Idaho spud fries. Burgers are made with buffalo or beef, and can come in lettuce wraps. Top it off with a shake, malt, beer, or wine.

At **Liberty Burgers** (160 N. Cache, 307/200-6071, http://givemelibertyburger. com, 11:30am-9pm daily, $6-13), you can get the standard burger, or order it doctored up with wild arugula, garlic aioli, avocado, specialty cheeses, and bacon. Burger options include beef, house-made vegetarian, lamb, ham, ahi tuna, turkey, and bison. Round it out with kale salad, sweet potato fries, stuffed roasted jalapenos, shakes, floats, malts, beer, wine, and cocktails.

Fine Dining

In a small historic house, the **Blue Lion** (160 N. Millward St., 307/733-3912, http://bluelion-restaurant.com, 5:30pm-10pm daily, $20-43) serves fish, meat, wine, and a dash of romance. It's the place for elk tenderloin, a rack of lamb, or rainbow trout. Some pasta dishes can be made vegetarian or vegan. Finish off the feast with the house mud pie.

At Spring Creek Ranch outside town, **The Granary** (1800 Spirit Dance Rd., 307/732-8112, www.springcreekranch.com, 7am-11am and 5pm-9pm daily, $12-20 breakfast, $27-45 dinner) has a dining location on Gros Ventre Butte that beats the views at Jackson

restaurants. Tall windows take in the Teton Mountains, best for dining around sunrise or sunset. The seasonal menu revolves around eggs Benedict for breakfast and elk, bison, or fish for dinner.

To watch food artistry in action, gather around the open kitchen at the chef-owned **Trio** (45 S. Glenwood St., 307/734-8038, http://bistrotrio.com, 5:30am-10pm daily, $18-48). An eclectic menu offers rabbit gnocchi, lamb chops, fish, and pork tenderloin. The wood-fired oven puts out pizzas and house-made s'mores.

Steakhouses

Across the street from the Jackson Town Square, **Local** (55 N. Cache St., 307/201-1717, http://localjh.com, 11:30am-close daily, $12-21 lunch, $21-48 dinner) serves steaks with a contemporary flair. Lunch is served until 2:30pm, while dinner starts at 5:30pm, but you can order appetizers and small plates in between. The chef-owned restaurant serves local and regional beer, wine, spirits, cheeses, steaks, lamb, and baked goods.

A block off the Town Square, **Snake River Grill** (84 E. Broadway, 307/733-0557, http://snakerivergrill.com, 5:30pm-10pm daily, $23-54) does creative fish, elk

croissant at Persephone Bakery

medallions, and Wagyu or Angus steaks, artfully presented and cooked to perfection. For lighter fare, share several small plates, including truffle fries.

Tapas and Small Plates

At ★ **Bin 22** (200 W. Broadway, 307/739-9463, www.bin22jacksonhole.com, 11:30am-10pm Mon.-Sat., 3pm-10pm Sun., $6-29), you'll think you're in a wine shop . . . which you are. Walk through the cases of wine to the back where delightful tapas and small plates are served with wines and craft beers. Choose a spot at the bar, outside on the patio, or at one of several big, shareable tables with stools that foster conversations between strangers. Tasty small-plate entrées are made to share: pancetta-wrapped dates, house-pulled mozzarella, and several Spanish dishes, with enough variety and substance to turn the whole dining adventure into a full, long, leisurely meal.

Vegetarian

For vegetarian, vegan, gluten-free, dairy-free, organic, raw, paleo, all-natural, or locavore cuisine, go to the **Lotus** (140 N. Cache St., Suite B, 307/734-0882, www.tetonlotuscafe.com, 8am-9pm daily, $9-32). Although a trifle spendy, you can get house-baked organic bread, egg-white breakfasts, organic tofu, kale, fresh greens, grass-fed beef, organic chicken, Southeast Asian specialties, noodle or rice bowls, cold-pressed juices, smoothies, espresso, beer, wine, and cocktails. Enjoy it all in their upscale atmosphere.

Cookouts

Cowboyland means cookouts in summer under the evening sky. Make reservations for all cookouts in advance.

Reaching the **Bar T 5 Cookout** (812 Cache Creek Dr., 307/733-5386 or 800/772-5386, www.bart5.com, 4:45pm or 6pm Mon.-Sat. mid-May-Sept., $46 adults, $38 kids) requires riding two miles in a covered wagon from Jackson to Cache Creek, where cowhands cook a meal of Dutch-oven roast beef under an outdoor pavilion. After dinner, the Bar

Bin 22 serves small plates.

T 5 band plays western music before guests ride the covered wagons back to town. In late August, departure times are earlier.

The **Spring Creek Resort** (1800 Spirit Dance Rd., Jackson, 307/733-9209, www.springcreekranch.com, 6pm Sun., Tues., and Thurs. in summer, $75 adults, $45 kids) wagon ride goes to the Sage Overlook for a three-course cookout. It's a classic outdoor barbecue with a s'mores bar around the campfire.

Located in Wilson (about 10 minutes from downtown Jackson), the **Bar J Chuckwagon** (4200 W. Bar J Chuckwagon, 307/733-3370 or 800/905-2275, www.barj-chuckwagon.com, 7pm daily late May-early Sept., Mon.-Sat. mid-late Sept., $25-35 adults, $12 kids) serves a western dinner for 750 people in cattle-call fashion. The gates open at 5:30pm with pre-dinner wagon rides and Dutch-oven biscuits. Claim your own seat for the barbecued beef, chicken, ribs, or steak dinner with sides. The Bar J Wranglers do a western show with a combo of twangy music and cowboy stories.

Groceries

Jackson has multiple supermarkets. **Jackson Whole Grocer** (1155 S. Hwy. 89, 307/733-0450, http://jacksonwholegrocer.com, 7am-10pm daily) has the biggest selection of fresh, local, and organic produce. For upscale market items, check out the **Pearl Street Market** (40 W. Pearl St., 307/733-1300, www.pearlstmarketjh.com, 7am-9pm daily). Heading north out of Jackson toward Grand Teton National Park, you can stop at **Creekside Market and Deli** (545 N. Cache Dr., 307/733-7926, www.creeksidejacksonhole.com, 6am-8pm daily).

TETON VILLAGE

Most restaurants in Teton Village open **late November-early April** and **mid-May-late September** in conjunction with Jackson Hole Mountain Resort lift operations. Only a few are open year-round, and they shorten their hours in spring and fall. Make reservations for dinner; otherwise, you are guaranteed a long wait.

American

Steaks, meat, fish, burgers, and bison (this is Wyoming, after all) are served at several casual and family-friendly Teton Village restaurants. Most have broad menus for light dining or multicourse meals that change seasonally. Patio seating is available in summer.

The **Spur Restaurant and Bar** (Teton Mountain Lodge, 3385 Cody Ln., 307/732-6932, www.tetonlodge.com, 7am-10pm daily year-round) serves breakfast (7am-10am, $7-17), lunch (11:30am-5pm, $12-20), and dinner (5:30pm-10pm, $22-30). House specialties include charcuterie of local cheeses and meats, buffalo short ribs braised in the locally brewed Zonker Stout, and Snake River Farms Kobe steaks. The cocktail menu has fun finds and innovative shared plates for après-skiing or hiking.

A longtime ski area classic, the **Mangy Moose Restaurant** (3295 Village Dr., 307/733-4913, www.mangymoose.com, 5:30pm-10pm daily mid-May-Oct., late Nov.-early Apr., $19-45) has grown over the years from its roots next to the party-hard après-ski bar (the famous saloon across the hall in the same building). The two-story restaurant is adorned with funky ski and western relics. The dinner menu serves up steaks, prime rib, Idaho rainbow trout, and elk chops. Go to the saloon for lunch (11am-2:30pm, $8-15) and its signature spicy margarita; live music cranks up most evenings.

In a casual beer-hall atmosphere with outdoor terrace seating in summer and winter, **The Handle Bar** (Four Seasons, 7680 Granite Loop Rd., 307/732-5000, www.fourseasons.com/jacksonhole, 11am-11pm daily May-Oct., late Nov.-early Apr., $12-40) is a modern take on an American pub. Sit in the restaurant, at the bar, or on the terrace flanked with gas flames in winter and enjoy views up to the summit of Rendezvous Mountain. The diverse menu features fish and chips, burgers, and sammies for lunch and steaks and fish for dinner. If you aren't walking or skiing to the pub, complimentary valet parking is available from the front of the Four Seasons.

International

An expansion from the original restaurant in Driggs, Idaho, ★ **Teton Thai** (7342 Granite Loop Rd., 307/733-0022, http://tetonthaivillage.com, 11:30am-9:30pm Mon.-Sat. mid-May-Sept.; 11:30am-9pm daily late Nov.-early Apr., $7-22) serves classic recipes from Bangkok—from pad Thai to roasted duck curry. Many dishes can be made vegan or vegetarian, and multiple curries can be customized for spiciness (and they can do HOT!). Beer, wine, sake, and specialty cocktails are available. The restaurant is located near Ranch Lot. Locals avoid waiting in lines by ordering take-out.

★ **Il Villaggio Osteria** (Hotel Terra, 3335 W. Village Dr., 307/739-4100, www.jhosteria.com, breakfast 7am-10am, lunch 11:30am-4pm, dinner 5:30pm-close daily year-round, $8-34) brings Italy to the Wyoming slopes with house-made pastas and an atmosphere that rings true to a bustling

Craft Coffee and Beer

Snake River Brewing

BEER AND WINE

- **Snake River Brewing** (265 S. Millward, Jackson, 307/739-2337, www.snakeriverbrewing. com): This brewpub staple whips up award-winning pale ale, lager, and Zonker Stout along with a host of specialty brews.

- **Roadhouse Brewing** (2550 Moose-Wilson Rd., Wilson, 307/739-0700, www.roadhouse-brewery.com): The brewery and restaurant offers hefty tastes of their Sweet Potato Porter, Brain Dead Double IPA, and Beautiful Buzz Espresso Stout.

- **Jackson Hole Brewing** (307/413-5459, http://jacksonholebrewingco.com): Find the few beers, such as Static Peak Stout, crafted by this brewery in local watering holes.

- **Grand Teton Brewing** (430 Old Jackson Hwy., Victor, ID, 888/899-1656, www.grandteton-brewing.com): Grand Teton Brewing's signature year-round brews include Old Faithful Ale, Howling Wolf hefeweizen, and Bitch Creek ESB, named for the creek on the Teton's west side.

- **Wildlife Brewing** (145 S. Main St., Victor, ID, 208/787-2623, http://wildlifebrewing.com): This Teton Valley staple puts out Mighty Bison Brown Ale, Buckwild Double Blonde, and Ale Slinger IPA.

- **Jackson Hole Winery** (2800 Boyles Hill Rd., Jackson, 307/201-1057, http://jacksonholew-inery.com): Make an appointment to taste the Tetons' home vintage.

ESPRESSO AND LOCAL ROASTERS

- **Jackson Hole Roasters** (50 S. Broadway, Jackson, 307/200-6099, www.jacksonholeroast-ers.com)

- **Cowboy Coffee Company** (125 N. Cache St., Jackson, 307/733-7392, http://cowboycof-fee.com)

- **Elevated Grounds** (3445 N. Pines Way #102, Wilson, 307/734-1343, http://elevatedground-scoffeehouse.com)

- **Snake River Roasting** (3610 S. Park Dr., Jackson, 307/734-9446, www.snakeriverroastingco. com, online only)

SWEETS

- **Moo's Gourmet Ice Cream** (155 Center St., Jackson, 307/733-1998, www.moosjackson-hole.com)

- **Cocolove** (55 N. Glenwood, Jackson, 307/733-3253) sells boutique gelato and artisan chocolates.

Il Villaggio Osteria serves Italian specialties.

filled with flavors from the Italian countryside plus American vineyards.

The **Alpenrose** (Alpenhof Lodge, 3255 W. Village Dr., 307/733-3242, www.alpenhoflodge.com, 5:30pm-close daily mid-May-Sept. and late Nov.-early Apr., $21-34) serves Swiss-German specialties that include raclette, schnitzel, sauerbraten, and strudel, plus multiple fondue courses of meats, seafood, cheese, and chocolate. For a casual option, eat lunch (11:30am-3pm, $10-20) or dinner (6pm-9pm, $12-24) in the **Alpenhof Bistro,** with deck dining in summer.

Fine Dining

For gourmet dining overlooking the ski slopes, the ★ **Westbank Grill** (Four Seasons, 7680 Granite Loop Rd., 307/732-5000 or 307/732-5156, www.fourseasons.com/jacksonhole, 7am-11am and 6pm-10pm daily May-Oct., late Nov.-early Apr., $34-70) combines professional service and knowledgeable sommeliers that can advise wine pairings with dinner. It's a romantic place for sinking into a leisurely multicourse dinner: appetizers, wine, entrées, and dessert. As a steakhouse, the grill serves regional Wagyu beef and succulent game such as buffalo, elk, wild boar, and duck, all with choices of sauces. For diners coming by car,

Italian eatery. The menu contains classic but fresh takes on antipasti, seasonal ensalata, primi pastas, secondi, and wood-fired pizza. The salumi bar serves up imported hand-sliced meats and cheeses, and the wine list is

Corbet's Cabin

the resort has complimentary valet service. Breakfast and a children's menu are available.

Jackson Hole Mountain Resort

Jackson Hole Mountain Resort (307/739-2675, www.jacksonhole.com) operates several on-mountain eateries accessed via lifts (tickets required). Reached via Aerial Tram at the top of Rendezvous Mountain, tiny **Corbet's Cabin** (9am-3pm daily late May-early Oct. and late Nov.-early Apr., $8) serves waffles. (It's more about the fun of eating waffles at 10,440 feet rather than exceptional food.) Located in Rendezvous Lodge at the top of the Bridger Gondola, **Piste Mountain Bistro** (daily June-Sept. and late Nov.-early Apr., $16-26) takes advantage of the views from 9,095 feet with huge windows overlooking Jackson Hole. Upscale seasonal menus emphasize regional sourcing, and wine, beer, and cocktails are served. Deck dining is available, as is grab-and-go food and pizza from the adjacent market downstairs. Hours change seasonally; sometimes dinner service is added.

Groceries

Teton Village has several small markets, but prepare for resort prices. The cheaper markets are in Jackson. The **Mangy Moose Market and Cellars** (3200 W. McCollister Dr., 307/734-0090 or 307/734-0070, www.mangy-moose.com, 10am-10pm daily late May-early Oct. and late Nov.-early Apr.) carries groceries, liquor, beer, and wine. The **Jackson Hole General Store** (307/732-4090, www.jacksonhole.com, 7am-5pm daily late May-early Oct. and late Nov.-early Apr.), located at the base of the Aerial Tram, carries a few grab-and-go items and serves espresso, hot chocolate, smoothies, and ice cream.

Accommodations

Visitors to Jackson Hole have considerable lodging choices. Jackson has moderate to inexpensive lodging, chain hotels, historic inns, and a handful of higher-end properties available year-round. Rates are highest in summer and in winter; spring and fall see lower prices. Count on more amenities than in the national parks: Air-conditioning, wireless Internet, and televisions are common.

Teton Village has the only remaining hostel in the valley but mostly offers upscale and luxury lodges. Rates are highest in winter and in summer. Seasonal lodging usually runs late November-early April and early May-October.

To scope out complete lists of lodging options, consult **Jackson Chamber of Commerce** (www.jacksonholechamber.com). For condos, townhomes, and vacation homes, check with **Jackson Hole Resort Lodging** (307/733-3990, www.jhrl.com) or Vacation Rentals by Owner (www.VRBO.com).

JACKSON

Staying in downtown Jackson offers a compact town where you can walk from lodging to restaurants, shopping, activities, and nightlife. To the west of town is a strip with motels that are beyond walking distance for many, but you can hop the START bus to downtown. Prices for familiar chains will be inflated due to the resort nature of the town. Rates listed are from the lowest off-season (spring and fall) to highest (summer).

Hotels

Two boutique hotels offer upscale lodging. ★ **Rusty Parrot Lodge** (175 N. Jackson St, 307/733-2000 or 888/739-1749 or 800/458-2004, www.rustyparrot.com, $220-800) has 32 luxury rooms. Rooms with a king bed or two queen beds feature high-end linens and amenities; some come with fireplaces, two-person whirlpool tubs, and sitting areas. The lodge is home to the Body Sage Spa and offers fine dining in the Wild Sage Restaurant. The historic ★ **Wort Hotel** (50 N. Glenwood St, 307/733-2190 or 800/322-2727, www.worthotel.com, $200-1,200) is the place to stay if you like character. The 59 rooms come in nine different styles with one king or two queen beds (or a mix of beds). Suites include sitting areas, two rooms, or theme decor. The Wort is also home to the famous Silver Dollar Bar, which rocks with live music.

Two other hotels come with extra perks. **The Lodge at Jackson Hole** (80 Scott Ln., 307/739-9703 or 800/458-3866, www.lodgeatjh.com, $140-400) has 154 mini-suites. Large suites feature one king or two queen beds, plus sitting areas with sofa sleepers, rain showers in the bathrooms, and electronics hubs. The hotel includes the Jackson Hole Spa, indoor and outdoor heated pools, hot tubs, sauna, fitness center, and restaurant. The three-story **Wyoming Inn of Jackson Hole** (930 W. Broadway, 307/734-0035, www.wyominginn.com, $140-360) greets guests with a stone fireplace, wood carvings of bighorn sheep at the check-in desk, saddle-leather couches, and a moose paddle chandelier in the lobby. Rooms have one king or two queen beds and custom window seats; some have fireplaces. The hotel has an on-site restaurant that serves organic, locally sourced breakfasts, as well as a fitness room and guest laundry.

Located on the strip away from downtown, the **Pony Express** (1075 W. Broadway, 307/733-3835, www.ponyexpresswest.com, $70-370) has 24 motel rooms and condos. Rooms include one queen bed, plus a kitchen or a twin bunk; some rooms allow pets. An outdoor heated pool is open in summer, and a guest laundry is available year-round. One block south of Jackson Town Square, the **Antler Inn** (43 W. Pearl Ave., 307/733-2535 or 800/522-2406, www.townsquareinns.com, $75-330) is a two-story hotel with outdoor stairs to the 2nd floor. Their 110 rooms have two double beds, two queen beds, or one king; some have fireplaces. The motel has a

25-person indoor hot tub, sauna, guest laundry, and fitness room.

Cabins

★ **Cowboy Village Resort** (120 S. Flat Creek Dr., 307/733-3121 or 800/962-4988, www.townsquareinns.com, $100-300) has 82 log cabins and kitchenettes. Cabins have one or two queen beds (some in bunks) plus a sofa bed and small porches with picnic tables and barbecue grills. The resort has an indoor pool, hot tub, laundry, fitness center, and business center. The same owners also run the **Elk Country Inn** (480 W. Pearl Ave., 307/733-2364 or 800/483-8667, www.townsquareinns.com, $75-340), which has 25 log cabins. The pine-walled cabins have two rooms and kitchenettes. The complex also has eight family units, each with three queen beds (one in a loft).

Resort and Condos

Located within seven blocks of Jackson Town Square, Snow King Hotel and Grand View Lodge are operated by the same owners and offer a resort atmosphere. Winter activities include skiing, snowboarding, tubing, ice-skating, ice climbing, and a mountain coaster, while summer has alpine slides, climbing walls, hiking, a mountain coaster, horseback riding, and kids' activities. Due to their location, both are a notch quieter than hotels in the downtown core.

The older, but revamped **Snow King Hotel** (400 E. Snow King Ave., 307/733-5200, www.snowking.com, $165-460) has hotel rooms with two queen beds and condos (1-4 bedrooms), with an outdoor pool (heated year-round), hot tub, spa, salon, fitness center, and lounge. The restaurant features large windows with a deck looking out at Snow King Mountain. In summer, lounging couches surround outdoor fire pits around the pool. Located on the hill above the hotel, the newer **Grand View Lodge** (537 Snow King Loop Rd., 307/734-3000 or 800/522-5464, www.grandviewjacksonhole.

com, $310-700, 3 nights min.) has one- or three-bedroom upscale condo units with access to all the resort amenities.

Bed-and-Breakfast

Sitting adjacent to Flat Creek, the **Inn on the Creek** (295 N. Millward St., 307/739-1565, www.innonthecreek.com, $150-300) has two types of rooms. Jacuzzi Fireplace Rooms have a king or queen bed, while Creek Side Rooms have a queen bed and sitting area. A full breakfast is served in the breakfast room, in bed, or to-go for hitting the road early. Summer guests can lounge on the creekside patio.

TETON VILLAGE

Teton Village is the resort complex at the base of Jackson Hole Mountain Resort. It is home to upscale and luxury hotels, a hostel, and a couple of mid-range hotels. Most hotels cluster around the base of the chairlifts, gondola, and Aerial Tram; for summer travelers, the lure is the village's one-mile proximity to Grand Teton National Park.

Peak season includes July, August, and winter holidays, when prices are highest and reservations are necessary 6-12 months in advance. Some hotels offer seasonal packages that combine lodging with activities: skiing in winter and outdoor activities in summer. Many lodges close for several weeks in early November and late April between summer and winter seasons.

Resorts and Lodges

The ★ **Four Seasons Resort** (7680 Granite Loop Rd., 307/732-5000, www.fourseasons.com/jacksonhole, May-Oct. and late Nov.-early Apr., $360-970 rooms, $560-1,800 suites, $2,700-3,900 residences) is the only Five Diamond, Five Star resort in Wyoming. It's a classy place with a professional, friendly atmosphere where casual outdoor attire is the norm. The layout of the resort's 156 guest rooms follows the contours of the mountain, yielding the atmosphere of a smaller, more intimate hotel.

Four Seasons Jackson Hole

Spacious guest rooms face the mountain, valley, or resort; most rooms have mountain or valley views. Rooms feature a gas fireplace, sitting area, and two double beds or one king; one-bedroom suites have a king and sofa bed. Suites and private residences have one to five bedrooms.

Concierge and valet services deliver seamless experiences for skiing and snowboarding in winter (they'll even put your ski boots on for you) and biking and hiking in summer. Naturalist activities take place in summer and winter. Outdoor pools and three hot pools offer fun for kids and adults. Clusters of outdoor fire pits complement the mountain scenery.

The Four Seasons houses the Westbank Grill, The Handle Bar, a spa, and a fitness facility with yoga classes, and offers ski and bike rentals. Guests can walk out the back door to the ski lifts (it's the closest hotel to the lifts). The hotel also caters to families, with childcare, baby amenities, and a Kids Club.

Two hotels, owned by Noble House, sit

adjacent to each other within a few minutes' walk from the Aerial Tram. Both have rooftop pools and hot tubs with big mountain scenery. They also manage multiple private luxury residences that have access to the hotel amenities. ★ **Teton Mountain Lodge** (3385 Cody Ln., 307/732-6865 or 855/318-6669, www.tetonlodge.com, $410-900 rooms, $700-3,200 condos, mid-Nov.-early Apr. and May-Oct.) turns mountain-style modern in its high-ceiling lobby. Hotel rooms include one king or queen bed or two double beds. Studios feature kitchens and gas fireplaces and have a Murphy queen bed; one-, two-, and three-bedroom condos have a king or queen bed or two double beds in separate bedrooms and a Murphy queen bed or sofa bed in the living room. On-site amenities include concierge services, Solitude Spa, Spur Restaurant, a fitness center with yoga classes, and indoor and outdoor pools.

Hotel Terra (3335 W. Village Dr., 307/739-4055 or 855/318-8707, www.hotelterrajacksonhole.com, $460-500 rooms, $700-1,810 suites, year-round) combines an urban indoor look with eco-features. The LEED-certified construction uses recycled products, water conservation, and low energy use systems. Hotel rooms have one king bed or two queens. Studios feature wall beds, and one-, two-, or three-bedroom suites come with full kitchens and gas fireplaces. All bathrooms have rain showers and air tubs. The hotel houses the Chill Spa, Terra Cafe, Il Villaggio Osteria, two hot tubs, and an outdoor infinity pool.

Wooden bear sculptures greet guests at the **Snake River Lodge** (7710 Granite Loop Rd., 307/732-6070 or 855/342-4712, www.snakeriverlodge.com, May-Oct. and late Nov.-early Apr., $210-990 rooms and suites, $1,850-2,400 residences), which has hotel rooms, one-bedroom suites, 2-3-bedroom residences with kitchens, and penthouse units. Some rooms have fireplaces and balconies. Most rooms have one king or two queen beds; some residences and penthouses have rooms with two twin beds for kids. The lodge has a restaurant, spa, fitness room, and a concierge for wildlife safaris, outdoor recreation, and gear rentals. The heated pool is swim-through indoor-outdoor; indoor and outdoor hot tubs are landscaped with waterfalls.

Teton Club (3340 W. Cody Ln., 307/734-9777, www.tetonclub.com, year-round, $450-2,100) has two- and three-bedroom luxury residences with gas fireplaces, balconies, laundry machines, and gourmet kitchens. Minimum stays of 4-5 days are required, but you don't have to be a member to stay here.

Hotels

Sitting adjacent to the Aerial Tram, **Alpenhof Lodge** (3255 W. Village Dr., 307/733-3242, www.alpenhoflodge.com, mid-May-Oct. and late Nov.-early Apr., $140-740) is one of the original hotels in Teton Village. The 42-room hotel was modeled after Swiss chalets in the alps, with small and cozy rooms featuring one queen bed, mid-size rooms with a king or two doubles, or large spacious suites that have fireplaces, decks, or Jacuzzi tubs. The hotel has a heated outdoor pool, hot tub, bistro, bar, and restaurant. Breakfast is included in the rates.

In a revamp of a chain motel, **The Inn at Jackson Hole** (3345 W. Village Dr., 307/733-2311 or 800/842-7666, www.innatjh.com, mid-May-mid-Oct. and late Nov.-early Apr., $110-420) offers a combination of hotel rooms and suites. Rooms include one king or two queen beds; suites feature kitchenettes, fireplaces, sofa beds, and one and two bedrooms or loft bedrooms accessed by circular stairs. Amenities include a heated outdoor pool, hot tub, and breakfast.

Hostel

The Hostel (3315 Village Dr., 307/733-3415, www.thehostel.us, year-round) has guest rooms that include private king or quad rooms ($80-140 summer/winter, $50-70 spring/fall) and male, female, or co-ed bunkrooms ($35-45 summer/winter, $20-32 spring/fall). Each room has a private bathroom and shower. Amenities include a washer, dryer, ski wax room, ski and board storage, and recreation room with refrigerator, microwave, freezer, and toaster. Pets are permitted for a fee.

JACKSON HOLE

Scattered across the valley floor of Jackson Hole are guest ranches, resorts, and cabins. Some sit between Teton Village and Jackson; others claim unique viewpoints.

Resort

Perched on East Gros Ventre Butte, the **Amangani** (1535 NE Butte Rd., Jackson, 307/734-7333, www.amanresorts.com, May-Oct., late Nov.-Mar., $800-2,500, two-night min. in summer) offers prime views of the Tetons from floor-to-ceiling windows in common areas and outdoor decks, pools, and patios. Sumptuous guest suites feature stone and wood styling, king beds, sitting areas, spacious bathrooms, and balconies to enjoy the views of the Tetons or Jackson Hole. The dining room serves breakfast, lunch, and dinner with a commanding view of the mountains. There is also a lounge, art gallery, library, and outdoor pool and hot tub.

Cabins

Located between Teton Village and Wilson, **Fireside Resort** (2780 N. Moose Wilson Rd./ Hwy. 390, Wilson, 307/733-1177 or 877/660-1177, www.firesidejacksonhole.com, year-round, $180-600) has 23 modern and compact cabins with fireplaces, kitchenettes, private decks, and bathrooms with glass showers. Rather than the traditional log cabin look, these modular cabins look like mini Frank Lloyd Wright structures and are sided with barn wood. Two cabin styles sleep 4-6 people: The basic one-bedroom has a king or queen bed, plus a sofa bed sleeper or an additional loft for twin beds. Front decks have picnic tables, grills, and fire pits. Three-night minimum stays are required in summer. Pets are allowed for a fee.

Bed-and-Breakfasts

In downtown Jackson, the historic **Huff House** (240 E. Deloney Ave., Jackson, 307/733-7141, www.huffhousejh.com, May-mid-Oct. and mid-Dec.-Mar., $150-520) has five rooms and three cabin suites, all with private baths. Landscaped grounds feature a hot tub and large gas fire pit. Stays include hot breakfasts and afternoon appetizers. It's a two-block walk to many restaurants and the Town Square.

The **Bentwood Inn** (4250 Raven Haven Rd., Wilson, 307/739-1411, www.

The Alpenhof provides old-world charm.

bentwoodinn.com, year-round, $230-440) is a rustic log inn with five guest rooms in a wooded setting. Western decor fills the inn and guest rooms. Four rooms have king beds; the Bunkhouse works for families, with a queen bed, a nook bed, and a ladder-accessed loft with twin beds and a skylight. The inn serves a full hot breakfast and evening hors d'oeuvres with wine, plus bistro dining two nights per week. Minimum stays of 2-3 nights are required.

With a covered deck soaking up views of the Tetons, the **Teton View B & B** (2136 Coyote Loop, Wilson, 307/733-7954, www.tetonview.com, June-Sept., $200-340) offers four guest rooms, a heated sheepherder wagon, a one-bedroom cabin with kitchen, an indoor whirlpool tub, and a large outdoor hot tub. Three guest rooms have queen beds; two of the larger rooms include queen futon couches for additional guests. Breakfast features a hot entrée, fresh fruit, and sides.

Guest Ranches

Jackson Hole is home to guest ranches that center around summer horseback riding. Activities also include fishing, rafting, and hiking.

With panoramic views of the Teton Mountains from its perch 1,000 feet above the valley floor, **Spring Creek Resort** (1800 Spirit Dance Rd., Jackson, 307/733-8833 or 800/443-6139, www.springcreekranch.com, year-round, $260-1,400) offers an upscale cowboy experience. Lodging spans hotel rooms, townhomes, and condos, some with outstanding views from decks. Amenities notch the resort up with an indoor hot tub, outdoor heated swimming pool, tennis courts, full-service spa, and restaurant. For extra fees, the ranch staff guides wildlife safaris (year-round), naturalist programs, national park tours, and summer trail rides.

At the 325-acre **R Lazy S Ranch** (7800 Moose Wilson Rd., Teton Village, 307/733-2655, http://rlazys.com, mid-June-Sept., $1,810-2,670 per person per week) on Grand Teton National Park's southern boundary near Teton Village, you feel like you're off in your own world. The ranch accommodates up to 45 guests in 12 log cabins; most sleep 2-4 people, but a few can sleep six. Rates include lodging, meals, and activities such as horseback riding and instruction, waterskiing on Jackson Lake, and fishing. Meals are a combination of dining in the lodge, cookouts, and buffets.

Remote **Flat Creek Ranch** (1 Upper Flat Creek Rd., Jackson, 307/733-0603, www.flatcreekranch.com, June-early Oct., $2,400-8,250 per person for 3-9 nights) requires a four-wheel-drive vehicle to handle the 15 miles of bumpy back road across the National Elk Refuge to get there. Or take the optional ranch shuttle and get dropped off to hike in to the ranch. Five renovated, historic log cabins have a bedroom, living room, private bath with clawfoot tub, wood-burning stove, and porch. Solar rays power the electricity. Activities include horseback riding, fishing, hiking, and backcountry trips. Meals feature gourmet meats and fresh produce from the ranch garden.

Camping

Jackson Hole has only a few private campgrounds, but national forest campgrounds are in the surrounding mountains. While many of the national forest campgrounds are attractions in their own right, they can also serve as backup when the national park campgrounds fill up.

JACKSON AND VICINITY

Three private campgrounds around Jackson have sites with full hookups (water, sewer, electric), picnic tables, flush toilets, showers, drinking water, laundries, camp stores, and wireless Internet. Rates are usually for 2-4 people ($8-12 per extra person, kids under 6 free). These are the only campgrounds that accept reservations, a must for midsummer. Only the KOA permits tent campers.

The **Virginian RV Park** (750 W. Broadway, Jackson, 307/733-7189 or 800/321-6982, http://virginianlodge.com, May-mid-Oct., $90-110) offers RVers a place to stay one mile from downtown Jackson. The campground is part of the Virginian Lodge, a motel complex with a restaurant, saloon, liquor store, hair salon, and heated outdoor pool and hot tub. The parking-lot-style campground has 103 sites; RVs are limited to 40 feet. Reservations are in demand since this is the only campground in town.

Located five miles south of Teton Village behind Fireside Resort, **Jackson Hole Campground** (behind Fireside Resort, 2780 N. Moose-Wilson Rd., Wilson, 307/732-2267, www.jacksonholecampground.com, mid-Apr.-Nov., $60-135) squeezes 63 grassy RV-only sites under mature cottonwoods and conifers. Facilities include a disposal station. During the ski season, the resort also can accommodate small RVs (by reservation).

Located 12 miles south of Jackson on U.S. Highway 26/89/189/191 (almost to Hoback Junction), the **Snake River Park KOA** (9705 S. Hwy. 89, Jackson, 307/733-7078 or 800/562-1878, www.srpkoa.com, mid-Apr.-Nov., $45-99 RVs, $32-50 tents) is operated by a white-water rafting outfitter on the Snake River. Tucked into a deep and narrow canyon, the campground squeezes between the busy two-lane highway (rumbling with commercial haul trucks) and the Snake River. Tent sites sit along Horse Creek and the river, and are held for river rafters in midsummer. Back-in RV sites (two-night min. midsummer, 30 feet max.) line up in parking-lot fashion, with mowed lawns between sites. Stairs connect to the sandy riverbank. Campers get 10 percent off white-water rafting trips. A horseback-riding corral is across the street.

Bridger-Teton National Forest

Bridger-Teton National Forest (Jackson Ranger District, 25 Rosencrans Ln., Jackson, 307/739-5400, www.fs.usda.gov/btnf, late May-Sept., $12-15 single site, $25 double site, $7 per extra vehicle) offers **first-come, first-served** campgrounds in the Gros Ventre Mountains, east of Grand Teton National Park or south of Jackson. Facilities include picnic tables, fire rings with grills, drinking water, bear boxes, and vault toilets. There are no hookups.

For boaters, **Atherton Creek Campground** (20 sites) has two loops of campsites on a sunny hillside of aspens and conifers above Lower Slide Lake. Some sites have tent platforms and a couple sites overlook the water. A boat dock and ramp aid launching onto the lake for fishing, paddling, sailboarding, waterskiing, or boating. To reach the campground, take the Gros Ventre River Road north of Kelly. Turn east onto Gros Ventre Road for 5.5 miles of bumpy but paved road to the campground entrance. If Atherton fills, drive 4.5 miles up Gros Ventre Road to **Crystal Creek Campground** (6 sites), a quiet older campground tucked on a trout-fishing stream.

The drive to **Curtis Canyon Campground** (11 sites) takes advantage of million-dollar views. At 7,000 feet on the east side of Jackson Hole, an overlook takes in Jackson Hole, the National Elk Refuge, and the Teton Mountains. The campground sits across the road in a small forest with one campsite claiming the million-dollar view; other campsites are in the trees (small RVs only). To find the campground from Jackson, drive the gravel National Elk Refuge Road north for 4.6 miles. Turn right onto the narrow, rocky Curtis Canyon Road for 2.6 miles to climb to the campground entrance on the right.

South of Jackson at Hoback Junction, multiple Forest Service campgrounds line the rivers. West of Hoback Junction along the Snake River, **East Table** (19 sites), **Station Creek** (15 sites), and **Wolf Creek** (20 sites) campgrounds are popular with white-water river rafters and kayakers. East from Hoback Junction, along U.S. Highway 191, **Hoback** (13 sites) and **Kozy** (8 sites) campgrounds flank the Wild and Scenic Hoback River. These campgrounds are highway roadside camps with fishing. To soak in nearby Granite Hot Springs, camp at **Granite Creek Campground** (51 sites) 11 miles north of U.S. Highway 191 on Granite Creek Road (Forest Rd. 30500).

Transportation and Services

DRIVING
Driving in Jackson Hole is on two-lane roads, with a handful of short stretches with four lanes around Jackson. From Jackson, it's 7 miles west to Wilson and 12 miles northwest to Teton Village. Highway 26/89/191 runs from Jackson north to Grand Teton National Park, reaching the Moose Entrance in 13 miles, the Moran Entrance in 30 miles, and the south entrance to Yellowstone National Park in 57 miles. From Jackson, Highway 189 travels 13 miles south to Hoback Junction, while Highway 22 crosses Teton Pass to become Highway 33 in Teton Valley, Idaho. The town of Victor appears in 25 miles; Driggs is in 33 miles.

Access to the Gros Ventre Mountains is via Forest Service roads around Jackson. Most are two-lane dirt or gravel roads; no one road tours the Gros Ventres.

Parking in Jackson is difficult. To head downtown to the Town Square, shopping, restaurants, and nightlife, walk from your hotel or hop the START bus. It's far easier, especially if you drive a big RV. Parking at Teton Village is in four pay lots (late Nov.-early Apr., $10-15/day) during the winter ski season. Overnight guests get free parking through their lodges.

Gas stations are located in Jackson, Wilson, and Teton Village.

Car Rental
Car rentals are available through three agencies at Jackson Hole Airport: **Avis** (307/733-3422 or 800/831-2847, www.avis.com), **Hertz** (307/733-2272 or 800/654-3131, www.hertz.com), and **Enterprise** (307/733-7066 or 800/261-7331, www.enterprise.com). Five more rental agencies are in Jackson: **Dollar** (307/733-9224, www.dollar.com), **Thrifty** (307/734-8312 or 800/367-2277, www.thrifty.com), **National** (307/733-0671 or 800/227-7368, www.nationalcar.com), **Alamo** (307/733-0671 or 800/327-9633, www.alamo.com), and **Leisure Sports** (307/733-3040, www.leisuresportsadventure.com).

AIR
Jackson Hole Airport (JAC, 1250 E. Airport Rd, Jackson, 307/733-7682, www.jacksonholeairport.com) is actually inside Grand Teton National Park, just north of Jackson. If the Tetons and Jackson Hole are your destination, fly in here. The airport also is easy for accessing Yellowstone's South Entrance. Three airlines service Jackson Hole: United, Delta,

and American. Fifteen flights or more have direct service to the airport from Washington DC, Newark, Atlanta, Chicago, Minneapolis, Salt Lake City, Denver, Dallas-Fort Worth, Houston, Seattle, Los Angeles, and San Francisco. Many flights run seasonally in winter or summer, and flights to Jackson Hole are usually more expensive than to other area airports. Taxis meet all flights.

Airport Transportation

Taxis through **AllTrans shuttles** (307/733-3135 or 800/443-6133, www.jacksonholealltrans.com, daily June-Sept. and Dec.-Mar., $40-140 for 1-7 people one-way) meet all incoming and outgoing flights at Jackson Hole Airport. In spring and fall, shuttles are by reservation only (by 7pm on the day before arrival or departure). If you make reservations earlier, call 24 hours ahead to reconfirm. A winter shuttle (by reservation only) runs from Jackson Hole Airport to Grand Targhee Resort.

Mountain States Express (307/733-1719 or 800/652-9510, www.mountainstatesexpress.com, $75 pp) also runs daily shuttles to and from the airport in Salt Lake City, Utah to Jackson (5 hours). **Salt Lake Express** (208/656-8824 or 800/356-9796, www.saltlakeexpress.com) services go between Salt Lake City Airport and Jackson, Wyoming, or West Yellowstone, Montana. Some of the destinations on this service are limited to summer months.

About 20 taxi companies operate in southern Jackson Hole. Costs vary depending on distance; for 1-2 people from the airport to Jackson costs $40-50 and to Teton Village costs $70-80. Add on $8-10 per person for extra riders. Several limo services also operate around Jackson. Find a complete list of companies online (www.jacksonholeairport.com).

BUS

Teton County runs a public bus system that allows visitors to travel around southern Jackson Hole. The Southern Teton Area Rapid

Transit, or **START** (www.startbus.com, daily year-round), changes schedules seasonally. Buses within the downtown core of Jackson run about every 30 minutes (6am-10pm, free). Bus connections between Jackson, Wilson, and Teton Village run at varied intervals (5am-11:30pm, $1-3 one-way). Be sure to have the exact fare in cash; drivers do not carry change. Maps and route schedules are available online.

Save yourself the nasty winter drive over Teton Pass with the **Targhee Express** (AllTrans, 307/733-3135 or 800/443-6133, www.jacksonholealltrans.com, daily in winter), the bus from Jackson or Teton Village to Grand Targhee Resort on the west side of the Tetons. Departure times vary (7am-7:50am) depending on pickup location. The bus arrives at Grand Targhee around 9:15am and departs the ski resort at 4pm with arrival back in Teton Village or Jackson by 5:30pm-6pm. Skiers and snowboarders can buy a combination round-trip bus ticket with a lift ticket for the day ($125 adults, $97 kids). Make reservations at least one day in advance.

SERVICES

Post offices are located in **Jackson** (220 W. Pearl St., 7:30am-5pm Mon.-Fri.; 1070 Maple Way, 8:30am-5pm Mon.-Fri., 10am-1pm Sat.), **Wilson** (5605 W. Hwy. 22, 8:30am-5pm Mon.-Fri., 10am-noon Sat.), and **Teton Village** (3230 McCollister Dr., 9:30am-12:30pm and 1pm-4pm Mon.-Fri., 9:30am-12:30pm Sat.).

ATMs are common in Jackson and Teton Village, available in many hotels and at banks in Jackson. In Jackson, the **Missing Sock Laundromat** (1325 U.S. 89, 307/733-9888, 7am-10pm daily year-round) has coin-op machines. For showers, head to the **Teton County Recreation Center** (155 E. Gill St., Jackson, 307/739-9025, www.tetonparksandrec.org, 6am-8pm Mon.-Fri., noon-8pm Sat., noon-7pm Sun. year-round, $7 adults, $5-6 kids and seniors), which has a swimming pool, fitness facilities, and locker rooms with showers. In Teton Village, **The**

Hostel (3315 Village Dr., 307/733-3415, www.thehostel.us, year-round, $5) allows non-lodgers to stop in for showers.

Media and Communications

Cell phone service is ubiquitous in Teton Village, Jackson, and Teton Valley. However, service will be interrupted in the surrounding mountains. Most hotels in Jackson and Teton Village have wireless Internet. Jackson also has several coffee shops and cafés with Internet access. In Jackson, **Teton County Library** (125 Virginian Ln., 307/733-2164, http://tclib.org) has free Internet access.

The local newspaper is the *Jackson Hole News and Guide* (www.jhnewsandguide.com). *Planet Jackson Hole Weekly* (http://planetjh.

com) contains events, music, art, and entertainment around town.

Emergency Services

The closest medical facility is **St. John's Medical Center** (625 E. Broadway, Jackson, 307/733-3636, www.tetonhospital.org). For other emergencies, contact the **Jackson Police Department** (150 E. Pearl Ave., Jackson, 307/733-2331, http://townofjackson.com) or **Teton County Sheriff Office** (180 S. King St., Jackson, 307/733-4052, www.tetonsheriff.org). For national forests, contact **Jackson Ranger District, Bridger-Teton National Forest** (25 Rosencrans Ln., Jackson, 307/739-5400, www.fs.usda.gov/btnf).

Teton Valley

Many people visiting Grand Teton National Park and Jackson Hole assume that the Teton Valley is just another name for Jackson Hole. But Teton Valley is on the less-traveled Idaho side of the Teton Mountains. Dotted with tiny towns like Victor and Driggs (bedroom communities for the high-priced Jackson Hole), Teton Valley accesses wilderness areas and Caribou-Targhee National Forest, which flanks the west side of the Tetons and Grand Teton National Park. Teton Pass connects Jackson Hole to Teton Valley.

VISITORS CENTER

The **Teton Valley Geotourism Center** (60 S. Main St., Driggs, ID, 208/354-2607, www.tetongeotourism.us, 9am-5pm Thurs.-Tues. summer; hours vary seasonally, free) has interpretive and interactive displays on winter activities, snow science, cultural history, Native American heritage, and summer activities. Information is available on camping, lodging, wildlife-watching, activities, events, and road conditions.

SIGHTS
★ Teton Pass

Driving up **Teton Pass** is one of the steepest climbs in the country, ascending at a 10 percent grade in places. The road curls around the 8,431-foot summit at the southern tip of the Teton Mountains. From Jackson, the curvy route to the summit ascends 11 miles west along Highway 22, then drops on Highway 33 about 12 miles to **Victor, Idaho.** On the east side, a few pullouts offer views that span Jackson Hole with the Snake River curving through its bowels and backdropped by the Gros Ventre Mountains. On the west side of the pass, the road follows the headwaters of the Teton River through a forested canyon of **Caribou-Targhee National Forest.** While the road is open year-round, it frequently closes in early mornings in winter for avalanche control work. Drive Teton Pass both directions, as the views are different.

Teton Canyon

Cruising up **Teton Canyon** toward **Grand Targhee Resort** yields in-your-face views of

Teton Valley

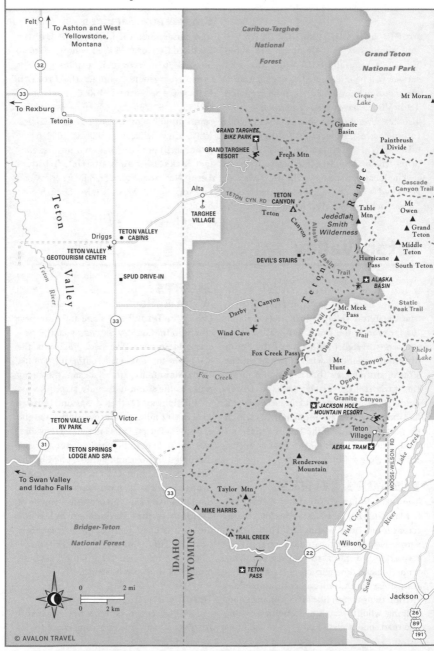

Felt

To Ashton and West Yellowstone, Montana

32

33

To Rexburg

Tetonia

Caribou-Targhee National Forest

Grand Teton National Park

Cirque Lake

Mt Moran

GRAND TARGHEE BIKE PARK

GRAND TARGHEE RESORT

Freds Mtn

Granite Basin

Paintbrush Divide

Teton Valley

Alta

TETON CYN RD

TETON CANYON

Teton

Cascade Canyon Trail

Mt Owen

Table Mtn

TARGHEE VILLAGE

Jedediah Smith Wilderness

Grand Teton

Driggs

TETON VALLEY CABINS

TETON VALLEY GEOTOURISM CENTER

DEVIL'S STAIRS

Middle Teton

Hurricane Pass

South Teton

Teton River

SPUD DRIVE-IN

ALASKA BASIN

Static Peak Trail

33

Darby Canyon

Wind Cave

Mt. Meek Pass

Cyn Trail

Phelps Lake

Fox Creek Pass

Fox Creek

Mt Hunt

Canyon Tr

Open

Granite Canyon Tr

JACKSON HOLE MOUNTAIN RESORT

Victor

TETON VALLEY RV PARK

Teton Village

AERIAL TRAM

31

TETON SPRINGS LODGE AND SPA

To Swan Valley and Idaho Falls

33

Rendezvous Mountain

Taylor Mtn

MIKE HARRIS

Bridger-Teton National Forest

TRAIL CREEK

Wilson

IDAHO WYOMING

22

TETON PASS

Snake River

Jackson

N

0   2 mi

0   2 km

26
89
191

© AVALON TRAVEL

Teton Pass climbs and drops at a steep grade.

the Cathedral Group in Grand Teton National Park from the west. Starting from downtown **Driggs,** head east on Ski Hill Road. After leaving the valley floor, the road climbs a couple switchbacks with eastward views of the Grand, Mt. Owen, Nez Perce, and Middle Teton. In eight miles, turn around at the overlook or at Grand Targhee Resort, 12 miles above Driggs.

Caribou-Targhee National Forest

Flanking the west side of the Teton Mountains and Teton Valley, **Caribou-Targhee National Forest** offers a back entrance into Grand Teton National Park, with hiking, mountain biking, and camping. **Grand Targhee Resort** offers lift-accessed skiing and snowboarding plus cross-country skiing in winter, and hiking and mountain biking in summer. Between the ski resort and Grand Teton National Park, the **Jedediah Smith Wilderness** contains unique karst limestone features including trail-accessible caves.

RECREATION

For trails in Caribou-Targhee National Forest, visit the **Teton Basin Ranger District** (515 S. Main St., Driggs, ID, 208/354-2312) for maps and information.

Day Hikes

Grand Targhee Resort (3300 Ski Hill Rd., Alta, WY, 307/353-2300 or 800/827-4433, www.grandtarghee.com) offers guided day hikes in summer.

BANNOCK TRAIL
Distance: 6.4 miles round-trip
Duration: 4 hours
Elevation change: 2,002 feet
Effort: strenuous
Trailhead: Grand Targhee Resort plaza

The Bannock Trail ascends the 9,862-foot Fred's Mountain at Grand Targhee Resort, where you can get views of the west side of Mt. Moran, the Jedediah Smith Wilderness, Grand Teton, and Cathedral Group. While **Grand Targhee Resort** (3300 Ski Hill Rd., Alta, WY, 307/353-2300 or 800/827-4433, www.grandtarghee.com) has multiple bike trails on the mountain, the Bannock Trail is for hikers only. You can take the lift (fee) either direction to cut uphill climbing or downhill pounding.

The trail climbs up open ski runs with wildflower meadows and broken forests to swing west into **Blackfoot Basin.** After crossing the basin, ascend along the ridge to reach the summit and the top of **Dreamcatcher Chairlift.** From the lift, a five-mile round-trip walk with 500 feet of climbing goes to **Mary's Saddle** for in-your-face views of the Grand Teton. Snow can cover parts of the trail into July.

★ ALASKA BASIN
Distance: 16.6 miles round-trip
Duration: 8-10 hours
Elevation change: 2,635 feet
Effort: moderately strenuous
Trailhead: South Teton Canyon Trailhead at the end of Teton Canyon Road

As the most popular hike in Caribou-Targhee National Forest, Alaska Basin provides a shorter, less demanding route to the Teton Crest than east side hikes. At 9,500 feet in elevation in the Jedediah Smith Wilderness, this collection of small, alpine Basin Lakes are rimmed with stunning wildflower shows in August. Prepare for changeable weather: common afternoon thunderstorms, potential high winds, and snowfields lingering through July. Some stream crossings require rock-hopping.

The trail starts off deceptively easy, wandering along the **South Fork of Teton Creek** through conifers that give way to wildflower meadows. After the junction with **Devil's Stairs Trail** at 2.7 miles, the path climbs more steeply through broken forests, rock slabs, and meadows until it crests into Alaska Basin. At the junction with the **Teton Crest Trail,** turn south and continue 0.1 mile to a junction, where two forks diverge around **Basin Lakes**. These idyllic lakes have views of Mt. Meek, Buck Mountain, Veiled Peak, and Battleship Mountain. Mirror Lake is the largest of the Basin Lakes.

DARBY WIND CAVE
Distance: 5.2 miles round-trip
Duration: 4 hours
Elevation change: 1,800 feet
Effort: strenuous
Trailhead: Darby Canyon Trailhead
Directions: Go 3 miles south of Driggs on Highway 33. At 0.7 mile past the Spud Drive In. Turn east onto Darby Canyon Road. Drive 3.2 miles east, turning south on Stateline Road for 0.1 mile, and then swinging left into Darby Canyon for 4.4 miles to the trailhead.

Wind Cave, tucked into 350-million-year-old dolomite, is a large cave on the west side of the Tetons. Its ceiling stretches up hundreds of feet in places, but exploring corners may force you to crawl through tight constrictions. Bring a headlamp for lighting. Just above Wind Cave, Darby Ice Cave requires technical climbing gear to explore.

From the trailhead, the path turns south to ascend the forested draw of **Darby Canyon** toward Fossil Mountain. After about one mile, the trail breaks into open meadows with views of the steep canyon walls. At the junction at 2.4 miles, continue straight on the right fork to climb up the west canyon wall to the cave.

Backpacking
ALASKA BASIN
23-29 MILES
In wildflower-rich **Alaska Basin**, backpackers can camp without a permit in the Jedediah

hiking Alaska Basin

Smith Wilderness on the Teton Crest Trail. Make a base camp for several nights at 9,500 feet in elevation at Basin Lakes, where rock slabs make good cooking sites (no fires allowed). Campsites are undesignated, but you can find well-used sites in spotty clumps of trees for wind protection. Pop your tent away from the lake shores and on durable surfaces rather than in the fragile meadows. Plan at least three days for this trip, which allows time for a day hike north on the Teton Crest Trail to 10,338-foot Hurricane Pass (6.5 miles round-trip) in Grand Teton National Park. Schoolroom Glacier below the pass is only one of the views; for the biggest, you will stare straight at the west side of three of the big Tetons: Grand, Middle, and South. Tack on another night at Basin Lakes to hike in the national park southeast over Buck Pass to Static Peak Divide (6.2 miles round-trip) or Death Canyon Shelf and Fox Pass (12 miles round-trip). Carry your food in a bear canister; bear boxes are not provided.

Biking

Old railroad lines have been converted to bike paths in Teton Valley. Maps of Teton Valley biking routes and pathways are available from **Teton Valley Trails and Pathways** (http://tvtap.org). A **paved bike path** runs between Victor and Driggs. The 104-mile **Yellowstone-Grand Teton Rail Trail** is a gravel and dirt trail that runs from Victor, Idaho, to West Yellowstone, Montana. As a rail trail, the riding is flat and easy, but a few sections are missing where you'll need to jump onto roads.

Habitat High Altitude Provisions (18 N. Main St., Driggs, ID, 208/354-7669, http://ridethetetons.com, $25-99) carries rental bikes, plus they do tune-ups. The shop also has rentals at Grand Targhee Resort.

★ GRAND TARGHEE BIKE PARK

At Grand Targhee Resort, the **Grand Targhee Bike Park** (3300 Ski Hill Rd., Alta, WY, 307/353-2300 or 800/827-4433, www.grandtarghee.com, mid-May-mid-Sept.) is becoming one of the most-lauded places to mountain bike in the Northern Rockies. Lifts service 13 miles of downhill trails, and 47 miles of cross-country multiuse single-track trails cruise through Caribou-Targhee National Forest. Targhee also has flow trails and a skills park. The park has a bike school, guided tours, women's camps, events, and rentals ($60-80). Combo bike park and lift passes cost $35 for adults and $30 for juniors.

mountain biking at Grand Targhee Resort

The annual **WYDAHO Rendezvous Teton Mountain Bike Festival** (http://tetonbikefest.org, Sept.), a three-day event on Labor Day weekend, attracts about 500 riders and caps the summer ride season with group rides, clinics, trials, demos, music, food, and beer.

Golf

Targhee Village Golf Course (530 Perimeter Dr., Alta, WY, 307/353-8577, www.targheevillage.com, May-Sept., $18-24) is a nine-hole community golf course. Amenities include a small clubhouse serving food, cart rentals, and club rentals.

Winter Sports
GRAND TARGHEE RESORT

Less crowded **Grand Targhee Resort** (3300 Ski Hill Rd., Alta, WY, 307/353-2300 or 800/827-4433, www.grandtarghee.com, late Nov.-late Apr.) skis like a much bigger mountain and gains big views of the Grand Teton when weather permits. The resort has five lifts spread across 2,602 acres and 2,176 feet of vertical, but much of its terrain is open glade skiing, prime on powder days. Targhee is known for dry, light powder snow; the average snowfall tops 500 inches. Intermediate skiers relish the long groomer runs, and the kids' learning terrain has special kid-zone tree trails that help improve skills while having fun. **Lift tickets** ($85-95 adults, $37-45 juniors, $62-70 seniors) are more affordable than Jackson Hole. The resort also has terrain parks, rentals, lessons, naturalist programs, restaurants, hotels, and cat skiing.

Snowcat Adventures (307/353-2300 ext. 1355, $450) runs full-day trips where you can get 12,000-15,000 feet of vertical per day in glades and open bowls outside the lift-served terrain.

Grand Targhee also has a big groomed **Nordic ski** area ($10-12 adults, $6-8 kids) with skate lanes and classic tracks. Fifteen kilometers (9.3 miles) of scenic trails loop through open meadows, aspen groves, and forest. The resort has lessons in skate or classic

Grand Targhee Resort

skiing, and the ski shop rents the gear. Fat bikes are allowed on the trails.

CROSS-COUNTRY SKIING

Teton Valley Trails and Pathways (http://tvtap.org) grooms cross-country trails multiple times weekly at several locations. Maps and grooming reports are online. Use of the trails is free, but donations are appreciated. Jackson Hole Nordic (http://jhnordic.com) also updates grooming reports and provides trail information.

ENTERTAINMENT AND EVENTS

In a throwback to the 1950s, the **Spud Drive-In** (2175 S. Hwy. 33, Driggs, ID, 208/354-2727, http://spuddrivein.com, summer) is recognizable with a huge potato on the bed of a 1946 Chevy truck. The outdoor theater is located between Victor and Driggs, and shows movies in double-feature format where you'll finish the second film around 2am. The snack bar is also a throwback to the 1950s with burgers, popcorn, and malts.

Festivals and Events

Grand Targhee Resort (3300 Ski Hill Rd., Alta, WY, 307/353-2300 or 800/827-4433, www.grandtarghee.com) hosts two long-running three-day music festivals every summer. **Targhee Fest** (Fri.-Sun. mid-July) brings together folk musicians from across the country. The **Targhee Bluegrass Festival** (Fri.-Sun. mid-Aug.) attracts well-known bluegrass bands from North America. Bring a lawn chair to enjoy the outdoor venue; camping for tents or RVs is in several parking lots. Food, drink, and retail vendors are on-site. Free buses run from Driggs to the festival site at the resort. Purchase tickets in advance online for single days, all three days, and camping. Pay for parking on site.

FOOD
Driggs

In a cozy red house tucked off Main Street, **Pendl's Bakery Café** (40 Depot St., 208/354-5623, http://pendlspastries.com, 7am-2pm Tues.-Sun., $4-13) serves espresso, crisp Austrian pastries, breakfast, and lunch. Sit indoors at the few tables in front of the wood stove, or outdoors in summer on the deck or in the yard around the fire pit.

Teton Thai (18 N. Main St., 208/787-8424, www.tetonthai.com, Mon.-Fri. 11:30am-2:30pm, nightly 4:30pm-9pm) lays on the heat with one to five stars in their classic Southeast Asian dishes (Pad Thai, Tom Kha Gai, and Crying Tiger) and fresh seasonal entrées. Veggies, rice, noodles, stir fry, soups, and curries come full of zesty flavors.

On the road heading up to Grand Targhee Resort, the small **Forage Bistro and Lounge** (285 E. Little Ave., 208/345-2858, www.forageandlounge.com, 11am-9pm Mon.-Fri. and 10am-9pm Sat.-Sun., $10-17) uses a European setting for small plates, unique salads, burgers, and sandwiches.

For groceries, **Broulim's Supermarket** (240 S. Main St., 208/354-2350, www.broulims.com, 7am-11pm Mon.-Sat.) carries fresh meats, produce, dairy, and baked goods, and has a deli. **Barrels & Bins Community Market** (36 S. Main St., 208/354-2307, http://barrelsandbins.market, 9am-7pm daily) is a deli and natural foods store that carries local, natural, and organic foods.

Victor

For huge burgers, the **Brakeman American**

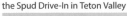

the Spud Drive-In in Teton Valley

Grill (27 N. Main St., 208/787-2020, www.brakemangrill.com, 11:30am-3:30pm and 5pm-9pm daily, $10-16) grinds their beef fresh daily. Half-pound burgers come with usual to unique toppings. You can order lighter quarter-pounders or get elk, bison, and turkey burgers. If the small restaurant is crowded, prepare to wait as the burgers are made to order.

Spoons Bistro (32 W. Birch St., 208/787-2478, www.spoonsbistro.com, Tues.-Sun. 5:30pm-close, $14-26) does a unique take on traditional pub food, Kobe sirloin, and Idaho trout. Vegetarians can revel in zucchini spaghetti with garlic marmalade. Appetizers such as tuna tartar and Roman artichokes start the feast.

ACCOMMODATIONS

Teton Valley offers reasonably priced, although limited, lodging and access to the west side of the Tetons through Caribou-Targhee National Forest. Compared to Jackson Hole, some people prefer its less trammeled feel with more breathing space. Guest ranches, cabins, and vacation rentals range up and down Teton Valley. There are even a few chain motels (Super 8, Best Western) in Driggs. Add on 8.5 percent for Idaho tax.

Alta

For a quiet mountain atmosphere with expansive scenery and access to viewpoints of the Grand Teton, Grand Targhee Resort (3300 Ski Hill Rd., Alta, WY, 307/353-2300 or 800/827-4433, www.grandtarghee.com, mid-May-mid-Sept. and late Nov.-late Apr., $120-580) has four lodging options: a two-bedroom tower condo, Teton Lodge economy rooms, Teewinot Lodge basic hotel rooms, and larger Sioux Lodge suites (studio, loft, and two-bedroom). Winter has the highest prices when lifts run for skiing and snowboarding, and activities such as cat skiing, Nordic skiing, and snowshoeing ramp up. Summer brings on scenic lift rides, mountain biking, hiking, and horseback riding. Both seasons have naturalist programs. The resort also has a restaurant,

bar, fitness center, heated outdoor saltwater pool, outdoor hot tub, and activities.

Driggs

Teton Valley Cabins (1 Mountain Vista Dr., Driggs, ID, 208/354-8153, www.tetonvalley-cabins.com, year-round, $70-115) takes advantage of the setting with cottonwoods and Teton views. Six small log cabins have 1-2 queen beds or bunks, and come with kitchenettes and private bathrooms. One cabin allows pets. The cabins are one mile up the road to Grand Targhee Resort.

Victor

Teton Springs Lodge and Spa (10 Warm Creek Ln., Victor, ID, 208/787-7235 or 888/451-0156, www.tetonspringslodge.com, year-round $195-900) has lodge rooms, suites, and luxury cabins that are really log homes with up to five bedrooms. A spa is on site, and the neighboring Headwaters Golf Club houses a restaurant.

CAMPING
Victor

On the west side of Victor, Teton Valley RV Resort (1208 Hwy. 31, 208/787-2647 or 877/787-3036, www.tetonvalleycampground.com, May-early Oct.) has RV hookups ($55-150), tent sites ($28-49), tepees and cabins ($60-100), and a swimming pool (summer only).

Caribou-Targhee National Forest

On the west side of the Teton Mountains, Caribou-Targhee National Forest (Teton Basin Ranger District, 515 S. Main, Driggs, ID, 208/354-2312, www.fs.usda.gov/ctnf, late May-late Sept., $12, $6 extra vehicle) has three campgrounds with picnic tables, fire pits with grills, bear boxes, drinking water, and vault toilets. Reservations (877/444-6777, www.recreation.gov) are accepted. On Teton Creek in Teton Canyon east of Driggs, Teton Canyon Campground has 20 campsites, but can fit only small RVs. A nearby trailhead serves as a leap-off point for hiking in the Jedediah Smith Wilderness and Grand Teton National Park. On Highway 33 on the west side of Teton Pass are two roadside campgrounds. **Mike Harris Campground** (10 sites), 3.8 miles south of Victor, and **Trail Creek Campground** (10 sites), 5.6 miles south of Victor.

TRANSPORTATION AND SERVICES
Driving
The route from Jackson crosses the scenic **Teton Pass** (open year-round, weather depending), reaching Victor, Idaho, in about 25 miles via Highway 22 (in Wyoming) and Highway 33 (in Idaho). Driggs, Idaho, is 8 miles north of Victor and 33 miles from Jackson. To reach Grand Targhee in Alta, Wyoming, follow Ski Hill Road another 13 miles east. Allow at least one hour for the drive from Jackson to Driggs, and another 20 minutes if continuing to Alta, Wyoming.

You can also reach Driggs from the west. The 73-mile route from Idaho Falls takes about 80 minutes. Head north on Highway 20 to Rexburg. North of Rexburg, take Exit 339 onto Highway 33 heading east. At Tetonia, the two-lane highway heads south to Driggs.

Bus
The Southern Teton Area Rapid Transit, or **START** (www.startbus.com, Mon.-Fri. year-round, schedules change seasonally, $8 exact cash fare) connects Driggs and Victor in Teton Valley with Jackson, Wyoming. Maps and route schedules are available online. Riders to Teton Village will need to debark in Wilson at the Village Road Transit Center and change to a bus going north. Two buses leave in the early morning and return in late afternoon.

Services
A **post office** (70 S. Main St., 8:30am-4:30pm Mon.-Fri., 10am-noon Sat.) is in Driggs. For emergencies, contact **Caribou-Targhee National Forest** (Teton Basin Ranger District, 515 S. Main St., Driggs, 208/354-2312, www.fs.usda.gov/ctnf, late May-late Sept.). Victor and Driggs have gas stations. The *Teton Valley News* (www.tetonvalleynews. net) is the weekly paper in Teton Valley.

Gateways

Big Sky, Montana 315

Red Lodge, Montana. 329

Cody, Wyoming. 340

Dubois, Wyoming 357

Several distinct gateways lead to Yellowstone and Grand Teton National Parks.

Big Sky, Montana, is the closest gateway to Yellowstone. With year-round access, a quick drive south reaches uncrowded trails in the park's northwest corner and the closest entrance to Old Faithful. In winter, the sprawling resort town attracts skiers. In summer, its upscale lodging lures vacationers.

Red Lodge, Montana, a cross between a mountain and western town, serves as the eastern springboard for the most scenic drive to Yellowstone. With gray granite snow-draped peaks, purple lupine, and clear shallow lakes, the Beartooth Highway climbs across the high Beartooth Plateau to Yellowstone's northeast corner. Due to snow burying the road in winter, it is only a Yellowstone gateway late May-mid-October.

Cody, Wyoming, relishes its cowboy heritage with everything related to founder Buffalo Bill Cody. In summer, nightly rodeos and staged gunfights erupt from its Wild West roots. Seasonal routes through Shoshone National Forest reach the East Entrance of Yellowstone or the Northeast Entrance of the park. But both routes are only viable May through early November, due to snow-buried roads in winter.

In Wyoming, the small gateway town of Dubois tucks below the Wind River Mountains. Popping year-round over Togwotee Pass delivers stunning first images of the Teton Mountains and entrances to both national parks.

While all of the gateway towns are open year-round, heavy snow closes down access roads between some of them and the national parks in winter.

Previous: cross-country skiing at Lone Mountain Ranch; the Beartooth Highway. **Above:** paintbrush blooms.

Look for ★ to find recommended
sights, activities, dining, and lodging.

Highlights

★ **Lone Mountain:** Ride a tram to the summit of this 11,166-foot peak, looming above Big Sky Resort (page 315).

★ **Big Sky Skiing:** Big Sky Resort offers more than 5,800 acres of skiing and snowboarding, while historic Lone Mountain grooms more than 85 kilometers for Nordic skiing (page 322).

★ **Downtown Red Lodge Historic District:** Browse this historic downtown's western storefronts (page 329).

★ **Beartooth Highway:** Drive far above tree line into alpine meadows with rugged scenery (page 331).

★ **Buffalo Bill Center of the West:** Visitors are catapulted back to the Wild West with five museums of exhibits on Native Americans, artists, natural history—and Buffalo Bill himself (page 340).

★ **Buffalo Bill Dam:** This National Civil Engineering Landmark squeezes into Shoshone Canyon (page 344).

★ **Cody Rodeo:** Experience rodeo thrills every summer night in this cowboy capital (page 348).

★ **National Bighorn Sheep Interpretive Center:** Learn about these wild icons of the Rocky Mountains (page 357).

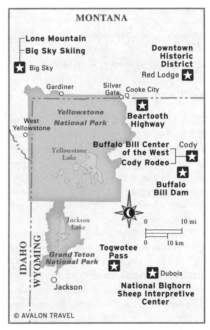

★ **Togwotee Pass:** This pass over the Continental Divide yields one of the most dramatic views approaching Grand Teton National Park (page 358).

Big Sky, Montana

While Big Sky started with old Montana ranching homesteads, today it is a huge, bustling, and upscale resort below Lone Peak. Summer and winter bring on the crowds, rocketing the population from 2,500 to 10,000. Due to the proximity to Yellowstone, some visitors prefer staying at Big Sky rather than the closer West Yellowstone simply because of the ambience, luxury accommodations, and breathing room. Big Sky draws the rich and famous with lodges, vacation homes, and shopping hubs sprawled across several miles. Big Sky links to Yellowstone via U.S. Highway 191 south.

SIGHTS

★ Lone Mountain

For Montana, the 11,166-foot **Lone Mountain** isn't one of the highest peaks, but its prominence gives it stature. The old volcano that blew out its side rises more than 4,000 feet from the Big Sky valley surrounding it. From several sides, you can see its alpine zone sweep up rugged, cliff-ridden ridges to its pointed summit. Skiers and snowboarders at Big Sky Resort take the tram to the summit to ski three sides. In summer, golfers can see it while teeing off, mountain bikers can ride on it, hikers can tour its trails, photographers try to catch its sunrise light, and sightseers can ride lifts to the summit.

For adventurous sightseers, the 2.5-hour **Lone Peak Expedition** (Big Sky Resort, 406/995-5769, www.bigskyresort.com, summer, from $85) goes to the 11,166-foot summit of Lone Peak. The guided expedition goes by chairlift, safari vehicle, and tram to reach the summit, where views take in three states and two national parks. Purchase tickets online in advance for the best rates.

Crail Ranch Museum

Big Sky is home to historic ranches. The **Crail Ranch Museum** (2110 Spotted Elk Rd., 406/993-2112, www.crailranch.org, noon-3pm Sat.-Sun. July-Aug., free) is housed in historic log buildings from the 1902 homestead of the Crail family. The small museum contains photos, documents, and artifacts that will give history buffs a taste of the early ranchers

Lone Mountain towers above Big Sky.

Gateways to Yellowstone

0 10 km

0 10 mi

Henry

Greys Lake

To Idaho Falls

Rexburg

St. Anthony

Ashton

Harriman State Park

Mesa Falls

26

33

32

Caribou-Targhee National Forest

Snake River

Wayan

34

Swan Valley

31

Victor

Tetonia

Driggs

IDAHO

WYOMING

Freedom

Palisades Reservoir

Alpine

Etna

89

Thayne

Bedford

Turnerville

To Evanston and Salt Lake City, Utah

Wyoming

22

JACKSON HOLE

Teton Village

Alta

GRAND TARGHEE

Grand Teton 13,772ft

Moose Junction

Jenny Lake

John D. Rockefeller Jr. Memorial Parkway

Grand Teton National Park

Jackson Lake

Bridger Teton National Forest

Mt Hancock 10,214ft

89

25

Hoback Junction

JACKSON

SNOW KING

National Elk Refuge

Kelly

191

89

26

Moran Junction

Bridger-Teton National Forest

Hoback Pk 10,862ft

Gros Ventre Range

Doubletop Pk 11,682ft

Mt Leidy 10,326ft

TOGWOTEE PASS

Merna

189

191

Bondurant

354

189

Daniel

Cora

Pinedale

Willow Lake

New Fork Lakes

352

Green River Lakes

Fremont Lake

To Rock Springs

Boulder Lake

WHITE PINE

Wind River Mountains

Continental Divide

Gannett Peak 13,804ft

NATIONAL BIGHORN SHEEP CENTER

DUBOIS

26

287

Pinnacle Buttes

Younts Peak 12,156ft

South Fork

Valley

Wind River

Shoshone National Forest

Wolverine Pk 12,360ft

Roberts Mtn 12,767ft

Bear Pk 10,755ft

Burris

Crowheart

Bull Lake

To Lander and Riverton

WIND RIVER INDIAN RESERVATION

Absaroka Range

To Evanston

To Evanston and Salt Lake City, Utah

© AVALON TRAVEL

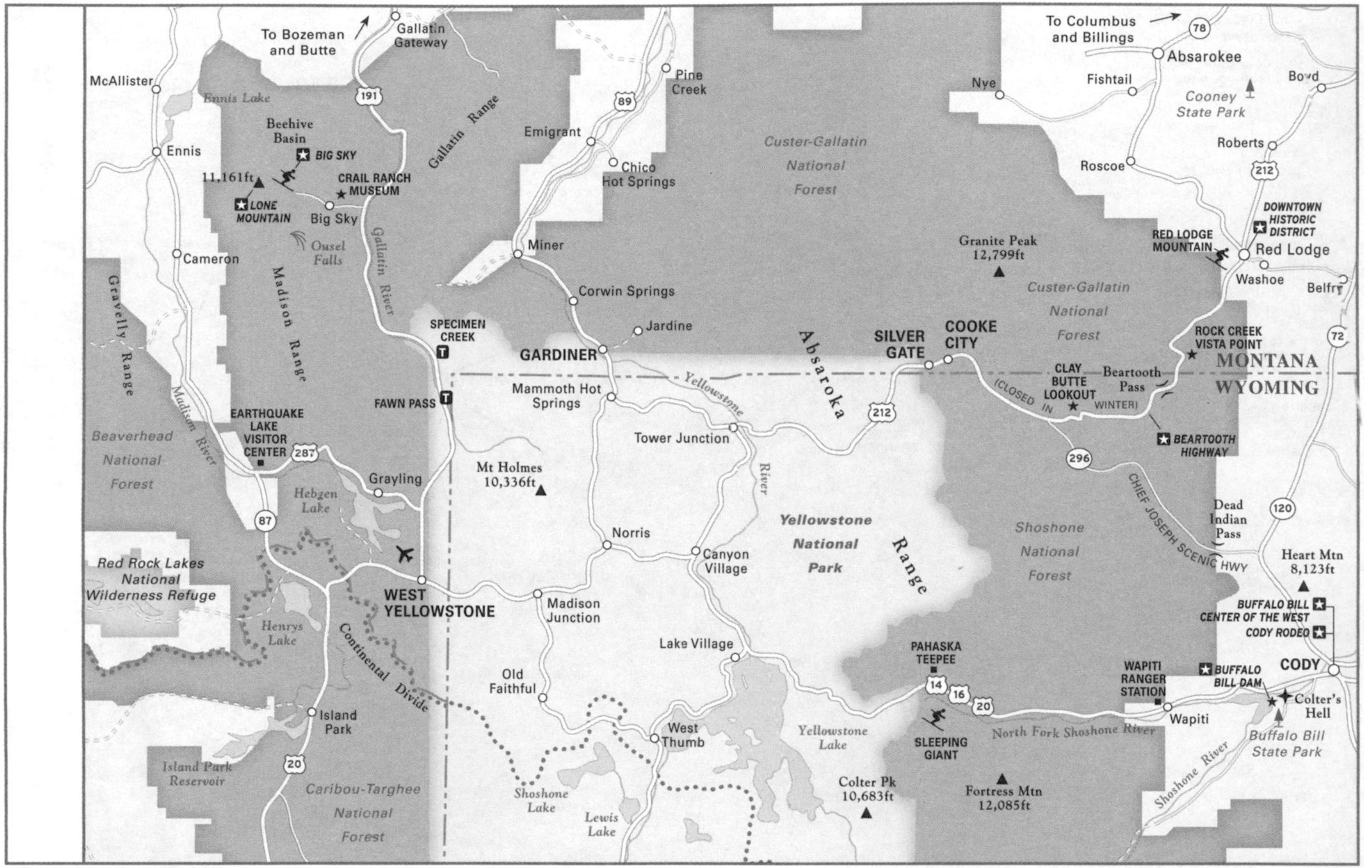

McAllister

Ennis

Cameron

Madison River

Gravelly Range

Beaverhead National Forest

Red Rock Lakes National Wilderness Refuge

Island Park Reservoir

Henrys Lake

Caribou-Targhee National Forest

Island Park

Continental Divide

20

87

287

EARTHQUAKE LAKE VISITOR CENTER

Hebgen Lake

Grayling

WEST YELLOWSTONE

11,316ft
LONE MOUNTAIN

Beehive Basin

BIG SKY

Ousel Falls

CRAIL RANCH MUSEUM

Madison Range

Gallatin River

To Bozeman and Butte

191

Gallatin Gateway

Gallatin Range

FAWN PASS

SPECIMEN CREEK

Mt Holmes 10,336ft

Mammoth Hot Springs

GARDINER

Miner

Emigrant

89

Corwin Springs

Chico Hot Springs

Pine Creek

Shoshone Lake

Old Faithful

Madison Junction

Norris

Tower Junction

Jardine

Lewis Lake

West Thumb

Canyon Village

Lake Village

Yellowstone National Park

Yellowstone River

Custer-Gallatin National Forest

Absaroka Range

Yellowstone Lake

Colter Pk 10,683ft

212

SILVER GATE

COOKE CITY

Granite Peak 12,799ft

Custer-Gallatin National Forest

Nye

296

CLAY BUTTE LOOKOUT

Beartooth Pass

Roscoe

To Columbus and Billings

78

Fishtail

Absarokee

PAHASKA TEEPEE

SLEEPING GIANT

14

16

20

Fortress Mtn 12,085ft

North Fork Shoshone River

Shoshone National Forest

CHIEF JOSEPH SCENIC HWY

Dead Indian Pass

(CLOSED WINTER)

RED LODGE MOUNTAIN

ROCK CREEK VISTA POINT

Cooney State Park

212

Roberts

Bord

WAPITI RANGER STATION

Wapiti

Shoshone River

BUFFALO BILL DAM

Colter's Hell

Buffalo Bill State Park

CODY

BUFFALO BILL CENTER OF THE WEST

CODY RODEO

BEARTOOTH HIGHWAY

Heart Mtn 8,123ft

120

MONTANA

WYOMING

DOWNTOWN HISTORIC DISTRICT

Red Lodge

Washoe

Belfry

72

Big Sky

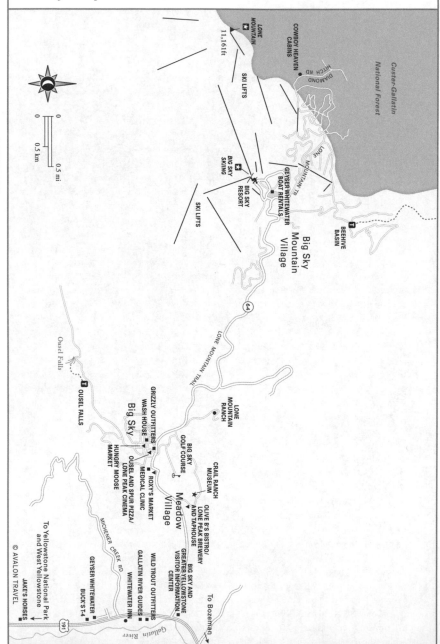

LONE MOUNTAIN

11,161ft

COWBOY HEAVEN CABINS

DIAMOND HITCH RD

Custer-Gallatin National Forest

SKI LIFTS

BIG SKY SKIING

BIG SKY RESORT

GEYSER WHITEWATER BOAT RENTALS

LONE MOUNTAIN TR

Big Sky Mountain Village

BEEHIVE BASIN

SKI LIFTS

64

LONE MOUNTAIN TRAIL

Ousel Falls

OUSEL FALLS

GRIZZLY OUTFITTERS

WASH HOUSE

Big Sky

HUNGRY MOOSE MARKET

LONE MOUNTAIN RANCH

BIG SKY GOLF COURSE

MEDICAL CLINIC

ROXY'S MARKET

OUSEL AND SPUR PIZZA/ LONE PEAK CINEMA

CRAIL RANCH MUSEUM

OLIVE B'S BISTRO/ LONE PEAK BREWERY AND TAPHOUSE

Meadow Village

BIG SKY AND GREATER YELLOWSTONE VISITOR INFORMATION CENTER

WILD TROUT OUTFITTERS

GALLATIN RIVER GUIDES

WHITEWATER INN

MICHENER CREEK RD

To Yellowstone National Park and West Yellowstone

GEYSER WHITEWATER

BUCK'S T4

JAKE'S HORSES

To Bozeman

Gallatin River

191

0   0.5 mi
0   0.5 km

© AVALON TRAVEL

in Big Sky. Visitors can take a self-guided or volunteer-guided tour.

Gallatin River

With headwaters in Yellowstone, the 120-mile **Gallatin River** runs north through the Gallatin Canyon. U.S. Highway 191 parallels the river, where calm stretches beckon anglers with blue-ribbon trout fishing. In the canyon, the rocky riverbed churns up white water for rafters and kayakers in a Class IV section known as the Mad Mile. Campgrounds also line the river corridor.

RECREATION
Hiking

Hiking trails tour Big Sky, Custer Gallatin National Forest, and Yellowstone National Park. While the Big Sky hikes are heavily traveled, the Yellowstone trails see very few hikers due to the lengthy walks needed to reach destinations such as passes or lakes. These trails all enter grizzly bear management areas, where the park service recommends hiking with at least four people; no off-trail travel is permitted. For hikers looking for shorter trails, the first few miles of these are enjoyable, especially in early summer with wildflowers.

OUSEL FALLS

Distance: 1.6 miles round-trip
Duration: 1 hour
Elevation change: 450 feet
Effort: easy
Trailhead: Ousel Falls Trailhead in Custer Gallatin National Forest
Directions: From Big Sky Town Center, take Ousel Falls Road 1.6 miles southwest to the trailhead parking lot on the right.

This short walk goes to a waterfall on the **South Fork of the West Fork of the Gallatin River.** The route is lined with wildflowers in July as the trail drops to a bridge across the river and then climbs along the south side of the river to the falls. At the falls, picnic tables offer places to sit. The falls, named for the American dipper, tumble down

stair steps, which toss up a cool mist. Pick up an interpretive trail guide at the trailhead.

BEEHIVE BASIN

Distance: 6.6 miles round-trip
Duration: 3-4 hours
Elevation change: 1,625 feet
Effort: moderate
Trailhead: Beehive Basin Trailhead in Custer Gallatin National Forest
Directions: From Lone Mountain Trail 1.4 miles north of the Big Sky Resort turnoff, turn right onto Beehive Basin Road for 1.7 miles to the trailhead parking lot on the left.

Trail #40 goes to scenic Beehive Basin, a bit of a grunt after the deceptively easy start. But the scenery more than makes up for it. In early June, you may encounter snow on the trail and ankle-deep streams to cross. But by July, wildflowers cover the meadows in rampant color. Later in summer, the meadow grasses turn gold. In the basin a small, narrow, shallow lake at 9,285 feet surrounded by meadows tucks below rugged Beehive Peak in the Spanish Peaks.

From the trailhead, cross the creek and ascend north through meadows with intermittent trees. After climbing several switchbacks, the trail enters the upper basin and works north to **Beehive Lake** at the base of **Beehive Peak.**

SPECIMEN CREEK AND SHELF LAKE

Distance: 15.4 miles round-trip
Duration: 8 hours
Elevation change: 2,300 feet
Effort: strenuous
Trailhead: Specimen Creek Trailhead on U.S. Highway 191 in Yellowstone National Park

This level, mostly forested trail follows Specimen Creek up valley to a small alpine lake surrounded by meadows. En route, it passes plenty of trees that have been clawed by grizzlies. At two miles, just after entering the 2007 Owl Creek Fire burn, the trail reaches a **fork.** Hikers out just to enjoy the creek with meadows of early summer wildflowers can turn around at this junction. Continue up the **Specimen Creek Trail** (left fork) following the **North Fork.** At 4.1 miles, the trail reaches a meadow where hikers must ford **Specimen Creek.** At 5.9 miles, the trail reaches a second **junction.** The left fork begins the steep climb 1,400 feet up switchbacks to the **Sky Rim Trail** and **Shelf Lake** at 9,194 feet. Sheep and Bighorn Peaks become visible as the trail breaks out of the trees.

FAWN PASS

Distance: 18 miles round-trip
Duration: 9-10 hours
Elevation change: 1,950 feet
Effort: moderate but long
Trailhead: Fawn Pass Trailhead on U.S. Highway 191 in Yellowstone National Park

This Gallatin Range trail is a sun-soaker. Between broad mosquito meadows and silvered blowdowns from forest fires, the trail can be a scorcher in midsummer and thick with black biting flies. It's also smack in the middle of a grizzly bear management area. In early summer, expect wildflowers galore in the huge sagebrush meadows. Shortly after starting, the trail reaches a couple of junctions. Stay right at both. About six miles in, a cutoff trail departs for the **Bighorn Pass Trail.** Head eastward, passing intermittent tiny ponds; before the pass, patchy forests appear. The final slope to the pass hikes straight toward Gray Peak. A sign marks the pass, which has a small lake for lunch just beyond and views of Crowfoot Ridge to the south.

BIGHORN PASS TRAIL

Distance: 21 miles round-trip
Duration: 11-12 hours
Elevation change: 1,885 feet
Effort: strenuous due to length
Trailhead: Bighorn Pass Trailhead on U.S. Highway 191 in Yellowstone National Park

Bighorn Pass Trail passes through a heavy bear area to follow the Gallatin River, making the route a favorite for anglers going after cutthroat, rainbow, and brook trout in the stretches close to the highway. The hike up valley hits intermittent forest, but much of it has broad open views of Crowfoot Ridge.

Soon, the trail crosses the Gallatin River on a bridge. At 4.2 miles, the trail reaches the junction with the **Fawn Pass Cutoff Trail.** Continue up valley instead, ascending through meadows and past **backcountry campsites**. Just before **Bighorn Pass**, the trail switchbacks up into bighorn sheep terrain. From the pass, at 9,110 feet, you can look down into Yellowstone's interior at Swan Lake and Bunsen Peak.

Biking

Big Sky has 40 miles of mountain biking trails. An easy 2.6-mile gravel trail tours **Crail Ranch Meadow.** Off Aspen Leaf Drive, the dirt single-track **Hummock Trail** (3 miles) rolls a triple loop over hummocks made by ice-age landslides; it's suitable for intermediate riders. A paved trail parallels **Lone Mountain Trail** (Hwy. 64, 6 miles) between Town Center and Hwy. 161.

Big Sky Resort (406/995-5849, www.bigskyresort.com, 9am-4pm daily in summer, from $40 bike haul pass) has three lifts that access 14 downhill trails, including an intermediate flow trail. In addition, nine cross-country single- and double-track trails for beginners and intermediate riders lead from Big Sky Village on loops across Andesite Mountain and through Moonlight Basin north of Lone Peak.

Located in the Big Sky Village Snowcrest Building, **Different Spokes Bike Shop** (50 Big Sky Resort Rd., 406/995-5849, www.bigskyresort.com, 9am-4pm daily early June-late Sept., $38-138) rents downhill and cross-country bikes (helmets and full pads included). Tours, lessons, and coaching are available.

Horseback Riding

Jake's Horses (200 Beaver Creek Rd., 406/995-4630 or 800/352-5956, www.jakeshorses.com, year-round, $45-150) guides horseback trail rides in Gallatin Canyon, the national forest, and Yellowstone. Rides last 1-4 hours or all day. They also offer winter rides; a two-hour dinner ride adds in a steak fry.

Water Sports

Tiny **Lake Levinsky** at Big Sky Resort offers a tame place for boating. **Geyser Whitewater Expeditions** (46651 Gallatin Rd., 406/995-4989, www.raftmontana.com, 10am-6pm daily summer, $15/hour) rents pedal boats, canoes, kayaks, and paddleboards from the shore. Day passes and Family Adventure Cards offer more economical rates.

FISHING

The **Gallatin River** ranks as one of the prime rivers to fish for trout in Montana. The waters hold brown and rainbow trout, and anglers are not permitted to float much of it, making wading the way to fish. You'll need a **Montana fishing license** (http://fwp.mt.gov, residents: $13-26; nonresidents: $25 for two days, $54 for 10 days, $70 season).

Four fishing guide services operate out of Big Sky: **Grizzly Outfitters** (11 Lone Peak Dr., 406/554-9470 or 888/807-9452, www.grizzlyoutfitters.com), **Gallatin River Guides** (47430 Gallatin Rd., 406/995-2290, www.montanaflyfishing.com), **Lone Mountain Ranch** (750 Lone Mountain Ranch Rd.,

406/995-4644 or 800/514-4644, www.lonemountainranch.com), and **Wild Trout Outfitters** (47520 Gallatin Rd., 406/995-2975 or 800/423-4742, www.wildtroutoutfitters.com). All fish the Gallatin River but offer a variety of trips, gear rentals, and instruction. Rates run $250-450 for a half day and $350-550 for a full day for two people. Fishing licenses cost extra. Tip 15 percent, but if you catch lots of fish, tip 20 percent.

RAFTING

The **Gallatin River** meanders and crashes through the Gallatin Canyon, creating prime white-water rafting. Through the canyon, the river goes from slow swirly pools to thundering wave trains of almost continuous Class II-IV rapids. Most of the rafting is north of Big Sky in the 13 miles between Greek Creek and Spanish Creek. Expert boaters hit House Rock rapid and bash through the rocky, rough current of the Mad Mile. The best water runs May-mid-July. Self-guided canyon rafting on the Gallatin is only for those skilled in strong currents, rapids, and obstacles.

Two companies guide half-day ($55-70) and full-day ($80-100) trips on calm, scenic float sections or white water. Boats depart multiple times daily. Plan to tip guides about 15

mountain bike trails at Big Sky Resort

percent. **Geyser Whitewater Expeditions** (46651 Gallatin Rd., 406/995-4989, www.raft-montana.com) is based in Big Sky. **Montana Whitewater Raft Company** (63960 Gallatin Rd., 406/995-4613, www.montanawhitewater.com) is based in Gallatin Gateway, about 16 miles north of Big Sky.

Golf

Golfing at Big Sky can be a challenge between the views of Lone Mountain and the wildlife that saunters out on the course. **Big Sky Golf Course** (2100 Black Otter Rd., 406/995-5780, www.bigskyresort.com, dawn-dusk daily late May-early Oct., $50 for clubs, $50-100 for greens fees and carts) is an 18-hole links-style par 72 Arnold Palmer course at 6,500 feet in elevation. The clubhouse offers rentals and instruction, and has a restaurant. Tee times are available online.

Spa

Located in the Huntley/Shoshone Lodge in Big Sky Village, the 3,000-square-foot **Solace Spa** (50 Big Sky Resort Rd., 406/995-5803, www.bigskyresort.com, hours vary daily Nov.-mid-Apr. and June-mid-Sept.) offers face and body treatments, massages, manicures, pedicures, waxing, tinting, and scrubs. The spa also houses a salon.

Thrill Sports

In summer, **Big Sky Resort** (406/995-5769, www.bigskyresort.com, 9am-4pm daily mid-June-mid-Sept., rates vary) brings on the thrill sports. You can fly through the air on ziplines, feel the rush of a giant swing, monkey around on a high ropes course or climbing wall, fling around on the bungee trampoline, or hop on a tamer scenic lift ride. Reservations are advised for ziplines and the high ropes course.

Winter Sports
★ DOWNHILL SKIING
Big Sky Resort (50 Big Sky Resort Rd., 800/548-4486, www.bigskyresort.com, 9am-4pm daily late Nov.-mid-Apr.), with

Big Sky Golf Course has big views of Lone Peak.

neighboring Moonlight Basin and Spanish Peaks, is one of the biggest ski areas in North America, with 5,800 acres of terrain across four mountains. With its summit on 11,166-foot Lone Mountain Peak, the ski area has 4,350 vertical feet full of broad groomers, gladed tree runs, and challenging steeps, plus 23 lifts, 11 surface lifts, 300 named runs, and 7 terrain parks. Rates for lift tickets ($85-140 adults) vary seasonally. Discounts are available in advance online, with lower rates for seniors, college students, juniors, and youth (youth often can ski for free with lodging through Big Sky Resort).

CROSS-COUNTRY SKIING
With one of the largest Nordic ski trail systems, **Lone Mountain Ranch** (750 Lone Mountain Ranch Rd., 406/995-4734, www.lonemountainranch.com, dawn-dusk daily late Nov.-mid-Apr.) grooms 85 kilometers (53 miles) of trails for skate and classic skiing.

Even though the trail system spans 2,200 feet in elevation, routes are designed on different loops for beginners, experts, and skill levels in between. The outdoor ski shop (8am-8pm) offers lessons, rentals, repairs, and guided cross-country ski trips into Yellowstone. Rentals cost $20-45 per day, and trail passes cost $15-20.

SNOWSHOEING

The trails at **Lone Mountain Ranch** (750 Lone Mountain Ranch Rd., 406/995-4734, www.lonemountainranch.com, dawn-dusk daily late Nov.-mid-Apr.) give snowshoers extensive touring options. The trails are separate from the Nordic ski trails. An outdoor shop (8am-8pm) offers guided tours on the ranch trails and in Yellowstone. Rentals cost $20 per day, and trail passes cost $15-20.

ICE-SKATING

A full-size hockey and ice-skating outdoor rink, plus a kids' rink, are available at the **Town Center** (Ousel Falls Rd. and Aspen Leaf Dr., http://bssha.org, noon-11pm daily in winter, $5). Helmets are required and can be rented from **Grizzly Outfitters** (11 Lone Peak Dr., 406/554-9470 or 888/807-9452, www.grizzlyoutfitters.com, $7-10).

ENTERTAINMENT AND SHOPPING

With so much outdoor activity, nightlife consists mostly of restaurants, but there are a handful of places to knock back a drink. In the village at Big Sky Resort, the Arrowhead Mall houses **Scissorbills** (406/995-4933, www.scissorbills.com, 11am-2am daily winter and summer only), a locals' hangout that hops with DJ tunes and dancing, plus live music on the weekends. For movies, head to **Lone Peak Cinema** (50 Ousel Falls Rd., 406/995-7827, www.lonepeakcinema.com), where two theaters show a revolving lineup of new releases.

The **Big Sky Classical Music Festival** (406/995-2742, www.bigskyarts.org, Aug.) invites guest soloists and ensembles to perform with the Big Sky Festival Orchestra. Big Sky Arts also sponsors the free summer **Music in the Mountains** (Thurs., July-Aug.) weekly series at the Center Stage in Town Center Park.

Shopping at Big Sky is separated into several different locations: **Town Center** (Ousel Falls Rd. and Aspen Leaf Dr., year-round), **Meadow Village** (Meadow Village Dr., Center Lane, and Little Coyote Rd., year-round), and **Big Sky Resort** (800/548-4486, www.bigskyresort.com, early Dec.-mid-Apr.

skiing from the top of Lone Mountain Ranch

and early June-Sept.). Shops carry upscale art, regional crafts, jewelry, furniture, and boutique and trendy clothing, but you can also find T-shirts, souvenirs, and sporting goods.

FOOD
Restaurants

Two restaurants at **Big Sky Resort** (50 Big Sky Resort, www.bigskyresort.com, early June-Sept. and early Dec.-mid-Apr.) are open seasonally. ★ **Andiamo Italian Grille** (406/995-8041, 4pm-10pm daily winter and summer, $18-44) serves Tuscan specialties, antipasti, Italian wine, and drool-worthy desserts that look more like artistry than food. Their Montana flair puts a twist on the housemade pastas and the lamb osso buco. Reservations are advised and can be made online.

Set on the summit of Andesite Mountain, **Everett's 8800** (406/995-8800, dinner 5:30pm-8pm Thurs.-Sat. winter, $32-56; lunch 10am-3pm daily winter and summer, $14-24) is an experience with a spectacular view. Pay to ride the lift up to the restaurant, then dine while gazing at Lone Peak before returning to the village (by snowcoach in winter). Reservations are recommended for lunch and are required in winter for dinner.

Lone Peak Brewery & Taphouse (Meadow Village, 48 Marketplace Dr., 406/995-3939, www.lonepeakbrewery.com, 11am-10pm daily year-round, hours shorten in spring and fall, $10-18) pours 12-14 craft beers on tap, including seasonal specialties, plus cocktails from the full bar. Dine on build-your-own burgers, bison quesadillas, salads, and rice bowls.

Olive B's Big Sky Bistro (151 Center Ln., 406/995-3355, www.olivebsbigsky.com, 11am-9pm Mon.-Fri., 4pm-9pm Sat., late May-mid-Oct. and early Dec.-mid-Apr., lunch $10-15, dinner $27-35) serves classic French bistro fare such as French onion soup and a blue-cheese crème Brûlée. Dinner includes a lobster mac and cheese, steaks, seafood, and elk, while lunch sees salads, burgers, sandwiches, and

dessert at Andiamo Italian Grille

appetizers. Go here for a huckleberry martini, whiskeys, and wine.

Ousel and Spur Pizza Company (Big Sky Town Center, 50 Ousel Falls Rd., 406/995-7175, www.ouselandspurpizza.com, 5pm-close daily year-round, $16-30) specializes in elk sausage pizza. Dine on classic pizzas and Italian pastas with local ingredients or gluten-free and vegetarian options. The **Lotus Pad** (3090 Big Pine Dr., 406/995-2728, www.lotuspadbigsky.com, 5pm-close daily year-round, shorter hours fall and spring, $14-30) serves vegetarian, gluten-free, and spicy Asian meals, including curries, stir-fries, noodle dishes, and seafood, plus specialty cocktails, sake, and beers from Japan.

The ★ **Horn and Cantle** (Lone Mountain Ranch, 800 Lone Mountain Ranch Rd., 406/995-2782, www.hornandcantle.com, late Nov.-mid-Apr. and early June-Sept.) has a dining room and saloon. Dinner (5:30pm-9:30pm daily, $26-88) includes artistic plates of farm-to-table meals with fresh, lively flavors. Elk, lamb, steaks, and trout are regionally sourced. Appetizers are a must and the desserts are exquisite. Reservations are highly recommended. The **saloon** (11:30am-10pm daily, $10-17) is the place to experience old Montana, with cocktails and homemade infusions or lighter dining.

On U.S. Highway 191, **Gallatin Riverhouse Grill** (45130 Gallatin Rd., 406/995-7427, http://gallatinriverhousegrill. com, 3pm-close daily year-round, $14-30) pumps out the barbecue—burgers, chicken, sandwiches, brisket, sausage, and ribs—and throws in live music for evening fun. Sampler platters serve 2-4 people and pile on the barbecue with traditional sides. **Buck's T-4 Lodging** (46625 Gallatin Rd., 406/995-4111 or 800/822-4484, www.buckst4.com, 5:30pm-9pm daily late May-mid-Oct. and late Nov.-mid-Apr., $13-40) serves burgers topped with duck bacon, sandwiches, a full line-up of steaks (including cauliflower for vegetarians), and specialty entrées with duck and fish. Try the huckleberry martini.

Cookouts

Reservations are required for cookouts. Most outfitters offer vegetarian alternatives to the main meal that can be requested when booking. Most events do not serve alcohol; some permit BYOB.

At Big Sky Resort, diners venture as a group on a snowcat to the **Montana Dinner Yurt** (1 Lone Mountain Trail, 406/995-3880, www. bigskyyurt.com, 6:30pm-10pm daily late Nov.-mid-Apr., $99-115). After arriving at the yurt (a huge round tent heated by a woodstove), guests can sled outside or drink cocoa around the fire before a three-course dinner is served. Musical entertainment is part of the gig.

From **Lone Mountain Ranch** (750 Lone Mountain Ranch Rd., 406/995-2783, www. lonemountainranch.com, 6:30pm-10pm daily mid-Dec.-early Apr., $135-160), a horse-drawn sleigh slides through the snowy woods to the cozy North Fork Cabin for dinner. Dress for the cold with hat and gloves; wranglers will also supply blankets for the 20-minute ride. A woodstove heats the cabin, which glows by the light of oil lanterns. Prime rib with all the trimmings and sides is served family-style, and live music and storytelling provides the entertainment. Sleigh-and-stay packages ($389 for two) are available.

At the **320 Guest Ranch** (205 Buffalo Horn Creek Rd., 406/995-4283, www.320ranch.com, Wed. mid-June-mid-Sept., horseback: $105 adults, $95 children; wagon: $55 adults, $35 children), you can opt to get to the ranch barbecue via wagon or two-hour horseback ride. Once at the Gallatin River, steaks and chicken come right off the barbecue. The ranch is located about 12 miles south of Big Sky.

Groceries

Big Sky has several markets for groceries, deli items, meats, fruits, veggies, beer, wine, and baked goods. Two outlets of **Hungry Moose Market and Deli** (209 Aspen Leaf Dr., 406/995-3045, 6:30am-10pm daily; Mountain Mall at Big Sky Resort, 406/995-3075, winter and summer only; www.hungrymoose.com) sell meals to go and premade grab-and-go items: espresso, breakfast sandwiches, salads, sandwiches, wraps, ice cream, and baked goods. They also deliver groceries. In Town Center, the larger **Roxy's Market** (20 Huntley Dr., 406/995-2295, http://roxys-market.com, 7am-9pm daily) carries a full lineup of groceries, plus specialty items.

ACCOMMODATIONS

Big Sky is an upscale resort community with more than 3,000 rooms, condos, townhomes, and vacation homes with modern conveniences such as wireless Internet. It has accommodations across the spectrum, from family hotels to ultra-pricey luxury vacation homes, but lacks chain hotels. Several property management companies rent condos, townhomes, and vacation homes. **Big Sky Luxury Rentals** (888/451-0156, www.vacationbigsky. com) has upscale vacation homes and a concierge service. **Big Sky Vacation Rentals** (888/915-2787, www.bookbigsky.com) has about 80 vacation homes across price ranges.

Big Sky Resort

For the largest number of hotels, condos, cabins, and townhomes, and especially slopeside options for winter and summer, check the listings with **Big Sky Resort** (50 Big Sky Resort Rd., 800/548-4486, www.bigskyresort. com, early Dec.-mid-Apr. and early June-Sept.). The resort offers lodging and activity packages during summer and winter, and summer lodging often includes free scenic lift rides. Lodging is in hotels, condos, townhomes, upscale cabins, and vacation homes. Many of the lodging properties have access to the outdoor swimming pool and fitness room at Huntley Lodge or have their own. Rates are highest in winter during the ski season and lower in summer. Book holiday lodging one year in advance. Resort fees will add 19 percent to rates.

Quiet and with views of Lone Mountain from a slopeside perch, the ★ **Cowboy Heaven Cabins** ($420-890, 3-5 night min.) are modern two-bedroom log cabins with full kitchens, fireplaces, two small bathrooms, living and dining area, and private outdoor hot tubs. They flank the Moonlight Basin side of Lone Mountain, and most have impressive views from their decks. The cabins sleep 4-8 people with one bedroom having a queen or king and the other twins or bunks. Some cabins also have a loft.

Big Sky Village hotels cluster around shops, restaurants, and lifts. The three-story ★ **Village Center** ($260-1,220) has luxury suites and condos to sleep 2-10 people with plush designer mountain decor. Studios have a queen bed, a sofa bed, and kitchen appliances. The one-, two-, and three-bedroom condos have a king or queen in the bedrooms. Some rooms also have sofa beds. Each unit has 2-3 full bathrooms with tubs and showers. The center has an outdoor pool, hot tub, and fitness room, and the rates usually include breakfast in neighboring Huntley Lodge. The high-rise luxury **Summit Hotel** ($262-4,200) has studios, hotel rooms with two queens or a king, condos, and penthouses. Rates usually include breakfast. Studios have queen beds. Condo suites have one, two, or three bedrooms, plus kitchens and 1-3 bathrooms. Penthouses, which have 2-4 bedrooms, have housed political notables such as the Obamas and Bidens. Some of the rooms have windows that frame Lone Peak. **Huntley Lodge** ($250-590) and **Shoshone Condominiums** ($455-1,175) were some of the early resort mainstays, but have seen several upgrades. Dining, shopping, the Solace Spa, an outdoor swimming

Village Center has condos slopeside at Big Sky Resort.

pool and hot tubs, fitness center, sauna, and tennis courts are in the complex. Huntley Lodge rooms have 2-3 queen beds with mountain views or lofts as options. The Shoshone condos come with one bedroom, with or without a loft. They contain various combinations of queen or king beds and sofa sleepers.

Guest Ranches

Historic ranches are one of the mainstays of Big Sky. They offer a way to experience the Old West with modern amenities. Secluded at Big Sky in a side canyon with a wilderness feel, ★ **Lone Mountain Ranch** (750 Lone Mountain Ranch Rd., 406/995-4644, www. lonemountainranch.com, late Nov.-mid-Apr. and early June-Sept., $475-650 pp summer, $350 pp winter, reduced rates for kids) has packages that include lodging, activities, and meals. Lodging is in quaint log cabins with no televisions, air-conditioning, or phones. Woodstoves ward off the chill on cold days. In winter, Nordic ski trails wind between the cabins, which scatter on both sides of the burbling creek, and sleigh-ride dinners head to a cozy remote cabin. Ranch programs include horseback riding, fishing, hiking, kids' programs, Yellowstone tours, and skiing (seasonal). The dining room serves outstanding meals. When available, single-night B&B stays start at $230 for two guests.

Located 12 miles south of Big Sky, the historic **320 Guest Ranch** (205 Buffalo Horn Creek Rd., 406/995-4283, www.320ranch. com, year-round, $140-500) flanks the Gallatin River. Lodging is in 29 small one-room duplex cabins, 12 two-bedroom cabins with efficiency kitchens, and seven three-bedroom luxury log homes. Summer stays include horseback riding, fly-fishing, and rodeos; winter offers sleigh rides. The restaurant is open in summer and winter only.

Motels

Two motels are located roadside on US 191 just south of the turnoff to the ski resort (15 minutes from the ski-area parking lots). An independent motel and a longtime Big Sky staple, **Buck's T-4 Lodging** (46625 Gallatin Rd., 406/995-4111 or 800/822-4484, www. buckst4.com, late May-mid-Oct. and late Nov.-mid-Apr., $170-270) has 72 motel rooms with two queens or one king bed. Stays include a hot breakfast. Owned by Big Sky Resort, **Whitewater Inn** (47214 Gallatin Rd., 800/548-4486, www.bigskyresort.com, year round, $200-280) has rooms with 2-3 queens or one king, as well as pet-friendly

Log cabins are part of the charm at Lone Mountain Ranch.

rooms, continental breakfast, a fitness room, a hot tub, and an indoor swimming pool with a 90-foot slide.

CAMPING

In **Custer Gallatin National Forest** (Bozeman Ranger District, 3710 Fallon St., Bozeman, 406/522-2520, www.fs.usda.gov/main/custergallatin), RV and tent campgrounds line the Gallatin Canyon along U.S. 191. They are popular with locals as quick getaways from Bozeman for fishing, river rafting and kayaking, and hiking. The campgrounds, open mid-May-late September, take **reservations** (877/444-6777, www.recreation.gov), which are mandatory in July and August. Facilities include picnic tables, fire rings with grills, vault toilets, drinking water, bear boxes, garbage service, firewood for sale, and wheelchair-accessible toilets and campsites. Campsites cost $15; extra vehicles cost $6.

The three of the most popular campgroundssit right on the highway and the Gallatin River, the first two located just north of Big Sky. In a loop around a sunny meadow, **Greek Creek Campground** packs out first with 14 campsites with RVs limited to 60 feet. Unfortunately, some campsites have views of the road, but campsites 14 and 15 overlook the river. **Moose Creek Flat Campground,** the closest campground to Big Sky, has 13 campsites with RVs limited to 60 feet. Located south of Big Sky in the Upper Gallatin Canyon, **Red Cliff Campground** is the closest to Yellowstone. Tucked in a young Douglas fir forest, the campground has 65 campsites with RVs limited to 50 feet; electrical hookups are at half the sites.

Two quieter campgrounds tuck up side canyons north of Big Sky. **Spire Rock Campground** huddles below Storm Castle Mountain with 19 campsites in clusters surrounded by lush undergrowth of thimbleberries, wild roses, and vine maples. RVs are limited to 50 feet. **Swan Creek Campground** is in the steep-walled Swan Creek Canyon. In grassy meadows with sun and views of the forested canyon walls, the campground has 14 campsites with RVs limited to 45 feet.

TRANSPORTATION AND SERVICES

Car

From Big Sky, **U.S. Highway 191** travels 20 miles south through several historic ranches before entering Yellowstone National Park. This 20-mile section of the park (no entrance station) is a good place to see bison, bears, or moose. After exiting the park, the road passes through Custer Gallatin National Forest as it descends south into West Yellowstone and to the **West Entrance** (47 miles south of Big Sky) to Yellowstone.

From the north, access Big Sky via **Bozeman** and the Gallatin Gateway down U.S. Highway 191. The two-lane road can be a nightmare: It's narrow and curvy, and locals who know all its curves drive it fast. It's also the most crowded access road to Yellowstone, with nonstop traffic in July and August. Because the road parallels the Gallatin River, scads of river rafters and anglers add to the traffic. If you pull off to let traffic pass, you may wait for quite a while to be able to pull back on. Winter can douse the road in snow or ice, which adds to the white-knuckle driving.

PARKING

Most first-time visitors to Big Sky expect a compact resort, but Big Sky is a sprawling unincorporated community. From the highway, it's a 20-minute drive through developments and forests to reach the Big Sky Resort and lifts. At the resort, most lodges have specified parking areas. Parking areas for day visitors to Big Sky Resort are located at Mountain Village and Madison Village, both marked on road junction signs.

Bus

The **Skyline Bus** (406/995-6287, www.skylinebus.com, hours vary seasonally year-round, free) connects the various base areas of Big Sky Resort with businesses on the highway, including motels. It makes about 15 stops around the Big Sky area. A bus also runs between Bozeman and Big Sky ($5 cash, purchase tickets at Base Camp in Big Sky Resort). Buses run daily in summer and winter, but only Monday-Friday in fall and spring.

Services

Located at the junction of U.S. Highway 191 and Lone Mountain Trail, the **Big Sky and Greater Yellowstone Visitor Information Center** (55 Lone Mountain Trail, 406/996-3000, https://visitbigskymt.com, 8:30am-5:30pm daily in summer, 8:30am-5:30pm Mon.-Fri. in winter) is a place to get oriented before driving up through Big Sky. Operated by the Big Sky Chamber of Commerce, the center has brochures, maps, and information for both Big Sky and Yellowstone.

Find **ATMs** at Big Sky Resort, Town Center, and Meadow Village. Meadow Village has the **post office** (5 Meadow Center Dr. #2, 406/995-4540), and Town Center has **The Wash House** (3415 Cedar Dr., 406/993-2822, www.thewashhousebigsky.com), with coin-op washers and dryers. No public shower facility is available.

MEDIA AND COMMUNICATIONS

Big Sky has all the modern services: wireless Internet in hotels and ubiquitous cell phone service. The **Big Sky Community Library** (45465 Gallatin Rd., 406/995-4281, www.bigskylibrary.org, hours vary Sun.-Thurs.) has computers available for public use, but call first to check on changeable hours.

Daily news comes from the *Bozeman Daily Chronicle* (www.bozemandailychronicle.com).

MEDICAL SERVICES

In Big Sky, call 911 for emergencies. The **Medical Clinic of Big Sky** (www.medicalclinicofbigsky.com) operates two urgent care walk-in clinics. The **Town Center Clinic** (11 Lone Peak Dr., 406/993-2797, 9am-5pm Mon.-Fri.) is open year-round. During the ski season, the mountain clinic (406/995-2797, 9am-5pm daily late Nov.-mid-Apr.) serves as the main location. The nearest hospital is in Bozeman: **Bozeman Deaconess Hospital** (915 Highland Blvd., 406/585-5000, www.bozemandeaconess.org).

Red Lodge, Montana

Red Lodge is a throwback to the Old West, but with a modern mountain vibe. It attracts visitors from the upper Midwest and the Canadian plains for skiing at Red Lodge Mountain in winter and driving the Beartooth Highway in summer. Downtown shop, hotel, and restaurant fronts retain the look of the Old West with two-story brick facades, but cater to tourists rather than horses. Part of the town's attraction is the mix of western tradition with outdoor sports. Ski joring (where a horse and rider pull a skier) is an annual competition as well as a recreational pastime. Red Lodge only serves as a gateway to Yellowstone **late May-mid-October,** when plowing opens the Beartooth Highway to the park's Northeast Entrance.

SIGHTS
★ Downtown Red Lodge Historic District

Downtown Red Lodge Historic District (Broadway Ave. between 8th and 4th Sts.) clusters a few blocks along the main drag through town. Some of the two-story brick buildings go back to 1887, and retro signs from the 1950s convey another historical era. Shops cater now to tourists rather than the Old West, and restaurants have modern sensibilities. In the evening, walk between western saloons that ramp up a hefty and sometimes raucous nightlife scene with live music, dancing, live poker, gaming machines, cocktails, and local microbrews. Free **wagon rides** (7pm-9pm daily Memorial Day-Labor Day)

Red Lodge

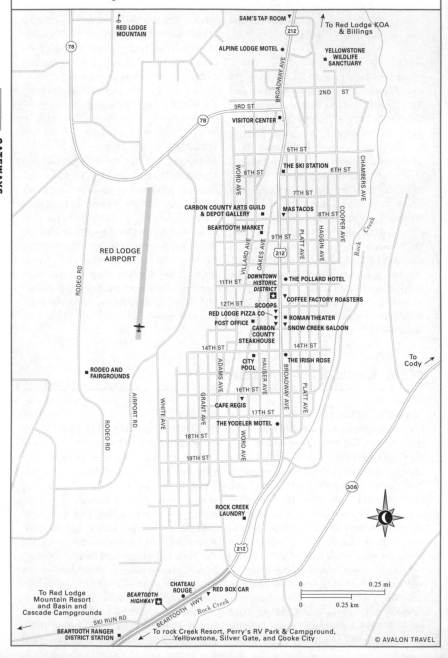

SAM'S TAP ROOM ▼
212
To Red Lodge KOA & Billings

RED LODGE MOUNTAIN

78

ALPINE LODGE MOTEL ●

YELLOWSTONE WILDLIFE SANCTUARY ■

2ND ST

BROADWAY AVE

3RD ST

78 VISITOR CENTER ■

5TH ST

CHAMBERS AVE

WORD AVE

6TH ST ■ THE SKI STATION 6TH ST

7TH ST

CARBON COUNTY ARTS GUILD & DEPOT GALLERY ■ ▼ MAS TACOS

COOPER AVE

8TH AVE

BEARTOOTH MARKET ■

9TH ST

PLATT AVE

HAGGIN AVE

Rock Creek

VILLARD AVE
OAKES AVE
212

11TH ST DOWNTOWN HISTORIC DISTRICT ● THE POLLARD HOTEL

✚ ▼ COFFEE FACTORY ROASTERS

12TH ST SCOOPS ▼

RED LODGE PIZZA CO ▼ ■ ROMAN THEATER
POST OFFICE ■ ▼ SNOW CREEK SALOON
CARBON COUNTY STEAKHOUSE

14TH ST ● 14TH ST

CITY POOL ■ ■ THE IRISH ROSE

ADAMS AVE

HAUSER AVE

BROADWAY AVE

PLATT AVE

RODEO AND FAIRGROUNDS ■

16TH ST ▼

GRANT AVE

WHITE AVE

CAFE REGIS ▼
17TH ST

THE YODELER MOTEL ●

WORD AVE

AIRPORT RD

RODEO RD

18TH ST

19TH ST

RED LODGE AIRPORT

RODEO RD

To Cody →

308

ROCK CREEK LAUNDRY ■

212

To Red Lodge Mountain Resort and Basin and Cascade Campgrounds

CHATEAU ROUGE ●
BEARTOOTH HIGHWAY ✚ ▼ RED BOX CAR

BEARTOOTH HWY

BEARTOOTH HIGHWAY

Rock Creek

0   0.25 mi
0   0.25 km

SKI RUN RD

BEARTOOTH RANGER DISTRICT STATION ■

To rock Creek Resort, Perry's RV Park & Campground, Yellowstone, Silver Gate, and Cooke City

© AVALON TRAVEL

Snowbanks line the Beartooth Highway.

August, the road yields 360-degree views of more than 20 peaks that top 12,000 feet. Red Lodge anchors the route on the northeast end and Yellowstone on the southwest. The road can close during summer for snowstorms, and frequent afternoon thundershowers are common.

From Red Lodge, the road squeezes through Rock Creek Canyon as it climbs slowly southwest following the creek. As the canyon widens, its walls heighten. From a meadow at a cluster of campgrounds, the road switchbacks up to **Rock Creek Vista Point,** a developed interpretive stop on the highway. From there, it switchbacks higher onto the Beartooth Plateau, rife with lupine in August. The road winds around the plateau's edge with the view growing to include more peaks in the Absaroka-Beartooth Wilderness. After crossing from Montana into Wyoming and rounding above Twin Lakes, the **Beartooth Basin Summer Ski Area** on the Twin Lakes Headwall appears. Scenic overlooks en route to Beartooth Pass are worthy stops; at the pass, you can spot the Beartooth Peak looking like a narrow cuspid. From the pass, the road descends through alpine meadows and bogs to pass Island and Beartooth Lakes. Between them sits **Top of the World,** a funky little seasonal store. A spur dirt road goes to **Clay Butte Lookout** (only open when staffed by volunteers). The road continues to drop via a couple switchbacks before reaching the Clarks Fork of the Yellowstone and climbing again to Cooke City and Silver Gate, and the Northeast Entrance to Yellowstone National Park.

travel Broadway Avenue, stopping at corners to pick up passengers.

Yellowstone Wildlife Sanctuary

In a wildlife-rich area such as the Greater Yellowstone Ecosystem, some animals need a little extra help. The **Yellowstone Wildlife Sanctuary** (615 2nd St. E., 406/446-1133, www.yellowstonewildlifesanctuary.org, 10am-4pm Wed.-Mon., $4-9) offers a way to observe rehabilitating wildlife up close. Residents include wolves, bears, raptors, and elk. Entry fees help support the rescue efforts.

★ Beartooth Highway

The 68-mile **Beartooth Highway** (www.beartoothhighway.com, late May-mid-Oct.), also known as the All-American Highway, climbs over Beartooth Pass at 10,947 feet, the highest drivable pass in the Northern Rockies. Above treeline, the alpine tundra runs for miles. Flanked by deep snowbanks in early summer and wildflowers in late

ROCK CREEK VISTA POINT

A stop on the east side of the Beartooth Highway, the **Rock Creek Vista Point** has a giant view. At 9,190 feet in elevation, the five-minute paved walk to the overlook can be lung-taxing for visitors from sea level, while golden-mantled ground squirrels skitter around unaffected. From the overlook, peer thousands of feet down Rock Creek Canyon and across to high-elevation alpine plateaus. Gray granite snow-draped peaks backdrop the scenery, with some mountains stretching above 12,000 feet.

CLAY BUTTE LOOKOUT

On the Beartooth Highway, **Clay Butte Lookout** (10am-5pm Tues.-Sun. early July-Aug.) offers one impressive view. Built at 9,811 feet in 1942 by the Civilian Conservation Corps, the volunteer-staffed lookout is on the National Register of Historic Places. Find interpretive information on the history of fire-fighting, the 1988 fires, geology, Beartooth Plateau wildlife, and local flora. But the view is so huge that your vision is constantly pulled away to the panorama of peaks. To reach the lookout, turn north onto the dirt and gravel Forest Road 142 (between Beartooth Lake and the junction with Chief Joseph Scenic Highway 296) and climb three miles.

RECREATION
Hiking

Hikers in the Beartooth Mountains need to be prepared for frequent afternoon thundershowers, copious mosquitoes, and altitude. Even short hikes can be challenging. For trail descriptions and directions, contact the **Beartooth Recreational Trails Association, Inc.** (www.beartoothtrails. org) or stop by the **Beartooth Ranger District Office** (Custer Gallatin National Forest, 6811 Hwy. 212 S., 406/446-2103, www. fs.usda.gov/main/custergallatin).

BASIN LAKES NATIONAL RECREATION TRAIL

Distance: 8 miles round-trip
Duration: 4 hours
Elevation change: 2,065 feet
Effort: moderately strenuous
Trailhead: Basin Lakes Trailhead in Custer Gallatin National Forest
Directions: South of Red Lodge, turn west onto West Fork Road for 7.8 miles. At the junction with the ski area road, stay left on West Fork Road for 4.1 miles to the trailhead.

The trail to Basin Lakes tops out at 8,995

Clay Butte Lookout on the Beartooth Highway

feet in elevation, which is actually low altitude for the Beartooth Mountains. Still, it's high enough that some flatlanders and sea level residents will feel lightheadedness or labored breathing. The trail also has several scenic turnaround points for those who want a shorter walk. At 0.5 mile with minimal elevation gain, you first reach **Basin Creek Falls. Lower Basin Lake** is at 2.5 miles, and the **upper lake** is at four miles. Anglers usually have more luck fishing small brook trout in the upper lake rather than the lower lake.

The trail ascends through a lodgepole pine forest, some of it burned in a forest fire, on routes once originally used for logging by horses. The first part of the trail is an **old logging road.** Switchbacks then gain elevation along Basin Creek to reach the lower lake, a mosquito pond surrounded by lily pads. After the trail circles the south end of the lake, it climbs again along **Basin Creek** to the shallow upper lake with views of the cliff faces flanking Silver Run.

PARKSIDE NATIONAL RECREATION TRAIL

Distance: 2.5 miles round-trip
Duration: 1.5 hours
Elevation change: 200 feet
Effort: easy
Trailhead: Parkside Picnic Area in Custer Gallatin National Forest
Directions: On the Beartooth Highway 10.7 miles south of Red Lodge, turn right onto the Main Fork Rock Creek Road (Forest Rd. #2421). Turn right again in 0.25 mile and park in the first lot.

Starting from the **Parkside Picnic Area,** this gentle trail parallels **Rock Creek** to reach **Greenough Lake,** a tiny lake stocked with rainbow trout for fishing (especially good for kids). A small peninsula, almost like a dock, extends into the lake's north end. The lake sits in a deep, scooped-out glacial basin between immense high plateaus of the Beartooth Mountains. The trail alternates between conifers and meadows, crossing back and forth over Rock Creek. It connects **Parkside, Limber Pine,** and **M-K Campgrounds**. A spur trail links **Greenough Campground** to the lake.

GLACIER LAKE

Distance: 4.2 miles round-trip
Duration: 3-4 hours
Elevation change: 1,400 feet
Effort: strenuous
Trailhead: Glacier Lake Trailhead in Custer Gallatin National Forest
Directions: From the Beartooth Highway 10.7 miles south of Red Lodge, turn right onto the Main Fork Rock Creek Road (Forest Rd. #2421). Drive past the three campground entrances, crossing the bridge over Rock Creek and continuing to follow the creek 7.7 miles to where it dead-ends at the trailhead.

After turning off the Beartooth Highway and crossing Rock Creek, a slow-going bumpy, washboarded and potholed dirt road leads to the trailhead. Vehicles should have high clearance. The trailhead also has a reputation for animal vandalism with marmots chewing car wires. Consult with the Forest Service on current road and trailhead issues before driving up. The parking lot fills up fast, so go early. Surrounded by immense gray granite cliffs at 9,709 feet, Glacier Lake is a two-state affair; it straddles Wyoming and Montana. While the trail is short, the altitude and climb up the difficulty. For anglers, the lake is stocked with Yellowstone cutthroat trout, and wildlife-watchers should see pika.

From the trailhead, the route switchbacks on a rocky trail up to a point where it crosses **Moon Creek** and climbs a side drainage. It works over the top of a rocky ridge before dropping to the **lake.** Once at the lake, you can explore shoreline trails, including adding on a walk to **Little Glacier Lake.**

BEARTOOTH HIGH LAKES

Distance: 6-8.4 miles round-trip
Duration: 4-7 hours
Elevation change: 200-2,130 feet
Effort: moderate to strenuous
Trailhead: Beartooth Lake Trailhead (in Beartooth Campground) or Island Lake Trailhead (at Island Lake Campground)

Starting from Beartooth or Island Lakes, trails loop back to countless lakes, from small ponds to larger scenic pools tucked into gray granite. The route in August is full of pink paintbrush and lush bluebells. But several things add to the challenge: altitude of 9,020-11,150 feet, swarms of mosquitoes and blackflies, soggy wetlands (your feet may get wet), and many stream crossings without bridges. The route from Beartooth Lake gains 2,130 feet during the 8.4-mile loop, while Island Lake, which starts at higher elevation, climbs 200 feet out and back to Beauty and Claw Lakes. Take a map, as side trails cut off to multiple small lakes on the Beartooth Plateau.

From **Beartooth Lake,** curve around through the wetlands at the head of Beartooth Lake and ascend the long meadow along **Beartooth Butte** to a junction with the **Island Lake Trail.** Head toward Island Lake, passing a string of small lakes and **Claw Lake.** At **Beauty Lake,** turn right at the junction to walk along the east shore and past **Crane Lake** to loop back to Beartooth Lake.

From **Island Lake,** the hike is better as an out-and-back to Beauty Lake (six miles) or Claw Lake (eight miles). It starts along the west shore of Island Lake, pops over a hill to **Night Lake,** and then traverses meadows, broken forest, and granite outcroppings to reach the junction at **Beauty Lake.** Continue around north of the lake to reach **Claw Lake.**

Biking

The coup for hard-core road cyclists is the Beartooth Highway. From Red Lodge to Beartooth Pass, the route climbs 5,379 feet in 31 miles. The best time for pedaling is late May, in the few days after road crews have plowed the road and before it is open to vehicles. Those days attract riders from across Montana, and it is a social event. After that, you have to contend with cars and no shoulders on the road. Prepare for rapidly changing weather, wind, squalls, hail, and lightning, but despite the conditions, most riders chalk the route high in lifetime achievements, and it's been heralded as one of the top five rides in the country.

The Ski Station (510 N. Broadway, 406/446-1086, www.theskistation.com, 8am and 5pm May-Sept., $60) shuttles riders to the **Top of the World** (26 miles one-way) at the summit of Beartooth Highway for the unguided trip downhill to Red Lodge. Reservations are required, and rentals are included. The company also rents bikes without the shuttle.

The Beartooth Mountains are loaded with trails for mountain biking, but many require at least intermediate single-track skills. Be prepared for fast-changing weather and afternoon thundershowers. Contact **Custer Gallatin National Forest** (Beartooth Ranger District Office, 6811 Hwy. 212 S., 406/446-2103, www.fs.usda.gov/main/custer-gallatin) for maps and trail descriptions. Note that bikes are not allowed in the Absaroka-Beartooth Wilderness. The **Silver Run Trails** (West Fork Rd.) have a variety of loops, steep, lung-busting climbs, and white-knuckle descents. Trails along the **West Fork Creek** are easier, with loops ranging 2.4-5.1 miles. The **Basin Lakes National Recreation Trail** (8 miles round-trip) is also a popular ride.

For families, the best ride is the **Rocky Fork Trail** (three miles), built by the Beartooth Recreational Trails Association, Inc. (www.beartoothtrails.org). The flat trail loops around the rodeo grounds, fairgrounds,

hiking into the Absaroka-Beartooth Wilderness from Island Lake

Beartooth Basin Summer Ski Area

Continental Dr., 406/446-3344, www.red-lodgemountain.com, dawn-dusk daily mid-May-mid-Oct., $33-47 greens fees, $15 club rental, $10-15 carts) is an 18-hole course with one island green on the back nine. Mt. Maurice and the Red Lodge Mountain ski area dominate the views. Discounts are available for tee times paid 48 hours in advance.

Skiing and Snowboarding

SUMMER

Due to the 10,900-foot elevation, the **Beartooth Basin Summer Ski Area** (23 miles west of Red Lodge on Beartooth Highway, 307/250-3767, www.beartoothbasin.com, 9am-3pm daily late May-early July, $20 one hour, $35 half day, $45 full day) operates two poma lifts for skiing or snowboarding near the summit of the Beartooth Highway in early summer. The steep, corniced Twin Lakes Headwall has advanced runs with 1,000 vertical feet, moguls, and an air and rails park. Operations depend on weather and snow. Groomed runs are rough due to above-freezing conditions. Pay cash at the trailer in the parking lot.

and the airport. Park at the rodeo grounds entrance located on Highway 78.

Fishing

Flowing from the Beartooth Mountains, **Rock Creek** (Montana fishing license required, http://fwp.mt.gov, $13-26 for residents, $25-54 for nonresidents, $70 per season) harbors rainbow, brown, and brook trout. These are bigger fish than the tiny ones in high-elevation lakes along the Beartooth Highway. Wade-fishing is best.

Lakes west of Beartooth Pass require a Wyoming fishing license (residents: $3 youth, $6 adult daily, $24 adult annual; nonresident: $15 youth, $14 adult daily, $92 adult annual). Wyoming fishing licenses are available at **Top of the World Resort** (307/587-5368, www.topoftheworldresort.com), between Island Lake and Beartooth Lake Campgrounds.

Golf

Located on the north end of town, **Red Lodge Mountain Golf Course** (828 Upper

WINTER

While Red Lodge may be cut off from Yellowstone in winter, it is still a destination for skiing. For downhill skiing and snowboarding, **Red Lodge Mountain Resort** (305 Ski Run Rd., 406/446-2610, www.redlodgemountainresort.com, 9am-4pm daily late Nov.-early Apr., $15-60) has 65 trails, six lifts, lessons, rentals, and a day lodge. The resort has a reputation for dry snow, steep chutes that attract diehards, and family-friendly prices.

Run by volunteers, the **Red Lodge Nordic Center** (Aspen Ridge Equestrian Ranch, Hwy. 78, www.beartoothtrails.org, dawn-dusk daily Dec.-Mar., $5 adults, kids and seniors free) grooms 15 kilometers of trails for skate and classic skiing west of Red Lodge. Rentals are available at **Sylvan Peak Mountain Shop** (9 S. Broadway, 406/446-1770, 9am-6pm Mon.-Sat., $15-25).

ENTERTAINMENT AND SHOPPING

Nightlife

Red Lodge nightlife is all about barhopping downtown. Since the bars fit within a several-block strip on Broadway Avenue, you can park and walk between them. Find live music and dancing at the **Snow Creek Saloon** (124 S. Broadway Ave., 406/446-2542, 11am-2pm daily), along with log stools at the bar and cold beer. The **Roman Theater** (120 S. Broadway Ave., 406/446-2233), built in 1917, shows movies nightly at 7:15pm.

Festivals and Events

In summer, the **Red Lodge Music Festival** (www.rlmf.org, early June) brings young classical musicians to town for a week. Faculty and student recitals for the public happen nightly. Cowboys and cowgirls compete in the **Home of Champions Rodeo** (www.redlodgerodeo.com, early July) for three days. The rodeo brings on all the classic western competitions, from bull riding to steer wrestling. A parade marches through downtown each day at noon.

Harley-Davidson bikers congregate to ride the Beartooth Highway during the annual three-day **Beartooth Rally** (https://www.beartoothrally.com, mid-July). Events include the Iron Horse Rodeo (a rodeo competition with motorcycles instead of horses), and black leathers are the clothing of choice at the rally's street dance.

Two March events celebrate activities on snow. Winter Carnival brings a parade to town followed by cardboard-box derby races on the slopes at **Red Lodge Mountain Resort** (305 Ski Run Rd., 406/446-2610, www.redlodgemountainresort.com, free). Horses pull skiers in the **National Finals Ski Joring Races** (101 Rodeo Dr., www.redlodgeskijoring.com, $5 adults, children free), a competition on the rodeo grounds that combines the Old and New West.

Shopping

Downtown Red Lodge has a few shops for souvenirs, art and photography galleries, and outdoor gear stores. The **Carbon County Arts Guild and Depot Gallery** (11 W. 8th St., 406/446-1370, http://carboncountydepotgallery.org, 10am-5pm Mon.-Sat., noon-5pm Sun., free) shows the works of local and regional artists. **Sylvan Peak Mountain Shop** (9 S. Broadway, 406/446-1770 or 800/249-2563, 9am-6pm Mon.-Sat.) carries hiking, backpacking, outdoor, and ski gear.

FOOD

Many of the Red Lodge restaurants cluster in the historic downtown area. Hours shorten in spring, winter, and fall.

★ **Café Regis** (501 Word Ave., 406/446-1941, www.caferegis.com, 6am-2pm Wed.-Sun., $7-12) serves meals indoors or out on a patio surrounded by organic gardens and greenhouses. They dish up fresh meals and house-baked goodies, and can handle vegan, vegetarian, and gluten-free requests, as well as food allergies. Breakfast (served all day) includes scrambles, omelets, and Mexican dishes. Lunch offers wraps, salads, and grilled or cold sandwiches.

The **Carbon County Steakhouse** (121 S. Broadway Ave., 406/446-4025, www.redlodgerestaurants.com, 4:30pm-9pm daily, $25-40) is the place to go for hand-cut ribeyes and beef tenderloins. **The Pollard Pub** (2 N. Broadway, 406/446-0001, www.thepollard.com, 11am-2pm and 5pm-close daily, $12-36) pulls live music into their pub on weekends. Dine on classic pub fare: burgers, mac and cheese, steak, and fish and chips. Drinks include beer from Red Lodge Ales, wine, or cocktails.

For lighter dining, Red Lodge has two local faves. **Sam's Tap Room** (1445 N. Broadway, 406/446-0243, www.redlodgeales.com, 11am-10pm daily, $8-10) serves salads, soups, and hot or cold sandwiches with indoor and outdoor dining. Mix dishes with Red Lodge Ales seasonal brews, classic Beartooth Pale Ale, or Glacier Ale. **Red Lodge Pizza Company** (115 S. Broadway Ave., 406/446-3333, www.

redlodgerestaurants.com, 11am-10pm daily, $10-25) offers a diverse menu of pizzas, salads, burgers, sandwiches, Italian dishes, and Montana rolls. They also have create-your-own pizzas, gluten-free crusts, and takeout.

For takeout and fast food, stop by **Mas Taco** (304 N. Broadway, 406/446-3636, 11am-9pm Tues.-Sat., 11am-4pm Sun., $4-10), a local Mexican eatery that serves fresh fare. Choose from pork, chicken, or beef tacos, empanadas, quesadillas, burritos, or taco salad. The taqueria also serves chiles rellenos, but they fly out the door fast. Housed in a century-old train car, the **Red Box Car** (1300 S. Broadway, 406/446-2152, 11am-9pm daily Apr.-Sept., $4-8) is the place to go for burgers, fries, and ice cream. Crowds on the outside picnic tables attest to its popularity.

Red Lodge even has its own coffee roaster. Drop in for a pick-me-up espresso at **Coffee Factory Roasters** (22 S. Broadway Ave., 406/446-3200, http://coffeefactoryroasters.com, 6:30am-6pm daily) and then take some beans home too: Beartooth Mountain Blend or Moose Joose. For old-fashioned ice cream, **Scoops** (205 S. Broadway Ave., 406/446-0160, 11am-9pm daily) serves sundaes, floats, and ice cream from its 1919 soda fountain.

Groceries

Beartooth Market (201 N. Oakes Ave., 406/446-2684, 7am-9pm daily) carries fresh produce and meats, beer and wine, and packaged groceries. It also has a deli.

ACCOMMODATIONS

Red Lodge has a few chain motels, but mostly independent hotels that are open year-round. Summer sees the most visitors and the highest prices. Reservations are highly recommended for July and August. Hunting season in fall and the winter ski season also bring in the visitors. Spring usually has the lowest rates. Add on a 7 percent bed tax.

For vacation home rentals, visit **AAA Red Lodge Rentals** (406/425-2125, www.aaaredlodgerentals.com) or **Red Lodge Reservations** (406/446-4700 or

877/733-5634, www.redlodgereservations.com).

Downtown, ★ **The Pollard Hotel** (2 N. Broadway, 406/446-0001, www.thepollard.com, $115-275) is a three-story brick affair that looks like a bank on the outside but retains restored historical Victorian features inside, including a triple-story gallery. The hotel has 39 rooms of several types. Standard hotel rooms have 1-2 queen beds; some queen rooms include small sitting areas. Queen and king suites feature one bed with a sitting area, jetted tubs, and a private indoor balcony overlooking the gallery. The hotel has an elevator, restaurant, pub, and fitness center, and breakfast is included.

The Yodeler Motel (601 S. Broadway, 406/446-1435 or 866/446-1435, www.yodelermotel.com, $70-160) is a historic two-story Bavarian lodge with 23 rooms, an outdoor hot tub, and a ski waxing room. Exterior stairs lead to (cheaper) downstairs and upstairs rooms. **Alpine Lodge Motel** (1105 N. Broadway, 406/446-2213, www.alpineredlodge.com, $70-160) has lodge rooms and cabins, kitchenettes, picnic tables, a grill, a laundry facility, and a bike wash station. Families go for the indoor pool and hot tub at **Chateau Rouge** (1505 S. Broadway, 406/446-1601 or 800/926-1601, www.chateaurouge.com, $70-160), with eight studio kitchenette rooms and 16 two-bedroom condos in a funky lodge.

Run by an artist, **The Irish Rose** (302 S. Broadway, 406/446-0303 or 877/446-0303, www.irishrosehost.com, $140-190) is a bed-and-breakfast with three rooms in a historic 1910 home.

Located five miles south of town on the Beartooth Highway, **Rock Creek Resort** (6380 Hwy. 212, 406/446-1111 or 800/667-1119, www.rockcreekresort.com, $140-420) offers a variety of lodging options: lodge rooms, condos, townhomes, and a log cabin. Some rooms overlook Rock Creek and include kitchenettes. The complex also has an indoor pool, hot tub, sauna, fitness room, and restaurant.

CAMPING

Red Lodge has two private campgrounds, one on each end of town. Each has hookups for water and electricity, picnic tables, flush toilets, showers, drinking water, camp stores, Wi-Fi, and disposal stations. Make reservations for July and August. Rates are for two people; add on 7 percent tax and $3-7 for each extra person. Located four miles north of town under cottonwoods and aspens, the **Red Lodge KOA** (7464 Hwy. 212, 406/446-2364 or 800/562-7540, www.koa.com, year-round, $31-70 RVs, $33-40 tents) has 68 RV and 19 tent campsites. There are sewer hookups for RVs, a laundry, playground, and swimming pool (summer only). On the south end of town, **Perry's RV Park and Campground** (6664 S. Hwy. 212, 406/446-2722, www.perrysrv.us, late May-Sept., $40 RVs, $20-25 tents, cash or check only) has 50 RV campsites close together on a large, sunny, and open parking lot, and 20 tent campsites under cottonwoods. A few campsites sit on Rock Creek. RVs are limited to 45 feet.

National Forest Campgrounds

Numerous national forest campgrounds are located between Red Lodge and Yellowstone; many are right on the Beartooth Highway. Facilities include picnic tables, fire rings with grills, drinking water, bear boxes, vault toilets, and firewood for sale. Many have campground hosts on-site. No hookups are available for RVs.

CUSTER GALLATIN NATIONAL FOREST

Campgrounds in **Custer Gallatin National Forest** (Beartooth Ranger District, 6811 Hwy. 212 S., Red Lodge, 406/446-2103, www.fs.usda.gov/main/custergallatin) are between Red Lodge and Beartooth Pass. **Reservations** (877/444-6777, www.recreation.gov) are highly recommended for July and August. Rates are $12-16; extra vehicles cost $8.

West Fork Rock Creek canyon is seven miles off the Beartooth Highway. It contains both the 30-site **Basin Campground** (mid-May-Sept.), popular for its paved access, nature trail around Wild Bill Lake, fishing, and national recreation trails; and the 30-site **Cascade Campground** (late May-early Sept.) overlooking the creek. RVs are limited to 30 feet.

Along the Beartooth Highway's east side, campgrounds line up on spur roads with easy access. At 6,282 feet, **Sheridan** and **Rattin** (Ratine) **Campgrounds** (mid-May-Sept., 30-foot RV limit) sit one mile apart on the dirt and potholed East Side Road, flanking Rock Creek. Farther along Rock Creek at 7,150 feet, three campgrounds cluster close together in Rock Creek Canyon: **Parkside, Greenough Lake,** and **Limber Pine** (mid-May-Sept., 40-45-foot RV limit) have 64 campsites straddling Rock Creek. They hide in the trees where the Beartooth Highway begins its 4,000-foot switchback ascent to Vista Point, Beartooth Plateau, and Beartooth Pass. If these campgrounds fill, free primitive first-come, first-served campsites (open as long as they are snow-free) line the rough, potholed dirt road following Rock Creek upstream.

SHOSHONE NATIONAL FOREST

On the west side of the Beartooth Pass, **Shoshone National Forest** (Clarks Fork Ranger District, 203A Yellowstone Ave., Cody, WY, 307/527-6921, www.fs.usda.gov/shoshone, July-mid-Sept., $15, 32-foot RV limit) runs two ultra-scenic campgrounds. All sites are **first-come, first-served;** no reservations are available. While in high demand, the campgrounds are also at high elevation, where breathing can be labored and sleeping fitful. Boat ramps access both of the lakes for fishing small trout that grow in the short ice-free season; voracious mosquitoes breed thick. Regular afternoon thunderstorms can pelt rain, hail, or snow, even in August. At 9,600 feet, **Island Lake Campground** is the highest. The campground loops 21 sites around a hillside of windblown pines and firs adjacent to a lake rimmed with fuchsia paintbrush and bluebells. **Beartooth Lake Campground** clusters 21 campsites at 9,000 feet in a lakeside forest with peek-a-boo views of the orange-streaked Beartooth Butte.

TRANSPORTATION AND SERVICES
Car

Red Lodge is 60 miles (1.15 hrs.) southwest of Billings, Montana, and 68 miles (2 hrs.) northeast of Yellowstone's Northeast Entrance via the Beartooth Highway (closed mid-Oct.-late May). Two-lane highways are the norm in Red Lodge. In summer, both the town and the Beartooth Highway are clogged with motorcycle clubs and road rallies jockeying for position. Throw in bicyclists and no shoulders on the road, and drivers need to pay attention.

Parking in downtown Red Lodge is mainly on the street on Broadway Avenue (between 8th St. and 13th St.), but it gets cramped. Campers driving large RVs should park at the visitors center (701 N. Broadway Ave.) or Lions Park (between 5th and 8th Sts.) to walk downtown.

Red Lodge Tour and Taxi (406/425-3091, www.redlodgetaxi.com) provides the town taxi service, but also runs shuttles on demand to Billings.

Services

The **Red Lodge Visitor Center** (701 N. Broadway Ave., 406/446-1718, www.redlodge.com, hours vary) is a small information center run by the Red Lodge Chamber of Commerce. Guides and maps on Red Lodge, Beartooth Highway, and the Absaroka-Beartooth Wilderness, Yellowstone National Park information, and a self-guided historic tour are available. The building has restrooms indoors and picnic tables, water, and an RV dump station outside, plus the historic log cabin of Liver-eating Johnston. For more Forest Service maps, road conditions, and trail information, visit the **Beartooth Ranger District Station** (Custer Gallatin National Forest, 6811 Hwy. 212 S., Red Lodge, 406/446-2103, www.fs.usda.gov/main/custergallatin).

Red Lodge has a **post office** (119 S. Hauser Ave., 406/446-2629, 8am-4pm Mon.-Fri., 10am-1pm Sat.), an **RV dump** station at the visitors center (Hwy. 78 and U.S. 212), and showers available at the **Red Lodge City Pool** (14th St. and Hauser Ave., 406/446-3727, daily June-Aug., hours are weather dependent). The **Rock Creek Laundry** (1101 S. Broadway Ave., 406/446-9890) has coin-op machines and wireless Internet in the waiting area. A public laundry is also at the **Alpine**

Liver-eating Johnston's cabin at the Red Lodge Visitor Center

Lodge Motel (1105 N. Broadway, 406/446-2213, www.alpineredlodge.com).

MEDIA AND COMMUNICATIONS

Cell service is available in Red Lodge. Verizon phones work the best; other services get spotty reception. Reception (both cell and Wi-Fi) disappears entirely up the Beartooth Highway. Most hotels and campgrounds in town have wireless Internet. Public computers are available at the **Red Lodge Carnegie Library** (8th St. and Broadway Ave., 406/446-1905, 10am-6pm Tues.-Fri., noon-6pm Sat.). Several cafés in town also have wireless Internet.

The Red Lodge newspaper is the weekly *Carbon County News* (www.carboncountynews.com), but the daily newspaper is the *Billings Gazette* (http://billingsgazette.com).

MEDICAL SERVICES

The **Beartooth Billings Clinic** (2525 N. Broadway, 406/446-2345 or 877/404-9442, www.beartoothbillingsclinc.org) has a 24/7 emergency department. The nearest hospitals are both about 60 miles away: **St. Vincent Healthcare** (1233 N. 30th St., Billings, MT, 406/237-7000, www.sclhealth.org) and **West Park Hospital** (707 Sheridan Ave., Cody, WY, 307/527-7501, www.westparkhospital.org).

Cody, Wyoming

Cody, Wyoming, is a cowboy relic on the western slopes of the Rocky Mountains. Designed and founded by Buffalo Bill Cody in 1895, the town hangs on to its Wild West heritage, which distinguishes it from towns that lost their sense of history in the evolution to modern day. Cody serves as a gateway to Yellowstone National Park half of the year. Two routes link into Yellowstone, but they are only open **May-early November.** During winter, access to Yellowstone is only by snowmobile.

Many visitors prefer using Cody as an airline gateway for Yellowstone. Though limited, flights can be cheaper than those into Jackson Hole. The **Buffalo Bill Scenic Byway** (U.S. Hwy. 14/16/20) connects Cody to the East Entrance of Yellowstone on a route than climbs through spires and crags of Shoshone Canyon and the Absaroka Mountains.

SIGHTS
★ Buffalo Bill Center of the West

The **Buffalo Bill Center of the West** (720 Sheridan Ave., 307/587-4771, http://centerofthewest.org, 8am-6pm daily May-mid-Sept., hours shorten mid-Sept.-May, $20 adults,

$12-17 kids) includes admission to five museums at the complex. It's a lot to take in (passes are good for two days), but provides a broad background. The **Whitney Gallery**

Buffalo Bill Center of the West

Cody

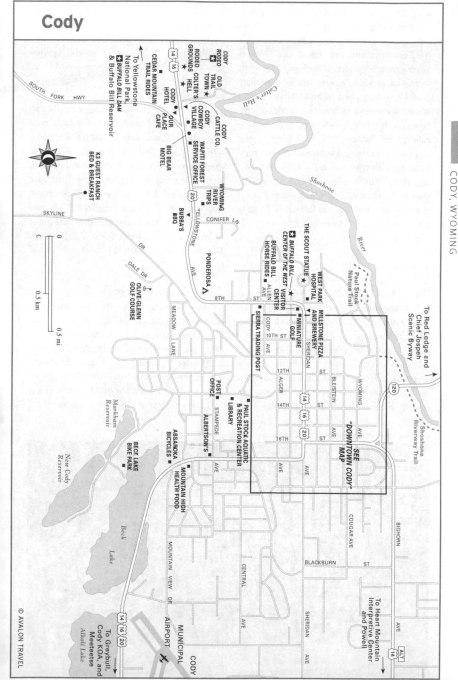

To Red Lodge and
Chief Jospeh
Scenic Byway

To Greybull,
Cody KOA, and
Meeteetse

To Heart Mountain
Interpretive Center
and Powell

To Yellowstone
National Park,
& Buffalo Bill Dam
& Buffalo Bill Reservoir

SOUTH FORK HWY

SKYLINE

Colter's Hill

Shoshone

River

Paul Stock
Nature Trail

Shoshone
Riverway Trail

CEDAR MOUNTAIN
TRAIL RIDES

K3 GUEST RANCH
BED & BREAKFAST

CODY
RODEO
GROUNDS

RODEO
HELL

CODY
TRAIL
TOWN

OLD
TRAIL
TOWN

COLTER'S
HELL

CODY
HOTEL

OUR
PLACE
CAFE

BIG BEAR
MOTEL

CODY
CATTLE CO.

CODY
COWBOY
VILLAGE

WAPITI FOREST
SERVICE OFFICE

WYOMING
RIVER
TRIPS

BUBBA'S
BBQ

CONIFER LN

PONDEROSA

BUFFALO BILL
CENTER OF THE WEST VISITOR
CENTER

THE SCOUT STATUE

BUFFALO BILL
HORSE RIDES

WEST PARK
HOSPITAL

MILLSTONE PIZZA
AND BREWERY

MINIATURE
GOLF

SIERRA TRADING POST

POST
OFFICE

LIBRARY

PAUL STOCK AQUATIC
& RECREATION CENTER

ALBERTSON'S

STAMPEDE

ABSAROKA
BICYCLES

BECK LAKE
BIKE PARK

MOUNTAIN
HIGH
HEALTH FOOD

OLIVE-GLENN
GOLF COURSE

SEE
"DOWNTOWN CODY"
MAP

Markham
Reservoir

New Cody
Reservoir

Beck
Lake

Alkali Lake

MUNICIPAL
AIRPORT

CODY

SKYLINE

DR

C

DALE DR

MEADOW

LANE

MOUNTAIN
VIEW

DR

CENTRAL

AVE

SHERIDAN

AVE

BIGHORN

AVE

COUGAR AVE

BLACKBURN

ST

WYOMING

AVE

BLEISTEIN

ST

ALGER

ST

SHERIDAN

ST

SHERIDAN

CODY

AVE

ALLEN

AVE

8TH

ST

10TH

12TH

14TH

16TH

0

0.5 km

0.5 mi

© AVALON TRAVEL

of Western Art houses famous artwork of the American West. The **Draper Museum of Natural History** has exhibits on wildlife, ecology, and raptors of the Greater Yellowstone Ecosystem. The **Cody Firearms Museum** contains a collection of American and European guns. The **Plains Indian Museum** celebrates Native American heritage. The **Buffalo Bill Museum** has memorabilia from Buffalo Bill Cody's life.

Exhibits even spill outdoors with several wildlife sculptures. Listed on the National Register of Historic Places, *The Scout* (between Sheridan Ave. and Monument St.) is a bronze statue of Buffalo Bill Cody. Built in 1924, the statue was designed by Gertrude Vanderbilt Whitney.

Old Trail Town

Old Trail Town and Museum of the Old West (1831 Demaris Dr., 307/587-5302, www.oldtrailtown.org, 8am-7pm daily mid-May-Sept., $10 adults, $9 seniors, $6 kids 6-12) conveys the visual ambience of a western ghost town—but it's not a true ghost town. A local historian and archaeologist built the town as a replica of the original town of Cody. The buildings and artifacts are real, but were all moved to this location. The site contains 26 buildings that date from 1879 to 1901. Strewn around the town are 100 horse-drawn rigs plus frontier and Native American artifacts. The site also contains the graves of several regional personalities, but those too were moved here.

Colter's Hell

Tucked between the Stampede Rodeo Grounds and Old Trail Town, **Colter's Hell** (U.S. Hwy. 14) is a barren, sunny, 0.5-mile interpretive loop that circles a field where the original town of Cody sat in 1897. Rock-cairn lot markers, wagon wheel ruts, and tepee rings are identified. Interpretive signs are named for geothermals on the Shoshone River and cover geology, flora, and wildlife. Parking is in a pullout on the north side of U.S. Highway 14. On hot days, walk this trail only in the morning.

Cody Mural Historic Site

Edward T. Grigware's 36-foot mural of Mormon pioneers fills the rotunda ceiling of the visitors center at the **Cody Mural Historic Site** (1719 Wyoming Ave., 307/587-3290, http://codymural.com, 9am-7pm Mon.-Sat., 4pm-7pm Sun. June-mid-Sept., free). Also on-site, the **Pioneer Museum** (free) includes exhibits of Mormon pioneers.

Old Trail Town and Museum of the Old West

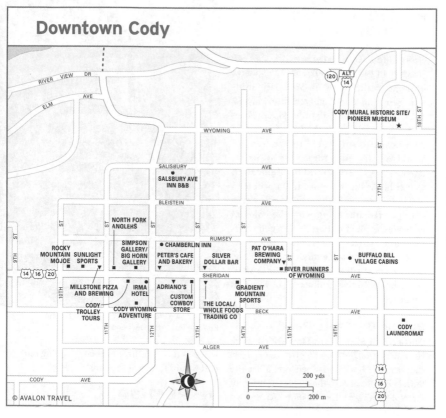

Downtown Cody

RIVER VIEW DR

ELM AVE

WYOMING AVE

CODY MURAL HISTORIC SITE/
PIONEER MUSEUM ★

18TH ST

17TH ST

SALISBURY AVE
SALSBURY AVE
INN B&B

BLEISTEIN AVE

NORTH FORK
ANGLERS

RUMSEY AVE

ROCKY
MOUNTAIN SUNLIGHT
MOJOE SPORTS

SIMPSON
GALLERY/
BIG HORN
GALLERY

CHAMBERLIN INN

PETER'S CAFE
AND BAKERY

SILVER
DOLLAR BAR

PAT O'HARA
BREWING
COMPANY

BUFFALO BILL
VILLAGE CABINS

RIVER RUNNERS
OF WYOMING

14 16 20

MILLSTONE PIZZA
AND BREWING

IRMA
HOTEL

ADRIANO'S
CUSTOM
COWBOY
STORE

SHERIDAN

GRADIENT
MOUNTAIN
SPORTS

AVE

CODY
TROLLEY
TOURS

CODY WYOMING
ADVENTURE

THE LOCAL/
WHOLE FOODS
TRADING CO

BECK AVE

CODY
LAUNDROMAT

ALGER AVE

CODY AVE

© AVALON TRAVEL

0   200 yds

0   200 m

14
16
20

Colter's Hell Interpretive Trail loops through sagebrush.

Heart Mountain WWII Interpretive Center

Located 14 miles northwest of Cody, the **Heart Mountain Interpretive Center** (1539 Road 19, Powell, 307/754-8000, www.heartmountain.org, 10am-5pm daily mid-May-Sept. and Wed.-Sat. Oct.-mid-May, $7 adults, $5 seniors and students, children under 12 free) records the life of Japanese Americans during their internment in World War II. In the three years of its existence, the Heart Mountain Relocation Center housed more than 14,000 people in 500 buildings. Only three buildings and a chimney remain, along with the colossal embarrassment of a country for such treatment of its citizens. The center uses replicas of barracks, a scale model of the camp, photographs, films, recorded oral histories, and interactive exhibits to convey what happened.

Buffalo Bill State Park

Buffalo Bill State Park (4192 North Fork Hwy., Cody, 307/587-9227, http://wyoparks.state.wy.us, $4-6 day-use) encompasses the Buffalo Bill Reservoir, the lower few miles of the North Fork of the Shoshone River, two campgrounds, Buffalo Bill Dam, and a few more miles of the Shoshone River. It's a place to camp, boat, fish, kayak, canoe, paddleboard, and sailboard.

★ BUFFALO BILL DAM

At 325 feet, the historic **Buffalo Bill Dam** (4808 North Fork Hwy., Cody, 307/527-6076, 8am-6pm Mon.-Fri., 9am-5pm Sat.-Sun. June-Aug., shorter hours May and Sept., free) was the highest dam in the country when it was built in 1910. Today it houses a visitors center with indoor and outdoor interpretive exhibits about local history and wildlife. It is also a National Civil Engineering Landmark due to how it squeezes into Shoshone Canyon.

From Cody, drive the North Fork Highway (Hwy. 14/16/20) 4.5 miles west. As the road climbs along the cliffs of Shoshone Canyon,

This ball plug was used to stop flow out of the Buffalo Bill Dam power conduit.

it passes through three tunnels, popping out of the third tunnel at the dam.

RECREATION
Hiking

In Cody, trails run along the Shoshone River. These two are close enough that you can connect them by walking a few blocks between.

PAUL STOCK NATURE TRAIL

Distance: 2.6 miles round-trip
Duration: 1.5 hours
Elevation change: 52 feet
Effort: easy
Trailhead: 801 Spruce Drive (west end of Spruce Street)

This sunny interpretive trail follows a gravel path upstream above the Shoshone River. It has benches for sitting and several short spurs to viewpoints. From the trailhead, the route drops to the river, where a short loop peels off to the right through a few trees. After the loop, continue upstream until the gravel ends at an overlook of an island. Return the way you came, gaining elevation back to the car.

SHOSHONE RIVERWAY TRAIL

Distance: 2.6 miles round-trip
Duration: 1.5 hours
Elevation change: flat
Effort: easy
Trailhead: end of 12th Street

A paved trail runs south along the Shoshone River for walkers and cyclists. The trail starts by crossing under the Belfry Bridge and then goes east for 1.3 miles through wetlands until it hits its lollypop-loop end. Return the same way.

Biking

Classic road rides are out-and-back trips on the Buffalo Bill Scenic Byway and the Chief Joseph Scenic Byway. **Buffalo Bill Scenic Byway** (Hwy. 14/16/20) is a century ride (100 miles round-trip) from Cody to the East Entrance of Yellowstone. It does not require as much climbing as the **Chief Joseph Scenic Byway** (Hwy. 296), which starts 17 miles north of Cody on Highway 120 and ends at the Beartooth Highway (Hwy. 212). Both routes are narrow two-lane roads with skinny shoulders; riders should be comfortable with large RVs whizzing past.

The local bike club **Park County Pedalers** (www.parkcountypedalers.org) has been developing mountain bike trails at **Beck Lake Bike Park** (2401 14th St.). Mountain bikers can ride for free on the single-track, pump track, skills features, flow trail, and jumps. Trails extend into adjoining BLM land. **Absaroka Bicycles** (2201 17th St. #7, 307/527-5566, 10am-6pm Tues.-Thurs., closes early Fri.-Sat.) rents mountain bikes ($40 with helmet) and guides tours. Ask them for details on the **Outlaw Trails,** about four miles north of town, for classic single-track and slickrock trails.

Horseback Riding

Cody has trail riding in town. Most of the wranglers rely on tips; plan to tip 15 percent. Wear sturdy shoes and long pants for safety and comfort. **Buffalo Bill Horse Rides** (720 Sheridan Ave., 307/250-7660, http://codywyominghorserides.com, daily June-Aug., $40) has one-hour trail rides from the Buffalo Bill Center of the West. Children under age five can enjoy pony rides ($20). **Cedar Mountain Trail Rides** (12 Spirit Mountain

Real McCoy Horses at Pahaska Tepee Resort

Dr., 307/527-4966, 8am-5pm daily mid-May-Aug., $35/1 hr., $50/2 hrs., cash only) offers one-hour or two-hour rides from one mile west of the rodeo grounds in Cody. Children too young to ride alone can join their parents. The trail is steep, rocky, and adventurous.

Ranches and other wranglers lead trail rides outside of Cody on the Buffalo Bill Scenic Byway. Located 26 miles west of Cody, **Bill Cody Ranch** (2604 North Fork Hwy., 307/587-2097 or 800/615-2934, http://billcodyranch.com, daily mid-May-late Sept., $55-275) leads two-hour horseback rides, four-hour lunch rides, all-day cookouts, and overnight pack trips. At Pahaska Tepee Resort, located 50 miles west of Cody, wranglers at **Real McCoy Horses** (183 North Fork Hwy., 307/527-7701, daily June-Aug., $40-165) lead one-hour, two-hour, half-day, and full-day rides.

Water Sports

Many days around Cody have calm air in the morning, but winds whip up in the afternoon, especially up on the Buffalo Bill Reservoir, located at 5,500 feet in the arid high-desert valley between raw mountains. Plan what you want to do on the water around what the winds deliver. It can be calm for paddleboarding in the morning, but perfect for sailboarding in the afternoon.

All boats, canoes, and kayaks require current **registration** for Wyoming residents or nonresidents (Wyoming Game and Fish, https://wgfd.wyo.gov, residents: $10 motorized, $5 nonmotorized; nonresidents: $30 motorized, $15 nonmotorized), and an Aquatic Invasive Species (AIS) sticker. The only exemption is for inflatable boats less than 10 feet long, paddleboards, and sailboards.

BOATING

The reservoir at **Buffalo Bill State Park** (47 Lakeside Rd., Cody, 307/587-9227, http://wyoparks.state.wy.us) has boat launches easily accessible from U.S. Highway 14/16/20. The easiest and biggest launch is at North Shore Bay Campground (May-Sept., $4-6 day-use), which has ample trailer parking, fish cleaning stations, cement ramps, restrooms, and water. You can also launch from the South Shore Boat Launch, accessed via Gibbs Bridge (same turnoff as the campground at the west end of the reservoir) and a dirt road.

Gradient Mountain Sports (1390 Sheridan Ave., 307/587-4659, www.gradientmountainsports.com, $30-50) rents touring, sit-on-top, tandem, and white-water kayaks, plus canoes and paddleboards. Paddles, spray skirts, life jackets, roof pads, and straps cost $5-8 extra.

FISHING

Anglers with boats can fish for rainbow trout, rainbow-cutthroat hybrids, Yellowstone cutthroat trout, brown trout, and lake trout in **Buffalo Bill Reservoir** (Buffalo Bill State Park, 307/587-9227, http://wyoparks.state.wy.us). Fly-fishing aficionados head for the North Fork of the Shoshone River (access is via Shoshone National Forest campgrounds and BLM campsites) after rainbow, brown, and Yellowstone cutthroat trout. Wade-fishing or float-fishing works in the river, and its tributaries also offer decent fishing. Anglers will need a **Wyoming fishing license** (Wyoming Game and Fish, https://wgfd.wyo.gov, residents: $6 day, $24 annual, $3 youth; nonresidents: $14 day, $92 annual, $15 youth).

North Fork Anglers (1107 Sheridan Ave., 307/527-7274, www.northforkanglers.com, daily May-Oct., Mon.-Sat. Nov.-Apr. $300-350 half day, $400-450 full day) guides floating trips and wade-fishing trips on the North Fork River. The outfitter also rents reels, rods, waders, and boots. Tip guides 10-20 percent.

RAFTING

The Class I-III **Shoshone River** floats through **Shoshone Canyon** below Cody. Families can take a splashy 5-12-mile ride during the May-September rafting season. Longer trips start with Red Rock Canyon, named for the dramatic red cliffs on both sides of the river, and work down through

Lower Shoshone Canyon; shorter trips put in for the lower canyon only.

West of Cody, the **North Fork of the Shoshone River** (Wapiti Valley, above Buffalo Bill Reservoir) has Class II-III white water. Most rafting floats 11-13 miles of river starting from Shoshone National Forest's east boundary through Wapiti Valley, or from river accesses just east of Pahaska Tepee Resort. Rafting season runs May-mid-July, before the water drops too low.

DIY river floaters can rent white-water and inflatable kayaks from **Gradient Mountain Sports** (1390 Sheridan Ave., 307/587-4659, www.gradientmountainsports.com, $30-50). Helmets, car-top carriers, paddles, and wetsuits cost $5-8 extra.

Guided trips run daily on both rivers. Companies provide transportation to and from the river, as well as life jackets and gear for nasty weather. Two-hour trips on the Shoshone River through Red Rock Canyon or Lower Shoshone Canyon run $33-50 for adults. Half-day trips on the North Fork cost $75-80 for adults and include lunch. When available, inflatable kayak trips cost $55-90. Make reservations to guarantee slots, and plan to tip your guide 15 percent. Three companies offer daily rafting trips

- **Cody Wyoming Adventures** (1119 12th St., 307/587-6988 or 800/293-0148, www.codywyomingadventures.com) guides trips through Red Rock Canyon, Lower Shoshone Canyon, and on the North Fork. You can also float inflatable kayaks, kayaks, and paddleboards ($10/hr. extra).

- **Wyoming River Trips** (233 Yellowstone Hwy., 307/587-6661 or 800/586-6661, http://wyomingrivertrips.com) guides trips through Red Rock Canyon and Lower Shoshone Canyon, plus one trip on the North Fork. Inflatable kayak trips go through Red Rock Canyon.

- **River Runners of Wyoming** (1491 Sheridan Ave., 307/527-7238 or 800/535-7238, www.riverrunnersofwyoming.com)

takes trips down the Lower Shoshone Canyon and one on the North Fork.

SWIMMING

Paul Stock Aquatic and Recreation Center (1402 Heart Mountain St., 307/587-0400, www.cityofcody-wy.gov, 5:30am-10pm Mon.-Thurs., 5:30am-8pm Fri., 8am-6pm Sat., noon-6pm Sun. year-round, $12 adults, $6 students and youth, children under 4 free) has an indoor lap swimming pool, leisure pool, therapy pool, aquatic climbing wall, diving board, and waterslide. Fitness equipment, a suspended track, a gymnasium, and racquetball courts are also on-site.

Golf

Olive Glenn Golf and Country Club (802 Meadow Ln., 307/587-5551, www.golfoliveglen.com, dawn-dusk daily Apr.-Oct., $50 greens fees, $20 club rental, $18 carts) is an 18-hole, par 72 public course with a pro shop, driving range, putting green, and restaurant. An 18-hole **miniature golf course** (9th St. and Sheridan Ave., mid-May-mid-Sept.) is at Cody City Park.

Winter Sports

SKIING

Sleeping Giant Ski Area (348 North Fork Hwy., 307/587-3125, www.skisg.com, 9:30am-4pm Fri.-Sun. mid-Dec.-Mar., $38 adults, $18-30 kids) is a small, resurrected community ski area with two lifts, a conveyer carpet, terrain parks, rentals, lessons, and a cafeteria. To get there, take Highway 12/14/20 west for 47 miles to Cody. Turn south at the signed entrance.

CROSS-COUNTRY SKIING AND SNOWSHOEING

Volunteers groom the **Park County Nordic Ski Association** (307/272-1509, www.nordicskiclub.com, Dec.-Mar., free, donations accepted) trails at **Pahaska Tepee Resort** (183 North Fork Hwy., 307/527-7701, www.pahaska.com). More than 19 kilometers (12 miles) are groomed for skate and classic skiing. Some trails permit snowshoers and dogs.

To reach Pahaska Tepee, drive 49 miles (1 hour) west of Cody on Highway 12/14/20. Cross-country ski and snowshoe rentals are at **Sunlight Sports** (1131 Sheridan Ave., Cody, 307/587-9517 or 888/889-2463, www.sunlightsports.com).

SNOWMOBILING
Guided snowmobile tours enter Yellowstone through the East Entrance and over Sylvan Pass. The owner of **Rimrock Ranch** (2768 North Fork Hwy., 307/587-3970, http://garyfalesoutfitting.com, late Dec.-early Mar., $375 for two people on one machine) guides full-day tours that stop at Old Faithful, the geyser basins, Lower Yellowstone Falls, and Yellowstone Lake. Reservations are required.

ENTERTAINMENT AND SHOPPING
Nightlife
Summer nightlife in Cody is at the rodeo. If you want to check out a few bars, sidle up to a stool in the Silver Saddle Saloon at the historic **Irma Hotel** (1192 Sheridan Ave., 307/587-4221 or 800/745-4762, 11am-2pm daily) to admire the ornate, wood-carved backboard. Shoot pool after ordering some burgers in the iconic **Silver Dollar Bar** (1313 Sheridan Ave., 307/527-7666, 11am-2pm daily), which has live rock-and-roll music on Friday and Saturday nights.

Guitars and fiddles boost the foot-stomping in live western music dinner theaters. **Cody Cattle Company** (1910 Demaris St., 307/272-5770, http://thecodycattlecompany.com, 5:30pm-7:30pm daily June-late Sept.) features music from Ryan Martin and the Triple C Cowboys Band. The show ends just in time for the rodeo. Ticket packages include the show plus an all-you-can-eat chuck wagon dinner ($30 adults, $15 kids), the show only ($16 adults, $8 kids), or show with dinner and rodeo ($47 adult, $25 kids). **Dan Miller's Cowboy Music Revue** (720 Sheridan Ave., 307/578-7909, http://centerofthewest.org, 5:30pm Mon.-Sat. June-early Oct.) is staged in the Dining Pavilion at the Buffalo Bill Center of the West. The entertaining family show mixes cowboy poetry, stories, humor, and well-known tunes with a dinner buffet. Ticket packages include the buffet and show ($40), the show only ($16), or buffet, show, and all-day admission to the center ($56).

The City of Cody puts on **free music concerts** in the downtown City Park (corner of 9th St. and Beck Ave., 6pm-8pm Thurs. July-Aug.), where musical talent spans the gamut.

Festivals and Events
CODY GUNFIGHT
A **Cody gunfight** (6pm Mon.-Sat. June-mid-Sept., free) bursts out in summer. Actors take to the street in front of the historic Irma Hotel (1192 Sheridan Ave.) with a 30-minute shoot-'em-up performance. Four different shows rotate throughout summer. Crowds pack the curbs with standing room only, so you'll want to nab your spot around 5:45pm. Reserve chairs from **Cody Trolley Tours** (307/527-7043, www.codytrolleytours.com, $2) at the trolley station or from their ticket booth at the Irma Hotel.

★ CODY RODEO
With traditional flag pageantry, the **Cody Rodeo** (519 W. Yellowstone Ave., 307/587-5155, www.codystampederodeo.com, 8pm-10pm daily June-Aug., gates open at 7pm, $20 adults, $10 children 7-12) whoops it up with bronc and bull riding, barrel racing, and a kids' calf scramble. Late June usually has one night of extreme bull riding, featuring top riders and top kicking bulls. The week of July 4th ups the rider caliber to PRCA heavyweights (reserved seats for July 4th finals cost $25). The stands are covered, but if the weather looks foreboding, bring layers—the rodeo goes on even in rain. **Tickets** are available in advance online (www.codystampederodeo.com) or at the ticket office (1031 12th St.) and visitors center (836 Sheridan Ave.).

Cody Cowboy Stages (307/272-5573 or 307/272-0616, www.codytransportation.com, $5 adults, $3 children 9-14, children under 8 free) runs a nightly shuttle to the rodeo grounds, stopping for pickups at most hotels and campgrounds. No reservations are needed; pay cash when boarding.

Shopping

Western art and clothing shops abound in Cody. For cowboy hats, boots, bandanas, buckles, jeans, and jewelry, stop by **Custom Cowboy Shop** (1286 Sheridan Ave., 800/487-2692, http://customcowboyshop.com, 9am-7pm Mon.-Sat., noon-4pm Sun.) or **Boot Barn** (1625 Stampede Ave., 307/587-4493, www.bootbarn.com, 9am-8pm Mon.-Sat., 11am-5pm Sun.). For western art, peruse **Big Horn Galleries** (1167 Sheridan Ave., 307/527-7587, www.bighorngalleries.com, 9:30am-5:30pm Mon.-Sat.) and **Simpson Gallagher Gallery** (1161 Sheridan Ave., 307/587-4022, www.simpsongallaghergallery.com, 10am-5:30pm Mon.-Sat.).

Sunlight Sports (1131 Sheridan Ave., 307/587-9517 or 888/889-2463, 9am-9pm daily) sells gear for climbing, hiking, backpacking, skiing, snowboarding, and Nordic skiing. The shop also rents camping gear ($3-30/day, discounts for multiple days) and skis, snowboards, Nordic skis, and snowshoes. The discount outdoor mail-order store **Sierra**

Trading Post (1402 8th St., 307/578-5802, www.sierratradingpost.com, 9am-8pm Mon.-Sat., 10am-6pm Sun.) has an outlet in Cody, right across from the Buffalo Bill Center of the West.

FOOD

In Cody, most restaurants are open year-round, but reduce their hours in fall, winter, and spring. In summer, make reservations for dinner or you may be waiting in line.

Western fare is a Wyoming staple. **Bubba's Bar-B-Que** (512 Yellowstone Ave., 307/587-7427, www.bubbasbar-b-que.com, 7am-8pm Sun.-Thurs., 7am-9pm Fri.-Sat., $10-28) uses a hickory-fired smoker to slow cook ribs, sausage, brisket, pulled pork, turkey, and chicken. This is one place you can try Rocky Mountain oysters (bull testicles).

Fine-dining restaurants offer something other than western food. ★ **The Local** (1134 13th St., 307/586-4262, http://thelocal-cody.com, 8:30am-2pm and 5pm-8pm, Tues.-Sat., $10-38) serves espresso and lunch in the morning, and dinner in the evening. Breads and pastries are house-baked; gluten-free, vegan, and vegetarian options made with local organic ingredients are a hallmark. An imaginative, upscale menu spans broad seasonal

Cody Trolley Tours

choices, from scallops, ceviche, and lamb burger to bison meatloaf.

Adriano's Italian (1244 Sheridan Ave., 307/527-7320, http://adrianositalianrestaurant.com, 11am-close daily, $10-28) serves what the owners term as "spaghetti western" food—steaks with pasta sides or burgers and subs with Italian toppings. Both lunch (11am-3pm) and dinner (5pm-close) include Italian pastas and thin-crust pizza, but dinner adds on veal, steak, chicken, sausage, and seafood.

Rocky Mountain Mojoe (1001 Sheridan Ave., 307/578-8295, htttp://rockymountainmojoe.com, 6am-6pm daily, $4-10) is a local espresso stop that serves huge cinnamon rolls and grab-and-go breakfast sandwiches for those looking to hit the road early to Yellowstone. Breakfasts feature scrambles, burritos, and stuffed hash browns, while lunch offers gourmet sandwiches, panini, and wraps. The restaurant is cramped inside, but has outdoor seating in summer.

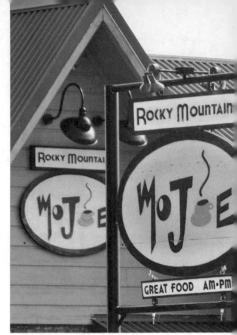

Rocky Mountain Mojoe

Peter's Café and Bakery (1219 Sheridan Ave., 307/527-5040, 6:30am-9pm Mon.-Sat., 7am-4pm Sun., $5-10) offers sandwiches to go and food made with fresh ingredients—breakfast items, espresso, scones, sticky buns, ice cream, salads, burgers, sandwiches, and sweet-potato fries. Peter's also doubles as an ice cream parlor. A locals' hangout, **Our Place Café** (148 W. Yellowstone Ave., 307/527-4420, 6am-2pm daily, $6-12, cash only), serves traditional breakfast and lunch; think biscuits and gravy or chicken-fried steak.

Pat O'Hara Pub & Grill (1019 15th St., 307/586-5410, http://patoharabrewing.com, 11am-close Wed.-Mon., $10-20) is a classic Irish brewpub with fish and chips, shepherd's pie, and bangers as the backbone of the menu. Beers on tap include their own craft brews, plus other regional ales. **Millstone Pizza Company and Brewery** (1057 Sheridan Ave., 307/586-4131, www.millstonepizzacompany.com, 11am-9pm Sun.-Thurs., 11am-10pm Fri.-Sat., $7-20) has a menu that goes far beyond pizza with Chicago dogs and oven-baked subs. Sixteen beers are on tap, including the company's own seasonal and mainstay brews

ACCOMMODATIONS

Summer is high season in Cody, when hotels pack out and prices are highest. To guarantee your choice of lodging, **make reservations four months in advance.** In fall, winter, and spring, reservations are not needed. Cody has several moderate hotel chains, plus a few of the budget variety, although budget rates in summer may be higher than average. Lodging is available year-round, except for guest ranches.

For a full list of hotels and lodges, contact the **Park County Travel Council** (www.yellowstonecountry.org); for vacation rentals, contact **Cody Lodging Company** (307/587-6000 or 800/587-6560, www.codylodgingcompany.com).

Hotels

Cody is full of history, and its hotels are part of that. ★ **Chamberlin Inn** (1032 12th St.,

888/587-0202, www.chamberlininn.com, $135-650) once served as the courthouse. Today it's a boutique hotel with fresh flowers, chocolates, and luxury linens in the rooms. The two-story redbrick building has 21 guest rooms; all are different and some have kitchenettes. Specialty rooms include the garden and historic courthouse residence. A library, sunroom, and enclosed lawn courtyard serve as communal spaces.

On the National Register of Historic Places, the **Irma Hotel** (1192 Sheridan Ave., 307/587-4221 or 800/745-4762, www.irmahotel.com, $80-200) radiates history down to the cigarette-scented front porch and saloon. Built by Buffalo Bill Cody in 1902 and named for his daughter, the hotel has historic and modern rooms in an old two-story brick building. Bed configurations include doubles, queens, or a king, with some rooms adding 1-2 single beds. The hotel includes a restaurant and a bar, where you can watch the famous gunfight six nights a week from the front porch.

Located 0.25 mile from the nightly summer rodeo, the modern **Cody Hotel** (232 West Yellowstone Ave., 307/213-4481, www.thecody.com, $115-295) has three types of suites, including Jacuzzi options. Rooms have a king or two queens, and breakfast is included. Amenities include a hot tub, indoor pool, and fitness room.

A 1950s motel that is good for families, **Big Bear Motel** (139 W. Yellowstone Ave., 307/587-3117 or 800/325-7163, www.codywyomingbigbear.com, $65-230) has rooms in combinations of queens, doubles, or one king, and an outdoor pool (in summer).

Cabins

Within walking distance of the nightly rodeo, **Cody Cowboy Village** (203 W. Yellowstone Ave., 307/587-7555, www.thecodycowboyvillage.com, May-mid-Oct., $100-220) is a collection of one- and two-story log buildings that house rooms and suites. The 40 cabin rooms include one king bed or two queens and bathrooms with tile showers. The 10 luxury suites feature two rooms with two queens and a queen-size sofa sleeper; bathrooms have tub-shower combos. The property has a giant hot tub fed by a small waterfall and offers concierge service, continental breakfast, and ADA rooms.

Located on the downtown strip, **Buffalo Bill Village Cabins** (1701 Sheridan Ave., 307/587-5544 or 406/587-3654, www.blairhotels.com, May-Sept., $145-200) includes 83 log-sided cabins that were built in the 1920s,

the historic Irma Hotel

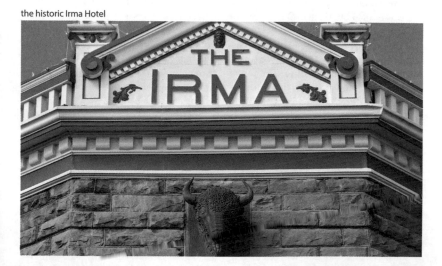

but are updated with pine-walled interiors. The one- and two-bedroom cabins with private bathrooms feature various combinations of king, queen, double, and twin beds. The cabins are tucked between a Holiday Inn, Comfort Inn, summer outdoor heated pool, and restaurant.

Bed-and-Breakfasts

About 10 minutes from downtown, the **K3 Guest Ranch Bed and Breakfast** (30 Nielson Trail, 307/587-2080 or 888/587-2080, www.k3guestranch.com, May-early Oct., $150-220) offers a western take on the usual B&B. Five guest rooms sleep 2-6 people each and include a private bath. Each is unique—one room has a bed in a 19th-century chuck wagon, while another bed is located inside a hay wagon. The Teton Room features a mural of its namesake mountains and a log bed. Other accommodations are located in a small house made from canvas tenting and an 1897 sheepherders' wagon with a cabin tent. A western-style breakfast is cooked on a campfire and served outdoors on a patio, or in the indoor dining room when the weather sours. Outdoor activities include hiking, fishing, rifle target shooting, and sitting around a campfire.

Near downtown and within walking distance to Buffalo Bill Center of the West, the **Salsbury Avenue Inn Bed and Breakfast** (1226 Salsbury Ave., 307/587-1226, www.salsburyinncody.com, $90-130) has four guestrooms in a home built in 1914. The rooms share three locking bathrooms that can guarantee privacy with Occupied signs.

Lodges and Guest Ranches

A lineup of historic summer lodges flanks the Buffalo Bill Scenic Byway (U.S. Hwy. 14/16/20) between Cody and Yellowstone's East Entrance. In Shoshone National Forest, halfway between Cody and Yellowstone, the 1925 **Bill Cody Ranch** (2604 North Fork Hwy., 307/587-2097 or 800/615-2934, http://billcodyranch.com, late May-late Sept., $130-270) features 17 rustic log cabins (no kitchens)

Pahaska Tepee Resort

on Nameit Creek below Ptarmigan Mountain. Some cabins have a two-night minimum. All-inclusive overnights add three meals plus horseback riding.

Located 18 miles west of Cody, historic **Wapiti Lodge** (3189 North Fork Hwy., 307/587-2420, www.wapitilodge.com, late May-mid Sept., $175-270) overlooks the North Fork of the Shoshone River. The 1904 lodge was renovated in 2012 and has six suites, two cabins, and kitchenettes or full kitchens. Amenities include a continental breakfast and fishing on the river.

Located three miles from Yellowstone's East Entrance, **Shoshone Lodge and Guest Ranch** (349 North Fork Hwy., 307/587-4044, www.shoshonelodge.com, late May-early Oct., $120-330) centers 18 cabins around a rustic 1920s log lodge that includes a restaurant and bar. Horseback riding is available. Acquiring its fame as the 1904 lodge built by Buffalo Bill Cody, **Pahaska Tepee Resort** (183 North Fork Hwy., 307/527-7701 or 800/628-7791, www.pahaska.com, mid-May-mid-Oct.,

$100-250) is a funky mountain resort with a main log lodge listed on the National Register of Historic Places. A mix of rustic A-frame motel-style cabins and two-story log cabins accommodates guests.

CAMPING
Cody

Cody's sunny campgrounds are the place for RVs (even the big rigs), full hookups (water, sewer, electricity, and cable TV), and action close to town. Amenities include flush toilets, showers, drinking water, picnic tables, camp stores, playgrounds, laundries, dump stations, and wireless Internet. Make summer reservations one month in advance.

Located near the airport, the **Cody KOA** (5561 Greybull Hwy., 307/587-2369 or 800/562-8507, www.codykoa.com, May-Sept., $40-80 RVs, $20-35 tents, $5-6 per person for more than two people) has 161 RV sites and 12 tent sites. Amenities include a swimming pool, hot tub, wading pool, game room, dog playground, and a shuttle to the nightly rodeo. Located on the west end of town, the **Ponderosa Campground** (1815 8th St., 307/587-9203, http://codyponderosa. com, mid-Apr.-mid-Oct., $35-60 RVs, $35 tents) has half of its sites under the shade of

big trees and half in open sun. In addition to the usual amenities, the campground has a cappuccino bar, six tepees, several cabins, and pickups for trolley tours, rodeos, and river rafting.

Buffalo Bill State Park

Located 9 and 13 miles west of Cody are two sunny campgrounds in **Buffalo Bill State Park** (4192 North Fork Hwy., 307/587-9227, http://wyoparks.state.wy.us, May-Sept., $10 standard, $15 hookups, $7 fee for nonresidents). Together, they comprise 99 campsites. Sites include those with hookups (water and electricity), primitive sites, ADA sites, and walk-in tent sites. Picnic tables, fire rings with grills, vault toilets, drinking water, disposal stations, coin-op showers, and campground hosts are available. The **North Shore Bay Campground** has a boat launch and overlooks Buffalo Bill Reservoir from a wind-blown arid slope between the highway and the water; some sites have windbreak fences. The **North Fork Campground** sits west of the reservoir and flanks the North Fork River. Sites are spread around a mowed green lawn. **Reservations** (877/996-7275, http://travel. wyo-park.com) are recommended for July and August.

North Shore Bay Campground at Buffalo Bill State Park

Shoshone National Forest

From Cody, campgrounds flank routes into Yellowstone in **Shoshone National Forest** (Wapiti Ranger District, 203A Yellowstone Ave., Cody, 307/527-6921, www.fs.usda.gov/shoshone, mid-May-Sept., $10-15 standard, $20 hookups). **Reservations** (877/444-6777, www.recreation.gov) are accepted for Big Game, Clearwater, Wapiti, Rex Hale, Threemile, and Hunter Peak.

Buffalo Bill Scenic Byway

A string of eight campgrounds lines the Buffalo Bill Scenic Byway (Hwy. 14/16/20) 28-48 miles west of Cody. Sites sit along or near the North Fork of the Shoshone River with access to fishing and floating. Located a 0.5-mile apart, brushy **Big Game Campground** (no water) and **Wapiti Campground** have 56 campsites between them. Wapiti can fit larger RVs and has electrical hookups; it stays open through hunting season until late November. The campgrounds are 29 miles west of Cody and 23 miles east of Yellowstone's entrance.

Four campgrounds cluster in sagebrush, junipers, and pines about midway between Cody and Yellowstone, with 85 campsites between them. **Elk Fork Campground** (30 miles west of Cody, no water) has river access. **Clearwater Campground** (43 miles west of Cody, no water) is popular with tent campers for its scenic walk-in sites on the river. Near Mummy Cave, **Rex Hale Campground** (35 miles west of Cody) has sites with electrical hookups, while sites at **Newton Creek Campground** (38 miles west of Cody) have views of dramatic pinnacles. Yellowstone's East Entrance is due west.

The more sought-after campgrounds are closest to Yellowstone, located 3-7 miles west of the East Entrance. **Eagle Creek Campground** and **Threemile Campground** scatter in cow parsnips and conifers with 40 campsites between them. Hard-sided units (no tents, tent pop-ups, or tent trailers) are required due to grizzlies frequenting the campgrounds.

Chief Joseph Scenic Byway

Chief Joseph Scenic Byway (Hwy. 296) leads to the Beartooth Highway and Yellowstone's Northeast Entrance. Located on the Beartooth Plateau between Chief Joseph Pass and Sunlight Canyon, **Dead Indian Campground** has 10 sites (no water). On the west end of the byway, **Hunter Peak Campground** (10 sites, water available) sits on the Clarks Fork of the Yellowstone River. After turning from the byway onto the west end of the Beartooth Highway (Hwy. 12), **Crazy Creek Campground** has 16 forested sites (no water). **Fox Creek Campground** has 33 sites with electrical hookups and drinking water and views of Index and Pilot Peaks.

TRANSPORTATION AND SERVICES
Car

The main highway cuts right through downtown Cody, and driving becomes clogged in summer. Street parking is minimal; explore side streets to find a spot. Those driving large RVs should head to the back lots at the Buffalo Bill Center of the West (720 Sheridan Ave.) and walk into town from there.

CHIEF JOSEPH SCENIC BYWAY

From Cody, the 80-mile route to the **Northeast Entrance** of Yellowstone travels the **Chief Joseph Scenic Byway** (Hwy. 296) over 8,076-foot Dead Indian Pass. To reach Chief Joseph Scenic Byway, drive north on Highway 120 for 17 miles and turn left, where the climb begins past red rock cuts and bluffs. At the pass, the view opens up to the **Clarks Fork of the Yellowstone River** dividing the Absaroka and Beartooth Mountains. Stop at the viewpoint to read about the **flight of the Nez Perce** who took this route while being chased by the U.S. Army. Drop down the switchbacks past Dead Indian Campground to **Sunlight Gorge** for another stop, looking down 300 feet into the dizzying narrow slot to Sunlight Creek. Continue heading northwest toward the distinctive toothy peak of **Pilot Butte.** When you reach the Beartooth

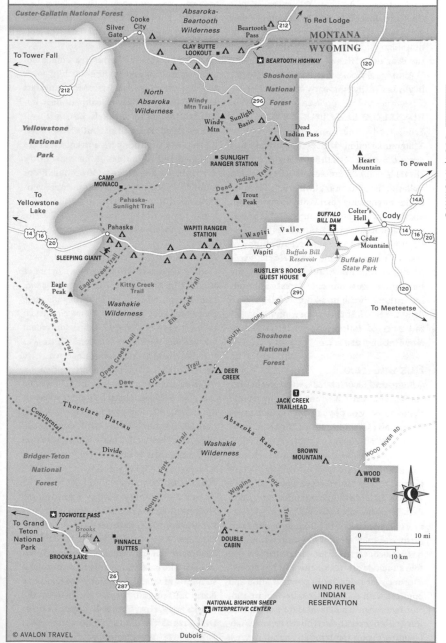

Shoshone National Forest

Custer-Gallatin National Forest

Silver Gate
Cooke City

Absaroka-Beartooth Wilderness

Beartooth Pass

212

To Red Lodge

MONTANA
WYOMING

120

To Tower Fall

212

CLAY BUTTE LOOKOUT

BEARTOOTH HIGHWAY

Shoshone National Forest

North Absaroka Wilderness

Windy Mtn Trail

296

Yellowstone National Park

Windy Mtn

Sunlight Basin

Dead Indian Pass

SUNLIGHT RANGER STATION

Dead Indian Trail

Heart Mountain

To Powell

CAMP MONACO

To Yellowstone Lake

14 16 20

Pahaska-Sunlight Trail

Trout Peak

14A

Pahaska

WAPITI RANGER STATION

Wapiti Valley

BUFFALO BILL DAM

Colter's Hell

Cody

14 16 20

SLEEPING GIANT

Eagle Creek Trail

Wapiti

Buffalo Bill Reservoir

Cedar Mountain

Eagle Peak

Kitty Creek Trail

RUSTLER'S ROOST GUEST HOUSE

Buffalo Bill State Park

120

Washakie Wilderness

Elk Fork Trail

SOUTH FORK RD

291

To Meeteetse

Thorofare Trail

Open Creek Trail

Deer Creek Trail

Shoshone National Forest

DEER CREEK

Thorofare Plateau

JACK CREEK TRAILHEAD

Absaroka Range

WOOD RIVER RD

Continental

Bridger-Teton National Forest

Divide

South Fork Trail

Washakie Wilderness

BROWN MOUNTAIN

WOOD RIVER

Wiggins Fork Trail

TOGWOTEE PASS

To Grand Teton National Park

Brooks Lake

PINNACLE BUTTES

DOUBLE CABIN

0   10 mi

0   10 km

BROOKS LAKE

26 287

WIND RIVER INDIAN RESERVATION

NATIONAL BIGHORN SHEEP INTERPRETIVE CENTER

Dubois

© AVALON TRAVEL

GATEWAYS
CODY, WYOMING

Highway (U.S. Hwy. 212), turn left to go through Cooke City and Silver Gate to reach the Northeast Entrance to Yellowstone. While the Chief Joseph Scenic Byway stays open year-round (except for temporary closures in heavy snowstorms), the eight-mile section of the Beartooth Highway—from Pilot Creek, Wyoming, to Cooke City, Montana—**closes in winter** (early Nov.-early May).

BUFFALO BILL SCENIC BYWAY

From Cody, the more direct route to Yellowstone follows the 52-mile **Buffalo Bill Scenic Byway** (North Fork Highway, U.S. Hwy. 14/16/20). The route goes west up Wapiti Valley to the park's **East Entrance**. The road begins by climbing narrow Shoshone Canyon via three tunnels to pop out at **Buffalo Bill Dam** and Reservoir. Continue driving west through the arid high desert flanking the reservoir and then follow the **North Fork of the Shoshone River** upstream as the terrain changes into pine forests alternating with sagebrush meadows. While you can drive the North Fork Road in winter, the **East Entrance of Yellowstone is closed early November-April.**

Bus and Taxi

Greyhound (800/231-2222, www.greyhound.com) buses reach Cody, but do not travel into Yellowstone. Cody has two taxi companies: **Cody Cab** (307/272-8364) and **Cody's Town Taxi** (307/250-8090).

Tours

Cody Trolley Tours (1192 Sheridan Ave., 307/527-7043, http://codytrolleytours.com, daily late May-late Sept., $27 adults, $25 seniors, $15 kids) carts visitors for a one-hour historical tour around town on a bus that has been converted to look like a trolley. The tours include stories of the Wild West heroes and renegades. Tours go out at 11am and 3pm, but 9am and 1pm tours add on in midsummer when needed. Make reservations. Purchase tickets at the trolley station, Cody Country Visitor Center (836 Sheridan Ave.), or online. The Buffalo Bill Center of the West (720 Sheridan Ave.) sells a combo ticket for the trolley and the center ($41 adults/seniors, $24 kids). The trolley company will pick you up at your hotel with a free shuttle to the trolley station.

Early May-late October, several companies guide sightseeing and wildlife-watching tours to Yellowstone National Park. Most tours last 10 hours. Reservations are required, and companies will pick up at hotels. Lunch is usually included. Rates run about $175-290 per person. Ask whether park entrance fees are included and tip guides 15 percent. **Cody Wyoming Adventures** (307/587-6988 or 800/293-0148, www.codywyomingadventures.com) tours the park in 15-passenger vans. **Yellowstone Tours** (307/527-6316, www.tourtoyellowstone.com) tours in SUVs.

Air

Cody's **Yellowstone Regional Airport** (COD, 2101 Roger Sedam Dr., 307/587-5096, http://flyyra.com) has service through United, Delta, and SkyWest from Denver and Salt Lake City. Flying through Cody is convenient for reaching the East or Northeast Entrances to Yellowstone May-October when roads are open for driving. It is not a winter option.

Rental cars are available at the Yellowstone Regional Airport: **Budget** (307/587-6066 or 800/527-0700, www.budget.com), **Hertz** (307/587-2914 or 800/654-3131, www.hertz.com), and **Thrifty** (307/587-8855 or 800/367-2277, www.thrifty.com).

Services

The **Cody Country Visitor Center** (836 Sheridan Ave., 307/587-2777, www.codychamber.org, 8am-7pm daily late May-late Sept., 8am-5pm Mon.-Fri. late Sept.-late May) has information, maps, brochures, and road conditions. The center also sells tickets to most summer events and attractions. For Shoshone National Forest information, stop by the **Clarks Fork, Greybull,** and **Wapiti Ranger Districts Office** (203A Yellowstone Ave., 307/527-6921, www.fs.usda.gov/shoshone).

Cody has a **post office** (1301 Stampede Ave., 307/527-7161, 8:30am-5pm Mon.-Fri., 9am-noon Sat.). **ATMs** are ubiquitous around town. For showers, go to the **Paul Stock Aquatic and Recreation Center** (1402 Heart Mountain St., 307/587-0400, www.cityofcody-wy.gov, 5:30am-10pm Mon.-Thurs., 5:30am-8pm Fri., 8am-6pm Sat., noon-6pm Sun. year-round, $12 adults, $6 students and youth, kids 4 and under free). The **Cody Laundromat** (1728 Beck Ave., 307/587-8500, open 24/7) has coin-op washers and dryers.

For emergencies, go to **West Park Hospital** (707 Sheridan Ave., 307/527-7501, www.westparkhospital.org).

MEDIA AND COMMUNICATIONS

Cell service is available in Cody and part of the Wapiti Valley toward Yellowstone. As the mountains close in, cell service becomes spotty to nonexistent. Do not expect service in the last 30 miles before Yellowstone's East Entrance.

Wireless Internet is common in Cody hotels and coffee shops. The **Park County Library** (1500 Heart Mountain St., 307/527-1880, http://parkcountylibrary.org, 9am-8pm Mon.-Thurs., 9am-5:30pm Fri., 9am-5pm Sat., 1pm-4pm Sun.) has public computers.

Founded by Buffalo Bill Cody, the Cody newspaper is the *Cody Enterprise* (www.cody-enterprise.com), published twice weekly.

Dubois, Wyoming

Most travelers whip past Dubois in a hurry to cross one of the most dramatic descents into **Grand Teton National Park**. From Dubois, Wyoming's Centennial Scenic Byway (U.S. Highway 26/287) cuts between the Wind River Mountains and Absaroka Mountains to summit the Continental Divide at Togwotee Pass. The western descent faces the implacable toothy Tetons before entering the park through the **Moran entrance**. From Moran, the road connects to the **South Entrance** of Yellowstone.

SIGHTS

Dubois has the distinction of a real cowboy frontier with fewer than 1,000 residents, making it a blip on the highway. For some, it offers a scenic gateway before entering the parks.

★ National Bighorn Sheep Interpretive Center

With one of the largest bighorn herds in the Lower 48 wintering near Dubois, this is a good place to learn about these icons of the Rockies. The **National Bighorn Sheep Interpretive Center** (10 Bighorn Ln., 307/455-3429, www.

bighorn.org, 9am-6pm daily late May-early Sept., 10am-4pm Mon.-Sat. early Sept.-late May, $3 adults, kids free) has information about the four species of wild sheep in North America. Exhibits include mounts, films, and interactive activities.

FOOD AND ACCOMMODATIONS

For dining in Dubois, the cafés are best. The older, homestyle **Cowboy Café** (115 E. Ramshorn, 307/455-2595, 7:30am-8pm daily, $11-30) serves pecan pancakes, elk skillets, bison burgers, sandwiches, and steaks. Their claim to fame is pie baked from scratch daily. **Nostalgia Bistro** (202 E. Ramshorn, 307/455-3528, www.nostalgiabistro.com, 11am-3pm and 5pm-9pm Tues.-Sat., $10-30) does a mix of Asian fusion meals and western food: smoked trout, beef stir-fry, tempura sweet chili chicken, eclectic burgers, Jenga-stacked pork ribs, braised kale, homemade soups, and fresh salads. Make reservations for dinner in summer.

The **Longhorn Ranch Lodge and RV Resort** (5810 Hwy. 26, 307/455-2337, www.

thelonghornranch.com, early May-mid-Oct.) is a 40-acre complex with motel rooms, cabins, and an RV campground. Motel rooms and cabins ($130-200) have private bathrooms and some include kitchenettes. Surrounded by cottonwoods, ponds, and a river, the campground has 42 RV sites ($50-75) with full hookups and 6 tent sites ($35-40). Rates are for two people; each additional person pays $10. The complex includes a store, coin-op laundries, fishing, kennels, massage services, and wireless Internet. In town, the **Stagecoach Inn** (103 Ramshorn St., 307/455-2303 or 800/455-5090, www.stagecoachmotel-dubois.com, $110-310) has rooms with 1-2 queens, king suites, and rooms with kitchenettes. The inn also has a hot tub, outdoor heated pool, laundry, and wireless Internet.

On the Wind River, the **Dubois/Wind River KOA** (225 Welty St., 307/445-2238, www.koa.com, late May-late Sept.) has 43 RV campsites ($45-75) with full hookups and 14 tent campsites ($30-45), plus showers, flush toilets, wireless Internet, fishing, and an indoor pool.

Services

Dubois has gas, ATMs, cell service, wireless Internet, and a **post office** (804 W. Ramshorn St.). For Forest Service information, contact **Wind River Ranger District** (1403 W. Ramshorn St., 307/455-2466, www.fs.usda.gov/shoshone).

★ TOGWOTEE PASS

From Dubois, the two-lane Wyoming Centennial Scenic Byway (U.S. Hwy. 26/287) ascends 30 miles to 9,658-foot Togwotee Pass (pronounced TOE-go-tee), with broad views of the valley and the eroded escarpment of **Sublette Peak** rising to the north during the climb. You'll barely know when you reach the summit, which has no significant pullout. But at the pass, the road crosses the **Continental Divide,** slicing between the summits of 11,010-foot **Breccia Peak** and 10,724-foot **Two Oceans Mountain.** On the westward descent, the full panorama of the Teton Mountains rises up with jagged spires, lit up by morning sunlight or backlit at sunset. The route is **open year-round,** but closes during blizzards in winter.

Sunset lights the Pinnacles near Togwotee Pass.

Accommodations and Camping

On the west side of Togwotee Pass, **Togwotee Mountain Lodge** (27655 Hwy. 26-287, 866/278-4245, www.togwoteelodge.com, late May-early Oct. and Dec.-Mar., $155-280) has 28 lodge rooms with two queens, six family bunk suites, 54 cabins, and a hot tub. The on-site **Grizzly Grill** (7am-10am, 11:30pm-2pm, and 5:30pm-9pm daily, $10-25) serves breakfast, lunch (winter only), and dinner. In summer, you can go horseback riding; in winter, snowmobiling is offered.

In the Absaroka Mountains north of Togwotee Pass, **Shoshone National Forest** (Wind River Ranger District, 1403 W. Ramshorn, Dubois, 307/455-2466, www.fs.usda.gov/shoshone, late June-mid-Sept., $10-20) has two coveted, ultra-scenic campgrounds: **Brooks Lake** (13 sites) and **Pinnacles** (21 sites). At 9,100 feet on the Continental Divide, sunrises and sunsets cast orange glows on the surrounding escarpments and pinnacles, yielding *National Geographic*-caliber photos. You can hike on the Continental Divide, or boat, paddle, and fish in Brooks Lake. The first-come, first-served campgrounds are for hard-sided vehicles only (no tents). Only Pinnacles has drinking water. They are located on Brooks Lake Road (Forest Rd. 515), five miles from Togwotee Pass, 28 miles north of Dubois, and 30 miles east of the Moran entrance to Grand Teton. Located adjacent to the highway near Togwotee Pass, **Falls Campground** has a few electrical sites and permits tents.

Background

The Landscape 361

Plants and Animals 374

History 380

Local Culture 387

The Landscape

GEOLOGY
Yellowstone

Why does Yellowstone National Park attract 3.5 million visitors a year? It is one of the few places on earth where people can watch supervolcano outbursts. Instead of eyeing only explosive aftermath, visitors can gape at volcanism in action with erupting geysers, bubbling mud pots, fuming vents, and steaming hot pools. All the action is due to Yellowstone's hot spot, a place where the molten magma rises near to the earth's surface.

SUPERVOLCANO

Volcanic activity in Yellowstone started with a supervolcano—far more than an ordinary volcano. The U.S. Geological Survey uses "supervolcano" for any eruption flinging more than 1,000 cubic kilometers of magma, ash, and pumice in one big eruption. Yellowstone's supervolcano qualifies with the Lava Creek eruption that took place 640,000 years ago. It left a caldera 34 by 45 miles, one of the largest calderas in the world, and shot ash to the Canadian and Mexican borders. See the tuff ash from that explosion at the Tuff Cliff Picnic Area.

The Lava Creek eruption was the last in a string of super blasts from the Yellowstone hotspot. Originally starting in Oregon 16 million years ago, the hotspot traveled northeast across Idaho's Snake River Plain as earth's plates shifted. Similar to the Hawaiian Island arc, the Yellowstone hotspot track contains evidence of 12 massive eruptions 8-12 million years ago. Nearer to Yellowstone were the more recent eruptions of Island Park Caldera (2.1 million years ago) and Henry's Fork Caldera (1.3 million years ago).

The action from Yellowstone's supervolcano changes constantly. Old Faithful has shifted from erupting about every hour before the 1959 Hebgen Earthquake to erupting on average every 91 minutes. In some of the geyser basins, boardwalks around thermal features have been moved as the action shifted. Even Firehole Drive west of Old Faithful closed temporarily in 2014 when a new hot spot started melting the road.

The supervolcano still has the potential to erupt again, but scientists don't know when. The Yellowstone Volcano Observatory (http://volcanoes.usgs.gov/observatories/yvo) monitors activity to keep tabs on heat, movement, and shifting thermals. Just think about something other than supervolcanoes erupting when you try to fall asleep at night.

TWIN CHAMBERS AND THE CALDERA

After eruptions, huge calderas, or cauldrons, remain at the volcano's site. In Yellowstone's case, two magma chambers pushed like oversized pimples toward the surface of the earth. As they hoisted the earth's crust upward into the monstrous supervolcano, giant circular fractures grew around the mountains apex. When the pressure became too much, the twin chambers exploded through the crust along the fracture rings, sending ash and pumice into the air and lava flowing down mountainsides. As magma depleted in the chambers, the roofs collapsed along the circular fractures, forming the rounded caldera, roughly one-third of the park. As smaller eruptions continued, lava flows dammed up places where streams drained from the caldera. The dams created Yellowstone's lakes: Shoshone, Lewis, and Yellowstone.

Since the supervolcano eruption, the twin chambers have refueled themselves with

---

Previous: Grotto Geyser; bighorn sheep, National Elk Refuge.

magma, bulging upward again. Today, these two bulges, called resurgent domes, are near Old Faithful and Hayden Valley. Magma continues to push to the earth's crust, sometimes producing uplifts. Over a six-year period ending in 2010, instruments recorded a large vertical push inside the eastern rim of the caldera. The land rose 11 inches, but then dropped more than 2 inches. Frequent earthquakes release pressure to let the uplifts ebb.

RECENT ERUPTIONS

Soon after the Lava Creek eruption 640,000 years ago, volcanic activity continued on a smaller scale. Magma flowed through labyrinths of underground cracks to ooze out over the caldera floor. The most recent lava flows occurred 60,000-75,000 years ago. Many contained rhyolite, the predominant light-colored rock inside the caldera today. In a few places, lava flows crested the caldera rim or surfaced along small fault lines, such as 180,000 years ago at Obsidian Cliff. Many of Yellowstone's trails are dotted with black, glassy obsidian from these more recent eruptions, formed from rapidly cooling lava.

Smaller eruptions have also occurred since the supervolcano. West Thumb Geyser Basin erupted 150,000 years ago. After the eruption, the volcano collapsed, creating the caldera. Water flowed into the caldera, turning it into a bay off Yellowstone Lake.

EARTHQUAKES

Yellowstone is active with earthquakes, caused when the crust slips against itself along fault lines. Each year, 1,000-3,000 earthquakes shake across the park; these brittle failures are daily occurrences, although most cannot be felt. The University of Utah Seismograph Station (www.seis.utah.edu) monitors the earthquakes. Check out recent earthquakes on the Yellowstone Volcano Observatory website (http://volcanoes.usgs.gov/observatories/yvo). Sometimes, swarms of earthquakes occur when numbers of quakes spike far above normal. Summer 2017 produced the longest earthquake swarm with more than 2,300 tremors.

Earthquakes perform an essential function in letting thermals release pressure. Thermals use heat, water, and a plumbing system that constricts gas bubbles to produce geyser eruptions. Earthquakes take the place of Drano in keeping the underground pipes open; shaking unseals cracks from minerals that are solidifying them closed. Between earthquakes and hydrothermal features, pressure releases to keep the caldera operating at a slow boil rather than building into a catastrophic eruption.

VOLCANIC SCULPTURES

Hydrothermal activity creates fantastical sculptures. But some sculptures are built from different components. Within the caldera, the landscape is built on rhyolite, formed from thick, liquid flows of the Lava Creek eruption 640,000 years ago. Beige-colored silicate minerals and silica solidified in the rhyolite. Since rhyolite is the underlying bedrock, many of the fountains and cones in the geyser basins are created from silica gushing up with water and clinging as building-block crystals on the sculptures. **Castle** and **Grotto Geysers** are two of these in the Upper Geyser Basin.

But the **Mammoth Hot Springs** terraces are different. They are made from calcium carbonate that comes from limestone underground. As the water comes to the surface, it brings calcium carbonate with it to spill out over the terraces. That's what creates the smooth-sculpted features that look more like frozen water.

PETRIFIED TREES AND BOBBY SOX TREES

A series of volcanic eruptions 40-50 million years ago petrified trees in Yellowstone. They were ancient redwoods, some up to four feet in width and 40 feet tall. They were swept along in lahars, flows of volcanic debris. Silica in the debris soaked into the living trees, petrifying them into rock. While redwoods no longer populate the park, their presence in petrified form indicates that Yellowstone once had a

Nature at Work

Yellowstone is a testament to the power of nature. In addition to geothermal features, geological upthrusts, and glaciation, other factors are still shaping the landscape.

Erosion: Wind, water, and ice conspire to whittle rocks and mountains. Winds tears particles off softer features. Water washes boulders downstream, and flooding reshapes water channels in the landscape. On lakes, wave action wears away shorelines. The freezing and thawing of ice pries shards of rock from cliffs.

Where can you see evidence of these forces? At the **Grand Canyon of the Yellowstone.** While the first scouring of the canyon started when lava flows dammed up lakes that overflowed, glacial lakes bursting their ice dams carved the canyon deeper and deeper until about 10,000 years ago when the dams melted. Winds carve away at the canyon sides, creating hoodoos, or pointed spires.

Earthquakes: Each year, the park has 1,000-3,000 quakes, most of which occur along faults in the earth's crust. The earthquakes help keep the plumbing systems of geysers and hydro-thermal features operational, while the shaking breaks up sinter that may clog water routes to the surface. In 2017, Yellowstone experienced its longest earthquake swarm in a series of local-ized quakes throughout summer. Many faults converge at **Mud Volcano,** making earthquake swarms common.

For real-time earthquake data, check the exhibits at the **Canyon Visitor Education Center** (307/344-2550, www.nps.gov/yell, 8am-8pm daily late May-mid-Oct., shorter hours in fall). The University of Utah Seismograph Station (www.seis.utah.edu) records earthquakes in Yellowstone; their online map shows earthquakes park-wide in the last hour, day, or week.

Fire: Every summer, lightning causes an average of 22 forest fires in Yellowstone. Most go out naturally. In 1988, Yellowstone experienced a monster fire season due to below normal pre-cipitation. That summer, wildfires burned 1.1 million acres in the Greater Yellowstone Ecosystem, including 36 percent of the park. Fires are key in creating wildlife habitat, diversifying vegetation, preserving grassland communities, and eradicating bug infestations. After a fire, the nutrients from ash added to the soil contribute to a burst of new plant life. Dead standing trees provide places for woodpeckers to chip holes, creating homes for cavity-dwelling birds and wildlife.

Where can you learn about wildfires? **Grant Visitor Center** (307/344-2650, www.nps.gov/yell, 8am-7pm daily late May-Sept.) hosts an exhibit on fire ecology. Around Grant Village, see stands of burned, silvered timber from the fire fast being replaced by a new forest of lodgepoles.

wetter, more tropical climate. Yellowstone's forest of petrified trees may be the largest in the world. To see them, stop at **Petrified Tree** or hike **Specimen Ridge.**

Lodgepole pines that populate the Yellowstone caldera today grow well in the sand-like sediments. But shifting thermal areas affect forests, killing the trees. Dead tree trunks stand erect in pools of hot water. Because many of the dead lodgepoles turn white around the base of their trunk due to soaking up silica in the water, they have garnered the name "bobby sox trees." Look in **Black Sand Basin** for the bottom foot or two of trunks appearing like they were painted white.

GLACIERS

Glaciers covered Yellowstone many times, starting two million years ago when the earth descended into a cooling phase in the Pleistocene Ice Age. While ice appeared and melted between bouts of volcanic spitfire, two late ice ages left tracks. The Bull Lake glacia-tion buried the park about 150,000 years ago. Then, beginning about 50,000 years ago, the Pinedale glacial era buried the park under 4,000 feet of ice. Yellowstone's high elevation and ice flowing down from the Beartooth Plateau created a localized island of ice dis-connected from the continental ice sheet shoving south from Canada. A glacier filled Yellowstone's caldera, forming an ice cap.

Hydrothermal Features

Of Yellowstone's 13,000 thermal features that have been mapped in the park, only four types exist.

GEYSERS

Geysers blow super-hot water into the air. Some erupt nonstop, while others blow on schedule, intermittently, or after long hiatuses of years. Eruptions result from big clogs of boiling water. After surface water percolates to a hot spot, it then boils toward the earth's surface. But gas bubbles get trapped in channels below water. Increasing bubbles push the water upward to make it overflow just enough to crank up fierce boiling that shoves water skyward. Eruptions finish when the gas bubbles reach air. Yellowstone's 500 geysers come in two types: Fountain geysers spray water in multiple directions, while cone geysers blast water upward in a narrow stream. More than half the earth's active geysers are in Yellowstone. Old Faithful Visitor Center and the Yellowstone Geyser App predict eruptions for **Old Faithful, Grand, Castle, Great Fountain, Daisy,** and **Riverside Geysers**.

HOT SPRINGS

Hot springs are created from underground channels just like geysers. But their larger channels don't clog up with steam bubbles, and cooler water is exchanged back down. Those factors prevent eruptions. At 199°F, most hot springs don't exceed the boiling point. Yellowstone's hot springs exhibit vibrant colors from two sources: Blues (the hottest on the color spectrum) come from the refraction of sunlight on the water, and other colors often fringing the pools are from thermophiles, or heat-loving life forms. See both of these at the park's largest hot spring, **Grand Prismatic** at Midway Geyser Basin.

MUD POTS

Mud pots form in depressions when hot water saturates clay-like sediments. Below the mud pot, as steam pushes upward into the saturated sediments, gaseous bubbles surface to pop and gurgle. Mud pots often have hydrogen sulfide gases that produce a rotten egg smell. Minerals tint mud pots different colors, like the pink and gray of **Fountain Paint Pot**.

FUMAROLES

Fumaroles are holes or vents in the ground, but instead of filling with hot water, they convert the small amount of water into super-hot steam. At Norris Hot Springs, **Black Growler** has reached 300°F. Often the steam creates noise as it rushes through the vent. It roars, hisses, or whistles.

Blue-colored pools have the hottest water.

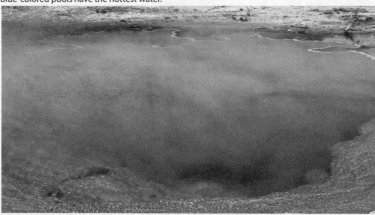

bobby sox trees

Most of the ice in the Yellowstone cap melted 13,000-14,000 years ago.

You'll find evidence of glaciers across the park. Moraines mark their sizes, and they left large boulders called erratics strewn about. The oldest evidence of glaciers is at Tower Fall in a sediment layer that is 1.3 million years old. Today, Yellowstone has no active glaciers.

YELLOWSTONE LAKE

Yellowstone Lake, the largest lake in the park, resulted from geologic forces. Part of the lake lies within the caldera and part outside. When lava flows dammed up caldera outlet streams, the lake formed. The portion inside the caldera still has active hydrothermal features, such as West Thumb Geyser Basin and Steamboat Point. But glaciers also reshaped the landscape on the southern half of the lake, in particular gouging out the South and Southeast Arms.

In addition, the lake basin is rising on the north end due to Sour Creek Dome north of

Fishing Bridge. That makes the lake basin tilt southward, creating larger sandy beaches on the north shore and more flood zones in the southern arms.

A five-year mapping project 1998-2003 gave scientists the first peek at the lake's floor. Sonar and an ROV (remotely operated vehicle) recorded volcanism: explosion craters, fissures and faults, vents, and siliceous spires. They make up the lake-bottom landscape in the north where volcanic processes are still active. But in the southeast, the lake lacks volcanic features, instead containing glacial debris such as erratics.

Using sonar and photo imaging, scientists also discovered strange spires on the floor of Bridge Bay. Hydrothermal vents emitted silica sinter that solidified into vertical sculptures. The spires contained a network of tubes that discharge steam and gases. Freshwater algae and sponges moved in to perch on the spires, creating underwater gardens. One spire was dated at 11,000 years old, forming after the last glacial age.

GRAND CANYON OF THE YELLOWSTONE

While fire and ice shaped most of the park, erosion also lent its artistry. The handiwork of wind erosion is evident in spires and hoodoos, while freeze-thaw cycles dislodged mountainsides into colossal talus piles. But water erosion is to thank for the **Grand Canyon of the Yellowstone**. While the canyon contains rusty oxidized rhyolite for a splash of color and steam escaping hydrothermic vents, its narrow V-shaped slot resulted from river cutting rather than glacial carving.

The canyon's formation is attributed to the ice damming that formed Yellowstone Lake 14,000-18,000 years ago. Ice dams typically melt and refreeze. During melt phases, torrents of water gushed downstream from the lake. The force of those repeated flash floods cut the canyon. Even today, the Yellowstone River continues to eat away at the canyon's depth.

Grand Teton

While Yellowstone represents ancient geologic forces, by comparison Grand Teton National Park is a young pup. The park hides ancient sea sediments, but its peaks are some of the newest in the Rocky Mountains. The wow factor comes from the extreme contrast between the flat plain of Jackson Hole and the Teton's sky-scratching teeth. A dose of faulting, glaciers, and erosion added the final brush strokes to the scene.

ANCIENT SEAS

Long before faulting shoved the Teton Mountains into existence, ancient shallow seas flooded portions of Wyoming. More than 2.7 billion years ago, their shorelines shifted over millennia eastward, but on the west side of where the Tetons now stand. As gravel, limey mud, clay, and sand washed into the sea basins, the debris settled in layers on the bottom. Over eons, the sedimentary layers compressed, and between the seabed layers, magma seeped in, adding volcanic rocks. Heat and pressure converted the sedimentary layers to gneiss, a metamorphic rock. The colorful rocks in Jackson Lake are from various sedimentary sea layers.

As recent as 510 million years ago, inland seas flooded the region. However, this time the sediment layers included fossils of sea plants and animals. Sea creatures such as trilobites, brachiopods, corals, and algae fossilized into layers of shales, limestones, and sandstones. Today, these ancient layers of sedimentary sea rock are exposed from fault thrusting. More than 1,000 feet of seabed layering is visible, particularly on the Teton's west side.

MOUNTAIN UPLIFT

Massive tectonic forces created the Rocky Mountains, starting 120 million years ago. When a Pacific Ocean plate slammed into North America, the resulting uplift of land shoved the Rocky Mountains upward. To the east of Grand Teton National Park, pressure from the tectonic movement created the Gros

Erosion carved the Grand Canyon of the Yellowstone.

Ventre Mountains about 70 million years ago. In comparison, they are much more weathered and rounded than the younger, jagged Tetons. As the mountain-building repercussions of the tectonic collision waned, volcanic activity kicked into action, including Yellowstone's supervolcano. Lava and volcanic debris built up to form the Absaroka Range opposite the north end of the Tetons.

TETON FAULT

The Tetons came late into the Rocky Mountains. It just took a while for the Teton Fault to wake up. About 10 million years ago, the fault's alarms went off, right where Jackson Hole abuts the Tetons today. As the two sides of the fault stretched apart, daring the other to tear away, massive 7.5 magnitude earthquakes rumbled. The fault's west side rose upward while Jackson Hole on the east side sank into a valley. Each violent earthquake shoved the mountains up about 10 feet while dropping Jackson Hole 30-40 feet, creating a new exposed scarp.

The Teton Fault is responsible for creating the prominence of the Teton Mountains. While the Grand Teton reaches 13,770 feet in elevation, it stretches 7,000 feet above Jackson Hole. Because the Jackson Hole side of the fault sank lower, no foothills formed. That vertical disparity, or prominence, between the peaks and Jackson Hole adds wow-worthiness. Geologists have also used the height of the Grand Teton to estimate the offset of the Teton Fault at 30,000 feet.

The last two major mountain-building earthquakes occurred 8,000 and 4,800 years ago. Today, very few earthquakes shake along the Teton Fault, but it is still active. Since Yellowstone's supervolcano erupted late in the Teton mountain-building process, gaseous lava clouds hit the north end of the range, where the mountains diverted them down Jackson Hole and Teton Valley. The summit of Signal Mountain has deposits from Yellowstone's explosions.

GLACIATION

As the earth's climate cooled two million years ago into the Pleistocene Ice Age, ice chewed

Falling Ice Glacier on Mt. Moran

on the landscape of the Tetons. The Bull Lake advance of ice that covered Yellowstone also buried the lower elevations of the Tetons. The ice stretched south in Jackson Hole nearly to Hoback Junction, burying what is today the town of Jackson with 1,500 feet of glacier. The Pinedale glaciation filled Jackson Hole, creating Jackson Lake but leaving the summit of Signal Mountain exposed. The melting of these glaciers flooded Jackson Hole with sand, gravel, and glacial debris to form the flat plain.

As the Tetons sat above the ice, the cooler temperatures piled up snow to compress over time into alpine glaciers. These glaciers are responsible for the artistic sculpting of cirques, horns, arêtes, and U-shaped valleys in the Tetons. Some of the glaciers descended to the valley floor where they deposited debris in moraines. These terminal moraines dammed up creeks to create lakes right at the base of the mountains: **Leigh, Jenny, Bradley, Taggart**, and **Phelps Lakes** are the handiwork of ice.

Grand Teton National Park still has about 12 named glaciers, but they are minuscule. From a recent ice age that plunged temperatures starting in 1400, they are responsible for carving cirques and hanging valleys. Known as the Little Ice Age, this glacier-building period was confined to higher elevations. In 1850, when warming began, the glaciers began to shrink. Annual accumulation of snow could not keep up with the amount of ice lost to summer melting. The past four decades have reduced the glaciers by 20-25 percent despite the annual 450 inches of snowfall. From different locations on the floor of Jackson Hole, you can see **Skillet** and **Falling Ice Glaciers** on Mt. Moran and the **Teton Glacier** on the Grand Teton. Plenty of static snowfields persist all summer, but due to their size and depth, they no longer move like glaciers.

EROSION

Wind, water, freeze-thaw cycles, and ice erode Grand Teton National Park. From high elevations surrounding Jackson Hole, streams descend to the **Snake River**. Cutting through glacial till, the river gradually carved a twisted trough through Jackson Hole. As it dug deeper, it left exposed terraces where channels ran in the past. The erosion continues slowly today as the river moves sediments downstream and digs lower.

CLIMATE

Yellowstone and Grand Teton National Parks experience four distinct seasons. Despite snowfall and the area surprises many with its semi-arid climate, forcing more water intake than at home. Higher elevations cling to winter longer, and weather can swing wildly during one day. Be prepared in all seasons for unpredictability. Skies may be blue and sunny in the morning only to turn into raging thunder or snowstorms by the afternoon. Hats, gloves, layers, and shells are needed year-round, and they must go in your day pack regardless of blue morning skies.

Northwest Wyoming is a land of extremes, with annual highs and lows separated by more than 100 degrees. Record highs range 93-99°F across both parks. The coldest temperature ever recorded was -66°F in Yellowstone near the West Entrance. Each summer swelters with several warm bouts of 90-degree heat, while each winter freezes with several periods of subzero temperatures made colder by windchill.

Spring

Springtime is moody in northwest Wyoming. Mild days with cool nights can ricochet with little warning into spitting rain and snowstorms. Sometimes a foot of snow can fall during a stormy cold front. Winds often accompany storms, which can make the temperatures seem colder. During April, May, and early June, daytime temperatures push into the 50-60°F range, but may barely top 30°F during storms. Overnight lows can sink to 5-20°F. June is mosquito season.

Summer

Summer is short, usually limited to July and August, with bugs prevalent in the early part of summer. Afternoons frequently see sporadic thundershowers, especially in the mountains. Likewise, winds tend to blow in the afternoons, turning lakes from placid flat water to raging whitecaps. Blue-sky days hang mostly around 70-85°F with a few spikes into the 90s. Nights are cool, dropping to lows of 35-45°F. High elevations may have below-freezing nights with frost in the early morning on trails.

Fall

While fall can be pleasant with warm bug-free days and cool nights, it can also be unpredictable with snow or rainstorms. Days of blue skies can alternate with several days of a wintry mix, dusting the higher elevations with snow. Winds accompany the arrival and departure of storms. Daytime warm-weather temperatures stay in the 50s-60s, but cold fronts can plummet the thermometer into the 30s. Overnight lows often drop into the teens or single digits.

Winter

White is the color of winter. From early November to late April, snow blankets the ground at all elevations. When the sun pokes out between storms, days are cold, and nights sink into frigid zones. Daytime temperatures range from zero to 20°F. Snowfall is common but varies from windy blizzards to lilting flakes. Nighttime lows often dive below 0°F. In winter, four-wheel- or all-wheel-drive vehicles handle snow better, and all-weather or studded snow tires are helpful.

Mountain Effects

Elevation plays a huge game with the weather, too. At higher elevations in the Tetons, for instance, temperatures can be 5-20 degrees cooler than on the valley floor of Jackson Hole. Winds can also amp up in strength. Frequent afternoon thundershowers douse hikers, and freezing temperatures, snow, and frost can show up on trails even in July and August. Heavy snowfall descends in November through April. While lower elevations may see 170 inches of snowfall in winter, upper elevations in the Tetons can accumulate 450 inches of snow.

Microclimates

Due to thermal activity in Yellowstone and extreme elevation differences in the Tetons, microclimates produce weather incongruities. In spring and fall, thermal areas often create intermittent fog that can roll out across nearby Grand Loop Road. On temperamental days, it's common to drive through a snow squall, fog, and sun within 10 minutes. In winter, cross-country skiers in Yellowstone's Upper Geyser Basin may encounter melt-outs in microclimates near hot features. Sometimes in shoulder seasons, Yellowstone and Jackson Lakes create their own wild squalls. No matter what season, higher elevations in the Tetons always have more extreme conditions than Jackson Hole.

ENVIRONMENTAL ISSUES
Pollution

Humans are one of the biggest threats to Yellowstone's thermal features. Some of Yellowstone's hot springs such as **Grand Prismatic, Sapphire,** and **Morning Glory** have changed color due to humans. Spectrometer evaluations show that water hues have altered from deep blues to greens due to visitors tossing coins and trash into the hot pools. The foreign objects partially block the water flow, which lowers the temperatures of the pools and changes the spectrum of color. It is impossible for the park service to remove these objects without causing further damage.

Air pollution is also affecting Yellowstone and Grand Teton. Both parks experience periods of air pollution that turn sharp, far-reaching mountain panoramas into hazy landscapes. Aspens, one species impacted by air pollution, are showing signs of decline. While anyone driving a vehicle into the parks contributes to emissions in the air, some of the pollution also comes from industry or

Morning Glory hot spring has changed color.

forest fires in the surrounding states. In the past decade, Yellowstone has made strides in reducing the smelly clouds of pollution along the road to Old Faithful during winter. By limiting numbers of snowmobiles and snowcoaches, plus requiring machines to have lower emissions, the winter air is now cleaner for visitors. During the other three seasons, all visitors can help reduce air pollution by turning off vehicles instead of idling, taking shuttles where available, and walking or riding bicycles for short-distance trips.

The **acoustic environment** is also important to protect in the park so visitors can hone in on the sounds of nature. Wildlife must be able to communicate with each other and hear predators. While the parks are studying noise levels, especially with motorcycles, visitors can minimize noise by turning vehicles off and opting for headphones to listen to music.

Climate Change

The current increase in global temperatures affects the Greater Yellowstone Ecosystem. Glaciers in Grand Teton National Park have shrunk in number and size since 1850 and will continue to melt into oblivion in the next few decades. Spring snowpack is melting earlier across both parks. In the 21st century, average annual temperatures have risen 1.4 degrees, while summers have been 2.3 degrees warmer.

These warming temperatures are already causing shifts in the ecosystem. **Whitebark pines** that grow at high elevations and play an important role in the grizzly bear diet have historically been protected by beetle-killing frigid winters. But now warmer temperatures have released tree-killing beetles in epidemic droves. Cold-water loving **cutthroat trout** are also declining due in part to climate change warming streams and changing snowmelt runoff patterns. With the reduction of pinecone and trout foods, **bears** are shifting toward a more meat-based diet.

Researchers are predicting warmer and drier conditions for Yellowstone and Grand Teton in upcoming decades. The impacts are already evident in less mountain snow, more catastrophic wildfires, and the reduction of native trees such as aspens, spruce, and pines. In turn, the Greater Yellowstone Ecosystem may shift from forest lands to desert shrublands. Animals requiring forested cover will see their habitat stripped. With fewer days of snow cover and thinner snowpack, the water feeding the Missouri and Snake Rivers will lesson.

With warming temperatures shifting floral habitats, wildlife may be forced to change elevation or latitude in search of food sources. Species such as the heat-intolerant pika may suffer extinction, and animals adapted to cold, such as **mountain goats, bighorn sheep, lynx,** and **wolverines**, may decline. **Ptarmigan, short-tailed weasels,** and **snowshoe hares** that molt with the amount of daylight to white in winter and brown in summer become easier prey when their colors fail to camouflage them on the ground. Melting glaciers, earlier snowmelts, fewer frost days, and hotter summers also contribute to rising stream temperatures that threaten the ability of cold-loving cutthroat trout to spawn.

Endangered Species and Areas of Concern
GRAY WOLVES

Now taken off the endangered species list in the Greater Yellowstone Ecosystem, gray wolves have seen a recovery in population. Once ranging throughout most of North America, gray wolves disappeared from the Yellowstone region in the early 1900s due to predator-control programs and loss of habitat. In the 1970s they were placed on the Endangered Species List. Two decades later, the federal government transplanted 41 wolves from Canada and northwest Montana to Yellowstone. While the return of the wolf helps keep the elk population in check, the introduction program met with resistance from some ranchers and landowners outside the national park. Wolf packs require huge territories, many of which range outside park boundaries. Today, about 500 wolves populate the Greater Yellowstone Ecosystem with 10 packs that use Yellowstone National Park. Winter counts inside the park usually tally around 100 wolves; numbers waffle based on the elk population, which makes up about 85 percent of their winter diet. While no hunting is permitted inside the park, wolves cross boundaries and can be hunted outside the park. Biologists keep radio and GPS collars on 25-30 wolves each year for tracking.

GRIZZLY BEARS

In the 1800s, more than 100,000 grizzly bears roamed grasslands and foothills in the Lower 48, but loss of habitat and predator extermination programs whittled their numbers down to a handful of small populations in the Northern Rockies. Greater Yellowstone's grizzly bears represented their southernmost stronghold, but the island population reduced genetic viability. In the 1970s, the isolated region's 136 grizzlies were listed as threatened on the Endangered Species List. With a recovery plan in place, biologists managed the rebound of grizzlies with the goal of sustaining the Greater Yellowstone population at 500. They have now expanded into surrounding ecosystem mountains: the Wind River, Gallatin, Absaroka, and Grand Tetons. Today, about 700 grizzlies populate the Greater Yellowstone Ecosystem. In 2017, grizzlies were delisted. While hunting grizzlies may be allowed by permit in specific locations outside the national parks as long as population numbers are maintained, no one can hunt bears inside the parks.

Despite the rebounding population, two issues concern biologists who monitor grizzlies by radio and GPS collaring. First, declining food sources such as whitebark pines and cutthroat trout threaten grizzly survival. In Yellowstone, seasonal trail and backcountry campsite closures protect feeding zones, particularly where sows take cubs in spring. Sometimes, the Moose-Wilson Road in Grand Teton closes for bears feeding on berries. Second, humans cause grizzly mortalities

through poaching, traffic, and improper storage of livestock grain, garbage, and bird feeders. In 2015, annual grizzly deaths in Greater Yellowstone topped a record 61.

CANADA LYNX

Recorded sightings of the Canada lynx have declined substantially in the Greater Yellowstone Ecosystem and it was listed as threatened on the Endangered Species List. Historically found in coniferous forests above 7,700 feet, the lynx follows its primary prey, the snowshoe hare, and the cat's cyclical population mirrors the ups and downs of hare numbers. However, fragmented forests threaten lynx: snowshoe hare populations are so small and dispersed that they cannot support the cat consistently to live, give birth, and rear kits. With scattered habitat, home ranges are huge, requiring long distance travel to find prey. DNA studies based on samples of scat and hair snags have revealed no lynx since 2014.

WOLVERINES

In 2015, the federal government declined proposals to place wolverines on the Endangered Species List, citing the need for more studies. In the Greater Yellowstone Ecosystem, they live above 8,000 feet with huge home ranges. Known as voracious eaters, the gluttonous weasels require deep, long spring snowpack for denning and rearing kits. Many biologists fear a warming climate threatens their survival. Since 2001, a study has radiotagged wolverines and located denning sites. It discovered the extreme distances wolverines travel: One walked 550 miles in less than six weeks, while another traveled from Togwotee Pass to Rocky Mountain National Park. Between that study and other hair snag studies, biologists estimate the Greater Yellowstone Ecosystem houses 60 wolverines.

BIGHORN SHEEP

Of all the ungulates, native **bighorn sheep** face the greatest risk. Once widely scattered across most western mountain ranges, the sheep today live in isolated pockets. The Tetons now contain less than 50, half the size of a decade ago. In the Greater Yellowstone Ecosystem, bighorns pick up disease from domestic sheep, which can decimate wild herds. A disease outbreak in 2009-2010 reduced populations by 50 percent. Fragmented habitat threatens the sheep's future.

BISON

Bison have rebounded from the small herd of 23 that remained in Yellowstone in the late 1800s. Today, the parks have some of the largest bison herds in the world; however, their numbers are of concern. Ranchers in lands surrounding the parks want to keep bison numbers down so that fewer migrate out of the park in winter to lower elevations. (This is due to a fear of brucellosis infecting the cattle and to reduce the trampling of ranchlands.) In winter migrations, Yellowstone's northern herd exits the park near Gardiner; the central herd heads out at West Yellowstone. While some bison winter inside the park, those that migrate outside the park return the following season. Herd numbers grow each year with more and more bison spilling out of the park.

The difficulty is that bison are wild animals that are managed like cattle. In order to avoid damage to grazing habitat and floral communities inside the park, wildlife managers keep the Yellowstone bison numbered at 3,000 animals. By 2016, the Yellowstone herd numbered 5,500. For the first time, the Interagency Bison Management Team and governor of Montana agreed to let some bison live year-round outside the park boundaries. About 40 bison were sent to Native American reservations to start herds. Licensed hunts culled herd numbers by 450. Numbers still weren't low enough, so winter 2017 saw another 750 bison shipped to slaughter—a controversial decision. The park service is investing in a brucellosis quarantine area outside the park in order to save bison or augment herds elsewhere.

In Jackson Hole, the herd goal is 500 animals; however, annual numbers frequently

Bighorn sheep are threatened by habitat fragmentation.

top that by 100-300. Hunting the Grand Teton herd that migrated onto the National Elk Refuge and Bridger-Teton National Forest resulted in a record 300 bison killed during the 2014-2015 season. To date, that herd is managed solely by licensed hunts.

Invasive Species

Yellowstone and Grand Teton's waters hold native cutthroat trout, one of the most sought-after fish for anglers. But the introduction of two species has reduced trout numbers. In Yellowstone and Jackson Lakes, lake trout have dwindled native trout populations. While lake trout were introduced as a sport fish, they out-compete native trout for food. Lake trout populations are kept in check by fishing creel limits to keep them from decimating trout populations into oblivion.

Aquatic invasive species such as the whirling disease parasite and New Zealand mud snails have now found their way into park waters in certain locations. By cleaning their gear, anglers can avoid transporting these creatures to uninfected waters. Boater permits require rigs to be cleaned before entering park waters.

Invasive plants can displace native vegetation. In fact, some introduced species even inhibit the growth of native plants that are vital to wildlife. Yellowstone has 218 species of invasive plants that include Canada thistle, toadflax, leafy spurge, ox-eye daisy, and spotted knapweed. The parks use targeted spraying programs to control the spread of these, especially along roadways.

Fire

Fires are part of the natural rejuvenation of the landscape, ensuring a patchwork of foliage to support a variety of wildlife and maintain biodiversity of plant species. Every summer sees lightning start small fires across the Greater Yellowstone Ecosystem. Nearly 75 percent of the annual fires in Yellowstone burn less than a quarter of an acre. They keep bug infestations in check, restore nutrients to the soil, open up forest understories, maintain grasslands, and improve wildlife habitat. But the amount and severity of fires are increasing.

Up until the 1990s, lightning ignited about 22 fires each summer. Since then, the average has been increasing due to warmer temperatures and drought—drying factors that reduce the moisture in fallen trees and dead limbs while increasing the fuel content. Severe drought can lead to catastrophic fires that burn a huge amount of acreage and pump smoke thousands of feet into the air. The drought-stricken summer of 1988 conflagrated into 250 fires across the region that burned 1.2 million acres. Inside Yellowstone National Park, about 36 percent (793,880 acres) of the landscape burned. While wildlife populations survived the fires, 67 buildings did not. In 2016, lightning ignited Grand Teton's largest wildfire; the Berry Fire burned 20,825 acres.

In general, most lightning fires are allowed to burn, while those near human structures are handled on a case-by-case basis. Check online (http://inciweb.nwcg.gov) to follow fires in Yellowstone and Grand Teton National Parks.

Historical Protection

Yellowstone National Park has more than 1,800 Native American and European American archaeological sites, more than 900 historic buildings, one National Historic Trail, and 25 sites listed on the National Register of

bison in the Yellowstone River

Historic Places. Grand Teton National Park likewise has historical resources that include homesteads, working ranches, and park service buildings, with 36 structures listed on the National Register of Historic Places. While the park service is charged with overseeing the preservation of these historical assets, it's up to visitors to treat them with respect and preserve them, too.

Tourists

Both Yellowstone and Grand Teton have seen record crowds in recent years. In 2016, Yellowstone topped 4.2 million visitors while Grand Teton surpassed 4.8 million visitors. Crowds stress the park's ecosystems, creating long lines, traffic jams, and frustration. Migratory animals must also contend with human occupation in zones that were once wild.

Plants and Animals

PLANTS

With its tremendous diversity, the Greater Yellowstone Ecosystem contains a mosaic of flora that in turn supports a broad spectrum of wildlife. Due to Yellowstone's thermal features, the park contains extremely unique flora, and because of Grand Teton's vertical relief, multiple elevations of plant communities are represented. The ecosystem houses more than 1,300 native plants, including seven conifers and 1,150 flowering species. Yet for those big numbers, only a few species are endemic, or found only in the region.

Geothermal Plants

A few plants can tolerate Yellowstone's geothermal zones. Mosses, for one, can endure the hot soil because they lack roots. The endemic **Ross's bentgrass**, which grows only in Shoshone Geyser Basin and the Firehole River geyser basins, clings to places that collect moisture, such as cracks. It takes advantage of a short growing season enhanced by hot temperatures that preclude other plants competing with it. It also accomplishes seed dispersal by hitching rides on the hooves of bison and elk. **Tweedy's rush** can grow in acidic hydrothermal zones that usually prove destructive to other vascular plants.

Wetlands

Eleven percent of Yellowstone's plants grow in wetlands. Some are unusual species. Due to thermally heated waters, warm spring **spikerush** proliferates in streams. Usually found in tropical and subtropical zones, it can survive the harsh cold winters because of the thermally heated water. One red-flowering **paintbrush** usually found in the Southwest grows in two wetlands in Yellowstone due to warm springs. Many of the wetlands also contain plants more commonly found in the boreal regions of Alaska and northern Canada.

Grasslands and Sagebrush Plains

Thousands of acres of grasslands and sagebrush steppes occupy Yellowstone and Jackson Hole. Receiving low moisture, they harbor grasses, wildflowers, and small shrubs that can tolerate arid, treeless environments and trampling from bison. **Idaho fescue** is one of the more dominant grass species, and mountain big sagebrush blooms with tiny yellow flowers in August. As snow melts, wildflowers start to bloom: **Spring beauties** and **glacier lilies** are the first to appear, sometimes even rushing to grow through lingering snow. As summer progresses, large **arrowleaf balsamroot** splash yellow across drier slopes, and more color comes from blue **lupine** and red or orange **paintbrush**. In August, **purple asters** and **goldenrod** dry into stiff yellow stalks.

Forests

The forests consist of seven conifer and several

Prairie smoke grows in sub-alpine meadows.

leafy deciduous species. In Yellowstone, 80 percent of the forest is **lodgepole pine**, one of the first tree species to grow after a fire. Its cones need the heat from fire to reseed. The species grows well in Yellowstone's rhyolitic soil because it can tolerate the poor sand-like conditions. Other conifers include Engelmann spruce, subalpine fir, limber pine, whitebark pine, Douglas fir, and Rocky Mountain juniper. All of them grow 75-100 feet tall, with the exception of junipers, which max out at 30 feet. **Whitebark pine** and **subalpine fir** grow at higher elevations. Deciduous species are birches, cottonwoods, and aspens. Because quaking aspen are joined underground with connected roots, entire groves in fall change to yellow or orange in unison. Their "quaking" name denotes their flat-leaf petioles, or stems, enabling them to quiver at the slightest breeze.

Subalpine

In the high-elevation subalpine around tree line, wetter meadows become lush oases that support rampant wildflowers. The short growing season forces them to bloom and disperse their seeds fast. **Prairie smoke,** yellow fritillary, yellow columbine, paintbrush, mountain heather, bluebells, gentian, and harebells are just a few of the subalpine wildflowers. In this upper elevation zone, conifers are stunted due to high winds and brutal conditions. Dwarfed, they often twist into contorted, low-to-the-ground shapes called **krummholz**. When firmly established, the krummholz can serve as an anchor for stunted subalpine firs to grow upright.

Alpine Tundra

Dry winds, extreme cold, lack of soil, no shade, and burning sunlight impede flora in the alpine tundra above tree line. From a distance the ground looks like bare rock, but tiny flowers cling low to the ground to survive, soaking up what moisture collects under rocks. **Sky pilot, alpine forget-me-nots,** and **Parry's primrose** bloom shortly after snowmelt to finish seed dispersal before snows return. Moss campion, which blooms with tiny pink flowers, grows in mats that can be a couple hundred years old.

Wild Berries

Succulent berries grow in the wild. Bears favor them, and so do humans. Thimbleberries, wild raspberries, and elderberries are just a few that bears and humans eat. But the **huckleberry** is the favorite—a small purple orb resembling a blueberry, but much sweeter. Other berries, such as serviceberry, chokecherry, buffaloberry, and twinberry, are food for mammals and birds. Berries may be on the upswing due to the reintroduction of wolves. Since the return of wolves to the ecosystem, berry bushes have been rebounding because the wolves keep elk populations in check, reducing herd sizes that used to decimate berry crops. Berries have now become a bigger part of the grizzly bear diet. Find lowland berries in late July, but mid-August-early September is known as huck season.

ANIMALS

The Greater Yellowstone Ecosystem houses one of the greatest concentrations of mammals in the Lower 48 with 67 species. In addition, the region harbors 300 species of birds, 16 species of fish, four species of amphibians, and five species of reptiles.

Megafauna

Megafauna, the big animals everyone wants to see, populate the Greater Yellowstone Ecosystem. **Black bears** and **grizzly bears** top the list along with members of the dog and cat families. Three elusive members of the cat family, **mountain lions, bobcats,** and **Canada lynx,** are quiet nocturnal hunters. With keen eyesight and hearing, they may see you while you can't see them. For mountain lions, elk calves top the menu, while lynx favor snowshoe hares. Both cat populations rise and fall with their prey populations. At the top of the dog family is the **gray wolf,** with packs that inhabit fairly large ranges of 100-300 square miles. In Yellowstone, the wolf diet is 92 percent elk and 8 percent bison, deer, and pronghorn. Each wolf eats about 22 elk per year, relying on carnassial teeth designed for tearing meat and chomping through bones. Wolf pups, born in April, weigh one pound and are blind. **Coyotes** are the biggest predator of wolf pups, but have lessened in numbers as wolf numbers rebounded. **Fox** populations also bounced back. More reclusive large carnivores are **wolverines** and **badgers.**

Ungulates crowd both national parks and spill outside their boundaries. **Bison** are the biggest, weighing in at 2,000 pounds for males and 1,000 pounds for females. **Elk** produce the largest antlers of the ungulates and provide a bigger food source than bison for wolves. Since wolf reintroduction reduced elk populations, aspens, willows, and cottonwoods have bounced back, bringing the return of beaver and moose. With a diet that is 60 percent water and 40 percent plants, **moose** feed mostly on willows around streambeds and lakes. Bighorn sheep opt to winter in lower elevations of the northern valleys of the Gardner,

Lamar, and Yellowstone Rivers. November-April, they feed on dry grasses exposed in the thin snowpack of windblown slopes. Breeding typically happens in November-December. **Mule** and **white-tailed deer** live throughout the parks in forests, while **mountain goats** and **bighorn sheep** cling to higher rocky slopes that have cliffs for protection. One herd of about 200 **pronghorn** populates the northern section of Yellowstone. As the second-fastest animal in the world, pronghorn can run 35 mph for 5-6 miles.

BEARS

Two bear species roam the Greater Yellowstone Ecosystem: the black bear and the grizzly bear. Omnivores and opportunistic feeders, bears will eat anything. Spending most of their waking time eating to gain 100-150 pounds before winter, bears feed on a protein-heavy diet of army cutworm moths, whitebark pine nuts, ungulates, and cutthroat trout. These foods supply the greatest nutrition for the least foraging effort. They also rely on seasonal supplemental foods: bulbs, roots, berries, shoots, flowers, ants, insects, carrion, and ground squirrels. Due to the waning of two of their traditional foods, whitebark pine seeds and cutthroat trout, bears are shifting toward meat from elk, bison, moose, and carrion. Contrary to popular opinion, humans are not on their menu of favorite foods.

Because bears learn fast, they adapt quickly to new food sources, be it a pack dropped by the side of the trail or dog food left out in a campground. For this reason, strict rules for handling food and garbage are enforced inside and outside the parks. All garbage cans and dumpsters are bear resistant. Bears that eat human foods and garbage often become more aggressive in repeating the behavior. As a result, bear managers are forced to move them to new habitat or, worse—destroy them.

Because grizzly and black bears are integral to the ecosystem, the National Park Service employs several bear rangers whose jobs entail monitoring bear and deterring them from trouble. To discourage bruins from lingering

Wildlife Facts

BISON

How can a 2,000-pound bison walk through deep snow? Herds walk in winter on groomed roads to avoid sinking in deep snow, and when they do travel in deep snow, they walk single file, allowing the bison in front to break trail. Although they seem docile, they can run up to 40 mph (more than three times faster than humans) and jump six-foot fences. Identify females by narrower heads and thinner curved horns that are often asymmetrical.

Bison cluster in smaller herds in winter, with about 20 members as opposed to 200 or more in summer. Because they feed mostly on grasses, geyser basins provide a refuge, as heat from geothermal activity keeps the snow thin or melted with patches of dry grasses. Bison also migrate in winter to lower elevations outside the park, where food is more readily attainable. Herds winter in the Lamar, Hayden, Firehole River, and Pelican Valleys.

GRIZZLY BEARS

Grizzly bears have a unique mechanism called delayed implantation. After mating in spring, the female's uterus hangs onto the fertilized eggs rather than letting them implant. The eggs wait until her body is ready in November. If she has not gained enough fat to survive feeding the cubs through winter, no implantation will occur. Grizzlies usually have 1-3 cubs; the number of eggs that implant correlates to the mother's health.

In winter, bears opt for denning. After bulking up on calories during hyperphasia in fall, grizzly bears dig dens on the north sides of slopes where deeper accumulating snows will insulate them from winter temperatures dropping below zero. While respiration, heart rate, and body temperature drop during winter sleep, bears do not eat, drink, urinate, or defecate. But females give birth while denning.

WOLVES

Wolf rules are strict. Packs of 5-10 animals form hierarchies led by the alpha male and female, the only breeders. After the alpha female gives birth to the pups, the other adults in the pack aid in caring for the young. They bring the pups pre-chewed food, which they regurgitate from their stomachs. Wolves are active year-round, with mating usually occurring in February. Ninety percent of their winter diet consists of elk—especially the young, elderly, and injured. Because of their dependence on elk, they often follow the herds.

WOLVERINES

Eating machines in the wild, wolverines have the Latin name *Gulo gulo*. Literally, it translates as "glutton, glutton," reinforcing their reputation for voracious appetites. They prey upon much larger animals such as elk. With powerful jaws and teeth, they can chomp right through bones. They eat everything, including teeth and bones.

ELK

What's all the bugling about? The park's most numerous large mammal puts on a stately show— during fall when elk breed, bulls bugle to attract cows into their harems. A bugle starts with a bellow that rises into a squeal and finishes with grunts. The bugle also shows the bull's prowess to other bulls, a statement that he's ready to fight for the harem and a warning for other bulls to steer clear.

Greater Yellowstone's nine elk herds migrate to lower elevations for winter and limit movement to preserve energy. Some migrate south to the National Elk Refuge in Jackson Hole where they are fed during winter. Smaller herds hang along the Madison and Firehole Rivers or head into Gardiner, Montana. Studies have also shown that elk are more at risk of transmitting brucellosis to cattle than bison.

near front-country campgrounds, bear teams uses hazing methods: loud noises, gunshots, pellet beanbags, and sometimes Karelian bear dogs. Nuisance bears are transplanted to remote park drainages or destroyed if their offenses warrant. "A fed bear is a dead bear," the truism goes. A bear that dabbles in human food often aggressively seeks more.

Bears are one of the least fertile mammals. Females must reach about seven years old to be fertile, and then they only give birth once every two or three years. Each birth usually results in 2-3 cubs born during winter's deep sleep.

Bears don't actually hibernate, as their respiration and pulse remain close to normal. Instead, they enter a deep sleep in which the body temperature drops slightly. Before crawling into their dens, they scarf down mountain ash berries, rough grasses, and twigs to form an anal plug, which inhibits eating, urinating, or defecating during winter. Bears emerge in the spring ravenously hungry, immediately heading out to rummage for snow-buried carcasses.

The pika is threatened by climate change.

Small Mammals

Members of the weasel family—fishers, pine martens, minks, and weasels—inhabit forests and waterways. The short-tailed weasel changes color in winter: Its fur becomes white, except for the small black tip of its tail. Snowshoe hares also change to white in winter, their large feet providing extra flotation on snow. In subalpine country, a chorus of eeks, screams, and squeaks bounce through rockfalls. The noisemakers are pikas, which look like tail-less mice, and the ubiquitous Columbian ground squirrel, recognized by its reddish tint. Looking like fat fur balls, yellow bellied marmots splay on rocks, sunning themselves. Scampering between high alpine rocks, golden-mantled ground squirrels look like oversized chipmunks with golden stripes.

Fish

Yellowstone and Grand Teton are home to 16 species of fish. Eleven are native, including mountain whitefish, arctic grayling, westslope cutthroat trout, and Yellowstone cutthroat trout. Nonnative rainbow, brook, brown, and lake trout were introduced to enhance sport fishing. Historically, about 40 percent of Yellowstone's rivers and lakes were barren of fish. Stocking programs converted many of those to fisheries with nonnative species. Those nonnative species now threaten native fish through predation, competition, and hybridization. In order to protect native fish, the park service has adopted stringent fishing guidelines.

Birds

The Greater Yellowstone Ecosystem has almost 300 species of birds: songbirds, waterfowl, shorebirds, and raptors. About 150 species nest in Yellowstone National Park. Two species of concern are the common loon and trumpeter swan. Yellowstone has about 28 loons, equating to 75 percent of the breeding and nesting loons in Wyoming. The trumpeter swan is more rare. In 2015,

Safety in Bear Country

Even though colors are used to name the bears, black and grizzly bears display a variety of hues. For instance, a reddish-black bear can give birth to three cubs of different colors: blond, black, and brown. Grizzlies, named for silvered hair, appear in all colors of the spectrum. Don't be fooled by color; look instead for body size and shape.

Grizzlies are bigger than black bears, standing on all fours at 3-4 feet tall and weighing in at 300-600 pounds. Black bears average 12-18 inches shorter on all fours. Adult females weigh around 140 pounds, while males bulk up to 220 pounds.

In profile, the grizzly has one notable feature: a hump on its shoulders. The solid muscle mass provides the grizzly's forelegs with power for digging and running. Black bears lack this hump. Their face profiles are also different. On the grizzly, look for a scooped or dished forehead-to-nose silhouette; the black bear's nose will appear straighter in line with its forehead. Note the ears: Grizzly ears look too small for their heads, while black bear ears seem big, standing straight up. Paw prints in mud reveal a difference in their claws and foot structure. Grizzly claws are four inches long with pads in a relatively straight line, while black bear claws are 1.5 inches long with pads arced across the top of the foot.

With a few precautions, you can eliminate bear scares. Although both bears have mediocre vision, they are fast runners. In three seconds, a grizzly bear can cover 180 feet.

- **Make noise.** To avoid surprising a bear, use your voice—sing loudly, hoot, or holler—and clap your hands. Bears tend to recognize human sounds as ones to avoid; they'll usually wander off if they hear people approaching. Make loud noise in thick brushy areas, around blind corners, near babbling streams, and against the wind.

- **Hike with other people.** Avoid hiking alone. Keep children near. Very few bear attacks happen to groups of four or more.

- **Avoid bear feeding areas.** If you stumble across an animal carcass, leave the area immediately and notify a ranger. Toward summer's end, be cautious around huckleberry patches.

- **Hike in broad daylight.** Avoid early morning, late evening, and night.

- **Never approach a bear.** Head swaying, teeth clacking, laid-back ears, a lowered head, and huffing or woofing are signs of agitation: Clear out slowly.

- **If you do surprise a bear, back away.** Contrary to all inclinations, do not run. Instead, back away slowly, talking quietly and turning sideways or bending your knees to appear smaller and nonthreatening. Avoid direct eye contact. Leave your pack on; it can protect you if the bear attacks.

- **Use pepper spray or play dead.** If you surprise a bear that attacks in defense, aim pepper spray at the bear's eyes. Protect yourself and your vulnerable parts by assuming a fetal position on the ground with your hands around the back of your neck. Play dead. Move again only when you are sure the bear has vacated the area.

- **If a bear stalks you as food, or attacks at night, fight back.** Bears rarely stalk humans as prey. If one does, use any means at hand, such as pepper spray, shouting, sticks, or rocks, to tell the bear you are not an easy food source. Try to escape up something, like a building or a tree.

- **Respect trail closures.** Trail and backcountry campsite closures are usually in heavy bear feeding areas. Staying out of these areas guarantees hikers a safer experience.

Two books with accurate information on bears include: Bill Schneider's *Bear Aware* and Stephen Herrero's *Bear Attacks: Their Causes and Avoidances*.

BACKGROUND
PLANTS AND ANIMALS

the park had 23 resident trumpeters, which includes two pairs of breeders. The swan is North America's largest bird, with a wingspan of eight feet.

Songbirds show up in spring, and the trees liven with their songs during breeding and nesting season. By August, the forests quiet as many begin migrating south. Mountain chickadees, gray jays, red-breasted nuthatches, and American dippers are year-round residents.

Waterfowl and shorebirds are common due to the big lakes, wetlands, and rivers. Visitors can see American pelicans, sandhill cranes, great blue herons, and a variety of ducks and geese.

Nineteen species of raptors nest in the Greater Yellowstone Ecosystem. These include golden eagles, bald eagles, osprey, peregrine falcons, and owls. The park service monitors nests, keeping tabs on 21 bald eagle nests in Yellowstone. Recoveries of bald eagles and peregrine falcons have removed them from the Endangered Species List.

Snakes

While several snake species inhabit the region, the prairie rattlesnake is the only venomous one. It is only found in the Black Canyon of the Yellowstone; most of Yellowstone and Grand Teton are too high and too cold for its survival.

History

NATIVE AMERICANS

Archaeological evidence in Yellowstone and Grand Teton National Parks shows that Native Americans appeared around 11,000 years ago after the Yellowstone Ice Cap melted. A few stone tools indicate their presence. One was an obsidian Clovis point. The obsidian matches the rock in Obsidian Cliff, which has an ancient quarry on top. Other points and projectiles were found around Yellowstone Lake in what was probably a summer camp.

Increased use of the Yellowstone area spiked about 3,000 years ago as many tribes found hospitable summer environments, wildlife for hunting, fish, and edible or usable vegetation. Some tribes used geothermal areas for ceremonies and medicine rites. Popular trade and travel routes brought multiple tribes through the area in the 1800s: Shoshone, Crow, Blackfeet, Flathead, and Nez Perce. The Bannock Trail, a route used by western tribes crossing the Rockies to hunt bison, traverses the northern part of the park.

The Sheep Eaters, or Tukudeka, members of the Shoshone, were assumed to be permanent residents of Yellowstone. They relied on bighorn sheep for survival. But their residential presence in the park may be myth. While conical timber lodges, wickiups, drive lines with sheep traps, and rustic structures are attributed to the Sheep Eaters, little evidence ties the constructions solely to this tribe. By the time Yellowstone became a national park, the Sheep Eaters had mysteriously disappeared.

Shortly after Yellowstone became a national park, it served as a temporary haven for the Nez Perce in 1877 on their flight toward Canada to escape the U.S. Army. The Nee-Me-Poo spent nearly two weeks in the park, bumping into a few visitors. The 1,170-mile Nez Perce National Historic Trail (http://www.nps.gov/nepe), which commemorates their flight, traverses the central part of Yellowstone.

TRAPPERS, EXPLORERS, AND HOMESTEADERS

In the late 1700s, European American fur trappers arrived in Yellowstone and Jackson Hole to trade with Native Americans and acquire beaver pelts. Shortly after, Lewis and Clark bypassed the Yellowstone area 50 miles to the north. On their return trip, one of their

Tipis are part of the the region's Native American culture.

the first scientific expedition with experts in botany, zoology, meteorology, ornithology, entomology, and mineralogy. Artists, a topographer, and a photographer came along to document the sites and terrain.

The Homestead Act of 1862 sent droves of settlers out West. But settlers avoided Jackson Hole with its sand and cobble soil, arid summers, and frigid winters. The first homesteaders who finally put down roots in 1884 struggled with farming and ranching.

CREATING THE FIRST NATIONAL PARK

The expeditions fueled fervor in the nation's capital, and explorers submitted a bill to preserve Yellowstone. Thomas Moran's paintings, William Henry Jackson's photographs, and Henry W. Elliot's sketches gave visual clarity to the written expedition reports. Even though Congressional legislation of the era supported westward expansion and resource exploitation, Congress agreed with the value of preservation, partially in the wake of preserving Yosemite as a California state park eight years earlier. In 1872, Yellowstone became the nation's, and the world's, first national park.

Legislating the creation of Yellowstone was one thing. But creating a park for people to visit was quite another. No park service existed to run Yellowstone, and the bill setting aside the land as a park included no government funding. No one really knew what a national park was, except that it was for people to enjoy rather than develop. No legislation protected its natural features and wildlife, and the park's first superintendent—who was unpaid—visited it only twice, the first time in 1872 with the second Hayden expedition. Several expeditions surveyed Yellowstone for science, mapping, and exploration, but the park floundered, unfunded and directionless.

Six years after the park's inception, Congress finally appropriated money to "protect, preserve, and improve" Yellowstone. The park's second superintendent, Philetus Norris, tackled the job. He built a few primitive roads

members departed the expedition to hook up with fur trappers. John Colter explored parts of Yellowstone including Yellowstone Lake in 1807-1808 and may have visited Jackson Hole and seen the Tetons. With only word of mouth, his stories amazed people but left little concrete documentation of his travels. Only the unverified Colter Stone bears his name and the 1808 date.

As the decline of beavers shifted fur trapping on to other pursuits, a small unofficial expedition in 1869 succeeded in documenting the Tower Fall, Mud Volcano, West Thumb, Shoshone Lake, and Firehole River geyser basins. The expedition's reports sparked the first official organized explorations. The 1870 Washburn-Langford-Doane expedition surveyed some of the same places as the previous exploration, climbed peaks, toured down the Grand Canyon of the Yellowstone, and tried to measure some of the natural features. This expedition named Old Faithful. A year later, the Hayden expedition ran concurrent with a U.S. Army Corps of Engineers survey. It served as

The World's First National Park

On March 1, 1872, the U.S. Congress made Yellowstone the first national park in the country. The park marked the first time that the federal government set aside land for the "pleasure of the people." Parkhood for Yellowstone came even before statehood for Montana and Wyoming. In addition to being the first national park in the United States, Yellowstone was also the first national park in the world.

On the tail of the Lewis and Clark expedition in 1806, exploration of the Northern Rockies put Yellowstone country on the map. Although the first descriptions of huge bubbling mud cauldrons and hot water shooting into the sky were dismissed as fantasy, multiple expeditions began to document the landscape.

While the concept of a national park got its foothold when Yosemite was deeded to the State of California to preserve for people to enjoy, Yellowstone benefitted from champions of preservation such as John Muir and George Bird Grinnell, who laid the groundwork. When the government deployed Ferdinand Hayden in 1871 with a cadre of artists and photographers to document Yellowstone, he filed a recommendation to make the area a national park, an idea suggested to him by Northern Pacific Railway lobbyist A. B. Nettleton, who saw the benefit to train ridership.

Hayden's report to Congress included details of Yellowstone's uniqueness, but also pointed out that the land was unsuitable for farming or mining, rendering it useless for development. With Hayden's recommendations also came a warning: to avoid the fate of Niagara Falls, a national treasure surrounded by private development.

At inception, Yellowstone had no funding, no staff, and no services. Refinement of the national park concept took several more decades. In the meantime, the U.S. Cavalry oversaw the park from Fort Yellowstone, today known as Mammoth. Finally, in 1916, the federal government created the National Park Service to operate the parks, a concept first enacted by Canada.

When Yellowstone first became a national park, 300 people visited during its first year, challenged with sightseeing on horseback and camping. A decade later when trains delivered visitors to Gardiner, that number climbed to 5,000. Today, Yellowstone sees more than four million annual visitors.

As the first national park, Yellowstone paved the way for 58 other U.S. national parks. Worldwide, almost 100 countries have set aside more than 6,000 national parks as places for protection of wildlife, landscapes, and resources plus the enjoyment of people.

and designed the Grand Loop Road. For headquarters, he constructed a rudimentary station at Mammoth Hot Springs. He hired the park's first gamekeeper to battle poachers. But political machinations swapped in a series of useless superintendents, and in its second decade, Yellowstone ran wild. Vandals destroyed natural features, poachers slaughtered wildlife, loggers harvested timber, squatters threw up shelters and camps for tourists, and hot springs facilities were erected as laundries and baths.

When Yellowstone was created, it looked like a big square on the map with no accommodation for topographical features. The northwest boundary was expanded in 1929 to include petrified trees, and the east boundary was reconfigured to match watersheds in 1932.

U.S. ARMY AND BISON

The public loved the idea of Yellowstone, but Congress trashed annual funding in 1886 due to ineffective management of the park. The solution to Yellowstone's management was the U.S. Army, already operating out of several forts in the territories of Montana, Idaho, and Wyoming. That year, the army took up residence in the park to enforce regulations. In 1891, Fort Yellowstone was erected at Mammoth Hot Springs, including the headquarters, officers' quarters, a guardhouse, and barracks. Many of the buildings were constructed of sandstone from a quarry located between Mammoth Campground and the Gardner River.

Outside the park, bison slaughters fed the booming fur and meat business. The federal government even encouraged them, especially as a means to subdue Native American tribes that relied on bison for food and to force them to move onto reservations. Inside Yellowstone, poachers likewise jeopardized the survival of bison. With eviction from the park as the maximum punishment, the army had no strong clout. After a journalistic outcry at one bison slaughter in Pelican Valley, Congress passed the National Park Protection Act in 1894 to protect birds, animals, and natural features in Yellowstone. Guilty violators faced fines and jail.

By 1910, the army stationed 324 soldiers at Fort Yellowstone. Soldiers were sent out on details to various outposts throughout the park. The army managed Yellowstone until 1918, when the two-year-old National Park Service took over.

EARLY VISITORS

When Yellowstone first opened as a national park with no services, roads, or lodging, only the hearty visited. To reach the park required riding a stagecoach. At the park, some visitors hired unsanctioned guides to sightsee via long hours on horseback and overnighting in canvas tents. Yellowstone's first year as a park logged 300 visitors.

In the park's fifth year, the Nez Perce came through en route to Canada while fleeing from the U.S. Army. In their two weeks in the park, they met up with 25 visitors and ended up killing two. Stories of wild Indians kept some would-be visitors away. Philetus Norris, the park's second superintendent, countered with fabricated stories that the Native Americans stayed away in fear of the geysers.

In the early 1880s, the Northern Pacific Railway added a train station at Livingston, Montana, 52 miles north of the park

boundary. A rail spur to Gardiner opened in 1883, increasing visitation to 5,000. By 1908, when park visitation pushed toward 20,000 annual visitors, the Union Pacific Railroad wanted in on the action, so the company built a line to West Yellowstone.

BUILDING LODGES

Immediately following the park's establishment, requests poured in from entrepreneurs who wanted to build hotels. A few rustic lodging facilities were constructed in the park's first decade, mostly on temporary 10-year leases. But the pressure to add more lodging came from the railroads, which needed facilities for their passengers. Nine small hotels were built in the early 1890s at Lower Geyser Basin, Norris, and Canyon. The Fountain Hotel introduced feeding bears for guest entertainment, a practice that lasted at garbage dumps in the park until 1970.

The Northern Pacific Railway bankrolled the biggest hotel venture. In 1891, the Lake Yellowstone Hotel opened on the shore of Yellowstone Lake. While the hotel boasted scenery and elegance, its boxy architecture was bland. Within 12 years, Robert Reamer, the architect of Old Faithful Inn, gave the hotel old colonial character with Ionic columns, false balconies, and extended rooflines.

Reamer's Old Faithful Inn, built in 1903-1904, has the rustic log-and-wood appearance that defines vintage parkitecture. The foundation is built from rhyolite from the caldera, and lodgepoles harvested nearby were used for the log walls. Posts, rails, and other details were crafted from knobby wood. The inn's shingles were painted with a red mineral thought to reduce flammability. Electric lights and steam heat made it modern, and elegance came from dining to the music of a string quartet. Later renovations added the east and west wings.

In 1897, the town site of Jackson was laid out around the town square, its central location selected for ease of access from ranches at all ends of Jackson Hole. By the early 1900s, homesteaders fed up with the toil required for farming such poor soil and managing cattle through long winters shifted to tourism, aiming to cash in on the desire of wealthy easterners to ride horses and experience the West. By 1920, dude ranches became vogue, piggybacking off the allure of Yellowstone National Park and Teton grandeur.

HISTORIC YELLOW VEHICLES

With the advent of the automobile, America grew infatuated with road travel, but the railroad and park transportation company dug in hard to maintain inside-park travel by horse-drawn surreys and painted yellow stagecoaches. When the political pressure boiled, Yellowstone admitted its first automobiles in 1915, with a Ford Model T as the first one, followed by 50 cars that summer. Drivers paid an exorbitant entrance fee of $5-10 ($116-232 in today's dollars) to take on the challenge of rough dirt roads at a maximum speed of 20 mph. Within two years, the park banned horse-drawn vehicles.

For summer 1917, the Yellowstone Park Transportation Company drove 116 snazzy new seven-passenger touring cars and 11-passenger sedans for toting affluent visitors around the sights. White Motor Company had leapt into the national park business of creating touring vehicles designed specifically for sightseeing. In addition to Yellowstone, their vehicles became iconic fleets in Glacier, Zion, and other national parks. Canvas tops allowed visitors to stand up to see wildlife and grab grander views. The fleet of 11-passenger touring sedans grew to more than 300 by the mid-1920s.

The touring sedans were replaced over the decades by updated White Motor Company models, all painted yellow and some holding 13 passengers. As private auto traffic increased in the wake of World War II, only 124 vehicles remained in service. The company sold off the vehicles in the 1950s. In 2007, Xanterra bought eight of the original White Motor Company Model 706 rigs, revamping them to modern safety standards for guided summer sightseeing tours of Yellowstone.

GRAND TETON NATIONAL PARK

As Jackson Hole attracted development in the early 1900s, the Teton Mountains became a backdrop for enterprises such as dancehalls, billboards, and racetracks thrown up in open fields. That horrified some longtime locals, who favored conservation and wilderness. Talk supported an extension of Yellowstone or a new park. In the mid-1920s, Yellowstone superintendent Horace Albright brought John D. Rockefeller to Jackson Hole. The scenery of the Tetons captured Rockefeller, who purchased 35,000 acres of land tracts under his Snake River Land Company with the aim of donating the land to the national park. Some locals, however, feared the loss of tax revenue if those valley land tracts became part of a national park. The battle over conservation landed in a Congressional hearing.

The process of making Grand Teton National Park sprawled across several decades. In 1929, Congress created Grand Teton National Park, but it consisted only of the mountains of the Teton Range and several moraine lakes along the base. In its first year, 51,500 people visited the park. In the 1940s, the federal government gained two large pieces of acreage in Jackson Hole: Franklin Delano Roosevelt converted the federal land in the valley into Jackson Hole National Monument, and John D. Rockefeller donated his land to the national park. In 1950, Congress combined the three into Grand Teton National Park. Later, Rockefeller's name was put on his donated land to honor his philanthropy. Today, the John D. Rockefeller, Jr. Memorial Parkway sits between Yellowstone and Grand Teton National Parks.

TOURISM TODAY

Following World War II, tourism skyrocketed. But travel patterns had changed. Train travel and the desire for elegant hotels waned in favor of private cars and camping, cabins, or moderate motels. In 1948, Yellowstone surpassed one million annual visitors; so did Grand Teton six years later. With visitation escalating every year, the parks needed more facilities. The National Park Service's Mission 66 program provided the answer. The 10-year program was designed to get park facilities nationwide up to snuff by the 50th anniversary of the park service in 1966.

In Yellowstone, Mission 66 intended to revamp older park developments and, in some cases, move them away from sensitive geothermal zones. The old Canyon Hotel was razed and replaced by Canyon Village. Grant Village was built two miles south of West Thumb to protect the geyser basin, which had encroaching development and a proposal for accommodations to house 2,500 visitors. Firehole Village was intended to replace Old Faithful Inn and Old Faithful Lodge, but that village project never materialized. In Grand Teton, Mission 66 built Jackson Lake Lodge and Colter Bay Visitor Center in the mid-1950s. John D. Rockefeller financially supported construction of the lodge and Colter Bay Cabins.

New facilities came just in time. By the 1960s, both parks hit the two million mark for annual visitation. The popularity of Yellowstone and Grand Teton continues to grow. Since 2015, both parks have continued to break annual records for attendance, each topping four million visitors.

WINTER TOURISM

Official organized winter tourism launched in Yellowstone in 1949 when snowplanes delivered passengers to the park's interior. By 1955, snowcoach trips started, carrying 500 people in winter to see Old Faithful. But overnight winter lodging did not open until 1971. Following the 1988 fires, the Snow Lodge was constructed at Old Faithful especially to accommodate winter visitors. Today, more than 30,000 people stay overnight in winter inside the park either at Old Faithful Snow Lodge or Mammoth Hot Springs Hotel. In winter, 5,000-6,000 visitors per month pass through the Roosevelt Arch, Yellowstone's North Entrance gate at Gardiner. The road from Gardiner to Mammoth and Cooke City is open year-round for private vehicles.

In Jackson Hole, the Snow King Ski Area launched on a hill cleared by a forest fire adjacent to the town of Jackson. Skiers hiked the hill to ski down until a cable tow powered by an old Ford tractor engine was installed in 1939. It was Wyoming's first ski lift. In the 1960s, Jackson Hole and Grand Targhee opened for skiing on opposite sides of the Teton Mountains, where some years they have received more than 500 inches of snowfall. Today, they are icons in the ski industry.

LANDMARKS AND DESIGNATIONS
National Historic Landmarks
Yellowstone has eight National Historic Landmarks. They are Old Faithful Inn, Fort Yellowstone District, Northeast Entrance Station, Obsidian Cliff, Lake Yellowstone Hotel, and the museums at Fishing Bridge, Madison, and Norris. Grand Teton National Park has two National Historic Landmarks: the Murie Ranch Historic District and Jackson Lake Lodge.

National Register of Historic Places
The National Register of Historic Places protects many sites in Yellowstone and Grand Teton. Walking tours are available in larger historic locations.

In Yellowstone, some of the 25 sites include districts: Mammoth Hot Springs, Old Faithful, and North Entrance Road including Roosevelt Arch, Roosevelt Lodge, and Lake Fish Hatchery. As districts they contain multiple buildings or structures that warrant preservation, and five of them influenced rustic park architecture. Other places on the national register include the Lake Hotel, Lamar Buffalo Ranch, Obsidian Cliff interpretive kiosk, Queen's Laundry Bathhouse, and Mammoth Post Office. Yellowstone has more than 900 historic buildings.

Grand Teton National Park has 36 sites listed on the National Register of Historic Places. Some are districts with many buildings such as Mormon Row, Murie Ranch, Menor's Ferry, Jenny Lake Ranger Station, and several ranch areas. Other sites are individual cabins, barns, and lodges.

Wilderness Designations

Since the creation of the Wilderness Act in 1964, huge swaths of the 20 million acres of the Greater Yellowstone Ecosystem have become part of the wilderness system. Two million of Yellowstone's 2.2 million acres are managed as wilderness. Much of the mountainous terrain in Grand Teton National Park has been recommended as wilderness. Despite lacking official designation, it is managed as de facto wilderness.

The Greater Yellowstone Ecosystem also contains multiple designated wilderness areas in the national forests surrounding and bordering the parks. These wilderness areas include Absaroka-Beartooth, North Absaroka, Lee Metcalf, Washakie, Teton, Jedediah Smith, and Gros Ventre. The Wind River Mountains, a southeast spur of the ecosystem, contain the Bridger, Fitzpatrick, and Popo Agie Wilderness Areas. These wilderness areas are key to the survival of many species, including wolves and grizzly bears.

Wild and Scenic River Designations

In 2009, Congress added the Snake River Headwaters to its list of federally recognized Wild and Scenic rivers. The designated river distance totals 387.5 miles, but that includes multiple tributaries. More than half is designated as wild with the remaining miles as scenic or recreational. Snake River Headwaters encompasses waterways in Yellowstone and Grand Teton National Parks, John D. Rockefeller, Jr. Memorial Parkway, the National Elk Refuge, and Bridger-Teton National Forest. The Wild and Scenic designation covers the Lewis River, the Snake River above and below Jackson Lake, and multiple tributaries including Granite Creek, Pacific Creek, Buffalo Creek, and the Gros Ventre River.

Yellowstone Biosphere Reserve

In 1976, Yellowstone was designated as a UNESCO Biosphere Reserve. Because it was created as the first national park in the world, it was one of the first places chosen to be a Biosphere Reserve. It gained the recognition due to its hydrothermal features, diversity of plant communities, wildlife, and outstanding opportunities for research on geology, fire ecology, vegetation, mammals, and fisheries.

Yellowstone World Heritage Site

In 1988, UNESCO also named Yellowstone as a World Heritage Site because it contains the world's largest concentration of geysers and is one of the few large intact northern temperate ecosystems. Many of the park's features contributed to its status as a World Heritage Site: scenery, evidence of natural history in fossils and geothermal activity, wild flora, and wildlife.

Local Culture

INDIGENOUS CULTURE

Located between Native American cultures from the Great Basin, Great Plains, and Plateau Indians, Yellowstone has 26 associated tribes with historical connections to the land. Since Yellowstone began its ethnographic program in 2000, the park service and the sovereign Native American nations have consulted together on mutual issues. Two concerns for Native Americans are the bison that leave the park and wickiup preservation. Four tribes have treaty rights to hunt Yellowstone bison. Collaborative work developed interpretation on the Yellowstone portion of the Nez Perce National Historic Trail, and the park service inventories culturally important and sacred sites. The Heritage and Research Center in Gardiner houses the immense Yellowstone collection of cultural and historical artifacts, including Native American items.

Three of the tribes that hunted, camped, fished, and held ceremonies in Yellowstone and Grand Teton National Parks have reservations nearby. None of the Shoshone, Crow, or Cheyenne reservations share boundaries with the national parks, but they are close enough for frequent visits. Some members still visit for religious, ceremonial, or medicinal purposes, and each celebrates their culture every summer with a powwow and rodeo.

Shoshone

East of Grand Teton National Park sits the 2.2-million-acre Wind River Reservation, home to the Eastern Shoshone (http://eastern-shoshone.org), who have established roots in the Wind River Mountains, and the Northern Arapaho (www.northernarapahoe.com), who were moved to the reservation when a treaty left them landless. One of the largest powwows in the region, Eastern Shoshone Indian Days, takes place the last week of June. The Arapaho celebrate a powwow in late August

or early September. Smaller powwows happen weekly in summer. The powwow schedule is available online (http://windriver.org). The grave and a memorial for Sacagawea, the guide for the Lewis and Clark Corps of Discovery expedition, are located on the reservation.

Crow

The Crow Nation (www.crow-nsn.gov) concentrates on the 2.3-million-acre reservation northeast of Yellowstone in Montana. The reservation is home to Little Bighorn Battlefield National Monument, which commemorates the Native American victory over Custer and the 7th Cavalry. The Crow Fair Powwow and Rodeo takes place during the third week of August to celebrate the heritage of the Apsáalooke, or "Children of the Large-Beaked Bird."

Cheyenne

To Yellowstone's northeast, a 444,000-acre reservation sits adjacent to the Crow Reservation in Montana. It is home to the Northern Cheyenne Nation (www.cheyennenation.com), two merged tribes known as the Tsitsistas and the Só'taeo'o. The Northern Cheyenne Powwow and Rodeo happens over Memorial Day weekend.

MODERN COWBOYS

Cowboy life in Montana, Wyoming, and Idaho has strong roots. Wyoming snagged the "Cowboy State" moniker for its 1890 statehood, and William "Buffalo Bill" Cody took his Wild West show on the road in the late 1800s to celebrate the lifestyle. But modern cowboy life is more than pulling on a pair of jeans, chaps, boots, hat, bandanna, and deerskin gloves. Being a real cowboy is physically demanding. It requires riding long hours in the saddle, wrangling cows, repairing fences, bucking wood, slinging hay bales, and putting up with arbitrary weather.

While many working ranches still operate in Jackson Hole, guest ranches have continued to meet the tourism desire to play cowboy for a week. As the popularity of Jackson Hole grew as a vacation paradise, developers began to buy up ranch lands for millionaire second and third homes. It is one of the fastest-growing rural areas in the U.S. Today, cowboys and cowgirls can no longer afford to buy homes in Jackson Hole, where the average price tops $1 million.

Yet the cowboy way of life persists, in part thanks to tourism. The world's longest-running shoot-out happens six nights a week in summer in Jackson. It keeps alive the lawless West in a theatrical performance, and rodeos give local cowboys and cowgirls a chance to show off their skills in summer. The Million Dollar Cowboy Bar even teaches country-western dancing to keep traditions alive.

Stirrups are still the trappings of a modern cowboy.

Essentials

Getting There 390
Getting Around............... 398
Recreation.................... 402

Visas and Officialdom.......... 410
Travel Tips..................... 410
Health and Safety............. 413

Getting There

SUGGESTED DRIVING ROUTES

Getting to Yellowstone and Grand Teton requires navigating wild country where gas stations are few and far between; sometimes 75 miles apart. Schedule gas fill-ups at major towns. Winter blizzards and icy roads can turn a two-hour drive into a four-hour nightmare. All times given below are for dry roads in summer. To get current road conditions, call 511 or consult state highway agency websites: **Idaho** (http://lb.511.idaho.gov/idlb), **Montana** (www.mdt.mt.gov/travinfo), and **Wyoming** (www.wyoroad.info). All driving routes are open year-round except where winter closures are mentioned.

I-90 to North and West Entrances

Interstate 90 crosses east-west through Montana north of Yellowstone. From the freeway between Billings and Butte, multiple routes drop south to reach the park's West, North, and Northeast Entrances.

FROM BOZEMAN, MONTANA

To reach **West Yellowstone,** drivers have two options: via the Madison River or Gallatin River, both north-south roads with the Madison Range separating them. Drivers of large RVs prefer Madison over Gallatin due to the straighter roadway and fewer vehicles. Both routes take longer in snow.

For the **Madison Valley** route (117 miles, 2.25 hours), leave I-90 at Exit 274 west of Three Forks between Butte and Bozeman. Head south on U.S. Highway 287. The two-lane route goes through several blink-and-you-miss-it towns and Ennis, a fishing mecca with multiple fly-fishing outfitters, guide

services, fly-fishing schools, and gear shops. Past Ennis, the highway parallels the Madison River, a headwater tributary of the Missouri River. Follow the river eastward up a canyon to Quake Lake, the site of the 1959 earthquake that caused a landslide. **Earthquake Lake Visitor Center** (206/682-7620, http://fs.usda.gov/main/custergallatin, 10am-6pm daily late May-Sept., free) is worth the stop. After passing Hebgen Lake, turn south onto U.S. Highway 191 to reach West Yellowstone. Once at West Yellowstone, U.S. Highway 191 becomes Canyon Street; follow it seven blocks to Yellowstone Avenue and turn left to reach the West Entrance.

The **Gallatin Valley** route (90 miles, two hours) clogs with more traffic as the most heavily traveled road to Yellowstone. From I-90 at Belgrade, take Exit 298 and drive south on Highway 85 (Jackrabbit Ln., Gallatin Rd.) through strip malls toward Gallatin Gateway. En route, U.S. Highway 191 from Bozeman joins the road. From then on, the road is U.S. Highway 191, squeezing between the Madison and Gallatin Ranges. Between Gallatin Gateway and Big Sky, locals speed along the narrow two-lane curves. After passing Big Sky and historic ranches, the road enters Yellowstone's northwest corner, which has no entrance station. After exiting the park, the highway drops straight south into West Yellowstone.

To reach Yellowstone's North Entrance at Gardiner, use **Paradise Valley** (53 miles, one hour) from Livingston, east of Bozeman. From I-90, take Exit 333 to head south on U.S. Highway 89. The two-lane highway follows the Yellowstone River upstream through bucolic valley ranch lands tucked between the Gallatin and Absaroka Ranges. Watch

---

Previous: hiking in Grand Teton; boardwalk around Yellowstone's hydrothermals.

out for pronghorn, bighorn sheep, and elk that frequently cross the road, especially in winter. About 20 miles south of Livingston, **Chico Hot Springs** (163 Chico Rd., Pray, MT, 406/333-4933, www.chicohotsprings.com, 8am-11pm daily year-round, $8 adults, $4 seniors and kids age 3-6) has two outdoor hot pools for soaking, as well as showers, changing rooms, a restaurant, saloon, lodge rooms, and cabins. Upon reaching Gardiner, the highway becomes the main road through town, curving right onto the bridge over the Yellowstone River. At the T intersection, turn right. Smaller vehicles can curve left around a 180-degree turn to drive through the narrow Roosevelt Arch, while oversized rigs can take the RV-friendly shortcut to reach the North Entrance Station.

FROM BILLINGS, MONTANA

The most scenic approach to Yellowstone is the **Beartooth Highway** (http://beartooth-highway.com, late May-mid-Oct., weather depending, 111 miles, 3 hours without stops) to the **Northeast Entrance.** At Laurel west of Billings, cut off I-90 at Exit 434 going south onto U.S. Highway 212. Drive 43 miles south to Red Lodge. If you are coming on I-90 from the west, leave the freeway in Columbus (Exit 408) to take Highway 78 instead to Red Lodge. Gas up in Red Lodge. Stay on U.S. Highway 212 through town, which becomes the 68-mile Beartooth Highway (All-American Highway). The climbing begins as the road gains elevation along Rock Creek. As the canyon opens up into a huge glacier-carved valley, the switchbacks begin. The highway climbs via switchbacks and curves to 10,977 feet at Beartooth Pass. Sightseeing stops and weather will add time. If snow-storms hit, which can be common in June or fall, the road may close until plowed. Driving in the morning will reduce the glare from the sun in your eyes as you cross the Beartooth Plateau. This route has multiple campgrounds en route, making it popular with RVers and tent campers.

I-15 to West and South Entrances

In Idaho, I-15 runs north-south along the west side of Yellowstone, Grand Teton, and Jackson Hole. This is the route to use when coming from Boise, Pocatello, Idaho Falls, and Salt Lake City. On I-15 in Idaho Falls is where the choices begin.

FROM IDAHO FALLS, IDAHO

To head to **West Yellowstone,** the most direct route to Yellowstone National Park, take the **Targhee Pass Highway** (80 miles, 1.75 hours). From I-15, use Exit 119 onto U.S. Highway 20. Go through Rexburg to head north, climbing on the two-lane road into the **Island Park** caldera and then pass Henry's Lake, both with many places to camp. After Henry's Lake, the route tops the Continental Divide at 7,105-foot Targhee Pass to cross into Montana. The highway ends in West Yellowstone where it becomes Firehole Avenue. Turn right onto Canyon Street and left onto Yellowstone Avenue to reach the West Entrance Station.

As an alternative from Ashton on U.S. Highway 20, fans of going remote on dirt roads can sneak in to Cave Falls, Bechler Trailhead, and the Bechler River Ranger Station in Yellowstone. Turn off U.S. Highway 20 onto the Mesa Falls Scenic Byway (Hwy. 47) for six miles, passing through Ashton and Marysville, then turn right onto Marysville Road, which becomes the dirt Cave Falls Road (Forest Rd. 5820). Follow that to its terminus at Cave Falls or its junction for the Bechler River.

To head to **Jackson Hole** and **Grand Teton National Park,** go via Teton Pass or Alpine-Hoback. The latter, often a preferred route for large RVs, avoids climbing the steep pass. They both start on the same route from Idaho Falls. From I-15, take Exit 115 to head east on U.S. Highway 26 through the Swan Valley. At Swan Valley, make your choice. The shorter **Teton Pass** (87 miles, 1.75 hours) connects Teton Valley with Jackson

Island Park

On U.S. Highway 20 from **Ashton, Idaho,** drivers climb the southern rim to drop inside the Island Park caldera en route to **West Yellowstone.** Sandwiched between the Craters of the Moon lava flows and the Yellowstone supervolcano, Island Park erupted 2.1 million years ago and the resulting 58-mile by 40-mile caldera sits partly inside Yellowstone. The smaller Henry's Fork caldera formed inside the Island Park caldera 1.3 million years ago, sharing a western rim. The residual heat produces warm springs that make for a rich habitat for wildlife and aquatic animals in Caribou-Targhee National Forest (208/558-7301, www.fs.usda.gov/ctnf).

- Highlights include roaring **Mesa Falls,** a 300-foot-wide drop of 114 feet, and **Big Springs,** an idyllic natural pool that stays 52°F year-round and provides wildlife habitat.

- The historic **Mesa Falls Visitor Center** (9:30am-5:30pm daily summer, $5/vehicle) has exhibits on history, geology, plants, and wildlife.

- Float the Warm River on a tube at **Warm River Campground** (nine miles north of Ashton on Warm River Road off the Mesa Falls Scenic Byway) or wet a line fly-fishing on the Henry's Fork in **Harriman State Park** (3489 Green Canyon Rd., Island Park, 208/558-7368, http://parksandrecreation.idaho.gov, year-round, $5/vehicle).

- Stay at one of 11 **campgrounds** (877/444-6777, www.recreation.gov, late May-Sept., $13-30 first vehicle, $7-8 second vehicle). Several campgrounds have electrical hookups and accept reservations.

Hole, but on a steep 10-percent-grade climb and descent. From Swan Valley, turn north onto Highway 31 to cross over the Big Hole Mountains into Victor, where a right turn puts you on the Teton Pass Highway (Hwy. 33) over the Teton Mountains into Jackson Hole. Use lower gears when descending Teton Pass and check road conditions before you go.

For **Alpine-Hoback** (109 miles, two hours), stay on U.S. Highway 26 through Swan Valley, passing Palisades Reservoir to reach Alpine Junction. Turn left onto U.S. Highway 26/89 through the Grand Canyon of the Snake River to Hoback Junction to continue north on U.S. Highway 26/89/189/191, paralleling the Snake River to reach Jackson.

VIA ASHTON-FLAGG RANCH ROAD

From Ashton on U.S. Highway 20, adventurous drivers with high-clearance vehicles can enter both parks via the **Ashton-Flagg Ranch Road** (a.k.a. Grassy Lake Road, 43 miles, 3-4 hours, snow-free June-Oct.), a narrow, rough cobble road through Caribou-Targhee National Forest in Wyoming with primitive campsites and solitude. Bumps, potholes, and washboards reduce speeds to 15-20 mph. It's not for large RVs or big trailers, but small RVs can handle the road most of the time. Drivers must be comfortable meeting oncoming vehicles in narrow stretches and backing up. Before driving, get current conditions from the **Ashton-Island Park Ranger District** (46 S. Hwy. 20, Ashton, ID, 208/652-7442, www.fs.usda.gov/ctnf). From Ashton, turn right onto the Mesa Falls Scenic Byway (Hwy. 47) and turn right after seven blocks onto Highway 32. Drive one mile and turn left onto the Ashton-Flagg Ranch Road. After 12 miles of pavement, the fun begins. The route ends in John D. Rockefeller, Jr. Memorial Parkway at the intersection with U.S. Highway 89/191/287. Turn left to Yellowstone's South Entrance or right for Grand Teton National Park.

FROM SALT LAKE CITY, UTAH

From **Salt Lake City** (288 miles, five hours), the fastest route heads north on I-15 to exit at

Brigham City. Take U.S. Highway 89 north to connect with the Alpine-Hoback route at Alpine Junction to reach Jackson, Wyoming.

I-25 and I-90 to East Entrances

I-25 running north from Denver meets up with I-90 in north-central Wyoming. These interstates connect to the east entrances for Yellowstone and Grand Teton National Parks. They are the routes to use coming from Cheyenne, Casper, and Sheridan in Wyoming, plus I-90 in South Dakota. Drivers from Denver should use this route for Yellowstone, but not for the Moran Entrance to Grand Teton, as the I-80 route is more direct. To get to Yellowstone's East Entrance requires going through Cody. To get to Grand Teton's east entrance at Moran requires driving through Wind River Indian Reservation and over Togwotee Pass. Check on road conditions (call 511, www.wyoroad.info) for driving over the passes. Be cautious of relying on a GPS, as it can select a more direct route through curvy byways or dirt backroads.

FROM CODY, WYOMING

Cody is accessed from the junction of I-90 and I-25 at **Buffalo** (169 miles, three hours). Follow U.S. Highway 16 west through Ten Sleep to Worland, U.S. Highway 16/20 north to Basin and Greybull, and then U.S. Highway 14/16/20 west to Cody.

From Cody, the **Buffalo Bill Scenic Byway** (U.S. Hwy. 14/16/20, 56 miles, 1.25 hours) passes Buffalo Bill Reservoir and goes along the North Fork of the Shoshone River through Shoshone National Forest with campgrounds right off the highway. A few minutes after Pahaska Tepee Resort, the highway reaches the **East Entrance** to Yellowstone (closed early Nov.-late May).

From Cody, **Chief Joseph Scenic Byway** (80 miles, 1.75 hours) accesses the **Northeast Entrance** of Yellowstone. Take Highway 120 north from Cody for 16 miles, turn left on Wyoming 296 for 46 miles, and turn left onto U.S. Highway 212 (closed mid-Oct.-late May)

for 16 miles to reach Yellowstone's Northeast Entrance.

FROM CASPER, WYOMING

Reach **Grand Teton's east entrance** at Moran via **Togwotee Pass** (256 miles, five hours) on I-25 to Casper. Take Exit 189 onto U.S. Highway 20/26 to Shoshoni. Turn left, staying on U.S. Highway 26 to Riverton, where the highway turns right toward Dubois. After U.S. Highway 20 joins U.S. Highway 287 from Lander, continue northwest through the Wind River Indian Reservation and Dubois to climb over the Continental Divide at 9,658-foot Togwotee Pass. The ultra-scenic route yields outstanding views of the Teton Mountains on the descent into Jackson Hole to Grand Teton's east entrance at Moran.

I-80 to Grand Teton

I-80 across the southern part of Wyoming provides the best access to get to the south entrances of Yellowstone and Grand Teton National Parks and Jackson Hole. From Denver (550 miles, 9-10 hours), routes go to the Moran Entrance of Grand Teton via **Lander** and Togwotee Pass or Jackson via **Pinedale.**

From Rawlins on I-80, **Togwotee Pass** (248 miles, five hours) leads to the **Moran Entrance** of Grand Teton, which connects to **Yellowstone's South Entrance.** Take U.S. Highway 287/Highway 789 northwest to Lander. From Lander, continue northwest through the Wind River Indian Reservation and Dubois to climb over the Continental Divide at 9,658-foot Togwotee Pass. Prepare for big views of the Teton Mountains descending the west side of Togwotee Pass into Jackson Hole to reach Grand Teton's east entrance at Moran.

To go to **Jackson, Jackson Hole,** and the south entrances to **Grand Teton** (177 miles, 3.5 hours), drive I-80 to Rock Springs. From there, take U.S. Highway 191 north along the Wind River Mountains to Pinedale. After Pinedale, stay on U.S. Highway 191 until U.S. Highway 189 joins it and swings north. Follow U.S. Highway 189/191 northwest through Bridger-Teton National Forest and along the Hoback River through Hoback Canyon, with a few roadside campgrounds. At Hoback Junction, turn north on U.S. Highway 26/89/189/191 to reach Jackson, Jackson Hole, and the south entrances of Grand Teton National Park.

TRAVEL HUB: BOZEMAN, MONTANA

Bozeman, Montana, a year-round hub for Yellowstone, has grown far beyond its cow town roots. As a college town, home of Montana State University, it has a young vibrancy, and hiking, skiing, snowboarding, mountain biking, and fishing are imbued in the culture. With the Bridger Mountains to the north and Gallatin Range to the south, accessing mountain activities is quick. The town is known for the **Museum of the Rockies** (600 W. Kagy Blvd., 406/994-2251, www.museumoftherockies.com), home of one of the largest dinosaur collections in the world and Dr. Jack Horner, whose legendary paleontology work garnered him fame as a character in the *Jurassic Park* books and movies. The town also serves as a base for skiing and snowboarding at **Big Sky Resort** (800/548-4486, www.bigskyresort.com) and **Bridger Bowl** (800/223-9609, www.bridgerbowl.com), and cross-country skiing on groomed trails at **Bohart Ranch** (406/586-9070, www.bohartranchxcski.com). From Bozeman, year-round roads go to Yellowstone.

Air

Bozeman Yellowstone International Airport (BZN, 406/388-8321, 850 Gallatin Field Rd, Belgrade, MT, www.bozemanairport.com) is the closest for reaching Yellowstone's entrances at West Yellowstone and Gardiner. Winter travelers planning to base out of Mammoth, Gardiner, Big Sky, and West Yellowstone should fly into Bozeman, and most visitors heading to Old Faithful to overnight use this airport. Arrivers by midafternoon can reach the park in the same day. Five airlines serve Bozeman: Alaska, Allegiant, Delta, Frontier, and United. The airport sees almost 30 flights per day from Newark, Atlanta, Chicago, Minneapolis, Denver, Salt Lake City, Houston, Las Vegas, Phoenix, Seattle, Portland, and Los Angeles. (The airport gets its international designation from charter flights to Canada.) Some service is seasonal: Flights correlate with the winter ski season or summer high season in the parks.

Bus and Shuttles

Greyhound (800/231-2222, www.greyhound.com) stops at Bozeman/Belgrade and Livingston. **Karst Stage** (406/556-3540 or 800/845-2778, www.karststage.com) operates shuttles or buses daily year-round to Big Sky and West Yellowstone and daily in winter and summer to Mammoth Hot Springs and Gardiner. The **Skyline Bus** (406/995-6287, www.skylinebus.com) to Big Sky runs multiple times daily summer and winter, but weekdays only in fall and spring. For skiers and snowboarders, free buses run weekends in winter to Bridger Bowl. **Bozeman Limo** (406/585-5466, http://bozemanlimo.com) also goes to Big Sky.

Tours

For wildlife-watching and sightseeing in Yellowstone, the Bozeman-based **Yellowstone Safari Company** (406/586-1155, http://yellowstonesafari.com, year-round, $690/1-2 people) guides full-day and multiday trips. They supply binoculars, spotting scopes, and lunch. Tip guides 15 percent.

Car and RV Rentals

Several car rental companies have desks in the airport: **Alamo** (406/388-6694 or 800/227-7368, www.alamo.com), **Avis** (406/388-4091 or 800/352-7900, www.avis.com), **Budget** (406/388-4091 or 800/527-0700, www.budget.com), **Enterprise** (406/388-7420 or 800/261-7331, www.enterprise.com), **Dollar** (406/388-1323 or 800/800-5252, www.dollar.com), **Hertz** (406/388-6939 or 800/654-3131, www.hertz.com), **Thrifty** (406/388-1323 or 800/847-4389, www.thrifty.com), and **National** (406/388-6694 or 888/868-6204, www.nationalcar.com).

Bozeman also has two other rental car companies in the area: **Journey Rentacar** (30 Homestake Dr., Bozeman, 406/551-2277, www.journeyrentacar.com) or **Phasmid Rentals** (32 Dollar Dr., Belgrade, 406/922-0179, www.phasmidrentals.com).

Cruise America (700 W. Madison Ave., Belgrade, 406/388-2330 or 800/671-8042, www.cruiseamerica.com) offers RV rentals and is close to the airport. **C and T RV Rentals** (501 N. 3rd, Bozeman, 306/587-0351 or 800/481-8610, www.ctrvrentals.com) is located in downtown Bozeman, about 10 miles east of the airport.

Equipment Rental

For outdoor gear, **Phasmid Rentals** (32 Dollar Dr., Belgrade, 406/922-0179, www.phasmidrentals.com) rents camping gear, sleeping bags and pads, camp cook gear and furniture, coolers, tents, fly-fishing rods and reels, binoculars, bear spray, bear canisters, baby car seats and cribs, car racks, GPS, and maps. Most items cost $2-14 per day.

Food

Bozeman's classic restaurants are downtown. In an old railroad freight house, **Montana Ale Works** (611 E. Main St., 406/587-7700, www.montanaaleworks.com, 4pm-11pm daily, $11-30) carries 40 beers on tap, many of them regional craft brews, and house cocktails and wine to accompany locally sourced beef and bison burgers, steaks, sandwiches, small plates, and salads. You can even get a gluten-free beer and meal. **Starky's Authentic Americana** (24 N. Tracy Ave., 406/556-1111, http://starkysonline.com, lunch 11am-4pm daily, dinner 4pm-9pm Tues.-Sat. $10-22) serves burgers, sandwiches, soups, big salads, comfort foods like mac and cheese, and classic dinner meat and pasta entrées that change daily. Many of their dishes can be dairy- or gluten-free, and their interpretation of Americana includes Mexican, Italian, and Asian flavors. Founded by media mogul Ted Turner, who has a bison ranch in the area, **Ted's Montana Grill** (105 W. Main St., Ste. B, 406/587-6000, www.tedsmontanagrill.com, 11am-10pm daily, $12-40) is an American steakhouse that specializes in bison: burgers, meatloaf, pot roast, and rib-eyes. For organic dining, the **Emerson Grill** (207 W. Olive St., 406/586-5247, http://emersongrill.com, 5pm-10pm Mon.-Sat., $13-37) goes Northern Italian: antipasto, insalata, pizza, pasta, and entrées of meats or eggplant Parmesan.

Accommodations

Bozeman has loads of chain hotels. Lodging is open year-round, with the highest rates in summer and around the college home football games. Winter sees the lowest rates. Find complete listings at **Bozeman Convention and Visitor Bureau** (www.bozemancvb.com).

In downtown Bozeman, **The Lark Bozeman** (122 W. Main St., 866/464-1000, www.larkbozeman.com, $150-260) has modern rooms crafted of leather, metal, and wood and spiffed up with individual pieces from local artists. **Gallatin River Lodge** (9105 Thorpe Rd., 406/388-0148 or 888/387-0148, www.grlodge.com, $160-680) is an upscale lodge with nightly B&B lodging. In summer, lodging includes meals on a ranch 12 miles outside of town on the Gallatin River. Run by two ex-Yellowstone rangers, **Bozeman Lehrkind Mansion** (719 N. Wallace Ave., 406/585-6932, www.bozemanbedandbreakfast.com, $150-260) has nine rooms, three in the mansion and six in the garden house, all decked out with antiques. The bed-and-breakfast is in a colorful 1897 Queen Anne-style Victorian mansion listed on the National Register of Historic Places.

In downtown Bozeman, the **Treasure State Hostel** (27 E. Main St., 406/624-6244, www.treasurestatehostel.com, from $28-34) has small dorm rooms with 2-5 twin/bunk combos and private rooms ($38-60). Rates include sheets, blanket, towel, Wi-Fi, and breakfast. Parking is $7 per day.

TRAVEL HUB: BILLINGS, MONTANA

As Montana's largest and fastest-growing city, Billings serves as a gateway hub to the parks. Connecting with Yellowstone requires driving over the **Beartooth Highway** (3-4 hours, open late May-mid-Oct.). For summer travelers, it's an utterly scenic drive. When the road is closed in winter, Billings is not a travel hub to reach Yellowstone.

If you have a few hours to kill, take in the **Yellowstone Art Museum** (401 N. 27th St., 406/256-6804, www.artmuseum.org), where you can see traveling exhibits and some of their permanent collection of modern art from the Northern Rockies and Plains.

Air

Billings Logan International Airport (BIL, 1901 Terminal Circle, Billings, MT, 406/657-8495, www.flybillings.com) is open year-round; however, road access to Yellowstone is open only in summer. The airport is served by more than 30 flights per day via Alaska, Allegiant, Delta, Cape Air, and United. Flights originate from Minneapolis, Salt Lake City, Denver, Las Vegas, Phoenix, Seattle, Portland, and several towns in eastern Montana. If you fly into Billings in the morning, you can make it to Yellowstone by dark, but otherwise, spend the night in Billings or Red Lodge to be able to drive the Beartooth Highway in daylight without rushing.

Bus

Greyhound (800/231-2222, www.greyhound.com) has a depot stop at Billings. But bus travelers are better off going to Bozeman for year-round connections into Yellowstone.

Car and RV Rentals

Eight car rental companies have desks in the airport: **Alamo** (406/252-7626 or 877/222-9075, www.alamo.com), **Avis** (406/252-8007 or 800/331-1212, www.avis.com), **Budget** (406/259-4168 or 800/527-0700, www.budget.com), **Enterprise** (406/294-2930 or 800/736-8222, www.enterprise.com), **Dollar** (406/248-9993 or 800/800-4000, www.dollar.com), **Hertz** (406/248-9151 or 800/654-3131, www.hertz.com), **Thrifty** (406/248-9993 or 800/847-4389, www.thrifty.com), and **National** (406/252-7626 or 800/227-7368, www.nationalcar.com).

Montana Happy Campers (2110 1st Ave. N., 406/294-2267 or 800/598-0241, www.montanahappycampers.com) offers RV rentals near the airport. Nine miles west of the airport, **Cruise America RV** (720 Central Ave., 800/549-2301, www.cruiseamerica.com) is on I-90 on the way to Yellowstone.

Equipment Rental

Sunshine Sports (304 Moore Ln., 406/252-3724 or 800/773-3723, www.sunshine-sports.com) rents inflatable rafts, canoes, touring and river kayaks, paddleboards, and all the accessories to go with them. Rentals for camping gear are not available.

Food and Accommodations

Billings (www.visitbillings.com) is a hub of chain motels and small conference center hotels. The historic **Northern Hotel** (19 N. Broadway, 406/867-6767 or 855/782-9589, http://northernhotel.com, $170-330) has upscale rooms and suites with 24-hour room service, a diner, and a fine-dining restaurant. **Ledgestone Hotel** (4863 King Ave. E., 406/259-9454, http://ledgestonehotel.com, $99-130) is one of the newer hotels in town with hotel rooms, suites, and kitchenettes. For families, the **Big Horn Resort** (1801 Majestic Ln., 406/839-9300, http://thebighornresort.com, $115-260) has an indoor water park.

Brewpubs show off craft beers and pub burgers, salads, and sandwiches. Go to **Montana Brewing Company** (113 N. Broadway, 406/252-9200, www.montanabrewingcompany.com, 11am-2am Mon.-Sat., noon-10pm Sun., $10-20) for wood-fired flatbread pizzas and Mac and Cheese. **Uberbrew** (2305 Montana Ave., 406/534-6960, http://uberbrewmt.com, 11am-9pm daily, $8-15) serves schnitzel, sausages, and beer cheese soup.

TRAVEL HUB: IDAHO FALLS, IDAHO

Idaho Falls, the largest city in eastern Idaho, sits on a high desert plateau about two hours from Grand Teton National Park and Jackson Hole. Most visitors using this hub head straight to their destination, but if you have time to spare in downtown Idaho Falls, take a walk along the **Snake River Greenbelt** (www.idahofallsidaho.gov) to explore where the Snake River goes after Grand Teton. Walking paths along both sides of the river go past a 600-foot-wide waterfall and historic downtown buildings to make a six-mile loop.

Air

The **Idaho Falls Regional Airport** (IDA, 2140 N. Skyline Dr., Idaho Falls, 208/612-8224, www.idahofallsidaho.gov) has flights via SkyWest/Delta from Salt Lake City and Minneapolis-St. Paul, United Express from Denver, and Allegiant Air from Las Vegas, Phoenix, Los Angeles, and Oakland. Some flights are daily, while others are weekly or summer only. The airport is still a two-plus-hour drive to Jackson Hole and Grand Teton National Park, but you can reach the park in the same day you fly in, unless winter snowstorms impede driving. Some people prefer flying into Idaho Falls as the flights are often cheaper than to Jackson Hole.

Bus and Shuttles

Greyhound (800/231-2222, www.greyhound.com) buses service Idaho Falls. The **Salt Lake Express** (800/356-9796 or 208/656-8824, www.saltlakeexpress.com) bus service runs between the Idaho Falls Airport and Jackson, Wyoming, twice a day for about $53 one-way.

Car and RV Rentals

Four rental car companies are located in the airport terminal: **Avis** (208/522-4225 or 888/897-8848, www.avis.com), **Budget** (208/522/8800 or 800/527-0700, www.budget.com), **Hertz** (208/529-3101 or 800/654-3131, www.hertz.com), and **National** (208/522-5276 or 800/227-7368, www.nationalcar.

com). Elsewhere in town are **Thrifty Rent-A-Car** (208/227-0444 or 877/283-0898, www.thrifty.com) and **Enterprise** (208/523-8111 or 855/266-9289, www.enterprise.com).

Two RV rental companies operate in Idaho Falls: **Smith RV** (1523 N. 25th E., 208/535-2500, www.smithrvidaho.com) and **American Carriage Rentals** (208/529-5535, www.rv-rentals-yellowstone.com).

Equipment Rental

Idaho Mountain Trading (474 Shoup Ave., 208/523-6679, www.idahomountaintrading.com) rents tents, sleeping bags, packs, bikes, kayaks, downhill skis, cross-country skis, snowboards, and snowshoes. Rates run $2-30 per item.

Food and Accommodations

Idaho Falls (www.visitIdahoFalls.com) is the land of chain hotels, from budget to mid-range. The **Residence Inn** (65 W. Broadway, 208/542-0000, www.marriott.com) sits at the falls, and **Hilton Garden Inn** (700 Lindsay Blvd., 208/522-9500, http://hiltongardeninn3.hilton.com) is right on the river. For uniqueness, the **Destinations Inn** (295 Broadway St., 208/528-8222, www.destinationsinn.com, $150-250) bed-and-breakfast has 14 upscale rooms, each themed from a different location around the world (think Thailand, Morocco, Paris, Athens, and Alaska) tucked into a 1905 building.

Despite the town's location in Idaho's high desert, you can find ethnic dining. **Tandoori Oven** (3204 S. 25th E., 208/522-8263, www.tandoriovenif.com, 11am-2:30pm and 4:30pm-9:30pm Mon.-Sat., $9-25) serves Indian specialties cooked in a tandoor, vegetarian dishes, and traditional Indian breads. You can choose your own spiciness. For American fare, the **SnakeBite Restaurant** (401 Park Ave., 208/525-2522, www.thesnakebiterestaurant.com, 11am-3pm Mon., 11am-9pm Tues.-Sat., $10-29, cash or check only) serves a large menu of stacked burgers (go for the Teton burger), steaks, fish, pasta, and salads. Twenty beers are on tap, including local and regional brews.

Getting Around

DRIVING

Yellowstone and Grand Teton National Parks have two-lane roads that are easy to drive. However, several factors escalate concerns. Wildlife uses the roads: Bison back up traffic as they walk down the yellow line, and traffic jams clog the road when bears feed nearby. Deer, elk, and coyote run out in front of cars, and they are especially difficult to see around dawn or dusk. For RV drivers, sections of curvy road demand more attention, especially climbing Dunraven Pass. Sections of road can be narrow with minimal shoulders. Due to wildlife, car jams, traffic, weather, and maximum speed limits of 35-45 mph, national park miles take longer to cover than the same miles at home. Watch for wildlife at all times: Both Yellowstone and Grand Teton see more than 100 animal deaths each year due to vehicles.

Junctions in Yellowstone can clog with cars. With each upcoming lane dividing into two lanes, each four-way junction has 11-12 lanes with stop signs, not lights, controlling the flow. First-time visitors can find the crowded junctions intimidating, and lines of RVs and cars can cover up the directional markers painted on the lanes. To turn right, get into the right lanes. To go straight or turn left, stay in the middle or left lane. When you reach the front of the line, use the rule, yield to the right.

GPS and Mobile Apps

Visitors can get around the parks with the use of GPS and map apps on phones. Be aware that you will have dead zones for phones, and the programs don't account for seasonal road closures. You'll still need to find out about these the old-fashioned way by inquiring at visitors centers or looking on the park websites (www.nps.gov/yell or www.nps.gov/grte).

National Park Service **mobile phone apps** for both parks contain information on visitor centers, hikes, geyser predictions, road construction, ranger programs, and interactive park maps. Download the apps before you begin your trip; there is limited Internet availability in the parks. Download the free **NPS Yellowstone National Park** or **NPS Grand Teton National Park** for travel information. The free **NPS Yellowstone Geysers** keeps track of geyser eruption predictions.

Follow a self-guided, go-at-your-own-pace GPS-audio road tour of Yellowstone and Grand Teton National Parks with **GaperGuide** (565 N. Cache St., Jackson, 307-733-4626, www.gaperguide.com, early May-Sept., $25-45). Reservations are recommended.

Maps and Planners

Topographical maps are best for hiking. Combined topographical maps with trail descriptions of Yellowstone and Grand Teton are available online (www.hike734.com, $12). **Day Hikes of Yellowstone National Park Map Guide** covers 65 day hikes while the **Day Hikes of Grand Teton National Park Map Guide** has 48 day hikes. **National Geographic Trails Illustrated** has maps of both parks that are a cross between a topographical map and a more detailed version of the National Park Service maps. Order them for trip planning through **Yellowstone Forever** (406/848-2400, www.yellowstoneforever.org) or **Grand Teton Association** (307/739-3403, www.grandtetonpark.org). Both parks also have trip planners available online (www.nps.gov/yell or www.nps.gov/grte). **Beartooth Publishing** (800/838-1058 or 406/585-7205, www.beartoothpublishing.com) makes topographical maps of the Tetons, Absaroka Beartooth Wilderness, Bozeman, Big Sky, and Yellowstone.

SHUTTLES
Bus

Yellowstone does not have a shuttle bus

system inside the park, but Grand Teton has **AllTrans, Inc.** (307/733-3135 or 800/443-6133, www.jacksonholealltrans.com), which runs between Jackson and Flagg Ranch with stops in between. It operates multiple times daily in summer with stops at Jenny Lake, Signal Mountain, Jackson Lake Lodge, and Colter Bay. In winter, the daily shuttle goes between Jackson, Teton Village, and Flagg Ranch. Rates cover unlimited use in one day. Park entrance fees are extra.

Boat

In Yellowstone, the only boat shuttle in summer is by reservation for hauling backcountry campers and kayakers from Bridge Bay to **Yellowstone Lake's southern arms** (Xanterra, 307/242-3893). In Grand Teton, a summer boat shuttle runs every 15 minutes all day long to convey hikers across **Jenny Lake** (Jenny Lake Boating, 307/734-9227, www.jennylakeboating.com).

TOURS
Bus

Sightseeing tours operated by multiple companies go out daily in summer in both parks. In Yellowstone, they depart from park lodges and West Yellowstone. In Grand Teton, they depart mostly from Jackson, but some will pick up riders at lodges. Some tours are sightseeing, making loops to take in the scenery, lodges, thermal hot spots, and natural wonders. Because both parks have substantial wildlife-watching opportunities, many companies guide wildlife-watching tours, some year-round. Find lists online (www.nps.gov/yell or www.nps.gov/grte) of all companies licensed to operate in the parks.

Boat

Daily summer boat tours operate on Yellowstone Lake in Yellowstone and Jackson Lake and Jenny Lake in Grand Teton. **Xanterra** (307/344-7311 or 866/439-7375, www.yellowstonenationalparklodges.com) runs the Yellowstone Lake tours. On Jackson Lake, **boat tours** (307/543-2811, www.gtlc.

com) go out from Colter Bay. **Jenny Lake** (307/734-9227, www.jennylakeboating.com) also has boat tours.

Snowcoach and Snowmobile

In winter, the only way to tour the interior of Yellowstone is by snowcoach or snowmobile, mid-December-early March. Launch points for day tours are from Flagg Ranch, West Yellowstone, and Mammoth Hot Springs. Multiple companies operate tours, and lists of licensed operators are online (www.nps.gov/yell). Grand Teton does not permit snowcoach tours or snowmobiling.

RVS

Traveling Yellowstone and Grand Teton by RV is a fun way to go. Most roads are easy to drive, although they are narrow and sometimes shoulder-less. In Yellowstone, Grand Loop Road in one section requires caution for RV drivers: For 19 miles, the road between Tower Fall and Dunraven Pass is steep, curvy, narrow, and along cliffs.

Restrictions

Unfortunately, RVs are not permitted everywhere. In Yellowstone, RVs, buses, and trailers are not permitted in some parking lots (Midway and Lower Geyser Basins) due to sharp, tight turnarounds or short-length parking stalls. They also are not allowed on Upper Terrace, Blacktail Plateau, Virginia Cascade, and Firehole Lake Drives. In Grand Teton, the Moose-Wilson Road is closed to RVs including trailers, due to the narrow, curvy road. Trailers are also not permitted on Signal Mountain Road.

Campgrounds

Most of the campgrounds inside Yellowstone and Grand Teton do not have hookups. However, a few do. In Yellowstone, Fishing Bridge Campground has hookups. In John D. Rockefeller, Jr. Memorial Parkway at Flagg Ranch, Headwaters Campground has hookups. In Grand Teton, hookups are at Colter Bay Campground

Driving Tips

Driving in Yellowstone and Grand Teton demands fortitude, especially around the congested geyser basins. Crowds of vehicles in summer, wildlife, and seasonal road construction put drivers in a precarious position. Adapt by settling into a slower mode. For trip planning and updates, consult the parks for road construction, seasonal closures, and other road issues.

- **Mileage, signage, and GPS:** The national parks do not have mileage markers. Use the park map received at the entrance for figuring out your location. Road junctions have directional signage with mileages. GPS will not show seasonal road closures.

- **Wildlife on the road:** Fences? Not here. Bison, elk, bears, deer, bighorn sheep, wolves, and moose cross roads anywhere. Wildlife crossings are not marked. Sometimes bison and bears walk straight down the yellow line in the middle of the road. Give them room (25 yards for most wildlife, but 100 yards for wolves and bears), drive slowly, and avoid honking at them. Just enjoy the show. You may be able to inch by them if they seem calm. Bison may look docile, but one kick can dent your vehicle.

- **Wildlife jams:** Wildlife jams are one of the biggest clogs on the park roads: Bear jams, wolf jams, elk jams, moose jams, and bison jams. When most of us see wildlife, we want to stop to watch as it's such a rare treat to see animals cruising the wilds. Jams occur all over the park, in any season, but are particularly bad during July and August when so many vehicles clog the roads. Whenever possible, use pullouts for wildlife viewing.

- **Speeds:** The speed limit on most park roads is 35-45 mph in Yellowstone and 35-55 mph in Grand Teton. Traffic congestion, wildlife, or road construction often makes driving slower. Plan for longer than usual driving time to cover even short distances.

- **Road construction:** Perennial road construction happens every summer. Long winters force road repairs and reconstruction to take place in the same season as high visitation. Look online before your trip to see where construction is planned and how it may affect your travel.

and Signal Mountain. Outside of the parks, you'll find private campgrounds with hookups in Gardiner, West Yellowstone, Moran, and Jackson.

Many of the campgrounds have campsites that are limited in the RV lengths they can fit. Check on these when making reservations. More options are available for 30-foot RVs rather than 40-foot RVs.

Rentals and Repairs

Two mobile RV repair services can come fix your rig, although it may be costly to cover the distance to where you are. **Mobile RV Tech** (406/682-4100) and **RV Fixit Pro** (801/831-8111) are based in West Yellowstone, Montana. **Mobile RV Repair** (307/699-1225) is based in Jackson, Wyoming. RV rentals are available in Billings and Bozeman in Montana, and also in Idaho Falls.

BICYCLES

Road cyclists in Wyoming's national parks must contend with huge RVs at their elbows and drivers gawking at scenery or wildlife instead of the road. For that reason, bikers should wear helmets, bright colors, and lights at dawn or dusk. Roads in Grand Teton tend to have paved shoulders, which makes cycling easier. Yellowstone's narrower roads lack shoulders in many stretches. Throw in blind curves, high snowbanks in spring, and heavy traffic in summer, and visibility of cyclists diminishes. Wildlife poses its own dilemmas with two-ton bison standing in the road. Maintain your distance, or use cars as shields when confronting them.

Most cyclists ride early in the day before traffic clogs roads. Afternoons often bring hefty winds or thunderstorms, another reason to ride early in the day. Most campgrounds

Be sure to give wildlife plenty of room to cross park roads.

- **Road closures:** Although roads may close temporarily in summer for various reasons, the National Park Service aims to keep all roads open May-early November. Some roads can open mid-April. Winter road closure for wheeled vehicles is November-mid-April.

- **Weather:** Due to high elevation, snow can show up every month of the year, even in summer. Sudden snowstorms, whiteouts, or fog can reduce visibility and slicken road surfaces. Adjust your speed accordingly.

in both parks reserve a few designated camp-sites for hikers and cyclists to share. Per person rates run $5-10. Bear boxes are available for storing food.

Bike Trails

In Yellowstone, several old roadbeds provide biking trails: Old Gardiner Freight Road, Fountain Flat Drive, Lone Star Geyser Road, and Natural Bridge Road. In Grand Teton, a paved bike trail parallels roads between Jenny Lake, Moose, Antelope Flats, and Jackson. In spring, after plowing is completed in both parks, some roads become prime cycling trails sans vehicles until they officially open for the season. Plowing and opening dates vary in different locations. Top roads to ride in early spring are the Teton Park Road (Inside Road) and Yellowstone roads between West Yellowstone and Mammoth.

MOTORCYCLES

Motorcyclists enjoy the scenery of the Wyoming national parks. But riding in the parks is not like riding at home. You can round a blind corner into a bison or grizzly bear. Animals can speed across the road in front of you, and traffic clogs the road midday. Riding shortly after sunup and in the evening will be less harried, but you also may encounter more animals. Since weather can mutate fast from a warm sunny day into a snowstorm, be prepared with the appropriate riding gear to handle these wild swings. Higher elevations can have icy roads in spring and fall, and unseasonable snowstorms can hit in August. Wyoming law requires helmets, but Montana and Idaho do not for anyone older than 18. Motorcycle rentals are available in Jackson Hole in Wyoming, Bozeman and Billings in Montana, and Idaho Falls.

Recreation

CAMPING

Camping in the national parks requires a bit of savvy. In summer, you cannot waltz in around sunset to claim a campsite. Campsites are filled up long before that.

In Yellowstone, you can make **reservations** (Xanterra, 307/344-7311 or 866/439-7375, www.yellowstonenationalpark-lodges.com) for five campgrounds one year in advance. These are Fishing Bridge, Bridge Bay, Madison, Canyon, and Grant Village. Fishing Bridge, which allows only hard-sided rigs (no tent trailers), is the only one with hookups for RVs. Seven campgrounds in Yellowstone are first-come, first-served: Mammoth, Slough Creek, Pebble Creek, Indian Creek, Tower, Norris, and Lewis Lake.

In Grand Teton, six campgrounds (Headwaters/Flagg Ranch, Lizard Creek, Colter Bay, Signal Mountain, Jenny Lake, and Gros Ventre) have first-come, first-served campsites. Full-hookup RV campsites, which should be reserved one year in advance, are at Colter Bay (800/628-9988, www.gtlc.com) and Headwaters at Flagg Ranch (307/543-2861 or 800/443-2311, www.gtlc.com). You can also reserve tent sites at Headwaters. Jenny Lake is for tents only.

HIKING

Miles of hiking trails tour the Greater Yellowstone Ecosystem. Yellowstone National Park has 900 miles (1,449 kilometers) of trails; Grand Teton National Park has 200 miles (320 kilometers) of trails. Surrounding the national parks are national forest trails, some of which connect with park trails. The 3,300-mile Continental Divide Trail goes northward through Bridger-Teton National Forest and Yellowstone.

Yellowstone has two types of trails: traditional dirt trails and boardwalk trails. The short boardwalk trails are designed for protecting visitors and sensitive features in high-traffic geothermal areas. In geothermal areas without boardwalks, stick to the trail to avoid scalding by boiling water. Grand Teton trails are traditional dirt trails, with the exception of the paved Multi-Use Pathway. In both parks, bridges do not span all streams. You

roasting marshmallows at Norris Campground in Yellowstone

Reservation Tips

Yellowstone is the fourth most visited national park in the country, and Grand Teton is the eighth. The onslaught of summer campers means that campgrounds fill up fast. Don't have reservations for camping? Here are a few tips for snagging a campsite in summer.

- Make a base camp and stay put rather than shuffling campgrounds every day or so. You'll spend a little more time driving to some destinations, but you'll experience the park more with the time you save from searching campground after campground only to be confronted with full signs.

- On any day you plan to move camp, change locations in early morning to get a campsite before campgrounds fill up. Make getting your next campsite the first priority rather than sightseeing.

- At campgrounds that allow self-selection of campsites, plan to begin prowling to nab a site when someone departs an hour or more before the fill times mentioned below.

YELLOWSTONE

- For a central location, claim a spot before 9am at Norris Campground. For Slough Creek or Pebble Creek, claim a campsite before 8am. For Indian Creek, Mammoth, or Lewis Lake, claim your campsite by 10am or earlier. These campgrounds have self-selection of campsites. Check online (www.nps.gov/yell) for fill times for yesterday and today.

- Unfortunately, most of the centrally located campgrounds in Yellowstone book full months in advance. Do not bother trying to get in line for a potential opening at the reserved camp-grounds at Madison, Canyon, Fishing Bridge, Bridge Bay, and Grant Village. Instead, call to check for last-minute cancellations (Xanterra, 307/344-7311 or 866/439-7375, www.yellow-stonenationalparklodges.com). They do not take names on a waiting list, so it's sheer luck that scores a campsite.

- Camp outside the park in West Yellowstone, Shoshone National Forest west of Cody, or in Custer-Gallatin National Forest near Big Sky, Gardiner, or Cooke City the night before entering the park. Then head in early to claim a campsite before going adventuring for the day.

GRAND TETON

- Jenny Lake (tents only) campground fills by 9am.

- Colter Bay Campground rarely fills up, but it can in July-August. If you arrive after the check-in station closes for the night, a sign usually lists open campsites and directions.

- At Signal Mountain, Colter Bay, Gros Ventre, and Headwaters, campsites are assigned at the entrance office rather than self-selection.

- Camp outside the park in Shoshone National Forest around Togwotee Pass, in Bridger-Teton National Forest on the west side of Teton Pass, or along U.S. Highway 26/89/191 or Highway 189 the night before entering the park. Then head in early to claim a campsite.

may need to ford creeks. In June, melting snow can raise water levels, making hiking poles helpful for stream crossings. Streams tend to be at their highest levels in the afternoon and lowest levels in the morning. Consult visitors centers on trail conditions before you go.

Hiking trails ban mountain bikes or motorized trail bikes in the parks, but many are open to horse travel. If you meet up with horses while hiking, step off the trail on the downhill side, if possible, to let them pass. Trail etiquette dictates that uphill hikers have the right of way; downhill hikers should step aside to let them pass, unless the uphill hikers opt to take a breather to rest. When planning hikes, consider the higher altitude. You may hike less far or more slowly than at lower elevations. Many trailhead parking lots pack out midsummer; plan for early starts to claim a parking space.

In winter, when snow buries trails, hikers travel by snowshoes or cross-country skis. Most trails are not marked with tree tags or other route-finding devices; navigation skills are required. Some trails also cross avalanche zones: Take beacons, probes, and shovels. Know how to use them and assess snow stability. Be aware of travel etiquette: On roads where snowcoaches and snowmobiles travel, skiers and snowshoers should travel on the right side to allow vehicles to pass. With skier-set tracks, snowshoers should blaze their own trails.

Hiking with kids can either be a nightmare or a hoot. To make it more fun, take water and snacks along to prevent hunger and thirst from zapping their energy. Take extra layers to keep kids warm if the weather turns. Help them connect with the environment while hiking by asking them about what they see and why things are the way they are. If you make hiking a fun experience for them, they'll want to do it again.

Trail Signs

All in-park trailheads and junctions have good signage. Some signs are just directional pointers with destination names. Others have multiple destinations with distances. Distances, when included, are listed in miles. Some signs add distances in kilometers, too. Geyser basin trailheads have large maps of thermal features and boardwalks posted, and Upper Geyser Basin adds "you are here" signs at every junction. Trail closures for seasonal bear management are permanently signed with the closure dates.

Bear Closures

With a high density of grizzly and black bears in the Greater Yellowstone Ecosystem,

Yellowstone National Park has implemented Bear Management Areas to prevent human-bear conflicts. During certain seasons of high bear use in these areas, the park service closes trails or does not permit off-trail hiking. Backcountry campsites close, too. Some trails require hiking with four or more people or during daylight hours only. These restrictions affect day hiker trails, paddle destinations on Yellowstone Lake, and backpacker routes.

Most of the Bear Management Areas are located around Yellowstone Lake, Hayden Valley, Pelican Valley, Tower-Roosevelt, the Firehole River geyser basin areas, and northwest Yellowstone. All restrictions are seasonal, but the seasons vary depending on the region. Lists of Bear Management Areas, seasonal dates of impacts, and a map of the regions are in the *Backcountry Trip Planner* (www.nps.gov/yell) or in visitors centers or permit centers. Grand Teton National Park and Jackson Hole also have annual seasonal closures (www.nps.gov/grte), such as Hermitage Point and Willow Flats in early summer.

BEAR BELLS AND PEPPER SPRAY

On trails, you'll hear sporadic jingle bells, sold in gift shops as bear bells. Locals call them "dinner bells," and many hikers hate them. While making noise best prevents surprising a bear, bells fail to carry sound the way a human voice does. To check their minimal effectiveness, see how close you get to hikers before you hear the ringing. Bear bells are best as a souvenir, not as a substitute for human noise on the trail in the form of talking, singing, hooting, and hollering. You may feel silly at first, but everyone does it.

Most hikers carry pepper spray with a capsicum derivative to deter bear attacks. Unlike insect repellents, do not use bear sprays on your body, in tents, or on gear; spray it directly into a bear's face, aiming for the eyes and nose. Wind and rain may reduce its effectiveness. Small purse-size pepper sprays are too small to deter bears; buy or rent an eight-ounce can.

Hiking Essentials

Hiking, especially in the Teton Mountains, demands preparedness. Unpredictable, fast-changing weather can mutate a warm summer day into wintry conditions in hours. Different elevations vary in temperature, wind, and visibility: Sun on the shore of Jenny Lake may hide knock-over winds barreling over Paintbrush Divide 5,000 feet higher. To be prepared in the backcountry, take the following:

- **Extra clothing:** Rain pants and jackets can double as wind protection, while gloves and a lightweight warm hat will save fingers and ears. Carry at least one extra water-wicking layer for warmth. Avoid cotton fabrics, which stay soggy and fail to retain body heat.

- **Extra food and water:** Depending on the hike's length, take a lunch and snacks, like compact high-energy food bars. Low-odor foods will not attract animals. Always carry extra water: Heat, wind, and elevation lead quickly to dehydration, and most visitors find they drink more than they do at home. Avoid drinking directly from streams or lakes. Due to the possibility of illness-inducing bacteria, filter or treat water sources before drinking.

- **Map and compass or GPS:** Although national park trails are well signed, take a map for ascertaining distance traveled and location. A compass or GPS will also help, but only if you know how to use it. In the deep, heavily forested canyons of the Tetons, a GPS may not pick up satellites.

- **Flashlight:** Carry a small flashlight or headlamp for after-dark emergencies. Take extra batteries, too.

- **First-aid kit:** Two bandages aren't enough. Carry a fully equipped standard first-aid kit with blister remedies. Many outdoor stores sell suitably prepared kits for hiking. Don't forget to add personal items like bee-sting kits and allergy medications.

- **Sun protection:** Altitude, snow, ice, and lakes all increase ultraviolet radiation. Protect yourself with SPF 30 sunscreen, sunglasses, and a sun hat or baseball cap.

- **Emergency toilet supplies:** Not every hike conveniently places a pit toilet at its destination. To accommodate an alfresco toilet stop, carry a small trowel, plastic baggies, and toilet paper, and move at least 200 feet away from water sources. For urinating, aim for a durable surface, such as rocks, logs, gravel, or snow. "Watering" fragile plants, campsites, or trails attracts animals that dig up the area. Bury feces 6-8 inches deep in soil. Do not bury toilet paper; use a baggie to pack it out.

- **Feminine hygiene:** Carry heavy-duty zippered baggies to pack out tampons, pads, and toilet paper.

- **Insect repellent:** Summer can be abuzz at any elevation with mosquitoes and blackflies. Insect repellents that contain 50 percent DEET work best. Purchase applications that rub or spray at close range rather than aerosols that go airborne onto other people, plants, and animals.

- **Pepper spray:** If you want to carry pepper spray, purchase an eight-ounce can, as nothing smaller will be effective; however, do not bother unless you know how to use it and what influences its effectiveness. Do not use it like bug repellent.

- **Miscellaneous:** A knife may come in handy, as can a few feet of nylon cord and a bit of duct tape (wrap a few feet around something small like a flashlight handle or water bottle). Many hikers have repaired boots and packs with duct tape and a little ingenuity.

Practice how to use it, but still make noise on the trail.

Weather Concerns

Weather in Yellowstone and Grand Teton is unpredictable. Warm summer days can disintegrate into rainy squalls or snowstorms. Afternoons see hefty wind gusts, bringing with them thundershowers and lightning. If lightning approaches, descend from peak tops, high ridges, and open meadows into forest for more protection. Hikers should plan on early starts in order to descend in elevation by the time afternoon storms hit. Pack layers and always take rain gear, even when the weather looks like a blue-sky day.

Guides

Yellowstone licenses companies to guide hikes and backpacking trips; Grand Teton permits no guided hiking. Lists of approved concessionaires for Yellowstone are available online (www.nps.gov/yell). National Park Service naturalists guide free day hikes in both parks. Consult the park newspapers for schedules and locations.

BACKPACKING

Yellowstone and Grand Teton National Parks have backcountry campsites that offer solitude, scenery, and unique experiences. Backcountry trip planners detail campsite locations, regulations, permits, and safety concerns. Only Yellowstone permits concessionaires to guide backpacking trips.

Permits

Both national parks require permits for backcountry camping. A percentage of backcountry campsites may be reserved in advance in Yellowstone ($25, with submission of form available online) and Grand Teton ($45, www.recreation.gov, early Jan.-mid-May). Permits are also available first-come, first-served. In Yellowstone, they are available 48 hours before departure ($3/person/night, $15/party maximum, children 8 and younger free). For more

information, access the online *Backcountry Trip Planner* (www.nps.gov/yell) for route and plan options. It also contains lists of areas that are closed annually in spring, early summer, or fall due to heavy bear concentrations.

In Grand Teton, backcountry camping permits are required and are available in advance online (www.recreation.gov, apply early Jan.-mid-May, $45/trip). Walk-in permits ($35/trip) are available first-come, first-served in person 24 hours before departure. Competition for walk-in permits is high in July and August; a waiting line usually forms at the Jenny Lake Ranger Station one hour before opening at 8am. Permits are also available at the Craig Thomas Discovery & Visitor Center in Moose. You may need an ice ax into early August for steep snowfields. Bear-proof canisters are required for food storage; the permit office has loaners.

Food Storage

Proper food storage while backpacking is essential in bear country. In Yellowstone, bear boxes are provided at a few backcountry campsites for storing food. In other places, hang food from bars or poles. Pack along a 35-foot rope and stuff sack to hang food. In Grand Teton, bear canisters are required for storing food. Permit offices have loaners, and rental gear shops in surrounding towns have them, too.

CLIMBING AND MOUNTAINEERING

If you want to stand on top of the Grand Teton, you can. Permits are not needed for mountaineering and climbing in the parks. But if trips require overnighting, then backcountry camping permits are needed. Several companies offer instruction and guided climbs in Grand Teton National Park. Two companies with worldwide reputations are **Exum Mountain Guides** (307/733-2297, http://exumguides.com) and **Jackson Hole Mountain Guides** (307/733-4979, www.jhmg.com).

Winter Safety Tips

Visiting the parks in winter is a whole different game than in summer. Frigid temperatures, strong winds, snow, blizzards, ice, and avalanches conspire to change a walk in the park into a life-threatening adventure.

- Be responsible: Know your skills, abilities, and limitations.

- Ski and snowshoe with other people.

- Prepare for changing weather conditions. Storms can move in fast, plummeting temperatures and bringing blizzards.

- Always leave a trip plan with a responsible person and check in upon your return.

- Plan to handle emergencies. Cell phones may not have service, and batteries can go dead in the cold.

- Watch for signs of hypothermia: slurred speech, stumbling, and uncontrolled shivering. Hypothermia can be fatal. Treat hypothermic victims by getting them out of the elements, adding clothing, administering warm liquids, and seeking help if incapacitated.

- Pack winter travel gear: first-aid kit with blister remedies; headlamp; high-energy snacks, bars, and drink additives; map and compass or GPS; ski or snowshoe and pole repair kit; sunglasses and sunscreen. Bring water in an insulated bottle (water hoses often freeze).

- Always carry extra clothing: wind protection, waterproof, and extra hat and gloves.

- Packets of hand warmers can aid in preventing and treating hypothermia.

- Only venture into potential avalanche terrain if you have the appropriate skills, knowledge, and gear. Carry a beacon, probe, and shovel, and know how to use them.

- Check on current avalanche conditions before you go; contact **Bridger-Teton National Forest Avalanche Center** (307/733-2664, www.jhavalanche.org) for Grand Teton and read the **climbing ranger blog** (http://tetonclimbing.blogspot.com).

FISHING

In Yellowstone National Park, more than 16 percent of the park's four million annual visitors go fishing. That high percentage compared to other parks speaks to the clean quality of the streams and lakes.

The epitome of Yellowstone fishing is fly-fishing. Hit up local fly shops to gain the best information on where the fish are biting, what flies are hatching, and what the fish are eating; then, purchase flies to match that scenario.

Anglers can fish sunrise to sunset, Memorial Day weekend through the first weekend in November. Park fishing regulations are strict: catch-and-release only of native trout, no fishing from docks or bridges,

no bait, no barbs on hooks, and no lead. Seasonal closures occur for bears, low water levels, or high water temperatures. Consult the nearest ranger station or visitors center for specifics regarding where you want to fish, as catch-and-release rules and creel limits vary between waters.

Inside Yellowstone, a **fishing permit** is required for anglers 16 years and older ($18 for three days, $25 seven days, $40 season). Kids under 16 can fish on their parent's permit or get their own free permit signed by a parent or guardian. Kids must be supervised fishing under a parental license, but can fish by themselves with the free permit. Purchase fishing permits and pick up regulations at park visitors centers.

Leave No Trace

To keep the national parks pristine, visitors to these parks need to take an active role in maintaining them.

- **Plan ahead and prepare.** Hiking in the backcountry is inherently risky. Three miles at the high elevations in Wyoming may be much harder than three miles through your neighborhood park back home. Choose appropriate routes for mileage and elevation gain with this in mind, and carry hiking essentials.

- **Travel and camp on durable surfaces.** In front-country and backcountry campgrounds, camp in designated sites. Protect fragile plants by staying on trails even in mud, refusing to cut switchbacks, and walking single file. If you must walk off the trail, step on rocks, snow, or dry grasses rather than wet soil and delicate plants.

- **Leave what you find.** Flowers, rocks, and fur tufts on shrubs are protected park resources, as are historical cultural items. For lunch stops and camping, sit on rocks or logs where you find them rather than moving them to accommodate comfort.

- **Properly dispose of waste.** Pack out whatever you bring, including all garbage. If toilets are not available, pack out toilet paper. Urinate on rocks, logs, gravel, or snow to protect soils and plants from salt-starved wildlife, and bury feces 6-8 inches deep at least 200 feet from water.

- **Minimize campfire impacts.** Make fires in designated fire pits only, not on beaches (except by permit at Jackson Lake). Use small wrist-size dead and downed wood, not live branches. Be aware: Fires and collecting firewood are not permitted in some places in the parks.

- **Respect wildlife.** Bring along binoculars, spotting scopes, and telephoto lenses to aid in watching wildlife. Keep your distance. Do not feed any wildlife, even ground squirrels. Once fed, they become more aggressive.

- **Be considerate of other visitors.** Particularly be aware of cell phones and how their use or noise cuts into the natural soundscapes of the parks.

For more Leave No Trace information, visit www.LNT.org.

Outside Yellowstone, you'll need a **Montana fishing license** (http://fwp.mt.gov, $13-26 for residents, $25-70 for nonresidents). East of Cooke City, you'll need a **Wyoming fishing license** (residents: $3 youth, $6 adults daily, $24 adults annual; nonresidents: $15 youth, $14 adults daily, $92 adults annual). When purchasing your license, pick up a list of current regulations for the state and the waters you plan to fish.

In Grand Teton, you'll need multiple permits for boating or paddling excursions. Purchase a Wyoming Aquatic Invasive Species (AIS) sticker and then successfully pass an AIS inspection in order to get a Grand Teton National Park boating permit. You will need additional permits if you plan to build a beach fire or camp overnight on Jackson Lake, or fish any lake or river while floating.

Native Species

National park fishing regulations enforce protection of native species through selected area closures and limits or bans on taking native species. Native trout include mountain whitefish, arctic grayling, and two cutthroat trout: the westslope and Yellowstone. Conserving these native species means relying on catch-and-release methods with barbless hooks and learning to recognize the fish. In particular with cutthroat, if you see a red slash along the throat, release it back into the water. You can also help protect these pristine fisheries by avoiding the use of lead and bait. By protecting native fish, you will also be aiding those animals such as bears and osprey, which rely on them as food sources.

Nonnative fish were introduced into Yellowstone to help populate some of the once fishless waters and boost recreational fishing. While no longer stocked, they now pose a threat to native species through competition, predation, and hybridization. Fishing regulations encourage the taking of nonnative species. In some areas, anglers are asked to kill nonnative fish even if they do not plan to consume them. Nonnative species include rainbow, brown, lake, and brook trout. Fisheries managers are removing nonnative trout and hybridized cutthroat from Soda Butte Creek in order to restock with native Yellowstone cutthroat.

Bear Concerns

Bears pose special considerations. Since smells attract bears that travel waterways, lessen your bear encounter chances by keeping fishy scents away from clothing. Catch-and-release fishing minimizes attracting bears.

For cleaning fish in the front country, dispose of the entrails in bear-resistant garbage cans. In the backcountry, do not bury or burn the innards, as that may attract bears. Instead, puncture the air bladder and throw the entrails into deep water where caught at least 100 feet away from a campsite, dock, or boat launch.

HORSEBACK RIDING

Dude ranches line the perimeters of the parks and offer a modern cowboy and cowgirl approach to exploring the sights. Cowboy hats are optional for horseback riding, which was the traditional way of touring the park in its early days. But wear long pants rather than shorts to prevent chafing, and hiking boots, cowboy boots, or tennis shoes rather than sandals. Make reservations for these trips, and tip guides 15 percent.

WINTER SPORTS

Be mindful of skier and snowshoer etiquette. On roads where snowcoaches and snowmobiles travel, skiers and snowshoers should travel on the right side to allow vehicles to pass. On groomed trails, snowshoers should stay off the parallel skier tracks. With skier-set tracks, snowshoers should blaze their own trails. Winter trail maps are available online (www.nps.gov/yell) and at visitors centers.

New regulations for quieter, cleaner snowmobiles and limits on numbers of winter rigs mean vehicles are not the ambience-wreckers they once were. To snowmobile on your own, you'll need a permit acquired in the annual **lottery** (www.recreation.gov, early Sept.-early Oct.). If you miss the lottery, you can pick up remaining or cancelled permits in November. If you bring your own snowmobile, it must be an approved BAT (Best Available Technology) snowmobile. All participants in your group must complete the **Yellowstone Snowmobile Education Certification** (www.nps.gov/yell) online training course, have driver's licenses, and be of certain ages to rent machines.

Visas and Officialdom

INTERNATIONAL TRAVELERS

Yellowstone has trip planning information in 10 different languages. Grand Teton has a selection of brochures in six languages. Ask for copies at visitors centers or online (www.nps.gov/yell or www.nps.gov/grte).

Entering the United States

International travelers entering the United States must have passports. One exception applies to travelers from Canada and countries in the Western Hemisphere Travel Initiative, who may use a U.S. passport card, enhanced driver's license, or acceptable alternate border crossing cards. In addition, visas are required except for countries with visa waivers (http://travel.state.gov). Except Canadians, international travelers entering the United States must have a current I-94 form ($6). You'll only need to show documentation at your international port of entry. Once in the United States, you will not need to show documentation when traveling between states except for commercial flights.

Money and Currency Exchange

International travelers should exchange currency at their major port of entry. As you travel, use ATM cards to get more cash. Smaller denominations ($50 and under) work best. Canadians who commonly use Canadian dollars in northern Montana should plan to convert to U.S. dollars instead. Businesses around Yellowstone are not prepared to handle other currency. Using a credit card while traveling will give you the best exchange rates.

Restricted Items

In general, the United States does not allow plants, drugs, firewood, or live bait to cross borders. Some fresh meats, poultry products, fruits, and vegetables are restricted, as are firearms. Pets are permitted to cross the border with a certificate of rabies vaccination dated within 30 days prior to crossing. Bear sprays are not allowed on airplanes in checked or carry-on luggage.

Travel Tips

TOURIST INFORMATION
Cell Phones

Cell phone coverage in Yellowstone and Grand Teton is not comprehensive, but around many of the larger developed areas, cell phones will work. Verizon is the predominant service. Cell phones using other services may have dropped calls. While hiking in remote terrain, canyons, or mountainous areas, you may not have coverage, so plan on self-rescuing rather than relying on a 911 call.

When using cell phones, be considerate. Turn off ringers, as phone noise catapults park visitors from a natural experience back into the hubbub of modern life. If you must make a call, move away from campsites and other visitors to avoid disrupting their experience. On trails, refrain from using phones in the presence of other hikers. Be considerate of other people in the backcountry and their desire to get away from it all.

Internet Access

Some of the park hotels have wireless Internet available, but not all. None of the visitors centers or campgrounds have wireless Internet, with the exception of the Craig Thomas Discovery & Visitor Center in Grand Teton

Enhance Your Park Experience

With expert instructors, **Yellowstone Association Institute** (406/848-2400, www.yellowstoneassociation.com) offers trips for wildlife-watching, bird-watching, hiking, cross-country skiing, snowshoeing, sightseeing, and natural history exploration. The institute runs single-day and multiday field seminars, learning programs, private tours, and programs for kids, youth, teens, college students, and families. In-park transportation is in 14-passenger buses. Lodging at the institute's Lamar Buffalo Ranch inside Yellowstone is sometimes included.

With three campuses, two in Grand Teton National Park and one in Jackson, the **Teton Science School** (877/404-6626, www.tetonscience.org) runs programs in Grand Teton, Jackson Hole, National Elk Refuge, and Yellowstone. They offer wildlife-watching trips, summer camps, and programs for kids, teens, adults, and families. Programs can be half day, full day, or multiday. Some programs add hiking, cross-country skiing, or snowshoeing.

Both Yellowstone and Grand Teton use volunteers to help out on a variety of projects with their **Volunteer-in-Parks** programs (www.volunteer.gov/gov). Projects can be working in visitors centers, doing maintenance, helping with office and clerical work, and rehabilitating abused campsites and trails.

National Park. Most hotels and private campgrounds outside the park have wireless Internet.

ACCESS FOR TRAVELERS WITH DISABILITIES

Yellowstone and Grand Teton National Parks offer **accessibility brochures** (www.nps.gov/yell or www.nps.gov/grte) at visitors centers and online. Both parks have TDD (Yellowstone: 307/344-2386; Grand Teton: 307/739-3400) and ADA facilities, although they are not ubiquitous. All lodging facilities have a few rooms or cabins that are accessible. Inquire about these through the individual concessionaires that run the lodging properties. Most campgrounds have a few wheelchair-accessible sites and restrooms. These are listed in the accessibility brochures for both parks.

Yellowstone and Grand Teton have some paved and hard-surface trails that are wheelchair-accessible. While some of the boardwalk trails at the geothermal areas in Yellowstone are wheelchair-accessible, many of the boardwalks have steps at some point. All accessible trails are listed in the accessibility brochures. Both parks also offer some interpretive activities that are accessible. Locate these in the seasonal park newspapers. While pet dogs are not permitted on backcountry trails, service dogs are allowed, although due to bears, they are discouraged. With service dogs, be safe by sticking to well-traveled trails during midday.

Blind or permanently disabled U.S. citizens and permanent residents can get a free lifetime National Parks and Federal Recreational Lands **Access Pass** (https://store.usgs.gov/pass/access.html). The pass admits the pass holder plus three other adults in the same vehicle; children under age 16 are free. Pass holders also get 50 percent discounts on federally run tours and campgrounds. Passes are available in person at entrance stations (proof of medical disability or eligibility for receiving federal benefits is required).

TRAVELING WITH CHILDREN

Yellowstone and Grand Teton were made for kids. Geysers, sputtering mud pots, fishing, and rampant wildlife are natural kid attractions. The National Park Service has designed ways to pique the interest of kids through educational activities online (www.nps.gov/yell or www.nps.gov/grte under "Learn About the

Park"), in-park activities, and visitors center hands-on activities.

Junior Ranger Programs (www.nps.gov/kids/jrRangers.cfm) mix educational activities with experiences for families to do in the park. Pick up Junior Ranger activity guides ($3) at any visitors center. Kids complete the activities and receive a Junior Ranger badge after stopping at a visitors center to get sworn in.

Yellowstone offers some **ranger programs** specifically geared toward kids. At the Madison Junior Ranger Station, 30-minute programs for families run multiple times daily during summer; 20-minute kids' programs take place daily at Old Faithful Visitor Education Center. Check with visitors centers, campground bulletin boards, hotel activity desks, and park newspapers for other seasonal park schedules.

Yellowstone also has a **Young Scientist** program. Kids can become a Yellowstone Young Scientist with booklets ($5) full of self-guided science activities sold at Old Faithful Visitor Education Center. Different booklets on volcanic activity are geared to specific age groups. Check out a Young Scientist Toolkit for the gear to do the science study. When finished, return to the visitors center for a Young Scientist patch or key chain. Grand Teton's Jenny Lake has a **Young Naturalist Program** (307/739-3392, 1:30pm Mon., Wed., Fri. June-Aug., free) for self-guided outdoor exploration that the whole family can do together. The online **WebRangers** (www.nps.gov/webrangers) program offers games, coloring pages, and quizzes that can help kids learn about wildlife, plants, geysers, and ecology in both parks.

Other park programs include **Wildlife Olympics,** where kids test their physical skills against wildlife skills. Summer drop-in programs happen several days each week throughout the summer at Old Faithful Visitor Education Center (www.nps.gov/yell). In West Yellowstone, kids can learn about being smokejumpers through the **Junior Smokejumper Program** (Yellowstone Nature Connection, 10 Yellowstone Ave.,

Take kids fishing on Yellowstone's streams.

406/646-7557, http://yellowstonenatureconnection.org, 10am or 3pm daily mid-June-Sept. and Mon.-Fri. mid-May-mid-June, $5). Kids get to jump out of a grounded plane and be sworn in as smokejumpers. Reservations by phone or online are recommended; parents can join in, too.

TRAVELING WITH PETS

Pets are allowed in the national parks, but only in limited areas: campgrounds, parking lots, and roadsides. They are not allowed on trails, boardwalks, beaches, in the backcountry, or on the Multi-Use Pathway in Grand Teton. Preventing conflicts with wildlife is the main reason. To hike with your pooch, go to surrounding national forests.

While outside a vehicle or in a campground, pets must be caged or on a leash six feet or shorter. Be kind enough to avoid leaving them unattended in a car anywhere. Be considerate of wildlife and other visitors by keeping your pet under control and disposing of waste in garbage cans.

Inside Yellowstone, several of the cabin complexes permit pets for a fee ($25). Check for additional restrictions when you make reservations. In general, lodging in Grand Teton does not permit pets, but many outside-park locales in Jackson do. For kenneling pets, Jackson Hole has **DogJax** (3590 Southpark Dr., Jackson, 307/733-3647, http://dogjax.com).

SENIOR TRAVELERS

National parks, plus lands run by the U.S. Fish and Wildlife Service, U.S. Forest Service, and Bureau of Land Management, offer a great bargain for U.S. citizens or permanent residents who are ages 62 and older. The **National Parks and Federal Recreational Lands Pass** costs $20 per year or $80 for lifetime. To purchase one, bring proof of age (state driver's license, birth certificate, or passport) in person to any national park entrance station. The card admits four adults in the vehicle, plus all children under age 16. The pass also grants 50 percent discounts on fees for federally run tours and campgrounds; however, discounts do not apply to park concessionaire services like hotels, boat tours, and bus tours.

SOLO TRAVELERS

Plenty of people travel solo to national parks, but hiking alone in the Greater Yellowstone Ecosystem is not recommended due to bears and mountain lions. Nevertheless, some hikers still venture into the backcountry alone. If you're one of them, make lots of noise while hiking, carry pepper spray, and brush up on your bear skills. Solo travelers looking for trail companions can join park naturalist hikes. For times and dates, check with visitors centers, in-park newspapers, or online. You can also connect with the Bozeman Adventure Club or Teton Sierra Club (www.meetup.com) for hikes. At popular trailheads, you can just hang out at the start and follow a larger group, staying close to them, or ask if you can join another few hikers. Many are happy to include additional hikers.

Health and Safety

WILDLIFE

Safe behavior can deter **bear** attacks. With strict food and garbage rules, the Greater Yellowstone Ecosystem has minimized aggressive bear encounters, attacks, and deaths, for both humans and bears. Bears are dangerous around food, be it a carcass in the woods, a pack left on a trail, or a cooler left in a campsite. Protecting bears and protecting yourself starts with being conscious of food, including wrappers and crumbs. Snack-mix tidbits dropped along trails attract wildlife, as do biodegradable apple cores chucked into the forest. Pick up what you drop, and pack out all garbage; don't leave a Hansel-and-Gretel trail for the bears.

Camp safely: Use low-odor foods, keep food and cooking gear out of sleeping sites in the backcountry, and store it inside your vehicle or inside bear boxes in front-country campgrounds. In front-country campgrounds, you'll find detailed explanations of how to camp safely in bear country stapled to your picnic table.

While hiking, make noise, go in groups of at least four people, stay on the trail, and carry and know how to use pepper spray. Be alert. If you come across a carcass, depart immediately. Avoid hiking at dawn or dusk, which are prime animal times. If you encounter a bear, remain calm. Back away slowly rather than running away like prey. Lower your eyes in deference and talk quietly. If a bear charges, use pepper spray in its eyes. Pepper spray should be sprayed directly at the sensitive facial tissues, not on people like bug repellent. If attacked, drop face down onto the ground and play dead, leaving your pack on to protect your back.

Mountain lions rarely prey on humans, but they can with small kids. Making noise for bears will also help you avoid surprising a lion. Hike with others, and keep kids close. If you stumble upon a lion, above all, do not run. Be calm, and group together to appear bigger. Look at the cat with peripheral vision rather than staring straight on, and back away slowly. If the lion attacks, fight back with everything: rocks, sticks, or kicking.

While **bison** appear docile, they are speedier than they look. They can head-butt or gore people.

LAND AND WATER HAZARDS

Drowning from falling into swift or scalding water is one of the top causes of death in the Greater Yellowstone Ecosystem. Be extremely cautious around lakes, fast-moving streams, and waterfalls. Rivers can be swift, frigid, clogged with submerged obstacles, unforgiving, and sometimes lethal. A second cause of injuries and death is falling while climbing off-trail on steep, cliffy terrain.

It's really cool to see geysers and mud pots, but they are dangerous in several ways. **Boiling geothermal waters** have scalded people stupid enough to think of them as hot tubs. They've even caused death. **Breakable crusts** surrounding features can hide boiling waters. Some thermals contain infectious parasites that can be fatal or emit toxic gases. To protect yourself, stay on boardwalks and trails. If gases make you feel sick, leave the area.

While **ice** often looks solid to step on, it harbors unseen caverns beneath. Buried crevasses (large vertical cracks) are difficult to see, and snow bridges can collapse as a person crosses. **Steep-angled snowfields** also pose a danger from falling. Use an ice ax and caution, or stay off

them. If you want to slide on the snow for fun, slide only where you have a safe run out away from rocks and trees.

Inhaling dust from deer mice droppings can lead to **hantavirus** infections, with accompanying flu-like symptoms. Avoid burrows and woodpiles thick with rodents. Store all food in rodent-proof containers. If you find rodent dust in your gear, disinfect it with water and bleach (1.5 cups bleach to one gallon water). If you contract the virus, get immediate medical attention.

Lakes and streams can carry parasites like *Giardia lamblia.* If ingested, it causes cramping, nausea, and severe diarrhea for up to six weeks. Avoid giardia by boiling water (for one minute, plus one minute for each 1,000 feet of elevation above sea level) or using a one-micron filter. Bleach also works (add two drops per quart and wait 30 minutes). Tap water in campgrounds, hotels, and picnic areas has been treated.

Bugs can carry diseases such as **West Nile virus** and **Rocky Mountain spotted fever**. Protect yourself by wearing long sleeves and pants, plus using insect repellent in spring and summer when mosquitoes and ticks are common. If you are bitten by a tick, remove it, disinfect the bite, and see a doctor if lesions or a rash appears.

PERSONAL SAFETY

Due to the high elevation and arid climate, winds, altitude, and lower humidity can add up to a fast case of **dehydration,** which often manifests first as a headache. While in the Greater Yellowstone Ecosystem and especially while hiking, drink lots of water. Carry enough water to consume more than you normally would. With children, monitor their fluid intake.

Some visitors from sea level feel light-headedness, headaches, or shortness of breath at the **high altitudes** of Yellowstone and Grand Teton. To acclimatize, slow down the pace of hiking and drink lots of fluids. If symptoms spike, descend in elevation as soon as possible. Altitude also

Wildlife Safety Tips

While there are no guarantees of spotting wildlife, huge broad meadows in the parks make it easy to see wildlife. You may get to see bison, elk, moose, deer, pronghorn, wolves, coyote, foxes, raptors, or bears. Remember that wildlife is just that....WILD. Though bison, elk, or even bears may appear tame, they are not and gorings are common. Here are a few hints to remain safe.

- **Do not approach wildlife.** Although our inclinations tell us to scoot in for a closer look, crowding wildlife puts you at risk and endangers the animal, often scaring it off. Seemingly docile bison and elk have suddenly gored people crowding too close. Sometimes simply the presence of people can habituate an animal to hanging around people; with bears, this can lead to more aggressive behavior. Stay at least **100 yards away** (the length of a football field) from bears and wolves. For all other wildlife, stay at least **25 yards away**. Both parks have volunteer Wildlife Brigades to help visitors along roadways and geyser basins maintain their distance.

- Safety is important when watching wildlife—safety for you and safety for the wildlife. For spying wildlife up close, use a good pair of **binoculars** or a spotting scope.

- Use **telephoto lenses** for photography rather than scooting in too close. Bison gorings have been getting more prevalent, all related to taking photos, especially selfies with tablets or cell phones. Since 2000, bison have injured 25 people, at least half when taking photos. **Avoid getting too close,** too while taking cell phone photos as bison have been known to charge.

- **Do not feed any animal.** Feeding can amp up their aggression. Because human food is not part of their natural diet, they may suffer at foraging on their own. If you see a carcass on a trail, move away and report it to park rangers. No doubt an animal is nearby protecting it.

- Follow instructions for **food storage.** They are designed to protect you and wildlife. Bears, wolves, and coyote may become more aggressive when acquiring food, and ravens can strew food and garbage, making it more available to other wildlife. Your actions may affect the next camper staying at your campsite.

- Let the animal's or bird's **behavior** guide your behavior. If the animal appears twitchy, nervous, or points eyes and ears directly at you, back off: You're too close. The goal is to watch wild animals go about their normal business, rather than to see how they react to disruption. If you behave like a predator stalking an animal, the creature will assume you are one.

- If you see **wildlife along a road**, use pullouts or broad shoulders to drive completely off the road. Do not block the middle of the road. Use the car as a blind to watch wildlife, and keep pets inside. If you see a bear, you're better off just driving by slowly (bear jams tend to condition the bruin to become accustomed to vehicles). Watch for cars, as visitors can be injured by inattentive drivers whenever a bear jam occurs.

increases UV radiation exposure. To prevent sunburn, use a strong sunscreen and wear sunglasses and a hat.

Insidious and subtle, **hypothermia** sneaks up on exhausted and physically unprepared hikers. The body's inner core loses heat, reducing mental and physical functions. Watch for uncontrolled shivering, incoherence, poor judgment, fumbling, mumbling, and slurred speech. Avoid becoming hypothermic by staying dry. Don

rain gear and warm, moisture-wicking layers, rather than cottons that won't dry and fail to retain heat. Get hypothermic hikers into dry clothing and shelter. Give warm, nonalcoholic and non-caffeinated liquids. If the victim cannot regain body heat, strip and use skin-to-skin contact with another person in a sleeping bag.

Incorrect socks and ill-fitting shoes cause most **blisters.** Cotton socks absorb water from the feet while you're hiking and hold onto it, providing a surface for friction. Synthetic or wool-blend socks wick water away from the skin. To prevent blisters, recognize "hot spots" or rubs, applying moleskin, blister pads, or New-Skin to sensitive areas. In a pinch, slap duct tape on trouble spots. Once a blister occurs, apply blister bandages or Second Skin, a product developed for burns that cools blisters and cushions them. Cover Second Skin with moleskin to absorb future rubbing, and secure it in place.

Resources

Suggested Reading

GEOLOGY

Bryan, T. Scott, *The Geysers of Yellowstone.* Boulder, CO: University Press of Colorado, 2008. A guidebook for geyser fans, the work has maps, photos, and cultural and historical information on visiting the park's 500 thermal features, including geysers.

Craighead, Charles, *Geology of Grand Teton National Park: How the Mountains Came to Be.* Moose, WY: Grand Teton Association, 2006. This 55-page book covers the geology behind the Tetons and Jackson Hole.

Good, J. M. M., and Kenneth L. Pierce, *Interpreting the Landscape: Recent and Ongoing Geology of Grand Teton and Yellowstone National Parks.* Moose, WY: Grand Teton Association, 1997. This 58-page book with photos and diagrams covers the basics for both parks, but does not include more recent geologic discoveries.

Love, J. David, John C. Reed Jr., and Kenneth L. Pierce, *A Geological Chronicle of Jackson Hole & the Teton Range.* Moose, WY: Grand Teton Natural History Association, 2007. Maps, photos, charts, and elevation graphs add to the discussion of the sinking valley and youngest peaks in the Rockies.

Smith, Robert B., and Lee J. Siegel, *Windows into the Earth: The Geologic Story of Yellowstone and Grand Teton National Parks.* New York, NY: Oxford University Press, 2000. The authors detail the volcanic and tectonic past of Yellowstone-Teton country with an emphasis on dynamic processes.

Thomas, Robert, and William Fritz, *Roadside Geology of Yellowstone Country.* Missoula, MT: Mountain Press Publishing Co., 2011. With color photos, diagrams, and maps, this classic geology guide covers Yellowstone and surrounding regions, including the Beartooth Mountains, Quake Lake, and the valleys of Gardiner, Wapiti, and Paradise.

GUIDEBOOKS

Schmidt, Jeremy, and Steven Fuller, *National Geographic Yellowstone and Grand Teton National Parks Road Guide: The Essential Guide for Motorists.* National Geographic, 2010. A handy 93-page guide to driving the roads in both parks. Each section has maps with roadside stops identified and detailed.

Walker, Carter, *Moon Montana & Wyoming: Including Yellowstone, Grand Teton & Glacier National Parks.* Berkeley, CA: Avalon Travel Publishing, 2014. A guidebook for traveling in Montana and Wyoming.

Yellowstone Association, *Yellowstone: The Official Guide to Touring the World's First National Park.* Yellowstone Association, 2014. The Yellowstone Association annually updates this cross between a top highlights guide to the park and a color photo book. It describes road tours, sights, hikes, wildlife, and flora.

HIKING AND CLIMBING

Anderson, Roger, and Carol Shively Anderson, *A Ranger's Guide to Yellowstone Day Hikes.* Helena, MT: Farcountry Press, updated 2013. Written by two park rangers, this guide covers 29 hikes, with details about geology, plants, and history.

Craighead, Charles, *Day Hikes and Short Walks of Grand Teton National Park.* Moose, WY: Grand Teton Association, 2005. A short guide to the best hikes in the Tetons with nature photos by Henry Holdsworth.

Duffy, Katy, and Darwin Wile, *Teton Trails: A Guide to the Trails of Grand Teton National Park.* Moose, WY: Grand Teton Natural History Association, 1995. Very detailed descriptions including natural history on trails in the park. Covers short hikes to overnighters.

Ortenburger, Leigh, and Reynold Jackson, *A Climber's Guide to the Teton Range.* Seattle, WA: The Mountaineers, 1996. This climbing guide details 800 routes on 200 peaks.

Rossiter, Richard, *Best Climbs Grand Teton National Park.* Guilford, CT: Falcon Guides, 2012. This new version of his 1994 Teton Classics book covers popular climbing routes on the Teton peaks, from easier ascents to technically challenging summits.

Schneider, Bill, *Best Easy Day Hikes in Grand Teton National Park.* Guilford, CT: Falcon Guides, 2012. Descriptions of day hikes in the park, including family-friendly options.

Schneider, Bill, *Best Easy Day Hikes in Yellowstone.* Guilford, CT: Falcon Guides, 2011. A trail guide covering 30 day hikes in Yellowstone for families. Includes geyser basin walks.

Schneider, Bill, *Hiking the Absaroka-Beartooth Wilderness.* Guilford, CT: Falcon Guides, 2015. For travelers on the Beartooth Highway, this is the hiking guide for the trails along the way.

Schneider, Bill, *Hiking Grand Teton National Park.* Guilford, CT: Falcon Guides, 2012. A comprehensive guide on trails in Grand Teton—from short jaunts to long ascents, including backpacking routes.

Schneider, Bill, *Hiking Yellowstone National Park.* Guilford, CT: Falcon Guides, 2012. A comprehensive hiking guide covering more than 100 hikes, from short flat trails to long traverses, including backpacking trips.

Woods, Rebecca, *Jackson Hole Hikes.* Jackson, WY: White Willow Publishing, 2009. A hiking guide for Grand Teton National Park, Gros Ventre Wilderness, Teton Wilderness, Snow King, and Teton Pass.

HISTORY

Barnes, Christine, *Old Faithful Inn: 100th Anniversary.* WW West, 2003. From the author of the Great Lodges books, this book celebrates the history of Yellowstone's historic lodge in photos and text.

Black, George, *Empire of Shadows: The Epic Story of Yellowstone.* New York, NY: St. Martin's Griffin, 2013. The story of the early explorations of Yellowstone until the establishment of the park and the flight of Chief Joseph and the Nez Perce.

Craighead, Charles, *History of Grand Teton National Park.* Moose, WY: Grand Teton Association, 2006. A short overview of park history with nature photos by Henry Holdsworth.

Miller, M. Mark, *Adventures in Yellowstone: Early Travelers Tell Their Tales.* Guilford, CT: TwoDot, 2009. A narrated collection of stories from early park travelers, with historical photos.

Miller, M. Mark, *The Stories of Yellowstone: Adventure Tales from the World's First National Park*. Guilford, CT: TwoDot, 2014. A collection of writing from early park visitors spanning 1807 to the 1920s.

Nabokov, Peter, and Lawrence Loendorf, *Restoring a Presence: American Indians and Yellowstone National Park*. Norman, OK: University of Oklahoma Press, 2004. Identifies Native American archaeology and ethnography in Yellowstone National Park.

Nerburn, Kent, *Chief Joseph & the Flight of the Nez Perce: The Untold Story of an American Tragedy*. San Francisco, CA: Harper One, 2006. Chronicles the 1,800-mile journey made by Chief Joseph and 800 Nez Perce from Oregon to northern Montana while fleeing the U.S. Army.

Righter, Robert W. *Crucible For Conservation: The Struggle For Grand Teton National Park* and *Peaks, Politics, and Passion: Grand Teton National Park Comes of Age*. Moose, WY: Grand Teton Natural History Association, 1982 and 2014. The first work recounts the history behind the creation of the park, a battle that stretched over 50 years. The second book, a continuation of the first, covers parkhood to the present day.

Whittlesey, Lee H., *Yellowstone Place Names*. Wonderland Publishing Co., 2006. Gives the background and trivia on about 1,000 names of places in Yellowstone.

NATURAL HISTORY

Johnson, Kurt F., *A Field Guide to Yellowstone and Grand Teton National Parks*. Helena, MT: Farcountry Press, 2013. Written by a Jackson Hole naturalist and photographer, this broad and well-rounded field guide gives details on rocks, minerals, plants, animals, birds, and fish.

Kershaw, Linda, Andy MacKinnon, and Jim Pojar. *Plants of the Rocky Mountains*. Auburn, WA: Lone Pine Publishing, 1998. A Lone Pine Field Guide for eight types of flora found in the Rocky Mountains: trees, shrubs, wildflowers, aquatics, grasses, ferns, mosses, and lichens. Although the pictures are small, the detailed descriptions of appearance, season, and habitat help in identification. Notes on each of the 1,300 species in the book include fun tidbits on the origin of names and Native American uses.

Shaw, Richard, and Marian A. Shaw, *Plants of Yellowstone and Grand Teton National Parks*. Helena, MT: Wheelwright Publishing, 2008. Written by botanists and veterans of 31 years as naturalists in Yellowstone, the book identifies wildflowers, shrubs, and trees.

Yellowstone Association. *Living Colors: Microbes of Yellowstone National Park*. Montana State University Biology Institute, and Montana Institute Ecosystems, 2013. A 52-page book with color photos of the park's geothermal microbes and information on where to see them.

Yellowstone National Park, Yellowstone Resources and Issues Handbook. Washington, DC: National Park Service, U.S. Department of the Interior, annually published. Heavy on current information, this 268-page compendium is produced and reviewed annually by the staff of Yellowstone. Covers current research on history, cultural resources, Greater Yellowstone Ecosystem, geology, thermal life, vegetation, fire, and wildlife.

RECREATION

Gollin Evans, Lisa, *Outdoor Family Guide to Yellowstone & Grand Teton National Parks*. Mountaineers Books, second edition, 2006. Contains 50 family outings including hiking, biking, paddling, and horseback riding.

Harrison, Melynda, *Ski Trails of Southwest Montana: 30 of the Best Cross Country &*

Snowshoe Trails Near Big Sky, Bozeman & Paradise Valley. Bozeman, MT: First Ascent Press, 2007. Covers cross-country ski and snowshoe trails surrounding northern Yellowstone.

Lomax, Becky, *Moon Montana, Wyoming & Idaho Camping: Including Yellowstone, Grand Teton, and Glacier National Parks.* Berkeley, CA: Avalon Travel Publishing, third edition, 2014. A camping guide for the northern Rocky Mountains, especially the national park corridor.

Nelson, Don, *Paddling Yellowstone and Grand Teton National Parks.* Guilford, CT: Falcon Guides, 1999. For kayakers and canoers, 38 paddle routes cover day trips to overnighters on park lakes. Some of the permit information is out of date, but routes are still doable.

Parks, Richard, *Fishing Yellowstone National Park: An Angler's Complete Guide to More than 100 Streams, Rivers, and Lakes.* Guilford, CT: Lyons Press, 2007. Written by a Montana fishing guide, the book tells you where and when to fish, plus tips on lures and tackle.

Retallic, Ken, *Flyfisher's Guide to Wyoming: Including Grand Teton and Yellowstone National Parks.* Belgrade, MT: Wilderness Adventures Press, revised edition 2012. Written by a local angler, this guide covers iconic rivers in Yellowstone and Grand Teton, plus famous rivers surrounding the parks.

Verderber, Gustav W., *Photographing Yellowstone National Park: Where to Find Perfect Shots and How to Take Them.* Woodstock, VT: Countryman Press, 2007. Part of The Photographer's Guide series, this 88-page book provides advice on where, when, and how to get stellar wildlife and scenery shots.

WILDLIFE

Craighead, Charles, *Wildlife of Grand Teton National Park.* Moose, WY: Grand Teton Association, 2006. A short, pithy guide to Teton wildlife with nature photos by Henry Holdsworth.

Fisher, Chris, *Birds of the Rocky Mountains.* Auburn, WA: Lone Pine Publishing, 1997. A Lone Pine Field Guide for birds found in the Rocky Mountains, from raptors to waterfowl, songbirds to woodpeckers. Large drawings help with identification, and descriptions include details on size, range, habitat, nesting, and feeding.

Fisher, Chris, Don Pattie, and Tamara Hartson, *Mammals of the Rocky Mountains.* Auburn, WA: Lone Pine Publishing, 2000. A Lone Pine Field Guide for 91 species of animals found in the Rocky Mountains. Each animal has details on physical description, behavior, habitat, food, denning, range, and young.

McMillion, Scott, *Mark of the Grizzly.* Guilford, CT: Lyons Press, 2011. This second edition of McMillion's top-selling book adds more recent stories on bear attacks to his original collection and digs deeper into why they happened.

Schneider, Bill. *Bear Aware.* Guilford, CT: Falcon Press, 2004. This handy little 96-page book is packed with advice on how to hike safely in bear country, debunking bear myths with facts.

Smith, Douglas, and Gary Ferguson, *Decade of the Wolf, Revised and Updated: Returning the Wild to Yellowstone.* Guilford, CT: Lyons Press, 2012. Written by a wolf biologist and nature writer, this book tells the story of the restoration of wolves to Yellowstone.

Steinhart, Peter, *The Company of Wolves.* New York, NY: Vintage Books, 1996. An analysis of wolf behavior: familial relationships, social ties, and predation.

Wilkinson, Todd, and Michael H. Francis, *Watching Yellowstone and Grand Teton*

Wildlife: The Best Places to Look from Roads and Trails. Helena, MT: Riverbend Publishing, 2004. This 96-page book describes the best places to spot 45 different species of wildlife in the parks.

Internet Resources

YELLOWSTONE NATIONAL PARK

Yellowstone National Park
www.nps.gov/yell
Official National Park Service website for the park.

Yellowstone Forever
www.yellowstone.org
Home of Yellowstone fundraising, educational institute, and bookstores.

Trail Guides Yellowstone
www.trailguidesyellowstone.com
A Yellowstone National Park concessionaire that guides hiking and backpacking trips, but also offers detailed trail descriptions with photos on their website.

GRAND TETON NATIONAL PARK

Grand Teton National Park
www.nps.gov/grte
Official National Park Service website for the park.

Teton Association
www.grandtetonpark.org
Information and bookstore for Grand Teton.

Teton Science School
www.tetonscience.org
Educational programs for Grand Teton, Yellowstone, and Jackson Hole.

Teton Hiking Trails
www.tetonhikingtrails.com

A new source of detailed information on hiking trails in Grand Teton National Park.

JACKSON HOLE

National Elk Refuge
www.fws.gov/nationalelkrefuge
Information on visitor activities and wildlife on the National Elk Refuge.

Jackson Hole Chamber of Commerce
www.jacksonholechamber.com
Businesses, activities, entertainment, lodging, and restaurants for Jackson Hole.

NATIONAL FORESTS

Recreation.gov
www.recreation.gov
Official site for campground reservations in the national forests surrounding Yellowstone and Grand Teton. Also the website for Grand Teton backcountry campsite reservations.

Bridger-Teton National Forest
www.fs.usda.gov/btnf
Official site for national forest land east and south of Grand Teton National Park and Jackson Hole.

Caribou-Targhee National Forest
www.fs.usda.gov/ctnf
Official site for national forest land west of Grand Teton and southwest of Yellowstone.

Custer-Gallatin National Forest
www.fs.usda.gov/gallatin
Official site for national forest land on the north end of Yellowstone.

Shoshone National Forest
www.fs.usda.gov/shoshone
Official site for national forest land on the east side of Yellowstone and Grand Teton.

IDAHO

Idaho Department of Commerce
www.visitidaho.org

Idaho Transportation Department
http://511.idaho.gov
For road conditions, construction disruptions, webcams, and travel information.

MONTANA

Montana Office of Tourism
www.visitmt.com

Montana Department of Transportation
www.mdt.mt.gov/travinfo
For road conditions, construction disruptions, webcams, and travel information.

WYOMING

Wyoming Travel and Tourism
www.wyomingtourism.org

Wyoming Department of Transportation
www.wyoroad.info
For road conditions, construction disruptions, webcams, and travel information.

Index

A

Absaroka-Beartooth Wilderness: 62
Absaroka Mountains: 55, 63
Abyss Pool: 147
Aerial Tram: 34, 273-274, 277
air travel: 394, 396, 397
Alaska Basin: 305-307
Albright Falls: 198
Albright Peak: 244
Albright Visitor Center: 45, 50
Amphitheater Lake: 37, 236-238; map 237
Anemone Geyser: 97
animals: 376-380
Antelope Flats: 39, 225-226, 233
Arch Park: 49
Artist Point: 31, 141, 143
Artists Paintpots: 38, 92, 100
Aspen Ridge-Boulder Ridge Loop: 242
ATMs: 410
auto travel: 390-395, 396, 397, 398, 400-401
Avalanche Peak: 157

B

Back Basin: 101-102
backpacking: general discussion 406; Canyon and Lake Country 162; Jackson Hole 279, 306-307; North Grand Teton 198-199, 203; North Yellowstone 62, 63; Old Faithful and West Yellowstone 111-112; South Grand Teton 228, 240, 244, 246, 250
Bannock Indian Ford: 62
Bannock Trail: 69, 305
Barronette Trail: 69
Basin Creek: 332
Basin Lakes: 306
Basin Lakes National Recreation Trail: 332, 334
Bearpaw Lake: 249
bears: 379
Beartooth Basin Summer Ski Area: 331, 335
Beartooth Butte: 333
Beartooth Highway: 69, 331-332
Beartooth Lake: 333
Beartooth Rally: 336
Beauty Lake: 333, 334
Beauty Pool: 97
Beaver Pond Loop: 57
Bechler Falls: 192
Bechler Ranger Station: 192, 198
Bechler River: 111-112, 192-193, 198-199
Beck Lake Bike Park: 345

Beehive Basin: 319
Beehive Geyser: 97
beer/breweries: gateways 324, 350; Jackson Hole 292; North Yellowstone 73
Berry Fire: 185
bicycling: general discussion 400-401; Canyon and Lake Country 162; gateways 315, 320, 334-335, 345; Jackson Hole 273, 279-280, 305, 307-308; North Grand Teton 189, 199; North Yellowstone 64; Old Faithful and West Yellowstone 105, 106, 112-113, 118; South Grand Teton 228, 248-249
Bighorn Pass: 320
Big Sky Classical Music Festival: 323
Big Sky, Montana: 315, 318-329; map 318
Big Sky Resort: 320, 322, 323, 324, 326-327
Bin 22: 36, 290
birds/bird-watching: general discussion 378, 380; Canyon and Lake Country 139, 140, 142, 143, 144, 145-146, 151, 156, 157, 165; Jackson Hole 273; North Grand Teton 188, 189, 190, 194, 197, 203; North Yellowstone 52, 53, 62; Old Faithful and West Yellowstone 113; South Grand Teton 233
Biscuit Basin: 99, 112
Biscuit Basin Overlook: 107
Black Canyon of the Yellowstone: 55, 59, 63; map 60
Black Dike: 186
Black Dragon's Cauldron: 143
Blackfoot Basin: 305
Black Growler: 38, 364
Black Opal Pool: 99
Black Sand Basin: 99-100
Blacktail Deer Creek: 59, 63, 66
Blacktail Plateau: 64, 68
Blacktail Pond: 53, 59
Blacktail Ponds Overlook: 233
Bliss Pass: 63
boating: Canyon and Lake Country 147, 163, 164, 165; gateways 344, 346; Jackson Hole 281; North Grand Teton 185-186, 187, 188, 189, 192, 200-203; Old Faithful and West Yellowstone 113-114; South Grand Teton 228, 249, see also kayaking/canoeing; rafting
boat transportation: 399
Bobby Sox trees: 99
Boiling River Hot Springs: 67-68
border crossings: 410
Boy Scout Antler Auction: 286
Bradley Lake: 230, 235-237, 249, 252, 253; map 236

Breccia Peak: 358
Bridge Bay: 158
Bridge Bay Marina: 163, 168
Bridge Bay Ranger Station: 164
Bridger-Teton National Forest: 191-193, 199, 274-276, 279
Brink of the Lower Falls: 32, 142, 155
Brink of the Upper Falls: 143, 152
Buffalo Bill Center of the West: 340, 342
Buffalo Bill Dam: 344
Buffalo Bill Museum: 342
Buffalo Bill Reservoir: 346
Buffalo Bill Scenic Byway: 340, 345
Buffalo Bill State Park: 344, 346
Buffalo Plateau: 59
Buffalo River Valley: 193, 199
Bunsen Peak: 52, 57-58, 64, 68
bus travel: 394, 396, 397, 398-399

C

Cache-Game Trails: 280
Calcite Springs: 53, 62
camping: general discussion 230, 399-400, 402, 403; Canyon and Lake Country 147, 163, 165, 166, 174-177; gateways 320, 328, 333, 338-339, 344, 353-354, 358, 359; Jackson Hole 300-301, 310-311; North Grand Teton 185, 187, 189, 192, 193, 202, 203, 213-216; North Yellowstone 63, 80-82; Old Faithful and West Yellowstone 103, 111, 113, 128-130; South Grand Teton 250, 259-260
Canary Spring: 51
canoeing: see kayaking/canoeing
Canyon and Lake Country: 133-177; map 136
Canyon Village: 31, 141-143, 149-156
Canyon Visitor Education Center: 137
Caribou-Targhee National Forest: 303, 305
car travel: 390-395, 396, 397, 398, 400-401
Cascade Canyon: 37, 38, 227, 232, 238, 241-242
Cascade Canyon Horse Trail: 239
Cascade Lake: 35, 111, 150-151, 152, 162
Casper Ridge: 278
Castle Geyser: 97, 104
Cathedral Group: 227
Cathedral Rock: 57
Cattleman's Bridge Site: 189
Cave Falls: 192
caves/caverns: 306
Celestine Pool: 94
cell phones: 410
Chain of Lakes: 35, 152, 162; map 153
Chapel of the Transfiguration: 228-229
Chasm Bridge: 239
Chief Joseph Scenic Byway: 345
children : 230, 411-412
Chittenden Trail: 150

Christian Pond: 196
Chromatic Pool: 97
Cinque Trail: 277, 278
Cistern Spring: 101
Claw Lake: 333, 334
Clay Butte Lookout: 331, 332
Clear Lake: 156
Cleopatra Terrace: 51
Clepsydra Geyser: 95
Cliff Geyser: 99
climate: 368-369, 370, 407
climbing: general discussion 406; Jackson Hole 279; North Grand Teton 186; South Grand Teton 227, 228, 246-247, 257
Cody Bowl Overlook: 278
Cody Firearms Museum: 342
Cody Gunfight: 348
Cody Mural Historic Site: 342
Cody Rodeo: 348
Cody, Wyoming: 340-347; maps 341, 343
Colonnade Falls: 198
Colter Bay: 34, 185-186, 187, 193-195, 201, 206; map 187
Colter Bay Lakeshore Trail: 34, 193
Colter Bay Visitor Center: 182, 185, 202, 203, 207
Colter's Hell: 342
Continental Divide: 109, 111, 148, 160, 358
Cooke City: 46
Corbet's Cabin: 34, 278
Cottonwood Creek: 252
Coyote Creek Trail: 59
Crackling Lake: 102
Craig Pass: 148, 159-160
Craig Thomas Discovery & Visitor Center: 34, 36, 222, 230
Crail Ranch Meadows: 320
Crail Ranch Museum: 315, 319
Crane Lake: 334
Crevice Creek: 59
cross-country skiing: Canyon and Lake Country 168-169; gateways 322-323, 335, 347-348; Jackson Hole 283, 305, 308; North Grand Teton 193, 206-207; North Yellowstone 68-69; Old Faithful and West Yellowstone 106, 115; South Grand Teton 253
Crystal Falls: 155
culture: 387-388
Cunningham Cabin Historic Site: 230
currency exchange: 410
Custer-Gallatin National Forest: 46, 334
Cygnet Lake: 186

D

Daisy Geyser Basin: 99
Dan Miller's Cowboy Music Revue: 348
Darby Wind Cave: 306

Deadman's Bar: 251
Deadman's Point Island: 192
Death Canyon: 39, 227, 232, 244; map 243
DeLacy Trail: 159-160, 161, 162
Devil's Stairs Trail: 306
disabilities, travelers with: 411
Ditch Creek: 252
Dogshead Trail: 161, 162
dogsledding: 284-285
Doublet Pool: 97
Downtown Red Lodge Historic District: 329, 331
Dragon's Mouth Spring: 143
Draper Museum of Natural History: 342
Dreamcatcher Chairlift: 305
Driggs, Idaho: 305
Dubois, Wyoming: 357-359
Duck Lake: 158
Dunanda Falls: 198
Dunraven Pass: 31, 141
Dunraven Pass Trail: 150

E

East Entrance Road: 137, 139-140, 162
Echinus Geyser: 38, 102
Elephant Back Mountain: 157
Elk Island: 186
Emerald Pool: 99
Emerald Spring: 101
emergencies: Big Sky 329; Billings 340; Bozeman 132, 329; Cody 83, 357; Cooke City 83; Idaho Falls 132; Jackson 303; Jackson Lake Lodge 217; Jenny Lake 261; Lake Village 177; Livingston 83; Mammoth Village 83; North Grand Teton 217; North Yellowstone 83; Old Faithful 132; Red Lodge 340; South Grand Teton 261
Emma Matilda Lake: 37, 188, 189, 197, 200, 203
environmental issues: 369-374
Excelsior Geyser: 96

F

Fairy Falls: 35, 105, 106-107
Falling Ice Glacier: 186
fauna: 376-380
Fawn Pass: 320
Firehole Canyon Drive: 93
Firehole Falls: 94
Firehole Lake Drive: 93
Firehole River: 32, 94, 108, 114
Firehole River Loop: 97, 99
fish/fishing: general discussion 407-409; Canyon and Lake Country 147, 151, 152, 160, 161, 163, 167-168; gateways 319, 321, 332, 333, 335, 344, 346; Jackson Hole 282; North Grand Teton 186, 187, 188, 189, 192, 193, 205-206; North Yellowstone 55, 58, 62, 63, 66-67; Old Faithful

and West Yellowstone 113, 114; South Grand Teton 228, 235, 238, 251-252
Fishing Bridge: 39, 144-145, 156-157
Fishing Bridge Museum and Visitor Center: 137, 144
Fishing Cone: 146
Flagg Canyon: 190-191
Flagg Ranch: 189, 190-193; map 191
Flagstaff Road: 199
flora: 374-375
45th Parallel: 31, 48, 49
Fountain Flat Drive: 93, 105, 107
Fountain Flats Road: 112
Fountain Geyser: 95
Fountain Paint Pots: 33, 38, 94-95, 105
Fox Creek Pass: 244

G

Gallatin River: 319, 321
Gardiner: 45-46, 49, 55; map 45
Gardiner River: 66
Gardiner Rodeo: 70
Garnet Canyon: 236-238; map 237
Garnet Hill: 55, 61-62
gateways to Yellowstone: 312-359, 390-397; map 316-317
geology: 38, 361-368
Geyser Basin: 92-93
Geyser Hill: 32, 108
Giant Geyser: 97
Gibbon Falls: 38, 100
Gibbon Meadows: 111
Gibbon River: 32, 110, 114
Glacier Lake: 333
Glacier View: 227
Golden Gate: 31, 51-52
golf: gateways 322, 335, 347; Jackson Hole 283, 308
Goodwin Lake: 279
Goose Lake: 107, 114
Grand Canyon of the Yellowstone: 31, 32, 35, 38, 55, 141-143, 168; maps 142, 154
Grand Geyser: 97
Grand Prismatic Spring: 32, 33, 38, 96, 105, 106-107
Grand Targhee Bike Park: 307-308
Grand Targhee Resort: 303, 305, 308, 309, 310
Grand Teton: 36, 37, 227, 232, 247; map 4-5
Grand Teton Brewing: 292
Grand Teton Music Festival: 286
Grand View: 142, 195-197; map 195
Grand View Point: 35, 37, 155, 188, 195-196, 197
Granite Canyon: 232, 245-246; map 245
Granite Canyon Entrance Station: 223
Granite Hot Springs: 275-276
Grant's Pass: 109, 111
Grant Village: 146-147; map 159

Grant Village Backcountry Office: 164
Grant Village Marina: 163
Grant Visitor Center: 137
Grassy Lake: 192, 206
Grassy Lake Road: 192, 193, 199, 207
Greater Yellowstone, map of: 6-7
Great Fountain Geyser: 32, 95-96, 104
Grebe Lake: 35, 111, 151, 152, 162
Greenough Lake: 333
Green River Overlook: 278
Grizzly and Wolf Discovery Center: 93, 117
Grizzly Bear Lake: 240
Grizzly Lake: 58
Gros Ventre Mountains: 274
Gros Ventre River: 282
Grotto Geyser: 97
Gull Point: 146, 167

H

Harlequin Lake: 103-104
Hayden Valley: 32, 33, 39, 143-144
health and safety: 413-416
Heart Lake: 161-162, 168; map 161
Heart Mountain WWII Interpretive Center: 344
Heart Spring: 97
Hebgen Lake: 113, 114
heli-skiing: 283
Hellroaring Creek: 59, 63, 66-67
Hermitage Point: 194-195
Heron Lake: 186
Heron Pond: 37, 194, 195
Hidden Falls: 34, 37, 230, 238-239
Hidden Lake: 241
hiking: general discussion 35, 37, 230, 402-406;
    Canyon and Lake Country 148-162; gateways
    315, 319-320, 332-334, 344-345; Jackson Hole
    276-279, 305-306; North Grand Teton 185-186,
    187, 189-198; North Yellowstone 55, 56-63; Old
    Faithful and West Yellowstone 102-111; South
    Grand Teton 227, 228, 232, 234-246
Historic Fort Yellowstone: 50
history: 380-386
Holly Lake: 240
Home of the Champions Rodeo: 336
horseback riding: general discussion 409; Canyon
    and Lake Country 163; gateways 320-321, 345-
    346; Jackson Hole 280; North Grand Teton 185,
    193, 199-200, 209; North Yellowstone 62, 64-
    65; Old Faithful and West Yellowstone 113
Howard Eaton: 108-109, 111
Huckleberry Mountain Lookout: 191-193
Hummock Trail: 320
Hurricane Pass: 241
Hurricane Vent: 102

I

Ice Box Canyon: 55
Ice Lake: 35, 111, 152, 162
ice-skating: gateways 323; Jackson Hole 284
Imperial Geyser: 105
Indian Creek-Bighorn Loop: 68
Indian Pond: 157
indigenous culture: 387
Indigo Spring: 96
Inside-Outside Loop: 184-185, 225, 248
Inside Road: 224-225, 227, 235-238
Inspiration Point: 34, 37, 142, 155, 238, 239, 241
International Pedigree Stage Stop Sled Dog
    Race: 286
international travelers: 410
Internet access: 410-411
Iron Horse Bar & Grille: 73
Isa Lake: 148
Island Lake: 333, 334
itineraries: 31-40

J

Jackson: 34, 36, 269-273, 276; maps 270, 272
Jackson Hole: 262-303; map 265
Jackson Hole and Greater Yellowstone Visitor
    Center: 266, 273, 276
Jackson Hole Brewing: 292
Jackson Hole Center for the Arts: 285
Jackson Hole Fall Arts Festival: 286
Jackson Hole Mountain Resort: 276, 277, 279, 280,
    283, 284, 285, 294
Jackson Hole Pathway: 279
Jackson Hole Playhouse and Saddle Rock
    Saloon: 285
Jackson Hole Rodeo: 286
Jackson Hole Winery: 292
Jackson Lake: 33, 36, 186-189, 192, 195-198, 200-
    201, 202, 206, 207; map 187
Jackson Lake Dam: 188, 189
Jackson Lake Lodge: 33, 187-188, 196, 205, 207,
    209-210, 212
Jackson Lake Overlook: 194, 195
Jackson Peak: 279
Jackson Point Overlook: 189, 198
Jackson Town Square: 34, 36, 269-273
Jedediah Smith Wilderness: 305
Jenny Lake: 34, 36, 227-228, 238-242, 241, 249,
    252; map 229
Jenny Lake Historic District: 228
Jenny Lake Loop: 34, 230, 238
Jenny Lake Ranger Station: 247
Jenny Lake Road: 225
Jenny Lake Scenic Drive: 248
Jenny Lake Visitor Center: 222, 238

Jewel Geyser: 99
John D. Rockefeller Jr. Memorial Parkway: 185,
    190-191
Junior Ranger Programs: 230, 412
Jupiter Terrace: 51

KL

kayaking/canoeing: general discussion 230;
    Canyon and Lake Country 147, 165-167;
    gateways 319, 344, 346; Jackson Hole 280-282;
    North Grand Teton 185-186, 187, 188, 189, 192,
    202-204; Old Faithful and West Yellowstone
    113; South Grand Teton 228, 249-250
Kelly: 226
Kepler Cascades: 110
Lake Butte: 38, 146
Lake Creek-Woodland Trail Loop: 242
Lake Levinsky: 321
Lake of the Woods: 192, 206
Lakeshore Trail: 34, 193
Lake Village: 144, 156-157, 162; map 147
Lake Yellowstone Hotel: 33, 144, 172, 173-174
Lamar River: 66
Lamar Valley: 31, 39, 54
Laurance S. Rockefeller Preserve: 34, 223, 230, 242
LeHardy's Rapids: 144
Leigh Lake: 239, 240-241, 249, 250, 252
Lewis Channel: 161, 162, 165, 166
Lewis Falls: 38, 147-148
Lewis Lake: 147, 163, 165, 166, 167
Lewis River: 33, 147, 168
Liberty Cap: 51
Lily Pad Lake: 156
Lion Group: 97
Little Glacier Lake: 333
Little Grassy Island: 192
Lizard Creek: 187
Lone Mountain: 315
Lone Peak Brewery & Taphouse: 324
Lone Star Geyser: 108, 109-110, 112, 115; map 109
Lookout Point: 32, 141, 142, 155
Lookout Rock: 197
Lost Creek Falls Trail: 61
Lost Lake Loop: 59, 61; map 61
Lost Lake Trail: 69
Lower Basin Lake: 332
Lower Falls: 31, 141, 143, 155
Lower Geyser Basin: 32, 33, 94-96, 104-107;
    maps 95, 106
Lower Grand Loop Road: 92, 140
Lower Slide Lake: 274-275, 281
Lunch Tree Hill: 188
Lupine Meadows Road: 249

Madison Arm Resort Marina: 114
Madison Campground Amphitheater: 117
Madison Information Station: 88-89
Madison Junction: 93-94, 103-104, 112
Madison Junior Ranger Station: 89, 94
Madison River: 32, 39, 94, 114
Mallard Lake: 108, 110
Mammoth Hot Springs: 31, 39, 50-51, 57, 112;
    map 50
Mammoth Hot Springs Hotel: 40, 70, 75-76
Mammoth Hot Springs Terraces: 50-51
Manor's Ferry: 228
Marion Lake: 245-246; map 245
Mary Bay: 157
Mary's Saddle: 305
Maud Noble Cabin: 228
Middle Fork Cutoff: 246
Middle Teton: 227
Midway Geyser Basin: 32, 33, 96; map 95
Miller Ranch: 273
Million Dollar Cowboy Bar: 34, 36, 269, 285
Millstone Pizza Company and Brewery: 350
Minerva Terrace: 51
Minute Geyser: 102
Minute Man Geyser: 109, 111
Monarch Geyser: 102
money: 410
Monument Geyser Basin: 110-111; map 111
Moon Creek: 333
Moose: 34, 36, 228-230, 242-246; map 231
Moose Entrance Station: 203
Moose Landing: 251
Moose Pond Loop: 238
Moose-Wilson Road: 34, 39, 226, 242, 248, 253
Mormon Row: 34, 39, 233-234
Morning Glory Pool: 33, 99, 105, 115
motorcycles: 401
Mound Spring: 105
Mound Terrace: 51
Mt. Holmes: 63, 111
Mt. Moran: 186, 227
Mt. Owens: 227
Mt. Sheridan: 161, 162
Mt. Washburn: 31, 35, 141, 149-151; map 150
Mud Volcano: 33, 143-144
Multi-Use Pathway: 248, 273
Mural Room: 34, 209
Murie Ranch: 229-230
Museum of the National Park Ranger: 102
Music in the Mountains: 323
Mustard Spring: 99
Mystic Falls: 107

N

Narrows of the Yellowstone River: 53, 55, 62
National Bighorn Sheep Interpretive Center: 357
National Elk Refuge: 39, 40, 268, 271, 273
National Finals Ski Joring Races: 336
National Museum of Wildlife Art: 34, 271
Natural Bridge: 158, 162
Night Lake: 334
Norris: 101-102, 110-111; map 101
Norris Campground: 111, 117
Norris Geyser Basin: 31, 38, 101, 105
Norris Geyser Basin Museum & Information
     Station: 89
Northeast Entrance Yellowstone: 46, 49, 54-55,
     62-63
North Entrance Yellowstone: 31, 46
North Fork of Cascade Creek: 241
North Fork of the Shoshone River: 347
North Grand Teton: 178-217; map 181
North Rim Drive: 32, 142
North Rim of Grand Canyon of the Yellowstone:
     142-143, 152, 155
North Yellowstone: 41-83; map 44

O

Observation Peak: 150-151
Observation Point: 108
Obsidian Cliff: 52
Obsidian Creek: 58
Old Bunsen Peak Road: 57
Old Faithful and West Yellowstone: 84-132;
     maps 87, 125
Old Faithful Geyser: 32, 33, 35, 38, 97, 108-110
Old Faithful Inn: 32, 100, 112, 115, 119, 123
Old Faithful Lodge: 109, 120, 123
Old Faithful Observation Point: 35
Old Faithful Visitor Education Center: 33, 89,
     104, 117
Old Gardiner Road: 64, 68-69
Old Pass Road: 280
Old Square Theatre Company: 285
Old Trail Town and Museum of the Old West: 342
Opalescent Pool: 99
Opal Spring: 51
Orange Spring Mound: 51
Osprey Falls: 57-58
Ousel Falls: 319
Outlaw Trails: 345
Outside Road: 36, 225, 230, 233-234
Oxbow Bend: 39, 188

P

Pacific Creek Road: 185
Paintbrush Canyon-Cascade Canyon Loop: 37,
     227, 232, 239-241, 246
Paintbrush Divide: 37, 240
Paintpot Hill: 100
Palette Spring: 51
Palpitator Spring: 102
Parkside National Recreation Trail: 333
passports: 410
Pat O'Hara Pub & Grill: 350
Paul Stock Aquatic and Recreation Center: 347
Paul Stock Nature Trail: 344-345
Pearl Geyser: 102
Pebble Creek: 55, 63
Pelican Creek: 39, 145, 156
Petrified Tree: 53, 61
pets, traveling with: 412-413
Phelps Lake: 230, 242, 244, 249, 252; map 243
Pinwheel Geyser: 102
Pioneer Museum: 342
Plains Indian Museum: 342
plane travel: 394, 396, 397
planning tips: 22-30
plants: 374-375
Playmill Theatre: 118
Plume Geyser: 97
Pocket Basin Mud Pots: 38
Point Sublime: 35, 155
Polecat Creek Loop: 190, 191, 207
Porcelain Springs: 102
Porkchop Geyser: 102
Potholes, The: 227
Punch Bowl: 99

QR

Queen's Laundry: 104-106
rafting: gateways 319, 321-322, 346-347; Jackson
     Hole 281-282; North Grand Teton 189, 204-205;
     North Yellowstone 55, 65-66; South Grand
     Teton 250-251
Rainbow Point Campground: 113, 114
ranger programs: North Grand Teton 207-208;
     North Yellowstone 70; Old Faithful and West
     Yellowstone 117; South Grand Teton 254
Red Lodge, Montana: 329-340; map 330
Red Lodge Music Festival: 336
Red Rock Point: 142, 155
Red Spouter: 95
Rendezvous Mountain: 34, 245, 277-278
Rendezvous Ski Trails: 113, 115
rental cars: 394-395, 396, 397
Rescue Creek Trail: 59
resources: 417-422
Ribbon Lake: 156
Riddle Lake: 160-161, 168
Riverside Geyser: 99, 104
Riverside Trail: 113, 115
Roadhouse Brewing: 292
Roaring Mountain: 31, 38, 52

Rockchuck Peak: 239
Rock Creek: 333, 335
Rock Creek Vista Point: 331-332
Rockefeller Parkway Visitor Information Center: 182
Rock Springs Loop: 278-279
Rocky Fork Trail: 334
Roosevelt Arch: 31, 39, 49
Roosevelt Lodge: 59, 61, 62, 76-77
Rustic Falls: 52
Rustic Geyser: 162
RVs: 394-395, 396, 397, 399-400

S

safety: 164, 379, 407, 413-416
Sapphire Pool: 99
scenic drives: Canyon and Lake Country 139-141; gateways 331-332; Jackson Hole 268; North Grand Teton 183-184, 193; North Yellowstone 47-48; Old Faithful and West Yellowstone 92-93; South Grand Teton 224-226
Schwabachers Landing: 233
Scout, The: 342
senior travelers: 413
Sentinel Meadows: 104-106
Sepulcher Mountain: 58
Sheepeater Trail: 68
Sheep Mountain: 274
Sheffield Creek: 192
Shelf Lake: 319-320
Shoshone Canyon: 346
Shoshone Geyser Basin: 108, 111, 162, 166
Shoshone Lake: 111, 159-160, 161, 162, 166; map 160
Shoshone National Forest: 354; map 355
Shoshone River: 346
Shoshone Riverway Trail: 345
shuttles: 394, 397, 398-399
Signal Mountain: 36, 189, 197-198; map 198
Signal Mountain Lodge: 189, 201-202, 204, 210, 212-213
Signal Mountain Road: 197, 199, 207
Silex Spring: 95
Silver Cord Cascade: 152
Silver Run Trails: 334
skiing/snowboarding: gateways 322, 335, 347; Jackson Hole 308
Skillet Glacier: 186
Skyline Trail: 280
Sky Rim Trail: 320
Sleeping Giant Ski Area: 347
"Sleeping Indian:" 274
Slide Lake Overlook: 274
Slough Creek: 54, 62, 63, 66
Snake River: 33, 36, 38, 188-189, 191, 203, 204, 206, 250-251, 252, 281, 282

Snake River Brewing: 292
Snake River Overlook: 233
Snow King Mountain: 269, 276, 282, 283
Snow King Trails: 280
Snow Lodge: 40, 112, 119-120, 123-124
Snowmobile Hillclimb: 286
snowmobiling: Canyon and Lake Country 169; gateways 348; Jackson Hole 284; North Grand Teton 207; North Yellowstone 69; Old Faithful and West Yellowstone 116
Snow Pass: 68
Snow Pass Trail: 58
snowshoeing: 323
snow tubing: 284
Soda Butte Creek: 55, 66
Solfatara Creek: 114
Solitary Geyser: 97, 108
Solitude Lake: 37, 232, 240, 241
solo travelers: 413
South Entrance: 33, 137, 147-148, 160-162
South Entrance Road: 139, 159, 162
South Entrance Station: 164
Southern Jackson Hole Loop: 268
South Flagg Canyon Trail: 207
South Fork of Cascade Creek: 241
South Fork of Teton Creek: 306
South Fork of the West Fork of the Gallatin River: 319
South Gate Boat Launch: 191
South Grand Teton: 218-261; map 221
South Rim Drive: 143
South Rim Trail: 35, 155
South Teton: 227
Spalding Bay: 201, 203
Specimen Creek: 319-320
Specimen Ridge: 62
spectator sports: gateways 336, 348; Jackson Hole 286; North Yellowstone 70; Old Faithful and West Yellowstone 118
Spouter Geyser: 99
Spring Creek: 110
Spring Lake Trail: 238
Static Peak Divide: 244
Steamboat Geyser: 38, 101
Steamboat Springs: 145
St. John's Episcopal Church: 229
Storm Point: 146, 157
String Lake: 239-241, 249, 252
Sublette Peak: 358
Sulphur Cauldron: 144
Summit Trail: 277
Sunset Lake: 99
Surprise Lake: 37, 237
Swan Lake: 31, 37, 186, 194
Swan Lake and Heron Pond Loop: 207
Swan Lake Flat: 39, 52

swimming: Canyon and Lake Country 168; gateways 347; Jackson Hole 282; North Grand Teton 206; North Yellowstone 67-68; Old Faithful and West Yellowstone 114; South Grand Teton 228, 252
Sylvan Lake: 168
Sylvan Pass: 162

T

Taggart Lake: 230, 235-237, 249, 252, 253; map 236
Targhee Bluegrass Festival: 309
Targhee Fest: 309
Teewinot: 227
tennis: 283
Terrace Mountain: 38, 58
Teton Canyon: 303, 305
Teton County Fair: 286
Teton County Recreation Center: 282
Teton Crest: 244
Teton Crest Trail: 246, 279, 306
Teton Fault: 38
Teton Glacier: 36, 227, 232
Teton Mountains: 33, 36
Teton Park Road: 34, 36, 39, 197, 224-225, 227, 248, 253
Teton Pass: 279, 284, 303
Teton Pines Nordic Center: 284
Teton Point: 227
Teton Range: 227
Teton Raptor Center: 273
Teton Science School: 230
Teton Valley: 303-311; map 304
Teton Valley Geotourism Center: 303
Teton Valley Trails and Pathways: 307, 308
Teton Village: 34, 273-274, 277-279
Teton Wilderness: 36
thrill sports: gateways 322; Jackson Hole 282-283; North Yellowstone 68; Old Faithful and West Yellowstone 114
Togwotee Pass: 185, 358-359
Top of the World: 331, 334
Top of the World Loop: 277, 278
tourist information: 410-411
tours: general discussion 394, 395; Canyon and Lake Country 138-141; Jackson Hole 266-268; North Grand Teton 183-185; North Yellowstone 46-47; Old Faithful and West Yellowstone 90-93; South Grand Teton 223-226
Tower Fall: 31, 39, 53-54, 69
Tower Junction: 59, 61-62
Tower Ranger Station: 61
transportation: 390-401
Trout Lake: 63
Turpin Meadow Ranch: 207
Turquoise Spring: 96

Twin Geyser: 147
Twister Falls: 198
Two Bit Saloon & Grill: 73
Two Ocean Lake: 37, 188, 196-197, 200, 203, 206
Two Ocean Plateau: 36
Two Oceans Mountain: 358
Two Top Trail: 116

U

Uncle Tom's Trail: 31, 35, 143, 155
Undine Falls: 52
Union Falls: 198
Upper Exum Ridge: 247
Upper Falls: 31, 141, 143, 155
Upper Geyser Basin: 32, 33, 96-100, 104-107; maps 98, 106
Upper Grand Loop Road: 48, 52, 141
Upper Terrace: 51
Upper Terrace Loop: 68, 69

VW

Victor, Idaho: 303
volcanoes: 104-105
Wall Pool: 99
Wapiti Lake Trail: 156
Warm Creek: 63
Warm Springs: 192
waterfalls: Canyon and Lake Country 141, 142-143, 147-148, 152, 155; gateways 319; North Grand Teton 192, 198; North Yellowstone 52, 53-54, 57-58, 61; Old Faithful and West Yellowstone 94, 100, 106-107; South Grand Teton 238-239
water sports: general discussion 230; Canyon and Lake Country 158, 160, 163-168; gateways 321-322, 344, 346-347; Jackson Hole 274-275, 280-282; North Grand Teton 185, 193, 200-206; North Yellowstone 65-68; Old Faithful and West Yellowstone 113-114; South Grand Teton 228, 235, 249-252, see also specific activity
weather: 368-369, 370, 407
West Entrance Road: 92, 94
West Entrance Yellowstone: 89-90, 112
West Fork Creek: 334
West Thumb: 33, 146-147, 158-159, 162; map 159
West Thumb Information Center: 137
West Yellowstone: 32, 84-132; maps 87, 125
West Yellowstone Old Faithful Cycle Tour: 118
West Yellowstone Visitor Information Center: 88, 117
Whirligig Geyser: 102
Whitney Gallery of Western Art: 340, 342
Wilcox Point: 192
Wild and Scenic Snake River: 204, 250-251
Wildflower Trail: 277
Wildlife Brewing: 292

wildlife refuges: gateways 331; Jackson Hole 271, 273
wildlife/wildlife-watching: general discussion 39, 230, 370-372, 376-380, 413-414, 415; Canyon and Lake Country 138, 140, 143, 145, 150, 156, 157, 160, 165; Jackson Hole 266-267, 271, 273; North Grand Teton 183, 188, 189, 190, 194, 195, 197, 203, 216; North Yellowstone 47, 50, 52, 53, 54, 55, 62; Old Faithful and West Yellowstone 91, 94, 103; South Grand Teton 224, 228, 233, 240, 242
Wilson: 273
windsurfing: 167
wine/winery: 292
Winter Creek: 63
winter sports: general discussion 40, 407, 409; Canyon and Lake Country 168-169; gateways 322-323, 335, 347-348; Jackson Hole 283-285, 305, 308; North Grand Teton 193, 206-207; North Yellowstone 68-70; Old Faithful and West Yellowstone 115-116; South Grand Teton 252-253, *see also specific activity*
Witch Creek: 161
Wolf Lake: 35, 111, 152, 162
World Snowmobile Expo: 118
Wraith Falls: 58
WYDAHO Rendezvous Teton Mountain Bike Festival: 308

XYZ

Yankee Jim Canyon: 55
Yellowstone Expedition's yurt camp: 40, 168-169
Yellowstone Forever Institute: 54, 56
Yellowstone General Store: 145
Yellowstone Giant Screen Theater: 117
Yellowstone-Grand Teton Rail Trail: 307
Yellowstone Heritage and Research Center: 49
Yellowstone Historic Center: 93, 117
Yellowstone Hotspot Plume: 104
Yellowstone Lake: 33, 145-146, 156, 163, 165-166, 167
Yellowstone Lake Overlook: 158-159
Yellowstone National Park, map of: 2-3
Yellowstone River: 53, 54, 55, 59, 65-66, 141-143, 168
Yellowstone Rodeo: 118
Yellowstone Wildlife Sanctuary: 331

List of Maps

Front Maps

Yellowstone National Park: 2–3
Grand Teton National Park: 4–5
Great Yellowstone Area 6-7

Discover Yellowstone & Grand Teton

Chapter divisions map 23

North Yellowstone

North Yellowstone: 44
Gardiner: 45
Mammoth Hot Springs: 50
Black Canyon of the Yellowstone: 60
Lost Lake Loop: 61

Old Faithful and West Yellowstone

Old Faithful and West Yellowstone: 87
Lower and Midway Geyser Basins: 95
Upper Geyser Basin: 98
Norris Geyser Basin: 101
Upper and Lower Geyser Basins: 106
Lone Star Geyser: 109
Monument Geyser Basin: 111
West Yellowstone: 125

Canyon and Lake Country

Canyon and Lake Country: 136
Grand Canyon of the Yellowstone: 142
Yellowstone Lake: 147
Mt. Washburn: 150
Chain of Lakes: 153

Grand Canyon of the Yellowstone Trails: 154
West Thumb and Grant Village: 159
Shoshone Lake: 160
Heart Lake: 161

North Grand Teton

North Grand Teton: 181
Colter Bay and Jackson Lake: 187
Flagg Ranch Trails: 191
Grand View Trails: 195
Signal Mountain: 198

South Grand Teton

South Grand Teton: 221
Jenny Lake Area: 229
Moose Area: 231
Taggart and Bradley Lakes: 236
Amphitheater Lake and Garnet Canyon: 237
Phelps Lake and Death Canyon: 243
Granite Canyon and Marion Lake: 245

Jackson Hole

Jackson Hole: 265
Jackson: 270
Downtown Jackson: 272
Teton Valley: 304

Gateways

Gateways to Yellowstone: 316–317
Big Sky: 318
Red Lodge: 330
Cody: 341
Downtown Cody: 343
Shoshone National Forest: 355

Photo Credits

Title page photo: Teton Crest Trail © Becky Lomax

All interior photos © Becky Lomax, except: page 8 © Zepherwind | Dreamstime.com; page 10 (top left) © Fotoeye75 | Dreamstime.com, page 11 (bottom right) © Mtilghma | Dreamstime.com; page 19 (top) © Lars4050 | Dreamstime.com, page 33 (bottom right) © Scukrov | Dreamstime.com; page 135 © Fyletto | Dreamstime.com; page 146 © Bennymarty | Dreamstime.com; page 178 (bottom) © Sburel | Dreamstime.com; page 271 © Rolf52 | Dreamstime.com; page 307 © Grand Targhee Resort

MOON NATIONAL PARKS

ACADIA
NATIONAL PARK
HILARY NANGLE

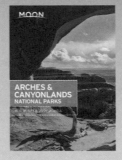

ARCHES & CANYONLANDS
NATIONAL PARKS
W. C. McRAE & JUDY JEWELL

BANFF
NATIONAL PARK
ANDREW HEMPSTEAD

DEATH VALLEY
NATIONAL PARK
JENNA BLOUGH

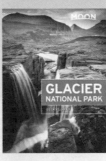

GLACIER
NATIONAL PARK
BECKY LOMAX

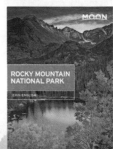

GRAND
CANYON
KATHLEEN BRYANT

GREAT SMOKY
MOUNTAINS
NATIONAL PARK
JASON FRYE

MOUNT RUSHMORE
& THE BLACK HILLS
Including the Badlands
LAURAL A. BIDWELL

ROCKY MOUNTAIN
NATIONAL PARK
ERIN ENGLISH

In these books:

- Full coverage of gateway cities and towns
- Itineraries from one day to multiple weeks
- Advice on where to stay (or camp) in and around the parks

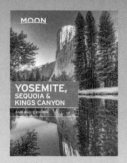

Craft a personalized journey through the top National Parks in the U.S. and Canada with Moon Travel Guides.

Join our travel community!
Share your adventures using **#travelwithmoon**

MOON.COM
@MOONGUIDES

MOON ROAD TRIP GUIDES

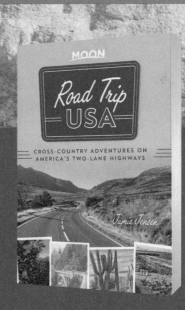

Road Trip USA

Criss-cross the country on America's classic two-lane highways with the newest edition of *Road Trip USA!*

Packed with over 125 detailed driving maps (covering more than 35,000 miles), colorful photos and illustrations of America both then and now, and mile-by-mile highlights